Christianity in North America

Editorial Team

Editors
Kenneth R. Ross
Grace Ji-Sun Kim
Todd M. Johnson

Associate Editor
Albert W. Hickman

Managing Editor
Danielle DeLong

Editorial Advisory Board
Margaret Bendroth
Peter C. Phan
Susan M. Shaw
John G. Stackhouse, Jr

Demographic Profile
Editor: Gina A. Zurlo
Data Analyst: Peter F. Crossing
Layout and Design: Justin Long
Cartography: Bryan Nicholson

EDINBURGH COMPANIONS TO GLOBAL CHRISTIANITY

Christianity in North America

Edited by

Kenneth R. Ross, Grace Ji-Sun Kim and
Todd M. Johnson

Edinburgh University Press is one of the leading university presses in the UK. We publish academic books and journals in our selected subject areas across the humanities and social sciences, combining cutting-edge scholarship with high editorial and production values to produce academic works of lasting importance. For more information visit our website: edinburghuniversitypress.com

© editorial matter and organisation Kenneth R. Ross, Grace Ji-Sun Kim and Todd M. Johnson, 2023
© the chapters their several authors, 2023

Edinburgh University Press Ltd
The Tun – Holyrood Road
12 (2f) Jackson's Entry
Edinburgh EH8 8PJ

Typeset in Palatino and Myriad
by R. J. Footring Ltd, Derby, UK, and
printed and bound in Poland by Hussar Books

A CIP record for this book is available from the British Library

ISBN 978 1 3995 0743 1 (hardback)
ISBN 978 1 3995 0744 8 (webready PDF)
ISBN 978 1 3995 0745 5 (epub)

The rights of Kenneth R. Ross, Grace Ji-Sun Kim and Todd M. Johnson to be identified as editor and the contributors to be identified as the authors of this work have been asserted in accordance with the Copyright, Designs and Patent Act 1988, and the Copyright and Related Rights Regulations 2003 (SI No. 2498)

Contents

Series Preface	viii
Volume Preface	x
Contributors	xv

Introduction

A Demographic Profile of Christianity in North America *Gina A. Zurlo*	3
Christianity in North America *Grace Ji-Sun Kim*	11

Countries

First Nations Canada *Terry Leblanc*	25
Anglophone Canada *John G. Stackhouse, Jr*	40
Francophone Canada *André Brouillette*	52
Western United States *Eliza Young Barstow*	64
Midwestern United States *David D. Daniels III*	76
Southern United States *Otis W. Pickett and Noah R. Karger*	88
Northeastern United States *Tyler Lenocker*	101
United States: Native American *Kimberlee Medicine Horn Jackson (Yankton Sioux)*	114
United States: Black/African American *JoAnne Marie Terrell*	125
United States: White *David P. Gushee and Isaac B. Sharp*	132

United States: Hispanic 144
Samuel Rodriguez

United States: Asian American 155
Timothy Tseng

Saint Pierre and Miquelon 168
Danielle DeLong

Greenland 172
Errol Martens

Bermuda 177
Kenneth R. Ross

Major Christian Traditions

Anglicans 183
Alan L. Hayes

Independents 197
Jeremy Paul Hegi

Orthodox 211
Anton C. Vrame

Protestants 219
Margaret Bendroth

Catholics 232
Christine Way Skinner

Evangelicals 245
Soong-Chan Rah

Pentecostals/Charismatics 258
Daniel D. Isgrigg

Key Themes

Faith and Culture 273
Miguel A. De La Torre

Worship and Spirituality 285
Grace Eun-Sun Lee

Theology 297
Dhawn B. Martin

Social and Political Context 310
Jim Wallis

Mission and Evangelism *Allen Yeh*	324
Gender *Susan M. Shaw*	337
Religious Freedom *Paul Marshall*	350
Inter-religious Relations *Peter C. Phan*	362
Immigration and Xenophobia *Jung Eun Sophia Park*	374
Christian Nationalism *Daniel D. Miller*	386
Ecology *Cynthia Moe-Lobeda*	398
Media *Zachary Sheldon and Heidi A. Campbell*	412

Conclusion

The Future of Christianity in North America *Robert Chao Romero*	427

Appendices

Christianity by Country	441
Methodology and Sources of Christian and Religious Affiliation *Todd M. Johnson and Gina A. Zurlo*	444
Index	462

Series Preface

While a number of compendia have recently been produced on the study of worldwide Christianity, the distinctive quality of this series arises from its examination of global Christianity through a combination of reliable demographic information and original interpretative essays by local scholars and practitioners. This approach was successfully pioneered by the *Atlas of Global Christianity 1910–2010*, published by Edinburgh University Press on the occasion of the centenary of the epoch-making Edinburgh 1910 World Missionary Conference.

Using the same methodology, the Edinburgh Companions to Global Christianity take the analysis to a deeper level of detail and explore the context of the twenty-first century. The series considers the presence of Christianity on a continent-by-continent basis worldwide. Covering every country in the world, it maps patterns of growth and/or decline and examines current trends. The aim of the series is to comprehensively map worldwide Christianity and to describe it in its entirety. Country-specific studies are offered, all the major Christian traditions are analysed and current regional and continental trends are examined.

Each volume is devoted to a continent or sub-continent, following the United Nations classifications. Through a combination of maps, tables, charts and graphs, each of the successive volumes presents a comprehensive demographic analysis of Christianity in the relevant area. Commentary and interpretation are provided by essays on key topics, each written by an expert in the field, normally an indigenous scholar. By the use of these various tools each volume provides an accurate, objective and incisive analysis of the presence of Christian faith in the relevant area.

The volumes (published and projected) in the series are:

1. Christianity in Sub-Saharan Africa (published 2017)
2. Christianity in North Africa and West Asia (published 2018)
3. Christianity in South and Central Asia (published 2019)
4. Christianity in East and Southeast Asia (published 2020)
5. Christianity in Oceania (published 2021)
6. Christianity in Latin America and the Caribbean (published 2022)
7. Christianity in North America
8. Christianity in Western and Northern Europe

9. Christianity in Eastern and Southern Europe
10. Compact Atlas of Global Christianity

As series editors, we rely heavily on the regional expertise of the dedicated third editor who joins us for each volume. Furthermore, each volume has its own editorial advisory board, made up of senior scholars with authoritative knowledge of the field in question. We work together to define the essay topics for the volume, arrange for compilation of the required demographic data, recruit the authors of the essays and edit their work. Statistical and demographic information is drawn from the highly regarded *World Christian Database* maintained by the Center for the Study of Global Christianity at Gordon-Conwell Theological Seminary (South Hamilton, MA, USA) and published by Brill. For each volume, a team of 35–40 authors is recruited to write the essays, and it is ultimately upon their scholarship and commitment that we depend in order to create an original and authoritative work of reference.

Each volume in the series will be, we hope, a significant book in its own right and a contribution to the study of Christianity in the region in question. At the same time, each is a constituent part of a greater whole – the 10-volume series, which aims to provide a comprehensive analysis of global Christianity that will be groundbreaking in its demographic quality and analytical range. Our hope is that the Companions will be of service to anyone seeking a fuller understanding of the worldwide presence of the Christian faith.

Kenneth R. Ross and Todd M. Johnson
Series Editors

Volume Preface

The landscape of North America is beautiful, pristine and wonderful. The land has majestic mountains such as the Rocky Mountains and the Great Smoky Mountains, and freshwater lakes such as the Great Lakes of North America and Lake Tahoe. North America is surrounded by the world's two largest oceans, the Pacific and the Atlantic. The vast continent is covered by deserts, forests, prairies, meadows, forests, canyons and wilderness. It has countless small towns as well as highly populated metropolitan cities. The land was first inhabited by Native Americans and First Nations, who lived off the land and in harmony with creation. It is a magnificent land, composed of only five countries, Canada, the USA, Saint Pierre and Miquelon, Greenland and Bermuda.

Just as the land is diverse and bountiful, so are the people who live in these five countries. Though their history is short compared with countries in such contexts as Asia, South America, Africa and Europe, it has been filled by devastation, horror and suffering. With the European conquest of Native land, the terror began for many Native and First Nations peoples as genocide was committed against them. The large-scale enslavement and importation of Africans brought further injustice, horror and suffering. During this horrific history, Christianity had a large presence and was part of the very fabric that caused the genocide of Native Americans and the enslavement of Africans. Christian adoption of the Doctrine of Discovery and the perception of Africans as heathens made it theoretically justifiable to enslave them. In addition, Asians were viewed as heathens and foreigners, a perception which white Americans used to indenture them. Throughout this history of immigration, enslavement and conquest, Christianity was deeply implicated in colonialism, subjugation and domination.

Due to increased immigration and the entrance of refugees during the last 70 years, North America is a very racially diverse place. This diversity means that various languages are spoken and different cultural customs are lived out. Many people who came from difficult situations found opportunities to build a new life in North America. Some refugees were able to start fresh lives and contribute to the wider society. Coming from many different backgrounds, they have formed an enterprising people who have built one of the world's strongest economies. North America has had the Civil Rights movement and recently the Black Lives Matter movement to fight racism, discrimination and prejudice. It has developed some strong and world-renowned academic institutions that have contributed enormously to scholarship in numerous fields of study. These developments, both the bad and the good, have had an impact on Christianity and its faith practices. It is not a homogeneous religion but rather is marked by diversity. There are several major denominations that have both flourished and declined in North America. Moreover, every region of North America has a slightly different perspective and practice.

The great variety of ethnicity and immigration history have influenced Christian practice, worship and understanding. The diversity and fluctuating outlooks within Christianity have also shaped the political landscape in North America. This in turn has impacted economic disparities among the people of North America. The concentration of wealth in the hands of a few and the wide gap between rich and poor has also impacted the practice of Christianity. Despite poorer individuals constituting the vast majority of the population, a small subset of rich people still controls the political, economic and religious landscape.

This seventh volume in the Edinburgh Companions series provides one lens through which to view the diversity of Christianity, not only within North America but also globally. It is not as innocent as white European Christians have claimed, as it has been implicated in colonialism, imperialism and other acts of injustice. Christianity changes, syncretises and transforms as cultures clash, people migrate and refugees move. As a result, new interpretations of Scripture continue to develop and impact how North Americans live out their Christian faith. It is this process of change and transformation that the present volume seeks to map.

In pursuit of understanding, the book offers four angles of analysis. The first is demographic, using the methodology of the highly successful *Atlas of Global Christianity* (Edinburgh University Press, 2009) to present reliable statistical information in an attractive, user-friendly format. Maps and charts depict the status of Christianity regionally and in terms of the principal church traditions. In this region all countries are majority Christian, though with a difficult history where Christianity came in conjunction with colonial conquest and the introduction of a slave-owning economy. Large-scale inward migration has brought increasing religious diversity while small but growing numbers profess a secular worldview. At the same time, new movements of Christian faith are changing the religious landscape and church life is marked by ever-increasing ethnic diversity. These trends are tracked in the demographic analysis.

The second angle of analysis is at the country level. Account is taken of the presence and influence of Christianity in each of the five countries of North America. Scholars who either belong to one of these countries or have long experience of the region have contributed interpretative essays that offer a 'critical insider' perspective on the way in which Christianity is finding expression in their context. Several essays are devoted to the two very large countries of Canada and the USA, which are considered in terms of geographic, ethnic and linguistic divisions.

Thirdly, Christianity in North America is considered in terms of its principal ecclesial forms or traditions. Five types of church are considered: Anglican, Independent, Orthodox, Protestant and Catholic. In addition, the Evangelical and Pentecostal/Charismatic movements, which cut across ecclesial affiliation, are examined. In each case, an author who is identified with the tradition in question brings a 'critical insider' perspective to the analysis.

Fourthly, selected themes are considered. Eight of these run through the entire Edinburgh Companions series: faith and culture, worship and spirituality, theology, social and political context, mission and evangelism, gender, religious freedom and inter-religious relations. A further four have been selected by the editorial board specifically for this volume on account of their salience in the context of North America: immigration and xenophobia, Christian nationalism, ecology and media. Each of these themes is examined on a region-wide basis, deepening our understanding of features that are definitive for Christianity in this part of the world.

As is evident from the short bibliography offered at the end of each essay, this book rests on the body of scholarship that has illumined our understanding of Christianity in North America. While there are many fine books about particular aspects of this topic, there are rather few that attempt to comprehend the whole. Most focus more on history and less on the contemporary context. More general works include: Paul Bramadat and David Seljak, *Christianity and Ethnicity in Canada* (Toronto: University of Toronto, 2016), which tackles the intersection between ethnicity and religion, a major emphasis in our volume; Thomas S. Kidd, *America's Religious History: Faith, Politics, and the Shaping of a Nation* (Grand Rapids, MI: Zondervan Academic, 2019), which assesses how faith has shaped American life and politics; Mark A. Noll, *A History of Christianity in the United States and Canada*, 2nd edition (Grand Rapids, MI: Eerdmans, 2019), which covers individuals, institutions and movements; and Nancy Koester's classic text with a focus on popular movements, *Introduction to the History of Christianity in the United States*, revised and expanded edition (Minneapolis, MN: Fortress Press, 2015). We are confident that our proposed volume will stand out from the existing literature on account of its attempt to bring a 'World Christianity' perspective to bear on Christianity in North America. Valuable steps in this direction have been taken by books that focus on particular communities within the region. These include: Michael Battle, *The Black Church in America: African American Christian Spirituality* (Oxford: Blackwell, 2006); Juan Francisco Martínez, *The Story of Latino Protestants in the United States* (Grand Rapids, MI: Eerdmans, 2018); and Fenggang Yang, *Chinese Christians in America: Conversion, Assimilation, and Adhesive Identities* (Pennsylvania, PA: Pennsylvania State University Press, 1999). The present volume owes much to these scholars and the many others whose work is acknowledged in the bibliographies, but it is distinguished by its local authorship, multidisciplinary perspective and comprehensive approach.

While resting on the preceding scholarship, this volume breaks new ground through its reliable demographic analysis, its contemporary focus, the local authorship of its essays and the originality of the analyses. The essay authors employ a variety of disciplinary approaches – historical, theological, sociological, missiological, anthropological – as appropriate to their topics. Taken together, the volume offers a deeply textured and highly nuanced account of Christianity in North America, one that will reward the attention of any who wish to deepen their knowledge of the subject.

The contributors to this volume represent the great ethnic, age and gender diversity of the region. Long-standing academics together with young researchers, coming from all corners of the immense North American geography, from various social and human disciplines, contributed to the knowledge of specific problems and realities. As an *ad hoc* community of scholarship, our privilege has been to explore the presence of Christianity in every part of North America at a pregnant moment in its history. There is currently a reckoning with the complicity of (white) Christians in historic acts of injustice on which the modern nations of North America have been built. Christianity formed a prominent part of the ideology that supported the dispossession of Native Americans and the importation of slave labour, mostly from Africa. The painful legacy of these injustices continues to shape North American societies today, with racism being named as America's original sin. The polarisation between those who espouse white nationalism and those who reject it is, in no small measure, a contest about the meaning of Christianity. Many of the pages that follow revolve around this contest. The culture wars by which much of current social reality is defined are, among other things, a battle about the interpretation of the faith. This struggle lies at the heart of this book. It is therefore not an easy read, nor one that invites complacency. We hope, however, that it will allow readers to undertake their own reckoning with an ambiguous and conflictive history.

Demographic trends reveal rapid change in the profile of North American Christianity today. They show decline in religious observance among communities that historically have been strongly identified with Christianity, with Canada providing a notable case in point. The rise of the 'nones' – people who do not identify with any organised religion – is the most striking demographic development, although in all the countries of the region a clear majority still identify as Christian. A major part of the explanation for this is the immigration that has brought many Christians from other parts of the world to make their home in North America. In the Catholic Church in Los Angeles, for example, Sunday Mass is offered in 42 languages, while in Toronto the number is 34. In terms of language, ethnicity and identity, Christianity is rapidly diversifying. Some have gone so far as to speak of the de-Europeanisation of American Christianity. While some long-familiar expressions of Christianity are suffering attrition and decline, there is nevertheless much evidence of vitality and renewal among new movements of Christian faith, often driven by relatively recent immigrants. The essays in the pages that follow seek to take account of these dramatic changes and to imagine what they will mean for the future. The book is offered as a contribution to understanding North American Christianity at a time of profound challenge and significant transformation.

Kenneth R. Ross
Grace Ji-Sun Kim
Todd M. Johnson

June 2022

Contributors

Eliza Young Barstow is Senior Instructor of Religious Studies and History at Oregon State University. She teaches in the areas of gender history, social reform movements in the USA and US religious history.
Western United States

Margaret Bendroth is a historian and scholar of American religion. Until her retirement in 2020 she served as Executive Director of the Congregational Library and Archives in Boston, Massachusetts.
Protestants

André Brouillette is a Jesuit priest from Quebec and the author of *Le lieu du salut: Une pneumatologie d'incarnation chez Thérèse d'Ávila* (Editions du Cerf, 2014) and *The Pilgrim Paradigm: Faith in Motion* (Paulist Press, 2021). He teaches systematic and spiritual theology at Boston College in Boston, Massachusetts.
Francophone Canada

Heidi A. Campbell is Professor of Communication, Presidential Impact Fellow and affiliate faculty in Religious Studies at Texas A&M University. She is also Director of the Network for New Media, Religion and Digital Culture Studies and author of numerous articles and books in the area of Digital Religion Studies, including *When Religion Meets New Media* (Routledge, 2010) and *Digital Creatives and the Rethinking of Religious Authority* (Routledge, 2021).
Media

David D. Daniels III is the Henry Winters Luce Professor of World Christianity at McCormick Theological Seminary in Chicago. An associate editor of the *Journal of World Christianity*, he is the author of more than 60 articles on global Pentecostalism and Black Church history.
Midwestern United States

Miguel A. De La Torre is Professor of Social Ethics and Latinx Studies at the Iliff School of Theology in Denver. He has published 40 books (five of which have won national awards). A Fulbright scholar, he served as the 2012 President of the Society of Christian Ethics and was the co-founder/first Executive Director of the Society of Race, Ethnicity, and Religion. He also wrote the screenplay for the documentary *Trails of Hope and Terror* (V1 Educational Media, 2017).
Faith and Culture

Danielle DeLong is the managing editor and a contributing author for the *Christianity in North America* volume of the Edinburgh Companions to Global Christianity series. She holds an MA in Theology and an MA in Intercultural Studies from Gordon-Conwell Theological Seminary, Boston, Massachusetts.
Saint Pierre and Miquelon

David P. Gushee is Distinguished University Professor of Christian Ethics at Mercer University and Chair of Christian Social Ethics at Vrije Universiteit Amsterdam. Widely regarded as one of the world's leading Christian ethicists, he is the author or editor of more than 25 books and approximately 175 book chapters, journal articles and reviews. Gushee was elected by his peers to serve as President of both the American Academy of Religion and the Society of Christian Ethics.
United States: White

Alan L. Hayes is Bishops Heber and Wilkinson Professor of the History of Christianity at Wycliffe College, University of Toronto. An ordained Anglican priest, he is author of numerous books and articles, including *Anglicans in Canada: Controversies and Identity in Historical Perspective* (University of Illinois Press, 2010).
Anglicans

Jeremy Paul Hegi is Assistant Professor of History of Christianity at Lubbock Christian University, Texas. A lifelong member of the Churches of Christ, his research interests include women and the formation of global denominational identities, the Stone-Campbell Movement, American Christianity and World Christianity.
Independents

Daniel D. Isgrigg is Assistant Professor and Director of the Holy Spirit Research Center at Oral Roberts University in Tulsa, Oklahoma. He is an ordained Assemblies of God minister and is the author of *Imagining the Future: The Origin, Development, and Future of Assemblies of God Eschatology* (ORU Press, 2021) and *Pentecost in Tulsa: The Revivals and Race Massacre that Shaped the Pentecostal Movement in Tulsa* (Seymour Press, 2021).
Pentecostals/Charismatics

Kimberlee Medicine Horn Jackson (Yankton Sioux) is faculty with the NAIITS: An Indigenous Learning Community (formerly the North American Institute for Indigenous Theological Studies), and co-editor of the *Journal of NAIITS: An Indigenous Learning Community*. She is a recipient of the 2022–3 Forum for Theological Exploration (FTE) Doctoral Fellowship.
United States: Native American

Todd M. Johnson is the Eva B. and Paul E. Toms Distinguished Professor of Mission and Global Christianity and Co-Director of the Center for the Study

of Global Christianity at Gordon-Conwell Theological Seminary in South Hamilton, Massachusetts. His most recent book is the *World Christian Encyclopedia*, 3rd edition (Edinburgh University Press, 2019). He also serves as a series editor for the Edinburgh Companions to Global Christianity (Edinburgh University Press).
Methodology and Sources of Christian and Religious Affiliation

Noah R. Karger is an MDiv student at Gordon-Conwell Theological Seminary, Boston, Massachusetts, where he works as a research assistant at the Center for the Study of Global Christianity.
Southern United States

Grace Ji-Sun Kim was born in Korea, educated in Canada and now teaches in the USA as Professor of Theology at Earlham School of Religion, Richmond, Indiana. An ordained Presbyterian Church (USA) minister, Kim has published 21 books, including *Invisible: Theology and Experience of Asian American Women* (Fortress Press, 2021) and *My Theology: Spirit Life* (Darton, Longman and Todd, 2022). She is the host of Madang podcast, which is sponsored by the Christian Century.
Christianity in North America

Terry LeBlanc is Mi'kmaq and Acadian, and together with Bev, his wife of 49 years, he resides in Epekwitk (Prince Edward Island), one of the seven districts of Mi'kma'kik. He holds an interdisciplinary PhD in Theology and Anthropology and is Director of NAIITS: An Indigenous Learning Community. He has accrued more than 41 years' experience as an educator and community development practitioner in global Indigenous contexts.
First Nation Canada

Grace Eun-Sun Lee holds a Master of Divinity with a focus on World Missions from Gordon-Conwell Theological Seminary, Boston, Massachusetts. She is a contributing author in the North America volume of the Edinburgh Companions as a Gordon-Conwell Rosell Scholar. A worship practitioner interested in ethnodoxology, she pioneered the Asian Heritage Chapel service, Global Chapel service, and Harp and Bowl worship initiative during her time in seminary.
Worship and Spirituality

Tyler Lenocker is a visiting researcher at Boston University School of Theology in the Center for Global Christianity and Mission, Boston, Massachusetts. With experience in cross-cultural parish ministry and university ministry, he has published peer-reviewed articles and book chapters on urbanisation, migration and the transformation of American Christianity in the twentieth century.
Northeastern United States

Paul Marshall is Wilson Distinguished Professor of Religious Freedom at Baylor University, Waco, Texax, and senior fellow at both the Hudson Institute and the Religious Freedom Institute, Washington, DC. He is the author and editor of more than 20 books on religion and politics.
Religious Freedom

Errol Martens, an ordained minister, has been Pioneer-Missionary-Coordinator of Youth With A Mission GREENLAND since 1984. He is presently writing a book on his experiences in Greenland for the YWAM International Adventure series.
Greenland

Dhawn B. Martin, PhD, is Executive Director of the SoL (Source of Light) Center, an inter-faith education centre at University Presbyterian Church, San Antonio, Texas. An ordained Teaching Elder in the Presbyterian Church (USA), she is a co-editor of the volume *Ecological Solidarities: Mobilizing Faith and Justice for an Entangled World* (Pennsylvania State University Press, 2019).
Theology

Daniel D. Miller is Associate Professor of Religion and Social Thought and Chair of the Department of Liberal Studies at Landmark College in Putney, Vermont. He is the author of *The Myth of Normative Secularism: Religion and Politics in the Democratic Homeworld* (Duquesne University Press, 2016) and *Queer Democracy: Desire, Dysphoria, and the Body Politic* (Routledge, 2022).
Christian Nationalism

Cynthia Moe-Lobeda is Professor of Theological and Social Ethics at Pacific Lutheran Theological Seminary (PLTS), Church Divinity School of the Pacific and the Graduate Theological Union, Berkeley, California, and is Founding Director of the PLTS Center for Climate Justice and Faith. She is author or co-author of six volumes, including the award-winning *Resisting Structural Evil: Love as Ecological-Economic Vocation* (Fortress Press, 2013), and more than 50 chapters and articles.
Ecology

Jung Eun Sophia Park, SNJM, is Associate Professor at the Holy Names University, Oakland, California. She has authored numerous books and articles, including *Conversations at the Well: Emerging Religious Life in the 21st-Century Global World* (Wipf and Stock, 2019).
Immigration and Xenophobia

Peter C. Phan is the inaugural holder of the Ignacio Ellacuria Chair of Catholic Social Thought at Georgetown University, Washington. He has earned three doctorates and written or edited more than 30 books on various themes of Christian theology.
Inter-religious Relations

Otis W. Pickett is the University Historian of Clemson University, Upstate South Carolina, on issues of historic interpretation, representation and commemoration. He has published widely on the history of the American South, including a chapter in *Southern Religion, Southern Culture: Essays Honoring Charles Reagan Wilson* (University Press of Mississippi, 2018).
Southern United States

Soong-Chan Rah is Robert Munger Professor of Evangelism at Fuller Theological Seminary in Pasadena, California. He is the author of *The Next Evangelicalism: Releasing the Church from Western Cultural Captivity* (InterVarsity Press, 2009) and *Prophetic Lament: A Call for Justice in Troubled Times* (InterVarsity Press, 2015).
Evangelicals

Samuel Rodriguez is President of the National Hispanic Christian Leadership Conference. CNN and FOX News have called him 'the leader of the Hispanic Evangelical movement' and *TIME* magazine named him among the 100 most influential leaders in America.
United States: Hispanic

Robert Chao Romero is Associate Professor of Chicano/Latino Studies and Asian American Studies at the University of California, Los Angeles. He is also an ordained minister and the author of *Brown Church: Five Centuries of Latina/o Social Justice, Theology, and Identity* (IVP Academic, 2020) and *The Chinese in Mexico: 1882–1940* (University of Arizona Press, 2012).
The Future of Christianity in North America

Kenneth R. Ross is Professor of Theology and Dean of Postgraduate Studies at Zomba Theological University, Malawi, and Extraordinary Professor at the University of Pretoria, South Africa. His most recent book, co-authored with Klaus Fiedler, is *A Malawi Church History 1860–2020* (Mzuni Press, 2020). He serves as a series editor for the Edinburgh Companions to Global Christianity (Edinburgh University Press).
Bermuda

Isaac B. Sharp is Visiting Assistant Professor and Director of Certificate Programming at Union Theological Seminary in the City of New York. He is the co-editor of *Evangelical Ethics: A Reader and Christian Ethics in Conversation* (Westminster John Knox Press, 2015), and author of the forthcoming book *The Other Evangelicals* (Eerdmans, 2022).
United States: White

Susan M. Shaw is Professor of Women, Gender, and Sexuality Studies at Oregon State University. She is the author of *Reflective Faith: A Theological Toolbox for Women* (Smyth and Helwys, 2015) and *God Speaks to Us, Too: Southern Baptist Women on Church, Home, and Society* (University Press of Kentucky, 2008).
Gender

Zachary Sheldon is a lecturer in the Department of Film and Digital Media at Baylor University, Waco, Texas, and is completing his doctorate in the Department of Communication at Texas A&M University. He has published numerous scholarly articles on religion, film and media.
Media

Christine Way Skinner is a doctoral student in ecclesiology at St Michael's College – Toronto School of Theology. A lay ecclesial minister for more than 30 years, she is the author of *The Joy of Living the Faith* (Twenty Third Publications, 2020).
Catholics

John G. Stackhouse, Jr, PhD, holds the Samuel J. Mikolaski Chair of Religious Studies at Crandall University in Moncton, Canada. He is the author of 10 books and editor of four more, including *Canadian Evangelicalism in the Twentieth Century: An Introduction to Its Character* (University of Toronto Press, 1998).
Anglophone Canada

JoAnne Marie Terrell is the Kenneth B. Smith, Sr Professor of Public Ministry and Associate Professor of Theology, Ethics, and the Arts at Chicago Theological Seminary. An ordained Christian minister and a Buddhist Lama, she is the author of *Power in the Blood? The Cross in the African American Experience* (Wipf and Stock, 2005).
United States: Black/African American

Timothy Tseng is Co-Executive Director of New College Berkeley, California, and Pacific Area Director of InterVarsity Christian Fellowship's Graduate and Faculty Ministries. An ordained American Baptist Churches, USA, pastor, he founded the Institute for the Study of Asian American Christianity and has published in the areas of Chinese American Christianity, race and American religion, and Evangelicalism.
United States: Asian American

Anton C. Vrame, PhD, is Director of Holy Cross Orthodox Press of Hellenic College-Holy Cross Greek Orthodox School of Theology, Brookline, Massachusetts, and Adjunct Associate Professor in Religious Education. He is an ordained presbyter of the Greek Orthodox Church, with the rank of archimandrite, and has published articles on the history of the Greek Orthodox Church in America.
Orthodox

Jim Wallis is a globally respected writer, teacher, preacher and justice advocate. He is the inaugural holder of the Chair in Faith and Justice at the McCourt School of Public Policy and the founding Director of the Georgetown University Center on Faith and Justice, Washington, DC. He is the founder

of Sojourners, host of The Soul of the Nation podcast and a *New York Times* bestselling author of 12 books, including *America's Original Sin: Racism, White Privilege, and the Bridge to a New America* (Brazos Press, 2016) and *God's Politics: Why the Right Gets It Wrong, and the Left Doesn't Get It* (Zondervan, 2005).
Social and Political Context

Allen Yeh is Professor of Intercultural Studies and Missiology at Biola University in southern California. He is the author of *Polycentric Missiology: Twenty-First Century Mission from Everyone to Everywhere* (IVP Academic, 2016).
Mission and Evangelism

Gina A. Zurlo is Co-Director of the Center for the Study of Global Christianity at Gordon-Conwell Theological Seminary, South Hamilton, Massachusetts. She is co-author of the *World Christian Encyclopedia*, 3rd edition (Edinburgh University Press, 2019) and co-editor of the *World Christian Database* (Brill).
A Demographic Profile of Christianity in North America; Methodology and Sources of Christian and Religious Affiliation

Introduction

A Demographic Profile of Christianity in North America

Gina A. Zurlo

Christianity by Province
269.5 Million Christians, 73.1% of Population

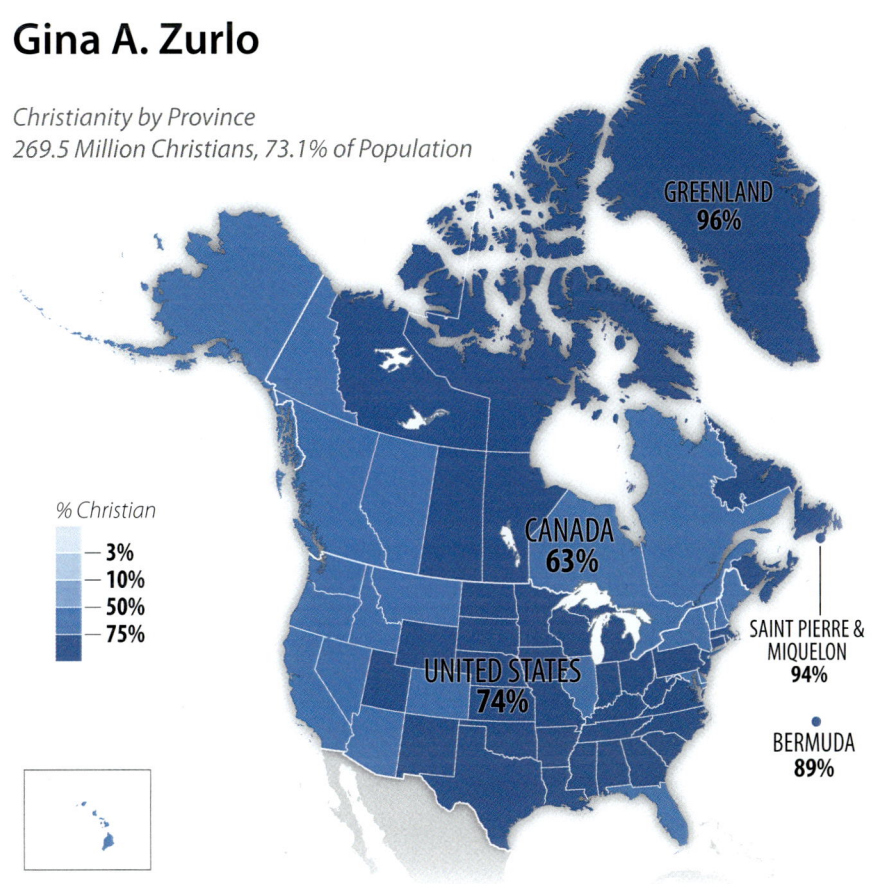

Religions in North America, 1970 and 2020

Religion	1970 Adherents	%	2020 Adherents	%
Christians	211,489,000	91.6	269,524,000	73.1
Agnostics	11,349,000	4.9	64,155,000	17.4
Atheists	300,000	0.1	10,587,000	2.9
Jews	5,700,000	2.5	5,940,000	1.6
Muslims	842,000	0.4	5,671,000	1.5
Buddhists	216,000	0.1	4,953,000	1.3
Other	1,095,500	0.5	8,040,500	2.2
Total	230,992,000	100.0	368,870,000	100.0

Source: Todd M. Johnson and Gina A. Zurlo (eds), *World Christian Database* (Leiden/Boston: Brill), accessed November 2021. Figures might not add to 100% due to rounding.

North America is a majority Christian continent consisting of five countries: Canada, the USA, Saint Pierre and Miquelon, Greenland and Bermuda. It is generally agreed that this region is secularising; Canada, for example, has experienced a substantial decline in its Christian percentage, dropping more than 30 percentage points in 120 years (from 98% to 63.5%). In the USA, there is less Christian affiliation in the Northeast and West than in the south and centre of the country.

Christianity in North America, 1970–2020

Major Christian Tradition by Province, 2020

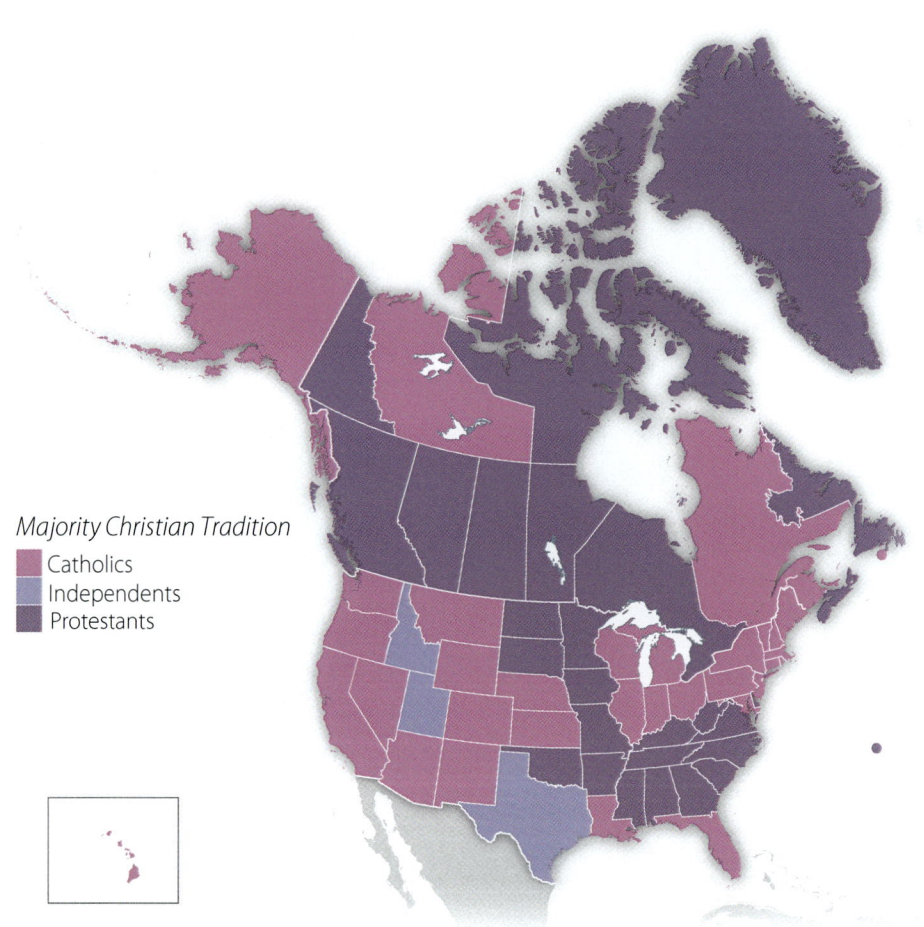

The diversity of North American Christianity is on full display when viewed from the perspective of the major Christian traditions. The region is home to sizable populations of the four major traditions. Catholics are the largest, with 88 million and 24% of the region's population, with the highest concentrations in Quebec and the Northwest Territories in Canada and in the USA throughout the Northeast, parts of the West, West Coast and Pacific Northwest. Protestants are the majority in all other Canadian provinces, the USA upper Midwest and the region known as the 'Bible belt' in the South. Independents form the majority in the US states of Texas (largely due to megachurches) and Utah and Idaho (due to the Church of Jesus Christ of Latter-day Saints).

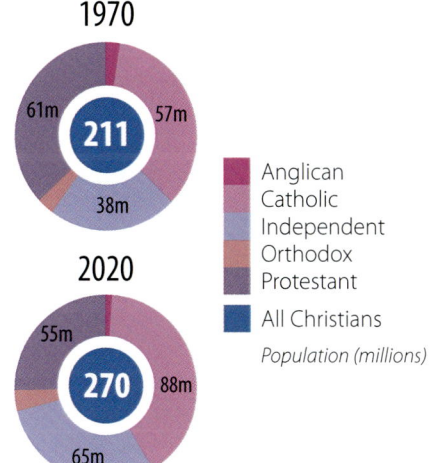

Major Christian traditions, 1970 and 2020
The internal makeup of Christianity in North America has changed slightly in the last 50 years. Catholics are still the largest tradition, with 88 million affiliates. The biggest change has been the actual and proportional decline of Protestantism, which dropped from 61 million in 1970 to 55 million in 2020.

Christians, 1970–2020
Christianity is the largest religion in North America, but it is experiencing a slow proportional decline. Christianity dropped from 92% in 1970 to 73% in 2020. Many Christians are becoming non-religious. Others are leaving institutionalised Christianity but continue to hold Christian beliefs.

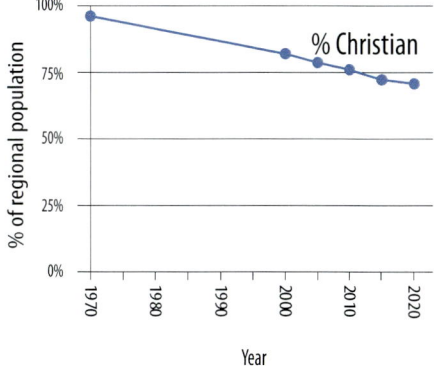

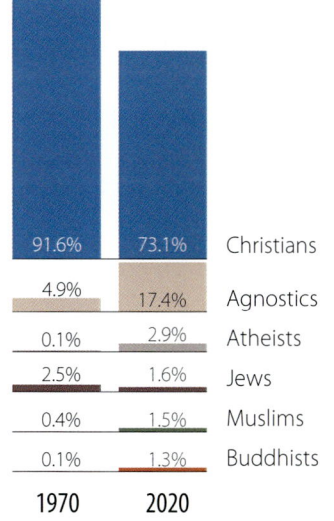

Religious affiliation, 1970 and 2020
North America is a religiously diverse region and is home to large populations of agnostics (17%) and atheists (3%), with smaller populations of other religionists, such as Jews, Muslims and Buddhists. Adherents of these other world religions have been increasing since the 1960s with changes in immigration law.

Note: For North America, traditions will not add up to total Christians because of double-affiliation and the unaffiliated. Only religions over 1% in 2020 are identified.

Major Christian Traditions, 1970 and 2020

Christians

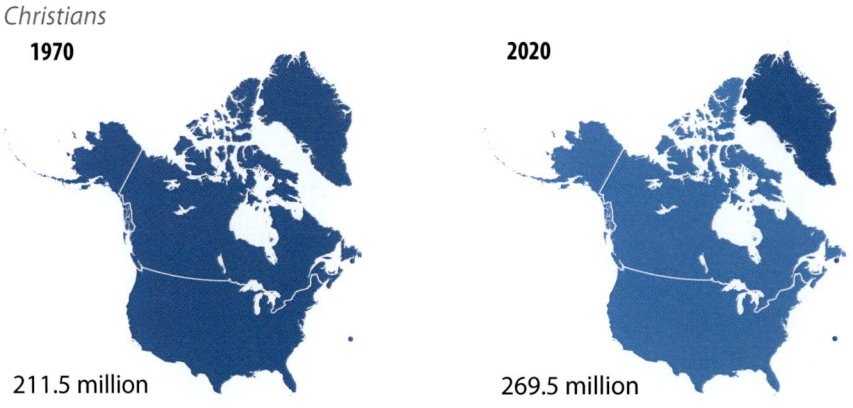

1970 — 211.5 million
2020 — 269.5 million

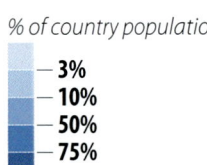

% of country population
- 3%
- 10%
- 50%
- 75%

Christianity in North America dropped from 92% of the population in 1970 to 73% in 2020. Every country in the region experienced decline over the 50-year period. Canada's was the most profound, from 94% to 63%, but the USA also dropped substantially, from 91% to 74%.

Anglicans

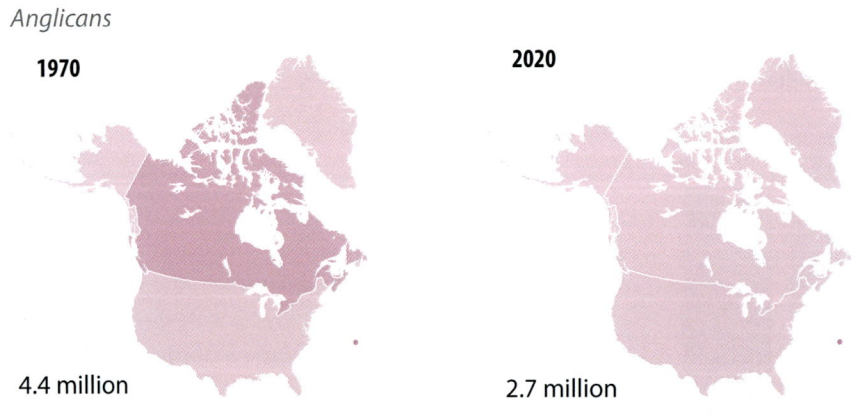

1970 — 4.4 million
2020 — 2.7 million

% of Christian population
- 3%
- 10%
- 50%
- 75%

Anglicanism has a long history in North America as the religion of the British upon colonisation, impacting both Canada and the USA. However, in the twentieth century, only Bermuda had a large Anglican population: 44% of all Christians in 1970, dropping to 20% in 2020.

Catholics

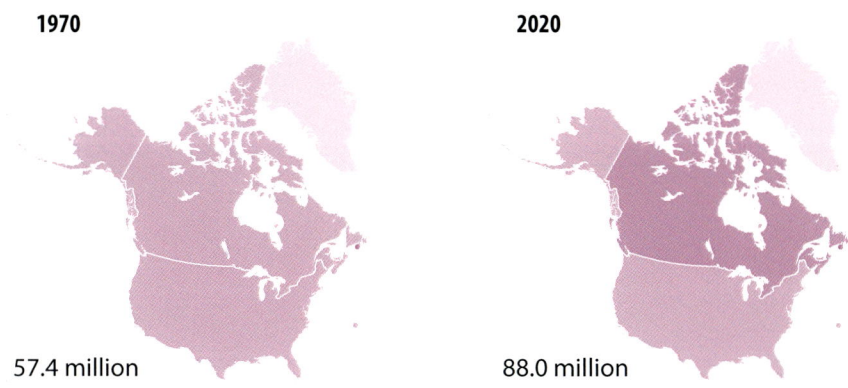

1970 — 57.4 million

2020 — 88.0 million

% of Christian population
- 3%
- 10%
- 50%
- 75%

Catholicism is a prominent Christian tradition in North America, with the highest share in Saint Pierre and Miquelon (97% of all Christians in 2020, but there are only 5,500 Christians in the country). Catholics are 59% of all Christians in Canada and 30% in the USA.

Independents

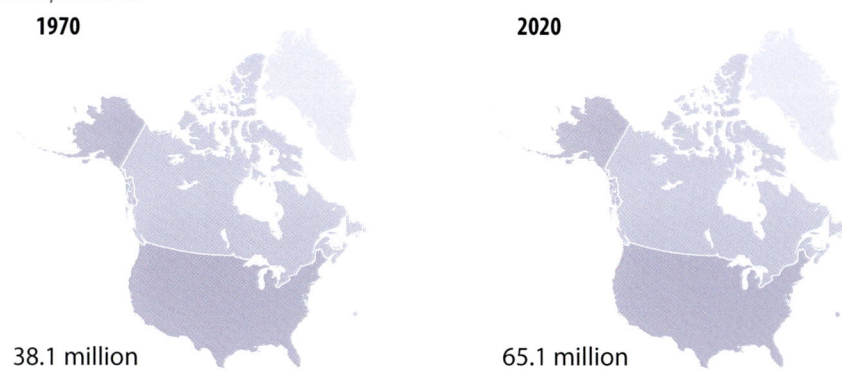

1970 — 38.1 million

2020 — 65.1 million

% of Christian population
- 3%
- 10%
- 50%
- 75%

Independent Christianity is unique in North America as the historic home and headquarters of the Church of Jesus Christ of Latter-day Saints (Salt Lake City, Utah, USA). The region is also home to numerous Independent Pentecostal/Charismatic churches, which have been growing.

Major Christian Traditions, 1970 and 2020

Orthodox

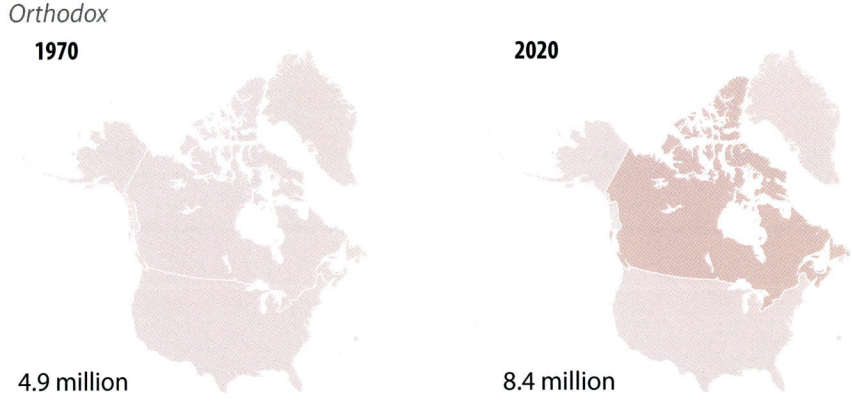

1970 — 4.9 million
2020 — 8.4 million

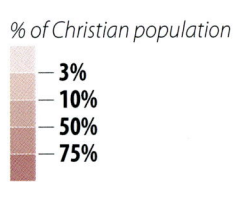

% of Christian population
- 3%
- 10%
- 50%
- 75%

Orthodox Christianity is a minority tradition in North America, despite a long history of missionary sending and church planting in Alaska. The highest share of Orthodox Christianity is in Canada, where they are 5% of all Christians.

Protestants

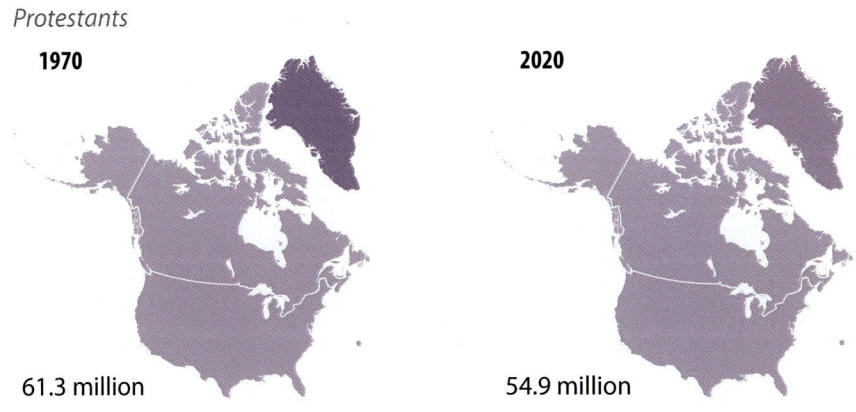

1970 — 61.3 million
2020 — 54.9 million

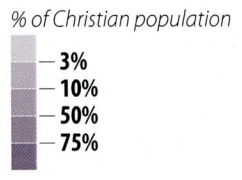

% of Christian population
- 3%
- 10%
- 50%
- 75%

Protestants are found in many different varieties in North America, including Baptists, Presbyterians, Lutherans and Methodists. These so-called 'mainline' churches have been in decline, especially in Canada. Greenland has the highest proportion of Protestants in the region, at 66% of all Christians.

Movements Within Christianity, 1970 and 2020

Evangelicals

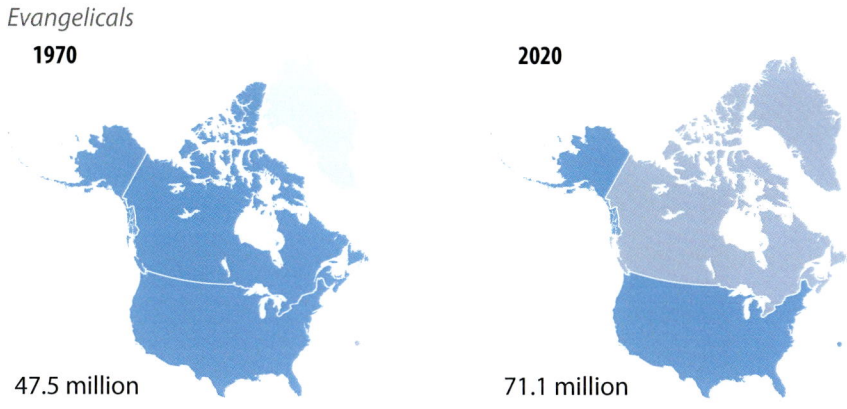

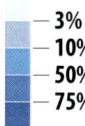

Evangelicalism has remained somewhat steady proportionally in the USA, home to the highest number of Evangelicals of any country in the world (69 million). Evangelicals were 24% of all US Christians in 1970 and 28% in 2020. Overall in the region, Evangelicalism increased proportionally as well, from 22% to 26%.

Pentecostals/Charismatics

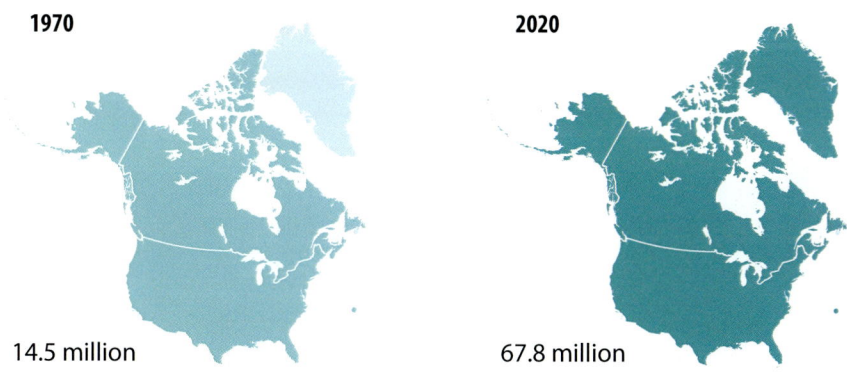

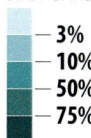

Pentecostal and Charismatic Christianity represents 25% of all Christians in North America, a substantial increase from just 7% in 1970. The region experienced many Charismatic revivals beginning in the 1970s, such as the Toronto Blessing in 1994. This kind of Christianity has grown proportionally in every country in the region between 1970 and today.

Future of Christianity in North America, 2020–50

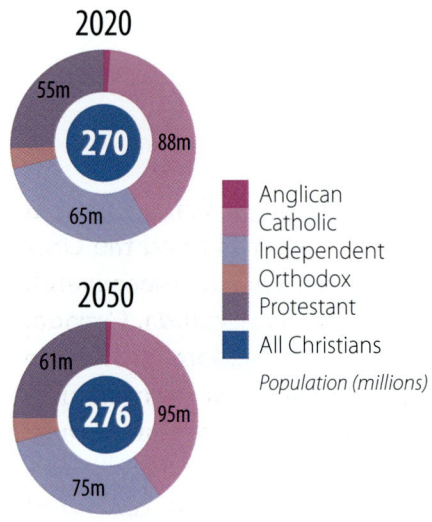

Major Christian traditions, 2020 and 2050
The internal makeup of Christianity in North America is not poised to change much. Catholics are likely to remain the largest tradition (95 million), followed by Independents (75 million) and Protestants (61 million).

Christians, 2020–50
Looking forward to 2050, Christianity is anticipated to continue its proportional decline to perhaps 65% of the region's population, with the most dramatic declines in Canada (down to 53%) and the USA (to 67%).

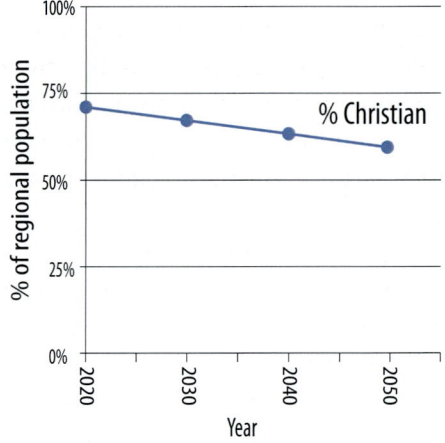

Religious affiliation, 2020 and 2050
The religious makeup of North America in 2050 is poised to remain diverse, but not significantly different from 2020. If current trends continue, the non-religious (atheists and agnostics together) could represent over 26% of the population (up from 20%), and Muslims could increase to 3% (up from 1.5% in 2020).

Christianity in North America

Grace Ji-Sun Kim

This volume attempts a comprehensive examination of Christianity in North America, which includes a large land mass (Canada and the USA are the second and fourth largest countries in the world, respectively). However, North America includes only five countries: Bermuda, Canada, Greenland, Saint Pierre and Miquelon, and the USA. Since some 90% of the region's population lives in the USA, this book focuses its major themes and issues within that country, while also taking account of Canada and the small nations to the east of the American mainland. The modern nations in North America were founded relatively recently, compared with European or Asian countries that are built on many centuries of history. However, North American countries are prominent in innovation and have become economic leaders, with influence around the world. The USA, in particular, wields great political and economic influence globally. As a result, how Americans practise or understand Christianity has a worldwide impact.

Christianity in North America is a vibrant, informative and challenging volume as it traverses various regions of North America to understand the origins, rise and impact of Christianity in the different areas. This volume examines pertinent themes and issues, such as gender, ecology and racism, as well as the different forms of church life in North America such as Anglicans, Independents, Protestants and Catholics. Through these various lenses of exploration and research, this volume seeks to challenge preconceived understandings of Christianity and to discern emerging trends in a land thirsting for spirituality, reconciliation, growth and flourishing.

Christianity in North America has taken on some distinctive cultural characteristics of the region. Some have argued that it is a highly individualistic culture. The Western culture of individualism has created churches and a theology that are highly individualistic in nature and less communal than in other parts of the world such as Asia and Africa. This individualism has consequences for our faith practices, as it tends not to promote communal worship and fellowship. The COVID-19 pandemic has not helped in building communities as, since March 2020, much interaction has moved online. This tends to isolate people further, especially the elderly, single people and other groups on the margins of society. Furthermore, COVID-19 has also led to an increase in hate crimes against Asian Americans as some in white society (following former US President Donald Trump) have continued to call COVID-19 the 'Chinese virus', which perpetuates racism and xenophobia. This has affected Asian American church communities and denominations as they try to cope with systemic racism within faith communities.

Its orientation to individualism might have made North America fertile ground for religious innovation, with movements like the Church of Jesus Christ of Latter-day Saints, Seventh-day Adventists and the Jehovah's Witnesses originating in the USA. These new religious movements were able to germinate and grow in a context where many had left Europe for a new world in pursuit of religious freedom. Also, individualism, which is the predominant way of life in North America, allows people to freely choose their own spirituality. There is little communal pressure to join a certain faith tradition. As such, new religious identities and practices can easily emerge and grow in North America. This climate also encourages the expression of Christianity through para-church organisations as opposed to the churches themselves. Such organisations do not have to negotiate the hierarchical power and authority that are found in the Roman Catholic, Episcopal or Presbyterian churches. Rather, they are organic and rise in response to the needs of students, communities and social movements.

In recent times, social media has heavily influenced North American Christianity. Conservatives and liberals argue on social media and thus it has become a powerful tool to convey Christianity to the masses. Christian churches and leaders use social media to share worship, sermons and church news. Some believe that without social media, they might feel isolated and out of touch with their church and faith communities. Social media has also been used to promote 'cancel culture' and expose those who have been abusive leaders. If social media is used positively, it can be a powerful tool to quickly disseminate news and prophetic messages to fight such evils as racism and sexism within the church.

The USA is a vast country with more than 330 million people. Due to the scale of the country and the different cultures in various parts of the USA, it is evident that Christianity is differently practised and exhibited in different areas. The South, for example, with its history of practising and defending slavery, is regarded as more fundamentalist and conservative. The Northeast is regarded as more liberal and progressive, though it was in favour of the extermination – or at least dispossession – of the Indigenous population and was also almost as covertly racist in certain ways during the twentieth century as the South was overtly racist. These conservative and liberal orientations are expressed today in relation to such issues as ordination and leadership of women, LGBTQ ordination, climate change and immigration laws. These regional variations are examined in a series of essays in this book.

Christianity is the most prevalent form of religion in the USA, with some 65% of adults viewing themselves as Christian. Presently, Christianity is prominent in politics, society and culture. It appears that every political leader running for office must share their faith, and the most desired faith tradition is Christianity. When a reporter asked the then presidential candidate George W. Bush who his favourite philosopher was, Bush answered, 'Jesus Christ'. The conservative Christians loved Bush's response as it confirmed for them that Bush was serious about Christianity and about his belief in Jesus.

A Fast-changing Situation
Perhaps what stands out most in the analysis assembled in this book is that Christianity in North America is undergoing rapid change. The continuous flow of immigrants and refugees entering North America has drastically altered the landscape of the continent in terms of demographics, politics, culture and religion. Immigrants are making North America a diverse, rich, beautiful and dynamic society. Furthermore, Christian immigrants from Asia, Africa and Latin America are also challenging and changing worship, faith practices and understandings of Christianity as it has historically been practised by white people in North America. Immigrants who have faith in other major world religions are also altering Christianity and Christian practices as the meeting of adherents of different religions encourages people to engage in inter-faith dialogue, which in turn tends to deepen their own Christian faith. However, there have also been negative attitudes towards people of different religious faiths entering North America, as some express fear and xenophobia towards immigrants of other faith traditions.

As people from all over the world come to live and work in North America, they also bring their own ways of being, living and believing. These different cultures, identities and individuals influence one another in terms of understanding of the Christian message. Christianity moves, adapts and transforms as it is affected by the surrounding culture and context. As Christianity changes, new ways of being, living and worshipping are emerging, such as intercultural ministry. Intercultural includes 'inter-racial' but extends more widely to include nationalities and ethnicities as well as races. An intercultural approach involves the interaction of people across races, ethnicities and nationalities so that people can grow to value, learn and celebrate each group's traditions.

Intercultural churches and ministries try to move beyond simply acknowledging diversity. Many churches welcome people of various races and take pride in the diversity of their membership, pointing to a scattering of people from races other than the dominant one. Intercultural churches and ministries bring people of various cultures together to learn from one another, giving equal value and power to each culture, preserving cultural differences and celebrating the variety of traditions. Some North American churches engage in intercultural ministries centred on justice, mutuality, respect, equality, understanding, acceptance, freedom, peace-making and celebration. As people from different cultures and ethnicities interact with one another and build relationships, they find that they grow together and transform.

The practice of Christianity is changing because North America is a land enriched by its many immigrants. It can be seen as a microcosm of the global situation: Christianity is receding among the white communities of the North while it is discovering new vitality among the peoples of the Global South. In North America this drama is being played out within one continent since in both the USA and Canada the population is composed largely of descendants of immigrants from all over the world. Hence some segments of North American Christianity are in decline while others are growing prodigiously. Many immigrant churches are growing as immigrants come to church not just to worship, but also to find friends, community, jobs and a flourishing life.

It is evident that many historic white churches are declining. Meanwhile, new church movements are undergoing rapid growth, many of them drawing their vitality from immigrant communities. Therefore, it is important to be inclusive of all voices when considering church and ministry in North America. The dominance of white Christianity is weakening and thus fresh attention is being paid to those on the margins of society. Christianity is changing and is being expressed in different ways. This has implications for its future in North America and for the catholicity of the faith. North American Christians are seeking ways to allow for diversity while still maintaining some kind of unity. This struggle is reflected in the pages that follow.

Immigration Changing the Landscape

When I was growing up in the 1970s in London, Ontario, we began elementary school each morning by reciting the Lord's Prayer, singing the national anthem and announcing school news. It was very clear to me as an immigrant child that Canada was a Christian country and that I needed to become a Christian if I was going to fit into this new country. Our family did not have any religious attachments when we immigrated, but we eventually became Christians as other Korean immigrants encouraged our family to attend church. We went to a Korean Presbyterian church on Sundays, but during the mid-week and Friday nights my parents dropped my sister and me off at a white Baptist church and a Missionary Alliance church for Bible studies, fellowship and worship.

Even though our family connection and regular attendance were at the Korean Presbyterian church, we still had a print image of the ever-popular *Head of Christ* by artist Warner Sallman in our living room. This image is a picture of Jesus as a nicely dressed white man, which reinforced the whiteness of God. My mother treated this print image as if it were a 'holy' art piece and carefully packed it every time we moved. That image was one of the first things unpacked. In every new place, she hung it up behind the living room couch so we could see the image of Jesus every day and any visitors to the home would see it immediately. My own family story is one of many.

The arrival of white settlers in North America began a continuous flow of different peoples from around the globe. Enslaved Africans were brought into the USA from 1619 to 1808 (when the importation of enslaved Africans was outlawed, although enslavement was still legal until 1865) to work in the production of crops such as tobacco and cotton. They worked in harsh conditions and were treated as sub-human. Immigrants slowly came from South America, Central America, Asia and Australia. Asians laboured as indentured workers and suffered discrimination due to their Asian looks and heritage. Many worked for low wages on the railway, paid much less than white workers and given more dangerous tasks, such as blowing up mountains, which cost the lives of many Asian workers.

Oppression, xenophobia and discrimination against immigrants of colour were evident from the beginning of migration and have continued until the present day. As immigrant Christians find their voice, they often expose the problem of racism in the USA and Canada, which is evident also in the life of the churches. Immigrants argue that a white Christianity, with a white God and a white Jesus, is promoted in order to keep immigrants of colour in their subordinate status within church and society.

American society is often described as a 'melting pot'. Immigrants were encouraged and expected to 'assimilate' into the dominant white Eurocentric society. This melting pot was not as easily created as initially expected and desired. Many immigrants wanted to maintain and hold on to their ethnic cultures, languages and faith practices. In Canada, immigration was viewed as a 'salad bowl' rather than a 'melting pot' as different individual cultural practices and ethnicities were expected to maintain their own specific identities rather than melt into the larger white, Eurocentric dominant culture.

World Christianity Lens

A special contribution of this volume is its use of the lens of 'World Christianity' to examine North American Christianity. World Christianity conveys the global nature of Christianity, and its focus is often on 'non-Western Christianity'. Over the past century, Christianity's centre of gravity has steadily shifted from Europe and North America to the global South as adherence to Christianity has dwindled in the former and grown in the latter. It is important to understand the movement, growth and decline of Christianity around the globe and how Christianity's practice, doctrines and worship change over time, place, context and circumstances. The study of World Christianity emphasises the diversity and the multiplicity of Christianity over the past 2,000 years. When these are not factored into the study of Christianity, Christianity can easily appear to be a white, male, Eurocentric and heteronormative religion that is static, claiming that its version of the faith represents truth for all times, contexts and cultures.

Through missions, the Christianity of Europe and North America has impacted many parts of the world as it spread white Eurocentric Christianity around the globe. World Christianity puts the focus on how native and Indigenous people respond, modify and adapt European Christianity in light of their own history, experience, culture and language. The impact of European Christianity has been substantial in the daily lives of people around the globe. The lens of World Christianity helps us understand and recognise the multiple components of a living theology and its impact around the globe. As various people have responded in their own way to the Christian message first brought by European missionaries, we see different forms and practices of Christianity emerging. This method of studying Christianity provides originality, depth and clarity. Its use of the World Christianity lens to consider North America makes this book the first of its kind. No longer can we do justice to the study of Christianity if we regard it only as a white, Eurocentric religion. World Christianity also sheds light on the future trajectory of North American Christianity.

Our study of Christianity in North America through the lens of World Christianity calls particular attention to the voices of the various immigrants who have come to this land and have made it their home. This volume includes Hispanic, Black, Asian American and Native American voices, as these different marginalised groups have all contributed to the development of a Christianity that stands in contrast to the white, dominant heteronormative Christianity. As the North American countries are becoming increasingly diverse through immigration and globalisation, a variety of voices bring richness and depth to the analysis. This richness expands our understanding of God, faith and the church, making these marginalised voices pivotal to attaining an accurate picture of North American Christianity today.

North America has been religious from its beginnings, with Indigenous people's spirituality and practice. Christianity has been part of the North American religious landscape since the beginning of immigration from Europe. World Christianity provides an enlightening pathway to explore North American Christianity. The chapters in this volume bring new perspectives to bear on contemporary Christianity in North America. Each chapter covers a wide timeframe and includes personal stories, statistics, new theologies and other relevant material to help us comprehend our present situation and gain a deeper understanding of Christianity. Much of the content in this volume is fresh, provocative and enticing. The voices of diverse writers of various educational backgrounds and differing ecclesial, gender, ethnic and racial identities make this volume interesting and essential reading.

With its commitment to cover all expressions of Christianity, the volume is also distinguished by its portrayal of the confessional diversity that marks North America. The variety is breath-taking. Pentecostal churches flourish in Bermuda as allegiance has shifted from traditional mainline churches to more Charismatic and Evangelical churches. Toronto is home to 28 Orthodox churches. Chinese churches are growing in size and number in Vancouver, swelled by large numbers of Chinese immigrants. Vibrant African churches in Manhattan are focused on justice issues and community service. Forty per cent of the Catholics in the USA are Hispanic. In addition, Latino Protestants form one of the fastest-growing sectors of American Evangelicalism. A conservative Catholicism holds its ground in Saint Pierre and Miquelon, while many in Greenland maintain their Lutheran identity. The diversity of churches in different parts of the region is part of the antidote to some of the historical and current challenges facing the region. In this sense, this volume (and the whole series) points to sources of renewal for Christianity.

Questions of Justice

The USA and Canada were built by dispossessing the Indigenous peoples, often violently. Many Native Americans were either murdered or killed by diseases brought by white European settlers. As a result, 98% of the population was wiped out and their stories were lost with them. This was an intentional action arising from the Doctrine of Discovery, promulgated by Pope Alexander VI on 4 May 1493 to provide justification for the Spanish to conquer the New World. The Doctrine of Discovery ensured Spanish rights to the lands discovered by Columbus in 1492. It provided a spiritual, political and legal justification for colonisation and seizure of land not inhabited by Christians. It gave a framework for Christian explorers to claim land in territories uninhabited by Christians. If a land did not have a Christian occupant, it was defined as 'discovered' and was claimed. This Doctrine led to the genocide of Native Americans. Today, North American Christians are reckoning with this very dark history and considering what will be needed to achieve reconciliation.

In addition, the USA imported enslaved peoples, mostly from Africa, and built its prosperity on their labour. Even as the white settlers professed their Christian faith and tried to convert Native Americans, they enslaved Africans as if it were quite acceptable and even scripturally sound. The prevailing racism and oppression were ignored. It was, rather, accepted as the norm, as if divinely ordained. The complicity of Christianity in this racism and enslavement of Africans is another painful reality that is brought into sharp focus in this book.

Not all American Christians, however, are prepared to recognise and acknowledge the wrongs of the past. Today, there is a rise of Christian nationalism, which has been influential in American politics, culture and church. Christian nationalism is the understanding that America is defined by Christianity and the government should take steps to keep it that way. Christian nationalists assert that America is and must remain a 'Christian nation' not merely as an observation about American history, but as a prescriptive programme for what America must continue to be in the future. As a result, Christianity should enjoy a privileged position in the public arena. A problem with Christian nationalism is its definition of who is and who is not part of the nation. In the past, it also used Christianity as a prop to support enslavement and segregation. Christian nationalism is a political ideology focused on the national identity of the USA as understood from an exclusively white perspective.

The dispersing of Christianity in Canada had negative consequences upon First Nations in many different ways. The people of the First Nations were colonised by white Europeans and their children were placed in residential schools from 1894 to 1947 with a goal of 'civilising' and assimilating them into Euro-Canadian Christian culture. The Christian influence on the residential school system isolated Indigenous children from their own culture and religion. The residential schools were supported and funded by the Canadian government's Department of Indian Affairs, and Christian teachers taught at these schools. The residential schools had negative effects on First Nations children as they separated them from family and loved ones, and they lost their own Indigenous culture, which was of great importance for their well-being and growth. The consequences of placing First Nations children into these schools are still felt today, as stories of abuse, isolation and death of these children are emerging. The

Canadian government and some churches that participated in organising and running these residential schools have publicly acknowledged their sorrow and have asked for forgiveness. However, much more needs to be done for reconciliation to occur.

The Preamble to the Canadian Charter of Rights and Freedoms refers to the supremacy of God, and the national anthem also refers to God, but Canada is becoming less and less a religious country. Presently, Canada is a religiously plural society with no official church or religion. The Canadian government's official ties to religion, specifically Christianity, are becoming scant and less relevant. This is in stark contrast to the USA, where politicians are desired to be Christians who publicly profess their faith in their campaigns and work as elected officials. In Canada, religion is becoming less relevant in politics, culture and society.

A haunting question in this volume is how to explain the prevailing racism and oppression in relation to the Christian faith that has been professed by the majority of the population in the USA. There can be no excuse for the sinful racist and xenophobic past and present situation in North America. This book highlights the need for the Christian church to reckon with its past and its present context of racism, oppression and xenophobia. The issue of racism has deeply affected church life and ministry. For African Americans, it led to enslavement, segregation and oppression. It still affects African Americans today – economically, socially and politically. Dr Martin Luther King Jr made the startling statement that eleven o'clock on a Sunday morning is the most segregated hour in America. In many ways, this is still the case as people of colour often do not feel comfortable in white churches and hence attend their own ethnic churches. As a result, Sunday mornings continue to be a segregated time in the USA. Therefore, some churches are trying to become more intentional in their practice of intercultural ministry. Racism has been a large problem in American history, as demonstrated by the genocide of Native Americans, enslavement of Africans, Asian indentured workers and the crisis along the US–Mexico border. Hence it is a recurrent theme in this book.

A Polarising Moment

It appears that this volume has been compiled at a polarised moment in North America, when some Christians are gravitating towards white supremacy while others are doing exactly the opposite. There has been an uprising of conservative Christians and white nationalism. The 6 January 2021 attempted insurrection in Washington, DC, is an example of the power of white nationalism advocated by those who seek to develop and maintain a white racial and national identity. Many white nationalists embrace various Christian denominational backgrounds. On the other hand, as this book will demonstrate, many Christians in North America strongly oppose white nationalism and imagine the future of church and nation very differently.

Another divisive issue among North American Christians concerns the understanding of gender and sexuality. Some wish to defend the patriarchal approach with which Christianity has traditionally been identified, while others offer a fundamental challenge to a patriarchal and sexist understanding of Christian doctrines. A particularly sensitive point has been gender-based violence. Through the courage of some of the victims it has been revealed that male leaders, priests and clergy have engaged in sexual violence and assault against women and children. The #metoo movement, which has extended to the #churchtoo movement, has brought it home to many Christians that sexual violence happens in the church and many of the perpetrators are male leaders, ministers and priests. As the Christian community reckons with this very disturbing reality, work is being done to reimagine Christian doctrines that have been understood in ways that undermine women or perpetuate the subordination of or violence towards women. Such imagination kindles a vision of a church that is marked by gender equality and safety for all.

Conclusion

Studying the region's Christianity provides many clues that help us to understand North American history, culture and identity. This volume therefore has much to offer to anyone seeking insights into the social dynamics shaping North America as a whole. Furthermore, North America is an important region for the study of World Christianity. The two major countries, Canada and the USA, have a big impact around the globe in terms of economy, politics, climate change and religion. Therefore, it is important for North Americans as well as the rest of the world to study carefully how Christianity is developing in the region. As the cultural and political situation changes in North America, so does its Christianity. Finally, the comprehensive portrayal of North American Christianity offered by this volume deserves study for its own sake. The following pages reveal that it is a dynamic movement. Intersecting with such salient issues as immigration, refugees, climate crisis and global health issues, it is apparent that Christianity in North America is in a period of rapid change and transformation. This volume is one attempt to interpret this dynamic change, which is likely to be a significant force in shaping our common future.

Bibliography

De La Torre, Miguel, *Burying White Privilege: Resurrecting a Badass Christianity* (Grand Rapids, MI: Eerdmans, 2018).

Gates, Henry Louis Jr, *The Black Church: This Is Our Story, This Is Our Song* (New York: Penguin Press, 2021).

Jones, Robert P., *The End of White Christian America* (New York: Simon & Schuster, 2016).

Kim, Grace Ji-Sun, *Invisible: Theology and Experience of Asian American Women* (Minneapolis, MN: Fortress Press, 2021).

Reuther, Rosemary Radford, *Sexism and God-Talk: Toward a Feminist Theology* (Boston, MA: Beacon Press, 1993).

Countries

First Nations Canada

Terry Leblanc

The Indigenous church in Canada covers a broad cross-section of geography, demographics and cultural beliefs. Moreover, it came into existence in different time periods, under varying colonial experiences, covering a wide variety of personal and ecclesial traditions. It also engages, perhaps most significantly, a broad range of Christian mission experience, including some good, some clearly bad and a significant amount that was outright ugly.

When I began this essay, I set out to describe the contemporary Indigenous church *in situ*, connected with the wider Christian church in Canada. After all, each of the denominations that find representation among the mainstream populations of Canada, particularly people of European origin, are also to be found among Indigenous peoples throughout Canada. I had imagined that if any mainstream denominations are not present among Canada's Indigenous populations, they have either not made a wide impact or they are so obscure as not to be readily found.

In the intervening months, however, events in Canada required, in fact demanded, that such an essay be revisited and rewritten to ensure that readers were provided with at least a glimpse of the historical context out of which the Indigenous church rose and in which the contemporary Indigenous church finds its existence. This essay, then, is the outcome of new and significant personal, extended family and community reflection. It is written not as an indictment but rather in the clear hope that what once was considered to be Indigenous Christianity is no longer, and hopefully never will be again – that the Indigenous church will not permit it to be so.

I have chosen to focus on denominational traditions that find a reasonably strong representation in the Indigenous Canadian landscape despite the history, and for some as a result of engaging the history in 'redemptive' ways. In some cases, this presence has been made strong by the increased presence of Indigenous leadership; in others, it is a result of risk-taking on the part of non-Indigenous denominational leadership; in still others, a renewed presence has come about because of a cooperative approach by Indigenous and non-Indigenous peoples to addressing the impacts of colonisation. This is not to say that other traditions and/or smaller representations of Christian faith and life are not to be found, or that they do not have Indigenous participation, even leadership, but, rather, that the ones described herein effectively capture the broad landscape of Indigenous Christianity in Canada.

A Necessary Retrospective

Historic mission had done a very good job initially of dividing what became the Canadian nation-state and its Indigenous peoples into neatly packaged groups to be missioned by one or another of the large denominational traditions. An examination of these endeavours appears to indicate 'equity' of opportunity and a guarantee that a particular version of Christianity would prevail in the land as the key motivators for what ultimately became a 'divide and conquer' strategy. Unfortunately, this approach frequently meant that Indigenous socio-cultural groups ended up being divided across artificial boundaries, either for ease of mission or to ensure comity. A concomitant, albeit 'unintended', impact often was that family, extended family and clan members were separated from one another by becoming either Francophone or Anglophone and, in the case of the two largest initial missions, being made either Catholic or Anglican.

In other cases, denominational missional divisions occurred in concert with the development of artificial nation-state boundaries established by colonial processes that demarcated one geographical territory from another. It was not uncommon to find an extended family divided in two or even more denominational traditions. Of course, the reader can imagine the potential, never mind real, conflicts that this would create among an otherwise highly communal, relational and ceremonial people whose identities, as Cree theologian Ray Aldred would note, were narrated, communal identities, inclusive of land.

We might have imagined Christian mission to have changed course following the Edinburgh 1910 mission conference. But that would not

Christianity in Canada, 1970 and 2020

Tradition	1970 Population	%	2020 Population	%	Average annual growth rate (%), 1970–2020
Christians	20,185,000	94.4%	23,952,000	63.5%	0.3%
Anglicans	1,177,000	5.5%	570,000	1.5%	-1.4%
Independents	761,000	3.6%	1,305,000	3.5%	1.1%
Orthodox	561,000	2.6%	1,220,000	3.2%	1.6%
Protestants	4,133,000	19.3%	2,900,000	7.7%	-0.7%
Catholics	9,066,000	42.4%	14,100,000	37.4%	0.9%
Evangelicals	2,566,000	12.0%	2,085,000	5.5%	-0.4%
Pentecostals/Charismatics	709,000	3.3%	2,750,000	7.3%	2.7%
Total population	**21,374,000**	**100.0%**	**37,742,000**	**100.0%**	**1.1%**

Source: Todd M. Johnson and Gina A. Zurlo (eds), *World Christian Database* (Leiden/Boston: Brill), accessed January 2022.

be at all accurate. Following the Edinburgh centenary, in their response entitled 'A Majority Report', the Indigenous and global Southern participants noted the following:

> An examination of the policies and practices that emerged from or were otherwise sanctioned by the 1910 gathering – either directly or, through inaction, indirectly – would show that the intent of missionary efforts from that point forward was an intensification of the on-going process of Christianizing and civilizing those of us in the global southern and Indigenous communities. The inescapable reality had this been completely successful is that we would have become 'Europeanized' and therefore completely comfortable in a Euro-centric setting. Our cultures and languages would have been absorbed into the body politic of the church and its surrounding society – at best tactically assimilated, becoming 'window dressing' to the historic and more 'authentic' culture(s) of the church; at worst our uniquenesses in the Creator's economy would have been eradicated entirely. Sadly, for some of the peoples we represent, the latter became their current reality. (Terry LeBlanc and Mark MacDonald, 'Statement by Indigenous Participants: Edinburgh 2010 – A Majority Report', in Kirsteen Kim and Andrew Anderson (eds), *Edinburgh 2010: Mission Today and Tomorrow*, Oxford: Regnum Books, 2011, p. 347)

It is all but inevitable, then, considering the philosophies of the times, that the missional duo of 'civilise' and 'Christianise' undergirded Christian mission almost entirely in Canada as it did elsewhere and was, for the most part, the driver of mission irrespective of the denominational or missional tradition. Indigenous people were prime targets since they were not in possession of a great deal of material wealth nor, it would seem, an appropriate social structure or spirituality.

Not unlike those in other global settings, colonial administrators in Canada believed Christianising and civilising went hand in hand. The plough and the Bible were considered mutually supportive. The notion of civilising took on a social and material betterment focus in many mission contexts as a result; that is to say, Christian mission and the development of Christianity among Indigenous peoples was significantly framed by the conversion of a people lacking material wealth and goods into those who had begun to acquire and then become dependent upon them. Mark Francis notes that this era relied solely on the most basic idea of 'civilisation' in the Victorian period – material culture.

Sadly, this was also the expectation Euro-Canadian missionaries held for Indigenous people in the church through the majority of the twentieth century and, in some cases, even today. We find it necessary still to differentiate between Christian traditions that have an authentically Indigenous cultural expression of faith and those that are more a mirror of the denominational tradition to which they belong. This wide array owes its existence to the protracted rejection of anything cultural within anything Christian – and the tradition did not matter. On more than one occasion over the past several decades, Indigenous people in ministry have reflected on the idea that, were you to be blindfolded on your entry to a service of worship, you would find no difference between an Indigenous church, irrespective of the tradition, and one that was mainstream Euro-Canadian.

It is easy, then, to understand why, with the release of the findings of the government of Canada's Truth and Reconciliation Commission in June 2015, Christian mission has finally and fully been confronted with its racist and assimilative attitudes, policies and practices. The implications for the church among Indigenous people in Canada are significant. Today, Christian traditions in Canada that are beginning to make a difference in the lives and communities of Indigenous people are those that have embraced the triple restorative mandates of right relationship with God and other spiritual powers, right relationship with one another in the human community and right relationship with and relatedness to the rest of creation, of which humanity is but a part. To put it in more classic theological jargon, these three areas, as deficiencies, describe the nature of sin and, as assets, their amelioration. For the follower of Jesus, this relationally restorative work is made possible only through the person, work, life, teaching, death, resurrection and ascension of Jesus Christ.

On the one hand, the legal and moral understanding of sin, handed down since Augustine, has not provided, and likely will not provide, a satisfactory framework for the theological expressions of the Indigenous church and Christianity. The results of this theology applied in mission to the Indigenous community are what the Indigenous church is, in fact, seeking to overcome. On the other hand, Christian traditions that are taking the above-noted spheres of relationship seriously in their engagement with Indigenous peoples appear to have better outcomes, whether the three are articulated precisely as I have done here or simply applied in their functional framework for ministries that are present within these churches.

Anglicanism

Perhaps one of the strongest Christian traditions in Canada at present, one that is thriving under Indigenous leadership, is the Anglican Council of Indigenous People (ACIP) under the auspices of its first national Indigenous archbishop, the Most Reverend Mark MacDonald, elevated to this position in 2019. The ACIP structure, created over time by Indigenous Anglicans and now facilitated by the archbishop, has become significantly framed by Indigenous ideologies, epistemologies, ontological frameworks, liturgical interpretations and missional applications.

The Anglican Church made its first appearance on the North American continent in 1578, when, as part of Martin Frobisher's Arctic expedition, an Anglican chaplain celebrated the Eucharist near present-day Iqaluit. However, it was not until the eighteenth century, as Anglicans spread across what is now called Canada, that the first Anglican missionary arrived, in 1752, among the Mi'kmaq. Seventy years later, in 1822, a Norway House Cree man, named Sakacewescam in his own language, was baptised with the English name Henry Budd. In 1850 and 1853, respectively, Budd was ordained deacon and priest, becoming the first ordained Indigenous Anglican. Although Budd worked with diligence among his own and other Indigenous people, realising significant fruit for his labours, the English missionaries who followed Budd when he left northern Manitoba for work among the Plains Cree in Saskatchewan and Manitoba complained of lack of evangelistic opportunity.

In the period of contemporary ministry with Indigenous peoples through the Anglican Church in Canada, what has become abundantly clear is that it has been its most fruitful and durable when undertaken by Indigenous peoples themselves. By 1993, when the then Primate of the Anglican Church, Michael Peers, delivered an apology for the church's complicity with residential schools, the Indigenous Anglican community-building was in full vigour.

Catholicism

The oldest organised church tradition among Indigenous people in Canada is Catholicism. Its original engagement with Indigenous peoples was with the Mi'kmaq of Atlantic Canada. While views differ about its birth in the early seventeenth century among the Mi'kmaq, a strong oral tradition exists that describes the first baptisms, by Abbé Jesse Fleché on 24 June 1610, as having a dual significance: allegiance to both Christ and France. Which one is to be understood as being of greater priority depends on who tells, and then interprets, the story. Like all church traditions engaging Indigenous people, it was birthed in a mixed experience of good and not-so-good.

For those Mi'kmaq who perceived it in a good way, Catholicism might have been viewed as being in continuity with their lifeways, spirituality and sovereignty. Mi'kmaw Saqamaw Membertou, for example, was purported to have linked his acceptance of baptism and faith in Christ to the Three Cross Vision. St Kateri was similarly known to have engaged in penitential practices drawn from Mohawk tradition alongside Catholic teachings and liturgies. These rich liturgical traditions – with bodily gestures, elaborate song traditions, long prayers and the use of incense and sacred language – were seen by many Indigenous people as being in continuity with Indigenous ceremony. The Catholic veneration of saints was also easily incorporated into the centuries-old tradition of Indigenous respect for and acknowledgement of the presence of ancestors.

Of note for Indigenous Catholicism are the annual pilgrimages in devotion to St Anne. In both Mi'kma'ki, the traditional homeland of the Mi'kmaw people, as well as Nakota and Cree territories in Alberta, St Anne, the mother of Mary, is believed to provide for healing and restoration. Adopted as patron saint of the Mi'kmaw people in 1628, just 18 years following the baptism of Membertou and his extended family of 21, St Anne is the principal focus of Mi'kmaw Catholic veneration on the last Sunday in July, set aside as St Anne's Day. Annually, as they have for hundreds of years, Mi'kmaq and other Catholics from across the Atlantic gather to pay homage to St Anne. Devotion to St Anne has continued throughout the centuries as a strong tradition particularly among Mi'kmaw women.

In Alberta, the first annual pilgrimage to Lake St Anne was held in 1889 on the shores of the lake, then known as Wakamne (God's Lake) by the Nakota Sioux nation dwelling on the west end and as Manito Sahkahigan (Spirit Lake) by the Cree living at the opposite end of the lake. Both the Nakota and the Cree had held the lake to be holy for many hundreds of years prior to its being 'renamed' Lac Ste Anne in the nineteenth century by a Catholic priest who had established a mission there. Many thousands journey to the lake each year seeking healing, visions, fellowship and spiritual restoration.

Even the best situations of Catholic ministry, however, continue to have Eurocentric and colonially framed complications. Many non-Indigenous church leaders will not accept the full sovereignty of Indigenous peoples. Adherence to European theology and church structures often still works against the development of Indigenous clergy and a fully contextualised faith and church. In addition, the individualistic, other-worldly tendencies of European Catholicism support Catholic social and cultural teachings that frequently fly in the face of Indigenous ways of knowing and being.

A major incursion of Catholicism that devastated Indigenous peoples, even as they expressed varying degrees of faith and dedication to Christian teachings, one which is only now beginning to be resolved, was the Catholic Church's participation in the 'Indian' residential school system. As a denomination, the Catholic Church ran the most schools over the widest geographical area. The uncovering of 215 unmarked graves at the largest Catholic school, Kamloops, in 2021 brought global attention to the unresolved legacy of the residential school era. While some suggest that positive exceptions exist, the residential school system nonetheless imposed an external, colonising faith that worked against the more integral faith many think of when considering Membertou and St Kateri.

Like all church traditions, Indigenous Catholicism is not static. Many questions remain about the nature of leadership and the relationship to a complicated but often vibrant past. Yet Indigenous Catholics continue to lead in charting their own way, drawing on the examples of those who went before them. In the case of St Kateri, for example, when told that she and her Mohawk sisters in Christ could not form a religious order, love of Christ led them to do so anyway.

The United Church
When the United Church of Canada (UCC) was formed in 1925, any mention of the Indigenous peoples and/or churches was absent from the founding documents, the Articles of the Basis of Union. This oversight, a result of colonial blindness, was corrected at the UCC's General Council 42 in Ottawa in 2012. Mention of the Indigenous churches was added to the document; the UCC crest was changed to include the four colours of the Indigenous medicine wheel; and the Mohawk phrase 'Akwe Nia'Tetewá:neren', meaning 'all my relations', was added. However, we need to be clear that since the United Church was an amalgam of Presbyterian, Methodist and Congregationalist denominations then in existence, this absence of mention extends much further back.

Beginning in 1965, Indigenous church leaders of the UCC recognised the harm some non-Indigenous clergy brought to their communities and decided to train their own people for ministry. Elders chose ministry candidates and evolved a system of training that included learning circles in centrally based training centres with on-the-job learning during church placements in Indigenous communities. The training needs for the 60 or more Indigenous communities of faith that currently exist are now served by the Sandy-Saulteaux Spiritual Centre (SSSC) in Beausejour, Manitoba, directed by Adrian Jacobs, a Cayuga clergyperson. Indigenous candidates are prepared at the SSSC for ordination, commissioning as diaconal ministers and recognition as designated lay leaders in the UCC.

In 1986, the UCC was the first church to apologise for its colonial Christianisation of Indigenous people through policies then in force that structured its historical approach to mission. In 1998, it also apologised for the policy of assimilation enacted by and through the UCC at the Indian residential schools it operated. The response of some within the Indigenous community of faith to these apologies was telling, receiving the apology while at the same time not necessarily accepting it. After 35 years of effort to 'live into' the apologies, the work continues.

Indigenous ministries within the UCC have met regularly over many decades and held deep and ongoing conversations about matters relating to the Indigenous work and their relationship with the broader UCC. This work has been evolving, struggling, adapting, growing and even losing ground at times. Indigenous elders, churches, presbyteries, conferences, circles, ministry training schools and now a national Indigenous region have carried on this important work of decolonisation and indigenisation. The Indigenous UCC includes 71 communities of faith, from the West Coast of British Columbia to Montreal, Quebec; regional bodies include BC Native Ministries and the Native Ministries of Ontario and Quebec, with the National Indigenous Council as the court of Indigenous governance. UCC Indigenous bodies employ staff across Canada, including at the SSSC, serving as the national Indigenous ministry training school. The Indigenous Studies programme at Vancouver School of Theology provides a Master of Divinity degree by extension.

This story of resistance to colonialism and renewal of Indigenous identity, with the locus of control recentring Indigenous communities, has taken place gradually over the decades, a colonial denomination blind to its own ethnocentrism coming to an awareness of its complicity with the colonial project. Today, active ministries can be found in scores of small Indigenous communities and in many urban centres. While these ministries do not always present as a classically described church body, pastoral care and sacramental ministry are nonetheless provided, as are culturally framed opportunities for worship.

Historically the largest Protestant mainline denomination, the UCC has often been viewed with suspicion and scepticism by other traditions of the Protestant faith, which perceived what it was doing to engage Indigenous peoples to be theologically liberal and religiously syncretistic. However, in several significant ways the UCC, in its Indigenous expression, has provided a role model and working example of how to re-engage culture alongside an authentic Christian faith.

Christian and Missionary Alliance

The formational development of the Christian and Missionary Alliance (CMA) clearly owes as much to Canadian personnel as to those from the USA, but, as with many such things, US governance took precedence, and the Canadian entity fell under its jurisdiction until the third quarter of the twentieth century. According to a timeline published by CMA's Ambrose University, it was not until 1972, when a Canadian federal charter was issued, and 1980, when its first general assembly was held, that the Canadian church gained autonomy from its US counterpart.

As can be seen by its approach to Indigenous ministry in Canada, even following the formation of the Canadian entity, US-framed missiology clearly influenced the approach to Indigenous ministry. Attitudes towards culture and faith quite obviously rooted in the more conservative values and practices of the US church impacted mission and ministry. Generally much more conservative and rigid, these attitudes and understandings prevailed for a lengthy period south and north of the Forty-Ninth Parallel. As the name suggests, the CMA's missionary focus was front and centre of its founding philosophy and continued existence through the twentieth century, and very much still is. Not surprisingly, however, mission to Indigenous peoples in Canada receives no mention in the founding timeline noted above.

Among Indigenous peoples, the work of the CMA has been undertaken primarily by a small gathering of Indigenous women and men seeking to give the church an Indigenous flavour. The First Nations Alliance Churches of Canada came into existence to gather in small assemblies – some on reserves, some in urban settings – under a common umbrella for fellowship, support, training and common evangelism. With churches in Edmonton, Regina, Winnipeg and elsewhere, it has an urban presence.

Pentecostal Assemblies of Canada
Perhaps the most widespread non-Catholic, non-mainline, ministry among Indigenous peoples in Canada is the work of the Pentecostal Assemblies of Canada (PAOC). Across two districts, the PAOC Indigenous work consists of a significant number of on-reserve congregations and fewer than a dozen urban congregations. Most of them have been in existence for several decades and most are in Central and Western Canada, as well as in the more northerly regions of the country. In describing the obstacles they have encountered to an authentic experience of Christian faith in the lives of Indigenous peoples, the PAOC notes the conflict with mainline Canadian values, as well as social issues such as suicide, substance abuse, past hurts and hopelessness. Nowhere in this description is one left with any sense in which the church in its broadest compass might own significant responsibility for the foundations of these social ills, if not their current expression.

Evangelism and discipleship are at the forefront of three critical priorities: leadership training, development of emerging leaders and church planting. These three, in turn, are predicated on the three values of culturally relevant evangelism, internal and external reconciliation, and the networking of resources through strong Indigenous leadership. While some churches, such as the Vancouver native Pentecostal church, have had a strong presence for many decades and have sought to engage the culture and faith conversation in legitimate ways, and while new young leaders are emerging who engage the culture and faith conversation very differently from their predecessors, much work remains to be done. As of this writing, no advertisements for positions with the Indigenous church can be found on the main PAOC website, and only a few in mission are described as being focused on Indigenous people, though Indigenous peoples are described as a priority for the PAOC's Mission Canada.

Baptists

While Baptists have a small Indigenous presence, most Indigenous people aligned with the various Baptist traditions in Canada attend churches that are not specifically Indigenous. Indigenous people are associated with various Baptists engaged in evangelism and other kinds of ministries, but Baptist congregations are scarce. Where such congregations do exist, they tend to be small gatherings of family members who hold to Baptist forms and theology rather than being directly associated with a formal Baptist tradition. Such gatherings are often in communities that are small and more isolated, often served by missionaries associated with US-based Baptist traditions. What does appear to be clear is that many of the more conservative mission organisations functioning in Canada, some for nearly a century, are aligned with Baptist theology, particularly as it pertains to mission and evangelism. Danny Zacharias, Cree New Testament scholar at Acadia, the Divinity College of the Canadian Baptists of Atlantic Canada (CBAC), notes that he is not familiar with any specific Indigenous Baptist congregations in Atlantic Canada.

Near the end of the first decade of the current century, several non-Indigenous Baptist ministers, out of concern for the tragic history of the church in Canada, began to reach out to Indigenous people, hosting small conferences, mostly in the southern Ontario region. These were helpful as a means of educating non-Indigenous Baptists and allowing for Indigenous people disposed to a Baptist theology and ecclesiology to gather for celebration, worship and learning. As far as research for this essay has determined, this has not led to any new congregations that are specifically Indigenous, though it appears to have strengthened Indigenous participation in Baptist churches in general. Unfortunately, evangelism may still be considered by some to be a civilising enterprise. Certain ministries in some of the more northerly areas of Canada, for example, until recently preached a gospel condemning Indigenous cultures as evil – and might still do so, albeit less obviously.

Presbyterian National Indigenous Ministry Council

According to former moderator, Peter Bush, two significant moments occurred in the life of the Presbyterian church and its Indigenous membership in Canada. The first was in 1908, when, during a gathering of Presbyterians who had been working with Indigenous people in both the residential school and the on-reserve contexts, Indigenous and non-Indigenous voices appeared to carry equal weight as discussions about Indigenous ministry were held. He notes, however, that the Edinburgh conference of 1910 and its dual mandates of 'Christianise and civilise' 'wiped out what was a promising move in the right direction'.

The second 'moment' lasted for about a decade, beginning in the late 1950s, with an on-reserve missionary contingent initiating a conversation about the direction and purpose of mission with Indigenous people. The focus was on the inculturation of the gospel – as challenging a topic then as it would be for decades to follow. Feeding this discussion was the fact that the federal government of Canada had begun steps to control residential schools, taking them out of the hands of the church with increasing frequency.

Bush also notes that Presbyterians, not unlike other denominations, used ministries in the context of Indigenous reserves, as well as Indigenous urban ministry settings, as a training ground to prepare people for other kinds of ministry. While this might have had the benefit of providing service to the reserve-based churches, once the supply of candidates dried up, reserve churches frequently found themselves closing, leaving Indigenous peoples who had been converted to Presbyterian Christianity to fend for themselves.

Some in the Presbyterian fold have described the current Presbyterian Indigenous reality as a 'worshipping handful' or a 'remnant of faithful', several of which are urban, one of which is a rural congregation and another of which is located on the Mistawascis reserve. Stewart Folster and other Indigenous people, such as Mary Fontaine, have worked to create a contextual approach to faith and life in urban settings. Folster oversees the Native Ministry Circle in Saskatoon and Mary Fontaine leads Hummingbird Ministries in Vancouver. Each of them cares for the range of ceremonies and sacraments of Christian faith, but all is engaged through the lenses of Indigenous cultural ways. Ministry in more rural settings exists in several expressions, such as the work of John and Shannon Wyminga in northern British Columbia.

Mennonites

While their embrace of cultural expressions of faith was not a great deal different from that in other traditions in the early years of their ministries, Mennonites, perhaps in keeping with their often more sedate approach to life in general, tended to engage anti-cultural theology and ministry, when it existed, with a less aggressive posture. The approach seems to have had an impact in some settings more than others, though it was not uncommon to find Indigenous women in northern reserve communities influenced by more conservative Mennonite mission traditions to wear ankle-length dresses, shawls and head coverings long after the mission had ended and the missionaries were gone.

As with other small Evangelical denominations in Canada, Mennonites, irrespective of the specific Mennonite tradition, tend to have initially engaged in mission among Indigenous peoples in smaller northern communities. Today, however, they reflect a variety of urban, rural and some on-reserve ministries and congregations. Of note in on-reserve congregations are the Evangelical Mennonite Church-affiliated Reserve Fellowship Chapel on the Sioux Valley reserve in Manitoba, the Pelly Fellowship Chapel on the Cote Reserve in Saskatchewan and the work at Birch River, Manitoba, using a Bible camp approach.

Mennonite Brethren (MB) mission work has been focused on evangelism, with the early expectation that converts participate in existing Mennonite congregations. This was subsequently supplemented with a wide array of evangelistic efforts and ministries, both urban and rural, making effort to train Indigenous leaders for credentialling, ostensibly either to plant or to lead existing congregations or ministries. Most of the current MB and affiliated work that has a significant proportion of Indigenous people is led by non-Indigenous missionaries or pastors.

The Mennonite Church Canada (MCC), not to be confused with the Mennonite Central Committee, has four Indigenous or at least mainly Indigenous congregations or gatherings in various stages of growth or decline, with one having dissolved its legal standing in late 2020. In urban settings, para-church ministries like Inner City Youth Alive and Healing Hearts Ministry are tied to Mennonite denominations – if not by direct denominational affiliation and oversight, then through a significant degree of funding and staffing. As with some other Christian traditions, numbers of Indigenous peoples who are members or affiliates of these churches are small and generally either static or in decline.

The Salvation Army
The Indigenous presence of the Salvation Army (TSA) varies across the country, depending on the geography. Northern British Columbia has the strongest contemporary representation. There, the history of the TSA's beginnings in these areas is different and hence the stronger representation. For example, in one village, a local Indigenous leader encountered TSA in the south (Vancouver area) and began work in their own village, so that when TSA officially went to begin ministry there, they were a bit surprised to find it growing and flourishing already. For many years, however, it was undertaken with more of an assimilationist perspective, so the people had to 'give up' their feasts and cultural expressions (as in many other places), although this began to change quite some time ago.

People will now participate in feasts and are beginning to integrate cultural practices a little more. For example, one Indigenous leader, Damian, will translate songs into Nisga'a because he sees the language as foundational to any other cultural expressions. TSA does have some local Indigenous leaders within the communities where it has a ministry presence, but numbers are still small. In other places, some non-Indigenous ministry leaders still have a 'ministry to' perspective while others are a little more open to cultural expressions. The latter, however, do not want to push their congregations/people but rather want the people themselves to come to this place on their own.

In 2017, together with Indigenous Pathways, a wholly Indigenous-led Christian non-governmental organisation, TSA struck out on a new trail for its ministry with Indigenous people, called Celebration of Culture. Now in its fifth year, the event unfolded after a year of planning. Indigenous and non-Indigenous peoples come together in a camp setting for a two-and-a-half day cultural learning event and powwow. The Celebration of Culture has been pivotal in increasing awareness among non-Indigenous leaders, but it has also been a huge encouragement to Indigenous peoples to embrace their identity and bring their gifts into their local and national contexts of Christian faith.

The Christian Reformed Church (Canada)
Unlike some of the larger mainline denominations, the Christian Reformed Church (CRC) has no Indigenous churches on reserve as they might be traditionally understood. The CRC presence among Indigenous people in Canada consists instead of a spotty representation of various Indigenous peoples, who initially became involved because they were part of the 1960s 'scoop' generation and were adopted by or married into a Christian Reformed family. According to CRC sources, a best guesstimate of the presence of Indigenous people in the CRC proper is only around 100 persons by adoption and a smaller number through intermarriage.

At the present time in Canada, the CRC operates three urban ministries to Indigenous people, two of which are Indigenous led. These Urban Indigenous Ministries (UIMs) are in Winnipeg, Regina and Edmonton. They were set up starting in 1973 as working and worshipping communities. The founding aspirations for these outreach ministries were that they would be Indigenous-led, self-governing and self-sustaining. Even today, these founding aspirations are not fully realised, though all have majority Indigenous staff and all are self-governing.

Sources within the CRC are clear that a decision appears to have been made to avoid the mission approach that the CRC had used in the Southwest USA among Navajo and Zuni communities. In the opinion of these sources, such an approach shared similarities in philosophy and methodology with mainline church missions to Indigenous communities in Canada, such as the use of residential schools. As a result, the UIMs in Canada appear strong and exhibit good leadership, providing excellent community-based ministry, community development initiatives and community-based pastoral care. They also provide strong cultural programmes and contextualised worship and prayer practices, employing the expertise and knowledge base of traditional Indigenous elders and community leadership.

Non-denominational groups
Non-denominational Christian gatherings and traditions of the church are often small, sometimes consisting only of family members, and are generally of two dispositions: Charismatic, including fringe groups such as the apostolic and prophetic manifestations of Christianity; or Baptistic, yet with a 'remnant' theological disposition expressed in an 'occupy until He comes' attitude. It is not at all surprising that members of each of these groups have been heavily influenced by US-centred populist theological and political teachings and attitudes. Many of the iconic figures of American populist, nationalist Christianity figure prominently in the highly esteemed teachers of such groups. These are as often as not movements and conference-focused gatherings, since few, if any, congregations meeting with regularity in any form or style reminiscent of the other expressions of Indigenous Christianity appear to be evident.

Where That Leaves Us
In all, there continue to be critical markers of the present state of Christianity and its varied expressions among Canada's Indigenous people, as well as requirements for its future existence. First, to the degree that it has been extricated from the confines of Western church traditions and structures, including modes of governance and worship, irrespective of the ecclesial tradition, Christianity among Canada's Indigenous people has had a better chance of continuity and longevity. Second, to the extent that Eurocentric theology, mission and biblical interpretation have been able to be circumvented, set aside or decolonised, an Indigenous expression of Christian faith and life has had a fighting chance to emerge and flourish. Finally, the degree to which Eurocentric ideals of faith and life continue to dictate the 'acceptable parameters' within which a genuine Indigenous Christian faith can emerge and grow is not to be underestimated. Being authentically Indigenous and authentically Christian is still a fight for many, if not most, Indigenous people.

Bibliography

Anderson, William H. U. and Charles Muskego (eds), *Indigenous People and the Christian Faith: A New Way Forward* (Wilmington, DE: Vernon Press, 2019).

Dickason, Olive Patricia and William Newbigging, *Indigenous Peoples within Canada: A Concise History*, 4th edition (Don Mills, ON: Oxford University Press, 2018).

Peterson, Wendy L., 'A Gifting of Sweetgrass: The Reclamation of Culture Movement and NAIITS: An Indigenous Learning Community', PhD thesis, Asbury Theological Seminary, 2018.

Twiss, Richard, *One Church, Many Tribes* (Ventura, CA: Regal Books, 2000).

Woodley, Randy, *Shalom and the Community of Creation: An Indigenous Vision* (Grand Rapids, MI: Eerdmans, 2012).

Anglophone Canada

John G. Stackhouse, Jr

'Canada emerged late from the Victorian period', declared historian John Webster Grant about the 1960s. 'And how!' we might say, six decades later. From the time of Confederation in 1867, Canada was among the world's most observant Christian countries, whose national motto ('From Sea to Sea') came from the Bible and implied God's dominion over the land (Psalm 72: 8), and whose day-to-day life was shaped in large part by the Christian church year. Within a few decades of Canada's centennial celebration in 1967, it was fast becoming one of the most secular countries in the world.

Canada indeed emerged late from a millennium and more of European Christendom: the official – or all-but-official – sanctioning of Christianity as the religion of the state, nation and society. Michael Gauvreau has termed the era beginning around Confederation and lasting until the 1960s Canada's 'evangelical century', and the cultural dominance of Roman Catholicism in Francophone Canada paralleled the influence of observant Protestantism in the rest of the country. Over the course of the first half of the nineteenth century, Canada went from being a country of colonists and native peoples who rarely, if ever, attended church to a country with one of the highest rates of regular churchgoing in the West. From the 1860s to the 1960s, two-thirds or more of Canadians attended church weekly, and the 1961 census recorded 96% of Canadians calling themselves Christians.

The largest religious bloc of Canadians, then and now, has been Roman Catholics: in Quebec overwhelmingly so, although in Anglophone Canada Catholic churches have maintained the nominal allegiance of about a third of the population. The Orthodox churches have made up 3–4% of the population. The Protestant sector used to take up the rest.

Canadian Protestantism has been constituted by two main groups: the four so-called mainline churches and then the congeries of groups known as Evangelicals. The two largest denominations have been the Anglican Church of Canada and the United Church of Canada (the latter formed in 1925 from an ecumenical combination of most Methodists, all the Congregationalists and roughly two-thirds of the Presbyterians). The remaining churches with a 'state church' heritage were the Presbyterians and Lutherans. In the 1960s, these churches together could claim a quarter or more of the national population. Most of the rest of the Protestant population have been Evangelicals (including Pentecostals and Charismatics, who generally identify with Evangelicalism in Canada), in the 1960s constituting perhaps as much as 15% of the country.

Since that time, however, Canadians have raced the Dutch – and, not coincidentally, the very similar populations of Australia and New Zealand – for the steepest secularisation since the French Revolution. By 2011, only two-thirds of the population even claimed to be Christian. In 1946, 6 out of 10 Anglophone Canadians attended church weekly (very high levels of attendance among Catholics in Quebec pulled up the national average to 2 in 3). By 2020, that ratio had levelled off at a little more than 2 out of 10, with a sharp rise in the number of young Canadians who never attended (from 30% in the mid-1980s to almost half two decades later). This pattern, moreover, held right across the country, with lower spots in Quebec and British Columbia but even the so-called Bible belts of the Prairie and Atlantic provinces not recording significantly higher figures. Again, these numbers looked very much like those in Australia and New Zealand, and they closely matched the lowest areas of church attendance in the USA: New England and the Pacific Northwest.

In general, therefore, Christianity has declined greatly in Canada, both in broad cultural influence and in the hold it has on the population's religious loyalty. Meanwhile, Canadians have manifested a new openness to the alternative religions brought by increasing numbers of immigrants with non-Christian backgrounds. And the religious 'nones' rose from barely noticeable in the 1960s to fully a quarter of the population by 2020, many of whom describe themselves as 'spiritual but not religious'. What happened? In short, the Baby Boom happened – and with it, the 1960s.

Post-war Promises Meet 1960s Disaffiliation

It seems impossible to believe nowadays, but not that long ago Canadian churches were struggling to keep up with their surging popularity. Catholic and Protestant churches alike saw post-war attendance come in like a tide, and when the little ones conceived in the reunion of military families and the stabilisation of national life started to appear, Christians realised they needed to adapt quickly.

Big building projects resulted, and churches became social centres for mothers and children, young people, women's and men's groups, and the elderly. Large additions were erected for classrooms, gymnasiums, kitchens and more in order to house not only burgeoning Sunday schools but also after-school kids' clubs, youth groups, Alcoholics Anonymous meetings, and Boy Scout and Girl Guide troops. Some denominations sponsored expansion in Christian schools from kindergarten through secondary education, whether with government support (especially in the case of Roman Catholics, as provided for in the national and several provincial constitutions) or without. As a welter of provincial universities were planned and planted, Christian denominations often sponsored constituent colleges on campus, offering dormitories, cafeterias, chapels, classrooms and faculty offices to assist the national project of higher education. And even as the Canadian state was expanding its social services, particularly into spheres (such as health-care and welfare) previously dominated by Christian organisations, the churches expanded their social services and other special-purpose groups still further, with support groups for single parents, service groups to various needy populations and fellowship groups for everyone from skateboarders to motorcyclists to hockey players.

The 1960s, however, brought a cultural revolution to the West. Churches felt it particularly in the liberalisation of divorce and in the sexual revolution facilitated by the pill. The new federal policies of bilingualism and biculturalism, which quickly metamorphosed into multiculturalism (in changes implemented between 1962 and 1976), opened up immigration quotas to non-European populations and brought the first significant numbers of non-Christians to Canada, as well as the beginning of an influx of non-European Christians. At the Montreal world's fair known as Expo '67, Canada welcomed the world to its new identity, even as churches sponsored not just one but two Christian pavilions.

These changes both shaped and strengthened the values of the baby boomers. The boomers (customarily characterised as those born between 1946 and the mid-1960s) emerged in a period of unprecedented stability, rapidly improving health-care and surging economic growth in North America. The boomers did what adolescents typically do: differentiate themselves from their parents. But they never outgrew that mode – because they never had to. Free of worries (war, depression or epidemics) that had forced previous generations to focus on a few sober priorities in times of scarcity and sacrifice, boomers were allowed to maintain an adolescent attitude as their permanent identity. Since Canada went on to enjoy a largely unbroken experience of peace, health and prosperity, the trends fostered by that cultural change have simply continued to the present day.

Those trends manifest a collection of themes that characterised the boomers and, because of their cultural dominance ever since, all of Canadian life: revulsion towards the conventions of their parents (which would have included allegiance to traditional Christianity); maximum individual liberty to pursue one's own life goals and, indeed, lifestyle; self-expression as an intrinsically virtuous act; and a consumerist attitude not only towards the burgeoning smorgasbord of goods and services but towards the rest of life as well, from employment to marriage. Aside from a few bumps in the road, such as the oil crisis of the 1970s, the dotcom crash of the late 1990s and the global economic crisis of 2008 – which Canadians rode out better than most because of their stable, conservative banks – Canadians since the 1960s have been able to push consistently forward with a progressive cultural agenda. And all poll data show that the generations subsequent to the boomers line up with them against the pre-boomers in marker after marker of cultural values, particularly of religious identity and observance.

Quiet Revolutions in Roman Catholicism

The story of how Quebec so rapidly, and mostly peacefully, abandoned its ultramontane Roman Catholic culture is detailed in the essay by André Brouillette that follows this one. Beyond Quebec, however, Catholicism in Anglophone Canada was undergoing a rapid and large-scale change as well. The Second Vatican Council (1962–5) offered global Catholicism a breath of fresh air – indeed, a strong wind of change – but Pope Paul VI subsequently made it clear that the most important things remained the same, including papal authority over every matter of human life. Guitars might now accompany hymns in a Mass offered in the vernacular. But with *Humanae Vitae* (1968) the Pope officially outlawed artificial birth control. At a stroke, millions of Catholics, including English-speaking Canadian Catholics, began to think of themselves as good Catholics – but that the Pope was wrong.

The decline of regard for papal authority expanded to a decline of clerical authority more broadly as sexual and financial scandals came into public view, none more notorious than the abuse of boys residing in the Mount Cashel Orphanage in St John's, Newfoundland, which closed in 1990 after a national uproar. In 2021, the Supreme Court of Canada refused to hear a final appeal by the Archdiocese of St John's to avoid liability in damage suits brought by victims from the 1950s and 1960s. So the Roman Catholic Church continued to pay for the sins of its workers in the midst of a continuing drop-off in church attendance – that reliable sociological proxy for religious seriousness – across the country. Outside Quebec, one in four Catholics no longer attended church at all, and the youngest adult group (15–24) had a church attendance rate of barely 11% in 2011.

The third revolution, however, came in the form of significant immigration. As Catholics of European descent were leaving by the back door, Filipinos led other immigrants in filling up the churches again through the front. By the 1990s, churches that had seemed on the brink of closing in some urban areas, and in Toronto especially, were adding services, and in the 2010s entire new churches were being built to accommodate the flood of interested newcomers. Indeed, some of Canada's largest congregations, at least in terms of parish rolls, were Roman Catholic (many had more than 1,500 families each), even though they did not typically show up on generic lists of large churches. Thus in the 2020s, the pattern of ebb and flow in Canadian Catholicism looks very different depending upon where you are in the country.

Quieter Revolution in Mainstream Protestantism

The baby boomers were the first Canadian generation in a century of which the majority did not go to church. Then, unlike previous generations, who generally reattached to the church once the first child came along, they largely did not send their children to church either. Canadian Christianity was in a decidedly new era.

Christianity was part of *l'ancien régime* for Anglophones, too. Going to a Christian church is what mom and dad did, and baby boomers determinedly refused to do whatever mom and dad did. The post-war attendance surge in Canadian Protestant churches turned out to be a form of cheerful social conformity in the interest of returning to a supposed 'normalcy' of stable middle-class life. The fact that the 1950s were the first decade in the history of the young country not marked by extremes of military engagement or economic stress meant that this 'normalcy' was largely an imaginary construct – but it was a compelling one.

What the post-war church attendance tide was not, however, was evidence of the genuine spiritual revival that had been sought by Canadian Christian leaders for decades. It proved to be hollow, even inflated. When the younger generation began to open the exits, the air went out of mainstream Protestantism at an increasing rate. The twin shadow establishment of the Anglican Church and the United Church of Canada, each of which had seen itself as custodian of and chaplain to English-speaking Canada, now shrank to the cultural margins. When once the mainline Protestant churches collectively could claim a quarter of the national population, they now claimed but 1 in 10. By the 2020s the main streams of Canadian Protestantism had been reduced to small creeks meandering through large and eroding beds, while the larger flows of Protestant churchgoers were Evangelical. As a sign of the times, both financial and theological, the United Church's flagship seminary, Emmanuel College at the University of Toronto, opened its doors to welcome an Islamic study centre in the early 2010s.

The Evangelicals Endure

By 'Evangelicals' in the accompanying table is meant the smaller, uniformly Evangelical groups (more than 100 such groups in Canada) led by the Baptists and the Pentecostals, even as there would have been many orthodox and observant believers also in the larger denominations. Evangelicals of both sorts established a small organisation in 1964 largely for the mutual encouragement of pastors: the Evangelical Fellowship of Canada (EFC). Some two decades later, in 1983, the EFC appointed a new, young executive director, Brian Stiller, to lead Evangelicals back into the public domain, just in time for Evangelicals to emerge as the new face of churchgoing Protestantism in Canada. The EFC was in the vanguard among Evangelical organisations of various stripes, particularly by representing Evangelical concerns to the federal and provincial governments and intervening in key cases before Canada's senior courts.

Evangelicals, including such disparate groups as the Mennonite Brethren, the Christian and Missionary Alliance, the Salvation Army and the Christian Reformed Church, quietly demurred from most of the progressive changes occurring in mainstream Canadian society. Notably, they supported alternative schools – from kindergartens to a handful of small universities (mostly undergraduate) and seminaries across the country. Christian clubs on public university campuses, furthermore, were almost entirely Evangelical, ranging from the doughty InterVarsity Christian Fellowship (started in Canada from Britain in the 1920s) and other transdenominational groups to denominational fellowships (notably the Pentecostal) to ethnic societies (especially among Chinese and Korean students), while mainstream denominational chaplaincies largely languished. This commitment signalled that Evangelicals grasped what other groups mostly did not: that retaining their youth was crucial to long-term viability, let alone vitality. Evangelicals invested heavily in the same kinds of building expansions evident in Catholic and mainstream Protestant edifices as well, adding multipurpose rooms, offices, classrooms and the like to their sanctuaries and Sunday school spaces. But they also invested in training Sunday school teachers, hiring full-time youth pastors, running summer camps, hosting kids' clubs and dominating popular Christian music so that contemporary Christian music basically *was* Evangelical by the 1980s. They thus outpaced all other groups in retaining a significant quota of youth as they passed into adulthood.

Evangelicals also increasingly found their public voice, particularly in the EFC but also in the Crossroads broadcasting group in Toronto (whose flagship television programme was *100 Huntley Street*, founded by Pentecostal pastor David Mainse in 1977), religious radio stations, and political and social ginger groups such as Citizens for Public Justice on the left and Focus on the Family on the right. Some secular journalists, looking at much bigger and more extreme developments in the USA, sounded the alarm that a new Religious Right now threatened the new post-Christian

Canada. But informed people recognised that Canadian Evangelicals were far milder and less focused on power politics than their US counterparts.

Canadian Evangelicals have in fact historically ranged across Canada's political parties. Some Evangelicals (notably in the Mennonite tradition) could be found on the progressive side of certain issues. Advocacy of same-sex marriage (passed by the Canadian parliament in 2005) temporarily drove many Evangelicals away from the Liberal and New Democratic parties into the arms of the Conservatives. And the later regime of Liberal Prime Minister Justin Trudeau did not help the situation, as he insisted on a strong pro-choice stance, support for physician-assisted suicide with little regard for conscientious objection, the legalisation of marijuana and other issues not likely to win over religious conservatives.

The previous Conservative government of Stephen Harper, however, eventually so thoroughly alienated many believers through Harper's lack-lustre support for and even foot-dragging resistance to their concerns about abortion, same-sex marriage and the other key elements of their social agenda that Evangelicals once again distributed themselves across the parties in the federal election of 2015, when fully half of Canadian Evangelicals supported other parties despite their antipathy to so many Liberal positions. Political scientists studying these matters have concluded that the influence of religiously motivated social conservativism is declining in Canada, both because the number of such people is declining and because Evangelicals refuse automatically and always to line up behind the most conservative party in an election. They instead consider a variety of issues and vote accordingly.

Indeed, the paranoia of alarmists belied Evangelicalism's small numbers in Canada. The relative rise to numerical prominence of Evangelicals versus formerly mainstream Protestant denominations was almost entirely due to the decline of the latter, not the increase of the former. The best the Evangelicals could do, in fact, was to resist the general downward trend of Canadian Christianity and hold their own – literally, in terms of retaining the loyalty of the next generation. Throughout this period, Evangelicals (again, including Pentecostals and Charismatics) claimed roughly 15% of the national population (although they ran one-third of Canada's 30,000 congregations), and the vast majority of Evangelicals were in English-speaking Canada. Even the increased immigration of Evangelical Asians, especially from Korea and China and most evident in several large congregations in suburban Toronto and Vancouver, did not change the overall complexion of Canadian Evangelicalism. By the 2020s, almost all the major Evangelical organisations, from schools to mission organisations to the EFC itself, were led by whites, and over 90% of the largest churches had a white man in the senior pastor position.

Indeed, those relatively big churches – which in Canada meant any congregation larger than 1,000, of which there were about 150 by 2020 and which were distributed across the country roughly in proportion to the general population – generally increased while most smaller churches correspondingly decreased. Prosperity-gospel Charismatic congregations such as Springs in Winnipeg, neo-Anabaptist churches such as The Meeting House in suburban Toronto and Centre Street Church in Calgary, and Baptist, Pentecostal and other large communities in Vancouver and the Fraser Valley of southern British Columbia grew mostly, in fact, from transfer of membership from other churches plus the retention their young people through large-scale programming and staffing. These churches typically foregrounded evangelism as a priority, and they did win some converts from Canada's unchurched or semi-churched population. The overall success – such as it was – of Evangelicals, however, was largely a story of maintaining their share of the religious market in Canada.

Religious Plurality

The first Christians in Canada were European explorers, fisherfolk, missionaries, soldiers and settlers. The last Christians in Canada might well be among the First Nations. As Terry LeBlanc's preceding essay on First Nations Canada in this volume indicates, the vast majority of Aboriginal people in Canada retain a Christian identity: upward of 80% in the National Household Survey of 2011. That Christian identity, to be sure, is held in widely varying measures alongside, and sometimes in creative mixture with, native traditions. Furthermore, investigation by the Truth and Reconciliation Commission (2008–15) into the compulsory education of thousands of native students in residential schools, in which some were subjected to abuse and many more to assimilation, indicated that the destiny of Christianity among Canadian First Nations remained unclear. Some early data, in fact, indicated a significant drop-off of allegiance to Christianity among young Indigenous people.

Meanwhile, Canadians encountered new options in the religious marketplace. Mormons and Jehovah's Witnesses continued to knock on doors and offer literature in public places. Each group was about a quarter the size of Baptists, Pentecostals or Presbyterians (roughly 140,000 each, with the latter three groups numbering about half a million each). But the 1980s saw the rise of New Age varieties, perhaps best understood as one of the more colourful aspects of the broad movement towards alternative therapies advanced by the authority-questioning attitude of the 1960s. Moreover, where New Age ideas and practices did not completely supplant Christianity or some other traditional religion for Canadians, they often combined with those proper-noun religions to form a remarkable postmodern religious phenomenon, variously termed 'DIY [Do It Yourself] Religion', 'religion à la carte', 'informal religion' and the like. In sociologist Reginald Bibby's helpful series of polls, a significant and increasing minority of Canadians were now telling his researchers both that they were Christians and that they believed in reincarnation or horoscopes or the benevolent power of crystals.

While disaffected Canadians could explore the various new religions and, indeed, the new mode of religion most obviously offered by the New Age, immigrants were bringing religions that were mostly new to the Canadian scene: Islam, Sikhism, Buddhism, Hinduism and more. As newcomers tended to find each other in their new country, they typically would band together to construct a house of worship. Thus mosques, gurdwaras and temples sprouted conspicuously across metropolitan areas – and a few rural places as well. Because major Canadian media are centred in urban areas, the arrival of new religions was sometimes over-reported: collectively they still constitute less than 15% of the national population. And while their numbers have grown, prudent observers have waited to see if their youth will go the way of most non-Evangelical youth in Canada – namely, deviating towards the growing cultural mean of vaguely 'spiritual, but not religious'.

The New Orthodoxy of 'No Religion'
What, then, has replaced Christianity as the default outlook of Canadians, in public and in private? Has Canada instead become simply a wide-open marketplace of ideological options? Many observers suggest that a new orthodoxy has emerged to dominate public life in Canada, from the legislatures to the courts to the universities to the mass media.

To be sure, some nervous Canadians, and particularly Catholics and Evangelicals who bemoan the loss of their cultural influence, have seen every expression of pluralism or even state neutrality as an alarming religious relativism, a state endorsement of the doctrine that 'all options are equally good'. Multiculturalism, the expansion of immigration quotas, secular school curricula regarding ethics and religion, and the featuring of non-Christians in public roles all point, some fear, to a progressive agenda that militates against Christians.

Several things, in fact, have happened at once. Yes, there has clearly been a dismantling of the Christian hegemony in Canada. And, yes, there has been a general, if not universal, public embrace of multicultural diversity and mutual celebration. But these developments are not intrinsically anti-Christian, and instead simply mark a new chapter in Canadian history that could indeed be a broadly free and diverse situation in which Christians can flourish alongside their neighbours of other outlooks.

Furthermore, few Canadians are strict, self-identified atheists (from 1% to perhaps 3% of the national population), but a rapidly increasing segment claim 'No Religion' on national surveys – by the 2020s, fully a quarter of the population. This fraction makes the Canadian scene comparable to the situations found in France, Sweden and the UK, and thus significantly higher than in the USA and even Australia.

About a quarter of these – and probably more than a third of the population who would still identify with a proper-noun religion – are 'Spiritual But Not Religious' (SBNR). These Canadians detach elements of religion and philosophy they find in the cultural marketplace and construct amalgams of individual experience and meaning. The vast majority of those SBNRs, therefore, are ex- or quasi-Christians (not ex-Muslims or ex-Hindus), so that a certain broad consensus remains in Canadian life about values such as honesty, compassion and the like. Still, national surveys have shown since the turn of the millennium that SBNRs are not discernibly different, in many measures of well-being in private and public life, from those completely uninterested in religion. For their part, the Christian minority who regularly attend church continue to set a strikingly higher standard by almost any measure of positive social behaviour, from lower rates of teenage pregnancy and drug abuse to higher levels of marital happiness and longevity and of civic and religious charitable giving and volunteering. The Canadian population is behaviourally dividing between observant Christians (along with, it is likely, observant members of other religions; the national numbers are still too small to track) and everyone else.

Some research has shown, moreover, that the lack of interest among the religious 'nones' runs deep. Most of this quarter of the population now claim not to believe in any sort of God or 'higher power' at all. Qualitative studies reveal that few, if any, would attend a nearby church no matter what changes that church might make to attract them. Indifference, much more than militant resistance, is therefore the posture of most non-Christians towards Christianity in contemporary Canada.

At the same time, however, the first decades of the twenty-first century have manifested an increasingly aggressive secularism. Broader questions of religious freedom, conscience rights and other basic issues of civil liberties have been raised and then answered in ways that might trouble anyone who does not share in the amorphous but discernible ideological consensus among the post-Christian, lightly spiritual and mostly secular members of Canada's governing classes. For example, Canada's largest Christian university, Trinity Western in British Columbia, won a Supreme Court case on behalf of its well-established school of education against the attempts of the provincial college of teachers to discredit it for incorrect views of sexuality (2001) – only to lose a case nearly two decades later (2018) before the same court on behalf of its proposed law school on essentially the same grounds. Furthermore, professional societies and courts across the country over the same period increasingly curtailed the conscience rights of medical professionals, insisting that pharmacists dispense abortifacients and physicians assist patients who opted for the newly authorised option of medical assistance in dying. Religious rights guaranteed by the Canadian Constitution in the Charter of Rights and Freedoms (1982) seemed to be acknowledged perfunctorily by legislators, jurists and others, only then to be set aside in the interest of a more compelling concern. So are these cases signs of a new hegemony?

What Happened – and What Will?
A number of North American sociologists – from Rodney Stark, Roger Finke, Wade Clark Roof and Laurence Iannaccone to Christian Smith – have usefully employed a marketplace model to explain religious patterns on this continent. In general, they suggest that religious traditions will do best in the competition for attention and adherence if they maintain a creative tension in a sort of 'sweet spot' that combines being different enough to offer something the broad culture is not already offering and being not so different as to be dismissed as implausible. Evangelicals in particular have done relatively well as they offer an outlook and a lifestyle that, for at least some Canadians, is attractively different from that offered by, say, Netflix or HBO, but not so outlandish or demanding that one recoils from it upon first encounter.

Still, what happens to Christian churches – or, indeed, to other religious traditions – if they provide answers to questions only a few are asking? If a majority of Canadians are reasonably secure and prosperous, and face no strong likelihood of losing that status, why would they devote their attention, their time, their talent and their money to a pursuit that emphasises deliverance from the travails of this life in a blessed world to come? Canadian culture in the last two generations has so insulated so many from the discomfiting questions of suffering and death (the great drivers of religious concern in India), social chaos (the great drivers of Daoist and Confucianist reflection in traditional China), political oppression (among the great drivers of Judaism and Islam) and moral guilt and its punishment (the great driver of Christian preaching) that the fall-off in religion across the board is largely explainable in this way.

Moreover, what accounts for the limited growth among even the two most orthodox communities of Christians in Anglophone Canada: Roman Catholics and Evangelicals? Two of the main social resources they traditionally have offered – morality to guide people away from vice and towards virtue plus community to cushion the shocks of life and promote wholesome and sustaining camaraderie – have been, respectively, exploded by scandal after scandal and eroded by the conformity of Canadian Christians to the individualism and hedonism of their neighbours – indeed, to the secular liberal freedom to engage wholeheartedly in the 'pursuit of happiness'. In the arms of an ever-increasing welfare state, if life in English-speaking Canada remains pretty good, with problems (such as pandemics or economic downturns) most likely to be solved by governments, why would most people bother with churches? The answer, increasingly, is that they do not.

Bibliography

Bibby, Reginald W., *Resilient Gods: Being Pro-Religious, Low Religious, or No Religious in Canada* (Vancouver: University of British Columbia Press, 2017).

Bibby, Reginald W., Joel Thiessen and Monetta Bailey, *The Millennial Mosaic: How Pluralism and Choice Are Shaping Canadian Youth and the Future of Canada* (Toronto: Dundurn, 2019).

Clarke, Brian and Stuart Macdonald, *Leaving Christianity: Changing Allegiances in Canada since 1945* (Montreal: McGill-Queen's University Press, 2017).

Noll, Mark A., *What Happened to Christian Canada?* (Vancouver: Regent College, 2007).

Stackhouse, John G., Jr, 'What Has Happened to Post-Christian Canada?', *Church History*, 87 (December 2018), 1152–70.

Francophone Canada

André Brouillette

Catholicism has for centuries played a central role in Francophone Canada. Even today, visitors notice the numerous villages and streets named after saints and the prominence of a large parish church at the centre of every community. The bond between language and religious identity was established naturally in the early years of French colonisation. Despite a rapid secularisation in recent decades, the imprint of Christianity on Quebec's society is still noticeable.

Francophone Canada refers *per se* more to a population than a place, though for the first century and a half of Christian presence in this land they tightly overlapped. The Francophone presence in Canada now extends to all provinces, but its institutional heart is in Quebec, which houses the majority of French-speakers in the country and is itself the only majority French-speaking province. For this reason, this essay focuses on the sociopolitical entity of Quebec, while leaving aside its Anglophone component.

In order to understand the contemporary reality of Christianity in Quebec, a journey through the various historical layers of Christian living is crucial. It will proceed in six stages. The first three uncover historical roots: the early presence in the seventeenth century, the regime change of the mid-eighteenth century, and the role as driving social force from the mid-nineteenth century to the twentieth century. The last three stages usher us into the contemporary period, from the 'Quiet Revolution' of the 1960s to the current realities.

Early Presence and Mystical Invasion

Although the French had already explored the territory of Canada in the sixteenth century, not until 1608 did Samuel de Champlain establish Quebec City as the first successful permanent colonial settlement. Religious communities soon came: first the Franciscan Récollets, then the Jesuits. These Catholic missionaries contacted the many Indigenous nations (Hurons, Algonquins, Iroquois), patiently making inroads among peoples who were often semi-nomadic and whose culture was fiercely different. Many natives converted to Christianity. One of them was Kateri Tekakwitha (1656–80), born at Ossernenon. To live fully her Christian faith, she moved to the St Francis-Xavier mission, a Mohawk village of converts near Montreal. There, while living as an Indigenous, she devoted herself to prayer and works of charity with like-minded women, refusing to follow the custom to marry. She was the first North American Indigenous woman to be canonised, in 2012. On the side of the missionaries, some encountered a violent fate. Among the important group of the North American martyrs, the figure of Jean de Brébeuf (1593–1649) stands tall. Brébeuf lived among the Wendats (Hurons), learning their language and culture, composing a carol in their language, and died in their midst as they were under attack. Some private writings of Brébeuf made public after his death show the mystical side of his commitment to his mission. Overall, the cultural and religious contacts between the Natives and the French were mediated mostly by the missionaries active among Indigenous communities. These relationships changed radically two centuries later through assimilationist policies of the Canadian government that resulted in a cultural trauma that lingers to our day.

Female religious played an important role in the early life of Canada. In 1639, two religious communities came from France to Quebec City: the Ursulines and the Hospitallers of St Augustine. The former established the first school for girls, while the latter founded a hospital (Hôtel-Dieu), both still in existence, securing a leadership position in education and healthcare for centuries. The Jesuits had already created a school for boys in 1635. While these institutions were intended to serve both the Native population and the colonists, they eventually served mostly the descendants of the French. Among the missionaries, Marie de l'Incarnation (1599–1672), an Ursuline nun, deserves special recognition for her spiritual writings.

The founding of Ville-Marie – modern Montreal – highlights the religious drive and enthusiasm in French Catholicism for the conversion of the Natives of North America. A group of devout laypeople and clergy connected with the Sulpician community devised the project of establishing at an important fluvial crossroads a mission to serve the needs of the Indigenous and gain their conversion. They financed the project and recruited the first colonists under the leadership of Paul de Chomedey de Maisonneuve (1612–76) and Jeanne Mance (1606–73), both of them laypeople. They set their sight on the island of Montreal and dedicated their mission to the Virgin Mary. Upon arriving on 17 May 1642, the colonists cleared some space to be able to celebrate a Mass the following day, marking the foundation of a city called to a great future. Montreal owes its existence to religious fervour and a desire for intercultural encounters.

In Quebec City, Bishop François de Laval (1623–1708) developed the structures of the Church after his arrival in 1659 as apostolic vicar, and more formally with the creation of the Diocese of Quebec in 1674. With indefatigable zeal, Laval created parishes, organised the clergy through the community of the Séminaire de Québec (1663) and instituted a minor seminary (1668). Laval University, established in 1852 as the first Francophone university in North America, emerged from the educational work of priests from the Séminaire and honoured the memory of Quebec's first bishop saint. The early presence of Christianity was driven by religious enthusiasm, encounters between French and Native cultures, and a number of exceptional mystical figures commemorated until the present.

Regime Change and New Challenges

Until the middle of the eighteenth century, the Church benefited from a close relationship with the political power in the colony of New France, financial support, and regular arrival of French religious personnel. The population numbered about 60,000 Canadian inhabitants – descendants of the French colonisers – in a territory covering half of North America, in addition to thousands of Indigenous.

The 1763 Treaty of Paris drastically changed the religious horizon. New France, already under British control for three years, was officially handed over. The English (and Anglican) king was to rule over the French-speaking Catholic inhabitants, posing an existential threat to their faith. To make matters worse, the Bishop of Quebec had died in 1760, leaving the Catholic community without their institutional leader. The British military government nonetheless had to accommodate the local population – too large to be displaced – and signs of unrest were to come soon enough from the other British colonies in North America. Despite an assimilationist policy to a different language – English – and a different Christian denomination – Anglicanism – the religious and linguistic allegiance of the inhabitants remained steady, though their political allegiance shifted. The new British masters and the local Catholic community reached a certain understanding. Jean-Olivier Briand (1715–94) was able to be ordained as bishop while journeying in Europe, and he in turn preached respect for the legitimate authority. For his part, the governor did not apply in the new colony most of the anti-Catholic measures common in Britain. Weakened by the loss of the connection with France – so important for personnel and funds – and the destruction of Church property that the military campaign of 1759–60 had brought, as well as the decline of the traditional elites, the Catholic Church nonetheless played a central role as catalyst of the voice of the Canadians, by that time overwhelmingly French-speaking and Catholic. The English-speaking population of Canada, mostly Protestant, grew steadily, especially with the arrival of Loyalists in the wake of the American War of Independence, introducing an element of religious pluralism in the colonial society.

A Driving Social Force

By the middle of the nineteenth century, the Catholic Church in Francophone Canada experienced a renewed dynamism. Bishop Ignace Bourget (1799–1885), who in 1840 became the second Catholic bishop of the recently established Diocese of Montreal, exemplifies the emerging new spirit. Montreal was by then the economic centre of Canada. Bourget's ultramontane ideology pushed him to look to Europe for new ideas and recruits to serve his growing flock. During the French regime, some religious congregations had been created in Montreal: the Congregation Notre-Dame in the seventeenth century by Marguerite Bourgeoys (1620–1700), for the education of girls, and the Sisters of Charity (nicknamed the Grey Nuns) in 1738 by Marguerite d'Youville (1701–71), to care for the sick. But Bishop Bourget unleashed a flurry of new establishments by calling on French religious communities to come to Canada in the 1840s. Moreover, the great religious fervour and the large families allowed for the creation of new local congregations. The religious personnel ran not only parishes but also schools and missions, and devoted themselves to the care of the poor and the sick. The feistiness of Bishop Bourget also extended to his fight against the liberal tendency evident among the local bourgeoisie, attacking frontally its newspapers and institutions. To respond to the threat posed by having French-speaking Catholics attend the only university in Montreal – McGill, both Anglophone and Protestant – Bourget fought to establish a Catholic university in that city. However, Laval University was established in Quebec City, with Montreal having to wait until 1876 to receive its branch. In a testament to his intrepid spirit, Bourget decided to make a bold statement after his cathedral burned down in 1852. Instead of rebuilding in the same location, he secured land at the heart of a fashionable district of the Anglophone Protestant elite and modelled his new cathedral after St Peter's Basilica in Rome. The statement was loud and clear. The place of Catholicism at the heart of Francophone Canada was secured for generations.

Brother André (1845–1937), *né* Alfred Bessette, is arguably the most popular religious figure in the history of Francophone Canada. Born into a poor rural family, he worked for some time in New England before joining the Congregation of the Holy Cross as a religious brother. He became the doorkeeper of the Collège Notre-Dame in Montreal. In that capacity, he assisted students, religious and visitors. Despite his limited education, small stature and humble employment, people recognised in him a spirit of holiness. Armed with an unflinching devotion to St Joseph, he would enjoin those seeking healing or advice from him to pray to his holy patron. He gained such a reputation as a miracle worker that his community asked him eventually to meet his numerous visitors in a nearby tramway station, then in a small chapel built on Mont Royal, in front of the school. The small wooden structure of 1904 progressively gave way to a magnificent basilica with a large dome looming over the island of Montreal, the largest sanctuary dedicated to St Joseph in the world. After the death of Brother André on 6 January 1937, newspapers claimed that a million people paid their respects to his remains over four days. St Joseph's Oratory stands among the three major pilgrimage sites of Francophone Canada, along with Notre-Dame-du-Cap (Our Lady of the Cape), in Trois-Rivières, and Sainte-Anne de Beaupré, near Quebec City. Each site features an impressive twentieth-century basilica witnessing to the centrality of Catholicism in Quebec at the time. Brother André was canonised in 2010, and a Mass of thanksgiving filled Montreal's Olympic Stadium with 50,000 worshippers to celebrate the event.

The convergence of religious fervour, renewed arrivals of religious personnel from France towards the end of the nineteenth century, an abundance of religious vocations and the missionary spirit of Christianity led to an international outreach by French-Canadian Catholics. After centuries of being on the receiving end of missionary movements, Francophone Canada was in a position to send missionaries abroad in the twentieth century. Even before that, some nuns, religious brothers and priests were sent from Quebec to other parts of Canada or even to the USA to minister to French-Canadians who had emigrated. International communities present in Canada, Canadian congregations, but also new missionary societies, such as the Missionaries of the Immaculate Conception (1902) and the Séminaire des Missions-Étrangères (1921), sent religious to China, Japan, Africa and Latin America especially. They built schools, colleges, parishes, dispensaries and dioceses. The necessary fundraising efforts among the laity widened the horizon of the many benefactors through a host of magazines and preaching endeavours. By the middle of the century, the missionary contribution of the Quebec Church also extended to the laity, as seen in the creation of the Centre d'études Missionnaires in 1958 to train religious and laypeople for international cooperation.

From 'Great Darkness' to 'Quiet Revolution'

By the middle of the twentieth century, Francophone Canada was a largely homogeneous population religiously. Few French-speakers were not Catholics. Society was ruled by traditions, emphasising the values of family, order, religion and hard work. Religious practice was high. Social conformity was high. Despite a mostly urban population, the ideal remained that of a resilient agrarian society, as romanticized by the novel *Maria Chapdelaine* (1913) by Louis Hémon (1880–1913). The Catholic

Church guided social mores and education. A spirit of unanimity reigned, befitting an isolated community that had had to fight adversity for centuries to ensure its survival. A heroic vision of Christendom permeates the historical work of Canon Lionel Groulx (1878–1967), an important intellectual and university professor of history. Maurice Duplessis (1890–1959) dominated the political scene for almost 20 years as Premier of Quebec. An ally of the Catholic Church, he favoured a conservative brand of small government, patronage, nationalism and anticommunism. Until the 1950s, female religious congregations were running most hospitals in Quebec, male and female religious managed and largely staffed most schools and colleges, and clergy headed Francophone universities – even as the number of laypeople working in these institutions was growing rapidly. Social services for the poor and the sick were under the leadership of nuns. A spirit of self-sacrifice and service on the part of religious personnel was rewarded with social status. For women in particular, religious life offered a greater variety of paths – as educator, nurse and missionary – than the motherhood of most laywomen. The osmosis between civil society and the Catholic Church had reached its apex.

Cracks had already started to appear in that unanimous facade, however. In 1948, a group of artists issued the *Refus global* (Total Rejection) manifesto, calling for changes in a suffocating society. Within the Church in the 1940s, tensions around attitudes towards labour issues pitted factions against one another, placing some at odds with the government. The outspoken Archbishop of Montreal, Joseph Charbonneau (1892–1959), was even exiled in Western Canada in the aftermath of turmoil. Cooperatives and unions were reconsidering their formal affiliation with the Church. The years following the Second World War brought economic development, increased urbanisation and sustained growth in population. The world was changing fast.

The election of the Liberal government of Jean Lesage (1912–80) in 1960 launched a forced march into modernity for Quebec. The state became the driving force in society, its workforce swelling to meet new challenges. In just a few years, most hospitals were taken over from the religious congregations and new hospitals were built. A Ministry of Education was established, the school curriculum was radically transformed, and new schools and universities were created, sometimes out of former religious institutions. Bureaucrats took over the management of state schools, while some religious institutions remained private. On the economic front, private hydroelectric companies were nationalised into Hydro-Québec, which became a powerful tool of development in further decades. The government created the Caisse de dépôt et placement du Québec to manage pension funds and spur economic growth. A new pride and hopefulness for the future was palpable. Francophone Canadians became more assertive of their rights, and the political horizon moved from that of a French Canada dispersed from coast to coast to that of the territory of the Province of Quebec, which was majority French-speaking. Emboldened by the rapid political and economic development of Quebec, a strong movement in favour of independence from the rest of Canada grew. In 1967, Montreal hosted the world for the International and Universal Exposition (Expo '67), and French President Charles de Gaulle declared in his state visit, 'Vive le Québec Libre!' (Long Live a Free Quebec!). Quebec was coming of age.

The rapid changes in the role of the state were not necessarily realised in opposition to religious authorities – hence the 'quiet' nature of the revolution. A member of the clergy headed the state commission on the reform of education. State schools remained denominationally religious (mostly Catholic for Francophones and Protestant for Anglophones). Numerous religious sisters, brothers and fathers became state employees as nurses, chaplains, teachers and professors. But the horizon had changed radically. The state had taken centre stage. Other paths were open to women. These transformations were also happening within an international context of changes, optimism and upheavals: the sexual revolution, the civil rights movement in the USA, liberation movements in Latin America, decolonisation in Africa, May 1968 in France. Change was the leitmotif, not tradition.

These profound changes affected the Catholic Church in Quebec. Amidst a diminished social role (and prestige), hundreds of priests and religious abandoned their vocations. Admissions to seminaries and congregations dried up abruptly. The Second Vatican Council (1962–5) with its *aggiornamento* also changed perspectives: the modern world was embraced, freedom of religion was recognised, the role of laypeople was elevated and the liturgical language shifted from Latin to the vernacular. The fight for social justice became paramount. In the midst of all those changes, the Archbishop of Montreal, Cardinal Paul-Émile Léger (1904–91), who was elevated as a 'Prince of the Church' in 1953, decided to embrace personally a call for change and left his position in 1967 to become a simple missionary in Africa.

The optimism of the Quiet Revolution and its rapid pace of change in turn created the myth of the *Grande Noirceur* (Great Darkness) of the previous regime of Duplessis. In subsequent decades, this myth would come to taint all dimensions of Quebec society prior to the 1960s, portraying it as a backwater. Religion, and especially Catholicism, would come to be associated with a dark force that had prevented the emancipation of modern Quebec for too long.

Changing Social and Religious Landscape

The changing status of Christianity in the social imagination of Francophone Canada happened more as a progressive erosion than a free fall. It is still unfolding, having started from a high point in the 1960s. No scandal, no single event, no outright rejection initiated that process; it was, rather, a slow erosion into distance and irrelevance. When Pope John Paul II came to Canada in 1984, he still drew crowds in the hundreds of thousands for Masses in Quebec City and Montreal.

The progressiveness – and radical character – of the change can be seen in the evolving place allocated to religious education in public schools. Even after the Quiet Revolution, school districts were confessional. Catechism was taught as part of the regular public-school curriculum. In 1984, catechesis was replaced by a Catholic Morality and Religion course, with the possibility to choose the Moral Teaching course instead, a decision left to each parent. Around that time, the sacramental preparation was entrusted to parishes. In 1997, school districts were no longer based on Christian denomination (Protestant/Catholic), but on language (English/French), although individual public schools continued to offer religious education. School chaplaincies were replaced in 2000 by an office for spiritual life and social commitment. In 2008, however, all religious connections were severed – despite the fact that a majority of parents were still choosing religious education for their children – and a common course was created on 'Ethics and Religious Cultures', presenting major religions in Quebec (including Christianity, Judaism and Islam) from a cultural perspective. During the past 50 years, the lived commitment to a religious faith has been progressively erased from the public-school system, and even a cultural presentation of religion is contested nowadays.

Until the second half the twentieth century, Catholicism faced little competition as a religious faith among French-speakers. During the French regime, Protestants (even the French Huguenots) were officially banned from setting foot in the colony. Some would come during the British regime, but they made few inroads as regards converting Catholics. Protestantism was largely kept at bay because of language. The same reality was true for other religions, especially the Jewish population present in Montreal, since they traditionally associated more with the English-speaking population – as most immigrant communities did. A linguistic difference accentuated the religious one.

In the 1970s, however, children of immigrants integrated massively into the Francophone school network in an effort to bolster the Francophone nature of Quebec's society. Religious diversity was becoming more visible. In Quebec, the Jewish population accounted for up to 2% of the overall population, but now the fastest-growing religious group (through immigration) is the Muslim community, accounting for 3% of the population of Quebec. According to the 2011 National Household Survey, Buddhists, Hindus and Sikhs each account for less than 1% of the total population. But already at that time, more than 12% of all Quebecers were claiming no religious affiliation, including many nominal Catholics, more than doubling the percentage in 10 years. The number of Francophone Quebecers who claim a Catholic identity is decreasing rapidly, and many of those who do claim it do not participate regularly in worship or believe in the central tenets of the faith. Some consider themselves culturally Catholics, detached from a faith commitment, like movie director Bernard Émond (b. 1951), who made three films based on the theological virtues in the 2000s. In this new religious environment, some Francophones discover – or rediscover – the Christian faith through the Catholic Church, but also through Evangelical or Protestant churches, or convert to another religion, although the majority of those who no longer identify as Catholics simply abandon any religious affiliation. Given immigration trends, the face of Christianity has also diversified, since many newcomers hail from various Christian denominations, adding through their participation in established communities or new ones a greater linguistic and racial diversity.

In a context of accelerated secularisation, the place of religion in the public square has been a hot-button political issue since the early 2000s. With the relative decline of religiosity among Francophone Catholics and the increase of the Muslim population through immigration, voices that advocate for curtailing any public expression of religion, and for limiting any 'reasonable accommodation' made for religious individuals or groups in light of the Charter of Rights and Freedoms have gained prominence. In 2008, a large government consultation spearheaded by noted philosopher Charles Taylor and sociologist Gérard Bouchard recommended a compromise proscribing religious symbols (hijab, cross, kippah, turban) for state employees who exercise coercive authority (such as judges and police officers). Nonetheless, the debate continued to rage between adherents of a France-inspired model of *laïcité* reticent to acknowledge and cooperate with religions – perceived as proper to the private sphere – and proponents of an open model of respect for individual religious liberty in a pluralistic society.

Transformations and Continuities

Since the beginning of the new millennium, two large events have mobilised Christians in Francophone Canada. The first was the World Youth Day organised in Toronto in July 2002. This last massive youth festival presided over by Pope John Paul II gathered 800,000 people for its final celebration. Before the time in Toronto, thousands of youth pilgrims from Canada and around the world had spent days in other parts of the country, housed in family homes and schools. Many were in Quebec. This encounter brought the international youth of the Church to Canada. The second event was the International Eucharistic Congress organised in Quebec City in 2008. Though smaller in scale than the World Youth Day, its location in the oldest city in Canada – which was celebrating that year its 400th anniversary – and at the heart of the Francophone area signified a certain dynamism of the Catholic community. The ordination of 12 young men of various religious communities to the priesthood by Cardinal Marc Ouellet, Archbishop of Quebec City, was a highlight of the event. Both happenings joined in the continued inscription of the Christian faith in the public square, though in a subdued key in the events organised in Quebec.

The Church in Francophone Canada has a long tradition of involvement in social issues. Religious congregations, in particular, support a variety of charitable institutions and social works. One good example is the Accueil Bonneau, in Montreal, which offers a variety of services for people in situations of homelessness. That tradition extends also to the world of reflection. From 1991 to 2017, the Journées sociales du Québec gathered socially committed Christians every other year to study and debate important social issues of the day, ranging from just development to the protection of the environment. In the same line, the magazine *Relations*, established in 1941, continues to animate the dialogue between culture and religion with respect to current social concerns.

The area of theological reflections has witnessed major transformations in recent years. In the context of college education in Quebec, schools of theology (traditionally Catholic) or religious science have been present in public universities. The institutional form of presence morphed recently in many universities (Montréal, Sherbrooke). The main Francophone school of theology is housed at Laval University in Quebec City. It developed innovative partnerships with different constituencies, such as academic institutions from various Christian denominations as well as dioceses. The school offers programmes in both theology and religious science within the context of a state-sponsored university, with some programmes oriented to ministry and ordination. Outside Quebec, the Dominican University College and Saint-Paul University, both located in Ottawa, offer bilingual programmes in theology. The life of research is sustained by journals such as *Science et Esprit* (Dominican University College), *Laval théologique et philosophique* (Université Laval) and *Théologiques* (Université Montréal).

One important feature of Christianity in Francophone Canada has been the strong presence of religious communities of women and men under vows. Despite a numerical diminishment, noteworthy initiatives emerged.

In the early twenty-first century, a Francophone community from Quebec, Famille Marie-Jeunesse, experienced growth and success. The spirituality of the community stressed the importance of Mary, Mother of Jesus, and centred on the joy and youth of the gospel. The joyful and fraternal way of experiencing Christianity attracted many followers, who participated in the various events of the community, for whom it became an important school of prayer and Christian life. Famille Marie-Jeunesse also branched out internationally in French-speaking parts of the world. More recently, as it aged, the community undertook a process of deep reflection regarding its future orientation. Other initiatives have emerged, such as the communal living of the Bande FM in Montreal, or the Youth Mass run by Emmanuel Community priests in Quebec City.

Among established religious communities, new circumstances called for innovations. When the Cistercian community of Oka decided to leave its former monastery – too large and too close to a noisy road – they commissioned a leading architect of Quebec, Pierre Thibault, to design a new monastery. The result is the Abbaye Val Notre-Dame, a 2005 building that won much acclaim and several architectural awards. The Trappists dared to reimagine their ministry of prayer and hospitality in a resolutely contemporary environment while anchored in their core mission and tradition. Val Notre-Dame has received a steady flow of visitors ever since.

For their part, the Augustinian nuns in Quebec City developed a legacy project. The presence of the nuns on the site of North America's oldest hospital goes back to the seventeenth century. Desirous to reorganise their real estate, they decided to embark on a multilayered project with public partners. The Monastère des Augustines project was to restore and develop the traditional nuns' monastery and transform it into a welcoming place for sojourns of wellness, either for patients or for visitors to the hospital next door, or indeed for anyone in search of a quiet time at the heart of the historical district of Quebec City. The project also integrated the historic chapel, still used by the hospital, an interpretation centre on a local saint, a bookstore, a cafeteria and a small space for the religious community. Inaugurated to great acclaim in 2015, the centre turned an ancient monument into a public space while commemorating the care for the body and soul that was central to the mission of the Augustinian nuns for more than three centuries. The organisational structure was built to be sustainable even after the departure of the founding religious community.

Despite an ambivalent relation with the Christian faith, Francophone Canadians hold some contemporary Christian figures in high esteem. Cardinal Jean-Claude Turcotte (1936–2015) was a beloved Archbishop of Montreal, perceived as a rounded people's man. Dominican Benoit Lacroix (1915–2016) was a writer, medievalist and intellectual who continued to build bridges with widely different people in his old age, writing for years the Easter editorial for a leading newspaper. Soeur Angèle (b. 1938) is a renowned Italian-born chef and nun who has been a media personality for decades. Iconoclastic priest Raymond Gravel (1952–2014) was well known for his unorthodox comments and his devotion to his parishioners, even being elected as a member of the Canadian parliament. Hence, some public figures clearly associated with the Christian faith have made their way into a secularised mainstream media panorama.

Looking Forward

In 2019, the National Assembly of Quebec removed from its chamber a successor to the crucifix installed in 1936 and confined it to a museum space. However, the white cross continues to appear on the flag of Quebec, and the statues of seven Catholic religious women and men remain on the façade of the building, witnesses to the inextricable link between Francophone Canada and Christianity.

The legacy of Christianity in Francophone Canada is rich, but its lived reality is undergoing tremendous changes. Its institutions are adapting to a highly secularised society that is often hostile to religious expression and lacks religious literacy. The personnel situation is transformed through a diminishing number of human resources and the arrival of international priests and missionaries. The architectural and artistic legacy of hundreds of churches is under threat because of maintenance costs, the diminishing resources of local congregations and the limited public funds available for historical preservation. The metrics of worship attendance are low, as is the rate of marriage, but a clear majority of Francophone Canadians still identify as Christians – with a wide variety of underlying understandings. By the measure of gospel values, however, the metrics are better, since generous social programmes (universal health-care, inexpensive higher education) demonstrate an ingrained care for the less advantaged. Adapting its structures for the twenty-first century, the Church has discovered that it must be missionary again, and strives to be so.

Bibliography

Dictionary of Canadian Biography, 15 vols (Toronto/Quebec City: University of Toronto/Université Laval, 1966–) <http://www.biographi.ca/en/index.php>.

Fay, Terence J., *A History of Canadian Catholics: Gallicanism, Romanism, and Canadianism* (Montreal: McGill-Queen's University Press, 2002).

Ferretti, Lucia, *Brève histoire de l'Église catholique au Québec* (Montreal: Boréal, 1999).

Lalonde, Jean-Louis, *Des loups dans la bergerie. Les protestants de langue française au Québec, 1534–2000* (Montréal: Fides, 2002).

Voisine, Nive (ed.), *Histoire du catholicisme québécois*, 4 vols (Montreal: Boréal express, 1984–91).

Western United States

Eliza Young Barstow

Within the American West, significant diversity characterises the religious experience of its inhabitants. Historical – and contemporary – immigration from almost every part of the world has brought a wide range of religious traditions to this part of the USA. Via missions and settler colonialism, Christianity has been shaped in new ways through interactions with traditions indigenous to the Americas. Moreover, the American West has also been the site of religious innovation, with altogether new forms of Christianity taking hold and thriving. Amidst this medley of religious ideas and practices, some areas of the West have high percentages of people who do not affiliate with a particular religion. It is within the context of this diversity – including the robust population of religiously unaffiliated Americans – that we can situate the diverse and religiously innovative forms of Christianity that thrive in the American West. This essay focuses on the area of the USA that includes California, Oregon, Washington, Alaska, Hawaii, Nevada, Arizona, Utah, Idaho, New Mexico, Colorado, Wyoming and Montana. Because of its vast size and population, California receives more attention than any other state.

According to surveys on religious affiliation, the 'nones' – people who do not readily identify with any religious tradition – have been the fastest-growing group in the USA in the twenty-first century. This growth was particularly dramatic in the second decade of that century. Because a majority of Americans are descended from families that once identified with Christianity, an increase in the 'nones' directly correlates with declining numbers of people identifying as Christians. While this reality is essential for understanding any portion of the USA, it is particularly important in the American West. This is because religiously unaffiliated Americans are found in the densest concentrations there, and more specifically within the Pacific Northwest: Oregon, Washington and Alaska. Mark Silk has argued that these three states likely offer us insight into the future of religion in the USA. That said, the American Religious Landscape Survey, collected most recently in 2020, indicates that the rate of religious non-affiliation is gradually slowing and the exodus from Christian communities is likewise slowing, particularly from the mainline Protestant churches, which had been haemorrhaging members since the 1960s.

When looking at the western regions of the USA, religious diversity is second only to parts of the East Coast (New York and Maryland). For instance, in a majority of states in the American West, the largest religion (after Christianity) is Buddhism. The exception is Arizona, where Hinduism is the second-largest religion after Christianity. In the western United States, the most religiously diverse counties are Navajo County, Arizona; Santa Clara County, California; and Maui County, Hawaii.

While Christianity emerged in the Middle East and spread to the USA via European settler colonialism, the United States has produced distinct varieties of Christianity, some of which have become global forces in their own right. Among those sects, the Church of Jesus Christ of Latter-day Saints (LDS), the Seventh-day Adventists and Pentecostals all have significant history in the American West; moreover, all of these groups likewise have thriving communities in the western United States today. This essay addresses those three groups as well as Catholics, mainline Protestants, Black Protestants, Evangelicals and Eastern Orthodox.

Catholicism

For much of US history, the Catholic experience has been dominated by people characterised as white (even as concepts of whiteness have changed over time). However, in the western United States today, it is people of colour who are growing the Catholic Church. From the mid-nineteenth century until the mid-twentieth century, the Catholic population in the USA evolved, in large part, because of immigration from Europe. English Catholics were numerically dominant until the mid-nineteenth century, at which point German Catholics began to migrate to the USA, soon followed by Catholic migrants from Ireland, who came to escape persecution and dire poverty. Later in the nineteenth century, Catholics began immigrating in large numbers from countries such as Poland and Italy. As these

Christianity in the United States, 1970 and 2020

Tradition	1970 Population	%	2020 Population	%	Average annual growth rate (%), 1970–2020
Christians	191,202,000	91.3%	245,457,000	74.2%	0.5%
Anglicans	3,196,000	1.5%	2,120,000	0.6%	-0.8%
Independents	37,285,000	17.8%	63,800,000	19.3%	1.1%
Orthodox	4,309,000	2.1%	7,150,000	2.2%	1.0%
Protestants	57,091,000	27.2%	51,915,000	15.7%	-0.2%
Catholics	48,305,000	23.1%	73,900,000	22.3%	0.9%
Evangelicals	44,883,000	21.4%	69,000,000	20.8%	0.9%
Pentecostals/Charismatics	13,833,000	6.6%	65,000,000	19.6%	3.1%
Total population	**209,513,000**	**100.0%**	**331,003,000**	**100.0%**	**0.9%**

Source: Todd M. Johnson and Gina A. Zurlo (eds), *World Christian Database* (Leiden/Boston: Brill), accessed January 2022.

Catholic communities grew, they were situated mostly in the Northeast and Midwest. Within the USA, many Protestants saw the entry of these Catholics as a threat to American identity and democracy. Specifically, they feared that Catholics would not fully participate in the democratic project but would instead default to whatever the pope instructed them to do. Also informing distrust of the new immigrants was a fear that they were of a lower racial status and would thus pollute the purity of white Protestant identity in the USA.

Racial categories are dynamic, and by the middle of the twentieth century most people with Irish, Polish or Italian heritage were no longer considered to be non-white. Including those once marginalised groups within the category of 'white', then, white Catholics comprised 12% of the US population in 2020. White Catholics continue to be found in the largest numbers in the Northeast and Midwest (and also Louisiana). The percentage of the population that identifies as white Catholic is declining from its high of 16% in 2008. Alongside this decline in white Catholics, the total number of Catholics in the USA is growing. This can be directly attributed to growing numbers of Latinx individuals. Since 1960, approximately 70% of the growth in Catholicism in the USA can be attributed to people who identify as Latinx or to Afro-Caribbean individuals who speak Spanish. Unlike the geographical locations in which white Catholics are numerically strong, Latinx Catholics are found most prominently in the Southwest of the USA. In addition to immigration, high birth rates among Latinx individuals have also contributed to the increase in this population. Much of the US Catholic hierarchy remains concentrated in archdioceses and seminaries in the Midwest and Northeast, but this might change in the decades to come.

Catholicism in the Caribbean and Latin America emerged out of settler colonialism and the enslavement of West African peoples who were taken to the Caribbean and the Americas. For the most part, the Europeans who took Catholicism to these regions were Spanish, Portuguese or French. Although missionaries, settlers and enslavers often foisted Catholicism upon those they enslaved and/or the people whose land they took, the forms of Catholicism that arose were far from identical to forms of Catholicism practised in Europe. Most notably, the figure of the Virgin of Guadalupe – understood to be an apparition of the Virgin Mary who appeared to a peasant in present-day Mexico in 1531 – merges Catholic and indigenous Aztec attributes in her identity. It is no exaggeration to say that the Virgin of Guadalupe is essential to Catholicism in places where Latinx individuals practise the faith. Throughout the Southwest and California, images of the Virgin of Guadalupe are pervasive in both public and private spaces.

Studies of Latinx Catholicism, such as Kristy-Nabhan Warren's *The Virgin of El Barrio: Marian Apparitions, Catholic Evangelizing, and Mexican American Activism* (New York: New York University Press, 2005), reveal the importance of Marian apparitions to contemporary Latinx Catholic identity in activism in the Southwest (her focus is on Arizona). Jonathan E. Calvillo, author of *The Saints of Santa Ana: Faith and Ethnicity in a Mexican Majority City* (New York: Oxford University Press, 2020), has written about the ways that Latinx Catholicism shapes community and ethnic identity in Southern California, and he argues that much of what counts as religious practice takes place outside of established churches. Family and community events, he demonstrates, are critical locations of lived religion, and thus these might well be the locations to which scholars should look in order to best understand the future of Catholicism in the USA.

Among Catholics registered to vote, approximately 60% of white Catholics identify as Republicans, whereas almost 70% of Hispanic Catholics are Democrats. That said, far more white Catholics are registered to vote than are Hispanic Catholics. Even with these disparities in voting registration, however, these affiliations help to provide one clear reason why California and many Southwestern states (although not Utah, which has a majority LDS population) lean towards the Democrats in elections. It is also worth noting that many Catholics identify with their political party's stance on political issues rather than the Vatican's stance. For instance, white Catholics tend to be less concerned about climate change and more vocal about immigration control; most also continue to oppose the legality of abortion. In contrast, a majority of Hispanic Catholics – who are, again, concentrated in the Southwest – are concerned about climate change, in favour of generous immigration policies and opposed to strict restrictions on abortion.

Protestants

Across the USA, the number of white mainline church members has been in decline for some time. According to the Public Religion Research Institute's 2020 Census of American Religion, however, the numbers appear to have stopped declining and are possibly even increasing. While the number of white mainline Protestants might be ever so slightly on the rise, their numbers are largest in the Midwest, not the West Coast. In Alaska, Hawaii, Washington, Oregon, California, Arizona, Idaho and Utah, in not a single county do as many as 25% of the population identify as mainline Protestant. Still in the West but moving towards the Midwest, the numbers begin to increase, as New Mexico, Colorado, Montana and Wyoming all have counties in which more than 25% of the population is mainline Protestant.

In the USA, the largest white mainline denomination is the United Methodist Church (UMC). In recent years, the denomination has been facing internal divisions over the understanding of LGBTQ rights and roles within the Church. At the 2019 Special Conference, the United Methodists passed 'The Traditional Plan', which upholds the denomination's ban on same-sex marriage and the ordination of LGBTQ Methodists. On the West Coast, many UMC clergy had already been marrying same-sex couples, and some pastors were openly gay. In fact, the Western Jurisdiction of the UMC had appointed a lesbian bishop in 2016. Across the country, both liberal and conservative churches are opting to leave the denomination. As of early 2020, it appears likely that the UMC might divide into two new groups, the Global Methodist Church, which will represent conservative ideas about sexuality, and the Liberation Methodist Connexion, which will represent progressive ideas about sexuality. It is likely that many West Coast churches would affiliate with the Liberation Methodist Connexion.

Black Protestants are typically categorised separately from mainline Protestants, in large part because historical discrimination and segregation resulted in the development of historically Black churches such as the African Methodist Episcopal Church and the National Baptist Convention of America. Black Protestant churches are overwhelmingly found in the Southeast of the USA. Solano County, California, has 9% of the population identifying as Black Protestant, but other than this, in only a handful of counties in California and Nevada do more than 5% of the population identify as Black Protestant.

Evangelicals and Pentecostals
In the western portion of the USA, Evangelical Protestants are more numerous than mainline or Black Protestants. While the numbers of Evangelicals in the western United States pales in comparison with the numbers of Evangelicals in the South or Midwest, nonetheless in parts of Colorado, Oregon, Northern California and Montana, well over 30% of the population identifies as white Evangelical. The Southwest is also home to many Latinx Evangelicals, a demographic that is growing quickly as increasing numbers of Latinx individuals – both in Latin America and in the USA – are leaving Catholicism for either Evangelical Protestantism or Pentecostalism (or some hybrid of the two).

In the West, some regions are very much associated with religious conservatism. For instance, parts of Colorado and Southern California gained large numbers of conservative Protestants during both the Great Depression and the Second World War. As people pursued jobs with the military industrial complex in places like Colorado Springs and Orange

County, California, numerous individuals moved from the American South and brought their Evangelical beliefs and culture with them. As such, although the American West is home to large numbers of religiously unaffiliated people, it is also home to a portion of the most religiously conservative people in the USA. For instance, at Influence Church in Anaheim Hills, California, the pastor rails against coronavirus precautions and calls the Black Lives Matter movement 'Black supremacy'. Among the most conservative Christians in the USA are the Christian Reconstructionists in Moscow, Idaho, about whom Crawford Gribben has written in his book *Survival and Resistance in Evangelical America: Christian Reconstruction in the Pacific Northwest* (New York: Oxford University Press, 2021). This group of postmillennial Evangelicals believe that Old Testament law should be implemented in the USA. While the group in Idaho is fairly small, they have a national influence, as members of the community have secured book contracts with Oxford University Press and Random House, and Douglas Wilson, lead pastor of the movement in Idaho, has a talk show that can be streamed on Amazon Prime.

Outside California, Colorado Springs, Colorado, has sometimes been called the 'Evangelical Vatican'. Beginning in the 1980s, a number of conservative Protestant groups – buoyed by the rise of the Moral Majority – situated themselves in the city. The largest of these groups, Focus on the Family, was led for many years by James Dobson, a proponent of male headship of the home and corporal discipline for children. The largest church in the city is the 10,000-member New Life Church, currently led by Brady Boyd. Featuring theatre-style seating that can accommodate up to 8,000 individuals, the church is also known for its worship music. New Life Church was once led by Ted Haggard, who was simultaneously president of the National Association of Evangelicals. Once an outspoken critic of same-sex marriage, Haggard received significant attention in 2006 when it was revealed that he paid a male prostitute for sex and also purchased and used methamphetamine. Since then, Haggard has asserted that the USA should be careful not to turn biblical law into civil law, and he has come to support same-sex marriage as a secular institution. More recently, at the Truth and Liberty Conference in Colorado Springs in September 2011, conservative Evangelicals discussed their belief that God should be more present in US public life. Invited speaker US Representative Lauren Boebert explained her belief that 'God wants us to be involved in the affairs of government'. While Colorado Springs represents a kind of headquarters for many Evangelical organisations, only 20% of people identify as white Evangelical in El Paso County, in which Colorado Springs is situated. Found in much larger numbers are people who identify as 'religiously unaffiliated', who comprise 32% of the population.

The origins of Pentecostalism in the USA lie in Los Angeles, with the Black preacher William J. Seymour. While Seymour had learned strategies to call upon the Holy Spirit from Charles Parham in Texas (where Parham required Seymour to sit outside of the room where white Christians were communing), it was at the Azusa Street Revival, led by Seymour, that Pentecostalism really took off, in 1906. Today, in the USA, the Church of God in Christ (COGIC) is not only the largest Black Pentecostal denomination but is also the largest Pentecostal denomination. Founded in 1897, COGIC became much more popular after the success of the Azusa Street Revival. While COGIC is now headquartered in Tennessee, it does have some very large communities on the West Coast. For instance, the West Angeles COGIC, located in Los Angeles, has approximately 24,000 members.

While Pentecostalism is now the fastest-growing form of Christianity around the globe and is seeing the quickest rise in numbers in Latin America and Africa, the USA remains an important home of Pentecostal growth and innovation. One of the largest Pentecostal churches there is King's Cathedral and Chapels, an Assemblies of God community in Kahului, Hawaii. Although this church is based in Kahului, it has numerous additional campuses in Hawaii, the continental United States and in diverse parts of the globe.

As scholars such as Philip Jenkins have noted, migration from the 'global South' is impacting religious demographics and practices in the North. Just as Catholicism in the USA has been transformed by immigration from Latin America, the Caribbean and the Philippines, Pentecostal communities are increasingly filled with immigrants from Latin America, the Caribbean, sub-Saharan Africa and Asia. Many Latin American Pentecostal communities now send missionaries to the USA. In his historical study of Latinx Pentecostals in the Southwest, Gaston Espinosa demonstrates the discrimination Latinx individuals faced in the historically white Assemblies of God denomination. Looking to recent years, Espinosa finds that many Latinx Pentecostals can be categorised as moderate voters, with their votes sometimes going to Republicans and sometimes going to Democrats. Overall, Latinx Pentecostals tend to have conservative views on abortion and same-sex marriage.

The line between Pentecostal and Evangelical is often blurry (and not always important in terms of lived experience) insofar as many Evangelical churches have incorporated Charismatic elements – such as speaking in tongues and divine healing – into their belief systems. One example of a significant California community that blurs these lines is Bethel Church in Redding, which identifies as a non-denominational, Neo-Charismatic church and has approximately 11,000 members. Bethel Church is the institution out of which the Bethel School of Supernatural Ministry (BSSM) was formed in 1994. Drawing from as many as 70 countries around the world, BSSM now has approximately 2,400 students, all of whom are training to become effective at producing miracles such as divine healing and even raising people from the dead. This church and academic community, then, do not identify with a particular Pentecostal denomination or a particular Protestant denomination. They do, however, express deep belief in the gifts of the Holy Spirit, as taught in all Pentecostal churches.

Another example of Neo-Charismatic religion is the Vineyard Movement, which got its start in Southern California in 1975 and continues to thrive in California. The Movement now has 1,500 branches worldwide. Anthropologists Tanya Luhrmann and Jon Bialecki have both written about their fieldwork in California Vineyard churches, and from their work it is obvious that those churches are home to Christians with a diverse range of views on sexuality, climate change, immigration and overseas military involvement. This does not mean that the leadership necessarily endorses socially progressive political stances, but it is clear that a sizeable portion of the people in the churches feel comfortable articulating these views.

The Church of Jesus Christ of Latter-day Saints

While the Church of Jesus Christ of Latter-day Saints (the LDS or, more colloquially, the Mormons) had its start in upstate New York in 1830, by the end of the 1840s, a majority of the LDS lived in Utah. Joseph Smith, the founder and first prophet, understood himself to be revealing truths about Christianity that gave the Christian tradition deep roots in North America. Through visits with the angel Moroni and inscriptions on tablets he found buried near his home in Palmyra, New York, Smith came to understand that Jesus Christ had visited North America after his resurrection. During that visit Christ ministered to the Nephites, a group the LDS believe to have emigrated to North America from Jerusalem in about 600 BC. Not only did Smith understand himself to have met with an angel and to have found holy tablets in upstate New York, but he also understood that Christian history in the USA was much older than most other Christians realised.

Today, in the American West, the states with the highest percentages of the population identifying as Mormon are Utah (55%) and Idaho (19%), and large populations also exist in Arizona, Wyoming, Nevada, Oregon, Montana, Alaska and California. In the twenty-first century, the Mormons in the western portion of the United States face the same issues as Mormons throughout the country. As the USA becomes increasingly racially diverse and people of predominantly European origin are likely to become a minority of the US population by 2050, the LDS has remained overwhelmingly white, with approximately 86% of American Mormons identifying as white. While the early Mormons sought out Black converts and actively discouraged slavery, all but the very earliest Mormons restricted the ways in which Black Mormons could participate within the religion. For instance, until the 1970s, black men were not allowed to become priests. Both Black men and all women were denied the right to participate in many temple rites until the 1970s. And while these rules changed in the 1970s, it was not until 2013 that the LDS officially apologised for these older laws of exclusion. In 2011 and 2012, building on the publicity they received when Mitt Romney, a Mormon, ran for President, the Mormons launched a campaign titled 'I'm a Mormon' in which they consciously promoted non-white members and thus presented their religion as one that was moving in a progressive racial direction.

The LDS has historically reserved positions of leadership for men, and the Church has long promoted a family structure in which men work and women stay home to take care of sizeable families. In recent years, women have launched some protests, such as Stephanie Lauritzen of Salt Lake City, who was the originator of the 'Wear Pants to Church' movement that mobilised Mormon women around the globe. Kate Kelly, a human-rights attorney and Mormon who grew up in Oregon, founded an organisation called Ordain Women. When she refused to attend a disciplinary session with the Church, she was excommunicated.

LGBTQ issues are also a source of tension within the LDS. While many younger Mormons no longer believe that God creates only heterosexuals, the leaders of the Church long taught this doctrine and advocated therapy for people who identified as homosexual. At the time of writing, the Church website read: 'The experience of same-sex attraction is a complex reality for many people. The attraction itself is not a sin, but acting on it is.' Some student activists at Brigham Young University (BYU) – located in Provo, Utah – have sought to create a safe and welcoming space for LGBTQ students within their community, and the short video *It Gets Better at Brigham Young University* tells the stories of LGBTQ youth at BYU who came to understand that God created them as they are and that they have every right to be open about their sexual identity.

Thus far, this section has discussed the Church of Jesus Christ of Latter-day Saints. Within the broader category of 'Mormonism', however, are some much smaller groups, such as the Fundamentalist Latter-day Saints (FLDS). Concentrated in Arizona, the FLDS – and some other smaller branches of Mormonism that are not part of the mainstream church – take issue primarily with the LDS's rejection of plural marriage. While Joseph Smith had a revelation calling for men to marry multiple women, the LDS formally brought plural marriage to an end in 1890, saying the practice was no longer needed. The FLDS criticises this change, saying it stemmed solely from a political desire to remove polygamy and thus allow Utah to become a US state. Members of Fundamentalist LDS communities tend to live in tight-knit communities on family compounds. Today, the FLDS has somewhere between 6,000 and 10,000 members.

Seventh-day Adventists

Another US-born variety of Christianity that has made a home in the West is the Seventh-day Adventists. Around the time when Joseph Smith was experiencing religious visions, William Miller, also in upstate New York, came to believe that his study of the Bible showed him when Jesus Christ would return to Earth – in 1844. When this did not happen, Miller's followers – the Millerites – experienced what became known as the Great Disappointment. For those who remained in the Millerite community, James and Ellen White became significant leaders. James authored a journal called *The Advent Review and Sabbath Herald* that helped unite this early community, who came to call themselves the Seventh-day Adventists. Ellen understood herself to have the gift of prophecy, and one of the teachings that she espoused was the need to maintain a vegetarian diet.

Vegetarianism has remained a key attribute of Seventh-day Adventists, and many associate this practice with the long lives of the Seventh-day Adventist community in Loma Linda, California. Today, Loma Linda is the only place in the USA that is considered a 'Blue Zone' – that is, a place where people have particularly long lives. All of the other Blue Zones (a concept introduced by Dan Buettner) are in other regions of the world. Nutritionist John Westerdahl is a Seventh-day Adventist with a PhD from the Loma Linda University School of Health, and he advocates veganism for reasons of health as well as for reasons of ethics, since factory farming tends to be abusive to animals. In addition to abstaining from meat, Seventh-day Adventists avoid coffee and alcohol. Finally, following the model of Judaism, Seventh-day Adventists understand the Sabbath to be from Friday evening until Saturday evening, and they tend to be quite observant about abstaining from work, shopping and use of electronic devices during this time. The tight-knit community, dietary practices and willingness to take a rest one day a week are all factors that likely contribute to the Loma Linda population of Seventh-day Adventists living, on average, 7–11 years longer than other people in North America.

Eastern Orthodox

While the previous section focused on traditions that emerged in the USA and are thus relatively young versions of Christianity, this section calls attention to the fact that some of the oldest forms of Christianity have also found a home in the USA. The first Eastern Orthodox missions to North

America were those carried out by Russian Orthodox individuals who wished to convert the Indigenous people of Alaska. These initial missions, in the mid- to late eighteenth century, took place while Alaska was under the control of Russia. Since then, both Indigenous people and individuals with Russian heritage have built Russian Orthodox churches in Alaska. Some parishes affiliate with the Orthodox Church in America, whereas others identify with the Russian Orthodox Church Outside Russia. In the small town of Eklutna is a small church that exhibits the merging of Indigenous and Russian Orthodox beliefs. There, spirit houses, built by the Dena'ina at St Nicholas Orthodox Church, offer a place for the spirits of the deceased to reside for 40 days after death, and they also allow people to leave personal items that the deceased might need during those 40 days.

Although Alaska has a high rate of people who do not affiliate with any particular religious tradition, it also boasts one of the most traditional religious groups that can be found anywhere in the USA: an old-order variety of the Russian Orthodox. Historian Jack Kollman likens these small, isolated groups of Russian Orthodox to the Amish insofar as they tend to resist the incursions of the modern world and promote a dedication to the Russian language, practices dating to the seventeenth century (before the Patriarch Nikon changed some aspects of Russian Orthodox liturgy) and traditional roles for women. Over the centuries, the ancestors of this community lived in Siberia, Manchuria, Brazil and Oregon before finally deciding that a remote part of Alaska's Kenia Peninsula was the ideal place to avoid outside interference. Within this small group, adherents take pride in maintaining beliefs and practices that they understand their ancestors to have followed for hundreds of years. The tiny size of the community, however, does mean that young people must sometimes look elsewhere – most often Woodburn, Oregon, which has a substantial Russian Orthodox population – for marriage partners. And in recent years, some changes have come to the community, as the youth are expressing less interest in the Russian language and increased interest in education for young women.

Older still in their origins, the Armenian Apostolic Orthodox churches of California can accurately state that they are descended from one of the most ancient Christian institutions in the world, as the Armenian Orthodox Church is understood to have originated in the first century. The Western Diocese of the Armenian Church in the United States was established in 1910 in recognition of the fact that the number of Armenian Orthodox in the USA was fast exceeding the capacity that the Massachusetts-based headquarters could handle. In 1928, the Diocese of California came into existence and was later renamed the Western Diocese of the Armenian Church of North America. Since then, waves of immigration – spurred by political unrest and wars – have brought many more Armenians to California. A particularly large wave came with the dissolution of the Soviet Union in the early 1990s. Churches are frequently the site of language and cultural education for the children and grandchildren of Armenian immigrants. And because Southern California boasts a large number of Armenian Americans, Glendale, near Los Angeles, will be the site of the new Armenian American Museum. In Glendale, the close-knit nature of the Armenian community can also be seen in the fear of COVID-19 vaccinations, particularly among people who get most of their news from sources in Armenia. Community leaders attribute this to an understandable fear of authority that grows out of years of persecution of Armenians in the Middle East and Soviet Union. Today, Armenian American physicians are working with churches to increase trust in the vaccine.

Conclusion

The American West possesses Christian groups that espouse vegetarianism, Christian communities who have hunkered down in rural areas to maintain ancestral traditions from hundreds of years ago, Charismatic Christians who fervently believe in divine healing and Christians who are willing to speak out against their denominations in order to support LGBTQ rights. Some of the very oldest forms of Christianity flourish in the American West, as do some of the very newest forms. Isolated areas of the American West have enabled small, insular groups to flourish. Major cities have offered homes to immigrants who have brought their own distinctive varieties of Christianity to the USA. Traditions indigenous to North America have sometimes merged with forms of Christianity to create unique versions of the faith. And contact with people with a wide range of beliefs has led to intellectual and theological diversity among the people who identify as Christians in the American West. Just as the American West has some of the highest rates of religious diversity in the USA, it also boasts immense diversity when it comes to varieties of Christianity.

Bibliography

Bowman, Matthew, *The Mormon People: The Making of an American Faith* (New York: Random House, 2012).

Calvilllo, Jonathan E., *The Saints of Santa Ana: Faith and Ethnicity in a Mexican Majority City* (New York: Oxford University Press, 2020).

Espinosa, Gastón, *Latino Pentecostals in America: Faith and Politics in Action* (Cambridge, MA: Harvard University Press, 2016).

Gribben, Crawford, *Survival and Resistance in Evangelical America Christian Reconstruction in the Pacific Northwest* (New York: Oxford University Press, 2021).

Luhrmann, Tanya, *When God Talks Back: Understanding the American Evangelical Relationship with God* (New York: Vintage, 2012).

Midwestern United States

David D. Daniels III

Christianity in the Midwestern United States captures the range of Christianity across the country: Catholic, Protestant and Orthodox. Twelve states form the Midwest: Ohio, Michigan, Indiana, Illinois, Wisconsin, Minnesota, North Dakota, South Dakota, Missouri, Kansas, Iowa and Nebraska. These states represent Middle America, standing between the two coasts, East and West, and the South.

By the early 2000s, the Midwest had become a major centre of Evangelicalism, an expression of conservative Protestantism. Collectively, the Midwest's Pentecostal and Holiness denominations along with non-denominational congregations constitute 26.1% of the Protestant population in the region. When one includes conservatives of Lutheran, Presbyterian, Reformed, Congregationalist, Baptist and other persuasions, the conservative Protestant population is even higher. With headquarters, publishing houses, schools, colleges and mega-churches in the region, they exercise a major presence.

After the Evangelicals, the Midwest is Baptist in a way that escapes the South's Baptist conservatism. Its breed is mainline Baptist in contrast to the popular style of the Southern Baptists. As mainline Protestants, the American Baptists reinforce the influence of mainline Protestantism in this part of the country. The Baptists are the region's second-largest community of Protestants. Of the Protestants in the Midwest, Baptists (23.1%) are followed by Lutherans (16.9%) and Methodists (12%). Whereas the Baptists (43.6%) in the South are mostly members of the Southern Baptist Convention, who along with other Evangelical Protestants reinforce the conservative tenor and church-going culture of the South, the mainline Baptists in the Midwest have more in common with other mainline churches such as Lutheran, Methodist and Presbyterian.

Lutheranism too makes its mark on the Midwest. The region was Lutheran country during much of the twentieth century. Demographically, the Upper Midwest still holds that distinction. The Upper Midwest states of North Dakota and Minnesota anchor Lutheranism for the region. In North Dakota, for instance, 56% of Protestants are Lutheran, and in Minnesota 49% are. The Midwest overall is the Lutheran epicentre of the USA. Lutherans, who are a defining religious factor in the Midwest, sponsor at least 20 denominations with headquarters in the region; these include the two largest Lutheran communions in the nation. Lutherans shape this region more than any other. American Lutheranism shapes the character of this part of the world.

The naming of towns and cities by Protestants in the Midwest during the nineteenth century registered the vital sites of the sixteenth-century Protestant Reformation, recalling the theological preferences of Lutheran and Reformed Christians. These town names range from Amsterdam (Missouri and Ohio), Augsburg (Illinois), Antwerp (Ohio) and Berlin (Wisconsin) to Geneva (Illinois), New Prague (Minnesota), Wittenberg (Missouri) and Zurich (Kansas). Cities deriving their names from the Protestant Reformation define the map of the Midwest. Cities in the Midwest are also named after Catholic saints such as St Louis (Missouri), St Paul (Minnesota), St Joseph (Missouri), St Anne (Illinois), St Clair (Michigan), St Peters (Missouri), St Francis (South Dakota), St Stephen (Minnesota) and St John (Kansas). The names of cities connected to the Protestant Reformation and Catholic saints dot the Midwest, located within states whose names were derived from First Peoples' terms, save Indiana (which means 'land of the Indians').

In addition to the Protestants, Catholics are a major presence in the Midwest, although the region is less Catholic than most of the USA, save the South. The population of the Midwest is 23% Catholic, whereas New England is 42% and the Middle Atlantic is 37%; the Midwest Catholic population is even somewhat less than that of the Pacific region (29%).

These five theological families – Evangelical, Baptist, Lutheran, Methodist, Catholic – have shaped the region in profound ways. Protestants have always been the most populous in this region. Together with Catholics and the Orthodox, they create a majority Christian society in the Midwest.

Of the 240 Protestant, Catholic and Orthodox seminaries and divinity schools accredited in the USA by the Association of Theological Schools, more than 25% are in the Midwest. These graduate theological schools reflect the diversity of American Christianity in the region; these institutions are affiliated with theological traditions ranging from Catholic to Lutheran to Methodist to Presbyterian to Episcopalian to Pentecostal to Mennonite. Included in the Midwest is a seminary located in Ohio that is sponsored by a Black Protestant denomination, the African Methodist Episcopal Church.

The Christian demographics of the Midwest are reflective of the nation. The Midwest's Protestant, Catholic and overall Christian populations approximate the national averages, but register slightly above them. The Midwest has a higher percentage of Christians than the West, the least-Christian region, and a lesser percentage of Christians than the most-Christian region, the South. Regarding Catholics and Protestants, it is more Catholic than the South and less Catholic than the Northeast, as well as being more Protestant than the Northeast and less Protestant than the South. This really is Middle America.

Being Middle America, the Midwest hosts the headquarters of at least 88 denominations. These include mainline Protestant denominations such as the United Church of Christ, the Disciples of Christ (Christian Church) and the Evangelical Lutheran Church in America. The national offices of the Presbyterian Church (USA) are located on the southern border of the Midwest in Louisville, Kentucky. The Pentecostal denominational headquarters of the Assemblies of God, the Pentecostal Assemblies of the World and the United Pentecostal Church are also located in the Midwest. The national offices of other conservative Protestant denominations in this region include those of the Lutheran Church–Missouri Synod, the Evangelical Covenant Church and the Church of God (Anderson, Indiana).

The history of Christianity in the Midwest can be understood in terms of four periods: mid-1600s to 1790; 1790 to 1890; 1890 to 1970; and 1970 to the present. These four historical periods frame a rich history. Each period is marked by particular features that contribute to the making of the Midwest as a distinct region of American Christianity.

The Catholic Era: Mid-1600s to 1790

Christianity was present in the Midwestern United States prior to the founding of the nation. During the colonial era of the mid-1600s, the First Peoples began embracing the Christianity introduced to them by French fur traders and Catholic missionaries. Christianity in the Midwest has a long history of interaction with the Indigenous people in the region. From this interaction emerged Ojibwe (also called Chippewa) and Oglala (part of the Lakotas) Christianity. Historically, the Ojibwe Christians inhabited the Upper Midwest from Michigan to Wisconsin and Minnesota over to North Dakota. They played a pivotal role in constructing the religious landscape of the Midwest. Native American Christianity was a contributing factor in the emergence and development of Christianity in the Midwest.

The First People who embraced Christianity were joined by European immigrants, especially from France during the colonial era. They established forts in St Louis and Detroit, places that would later develop into towns, and opened Catholic chapels like Immaculate Conception in Kaskaskia in 1675 and St Anne de Detroit in 1701. The children born of French fathers and First People mothers became known as the Metis; most of them would grow up as Catholics, becoming vital members of the emerging Catholic communities that they would establish.

The Methodist Era: 1790 to 1890

Protestantism would join Catholicism during the second historical moment of the Midwest. Among Native peoples of the Midwest, Protestantism emerged during the early 1800s. The first mass Protestant conversion of Native peoples occurred in Ohio. During this period, migration would mark First People as they were forced to relocate away from the East Coast to the Midwest or within the region due to the occupation of tribal lands by white settlers, war with whites and war between tribes.

Nineteenth-century Protestantism in the Midwest commenced with the arrival of Methodists, Presbyterians, Baptists and Congregationalists. By 1850, the Methodists dominated the Christian landscape of the Midwest, outnumbering the combined total of all other Protestants and Catholics. The Midwest would become known for innovative religious experiences such as the establishment of Oberlin College in 1833, a co-educational and inter-racial institution, during the era when education was segregated by gender and race. The College and town by the same name became a thriving community committed to abolitionism, the ending of slavery. The novel social vision of Oberlin was ignited by the revivalism of the era which among Protestants promoted Christian conversion and activism. The Presbyterian turned Congregationalist clergyperson Charles Grandison Finney joined the faculty of Oberlin in 1835, serving as president from 1851 to 1865, while pastoring the town's First Congregational Church from 1844 to 1872.

During most of the nineteenth century, the Midwest was Methodist country. By 1890, the religious landscape was changing. Catholic and Lutheran immigrants reshaped the region. Catholic immigrants revived the Catholic population that had emerged during the colonial era. Lutheran immigrants introduced a new communion to the Midwest. While Catholics never outpaced Protestants, as would happen in the Northeast, the Catholic presence was strong in the region, though Protestants still dominated the religious landscape. By 1890, Methodists had ceded ground to Lutherans and others. Among Protestants, the Methodists remained the largest Protestant tradition in seven of the 12 Midwestern states – Ohio, Michigan, Illinois, Iowa, Nebraska, Indiana and Kansas – while Lutherans had emerged as the largest Protestant tradition in four upper Midwest states – Wisconsin, Minnesota and the Dakotas.

By 1890 the vast majority of the Christians were American-born whites and European immigrants. Nonetheless, African Americans did establish congregations, often Protestant, during the nineteenth century. The Christianity of the Ojibwe and Oglala still grew. African American Protestant denominations opened in the Midwest in Ohio and Michigan during the early 1800s. These denominations included the African Methodist

Episcopal Church and African Methodist Episcopal Zion Church as well as Baptist congregations that belonged to the newly established Providence Baptist Association and the Woods River Baptist Association, the first Black Baptist associations in the whole country. Congregations associated with predominately white denominations within the Methodist and Presbyterian traditions, among others, also were founded.

Charles Grandison Finney was hailed as the leading clergyperson and revivalist during the middle years of the nineteenth century, not only for the region but for the whole country. In the late nineteenth century, Dwight L. Moody, a lay preacher, emerged as the leading revivalist. In 1864, Moody turned the 500-pupil Sunday school that he had begun in 1856 into the Illinois Street Church, which would be renamed Moody Church in the next century. Moody's partnership with Ira Sankey combined preaching with robust hymn-singing to create a new form of revivalism. Sankey popularised the new gospel hymns of composers such as Frances (Fanny) Cosby. He made her 'Blessed Assurance' and the new sound of gospel hymns a sensation. He also compiled and published songbooks of gospel hymns, including those with his musical settings of hymns; by 1908, he had sold over 50 million copies of these hymnals. The larger revival movement of Moody, Sankey and Cosby, with its message of conversion, holiness, restorationism, Bible prophecy and healing, found ready audiences in the Midwest.

Chicago was also the site where Frances Elizabeth Willard, a Methodist layperson, led the Women's Christian Temperance Union (WCTU), an organisation that advocated the closing of saloons, women's right to vote and the rights of the workers. With its holistic approach, the WCTU mobilised thousands of women. Before women received the right to vote, many Protestant women expressed their 'political' views through their rallies, community-organising and lobbying male elected officials. Founded in 1883, the WCTU was the leading women's social movement in the region and the country.

The Mainline Protestant Era: 1890 to 1970

By 1890, the Roman Catholics were outpacing the Methodists, becoming the largest denominational family in most of the Midwest, except Indiana and Kansas. Yet combined, Protestantism outnumbered the Midwest's Catholic community. In Indiana and Kansas, the Methodists remained the largest church tradition. Lutherans, however, became the most numerous Christian community in the Upper Midwest. Mainline Protestants dominated the landscape.

During the late nineteenth century, mainline Protestants organised major conferences such as the 1893 World's Parliament of Religions. It was an overwhelmingly Protestant event, being organised, led and attended mostly by Protestants. The 16-member steering committee consisted of 14 mainline Protestant clergymen, a Roman Catholic bishop and a Reformed Jewish rabbi, and it had a prominent Presbyterian pastor as chair. The leadership of the Parliament were persons who led religious communities that were all located in the Midwest, specifically metro Chicago. While the conference has been characterised by some scholars as the first major conference in North America where Eastern religions such as Hinduism and Buddhism were able to present their respective faiths in their own words, these leaders of Eastern faiths were invited to the conference based on the interests of the Protestant-dominated leadership of the Parliament who designed the conference. The Lord's Prayer, deemed the 'Universal Prayer', was recited at the voluntary daily morning worship events as well as the Opening Worship, where the doxology was also sung.

The 1893 Parliament was informed by the Christian 'fulfilment theology' which recognises that all major religions possess worth but maintains that the completion or fulfilment of all religions is found in Christianity. While the most prominent African American Christian leader of the era, Frederick Douglass, addressed the conference, African American Christian clergy who were key religious leaders in the Midwest in general and Chicago in particular were absent from the leadership of the Parliament. It was a predominately white American Protestant event.

The social gospel was a mainline Protestant theological innovation that focused on the salvation of society as well as individual lives. How to apply the gospel to political, economic and civil reform became its project. Protestant 'institutional congregations' were a particular expression of a social gospel. Inspired by social Christianity, these institutional churches understood salvation as social and personal, envisioning congregations as agents of social change within communities. This model of church introduced the 'social settlement' model to parish ministry, inspiring congregations from Columbus (Ohio) to Detroit to Chicago to St Louis to expand their religious activity to include sponsoring job-related services such as employment bureaus, consumer cooperatives and credit unions, along with hosting labour union meetings in addition to other social services. Among the leading institutional congregations were First Congregational Church of Columbus and Institutional African Methodist Episcopal Church of Chicago. All of these institutional congregations became community hubs that advanced social reform. They were vital community centres that not only intersected with social service agencies but in some instances became providers of job-related and consumer services themselves.

Urban mainline white Protestant and leading Black Protestant congregations in the Midwest distinguished themselves for their musical productions, ranging from classical concerts to operas in Chicago after the First World War. Choirs and choral study clubs became the primary vehicles for cultural advancement. Historian Michael Wesley Harris notes that the culture clubs advertised that they were 'organized to create a desire for better music' within these churches. These choirs and clubs excelled in classical and choral music such as Handel's *Messiah*. Congregations like Bethel African Methodist Episcopal Church in Chicago mounted the first opera sung by African Americans in that city with the choir's performance of Von Flotow's *Martha*. These choirs and clubs would sing in Latin and English compositions ranging from Rossini's *Stabat Mater* to Mendelssohn's *Elijah*, Bach's Cantatas, Haydn's *Creation* to *The Seven Last Words* by Theodore Dubois. The complete performance of these works occurred at concerts advertised as 'monthly musicales'. In addition to European classical music, the choirs at leading Black Protestant congregations in the Midwest sang new choral arrangements of Negro Spirituals by composers such as Nathaniel Dett, Hall Johnson and Harry T. Burleigh.

Chicago became the centre of the African American gospel music movement, marked by two major sounds: Baptist and Pentecostal. Thomas Dorsey, a Baptist clergyperson, was recognised as father of the gospel music movement, noted for his composition 'Precious Lord'. He and Sallie Martin travelled across the country organising gospel choirs in Black congregations with his solo and choral compositions. Under the auspices of the National Convention of Gospel Choirs and Choruses, Dorsey and Martin popularised a major sound of gospel music. Mahalia Jackson would become of most famous gospel singer from the 1930s until the early 1970s. While Dorsey was deemed the 'father of gospel music', Arizona Dranes has been called the 'mother of gospel music'. Dranes along with Rosetta Tharpe and F. W. McGee crafted the Pentecostal sound alongside Dorsey's Baptist sound. The Pentecostal sound was noted for its call-and-response, improvisation, poly-rhythms and diatonic harmonies, a sound often associated with New Orleans jazz style and ragtime-styled piano accompaniment.

African American ecumenism found expression in the establishment of the National Fraternal Council of Negro Churches in Chicago in 1934 with an ecumenical leadership that was mostly based in the Midwest. With its headquarters in Chicago, this national ecumenical organisation brought together seven African American denominations, later increasing to 12, ranging from Baptist to Methodist to Pentecostal, along with African American representatives of predominately white denominations. Channelling their political activism through the Council, Black activist clergy challenged the legal system of racial segregation and promoted racial justice during the 1930s and 1940s.

The five largest African American Baptist and Methodist denominations were members of both the Fraternal Council of Negro Churches and the Federal Council of Churches, a white-led organisation with a majority white membership representing approximately 30 predominately white mainline Protestant denominations. The representatives of the five African American member denominations promoted the Fraternal Council's vision of racial justice within the Federal Council. In 1946, the Federal Council adopted a statement renouncing racial segregation and calling for an inter-racial church and an inter-racial society.

In 1942, the National Association of Evangelicals (NAE), a predominately white Protestant ecumenical body, was founded in St Louis to provide a distinct voice for conservative Christians which could be differentiated from the separatist or militant stance of fundamentalists. The NAE brought together conservative Presbyterians, Congregationalists, Baptists, Pietists, Anabaptists, Holiness and Pentecostals. While being a national organisation, it brought within its fold denominations headquartered in the Midwest such as the General Association of General Baptists, the Mennonite Brethren Churches (USA), the Evangelical Free Church of America and the Assemblies of God. The NAE became a larger institutional network with the Midwest flagship institutions like Wheaton College and religious publications such as *Christianity Today*. This network charted an ecclesial trajectory that distinguished itself from what it called militant fundamentalism and mounted a new conservative theological movement it named Evangelicalism.

Martin Luther King, Jr brought the attention of the national civil rights movement to the Midwest, specifically Chicago. Activists in Chicago addressed the problem of overcrowded public schools in Black communities. *De facto* school segregation occurred throughout the Chicago school district. A one-day school boycott was held on 22 October 1963 to spotlight the problem. A second school boycott was in the planning that was contested by community leaders. Abstaining from supporting the boycott were the Chicago branches of the National Association for the Advancement of Colored People (NAACP) and the Urban League, Chicago's Black Democratic leadership, and many prominent African American congregations, including the historic Olivet Baptist Church pastored by Joseph H. Jackson. Support for the boycott included representatives of other congregations, including Vernon Park Church, Quinn Chapel AME and First Congregational Baptist Church. During the second school boycott, held in 1964, a number of Black congregations housed the 'Freedom Schools'. At a July 1964 rally, there was a march of more than 30,000 protesters.

During the summer of 1965, King began conversations about the possibility of shifting the civil rights movement's focus beyond the South to the Midwest, specifically Chicago. A Chicago chapter of the Southern Christian Leadership Council was established with its headquarters at the Warren Avenue Congregational Church, a congregation on Chicago's West Side pastored by a white clergyperson, William Briggs. King spotlighted the travesty of northern *de facto* segregation in cities like Chicago with the harsh poverty of the Black poor in 'urban ghettos' like Chicago's West Side. Pivotal in securing support from African American congregations was Clay Evans, a famous radio preacher and pastor of Chicago's Fellowship Baptist Church.

Through the efforts of King, Evans and the Chicago chapter of the Southern Christian Leadership Conference (SCLC), various congregations and community organisations joined King's Chicago campaign. During the summer of 1966 Black congregations were drawn on for mass meetings. Violence against the Chicago civil rights campaign was seen in a bomb being detonated at the New Friendship Baptist Church on Chicago's West Side as well as bomb threats directed at affiliated sites. The 1966 marches for open housing that King led through Marquette Park received attention from the national media; these marches were met by counter-protests, seeking to maintain restrictive covenants that prohibited houses in certain neighbourhoods from being rented or sold to African Americans.

While the campaign for open housing would secure little success, Chicago's Operation Breadbasket, led by Reverend Jesse Jackson, Sr, originally an arm of Chicago SCLC, experienced larger Black clergy support as well as later success in its economic boycott of corporations and lobbying for Black ownership of franchises, distributors and car dealerships. In 1966, Operation Breadbasket relocated from Atlanta to Chicago with the objective of abolishing job discrimination by white companies with stores in Chicago's Black communities. The strategy included Black clergy collecting statistics about the hiring of Black employees in Black neighbourhoods. From these surveys, Operation Breadbasket identified the stores where Black employees were non-existent, underemployed or excluded from managerial positions. It negotiated with the store to rectify the inequality. For those stores that refused to institute fair employment practices, it launched a selective patronage campaign: picket and boycott the stores as well as boycott the parent companies.

The Chicago campaign was successful. Over 2,000 new jobs were created. In addition to the hiring of Black employees, Operation Breadbasket also secured agreements from major companies to buy products from African American companies and deposit capital funds in Black-owned banks. Among the parent companies successfully engaged in the Chicago selective patronage campaign during 1966 were: dairy companies such as Borden, Bowman Dairy, Country Delight Dairy,

Hawthorn-Mellody and Wanzer Dairy; beverage companies such as Coca-Cola and Pepsi-Cola; and supermarkets such as National Team Company, Jewel Foods, A&P and High Low Food (Hi-Lo). The selective patronage campaign with its focus on Black employment, contracts and products, and capital investment in Black-owned banks leveraged the 'purchasing power' of African Americans. Organisations like Operation Breadbasket as a Christian activist organisation could persuade or 'force' companies to be socially responsible towards the Black community.

The Evangelical Era: 1970 to the Present
By the 1970s, the decline in the membership of mainline Protestant denominations became noticeable and the growth in Evangelical congregations and denominations became pronounced. The rise of the Evangelical megachurches marked the era, with congregations of over 2,000 attendees at worship services held on either Saturday or Sunday. Evangelical megachurches in the Midwest that gained national attention included Willow Creek Community Church in the Chicago suburb of South Barrington, Apostolic Church of God (Chicago), Moody Church (Chicago), First Baptist Church (Hammond, Indiana), Bethlehem Baptist Church (Minneapolis), and The Chapel (Akron, Ohio). Mainline Protestants led progressive efforts that defined this period. From civil rights, the peace movement's anti-Vietnam campaign, women's rights, rights of gays and lesbians, environmental justice, free South Africa and pro-Palestine, progressive Christian movements had bases in the Midwest.

During the 1970s, Black church-based campaigns, in alliance with progressive whites, were mounted to elect African American mayors in cities like Gary (Indiana), Cleveland (Ohio), Detroit and Chicago. Massive voter registration drives were launched in different cities at different times. For instance, during a 1982 multiracial voter registration campaign in Chicago, 230,000 new registrants were added to the voting rolls.

A prominent conservative Protestant laywoman during this era was Phyllis Schlafly, an attorney by training. She was a forerunner of the Christian Right led by Jerry Falwell's Moral Majority and supported Pat Robertson's Christian Coalition, having founded the Eagle Forum in 1972 as an organisation opposed to the passing of the Equal Rights Amendment (ERA), a proposed amendment to the US Constitution guaranteeing gender equality for women; the amendment was ratified by 35 states, but was defeated by failing to achieve ratification by the required 38 states. Schlafly would also oppose reproductive rights for women and rights of sexual minorities.

By the 1970s, in urban centres of the Midwest such as Chicago, Detroit and St Louis, Roman Catholic parishes built by Irish, Polish and other immigrants sometimes became African American congregations. St Columbanus, a previously white parish, was located on Chicago's South Side. Having been created in 1909 for upwardly mobile Irish-American residents, by 1970 the parish was becoming predominately African American. With two priests and two deacons, the parish offered a daily Mass during the week and three Masses on Saturdays and Sundays during this period. It also operated a highly respected and growing parochial school whose students came from throughout the South Side of Chicago.

The 1993 Parliament of the World's Religions (renamed since 1893), according to Seager, reflected the spirit of religious pluralism rather than the primacy of Christianity. While the chairperson of the council for the Parliament was a Protestant clergyperson, David Ramage, Christians, for instance, comprised only 4 of the 14 host committees which organised the vast majority of the sessions. The Christian host committees were Anglican/Episcopal, Pan Orthodox, Roman Catholic and African American Protestant. The other nine host committees represented world religions beyond Christianity, including Native American. Similar to the 1893 Parliament, the members of each host committee were Midwestern religious leaders, specifically from metro Chicago.

The Christian delegates to the 1993 Parliament included Roman Catholics and mainline Protestants who supported the event, whereas white Evangelicals and Fundamentalists boycotted it. Embodying the ecumenical and inter-faith spirit of African American Christianity in the Midwest or, at least, in metro Chicago, the African American host committee included representatives from Wesleyan and Pentecostal dominations, including the Pentecostal Assemblies of the World and the Church of God in Christ. A Pentecostal clergyperson from New York City served as one of the 25 presidents, two Chicago Pentecostal clergypersons served as trustees and three Pentecostal churches were among the co-sponsoring congregations.

The new era of immigrant Christian congregations in the Midwest is a product of the 1965 Immigration Act. The advent of Korean, Asian Indian, Brazilian and Nigerian immigrant churches, specifically denominations, in the USA during the post-1965 era created a new moment in the Christianity of the Midwest. While Mexican, Afro-Caribbean and Ethiopian immigrant congregations emerged in the Midwest prior to 1965, even prior to 1940, Christianity in the Midwest during the opening decades of the twentieth century was more shaped by Christian immigrants from Europe.

During 2000, in greater Chicago 40 African immigrant congregations were identified. Out of the various denominations, it appears that a significant number of congregations, 21, belonged to the Pentecostal-Charismatic wing of Christianity. The second largest group, nine, fitted within the orbit of the spiritual churches such as the Cherubim and Seraphim. The third largest sector, six, was affiliated with mainline denominations. The national origin of congregations reflects the immigration pattern to the Midwestern city of Chicago: 16 Nigerian, 9 Ghanaian and one each among Senegalese, Ethiopians and Eritreans.

By the early 2000s, the Roman Catholics became the largest denominational family, larger than the Evangelicals, Baptists, Lutherans or Methodists in most of the Midwest, except Minnesota and the Dakotas, where the Lutherans were the largest. However, Protestantism remained the largest branch of Christianity in the Midwest.

Conclusion

Christianity in the Midwest United States exhibits the shape of Middle America. From the colonial era to the twenty-first century, it has been heavily Catholic, Methodist, mainline Protestant and Evangelical. It is the epicentre of American Lutheranism. It has been at the centre of various social initiatives led by Christians: temperance, women's right to vote, against the Equal Rights Amendment, and reproductive rights. When Martin Luther King, Jr took the civil rights movement beyond the South, he moved it to the Midwest, specifically Chicago. Leading Evangelical denominations, congregations and institutions operate out of the Midwest. Some of them clearly anchor the Evangelical movement. Two Parliaments of World Religion were convened: the first in 1893, by mostly mainline Protestants; and the second in 1993, by an inter-religious group with a mainline Protestant as the conference chair and Pentecostals included in the African American host committee. Christianity in the Midwest possess a religious character of its own.

Bibliography

Barlow, Philip and Mark Silk, *Religion and the Public Life in the Midwest: American Common Denominator?* (New York: Alta Mira Press, 2004).

Ezra, Michael, ed., *The Economic Civil Rights Movement: African Americans and the Struggle for Power* (New York: Routledge, 2013).

Livezey, Lowell W., *Public Religion and Urban Transformation: Faith in the City* (New York: New York University Press, 2000).

Loveland, Anne C. and Curtis B. Wheeler, *From Meetinghouse to Megachurch: A Material and Cultural History* (Columbia, MO: University of Missouri Press, 2003).

Sisson, Richard, et al., eds, *American Midwest: Interpretive Encyclopedia* (Bloomington, IN: Indiana University Press, 2007).

Southern United States

Otis W. Pickett and Noah R. Karger

The Southern United States includes the states of Alabama, Arkansas, Delaware, Florida, Georgia, Kentucky, Louisiana, Maryland, Mississippi, North Carolina, Oklahoma, South Carolina, Tennessee, Texas, Virginia and West Virginia. Though in slight decline, according to Pew Research, the Christian proportion of the population of the South was 76% in 2014, still higher than that of any other US region. Its makeup is predominantly Evangelical Protestant, with the vast majority of the country's Baptist churches, including the country's second-largest denomination, the Southern Baptist Convention. Largely due to a burgeoning Hispanic population, the South has become home to 27% of the country's Catholics, more than any other region. Areas with a high concentration of Catholics include south-east Florida, southern Louisiana and throughout Texas, especially along its border with Mexico. However, the South is still overwhelmingly Protestant. Nearly 100 years ago the South (excluding areas in its south-west and the southern-most part of Florida) was given the epithet of the 'Bible Belt', a designation that remains relevant today. The Bible Belt denotes not only the preponderance of religious affiliation but also cultural-political affiliation with conservative Protestant Evangelicalism.

Historical Background

Landing in Florida in 1538, European explorers violently conquered Indigenous American peoples, invoking Catholicism to rationalise their cruelty. It was here that amassing land, wealth and power at the expense of Indigenous American and African peoples became intertwined with Christianity in the South. In the hands of land-hungry Europeans, Christianity was a tool for justifying land expropriation and the exploitation of labour for centuries. Although Southern Christian history has often been studied through white lenses, its multi-ethnicity and global impact are of increasing interest in academia. As European Christianity became the predominant religious expression in the eighteenth and nineteenth centuries, its diversity influenced the US South profoundly. For instance, while Catholicism in the colonial South was influenced mostly by Spanish explorers, its lasting imprint is more Irish, due to the arrival of immigrants in the nineteenth century.

The Eighteenth Century

The brand of Christianity that would come to distinguish the Southern Church emerged with the First Great Awakening (1730s–1740s). This highly evangelical and individualistic expression of the faith developed amidst widespread isolation and chaos. It emphasised the weight of personal sin and consequent likelihood of hell, intending to inspire urgent interest in salvation and resultant confessions of faith. Eschewing liturgy, hierarchical church government and systematic theology, this movement stressed individual experience and emotion in interpreting the will of God. Confessions of faith were preferably public, which allowed preachers and their acolytes to count converts, the metric for an evangelist's success. Accordingly, the focus was not instructing the newly converted on how to live as such but the conversion of non-Christians. Employing a numbers-driven metric evinced broader economic desperation throughout the colonies. Every shipment of tobacco and cotton was calculated for maximum profit. Just as the maximisation of profit determined a merchant's success, the maximisation of converts determined a preacher's.

Churches influenced by the First Great Awakening provided more freedoms to enslaved people, women, young non-landed men and children. This could be attributed to these communities' emphasis on (1) all individuals being 'created in God's image' and (2) their numbers-driven metric of evangelistic success. Elite, landed Anglicans recoiled against the challenge these new expressions of Christianity posed to the existing power structure. However, after the American Revolution (1775–83), this new Evangelical movement began embracing the values held by the elite. In the latter part of the eighteenth century, immigration became the main driver of denominational plurality in the South. New settlement from France, Germany, Scotland and Ireland brought Huguenots, Lutherans, Quakers, Presbyterians and Methodists. As settlers wrestled to find their place in this new land, their Christian identities helped forge a robust and multifaceted Southern religious experience. Enslaved Africans were exposed to Catholicism, Anglicanism, Islam, African-based polytheism, nature-based practices and New Light Evangelicalism. With the Second Great Awakening and Reform Era (1830s–1850s), robust Evangelical Protestantism came to dominate the South by way of Baptists and Methodists.

The Nineteenth Century

The Second Great Awakening (1795–1835) began with revivals among Presbyterians in Cane Ridge, Kentucky, moving through Tennessee, Mississippi and the 'old south-west'. Highly disorganised and even more emotional than those of the First Great Awakening, these revivals attracted numerous worshippers from every social stratum. The revivals engendered new communities across the South, which provided women and non-landed men spaces for the expression of agency, often taking the form of political activism. During the 1820s and 1830s, as congregationalist churches began voting on their pastorates and budgets, a spirit of democratisation crept into churches. An ethos of self-advocacy increased in churches and states, as Southerners sought to reform their chaotic, frontier existence. The 1820s and 1830s also brought about the Reform Era, during which the temperance movement gained chief importance among Christians. As Southern congregations were of a female majority, women led the temperance reform, using the Church as a space to organise and build consensus across municipalities. Christian women's leadership in the temperance movement set a precedent for their participation in later suffrage movements.

Christian responses to the abolitionist movement varied. While Northern abolitionists presented slavery as unbiblical, Southern theologians like James Henley Thornwell and Robert Lewis Dabney argued the opposite. They equated slavery in the Ancient Near East and Roman Empire to that of nineteenth-century America. They further argued that it was beneficial for enslaved people, as they could be 'liberated from an uncivilised African continent'. Adopted by churches throughout the South, these theological positions were the impetus to 'missionise the enslaved'. Charles Colcock Jones of Liberty County, Georgia, for example, founded 'slave mission churches'. He travelled to different plantations, preaching on Sunday to enslaved people. By the 1850s, these efforts had grown into establishing local churches that often were led by white people. Southerners had to create new categories for enslaved memberships, as Blacks were mostly prohibited from reading the Bible. Performing baptisms and weddings wove slavery into the ecclesiastical structures and thus accommodated slaveholder hegemony.

Enslaved people used these spaces in unique ways. For instance, Denmark Vesey, who was likely married in a white Presbyterian church as an enslaved person, later purchased his freedom and became a member of an all-Black African Methodist Episcopal church in Charleston, South Carolina. He leveraged his position in the church to help free his enslaved brothers and sisters. For Vesey, Christianity and freedom were synonymous; ergo, the institution of slavery was an abhorrent deviation from its doctrine. Autonomous Black congregations continued cropping up across the South. However, Black preachers were treated with suspicion and were severely limited in their opportunities to preach. Historians like Albert Raboteau have underscored the myriad ways in which enslaved Black people worshipped under the watchful eyes of white overseers. In what has been called the 'invisible institution', they met in the woods, swamps and brush arbours in and around isolated plantations.

On the eve of the Civil War, the South believed God was on their side and would surely bring victory. Historian Mark Noll has labelled the Civil War a 'theological crisis' for the USA, particularly the South. In addition to overturning the Southern 'way of life' (one directly tied to slave-holding), God had chosen their enemies to conquer them. In 1865, this crisis was brought to the fore with Lee's surrender at Appomattox, Virginia, followed by the beginning of Reconstruction. Reconstruction revealed not only a theological crisis for the defeated Confederacy, but also crises in politics, transportation, infrastructure and food. Southerners compared themselves to the Israelites, as hordes of Northern Assyrians, Babylonians and pagan 'Yankees' occupied their land. Seeing themselves as God's people, white Southern Christians interpreted their defeat as God's discipline, proving that God still ultimately loved and sided with them. Insulting to white Southerners was that Northern white missionaries were moving south to educate and support freed slaves, which was interpreted as an expansion of the Union's control.

During Reconstruction, white Southern Evangelicals adopted a nationalistic Christianity that commemorated the Confederate 'lost cause'. These efforts were led by clergy, former Confederate chaplains and women active in organisations like the United Daughters of the Confederacy. From this political-religious fervour emerged memorials, rituals, literature and even a catechism, editing American history to portray the Southern cause as one similar to that of the Founding Fathers, evading the topic of slavery. This portrayal of the Confederacy came to typify the political and racial views of white Southern Christians. They sought to 'redeem' their land by opposing Reconstruction and recreating slavery, seeing it as God-ordained.

Freed Blacks began leaving white denominations and slave mission churches in large numbers. A kind of 'religious exodus' occurred during Reconstruction that gave them true, public religious autonomy. They developed schools, burial societies and benevolence organisations. They used their churches for political mobilisation and voting, often holding rallies. Some Black Americans chose to stay in white Evangelical churches, and by the mid- to late 1870s, these denominations were leading the culture on segregation. For instance, in 1874 Southern Presbyterians voted for what was called an 'organic separation' along racial lines. The result was that churches with Black members could no longer be a part of the Presbyterian Church of the United States (the Southern branch). In some ways, this church led the region in what would later become legalised segregation.

The Twentieth Century

Rather than addressing centuries of institutionalised racism, white Christians at the turn of the twentieth century chose to emphasise perceived personal sins like gambling, dancing and drinking. Meanwhile, Black Christians began objecting to racial violence and their lack of access to voting and education. By 1900, the African Methodist Episcopal Church, National Baptist Convention, African Methodist Episcopal Church Zion and Colored Methodist Episcopal Church had nearly three million members. The church was central to the Southern Black American way of life, not just as a religious institution, but as the centre of Black life, community, family and belonging.

White Southern Evangelicals rejected two major shifts in the early twentieth century: the influence of science and the anti-lynching movement (1890s–1930s). Their rejection of modern science is famously exemplified by the 1925 Scopes trial, where William Jennings Bryan argued that Charles Darwin's theory of evolution contradicted the biblical account of creation. The case inspired many in conservative-majority counties to remove evolution from public school curricula. Despite repeated calls for an anti-lynching bill by Christian advocates such as Ida B. Wells, Francis James Grimké and Booker T. Washington, most white Southern Evangelicals remained silent. Many even attended and participated in lynchings. Though odious, extra-legal murder was acceptable to most white Evangelicals, as it protected the racial status quo and maintained their hierarchical understanding of race. Southern representatives worked to prevent a federal anti-lynching bill, knowing it would upset their constituents who preferred a rougher, more Southern, 'frontier justice'. The justice system's racism was evinced, for example, by the over-representation of Black Americans in prison and the convict lease system. Segregation protected white Southerners from what they called 'miscegenation', the prospect of their children dating, dancing with, having intercourse with and/or marrying Black people.

During the Great Depression (1929–41), churches were unable to meet the needs of the poor and unemployed. Southern Christians prayed to God but ultimately looked to the federal government to provide relief. The New Deal (1933–9) garnered overwhelming support, not only because of the aid it provided but also because Franklin D. Roosevelt maintained the racial status quo. He let the New Deal mostly benefit white Southerners while protecting the right to 'lynch'. FDR never promoted an anti-lynching bill, although First Lady Eleanor Roosevelt spoke often about its need, openly challenging segregation laws. After the Second World War, however, Southern white Christians hardened their position on another set of racial issues: civil rights.

In the South, the civil rights movement was led by Black American Christians, men and women like Ella Baker, Daisy Bates, Martin Luther King, Jr, Ralph Abernathy, Jesse Jackson and Fred Shuttlesworth. These were pastors who perceived an inherent connection between civic equality and Christian ethics. Black Southern Christians had suffered discrimination since before the Civil War, and so faith became essential to their profound endurance. This was embodied by the life of Fannie Lou Hamer, who was nearly beaten to death for asserting her right to vote. Hamer was known for her constant singing of Christian spirituals and quoting of Bible verses. She taught Sunday school and cared for her neighbours. She peacefully spoke, marched and advocated for her right to be a first-class citizen in America. Amid the affliction experienced as a Black woman in the South, she has been hailed as an example of what it means to truly follow Christ.

Most white Evangelical Christians were hesitant to support civil rights. In his 'Letter from Birmingham Jail', King wrote to the 'white Christian moderate', who chose the racial status quo despite the suffering it caused their Black American brothers and sisters. White Christian colleges maintained segregation much longer than Southern public universities. They posited it as biblical, using accounts from Genesis like the Tower of Babel to prove how God desired to keep the races separate. Few white pastors across the South oversaw integrated churches. During the 1960s, many churches had deacons or hired guards standing at their front doors, ready to prevent 'kneel-ins', which were visits by Black Americans to prominent white churches to test their tolerance for integration.

The Twenty-first Century: Evangelicals

Although it is prevalent throughout the USA, Evangelicalism is concentrated in the South. Historian David W. Bebbington defined Evangelicalism in terms of four characteristics: biblicism, conversionism, crucicentrism and activism. Essentially, Evangelicals emphasise the atoning work of Christ as attested in the Bible and the importance of responding via conversion and subsequent obedience. The centrality of Scripture and the individual's personal relationship with Jesus Christ have been distinguishing features of Southern churches. Placing spiritual authority mostly in Scripture and individual experience, Southern Evangelicals have tended to adopt ecclesial polities which permit considerable independence, and often complete independence. This helps explain the over-representation of Baptists in the South. Southern Evangelical churches tend to integrate with highly localised communities, becoming a central feature of the Southerner's way of life. Southern Evangelical churches often work against seeming overly formal, actively seeking to harmonise with the unpretentious facts of one's life.

Southern Evangelical churches' integration into their congregants' weekly rhythms and local culture creates space for the intermingling of theology and politics. In this regard, the words of Martin Luther King, Jr, are still true: 11 o'clock on a Sunday morning is one of the most segregated hours in Christian America, if not the single most segregated. The South confronts issues of race today that have long determined its history. These matters have become increasingly politicised, dividing the Church along partisan lines. In the 2016 and 2020 US presidential elections, the overwhelming majority of white Evangelical Protestant voters chose the Republican candidate, while the overwhelming majority of Black Protestant voters chose the Democrat. The centrality of race relations in Southern churches became heightened with the election of Donald Trump in 2016. Trump was in many ways a spokesperson for a poor, white, Evangelical working class. This demographic, who felt their issues were muffled by a public discourse concerned with race relations, gender equality and LGBTQ+ rights, found representation in Trump. However, feelings of neglect often evolved into deep-set resentment, sparking blatant prejudice towards Black Americans and other minorities.

This culminated in the racially motivated murders of two unarmed Black Southerners, Breonna Taylor and George Floyd, by white police officers during the spring of 2020. Around the same time, Russell Moore, a renowned Southern Evangelical who presided over the Ethics and Religious Liberty Commission of the Southern Baptist Convention (SBC), sent a letter to his board of trustees. In it, he charged the SBC's executive committee with egregious sexual abuse and racial discrimination. Moore's repeated attempts to confront such issues were met with belligerence. The response to Moore demonstrated the issue's depth and breadth in the SBC and Bible Belt in general. Later that year, the SBC's seminary presidents released a statement declaring critical race theory unbiblical and therefore incompatible with Christian doctrine. Ralph D. West, the Black senior pastor of a Houston mega-church, responded by announcing his church's exit from the SBC alongside several others. This initiated an exodus which continues in the present. The SBC's membership declined from 16.6 million to 14.1 million between 2005 and 2020.

The worldwide Women's March on 21 January 2017 communicated a ubiquitous frustration regarding the state of issues such as women's rights, reproductive rights and LGBTQ+ rights. It was the largest single-day march in US history. This spirit of unrest has been especially present in Southern churches, concerning, for instance, the polarising issue of female ordination. While most mainline Protestant traditions now allow it, the majority of Southern Evangelical churches do not. However, even among mainline churches that permit female ordination, women are still underrepresented in top positions. These differences are hashed out theologically in the ongoing debate between complementarianism and egalitarianism. Complementarianism posits that men and women are given unique but complementary roles by God: men are given the role of headship and women that of submission, in both domestic and ecclesial affairs. While historically Southern Evangelicalism has been dominated by a complementarian view, there appears to be a recent groundswell of support for egalitarianism.

The shifting zeitgeist cannot be attributed to a single cause, but the widespread and increasingly publicised abuse of women in churches has contributed in a major way. In 2019, the *Houston Chronicle* published a six-part series on sexual abuse within the SBC, counting 700 victims over 20 years. It detailed stories of sexual abuse by pastors and other leaders, predominantly against teenage girls. The SBC's response was alarmingly dismissive. Prominent Evangelical Bible teacher and former Southern Baptist Beth Moore has been an advocate for victims of sexual abuse within the denomination. She was also an outspoken critic of Donald Trump, labelling his behaviour sexist. Her criticism of Trump and exposure of sexual abuse in the SBC were met with hostility from SBC leaders. She left the SBC in March 2021. The impact of her departure is difficult to fathom, as she held a unique representation amidst an otherwise male-dominated denomination.

The frequency of sexual abuse within Southern Evangelical churches may be connected to an unresolved tension within the culture and theology. Purity culture, most popular at the turn of the twentieth century, is an offshoot of Southern Evangelical conservative sexual values. Its chief symbol is a 'purity ring', given to a pre-teen or teenage girl by her father, signifying her commitment to abstaining from premarital sex. This model often frames young women as a temptation to their male peers, needing to dress modestly, for instance, to counteract this. The SBC championed this movement with its True Love Waits campaign, which encouraged young adults to abstain from sex before marriage. Framing the social-sexual dynamic like this is unlikely to prove benign. In 2021, Robert Aaron Long, aged 21, went on a shooting spree in spas in Atlanta, Georgia, killing eight people, six of whom were Asian women. He claimed to have done so to eradicate what he perceived as the cause of his sexual temptation.

Southern Evangelical churches have responded to contemporary ethical issues by focusing on the individual's culpability or lack thereof. This interest in individual rather than corporate sin and faith dates back to the First and Second Great Awakenings. The South has a long history of prioritising the individual's relationship with Christ. The priority of that relationship over and above issues of social justice are seen in Billy

Graham's response to Martin Luther King, Jr. Graham perceived his primary task as saving souls, addressing the human heart rather than the systems wherein they operate collectively. This resulted in the refusal to join, or support, civil rights marches. The same reluctance to explicitly support social justice is still present in white Southern Evangelicalism. The exit of Russell Moore, Beth Moore, Ralph D. West and others from the SBC provides evidence of this.

The emphasis on the individual believer is also apparent in their worship. The majority of popular Southern Evangelical worship music is written in the first person. Music and sermons alike tend to be more emotive. While traditional tent revivals still occur in rural areas of the South, the worship conference is a kind of contemporary version. Worship conferences occur all over the region throughout the year. Louie Giglio, pastor in Atlanta, Georgia, founded Passion Conferences in 1997. Passion Conferences have been held around the world but are headquartered in Atlanta and are usually organised in the Southern states. These annual conferences feature famous Evangelical (and mostly Southern) speakers, pastors and worship leaders, attracting as many as 50,000 participants.

While Evangelical churches have assimilated into the social fabric of small towns across the South, they have also featured prominently in its cities. Southern Evangelical churches scale with their demand, a demand that seemingly has no ceiling. Lakewood Church in Houston, Texas, has the country's largest weekly attendance, at 43,500. Lakewood is followed by North Point Community Church in Alpharetta, Georgia, and Gateway Church in Southlake, Texas. These churches meet in stadium-like arenas, televising their services. The Southern mega-church is a product of the consumer-driven, capitalistic model of the American economy and an independent ecclesial polity common in Evangelical churches. The cultural integration that small Evangelical churches accomplish in rural areas is achieved at the regional level by the mega-church. Mega-churches have spawned Christian celebrities and entertainment, basically a Christian pop culture. This Christian pop culture does not exist harmoniously alongside secular pop culture. Rather, Christian pop culture emerges as a competitor, its target market being made up largely of Southern Evangelicals. While small, rural Evangelical churches exist at the periphery of American media, mega-churches have oriented themselves inversely.

A consequence of the massive attention garnered by mega-churches is that instances of moral failure are known readily and widely. In February 2021, Ravi Zacharias, a licensed minister in the Christian and Missionary Alliance and founder of the global evangelism organisation Ravi Zacharias International Ministries (RZIM, based in Atlanta, Georgia), was posthumously indicted for a pattern of sexual abuse. As a massively influential Evangelical apologist, he was lauded by culturally prominent Southern Christians like rapper and songwriter Lecrae Moore and NFL player Tim Tebow; the allegations of his misconduct came as a complete shock to the Southern Evangelical establishment. After confirming the veracity of the allegations, RZIM changed its name and renounced all content related to Zacharias.

Black Protestant Churches

Most Black churches belong to historically Black denominations such as the African Methodist Episcopal (AME) Church, the African Methodist Episcopal Zion (AMEZ) Church, the National Baptist Convention (NBC), the National Baptist Convention of America (NBCA), the Progressive National Convention (PNBC), the Christian Methodist Episcopal (CME) Church and the Church of God in Christ (COGIC). Black Southern Christians are generally less insular than white Southern Christians in their concern for and identification with the South. This is likely due to the dissimilarity of their relations with its history. While white Southerners cling to vestiges of Confederate culture and politics, seeking to preserve a disappearing way of life, Black Southern Christians are motivated by ways to overcome it. The political identities of Black Southern Christians are thus less often delineated by a single party.

Black Southern churches show special concern for issues of systemic and social injustice. While opposing racism might seem of secondary importance to many white Southern churches, Black Southern churches were founded and exist under this very condition. While Black American church membership dropped from 78% in 2000 to 59% in 2020, Black Americans are still more religious than any other demographic in the USA. Even though younger generations are less involved in the Black Southern Church, the Reverend Tyshawn Gardner, historian at the University of Alabama, posits that the church remains an epicentre for Black life. With many Black Southerners living in substandard urban infrastructure, churches play a unique role in protecting and maintaining people's livelihoods. Making up the majority of Democratic voters in the South, Black Christians also have a distinct role politically.

Despite voting Democratic, most Southern Black Christians hold socially conservative views on issues such as LGBTQ+ rights and same-sex marriage. However, there is still ample participation in the leadership of Southern Black churches by LGBTQ+ people, operating with the dictum 'don't ask, don't tell'. Twenty-first-century Black Southern churches are also largely conservative on the issue of female ordination, even though they have historically embraced female preachers, such as Jarena Lee, Zilpha Elaw and Julia Foote. However, Teresa Elaine Jefferson-Snorton was elected the first ever female bishop of the CME Church in 2010. She presides over churches in Alabama and Florida. Likewise, Vashti Murphy McKenzie became the first female bishop in the AME Church in 2000 and presided over churches in Kentucky and Tennessee. Later, she became titular head of the AME Church. In her book *Red Lip Theology: For Church Girls Who've Considered Tithing to the Beauty Supply Store When Sunday Morning Isn't Enough* (Colorado Springs, CO: Convergent, 2022), public theologian Candice Benbow of Atlanta, Georgia, offers an invitation to Black women to seek God as Black women, to embark on a personal, spiritual journey which affirms their femininity.

First advocated by theologians like Dwight Hopkins of Richmond, Virginia, Black liberation theology understands the Christian narrative in light of the oppressive realities that have long plagued Black Americans. Its aim is to liberate non-white (especially Black) people from unjust social, economic and political systems. It is a theology concerned, like Jesus, with the poor and needy. Perhaps in part because fewer young Black Southerners are attending church, the protests that followed George Floyd's death were led by Black Lives Matter rather than a modern-day Martin Luther King, Jr. While Black Southern churches routinely address issues of social justice, the intensity of recent events and increasing secularisation of younger generations has meant social justice is sought elsewhere. However, in *Reading While Black* (Downers Grove, IL: IVP, 2020), Esau McCaulley, an Anglican priest and New Testament scholar, outlines the US history of racist biblical interpretation and its present consequences, with which he is intimately familiar, having grown up in Huntsville, Alabama. He proffers a Black ecclesial hermeneutic as a means of responding to this tragic reality. McCaulley's reflections provide space for simultaneous lamentation and hope regarding issues of race within Southern churches.

Hispanic Churches

According to the 2020 US census, Hispanics accounted for 51.1% of the country's growth in population since the previous (2010) census. In Texas, Hispanics make up 39.3% of the population, while non-Hispanic whites make up 39.7%. The USA declared a crisis at its border with Mexico in 2014, as border patrol agents became unable to handle the volume of immigration and its accompanying calamities. While the Trump administration enacted the harshest anti-migration laws, even erecting a wall on the border, immigration continued to balloon. Mexican-Americans, or Tejanos, influenced the south-west long before the USA emerged. While Spanish missionaries of the sixteenth century brought Catholicism, American missionaries of the twentieth brought Pentecostalism. Now, Latino/as bring a unique form of each across the border.

American Catholicism is more Hispanic than ever. According to the Public Religion Research Institute, Hispanic Catholics made up 8.2% of the US population as of 2020, up from 7.4% in 2013–19. Eight out of the 10 counties with the highest concentrations of Hispanic Catholics are in Texas. There are currently 25 active Latino bishops in the USA, with five in Texas and two in Florida. In 1970, Archbishop Patrick Flores became the first Mexican-American bishop in the USA, serving the Archdiocese of San Antonio, Texas. Historian Timothy Matovina posits that, while Catholic leaders of European descent often focus on the Church's intersection with American culture, those of Hispanic descent tend to be preoccupied with equipping it to aid the suffering of Latino/a members. He argues that the American Catholic Church is divided not only politically, but culturally and socioeconomically, which becomes increasingly clear as it gives Latino/a Catholics a platform. Developed in Spain in 1944, Cursillos de Cristiandad (Short Courses of Christianity) have spread across the Southern United States via Latino Catholics. Cursillos are intended to foster spiritual maturity and leadership among laity, promoting a widespread sense of community among Latino/a American Catholics. Its national headquarters is in Jarrell, Texas.

Simultaneously, Hispanic Americans are less Catholic than ever. According to Pew Research, Hispanic Americans went from 57% Catholic in 2009 to 47% in 2018/19. Two major trends can account for this: increasing conversion to Evangelical Protestantism and an increasing lack of religious affiliation ('nones'). Though many are leaving Catholicism, the tradition is embedded in Latino/a culture. Take, for example, the ubiquity of the Virgin of Guadalupe's image in homes (a Marian apparition to Aztec people in the sixteenth century and current patron saint of Mexico). Southern Latino/a culture has long been dominated by the traditions and symbols of Catholicism. Hispanic American communities have normally emerged in and around shared religious belief or custom. Because of this, Latino/a Americans who lack religious affiliation are forming new ways to engage in a community. Groups like the Hispanic American Freethinkers, formed in 2010 and based out of Reston, Virginia, exist for the growing number of Hispanic American 'nones'. Its website defines its mission as serving Hispanics in their search for truth via science, reason, logic and humanism.

According to Pew, more than a quarter of Protestant Latino/as in Texas and about a third in Florida identify as Evangelical Pentecostal. The growing number of Pentecostal Hispanics in the South come largely from Catholicism. However, according to Archbishop Thomas Wenski of Miami, many of these are 'cultural Catholics'. Perhaps Pentecostalism's profound influence in these communities is precisely because Catholicism became so interconnected with their culture, seemingly commonplace. The two are drastically different in their liturgies; while Catholicism emphasises tradition, Pentecostalism emphasises experience. Catholicism's polity is hierarchical, but Pentecostal churches tend to be independent. This might be of pressing interest to Hispanic immigrants, feeling underrepresented in American Catholic leadership. According to Luis Lugo, director of the Pew Forum on Religion and Public Life, this shift to Pentecostalism could also be due in large part to a growing number of immigrants who are already Pentecostal. Pentecostal missionaries from the USA have been travelling to South America since the early twentieth century. According to a study by religious studies professor Gastón Espinosa on Latino/a American voters in the 2020 election, Latino/a Evangelicals (a demographic that is largely Pentecostal) were a significant aid to Trump in both Florida and Texas.

Conclusion

Churches in the South continue to wrestle with questions regarding their relation to public policy, science and technology. Among liberals and conservatives alike is an increasing distrust of government, news and even church polity. For instance, the growing 'Exvangelical' movement is marked by scepticism regarding the authority of the mega-church, a hallmark of Southern Christian culture. With increasing visibility of moral failure in the pulpit, Southern Christians are becoming disillusioned about the capacity of any one individual or church to adequately proclaim the Christian gospel. Ironically, with the increasing availability of information, dialogue both internal and external to the Southern churches seems to become only more strenuous. The South has long placed a premium on its autonomy, a spirit that continues shaping its churches in an ever-changing manner.

Bibliography

Brekus, Catherine A., *Religious History of American Women: Reimagining the Past* (Chapel Hill, NC: University of North Carolina Press, 2007).

Butler, Anthea, *White Evangelical Racism: The Politics of Morality in America* (Chapel Hill, NC: University of North Carolina Press, 2021).

Harvey, Paul, *Christianity and Race in the American South: A History* (Chicago, IL: University of Chicago Press, 2018).

Noll, Mark A., *A History of Christianity in the United States and Canada* (Grand Rapids, MI: Eerdmans, 2019).

Tisby, Jemar, *The Color of Compromise* (Grand Rapids MI: Zondervan, 2019).

Northeastern United States

Tyler Lenocker

The states of New Jersey, Pennsylvania, New York, Connecticut, Rhode Island, Massachusetts, Vermont, New Hampshire and Maine comprise the Northeastern United States. The story of Christianity in the region is one of shifting global and regional migrations entangled in European imperialist expansion and its aftermath. From the turn of the twentieth century, mass Western and then global urbanisation began to transform Christianity in the Northeast. Settler colonialism from Western Europe introduced a diverse array of post-Reformation traditions to the area. Missionary endeavours to the Native American population remained mostly peripheral to the colonial projects, aside from notable initiatives from Puritan John Eliot and French Jesuits led by Jean de Brébeuf. European diseases, along with occasional military conflicts, cleared most of the Native population from the region. The First and, especially, Second Great Awakenings of the eighteenth and nineteenth centuries further Christianised the region's European and small African-descendant population. Expanding mercantile connections combined with religious revival made the Northeast the nation's missionary-sending centre across the nineteenth and early twentieth centuries. Revival fervour and migratory mixing generated an environment of religious creativity and conflict, producing figures like Charles Grandison Finney and Sojourner Truth, as well as movements like Mormonism, led by Joseph Smith, that which became the Jehovah's Witnesses, led by Charles Taze Russell, and the Christian Scientist Association, led by Mary Baker Eddy. The movements coincided with Catholic migrations to Northeastern cities, migrations that maintained while also diversifying the region's Christian population. The religious tumult of the nineteenth century produced groups that migrated out of the area, like Smith and the Mormons. Others, including the Jehovah's Witnesses and Christian Scientists, maintain their international headquarters in the region to this day.

From the last century until the present, the Northeast remains a place of religious creativity and contradictions. The region is a centre of de-Christianisation, containing the nation's least Christian region, Northern New England. Countless urban neighbourhoods, conversely, are hubs of Pentecostal revival and Christian pluralisation. In the twentieth century, migration patterns shifted from east–west transatlantic crossings to north–south hemispheric entanglements, connecting urbanising populations from the American South, the Caribbean and Latin America to the Northeast's deindustrialising and depopulating cities. More than in any other global region, religious developments in the Caribbean continue to shape Christianity in the urban Northeast. However, as cities gentrify with the de-Christianising white middle and upper classes, the urban environment and its religious trajectories continue to segment based on race and class. Northeastern cities are becoming simultaneously more Christian and less, depending on the neighbourhood and its rising or falling property values. Recent decades of growing Asian migration create even more complicated trajectories, adding both greater Christian and greater religious diversity to the region. Through transnational inter-urban networks, global Christian developments shape Christianity in the Northeast, and the reverse. If a single trend cuts across traditions, a certain Pentecostalising of Christianity in the region is underway. Whether through migrant conversion into Pentecostal denominations; the Catholic Charismatic Renewal movement; the rise of Neo-Pentecostal worship in mainline, Evangelical and African American Protestant congregations; or even the drift away from institutionalised forms of Christianity to personalised, experiential forms of religious devotion, a mobile and unsettled pietism increasingly characterises Christianity in the Northeastern United States.

Catholicism

Despite its marked decline in recent decades, Catholicism remains the dominant Christian tradition in the Northeastern United States. The region was the first in America to have a Catholic majority when Catholics eclipsed Protestants in the middle of the twentieth century. Small Northern and Western European migrant Catholic communities were founded in the early colonies and first decades of the new Republic. The shift towards a Catholic majority, however, began with mid-nineteenth century mass Irish migration to cities like New York, Boston and Philadelphia. The trend continued with Italian migration to the same cities – and smaller industrial hubs – at the turn of the twentieth century. The new Catholic migrants helped create Northeastern urban culture and its social structures, as the migrations fuelled and coincided with the industrialisation and urbanisation of the region. Protestants fled to the suburbs, making Catholicism the religion of the city. Urban parishes were ethnic in nature – Italian, Irish, Polish, Portuguese – with spatially concentrated Catholic schools and social services providing a cushion against the travails of transatlantic migration. Catholics were long America's 'religious other', stoking waves of nativism among Protestants. Anti-Catholicism lasted for centuries, from the notorious burning of the Ursuline Convent outside Boston by a Protestant mob in 1837 to widespread suspicions of John F. Kennedy's commitment to democratic principles prior to his momentous election – the first ever for a Catholic – to the American presidency in 1961.

By the middle decades of the twentieth century, and continuing today, Catholic descendants of European migrants began leaving deindustrialising cities – larger cities like New York and Boston, but also smaller former industrial hubs like Buffalo, New York and Lowell, Massachusetts. Catholic suburbanisation, however, occurred at a slower pace than for Protestants or Jews. The parish system, wed to a Catholic theology of place, encouraged higher rates of home ownership in urban neighbourhoods and made it more difficult to close parishes to follow upwardly mobile white Catholics to the suburbs. The slow Catholic march out of Northeastern cities also made white ethnic Catholics the face of urban racial conflict as urban demographics shifted with a rise in Black migrants from the South, Puerto Rican migrants and later other foreign migrant communities. The conflicts were most starkly epitomised in the violence occasioning Boston's Busing Crisis in the 1970s. That white Protestants – conservative or liberal – were not the face of these conflicts was mostly due to their urban absence, as well as racialised housing covenants developed by white Protestants that long kept African Americans out of the suburbs. Christianity in the Northeast still carries the consequences of funnelling people of colour – most of whom were and are Christians – into cities while restricting them from the suburbs.

The suburbanisation of European-descendant Catholics has coincided with Church division and decline. White Catholic disaffiliation, especially among younger generations, is among the most significant religious trends in the Northeast. Some ex-Catholics turn to more personalised, Evangelical or Pentecostal forms of Christianity, but most abandon institutional connections to Christianity altogether. The clergy abuse scandal that peaked in 2002, with its epicentre in the Boston archdiocese, exacerbated Church division and decline. The scandal led to the famed resignation of Cardinal Bernard Francis Law. Catholic laity further divided itself from clergy and thus from the broader institutions of the Church. Divisions also grew among Catholic leadership, between more liberal supporters of Vatican II reforms and a conservative movement that grew in the 1970s and 1980s in reaction to the social and sexual revolutions of earlier decades. The conservative wing of the American Catholic Church exerts significant influence, both in the USA and overseas. As with conservative Evangelical Protestants, wealthy conservative Catholic donors fund initiatives to disseminate conservative ideas abroad. The recent global expansion of US-based Eternal Word Television Network (EWTN) is one such example.

The pronounced liberal–conservative divide – sowed in an earlier generation – is less evident among younger Catholics. They hold fewer ties to the institutions of the Church, whether local or global, and practise a more privatised faith.

Despite deinstitutionalising trends, Catholic institutions – especially schools – still play a prominent role in religious formation. Private elementary and secondary schools, along with scores of colleges and universities – Boston College, Fordham University, St John's University and Villanova University, among the more notable – testify to the still robust institutional Catholic presence in the Northeast. The schools, along with college ministries like Newman Centers found at non-Catholic colleges, remain vital in the religious formation of younger generations. Many of the schools are run by religious orders, Jesuits most prominently, but also Dominicans, Franciscans, Sisters of Mercy and many others. Religious orders are often at the forefront of innovation in the Catholic Church, connecting Catholic laity to pioneering ministries ranging from social justice initiatives to eco-mission projects to social media outreach. Examples include 'The Busted Halo' website pioneered by New York City-based priest Dave Dwyer CSP and 'The Jesuit Post' blog maintained by young Jesuits in the Northeast and throughout the country. At the parish level, church leadership has adapted Church structures in sanctioning 'personal parishes' within dioceses. Personal parishes are defined not by geographic proximity but by purpose. Shared liturgical preference and practice, cultural belonging or even social action initiatives can all constitute a Catholic 'parish'.

The Catholic Church has also been transformed in the twentieth and twenty-first centuries by non-European migration. Already by 1955, Puerto Ricans made up a quarter of all Catholics in the New York archdiocese. By the 1980s, the archdiocese was majority Hispanic, primarily Mexicans and Puerto Ricans. The Hispanic share of urban dioceses continues to grow with new migrants from the Dominican Republic, El Salvador, Guatemala and Honduras. With the inclusion of large communities of Haitian Catholic migrants, urban Catholicism in the Northeast is increasingly connected to the Caribbean Basin and defined by religious movements in the region. The mixing of Catholic devotion with Vodou and Santería practices is common among Caribbean migrants. Asian migrations from Vietnam and the Philippines add to the diversity of urban Catholicism in the region. Compared with Western and Southern states, however, the Catholic Church in the Northeast is still dominated by populations of European descent.

Catholic parishes formally integrated in the 1970s, officially ending the practice of encouraging the ethnic parishes that dominated Northeast urban life in the first half of the century. Integrated parishes now often have multiple Masses, each in a different language. Ethnic mixing at the parish level – even in the now-integrated parishes – is measured. Some parishes are *de facto* ethnic parishes, like St Jerome's in Brooklyn's Flatbush neighbourhood, once an Irish ethnic parish but now known locally as the 'Haitian Cathedral'. Devotional practices among urban Catholics are as diverse as their countries of origin, but newer migrants show higher rates of religious devotion than second- or third-generation immigrants. Migration also encourages devotional mixing, as devotion to the Virgin of Guadalupe – a traditionally Mexican practice – has become a pan-Hispanic phenomenon in some Northeastern parishes. The urban context, with its demographic volatility and persistent inequalities, has proved a fertile environment for Catholic devotional and social innovation. The innovation is found in Dorothy Day's work among the poor in Depression-era New York City, Ivan Illich's transformation while working as a priest among the city's Puerto Rican community and young Hispanic laity working today with the Catholic Climate Covenant and Catholic Action Team to advocate and organise for environmental sustainability.

Mainline Protestants

While affiliation rates have declined for decades, mainline Protestant denominations maintain a public and institutional presence in the Northeast not found in other US regions. Such presence has been built over centuries, as the Northeast served as a hub for social and religious innovations pioneered by Protestants in historic denominations, such as the abolition movement, universal education, women's suffrage, the modern Protestant missionary movement and missionary societies, turn-of-the-twentieth-century evangelistic crusades, the social gospel movement, the ordination of women, the modern ecumenical movement and the ordination of gay and lesbian ministers. By the twentieth century, a constellation of 'establishment Protestant' denominations coalesced into a network now represented by denominations like the United Churches of Christ, Episcopal Church (US), United Methodist Church, Presbyterian Church (USA), Evangelical Lutheran Church in America and American Baptist Churches (USA).

While mainline laity and clergy are theologically eclectic and diverse, the region and its institutions have served as centres for liberal and progressive expressions of Protestant Christianity for the USA since the nineteenth century. The fundamentalist–modernist controversy of the early twentieth century proved most divisive for denominations centred in the Northeast. Theological moderates and liberals remained in the denominations while many conservatives left and formed alternative religious bodies. Major institutions of theological learning remained within the mainline denominations, and these institutions – like Yale Divinity School, Boston University School of Theology, Princeton Theological Seminary and Drew Theological School – continue as centres where Christians of diverse theological backgrounds go to be trained as educators and scholars for Christian institutions in the USA. The institutions also draw Christian leaders from the global South, especially leaders with denominational ties to the schools. Northeast theological schools are innovators in Christian thought, pioneering trends in postcolonial theology, Christian feminism and queer studies, and integrating theological movements from abroad, like Latin American liberation theology, into Protestant theological education. Even as adherence to mainline churches declines, robust financial endowments and institutional ties to research universities sustain Northeast mainline educational institutions and their national and global influence.

Northeast mainline leaders have also been pioneers in ecumenical and inter-faith partnership. Most inter-faith networks, like the Interfaith Center of New York, organise faith leaders for local initiatives in social, legal or educational reform. Some coalitions, like New York City-based GreenFaith, led by Episcopal priest Fletcher Harper, have shifted to global inter-religious activism to fight climate change. The Northeast's early experience with nascent religious diversity through migration – along with the region's once robust ties to the Protestant missionary movement – made the region's mainline theologians intellectual leaders in the promotion of religious pluralism. In an earlier generation, the phrase 'Judeo-Christian tradition' emerged from this Northeast milieu. More recently, Methodist and religion scholar Diana Eck has developed the Pluralism Project at Harvard Divinity School. Northeast inter-faith networks also played a central role in navigating the religious tensions following the 9/11 attacks in the region. The networks provided forums for many Muslims to display their commitment to the USA. Since the social ruptures of the 1960s and 1970s, many mainline leaders have shifted from the promotion of social and religious consensus to the promotion of issue-specific social activism. Northeast mainline clergy are often on the front lines of the Black Lives Matter movement, advocacy for LGBTQ rights, advocacy for refugees and immigrants, and promotion of environmental justice. Earlier mainline emphasis on social cohesion can still be found in towns and small cities throughout the region, where mainline congregations and their facilities serve as community centres and promoters of local civic engagement.

Mainline laity are typically less activist and more theologically and politically conservative than their ministers. Also, within mainline denominations, larger numbers of theologically conservative and

Evangelical congregations are found on the western side of the Appalachian Mountains, in western New York and western Pennsylvania. The regions often reflect Middle America and its religious trends more than the East Coast. Conservative congregations, most notably in the Episcopal and United Methodist denominations – both with episcopal polities and thus robust international connections – have become more globally networked in recent decades. Conservative clergy and churches have joined with leaders in the global South, most notably in Africa, to resist moves by progressive Western leadership to allow for church endorsement of same-sex marriage and ordination of gay and lesbian clergy in the USA. The conflict has created complicated partnerships, with US congregations temporarily existing under the jurisdiction of African bishops, large financial investments flowing from US congregations to African religious institutions, and even the adoption of African liturgical elements into conservative middle-class US churches.

Evangelicalism and Pentecostalism
Migration, notably from Latin America and the Caribbean, has Pentecostalised Christianity in Northeastern cities. While white, middle-class Evangelicals have long been marginal in the region, the Northeast emerged as an early centre for the nation's burgeoning Hispanic Protestant community. Due in part to the small white Evangelical population, Pentecostalism makes up a larger share of the Northeast's Protestant population than in any other region of the USA. Puerto Rican Pentecostal pioneer Juan Lugo – converted in a migrant labour camp in Hawaii – moved to New York City in the final decades of his ministry and started the Spanish American Bible Institute there in 1935. The Institute produced Ricardo Tañon, who founded Iglesia Juan 3:16 in the Bronx, which had become the nation's largest Hispanic congregation by the Second World War, with membership in the thousands. By the year 2000, New York City had more than 1,000 Hispanic Pentecostal churches, many of them storefronts. The growth was fed by itinerant revival preachers like Mexican Francisco Olazábal in the first half of the twentieth century and Puerto Rican Yiye Ávila in the second half of the century, who preached to hundreds of thousands of Spanish-speaking migrants in the region and millions in North and South America.

In recent decades a Hispanic community dominated by Puerto Rican and Mexican migrants and their descendants has been diversified with newer movements from El Salvador, Honduras, Guatemala and the Dominican Republic. Dominicans, notably, have become the most prominent new Hispanic community, now rivalling Puerto Ricans in the region. Unceasing migrant flows throughout the twentieth and twenty-first centuries has meant that Hispanic Pentecostalism in the region has been transnational and multicultural from its origins. New York City, in particular, has produced nationally and internationally recognised Hispanic leaders, like theologian and educational pioneer Eldin Villafañe and Gabriel Salguero, an Assemblies of God minister and founder and president of the National Latino Evangelical Coalition. Urban-based Hispanic Pentecostalism largely remains, however, a popular movement among the poor and working classes, and thus marginal to most national Christian organisations. The movement provides a means for local, communal survival and spiritual vitality as well as belonging to global and diasporic networks extending throughout North and South America. While most pastoral roles are taken by men, women leaders often sustain congregational life and local ministries. Boston-based Puerto Rican minister Ramonita Díaz has led a Spanish-speaking house church planting movement for decades that has extended throughout the region. Lay-led evangelism remains robust across all migrant Pentecostal communities, with church growth fed regularly by new conversions. Evangelistic initiatives among white Evangelicals, however, are more limited, and mass evangelistic meetings like those led by Billy Graham have fallen out of style. For mainline Protestants and Catholics, efforts to evangelise beyond their communities are largely absent.

In the latter decades of the twentieth century, continuing to today, migration has expanded, diversifying the Northeast's Evangelical and Pentecostal communities with new residents from Asia, Africa and Latin America. The migration has been driven by the combination of the rapid industrialisation and urbanisation of non-Western societies, the connected incursion of capitalist economic systems into these societies, the Cold War and US military involvement in the Middle East, advances in technology(most importantly, the aeroplane), rising economic inequality between countries and, finally, the passage of less-restrictive immigration laws like the Hart–Cellar Act of 1965. Discussed further below, a diverse array of Asian migrants, most notably Chinese and Koreans, are restructuring Evangelicalism in metropolitan areas throughout the region. Less Pentecostal than other migrant groups, Chinese and Korean Protestant congregations can be found in mainline and Evangelical Protestant denominations. Chinese and Korean Protestants also found their own separate congregations, with typically robust ties to church networks in their home countries.

New migration from sub-Saharan Africa, most prominently Nigeria, Ghana, Kenya, Liberia and South Africa, adds further Christian diversity to the region. Many African migrants bring independent and Pentecostal networks and organisations founded in Africa to the Northeast. The

Nigerian neo-Pentecostal Redeemed Christian Church of God (RCCG) has planted churches throughout the region, and one of its former Brooklyn-based pastors, Nimi Wariboko, is now professor of social ethics at Boston University School of Theology. Migration from the Caribbean and Latin America has also diversified. Haitians and Brazilians are prominent in the region, with many declining mainline or white Evangelical congregations selling or sharing their buildings with the new, growing migrant churches. Mirroring integrated Catholic parishes, many urban Baptist churches host multiple Baptist congregations with separate worship services in English, Portuguese, French-Creole and Spanish. Across all ethnic groups, migrants to the USA tend to be more Christian and more Protestant than in their countries of origin. Most Haitians on the island are Catholic, but most Haitian immigrants are Protestant – primarily Baptist or Pentecostal.

White Evangelicals are marginal in the Northeast when compared with their more conspicuous presence in other US regions. And while at a slower rate than mainline Protestants or Catholics, Evangelicals are also declining in the region. White Evangelicals are most common west of the Appalachian Mountains, in western Pennsylvania and western New York. Evangelicals – of any ethnicity – are least likely to be found in Northern New England. They maintain a small network of educational institutions, many with roots in earlier Holiness, fundamentalist or neo-Evangelical renewal movements. The institutions include Eastern University, Grove City College, Houghton College, Gordon College, Nyack College, Gordon-Conwell Theological Seminary and Westminster Theological Seminary. Evangelicals also remain influential through robust para-church college ministries like Cru (formerly Campus Crusade for Christ) and InterVarsity Christian Fellowship. With less demographic and institutional influence than other regions, Evangelicals in the Northeast tend to be more apolitical or more politically progressive than in other parts of the country. Nearly half of Evangelicals in the Northeast support legalised same-sex marriage and expansion of rights and inclusion of LGBTQ persons.

Evangelical trends have followed the movement of the white middle class, first out of the city to the suburbs and then returning through gentrification. Recent decades have seen a rise of 'creative class' church plants among upwardly mobile gentrifiers. The most influential has been Redeemer Presbyterian Church in Manhattan, started by pastor and author Timothy Keller out of the Southern-based, theologically conservative Presbyterian Church in America. Churches like Redeemer draw some new converts disillusioned with the dehumanising forces of modern urban life. Much of the urban congregational growth, however, is driven by suburban Evangelicals moving to the city – as well as Southern or Midwestern internal migrants moving to Northeastern cities for professional or educational reasons. In recent years, an average of 100 Evangelical church start-ups have been launched per year in New York City. While some Evangelical urban initiatives have remained within the upwardly mobile white gentrifying population, other initiatives have promoted intercultural partnership. The Redeemer City-to-City church planting network, pioneered by Keller, now has leaders from multiple migrant communities and has branches in cities throughout the world. Urban initiatives like City Seminary New York, Gordon-Conwell's Center for Urban Ministerial Education and the Emmanuel Gospel Center in Boston are products of a diversifying urban Evangelicalism. The initiatives represent a localised 'neo-ecumenism' spurred by the new global migrations and back-to-the-city white Evangelicals. Multi-ethnic Evangelical congregations continue to grow in coastal metropolitan areas as well. These churches remain within the middle and upper classes and often are composed of a mix of white and Asian professionals. As economic inequality increases in Northeastern cities, the class divide among Christians will remain a most pressing ecclesiological challenge.

African American Christianity
The Catholic Church and African American Protestants are often the primary public face of Christianity in the cities and inner suburbs of the Northeast. Black mega-churches are often the largest congregations in metropolitan areas – like Enon Tabernacle Baptist Church in Philadelphia or the Christian Cultural Center, with nearly 40,000 members, in Brooklyn. While the mass urbanisation of America's Black population did not occur until the twentieth century, Northeastern cities served as early sites for the development of independent free-Black congregations and denominations. Philadelphia minister and ex-enslaved Richard Allen pioneered the African Methodist Episcopal (AME) Church, which separated from the Methodist Episcopal Church in 1816. Mother Bethel AME Church in Philadelphia and Abyssinian Baptist Church in New York City – both with large congregations to this day – were early initiatives by free Blacks to found Black-led fellowships in resistance to segregated white-led churches and denominations.

The Northern Black population remained small until the 'Great Migration' of African Americans from the South that began in the inter-war years and then peaked from 1940 to 1970. More than eight million African Americans, mostly rural migrants accompanied by their families, moved to Northern cities, with New York and Philadelphia as dominant destinations. Complementing migration from the South was simultaneous Anglophone West Indian migration, principally from the industrialising Caribbean-island nations of Jamaica and Barbados. The migrations mixed Northern

Black Christians, often more highly educated and wealthier, with Southern rural migrants bringing an array of Baptist and Wesleyan traditions, along with Caribbean migrants with Moravian and Anglican roots. Pentecostalism was also growing in the Northeast. Storefront congregations began to dominate in poorer Black neighbourhoods. The dense, diverse, mobile urban Black population created a context of religious porosity, with many urban migrants switching Christian traditions or leaving the faith altogether. Women, especially, turned to Pentecostalism – and still do today – finding in the congregations the relational, social and spiritual support and dignity denied to them in the surrounding culture. The urban migrations created new religious movements tied to Christianity, like the International Peace Mission led by Father Divine and the United House of Prayer for All People led by Marcelino Manuel da Graça (Daddy Grace).

Black Christianity in the Northeast has continued to diversify in the twenty-first century. Many new migrants from the Caribbean or Africa will first attend an African American church, but then often seek greater cultural affinity and belonging in immigrant churches from their home country or region. Second-generation Haitian or African immigrants are more common in historically Black denominations: the African Methodist Episcopal Church, African Methodist Episcopal Zion Church, National Baptist Convention, Progressive National Baptist Church and Church of God in Christ. Many churches in these denominations carry on the historic blending in African American Christianity of Evangelical piety with social gospel ethics. James Cone, the pioneer of Black Liberation Theology and ordained AME minister, taught for decades at Union Theological Seminary in New York City. Prominent Black clergy and their formal ministerial alliances are often leaders in promoting educational, housing and police reform in their cities. Michael A. Walrond, Jr, pastor of First Corinthian Baptist Church in Harlem, has worked on the forefront of social justice initiatives in concert with his 10,000-member congregation. Beyond their political influence, Black churches also continue to shape US popular music with artists Marvin Gaye, Donna Summer, Faith Evans and John Legend all nurtured in gospel music traditions in churches in the Northeast.

Despite the continued prominence of the African American population in Northeastern cities, the last two decades have witnessed the deurbanisation of that population across the entire country. In the face of white gentrification and a rising cost of living, some African Americans have suburbanised or moved to smaller cities. Many notable African American churches have likewise been forced to move out of their historic urban locales with their congregants. Large numbers of African Americans are leaving the Northeast altogether, typically relocating to the more culturally and financially amenable cities and suburbs of the American

South. The continued influx of African and Caribbean migrants combined with the African American exodus to the South further diversifies Black Christianity in the Northeast.

Emerging Trends

The rise of those unaffiliated with any religious tradition, the 'nones', dominates all religious trends in the region. Mass disaffiliation of white Catholics in recent decades remains the chief cause, with mainline and Evangelical Protestant disaffiliation also contributing to Christian decline. Most 'nones' are not atheist or even self-consciously agnostic but, rather, religiously identify as 'nothing in particular'. To describe 'nones' as 'non-Christian' is a misnomer, as most continue to believe in God and hold distinctly Christian ideas about God. The rise of 'nones' is in part a story of Christian institutional and organisational decline, linked to increased state and commercial involvement in all areas of life. The expanded commercial and governmental ties weaken the need for broad social networks and supports, thus heightening the individuating, particularising power of modernity. 'Nones' have less diverse relational connections than religious adherents: they spend more time with people in their generation and less across generational divides, marry less, have fewer children and spend less time with their families. Atheists remain a small proportion of the region's population, at less than 5%, and are most likely to be male, white, wealthy and highly educated.

While the rise of 'nones' dominates religious trends in the region, the growth of Asian immigration will add increasing religious diversity to the Northeast. The region is already the nation's most religiously diverse, even though it lacks the religious parity of many multireligious nations. Only 10% of the Northeast population adhere to non-Christian religions. Asians are the most religiously diverse group in the country, with one-third Christian, one-third unaffiliated and the rest a mix of religious traditions, with Hinduism the most prominent, at 15%. Such diversity is concentrated in neighbourhoods with high rates of Asian immigration, like Flushing in New York City. Asian immigrants are the fastest-growing migrant group in the USA and are anticipated to surpass Hispanic migrants as the nation's largest immigrant population by 2050. Asian migration also continues to diversify the region's Christian population. Along with Protestant and Catholic traditions, Asian migration from the Middle East adds diverse Orthodox traditions to the region. The Northeast became an early centre for Greek and Russian Orthodox migration to the USA, marked by the continued importance of St Vladimir's Seminary in Yonkers, New York. However, even with newer migrants, the Orthodox population in the Northeast makes up only 1% of the total population.

Of final growing significance to Christianity in the region is the rise of digital media in every area of religious life. The COVID-19 pandemic accelerated the digital mediation of music, Bible reading, prayer, preaching, evangelism, missionary outreach, theological education and even baptism and the celebration of communion. Use of digital media has increased global connections, especially among diaspora communities, while also attenuating connections to neighbourhood and one's local church. Ministries and churches with resources can expand their global and national reach, while many small congregations have closed due to the lack of such capabilities. A trend that began with private book ownership, the rise of religious periodicals and the invention of the radio and television has further allowed Christian laity both to challenge and to disconnect from the authority and influence of local clergy. Akin to other responses to globalisation, some movements across Christian traditions have reacted against de-localising trends by emphasising a turn towards the neighbourhood and local parish. Reactions against the digitisation of faith include a growing sacramentalism among many Protestants – mainline and Evangelical – with increased frequency of communion and other material liturgical practices. The interplay and tension between material and digital, global and local, will continue to shape Christian traditions in the Northeast throughout the remainder of the twenty-first century.

Bibliography

Butler, Jon, *God in Gotham: The Miracle of Religion in Modern Manhattan* (Cambridge, MA: Harvard University Press, 2020).

Drescher, Elizabeth, *Choosing Our Religion: The Spiritual Lives of America's Nones* (New York: Oxford University Press, 2016).

Espinosa, Gastón, *Latino Pentecostals in America: Faith and Politics in Action* (Cambridge, MA: Harvard University Press, 2014).

Gaustad, Edwin S., Mark A. Noll and Heath W. Carter, *A Documentary History of Religion in America*, 4th edition (Grand Rapids, MI: Eerdmans, 2018).

Hanson, R. Scott, *City of Gods: Religious Freedom, Immigration, and Pluralism in Flushing, Queens* (New York: Fordham University Press, 2016).

United States: Native American

Kimberlee Medicine Horn Jackson
(Yankton Sioux)

In the past, the American Christian church and its denominations operated as tools of colonisation, aiming to erase Native culture and to dehumanise Indigenous people unless they buckled under the oppressive coercion and converted to Christianity. This is evident in the myriad methods of Indian removal or, as the government was wont to call it, 'the Indian problem'. For example, the Native American boarding school era of the nineteenth and twentieth centuries, when genocidal practices of abuse were effective tools of coercion, was marked by spiritual, intellectual, physical and emotional abuse, along with displacement of persons on the land and disruption of language and culture. These developments are still not widely known or taught within US history. Yet it is imperative to know the boarding school was just one method of removal. For so many Native Americans, roots of bitterness are embedded in generations of their families because of these abuses, and they refuse to have anything to do with any churches. Today, science recognises the effects of intergenerational trauma as passed down genetically. There is much concern about the generational consequences of colonisation, not just for Indigenous people but for the Christian church as well. People often incorrectly refer to Indian removal as harsh treatment and this diminishes the truth of genocide. When non-Native Christians learn about the complicity between church and government, some do not know how to process this legacy of sin and shame passed on to them.

It is necessary to discuss how some church denominations are enthusiastic or feel compelled to be multicultural churches, but if the cultures remain segregated inside of the church walls, out of a need for continued hierarchy, how far have we come and what needs to change? If one attends a conference about building multicultural churches but the white church is missing from the conversation, what change is possible? The very people who need to do the arduous work of learning new ways to grow the body of Christ are absent from the conversation and addressing the major obstacles. The conference might provide insights that can help to end the struggle by offering practical asset-based teachings to help churches rise from the ashes of misguidance and false prophets that started the problem.

It follows that the well worn weaponising of Scripture appears as a default way of problem-solving when addressing racism in the Christian church. Anyone who dares to challenge white superiority in the church risks the label of a hopeless sinner embedded in judgemental postures and is considered a divisive threat. Thus, they are swiftly discredited, and the church members continue to wring their hands as to why Indigenous families are not flocking to their church. The church is reluctant to peer too closely into the ways in which they practise racism and prefer to dismiss any accusation. This has been the great weakness of the church over centuries. One of the most popular defences by Christians when they begin to think about why some Native people outrightly reject Christianity is that they were not there when any atrocities occurred and therefore feel absolved of any perpetuating of wrongdoing. A better response includes an exploration of the roots of how Christianity began to go askew from the intention of the good news of salvation.

The Doctrine of Discovery

In their book *Unsettling Truths: The Ongoing Dehumanizing Legacy of the Doctrine of Discovery* (Downers Grove, IL: InterVarsity, 2019), Mark Charles and Soong-Chan Rah examine the Doctrine of Discovery as a point of origin. In 1452, a papal bull was issued that gave Christians the permission, as they interpreted it, to call people pagans (among other names) if they did not profess Christian beliefs. Further papal bulls included wording that the land in what is now called the USA was empty because the Indigenous people were not Christians and were therefore non-existent and not human. Charles has studied this topic extensively. The authors show how the Doctrine of Discovery set the tone for legal provisions that work against self-determination for the Tribal Nations, whether federally recognised or outside the USA.

The complexities that add to building what is often called right relationship between Indigenous people and Christian churches is the same problem Native Nations have encountered for centuries. The church thinks it knows best how to solve the problem of colonisation yet is reluctant to give up the sense of pride that comes with feeling like a dominant population wielding power without accountability. Yet the day(s) of reckoning are on the horizon.

While this is a brief mention of the topic, it is of great concern to Indigenous Christians and other social justice activist groups like the Methodist Federation for Social Action or the Center and Library for the Bible and Social Justice. Some denominations discern a need to dismantle the Doctrine of Discovery or rescind it in an effort to move towards conciliation between white and Indigenous Christian and with those outside of

Christian faith. An example of this occurred at Standing Rock Reservation in 2016 when the Indigenous Water Protectors fought against corporate oil pipelines contaminating drinking water supplies for Indigenous and non-Native alike. This was a historic event in which Indigenous Nations the world over converged in solidarity and engaged in sacred ceremony and prayer to stay the hand of corporate greed. One day during the encampment, hundreds of clergy people appeared as allies standing in solidarity with Indigenous people and destroyed a copy of the Doctrine of Discovery to expose the Doctrine as unsound and unbiblical. The implementation of the Doctrine shows misuse. Even today, countless Christians are unaware of the Doctrine of Discovery. Many Christians hold sacred the Declaration of Independence that identifies Indigenous people as 'merciless Indian savages'. The church needs to decide whether or not to treat human-made documents with the same reverence as they do the Bible.

Mark Charles expresses how conciliation must come before reconciliation because the church has yet to demonstrate a clear understanding of a healthy relationship with Indigenous people. A clear example is how a Christian church expects Native people to assimilate to white cultural and religious practices.

Countless Native people are coerced into denying their Native personhood if they want to follow Jesus. The same assimilative practices evident during the boarding school era continue to be prominent in churches today. Membership into the fold is based upon the erasure of any hint of Indigeneity. This lived experience is still common. Native people must burn any regalia and not sing or dance their prayers to the Creator because it is considered to be demonic. A new church attendee may repress these natural forms of worship in order to enter the gates of heaven. What the white Christian neighbour does not know, but could know if they would listen, is the prayer that goes into the preparation of any regalia and the prayer and honour songs that are expressed by Indigenous people through the use of the sacred drum and dance. Since white Christians misunderstand this form of worship they assume it to be nothing more than an entertaining novelty. The church family may oust them from the interior of their building permanently.

As Richard Twiss (Sicangu Lakota) writes in *One Church Many Tribes*, 'I believe the Christian Native community must be recognised as a vital and integral part of the God-given destiny of America. We as a church must ask our Creator Father to help us look back, repent and honestly seek reconciliation for the injustices of five centuries imposed by Euro-American immigrants on the First Nations Peoples of North America'. Twiss's book was published in 2000, that is, 19 years before Charles and Rah's exposition of the Doctrine of Discovery, and shows the complexities of being Native and Christian. The church asks us to choose either/or while Indigenous people consider how both/and is in line with the Creator. In 1997, Richard and Katharine Twiss's ministry, Wiconi International, invited Native followers of Jesus into the dance arena and encouraged them to accept wearing their regalia, singing with the drum and smudging (burning sage or other medicines such as cedar and sweetgrass and directing the smoke to areas of the body) as a symbol of cleansing the mind, heart and body before times of praise and worship as ways to honour the Creator. This acceptance freed many Native people from the utter shame and degradation with which they had been burdened within white Christian churches. The Twisses' ministry demonstrates how Indigenous Christians belong in the body of Christ without any expectation of assimilation.

Twiss also conducted a cross-cultural immersion class for many years. One of the purposes of this class was to help non-Native people understand who Native people are and how their tribe functions daily. The week-long immersion class also welcomed Native attendees. In particular, people who want to minister to Native people could gain insights from the class that a person in the mission field might not be privy to, even after years of contact with an Indigenous community, because of the high level of mistrust some Indigenous people have towards any representative of any church that professes Christian beliefs. One exercise in a class held in 2008 assigned students to attend a local church's Sunday service. The groups discussed if there were visible signs of Indigenous presence inside the church. Who attended the service? Who led the service? Were the churches assimilative? The group travelled over two reservations and observed a tribal council meeting. They also toured the tribal college and a working Native American ministry that had a food pantry, a place to acquire household goods and a place to sell Native jewellery. The immersion class was particularly attentive to teaching about the history of the tribe and offered voluntary participation in a sweat lodge or *inipi*, which is a time of cleansing and prayer. The most profound outcome of the immersion class was for Christians to learn how to actively listen to people from communities different from their own. The group visited Wounded Knee cemetery and the mass grave created after the Wounded Knee massacre. One participant, upon reading the names of the deceased in the mass grave, sobbed brokenly, which accurately captures the layers of grief in the land.

Missions to Native Americans

Often, when people think of Native American ministry or missions, they are non-Native Christians who come to reservations in droves and, as Twiss explained, the locals call it 'missions season'. Mission groups can be problematic for Tribal Nations. Many groups are unaware of the tribal council and the protocol of contacting them to ask for permission to come to the reservation. Some church groups feel led to bring an inordinate amount of clothing or to do 'good works'. There is nothing wrong with feeding people and helping to repair houses, but what makes better sense is asking what a tribal community needs instead of assuming they do not know how to help themselves. A church group might spend more time in rescue mode than in building relationships with Indigenous people. Some Tribal Nations have reported never seeing the same person or people twice or having to explain the proper behaviour in a cemetery, for example not eating or littering the sacred ground. Sadly, there have been cases of more serious harmful behaviour, in the form of the abuse of children. One Native Nation described how a white van patrolled the streets looking for children to take to vacation Bible school. If this occurred in a mainstream church community, someone would call the sheriff to report a threat to their children and no one would question the wisdom of protecting their children.

If church members are interested in helping to build an Indigenous community, they will need to learn how to be satisfied with being invisible, working behind the scenes, and not worry about how many souls they led to Christ for the report to their home church and to show how efficiently their missions money was spent. The church might learn how to sit down with and share a meal in Indigenous communities rather than serving a meal to them with little interaction. It is easy to rescue, but the greater commitment relies on building a consistent relationship with Indigenous communities by practising reciprocity. A church on its knees with outstretched hands intent on building relationships that does not include giving possessions as a quick fix is a church after God's heart. If the conditions for accepting food for their family is to hear the Good News, then the priority is troublesome. If a group of people is labelled as incapable of caring for themselves due to the ravages of colonialism and it is not permissible to share the trauma they have incurred, how can an honest relationship form? These are just some of the questions Indigenous communities contend with daily. Some Native Nations are more interested in protecting their communities from more harm than converting to a religious belief steeped in the practices of colonialism.

Any church planning a short-term mission trip to a reservation would exercise wisdom by learning the history of the Indigenous community and ongoing methods of Indian removal for the sake of land or acquiring resources before their trip. The church should remember they are a guest for a finite period of time. A church would be wise in addressing their motives before they go. For example, do they, as a body of believers, feel they can evangelise Indigenous people better than an Indigenous member of the community? Ethnocentrism is still alive and well in churches, but they are blind to their own perspective. Education should be a priority, with a preference for learning an accurate Indigenous perspective from an Indigenous instructor rather than a white researcher from outside an Indigenous community. There is concern in today's Christian church over the low percentages of Christian Native Americans and a prevailing assumption that Native Americans are ignorant of who Jesus is, which is inaccurate.

Towards Contextual Christianity
While a flurry of concern persists over lost Indigenous souls, rest assured, Native Christians do exist, and they have been busy trying to build bridges where peaceful relations can form and persist. In Randy Woodley's (Keetoowah Cherokee) book *When Going to Church Is a Sin* (Scotland, PA: Healing the Land Publishers, 2007), he chronicles a timeline of the Native American Contextual Movement, which finds its origin in the mid-1980s. It was in the mid-1990s, Woodley notes, that the inaugural World Christian Gathering of Indigenous People occurred in New Zealand, and he observes that at this time some key national leaders like Richard Twiss and Terry LeBlanc began to find each other and allow the Creator to use their common unity to promote God's kingdom and the contextual gospel in a public way. Woodley goes on to observe that at the second World Christian Gathering of Indigenous People, hosted by Native Americans in Rapid City, South Dakota, participants began to realise that more like-minded Native Christians were becoming active in the USA and Canada with the aim of arriving at a culturally contextual gospel. This gathering helped unify Christian Native Americans together in a common place where productive conversations on such matters as contextualisation could take place. The praise and worship of contextual Native American Christians begins with a smudging ceremony, presenting a sacred pipe ceremony and using a hand drum or a large sacred drum depending on the number of worshippers. A Native American flute offers a soothing path for healing and they sing songs in their home language, including hymns, and they dance before the Lord in regalia. These are considered to be acceptable, appropriate ways to express praise and worship, received as gifts to Indigenous people from the Creator. There has always been pushback from the white Christian church that contextualisation is nothing more than syncretism and of the devil. This is why attempts to achieve right relationship continue to limp along.

In 1999, the North American Institute for Indigenous Theological Studies (NAIITS) was founded, and it held its first symposium in 2001. The nineteenth symposium met in 2022 in the Indigenous learning community, which is inclusive of Native and non-Native academics, Christians from a variety of denominations, practitioners, community leaders, social justice activists and other interested people. Each symposium explores a different topic, for example the meaning of treaty and covenant or racism in the church. A call for papers or panels goes out and the *Journal of NAIITS: An Indigenous Learning Community* publishes them. NAIITS offers graduate and postgraduate degrees and awards and has been accredited by the Association of Theological Schools and the Commission on Accrediting.

In addition, iEmergence, a non-profit/non-stock organisation focusing on holistic community and leadership development in Indigenous and tribal communities, offers another place for emerging Indigenous leaders to sharpen their skills. At present, the Indigenous Pathways and NAIITS Learning Community serves a global Indigenous community and is unique in its structure, which speaks to Indigenous Christians and non-Native Christians alike. It serves as a model for building relationships with and for Indigenous communities by an Indigenous community and is attentive to sustaining relationships.

A long way still lies ahead in Native American Christian ministry by and for Native Americans in the USA, but fruitful progress has been made. One current ministry resource is Terry Wildman's (Ojibwe and Yakima ancestry) *First Nations Version: An Indigenous Translation of the New Testament*. In the introduction, Wildman explains the purpose 'was birthed out of a desire to provide an English Bible that connects, in a culturally relevant way, to the traditional heart languages of the over six million English-speaking First Nations people of North America'. At first, the concern for pan-Indianism was a relevant discussion among Indigenous people from a variety of tribal affiliations. Pan-Indianism overgeneralises distinctive Tribal Nations to the point that they disappear. Pan-Indianism 'others' Indigenous people and their communities, which does more harm. Certainly, the First Nations versions might not speak to every reader, but to date testimonies from Indigenous readers becoming followers of Jesus indicate positive outcomes.

Wildman's deep desire to honour the traditional storytelling of Indigenous peoples is what helps to build a meaningful connection with Indigenous readers. His aim was to create not a word-for-word translation but a thought-for-thought translation. A traditional translation of the Bible completely overlooks the more linear way of writing for non-Native audiences. When Indigenous people gather in community to solve the problems of how white Christianity assumes they are the only ones who know about Jesus, this is what they accomplish. The new Bible translation is an excellent example of defining contextualisation. *First Nations Version* is used in Bible studies and in other Native Christian gatherings, when a copy is available. It sold out for a time due to its enthusiastic reception. Wildman and his wife, Darlene, are the founders of Rain Ministries, a Native American music ministry in the USA. They have travelled extensively for many years, providing Native American Christian worship music to many churches, Indigenous communities and conferences.

Trauma from the Past

When church denominations first built their missions across the USA, before the Civil War, some missionaries took the time and spent the effort to learn the language of the Indigenous people they were serving. This often required years of commitment. Some of the denominations were assimilative even then, demanding any Native children quit speaking their own language forever and defer to speaking only the English language. One of the reasons Wildman uses English in *First Nations Version* is that so many Native people do not speak their original languages. The Civil War disrupted mission schools, because often the buildings were put to other uses. After the war ended, church denominations opened schools once again, only now they were funded, in part, by the federal government as a way to solve the 'Indian problem'. The guiding idea was that educating Native children was cheaper than acts of war. Government support might include paying for books, tuition or buildings.

Today, in churches across the USA, one can find Native Christians who are boarding school survivors and might carry severe trauma with them. After the boarding schools shut down because the government pulled the funding for them, some schools went on to be controlled by the states. Finally, Tribal Nations controlled their own schools if they had the funds. Today, some non-assimilative Native-operated boarding schools still exist. The extreme abusive environment Native children endured is something Native elders might have never yet voiced because of trauma impact. When churches want to minister to Native people, they must educate themselves about trauma and triggers of trauma and offer safe havens in which to begin healing processes.

Of major concern was the news in 2021 in Canada of the remains of children found in the residential schools in mass graveyards. In Indian country in the USA, the question Native people ask non-Native people is 'Did your school have a cemetery?' The terrible genocidal practices of abusing children and neglecting them with inadequate sanitation and other public health practices such as overcrowding and malnutrition, not to mention stealing the children from their families, set the precedent for other methods of removal. One thriving method was adopting Native children off the reservation and placing them with white families as a way to completely sever the cultural practices in Native families by disrupting the generations. Removing or relocating generations of Native children from the reservations so they would never find their way back home has been deeply traumatic. Since many denominations have had their hand in Indian removal, this is a starting place to closely examine before the desire to see rising numbers of Indigenous converts to Christianity.

Another removal method was laid down in the Relocation Act of the 1950s in which the government paid Native families a small stipend to move into urban cities to learn a low-wage trade under the condition they would not return to the reservation. Another method is the foster care system, which is reluctant to place at-risk Native children with trained and certified Native foster parents but rather chooses to remove Native children to place them in institutional groups or completely out of state with non-Native parents. The records will show this happens to a disproportionate number of Native children even to this day. These methods of removal show the continued attempts to solve the 'Indian problem' today. Mainstream society looks at Native people as a problem, and while Christian churches want to help, they see only the poverty-ridden, alcoholic Native Americans incapable of helping themselves and in need of a rescuer. The church rides in on a perceived white stallion yet still fails to see the effects of the colonisation brought on by themselves.

Methods of removal still exist today in other forms such as the Missing and Murdered Indigenous Women. Some of this is due to the transitory male camps built to house pipeline workers. A transitory community brings drug and sex trafficking. Christian churches outside of these types of communities might never have any knowledge of them. When churches become healthy, multicultural bodies of Christ, the struggles Native Nations face daily can become a shared burden to solve.

Currently, many studies are following methods of decolonisation for Indigenous people and some groups of Native Christians are interested in decolonising the church. This is a difficult challenge because the Christian church wants revival more than anything else and to save as many souls as possible in the process. The facts of how the church has treated Native Americans remain a point of separation. White Christians do not know what to do when confronted with the patterns of their behaviour, and this leads to a contentious relationship on both sides simply because it has taken centuries of waiting for resolution of conflict for Indigenous people. Because organisations like the National Native American Boarding School Healing Coalition and the federal investigation of the Native American boarding schools are at the forefront, now would be an excellent time for the church to open sealed records and to ask what they can do to right the wrongs, but the waiting continues.

Processes of decolonisation can include giving back stolen land, returning the remains of Native children's bodies to their tribal communities, reclaiming Native language, resurgence of Native cultures and finding voice and place within the academy and the church. All of these can position the church in a variety of ways to build relationships behind the scenes. Some Native Christians are helping to decolonise the church by keeping alive the discussion of the history of what has happened to Native people. Native Christians face push-back from non-Native Christians and from people in their own communities who cannot understand why any Native person would want to practise Christianity – the ways of the colonisers. The challenge is to show that colonisation is an act of man, not of God.

Signs of Hope

Although it seems a daunting task to explore the current state of affairs in Christianity and Native American people, there is hope. There is hope when people actively listen to the consequences of colonisation in Christianity. There is hope when the Christian church laments with Native Nations. To bypass the sacred time of grieving over what has happened is to sacrifice healing. Many Christians respond too quickly to the facts of the genocidal practices as something they did not do and therefore attempt to bypass guilt or to deny wrongdoing rather than move to disrupt the patterns of human behaviour. This is a reason why a low percentage of Native people practise Christianity.

Other considerations exist as well. How is Christianity defined, and which definition is correct? Many people outside of Native America profess Christianity but do not have a home church, are not involved in their home church, do not read their Bibles or have a close relationship with Jesus, and yet feel they are good Christians. Some Native people are leaders in their church; they are pastors, pastors' wives, pastors' kids; they instruct the children; they are worship leaders and host Bible studies; and small groups gather in their homes. Some Native Christians are theologians. Some Native people might follow Jesus but not disclose this to their family or friends for fear of losing relationship with them. Christianity inside Native communities can look similarly sacrificial as in mainstream society among both marginalised and dominant people.

It appears Christians, no matter what their denomination or culture, have more in common than they think. All suffer varying degrees of the human condition that leads to brokenness. Throughout the centuries of contact with Indigenous people, drastic loss of life has resulted. The constant losses seem to outweigh the good, and yet Native Americans are still here. They have been observing the profession of Christianity in conjunction with the action of Christians and continue to wonder, in many cases, what must have happened to white Christians to cause them to behave in the ways they do. Having survived genocide and the historical trauma passed down through the generations, Native Americans are still here. Now that newer methods of healing have begun within Native Nations, heavy spiritual lifting must be done.

Throughout the centuries, in the middle of the experience of removal, there have been conversions of Indigenous people to Christianity. There always will be, regardless of the pride and superiority of the white church. This teaches us who is control, and it is not us. There will continue to be Indigenous praise and worship music made by people like Cheryl Bear or Jonathan Maracle and Broken Walls. These Christian Natives can reach Indigenous people in more compelling ways not embedded in colonisation. Many older Native Americans will continue to sing their favourite gospel hymns or sit in the church pew every Sunday morning in their favourite church.

More communities, such as NAIITS, will offer a place at the table that is more inclusive to discuss what people can accomplish together or how to find a way forward. Writers like Randy Woodley (Keetoowah Cherokee), Richard Twiss (Sicangu Lakota), Casey Church (Pokagon Band Potawatomi), Terry Wildman (Ojibwe and Yakima ancestry), Dr T. Christopher Hoklotubbe (Choctaw) and Dr Negiel Big Pond (Euchee/Yuchi), and more, continue to challenge readers how to connect with creation and what it is like to worship as a Christian Native. It is important that white Christians begin to understand that Native Christians have moved forward without their help in professing Jesus. For any Christian church that still sees only the poverty-ridden Native American and knows nothing of the fullness of the identity of Indigenous people in the USA, they miss so much vibrancy and lose opportunities to gain experience from a people who have emerged victoriously from the brink of destruction.

Bibliography

Charles, Mark and Soong-Chan Rah, *Unsettling Truths: The Ongoing Dehumanizing Legacy of the Doctrine of Discovery* (Downers Grove, IL: InterVarsity Press, 2019).

First Nations Version: An Indigenous Translation of the New Testament (Downers Grove, IL: InterVarsity Press, 2021).

NAIITS: An Indigenous Learning Community (2021) <https://www.naiits.com>.

Twiss, Richard, *One Church Many Tribes: Following Jesus the Way God Made You* (Ventura, CA: Regal, 2000).

Woodley, Randy, *When Going to Church Is a Sin: And Other Essays on Native American Christian Missions* (Scotland, PA: Healing the Land Publishers, 2007).

United States: Black/African American

JoAnne Marie Terrell

I've got the blues
I've got the blues
I've got the deep purple
Womanist consciousness
Self-loving
Superwoman
Brokenhearted black woman blues
Deep purple blues
Every day I gotta pray …
'Cause I don't wanna be
Tomorrow's bad news
Day and night we gotta fight …
If we don't wanna be
Tomorrow's bad news.

JoAnne Marie Terrell, 'Purple Blues', unpublished song

What did I do
To be so black and blue?

Fats Waller, 'Black and Blue'

Racism is a world-defining byproduct of capitalism. It is the scientific justification for the violent accretion of the Earth's abundant natural resources in the coffers of European nations and white North Americans after centuries of their enslavement of Black Africans and after their imperial conquest and colonial oppression of Africa, Asia and the Americas, that is, the 80% of the world that is non-white. Racism is not merely a stratifying ideology that is based on the presumption of white supremacy, the reverse claim of Black inferiority, and the relative inferiority/superiority of other people of colour. It did not originate in the realm of poorly framed, impious, prejudicial, hierarchical thoughts but in the concrete motives of European imperialism and the failed intention to establish, in perpetuity, chattel slavery as its means of wealth production.

Racial violence characterised the founding of North America and the colonisers' structuring of the social order, labour force and police powers to advantage themselves; therefore, race, socioeconomic class and the nature of the justice system are linked in the lived experiences of Black, Indigenous and citizens of colour. In the USA, racist policies drive discriminatory practices in all its institutions of socialisation: the economy, government, education, religion and family, where the quirks of colourism allot each member metrics of worth based on degrees of brownness. Conscious and unconscious racism, especially the inclination to preserve its privileges (and, for some, the determination to defeat it), remains at the epistemological centre of all social relations in the postmodern era.

Racism has been sustained by the European colonisers wresting control of religious ideas, discourses and imagery from the peoples of colour who produced both the principles and principals of many of the world's religions and by religious supremacy accorded to white, Western versions of Christianity. From the hijacking of the spiritual and moral trajectory of Palestinian Christianity to cultivate Orthodoxy by Roman Emperor Constantine I (c. 280–337); from the gradual whitening of the image of Jesus of Nazareth, a Palestinian Jew, and his mother, Mary, in iconography to the whitening of the images of Lord Krishna (etymologically, 'black' or 'all-attractive', 'the Dark Lord'), Radha, his consort, and Shakyamuni Buddha (563–483 BCE) during the Age of Empire; and from the dislodging of the concept of salvation from its collective, liberative moorings in Jewish messianism to the advancement of individualism and pious religious sensibilities in North American Evangelicalism, the experience of racism is fraught with implications not only for the ways that Black, Indigenous and people of colour are regarded but also for the ways they regard each other and are compelled to regard themselves: from the vantage point of the white gaze, through which white people are affirmed as standard-bearers of every good gift, from intellect, to creativity, to beauty, to morality. Racism thus compels Black, Indigenous and people of colour to simulate the imago whiteness in order to gain religious credibility as well as social, political, cultural and economic access.

The presumption of white people's fitness to rule the world was a pretext for their imperial incursions into Africa, the Indian subcontinent, the Pacific Rim, Latin America and the Caribbean. They fortified their ill-gotten gains from slavery by shaping capitalism into a system that sanctions perpetual exploitation of the natural resources of those continents and island nations and their peoples. Debt structuring, political destabilisation, military occupation, perpetual war, proxy wars that benefit white superpowers and multinational corporations, and the denigration of natural environments through the literalist claim to 'dominion' over the rest of creation are part of the political calculus that renders life on wondrous, imperilled planet Earth, principally stratified by race, gender and class, simultaneously a 'sweet dream' and a 'beautiful nightmare', as Beyoncé has sung – a potential utopia and an experienced dystopia.

In the late modern era, Enlightenment science and the advent of historical critical methods challenged this reliance on literal biblical interpretation to justify all elements of the status quo. The early twentieth century saw the rise of fundamentalism to counter this liberalising trend; yet historical criticism, specifically the 'quest of the historical Jesus', also enabled the theological enterprise to reclaim Jesus by social gospel theologians such as Walter Rauschenbusch (1861–1918) and Washington Gladden (1836–1918) as the bearer of 'good news' to the poor and marginalised. With neo-Orthodox theologians such as Karl Barth (1886–1968) and Reinhold Niebuhr (1892–1971), who emphasised the sovereignty of God, they paved the way for the emergence of liberation theologies in North America that would unequivocally proclaim Jesus Christ as Liberator of the oppressed, initially, the Black oppressed, who found their most vociferous advocate in James Hal Cone (1938–2018), widely recognised as the 'father of Black liberation theology'.

The significance of Cone's life and witness for the theological academy cannot be overstated. By situating himself in his own particularity as a Christian, Black man seeking freedom for his people from dehumanisation and death, his sources were the Bible and Black creativity: the spirituals and the blues, poetry, the visual and performing arts. As a Christian apologist, with North American Blacks ever under threat from white violence, Cone asked, 'How do I remain Black and Christian?' and another poignant question from his jazz and blues heritage, 'What did I do to be so black and blue?'

Cone helped shape theologies in West, Central and Southern Africa. He influenced theologians from places as far ranging as South Korea and Indonesia and was a charter member of the Ecumenical Association of Third World Theologians (EATWOT). In North America, he was a charter member of Theology in the Americas and the Society for the Study of Black Religion, a cadre of Black academicians who were helping each other refine their theologies, focusing on the relationship between liberation and the theme of reconciliation.

A significant number of Black women who began entering the religious academy in the early 1980s adopted the moniker 'womanist' in order to characterise the intersectional voices they were compelled to raise in contradistinction to Cone and other Black theologians who focused on the issue of race as well as to white feminist scholars who focused on the issue of gender, such as his colleague Beverly Harrison (1932–2012). Delores S.

Williams, Katie Geneva Cannon, Jacquelyn Grant and others broadened the discourse to include their voices, unique experiences and specific focus on the norm of survival, as distinct from that of liberation. Williams also challenged Rosemary Radford Ruether, a Roman Catholic feminist theologian who, in a series of articles published in *Christianity and Crisis*, had resisted Black women's naming of their take on the theological enterprise as 'womanist' in contradistinction to 'feminist'.

'Womanist is to feminist as purple is to lavender'. Alice Walker proffered this fourth and last instance of the definition of womanism in *In Search of Our Mothers' Gardens* (Orlando, FL: Harcourt Brace Jovanovich, 1983). The analogy suggests an intensified experience of sexism that Black, Indigenous and women of colour face, and argues that the analysis of sexism must be complicated by the intersecting, collective oppressions of racism and classism, the social, cultural and religious strictures of heterosexism; and the violence in misogynoir, misogyny, transphobia and homophobia that they suffer, witness and/or internalise.

Although Walker signalled an inclusive spirit and a commitment to feminist unity in crafting the first instance of her definition of a womanist as a 'Black feminist or feminist of colour', in the North American academy, some Black women resist the nomenclature and call themselves 'Black feminists', while other women of colour have assumed the task of naming themselves as mujerista and/or Latinx, or as Korean or Korean-American feminists. Cuban-born Ada Maria Isasi-Diaz (1943–2012) coined the term 'mujerista' and suggested the *cotidiano*, the quotidian or day-to-day life experiences of Latina women, as abundant resources for doing theology. Teresa Delgado and Robyn Henderson-Espinoza are Latinx theo-ethicists who focus on bodily redemption, deconstructing and queering gender norms. Choi Hee An, Chung Hyun Kyung, Wonhee Anne Joh and Grace Ji-Sun Kim are Korean and Korean-American feminists whose work in practical and systematic theology highlights Korean women's historical and immigrant experiences.

In the nearly 40 years since Walker articulated her womanist vision, womanist and Black feminists have engaged in unmasking the sexism disguised in the interdictions of paternalism and decried its dominating, rapacious and death-dealing forms. They have also confronted the pernicious racism that Black people experience, the recrudescence of the violence of their enslaved past in the unfolding present – in extrajudicial police and vigilante killings and acts of maiming, in mass incarceration and medical malfeasance, including the impact of protracted systemic oppression on Black folks' mental health – as well as in the abject poverty that attends Black life everywhere. These demonstrable truths are not a divine indictment of Black creatureliness based on dubious biblical interpretive schemas and pseudoscientific ratiocinations. Rather, their debased condition is a result of the systematic, centuries-long, violent accretion of wealth and power in the hands of European peoples, derived from the transatlantic slave trade, that massive scheme of coerced surrogacy that, for nearly three centuries, enabled the rise of agrarian capitalism in North America. While stripping human beings of their 'unalienable' rights, depriving them of the civil rights they were forging for themselves against monarchical governments, such as the English, French, Portuguese and Dutch, they did so at the expense of Indigenous populations in present-day Canada, the USA, Mexico, Central America and the Caribbean, whom they subjected to genocide, the survivors of which were removed to reservations, whose posterity remain at the bottom of all social and economic indicators and are rendered almost invisible in national discourses about race.

Cone's emphasis on theology done from within one's particularity assisted others in articulating Indigenous and LGBTQ theologies. Vine Deloria (1933–2005), a Standing Rock Sioux activist and theologian, George E. 'Tink' Tinker (Osage), retired professor from the Iliff School of Theology, and Clara Sue Kidwell (White Earth Chippewa and Choctaw) were among the first Native Americans to enter the mainstream of the liberal religious academy.

Racism is projected against Black, Indigenous, women, girls and gender non-conforming persons of colour differently from that against men, according to reified notions of gender. Feminist sensibilities among white women, however attuned to the plight of women and girls generally, never automatically guarantee racial sensitivity. Their racial privilege has been a barrier to sisterhood with Black women, whose moral momentum for abolition and civil rights they rode during their common fight for suffrage and reproductive rights.

'Black-fishing' and 'Asian-fishing' are attempts white women make to simulate the imago Blackness and Asian identity through the use of cosplay, accent manipulation, hairstyling, tanning and make-up techniques in order to eroticise themselves in their own and others' eyes without having to participate in the actual empowerment of Black and Asian women. In addition, the tenacity and ubiquity of 'Karen' – whom the *Slang Dictionary* defines as 'an obnoxious, angry, entitled, and often racist middle-aged white woman who uses her privilege to get her way or police other people's behaviors' – stake the racial insensitivity of white women against the safety of Black, Indigenous and people of colour from potentially aggressive police reaction and other repercussions, even as they are doing ordinary things.

Beating the 'purple blues' is the quotidian lot of the children, women and men who struggle for equal educational opportunities, equal protection under the law (to include the presumption of innocence), equal treatment by the banking system, health-care and housing industries, the right to vote and to traverse cities, roads and paths unmolested; for the right to breathe, whether due to the impact of environmental racism or unyielding police. In the zeitgeist that grips North America and the world, insensitivity to the effects of these everyday terrors makes some fellow citizens reluctant to utter the basic proposition 'Black lives matter', as if by arithmetical calculation saying so would render white, Asian, Latinx and Native lives moot.

The coronavirus that to date has claimed more than six million lives worldwide persists in a zeitgeist swirling with utter inhospitality, the un-neighbourliness that leads from trespass to violence to war, exacerbating the already dystopian mood of the country as well as the life prospects for Black people. Indigenous people, who have least access to health-care, experience 'poverty, food insecurity, and poor housing conditions' and are disproportionately impacted by the virus. In addition, in the USA, between March 2020 and September 2021, anti-Asian violence and 'hate incidents' rose to more than 10,000 and violent attacks rose from an average of 8.1 per year to 81.5 per year, more than 10 times the previous average. Such is the toll of racism, the human cost of maintaining a philosophy that holds one race superior and all others inferior, in relative terms.

In Christian signification, the rich imagery of 'the colour purple' – the name of Alice Walker's Pulitzer Prize-winning 1982 novel – connotes the royal suffering of Jesus Christ, eliciting comparisons with human suffering. It is thus used to demarcate the Lenten season on liturgical calendars. Although Walker was raised in a Christian household, her deeper intentions were to expand the god-concept to which North American Evangelical Christians often resort, beyond the image of the 'big and old and tall and graybearded and white' man who 'wear[s] white robes and go[es] barefooted'. In the novel, the colourful character Shug Avery prompts Celie, the central protagonist, to re-imagine God as relational, delightful and engaging, saying, 'I think it pisses God off if you walk by the colour purple in a field somewhere and don't notice it'.

Walker sought to empower Black women, connect Black people intergenerationally, brook the socially, culturally and religiously reinforced divide between Black women and men, and elevate all people of colour in their own estimation by empowering them to see the giftedness of their cultures and ways of being in the world, despite the ways the world treats them. Accordingly, the theological work required for beating the purple blues is manifold: demystifying the relationship between racism and capitalism; extricating themselves from the white gaze; accepting diversity as the standard of beauty; honouring the intersectionality of persons and persons in community; embracing liberative spiritual and intellectual traditions; leaning into creativity; emulating the *imago Dei*.

Bibliography

Cone, James H., *The Cross and the Lynching Tree* (Maryknoll NY: Orbis, 2011).

Morrison, Toni, *Playing in the Dark: Whiteness and the Literary Imagination* (Cambridge, MA: Harvard University Press, 1992).

Ringer, Christophe D., *Necropolitics: The Religious Crisis of Mass Incarceration in America* (Washington, DC: Lexington Books, 2020).

Walker, Alice, *The Color Purple* (Boston, MA: Houghton Mifflin, 1982).

Washington, Harriet A., *Medical Apartheid: The Dark History of Medical Experimentation on Black Americans from Colonial Times to the Present* (New York: Doubleday, 2007).

United States: White

David P. Gushee and Isaac B. Sharp

In the wake of his 2016 election and throughout his presidency and most especially in the lead-up to and wake of the 2020 election, Donald Trump made near constant reference to 'fake news', 'rigged' outcomes and 'stolen' elections. His false claims about stolen elections predictably reached a crescendo when Joe Biden was elected as the forty-sixth President of the United States in November 2020. In early 2021, crowds of Trump supporters descended on Washington, DC, to protest against Congress's certification of the election results. On 6 January, with Trump's encouragement, thousands of those who had gathered in DC marched to the US Capitol grounds in an attempt to overturn the results of the election. Quickly overwhelming security, hundreds of the rioters broke into the Capitol building, which they occupied for much of the afternoon.

Republican Party lawmakers and donors, US military members and various rogue militia groups, QAnon supporters and other conspiracists, Proud Boys and Boogaloo Boys, along with an array of other far-right and white-nationalist groups, from neo-Nazis to neo-Confederates, were represented in the coalition that stormed the Capitol. So too were members of one of Donald Trump's most faithful and devoted groups of supporters: white Christians. Religious iconography in general and Christian imagery in particular were well represented. Flags, banners and posters bearing crosses and Christian messaging marched lockstep alongside the kinds of Norse mythological symbols often appropriated for contemporary white supremacist purposes; a variety of marchers wore clothing emblazoned with a range of racist and anti-Semitic slogans, memes and ideas.

When pressed, some of the white Christian leaders who otherwise supported Trump throughout his presidency and re-election campaign denounced and distanced themselves from the Capitol rioters. Others were either actually there or at least close by. Some supported the messaging but not the methods. As it became clear that Christianity was in some way implicated, some merely demurred for one reason or another.

Whatever else it might currently signify or encompass, white Christianity in the context of the contemporary USA cannot be divorced from its militantly ethno-nationalist representation, which was on display during the 6 January siege. Nor can contemporary white US American

Christianity be properly understood apart from the broader reality of the large numbers of aggrieved white Christians who might not have participated directly or even approved of what transpired, but who similarly consider themselves an oppressed, persecuted or at least beleaguered minority in a rapidly changing culture bent on undermining their way of life. As a racialised tradition that has been historically accustomed to taking for granted its own normativity and pre-eminence as the nation's default version of mainstream religiosity, white Christianity in the contemporary US context has increasingly become defined by widespread collective anxiety over its diminishing social control and waning cultural relevance. Whether that is all that it now is, it is at least that. To understand how it got there, a brief historical overview is in order.

Historical Background

One way of telling the story of twentieth-century white Christianity in the USA is as the rise and fall of white Protestantism as the presumptively predominant religious tradition in US life, and of the triumphant rise and unhappy fall of the white Protestant self-perception as guardians of the national soul along with it. Another way of telling the story is of the proliferation of nationalistic forms of Christianity, the fusion of white Protestantism with American patriotism, and the establishment of a mythic Judeo-Christian (though primarily white Protestant) national heritage.

This external presumption of cultural and religious normativity intensified the various internal battles for pre-eminence within white Protestantism itself, because it was the fate of US culture and not just the church that was presumed to be at stake. For the first few decades of the twentieth century, theologically progressive, socially reformist and politically liberal elements within white Protestant Christianity seemed to be winning the intra-Protestant tug-of-war. From the social gospel of figures like Walter Rauschenbusch to the realist social ethics of figures like Reinhold Niebuhr, the left hand of white Protestantism that eventually became known as the mainline enjoyed massive influence within the nation's churches and in the halls of national power until at least the middle of the century.

Early twentieth-century struggles between fundamentalist and modernist white Protestants had apparently resulted in a resounding victory for the liberals. The established Protestant churches remained securely in the hands of those who believed that the fruits of modern knowledge – the historical-critical study of the Bible and the reality of Darwinian evolution, in particular – were perfectly reconcilable with Christian faith. Fundamentalist white Protestants, on the other hand, had been forced to retreat. As later histories would eventually retrieve, however, fundamentalist white Protestants had not so much disappeared as they had retreated into sectarian enclaves, where they busily worked to build their own networks of schools, ministries, interdenominational organisations and publishing houses.

Building upon the work of their fundamentalist forebears, in the years following the Second World War, a new generation of white Fundamentalists burst forth on the scene with a less bellicose, putatively more culturally engaged vision of Protestant conservatism, positioning it as a direct rival of and challenge to liberal-mainline Protestantism's apparent pride of place as the self-appointed caretaker of the national soul. Rebranding their culturally reengaged fundamentalism as neo-Evangelicalism – and eventually just Evangelicalism – the architects and founders of older fundamentalist Bible colleges and publishing houses, along with newer groups and institutions like the National Association of Evangelicals, Fuller Theological Seminary and *Christianity Today*, began rallying an enormous coalition of conservative white Protestants that would soon surpass organisations like the National Council of Churches and publications like the *Christian Century* in terms of both scope and influence. Whereas mainline leaders like Harry Emerson Fosdick or the aforementioned Reinhold Niebuhr were arguably the most influential white Christian figures until at least the middle of the century, the balance of power shifted in its later decades with the rise of conservative white Christian figureheads – including one of the most famous and influential Christians of the twentieth century, evangelist Billy Graham – to new levels of prominence in national life.

Both the Protestant soul-of-the-nation mythos and the struggle for pre-eminence within white Protestantism for control of the narrative included anti-Catholic, anti-Semitic and anti-immigrant animus, whether open or thinly veiled. The obvious presumed rightness of white, native-born Protestantism's status as the predominant form of American religiosity was part and parcel of much of twentieth-century Protestantism's official and unofficial theological, social and political positioning, despite the fact that many twentieth-century white Protestant leaders were themselves only a generation or two away from immigrant ancestors.

Over time, the presumption of white Protestant normativity softened to include space for Catholicism and Judaism within the range of acceptable forms of American religiosity. But for the most part, Catholics and Jews would be considered as safely within the bounds of a vague, newly regnant Judeo-Christian heritage only if they were successfully assimilated. The eventual measure of toleration for the Judeo-Christian rendering of suitably American religious identities depended in large part, in other words, on the ability of Catholics and Jews to become 'white/American' in their self-perception and self-presentation – and to be accepted as such from the perspective of those whose white Americanness had already been established. Jewish theologian Will Herberg's 1955 work *Protestant Catholic Jew* is famous at least as much for its timing and title as for its contents. The idea that the bounds of religious America had now stretched, however uneasily, to include not just white Anglo-Saxon Protestants but also other kinds of Protestants, and not just Protestant Christians but also Catholic Christians, and not just Christians but also Jews, seemed like a major step forward in inclusivity as well as perhaps a tolerable stopping point for American religious diversity. America would be a (white) Judeo-Christian country, with Protestants pre-eminent but Catholics and Jews also included. Notice that Eastern Orthodoxy did not make that list, nor did people of any other religious tradition.

By the later years of the twentieth century, it nonetheless had become increasingly clear that nothing would be able to prevent an emerging tide of social and political change from eroding the foundations of white Protestantism's majoritarian status. As waves of mass immigration and changing national demographic, geographic and religious patterns, as well as an increasingly globalised world, slowly chipped away at the presumption of WASP normativity, panic over the breakdown of white Christian dominance resulted in widespread resistance to some of the twentieth century's most significant social and political movements. Perceiving the civil rights, feminist, anti-Vietnam, anti-nuke and early gay rights movements as direct threats to white, straight, male, Christian hegemony over the collective national morality, white Christians – both Catholic and Protestant – consistently (though never universally) positioned themselves in direct opposition to struggles for major social change. A religion founded by a radical Jewish prophet had become the most predictably and stubbornly conservative force in American life.

Throughout the twentieth century, a variety of major internal theological, political, institutional and ecclesiological changes within both white Protestantism and white American Christianity more broadly also made monocausal narratives of either ascension or decline increasingly impossible. While establishment and/or mainstream versions of white Protestantism waxed and waned, for example, Pentecostal and Charismatic versions of Christianity came roaring in from the margins with explosive growth. The long, slow death of denominationalism was similarly paralleled by the proliferation of various non-denominational groups, small independent church traditions and a slew of individual mega-churches and multi-site church networks. Both trends represented iterations of a perennial theme in US religious history in general and in white Protestantism in particular: the prevalence of disestablished, initially anti-institutional, popular religious movements, and the frequent success of charismatic, personality-driven, wildcat expressions of Christianity.

But even the significant growth of various Pentecostal, Charismatic, non-denominational and mega-church versions of (mostly Evangelical) white Protestantism would not be enough to stave off the precipitous demographic decline of white Christianity. By the end of the twentieth century, white Protestantism's dominance as the majority faith of the nation had already come to an end. White mainline Protestantism had declined to a shell of its former self, and white Evangelicalism had plateaued before beginning its own decline in the first decades of the twenty-first century.

The changing relationship between US Protestantism and Catholicism in the last third of the twentieth century reveals much about shifting power dynamics as well as religious realignment. Roman Catholicism had seemed frighteningly 'Roman' – that is, alien, foreign, anti-democratic and wholly other – until the historic Vatican II conference (1962–5) began a modernising of Catholicism that in many ways brought its spirit into alignment with then current mainline Protestantism. Much of the perceived foreignness abated with the shift to the vernacular Mass and the overall modernisation of Catholic worship and education. The sense that Catholic theology was archaic and backward-looking was exploded by new currents in Catholic theology, including respect for other Christian and non-Christian faiths, that suddenly appeared in Vatican II documents. The peace and justice themes that predominated in the ethics documents of Vatican II were highly congenial to the increasingly progressive mainline moralists and denominational leaders.

Thus, the first serious rapprochement between US Catholics and Protestants occurred on the left end of the spectrum. A generation of post-Vatican II Catholic and mainline Protestant theologians, ethicists and church leaders formed new working relationships as confessional hostility dissolved. But then, beginning in the 1980s, conservative white Evangelicals fell hard for Pope John Paul II, who reigned from 1978 to 2005 and whose anti-Communism, conservative positions on family-related and sexual issues, along with his political dexterity, proved highly attractive. Moreover, as Evangelicals fixed on opposition to abortion as a central part of their US electoral and policy agenda, they found intellectual resources and co-belligerents especially on the conservative side of the US Catholic Church. This foreshadowed a development that by now is in full flower – theological and especially political conservatism, and liberalism, would become so salient that 'right' or 'left' would eventually overwhelm confessional identity in significance for many US Christians.

Twenty-first-century Developments

With the dawn of the twenty-first century, the decline of white Christian pre-eminence more broadly was only getting started. Within a few short years, white Protestants and white Catholics combined would no longer represent a majority of the population. The last year that more than half of Americans (50.5%) were white Christians was 2011. By 2012 their numbers had fallen to 48%. By the end of the 2010s white Christians made up only 42% of the population. All indications suggest that these patterns of demographic decline will continue into the near and distant future. For weal or for woe, this ongoing pattern of decline will likely remain among the most significant contextual realities affecting white Catholicism and white Protestantism alike. The current and future shape of white Christianity in the contemporary US context will undoubtedly be determined in large part by the nature of white Christian groups' responses to these changes. It is not easy for any religious group to face losing almost one percentage point of market share every year, especially one that has always considered itself the properly dominant religious community in a 245-year-old nation.

Due in large part to enormously effective marketing across the final decades of the twentieth century – orchestrated in most cases by conservative white Christian groups – the mythos of a white Judeo-Christian heritage as the religious wellspring of the national soul has remained persistent despite white Christian numerical decline. The power and pervasiveness of the myth has so thoroughly imbricated white Christianity with national life that it is often hard to tell whether a ritual, practice, belief or idea is an example of Christianity or Americanism. (Consider the US Pledge of Allegiance, the references to God in political speeches or presidential inaugural ceremonies structured along the lines of worship services.) The intertwining of Americanism and Christianity used to be called civil religion, evidence of which was seen as intellectually interesting, perhaps a bit troubling from the perspective of Christian theological integrity, on the one hand, or separation of church and state, on the other. But today, in a more frightened and reactionary white conservative Christian community, this religio-political intertwining looks more like white Christian ethno-nationalism and now appears uncomfortably like Peronist Catholicism in mid-century Argentina or Christian Nazism in 1930s Germany. Apparently, the mid-twentieth-century German theologians Karl Barth and Dietrich Bonhoeffer were right in warning against racist-nationalist-quasi-Christian idolatry.

Major twenty-first-century events and major figures in the life of white American Christianity have thus been inextricably tangled up in major events in the nation writ large. To a large extent, the history of US politics since 2001 just is the history of US white Christianity, as narrowly theological or ecclesial developments have been dwarfed in significance by political developments with religious connections, implications and interpretations.

At the outset of the century, the 9/11 attack on the USA and the events in its wake were a prime example. Political leaders successfully cast the subsequent beginning of the never-ending 'war on terror' as a civilisational clash between the good forces of Western, white, democratic, Judeo-Christian America and the evil forces of Middle Eastern Islamic terrorists. White Christians in the USA were particularly susceptible to and adept at popularising narratives that painted Muslims and Islam as an inherent threat to the American/Judeo-Christian way of life. Many of the worst atrocities of the ensuing years – from anti-Muslim bigotry and anti-immigrant backlash to US war crimes, human rights violations and the use of torture – received enthusiastic support from white Christians in particular. Indeed, on torture, white Evangelical Christians polled higher than any other religious group in supporting the torture of suspected terrorists. White Christian anxieties about waning national influence mixed with broader American anxieties about the nation's role in international affairs made the remaining years of the presidency of George W. Bush a particularly fertile ground for widespread expressions of religious patriotism and patriotic religion.

The George W. Bush years were also memorable because of that president's explicitly Evangelical faith. Unlike his father, former President George H. W. Bush, the younger Bush was a Texas-raised born-again Evangelical who credited faith with freeing him from addiction and getting his life on track. He came into office promising a 'compassionate conservatism' while also elevating the role of faith – and partnerships with faith-based organisations – in the official work of the US federal government. Bush's first major policy initiative, almost forgotten now, was to ban federal support for most embryonic stem-cell research, because he said this technology required the destruction of human life. This was a maximalist kind of anti-abortion position made into US science policy, a move pleasing to conservative Catholics and Evangelicals alike. Bush made a major speech to this effect in August 2001, a month before the terrorist attacks that drove his administration in a very different direction. Thus the 'embryonic' first months of the Bush administration presaged a certain kind of white conservative Christianity at the helm of American public life, which combined conversionist piety, faith–government partnerships, even more 'pro-life' policies than had been championed by Ronald Reagan and a faith-infused softheartedness towards, for example, immigrants and refugees.

The 2008 election of Barack Obama as the first Black US President seemingly signalled a watershed moment for a nation that has never truly reckoned with its long and ongoing legacy of white racism. For all the vaunted rhetoric about the putatively post-racial era his election symbolised, Obama's two terms in office wound up giving the lie to collective myths about American progress on race. A moderate Democrat politically, who sought compromise with Republicans and also reached out to conservative and progressive Christian leaders alike, Obama nonetheless inspired – or simply uncovered – a tide of racist vitriol among white Christians in particular. White racial anxiety combined with conservative Christian anxieties over waning cultural relevance made the reactions of the white Christians associated with the religious right especially hysterical. The 'birther' conspiracy movement claimed that Obama was not born in the USA and was therefore ineligible to be President. Grotesque racist insults and innuendos proliferated, including on Christian social media sites. Charges that Obama was secretly a Muslim rather than a Christian found common currency among certain subsets of the white Christian population, despite his longstanding Christian self-identification and church involvement. And Obama's occasional efforts to gingerly address US racial problems directly ran into frantic opposition.

For conservative white Protestants and Catholics alike, one of the era's most significant cultural developments was the relatively rapid shift in the general population's support for same-sex marriage, its eventual nationwide legalisation in 2015 and the broader societal acceptance of LGBTQ persons more generally that went hand in hand with such changes. In the early years of the gay rights movement, in the 1970s and 1980s, conservative white Christian organisations and lobbying groups had utterly opposed that movement, sometimes with the most hateful and degrading rhetoric. Twenty years later, when the issue became marriage, these same groups or their successors threw their weight behind opposition to the legalisation of same-sex marriage at both the state and national level. They lost, relatively quickly, and the loss stung. Today, some white Christian groups have shifted their focus to fighting for religiously based exemptions to laws requiring equal treatment of same-sex couples in business and commerce – and, of course, in their churches. This approach to religious liberty remains a major issue in US jurisprudence today. Meanwhile, most conservative white Christians would certainly welcome the (unlikely) reversal of gay marriage.

Even as conservative white Christian leaders drew a line in the sand of the culture wars on the question of same-sex marriage, signs of internal change simultaneously began piling up. Higher levels of support among younger conservative white Christians for gay rights, tentative steps towards equal treatment for same-sex couples by certain white Evangelical institutions – though never without significant backlash – as well as broad support for LGBTQ persons and their relationships among the historically mainline white Christian denominations, have all made clear that white

Christianity is by no means monolithic on these questions. But the frustration of white conservative Christian leaders about the erosion of what they believe to be the clear 'biblical' position on sexuality is intense.

In recent years, conservative white Christian power-brokers have lost some of the influence that they once wielded over the white Christian Protestant and Catholic laity. Driven in part by rising distrust in white Christian leaders, disappointment with white Christian clergy and dismay over ongoing revelations of abuse within white Christian power structures, white Christian disaffection with the institutional representations of their respective traditions grew significantly in the opening decades of the twenty-first century. The revelations of rampant sexual abuse and the widespread covering up thereof dating back decades in the Catholic Church were among the earliest examples of the scandals that have combined to form a crisis of trust in white Christian institutions and leadership.

Inspired in part by the untold millions of women who began publicly sharing their stories of rape, assault and sexual abuse under the social media hashtag #MeToo, the past few years have also witnessed the beginnings of a yet ongoing reckoning over the prevalence of abusive behaviour in general and sexual abuse in particular in white Evangelical church hierarchies. Denominations like the Southern Baptist Convention, multi-site mega-church networks such as Willow Creek and Mars Hill, and para-church organisations like Ravi Zacharias International Ministries have all been disturbed by revelations that they enabled and, in some cases, covered up all manner of abusive behaviour by their almost universally white male leadership. Conservative white US Protestants had once pointed to Catholic sex abuse scandals as evidence for the superiority of their version of Christian faith, but they can no longer do so. At the same time, and perhaps in consequence, a number of women raised in Evangelical circles and/or scholars of this part of the US white Christian world have been analysing and attacking patriarchal theology and toxic masculinity within their former (or current) faith communities. Kristin Kobes Du Mez's work *Jesus and John Wayne* (2020) tore through the Evangelical reading public like wildfire, as did news of superstar Bible teacher Beth Moore deciding to abandon the Southern Baptist Convention.

White Christianity's apparent toleration of abusive male leaders likely played at least some role in the 2016 election of Donald Trump and has contributed to the fallout at the time of this writing. Despite openly flouting almost every conceivable item on the usual list of contemporary white Christian positions on personal morality and differing profoundly in character and spirit from George W. Bush, Trump's election would not have been possible without the support of the same white Christian voters who elected Bush. Majorities of each of the major subgroups of white

Christian voters – including white Catholics, white mainline Protestants and white Evangelicals – chose Trump in 2016. White Evangelicals, in particular, overwhelmingly voted in his favour, remained his most loyal supporters throughout his presidency and voted for him once again in 2020 at the same levels as the first time.

Even after Trump's incitement of the 6 January 2021 insurrection, with dozens of lawsuits and potential criminal prosecutions looming, he remains the single most popular figure in the white US Evangelical Christian world. This presents something of a dilemma for conservative white religious leaders who wish to remain relevant or even viable with their constituencies. Like Republican politicians, these religious figures must decide whether to (continue to) embrace Trump or to place some distance between themselves and him. Figures like Eric Metaxas and Franklin Graham remain all in with Trump, while Southern Baptist Theological Seminary president R. Albert Mohler, Jr, tacks in his direction and former SBC Ethics and Religious Liberty Commission head Russell Moore's opposition to Trump led eventually to his resignation in 2021. Examining this situation nearly 80 years after the birth of the modern US white Evangelical movement, the contrast is stark indeed. White Evangelicalism had wanted to transform US culture for Christ. By 2020, it had become deeply enmeshed with a decadent US cultural figure like Donald Trump.

Looking to broader trends in US white Christianity, a place to begin is to note that the US white population appears increasingly indifferent to organised religion, with its refugees sometimes reporting weariness with the politicising of Christianity as a primary reason. To the extent that US Catholicism is holding its own numerically, this is clearly due to the influx of more devout immigrant populations, especially from Latin America. At the time of the COVID crisis, which began in March 2020, white Evangelicals did continue to boast some of the largest and most well attended mega-churches, though critics noted their reliance on a rock-concert and celebrity-culture ethos susceptible to both the abuse of power and the neglect of pastoral care and discipleship.

Whether such trends are particularly acute in contemporary white Christianity or are merely the white Christian version of broader cultural developments is perhaps an open question. But at this juncture in history, it has become abundantly clear that white (mostly Evangelical) Christians have developed their own cultural ecosystem comprising an extensive network of publishers, producers, writers, artists and popular figures who make and distribute media targeted at and consumed by a still sizeable, white, mostly Evangelical Christian populace. In fact, white, mostly Evangelical Christians are arguably most clearly distinguishable by the media that they consume. To be a white Christian in the contemporary US context often means participating above all else in a subculture with its own linguistic idioms, media diet and patterns of consumption. White Christians have their own set of internet celebrities, popular pastors, bloggers, podcasters, influencers, musicians and authors whose products sometimes become best-sellers based solely on their appeal to generally conservative white Christians. There is a real sense, in other words, in which contemporary white Christianity in the USA has become an industry that most directly catechises its people via the media products that it sells them, rather than through congregational life.

The contemporary Christian music (CCM) genre is a prime example. CCM has developed its own industrial complex that simultaneously draws from, reflects and drives trends in the ecclesial, liturgical and personal devotional practices of millions of white Christians. Mega-churches with in-house bands and high-level production capabilities write and record 'praise and worship' songs that reach considerable audiences via both traditional outlets like Christian radio stations and newer formats like streaming platforms, where they are then heard, absorbed and eventually played in innumerable smaller (mostly white Evangelical) churches throughout the country. Though some critics point out that the mass consumer nature of the CCM industry tends to produce derivative, trendy and hackneyed material that is slickly produced but theologically thin, the genre remains incredibly popular.

The white Christian media industry often replicates the in-group/out-group border-guarding of white Evangelical culture writ large. CCM artists, pop theologians and various Christian celebrities, for instance, occasionally run foul either of their distributors or of their consumers by stepping outside the acceptable bounds of regnant Evangelical orthodoxy on a host of theological or political issues. Christian bookstores have withdrawn the work of popular authors, pastors, artists and musicians for, among other sins, advocating for the acceptance of the moral legitimacy of LGBTQ persons and their relationships, questioning the eschatological reality of the eternal conscious damnation of non-Christians, and challenging the *de facto* political orthodoxy of the white Evangelical establishment.

No one yet knows what post-COVID church life will look like, and whether scarred, perhaps frightened US Christians will want to gather in massive indoor worship centres any time soon. But in the meantime, white Christian media culture continues discipling white mostly Evangelical Christians apace.

Mainline white Protestantism as of 2020 had few culturally visible leaders, though if one adds the post-Evangelical exiles and refugees, the number of visible figures swells a bit: Brian McLaren, Jim Wallis, Diane Butler Bass, Nadia Bolz-Weber, Peter Enns and Rob Bell. Increasingly, the energy on the religious left, and the dominant voices, are coming from non-white, non-male, non-straight figures, and the justice commitment of the white Christian left encourages them to cede pride of place to such leaders in conference and church venues. The white Evangelical left has also become heavily politicised. Though without the numbers or visibility of white conservative leaders, many on the white Evangelical left worked just as hard and explicitly for the election of moderate Catholic Democrat Joe Biden as the other side did for Donald Trump. The discovery that America's white Christians were just as politically divided as everyone else, and that their supposedly shared religion failed to provide meaningful common ground, frightened many observers who fear further political violence.

Ultimately, America's original sin of racism seems the issue that most profoundly defines this period in American history and the divisions that persist. The difference today, perhaps, is that a growing number of white US Christians are committed to the #BlackLivesMatter fight, while others dig in their heels against it. The year 2020 in the United States of America saw the murder of the Black man George Floyd by white Minneapolis police officer Derek Chauvin, the massive street protests that followed, the deepening of #BlackLivesMatter activism on the progressive side and the doubling down of opposition to even the study of critical race theory among white conservative Christians. America's oldest moral problem manifested in yet one more way, illuminating the extent to which the nation, and its white Christians, were utterly divided.

Bibliography

Burge, Ryan, *The Nones: Where They Came From, Who They Are, and Where They Are Going* (Minneapolis, MN: Fortress Press, 2021).

Jones, Robert P., *The End of White Christian America* (New York: Simon & Schuster, 2016).

Kobes Du Mez, Kristin, *Jesus and John Wayne: How White Evangelicals Corrupted a Faith and Fractured a Nation* (New York: Liveright, 2020).

Kruse, Kevin M., *One Nation Under God: How Corporate America Invented Christian America* (New York: Basic Books, 2015).

Whitehead, Andrew L. and Samuel L. Perry, *Taking America Back for God: Christian Nationalism in the United States* (New York: Oxford University Press, 2020).

United States: Hispanic

Samuel Rodriguez

The broad horizon of Christianity in the USA shows an increase in Hispanic Christians so far out of proportion to every other group that Christian leaders project Hispanics will one day be the heart and soul of the American Church. The nation's largest minority group is not just exploding in numbers, it is influencing culture and, in many ways, creating culture through media behemoths such as Telemundo and Univision, Latin holidays and traditions, and wide distribution of works by Spanish-language authors and music artists. Social scientists agree that we are entering an era some call a 'Brown Millennium', when Hispanics will profoundly shape the religious climate, culture, politics and very likely the direction of the entire nation.

Hispanics in the USA number roughly 60 million. Non-Hispanic whites (hereinafter referred to simply as 'whites') will shift from being the majority to being a minority by 2045, according to census projections. Yet the younger the demographic, the sooner the tipping point will be reached. In 2020, whites under the age of 18 were already a minority and Hispanics the second-largest minority. By 2026, whites will be in the minority in the 14- to 29-year-old demographic. Hispanics will make up more than 21% of the total US population by 2030 and one-third by 2050. Some experts believe Hispanics will make up the majority of the total US population by 2100.

Hispanics as a group are not only the fastest growing but also have the greatest adherence to Christianity, with 93% self-identifying as Christian. The opportunity for the American Church is evident. Any organisation that is not including Hispanic leaders in its foundation will be poorly positioned for the future. Already, many Christian organisations are seizing this present time to invest in greater evangelism and discipleship in the Hispanic community.

The Hispanic Population's Distinctive Features

To understand the faith of Hispanics in the USA it is necessary to trace the origins of this massive population. Spanish-speaking peoples in the United States pre-date the formation of the nation by more than 250 years. The first Spanish missionaries to North America established a post in Puerto

Rico in 1511, roughly 100 years before Jamestown. Between 1598 and 1769, they created the nation's oldest city – St Augustine, Florida – and established missions in Arizona and Texas and along the coast of California.

In the 1800s, as the USA extended its borders westward through wars and land purchases, Spanish-speaking peoples who had lived there for decades or even centuries became US citizens. In the 1890s, their population was boosted by as many as 100,000 Latin Americans immigrating each year to fill jobs in southwestern agriculture and mining industries. The Mexican Revolution 20 years later drove thousands more immigrants across a border that has ebbed and flowed for decades.

Pressured to isolate research about this fast-growing minority, the US Census Bureau in 1980 added the term 'Hispanic', and by so doing identified a group for the first time based not on 'race' but on ethnicity and culture. The Bureau later added 'Latino'. Latino references people from Latin America, while Hispanic references having roots in Spain (ancient Hispania). The terms have blurred both in academic papers and in the common vernacular, but according to polls, 72% of US Spanish-speakers now prefer the term 'Hispanic'.

Research on Hispanics has produced fruitful results. Today we know that immigration is still an important factor but is no longer the greatest factor in population growth; that 81% of Hispanics under the age of 35 years were born in the USA and live predominately in the southern and southwestern United States, specifically in California, Texas and Florida; and that Hispanics are young, with 61% under the age of 35. We also know that they tend not to identify with umbrella terms – only 21% self-identify most often as 'American' – identifying instead with their nation of origin, such as 'Puerto Rican', 'Cuban' or 'Mexican', regardless of how many generations of their family have lived in the USA. These diverse subcultures from various national origins are tethered together by a Catholic religious tradition and a common language. However, the very ties that bound also contributed to a bias against Hispanics.

First, Hispanic religion seemed suspicious. Early Americans did not believe Catholicism was even Christian. This bias worsened in the 1800s when floods of European Catholics escaped famine by immigrating. By 1906, 17% of the US population was Catholic, making it the largest Christian Church in the USA, and possibly the most maligned. To stop Catholic growth, a 1924 law limited European Catholic immigration yet ironically exempted Latin America Catholic immigration, thereby strengthening the Catholic Church. As waves of Latin American immigrants arrived, the Catholic Church served as a hub, assisting with housing, jobs and cultural assimilation, such as learning English. The growing Church gained respectability by building schools, hospitals, charitable institutions and major universities. Then came the 1960 presidential election of the very likable Irish Catholic John F. Kennedy. His election muted Catholic intolerance, and his enduring legacy helped move Catholicism finally into the mainstream. By the turn of the millennium, 57% of the US population had a favourable view of the Catholic Church.

Second, the Spanish language produced prejudice, because broken English was interpreted as ignorance, rather than bilingualism appearing as intelligence. Spanish today, however, is the unrivalled second language of the USA and the principal language of the western hemisphere. In the USA, fully 41 million people speak Spanish at home and prefer to retain their language, even while learning English, because the vast majority believe English is necessary for success. Foreign-born Hispanics remain Spanish-dominant and US-born Hispanics are English-dominant, although more than 50% still speak Spanish at home. Among young Hispanic parents, 86% speak Spanish to their children. Although some studies indicate that Hispanics lose Spanish by the third generation, bilingualism among Hispanics is far more common than in any other immigrant group.

Hispanic Religious Life
Hispanics have overcome prejudice and stepped out of history's shadows to exercise voice, agency, leadership and self-determination. Having been 'adopted' into the USA – although being, as a point of fact, some of the earliest founders of the nation – Hispanics were largely written out of history books that favoured the Euro-American immigrants who assimilated quickly into the population. Such blatant condescension created a paternalistic system much like the plantation system, which immigrants at one time accepted, depending first on the Church, then on the government. But as Spanish terms bled into English, and Spanish food, Latin traditions and Catholicism went mainstream, Hispanics achieved cultural significance. The paternalistic approach by government, educators and churches diminished as the Hispanic population became less marginalised. Today, instead of kneeling with hands out, imploring, Hispanics stand strong with arms wide, inviting. Institutions are scrambling to embrace this gigantic population group. Most secular and Church leaders understand that either any paternalistic patterns remaining will die or the institutions perpetuating them will. They have come to realise that they ignore the Hispanic population at their own peril.

For Church institutions, the intractable Spanish language and large population of young, bilingual Hispanics mean that to survive, churches must either adopt Spanish-language services or help plant Spanish-language churches, and at the same time, learn to accommodate second- and third-generation English-dominant Hispanics. Spanish-only churches must find ways to accommodate the ballooning numbers of young English-speaking Hispanics, conduct services that minister to multi-generational needs, and include the lasting cultural distinctiveness of congregation members' nations of origin. Some church streams are faring better than others.

In Catholicism, the massive Hispanic population in church has changed the face of the Church in the USA and, in many ways, the world. US Hispanics now account for 40% of all Catholics in the USA and 71% of Catholic Church growth. Almost three-quarters of all US Hispanics self-identify as Catholic. Of US-born Hispanics, half self-identify as Catholic. Observers believe that the tremendous growth in the number of Hispanic Catholics is one reason why the Church broke with tradition in 2013 and elected the first Pope from the Americas, the Argentina-born Pope Francis.

US Hispanics have held to their traditional Catholic values even as many Catholics globally recoiled against Church policies following the Second Vatican Council and were disillusioned by later sex scandals. As America's secularism rose in the 2000s, Hispanics continued to hold firm, rejecting the idea that religious faith is a private matter, seeing instead that faith affects every aspect of life. It is understandable why even US-born Hispanics hold fast to the traditions of the Catholic Church. It provided comfort to immigrants in a foreign world. And still today, many Hispanics attribute the growth of their social status and bank accounts to the help of the Church, prayers to God and the intervention of the saints. Most see the Church as a safe place where everyone, regardless of socioeconomic background, can take part in celebrations, rites and traditions. Their faith is a religion, a habit, their culture, a social remedy and their identity.

Catholic leadership is working actively to meet the needs of the growing Hispanic population. Roughly 4,800 parishes, one-quarter of the total, have Hispanic ministry. Most include Spanish-language Masses in their weekly schedules. Two-thirds of all Hispanic Catholic baptisms are celebrated in Spanish. Catholic leaders are accepting more Hispanic traditions and creating more Hispanic resources. The *quinceañera* celebration of a girl's fifteenth birthday and the feast day of Our Lady of Guadalupe are some customs appearing in US parishes. So many priests and parishioners speak or are learning Spanish that the US Catholic Church, in effect, is becoming bilingual. For example, in Philadelphia, a Spanish parish merged with an English one. In Georgia, a disappearing parish in a factory town grew again when it became 90% Hispanic. In Lawrence, Massachusetts, all three Catholic churches celebrate Masses in Spanish every week, and one employs two Hispanic staff members with advanced theology degrees and pastoral skills.

Catholic Hispanics are mostly young, but retaining them is proving to be a challenge. Hispanics make up 60% of Catholics under the age of 18, almost half of all Catholics aged 18–29 and half of all Catholic millennials. The median age of Catholics by race or ethnicity is 43 for whites, 36 for Asians, 33 for Blacks and just 27 for Hispanics, which correlates to figures in the total US population. Parishes with Hispanic ministry enjoy larger attendance at Mass than the national average. Overall, however, devotion to the Church is declining, with 86% of Catholics still claiming their faith is important even though their attendance does not show it. In 1965, 71% of all Catholics attended Mass regularly. By 2018, only 39% of Catholics did so. Hispanic Catholics proved to be more faithful, with 55% attending at least monthly and 26% attending weekly. By way of comparison, 85% of Hispanic Protestants say religion is important and 61% attend weekly religious services. For Evangelical Hispanics, 92% say religion is important and 70% attend weekly religious services.

Declining attendance bodes poorly for the growth of the Catholic Church. For one thing, Catholics have fallen behind at every level of education. Few Hispanics are prepared to fill positions in parishes or in the upper echelons of the Church. Out of 37,300 US-based priests, only 3,000 are Hispanic. Of those, only 1,000 are US-born. Most seeking leadership training are Hispanic, but only 17% of Hispanics are in programmes that grant degrees. The Catholic leadership is trying to speed up training, in part by identifying more than 20,000 new Hispanic pastoral leaders through what is called the Fifth National Encuentro of Hispanic/Latino Ministry, or 'V Encuentro'. The Catholic leadership is also seeking to add more Spanish congregations to existing parishes as well as to new parishes, schools, universities and seminaries in locations of high Hispanic population growth.

Parochial schools have been particularly hit by a massive slide in attendance. Since 2005, a quarter of Catholic schools have closed. Just half the schools operating 50 years ago still operate, with a total student enrolment of less than two million. The decline of Church schools is most extreme in urban areas, the very cities where great numbers of Hispanics live. Of Catholic school students, 15% are Hispanic, which sounds good – except it means that only 4% of Catholic Hispanic children attend Catholic schools. This puts the burden solely on parishes to educate 96% of Catholic youth; however, only 10% of Hispanic children are enrolled in parish education programmes. The cost to rectify this downward slide is staggering. If Catholics aspired to educate the half of all US Hispanic children whose parents are most likely Catholic, they would require roughly 21,000 schools. With just over 6,500 Catholic schools in total operating today, the task of educating Hispanic children seems insurmountable. This dearth of education is even more lamentable in view of the trend for Hispanic young people to be more highly educated and to boast higher graduation rates than the general US population. The result is seen in Catholic colleges and universities, where only 11% of students are Hispanic.

Other issues facing the Catholic Church are seen in the numbers. In 2010, 67% of Hispanics self-identified as Catholic. Within three years, this fell to 55%. By 2021, fewer than 50% self-identified as Catholic. The result is that while the Catholic Church has grown numerically, it now makes up a lower percentage of the overall population. In 2015, roughly 81.6 million Americans, or one quarter of the entire population, identified as Catholic. In 2018, roughly 51 million Americans, or one fifth of the entire population, identified as Catholic. After generations of tradition, culture, community and loyalty, the Catholic Church today is shedding Hispanics.

The Hispanic Protestant Reformation
'Religious switching' is the term experts have given for people who leave one church for another. Catholics have experienced a greater net loss due to religious switching than any other group. So many Catholics have left their Church that pollsters have made 'formerly Catholic' its own subgroup. Some call it the second-largest religious group in the USA. Presently, roughly 600,000 Hispanic Catholics switch to Protestantism each year. Census experts call it the 'de-Europeanisation of American Christianity'. Members of the National Hispanic Christian Leadership Conference (NHCLC) call it the first generation of a 'Hispanic Protestant Reformation'.

Religious switching is a youth movement. Of the Catholic parishioners who leave, 70% make that decision before the age of 24. Hispanics aged 30–49 who leave Catholicism are split between ending religious affiliation altogether and joining Evangelical Protestantism. Those a decade younger are more likely to change to 'no religious affiliation'. Between 2009 and 2017, Hispanics leaving Catholicism to self-identify as Protestant rose from 23% to 26%. Switching has caused inverted growth, with 69% of foreign-born Hispanics identifying as Catholic and only 16% identifying as Protestant. But by the third generation, only 40% identify as Catholic while 30% identify as Protestant. As a result, Protestant churches have grown by targeting third-generation Hispanics who might otherwise have switched to 'no religious affiliation'.

Catholics are switching not just to Protestantism in general but to Evangelicalism in particular. In the 1970s and 1980s, the rise of televangelism and contemporary Christian music gave alternatives to Hispanic Catholics, who became more inclined to break from tradition than previous generations. The first Catholics switching to Evangelicalism were met with discrimination, ridicule and even persecution in their communities. Today, Evangelical Hispanics are one of the fastest-growing groups in US religious life.

In 1993, Protestant Hispanic congregations in the USA numbered more than 10,000. Of those, the Assemblies of God led, with more than 1,200 churches. By the turn of the millennium, Hispanic Protestant numbers had mushroomed, including a 50% increase in Spanish congregations of the Assemblies of God, a 100% increase in members of the Seventh-day Adventist Church, a 40% increase in churches and members of the Apostolic Assembly of Faith in Jesus Christ, and 150 more Nazarene Hispanic congregations. Hispanic Protestant churches now number more than 23,000. By 2003, the number of Hispanic Protestants in the USA was greater than the populations of Jews, Muslims, Episcopalians or Presbyterians. By 2014, roughly 12 million Hispanics identified as Protestant. Of those, 8.8 million were Evangelical/Pentecostal. Today, more than 35% of Hispanics use the term 'born again' to describe their religious identity. Of the 23,000 Hispanic Protestant churches, 88% are Evangelical, including Pentecostal or Charismatic. The new term emerging for Hispanic Evangelicals is *evangélicos*.

Pastors of successful Hispanic congregations state that parishioners are looking for a place where they feel welcome, where they can have a family, and where they can belong, with some also claiming their new members want a deeper experience with God. Of Hispanics who were raised Catholic and became Protestant, 49% say an important factor is finding a church that reaches out to help its members. Evangelical churches have responded in various ways. 'You're Mexican and want to worship at our church? We'll show you mariachi music. You're Puerto Rican? We'll show you how we salsa. Dominican? We'll have merengue. Colombian? We'll have cumbia.' A conference of Southern Baptist Hispanic pastors set goals to bring back the 'apartados', the groups of Hispanics who once went to church but stopped. Southern Baptist Convention leaders set goals to add 7,000 new Hispanic churches. By 2022 they had more than 3,200 Spanish congregations, up from around 2,100 at the start of the century. Pastor Rick Warren's Saddleback Community Church alone has planted three dozen Hispanic churches near its base church.

In the move to Evangelicalism, 64% of Catholics who switched have become Pentecostals. Of 'formerly Catholics', 28% became Pentecostals. One reason for the allure of Pentecostal churches is that 52% of Hispanic Catholics have experience with the 1970s Catholic Charismatic Renewal, which still holds meetings that resemble Pentecostal services. Also, Pentecostalism has proliferated for a century in Latin America. For Hispanics originating from those nations, Pentecostal churches seem non-threatening, if not intriguing. Today, at least 225 Hispanic Pentecostal or Charismatic denominations and Spanish-language branches of denominations accommodate the flood of Hispanics. Of them, the Assemblies of God is the largest, with 9% of all Protestant Hispanics attending Assemblies of God Hispanic churches.

The first US Hispanic Pentecostal ministers were ordained in 1909 at the Azusa Street Revival in Los Angeles. At first, Euro-American churches governed Hispanic churches and ministers. In 1926, the Latin American Council of Christian Churches convened in Houston and asserted their ability to self-govern, but it was not until 1973 that the Assemblies of God became the first fellowship to form a 'foreign-language district', Las Asambleas de Dios, with 'the same privileges and responsibilities' as English-language districts. Today, that 'foreign language' movement has grown to 14 independent districts that pioneer new works, raise resources to plant churches, engage in friendly competition with each other and enjoy phenomenal growth. As a result of leaving paternalistic governance, the Assemblies of God now has more than 3,000 Hispanic congregations and 4,000 Hispanic ministers, with more than one million Hispanics self-identifying with the Assemblies of God. Of Hispanic ministers, roughly a third are women, the largest group of women serving in any Hispanic Protestant fellowship.

An old assumption was that by leaving the Catholic Church, Hispanics would leave part of their culture, but studies reveal that Hispanics who adopt Protestantism are even more likely to maintain their unique ethnic identity, as well as their devotion to the faith. Hispanic Evangelical churches seem to provide the deeper connection to God that 'formerly Catholics' desired. Services tend towards vibrant worship, up-tempo music, prayer sessions, spontaneous prophecies or testimonies, and charismatic sermons. For example, New Life Covenant in Chicago has 17,000 people attending each week. The pastor, Wilfredo 'Choco' De Jesús, specifically targets third-generation Hispanics, the group statistically most likely to leave Catholicism and join a Protestant church. Nine of the church's weekly services accommodate Hispanic distinctives in a bilingual and bicultural format.

Rising Influence of Hispanic Christians

When Hispanics find agency and voice, the culture shifts. However, it shifts in ways that do not follow strict lines of common ideologies. Socially, Hispanics are likely the most researched group in America, and perhaps the least understood. Racially, Hispanics demand to be included in history books, yet they do not carry the pain, grievance and tragedy of past wrongs and therefore tend not to accept public policies for racial remedies. Hispanics are proud of their ethnicity and yet have high intermarriage rates, with 28% of marriages under the age of 35 being inter-racial or inter-ethnic. Hispanics are vocal about racial dialogue revolving around blacks and whites but omitting Hispanics and Asians. Hispanic church leaders believe the church and not the government should administer remedies for the soul, including empathy, understanding and love for one's neighbour. NHCLC leaders wrote an open letter to President George W. Bush during his presidency for allowing racialised sentiments. In 2020, they openly recommended to the Trump administration that the impartial eye of justice should guide legislators and judges. Overall, Hispanics attribute racial economic inequities more as a function of individual achievement than public policies and see economic success as a cure for racism, placing economic lack more on the individual than on systemic problems. Among Hispanics aged 18–35, 77% say people who want to get ahead can make it.

In education and economics, well-educated US-born Hispanics are blowing up standard demographics. Hispanics are the fastest-growing group in the middle class. They now make up 18% of the middle class and are more educated than ever before. The US post-millennial generation is the most racially and ethnically diverse generation, and one-quarter of them are Hispanic. Their dropout rates are lower than those of millennials and they have a higher college enrolment rate – 59%. Among 18- to 20-year-old Hispanics no longer in high school, 55% are in college. And of these post-millennial Hispanics, just 12% were born outside the USA.

Political parties are struggling to pin down the preferences of this, the fastest-growing religious group in the USA, the largest minority to vote in recent elections and one of the nation's largest voting blocs. The Hispanic Protestant electorate is about the same size as the Asian American electorate, 50% larger than the Jewish electorate and three times larger than the Muslim electorate. Of Hispanic Protestant voters, 65% are Pentecostals, and of those Pentecostal voters, the Assemblies of God makes up almost 25%. This makes Hispanic church leaders valuable allies to secure during any election season.

The Hispanic population voted decisively against Republicans in almost every US presidential election until the George W. Bush team courted Hispanic church leaders in 2004 and won 40–44% of the Hispanic vote. Every presidential campaign since has worked hard to get the Hispanic vote. The late Reverend Jesse Miranda, former president of the NHCLC, met with every US President from Reagan to Obama and led the push for comprehensive immigration reform on Capitol Hill from 2006 to 2014. It was not just talk for Hispanic leaders, who later openly chastised President Obama for not fulfilling his 2008 campaign promise on immigration. Nevertheless, they voted for him as a group in 2012.

In the 2020 presidential election, Hispanics were forecast to be 'the' group that would determine the outcome. Political parties actively courted them, and Hispanic leaders actively demanded to be heard. Of the 32 million Hispanic people who actually voted, 66% went with the winning Democratic candidate. Political prophecies were confirmed. The trend for Hispanic voters to determine elections will increase as 18.6 million Hispanic people who were not yet 18 in 2020 become eligible to vote in 2024. However, Hispanics as a group will remain difficult for politicians to corral. They are evenly split, with 47% leaning Democrat and 46% leaning Republican, but their affiliation does not denote acceptance of the party's platform. Among Hispanics, 30% describe themselves as liberal or very liberal, compared with 21% of the voting public. Yet issue by issue, their views do not hold to the category they claim. Hispanics are strong on marriage and family but neutral about homosexuality. They are strongly opposed to racism, yet believe racism is solved more by individual effort than by government interference. On abortion, 51% of Hispanics say it should be illegal in most cases. They have influenced foreign policy in Latin countries and are adamant about immigration reform. The weight of Hispanic convictions rests heavy on lawmakers concerned about winning votes. And yet, the power of the rising *evangélico* population has not been fully realised. It cannot be underestimated in coming years.

The Future of Hispanic Christians
Hispanic Christians have a powerful voice. Contemporary Spanish Christian music is sought by record labels and Hispanic musicians become virtual superstars. Christian magazines and publishers distribute in Spanish as well as English. Hispanic Christians no longer wait for denominations to plant or adopt *iglesias*. Hispanic congregations spring up in many places and are involved in evangelism, compassion ministry, social justice and community. Looking to the future, to minister to the growing needs of this burgeoning population will require building up Christian leaders in all streams who are educated theologically, mission driven and ready to accept their places as thought leaders for the nation. Three challenges can be identified that are likely to shape the future.

First, Hispanic churches will need to develop new forms of leadership, geared not only to spiritual qualities but also to effective administrative and financial management. As well as nurturing the spiritual life of the community, Hispanic Christian leaders will require the skills that enable them to play a full part in the wider culture and society. Top-down, paternalistic relationships will need to give way to fraternal fellowship and partnerships with others.

Second, Hispanic ministry will need to become multilingual, multi-generational and multi-ethnic. This will involve building cultural and linguistic bridges between generations with leaders who understand the culture and values of the previous generation as well as the generation coming up, recognising that monolingual churches no longer fit the multigenerational needs of the Hispanic community. As neighbourhoods transition from first-generation to second- and third-generation, churches will need to learn to minister to future generations that prefer English but do not fit culturally into Anglo-English churches.

Third, Hispanic Christians will need to accept their own missional call to act as missionaries to the world around them. This will involve learning to minister to others in a holistic way, balancing discipleship, social responsibility and evangelism to meet the needs of the whole person and the whole community. Rather than occupying a passive role as targets of mission, for the future Hispanic American Christians must become active agents of mission within the life of the country as a whole. Hispanic Christians can be seen as the firewall of the nation's moral future. The USA was built on a foundation begun by Hispanics, and perhaps its future too will rest on pillars built by Hispanics.

Bibliography

Avalos, Hector, *Introduction to the US Latina and Latino Religious Experience* (Boston, MA: Brill, 2004).

Espinosa, Gaston, *Latino Pentecostals in America: Faith and Politics in Action* (Cambridge, MA: Harvard University Press, 2014).

Gonzalez Rudolph, *Then Came Hispangelicals: The Rise of the Hispanic Evangelical and Why It Matters* (Sisters, OR: Deep River Books, 2020).

Martinez, Juan Francisco, *The Story of Latino Protestants in the US* (Grand Rapids, MI: Eerdmans, 2018).

Ramirez, Daniel, *Migrating Faith: Pentecostalism in the United States and Mexico in the Twentieth Century* (Chapel Hill, NC: University of North Carolina Press, 2015).

United States: Asian American

Timothy Tseng

Asian American Christians in the twenty-first century, like the more than 24 million Asian Americans, reflect a wide range of educational attainment, economic status, political orientation and diversity of language. They also experience fraught intergenerational dynamics and occupy an uneasy interstitial space in the American racial landscape. Identifying with a religion that continues to be associated with Euro-American culture and white racial privilege complicates the picture. Given the Euro-American perception of Asians as quintessentially 'not Christian' (or 'heathen'), Christianity among Asian Americans has been a confounding idea. But the ground is shifting in the study of American Christianity and in Asian American studies; thus, many of this essay's conclusions necessarily will be provisional.

We begin with a discussion of the evolving meaning of the term 'Asian American'. The origins of the moniker can be traced to the Third World Liberation Front student strikes at San Francisco State University (1968) and the University of California, Berkeley (1969). Prior to this, 'Oriental' was commonly used by missionaries and social scientists to identify people from Asia. Originally considered a descriptive term, 'Oriental' became problematic when it was rejected by Asian American activists and critiqued by postcolonial scholar Edward Said. 'Asian American' seemed to be a better description of the diversity of peoples with Asian origins and escaped the Western and white 'gaze'.

Most Asian Americans, however, connect primarily to their ethnic communities. From the 1970s, ethnic identity – rather than Asian American consciousness – heightened as immigration from Asia swelled dramatically. Asian American organisations became tertiary spaces for pan-ethnic coalitions. But these efforts were often fraught as Filipinos, Southeast Asians, South Asians and other groups challenged the dominance of East Asians in the early 1970s. Each subsequent wave of Asian immigration has required Asian American organisations to broaden their coalition and stretch their definition of Asian American. For example, after the 9/11 attacks and anti-Muslim backlash, the inclusion of Middle Eastern and West Asian peoples under the 'Asian American' umbrella has been debated extensively.

The US Census Bureau's efforts to classify Americans by race has both fuelled uncertainty about and placed limits on the term 'Asian American'. In 1980 and before, the census forms listed specific Asian ancestries as separate groups, along with White and Black or Negro. But in 1977 the US federal government required government agencies to maintain statistics on racial groups, including on 'Asian or Pacific Islander'. In the 1990 census, 'Asian or Pacific Islander (API)' was included as a racial category (respondents were still required to select one particular ancestry as a subcategory). This led to protests from Native Hawaiian and Pacific Islander leaders who did not want to be lumped into the Asian American racial category. So, beginning with the 2000 census, 'Native Hawaiian and Other Pacific Islander' and 'Asian American' were separate categories. People with ethnic origins in West Asia were also excluded from the 'Asian American' classification. In the 2020 census 'Middle Eastern Americans' and 'Central Asian Americans' were included as sub-categories of that classification. Today, the Census Bureau's 'Asian' category includes people who indicate their race on the census as 'Asian' or report entries such as 'Chinese, Indian, Filipino, Vietnamese, Indonesian, Korean, Japanese, Pakistani, Malaysian and Other Asian'. Based on this definition, Asian Americans comprised 5.4% of the US population in 2018 (that proportion increases to 6.5% when multiracial Asian Americans are included). In 2020, the estimated number of Asian Americans was 24 million.

Scholars have continued to debate the definition of Asian American with increasing rigour and sophistication. This essay, however, will limit itself to the Census Bureau's definition (which will exclude Native Hawaiian and Pacific Islanders, communities with majority Christian presence). Based on the most recent data, the largest shares of the Asian American population are Chinese (5.4 million), Indian (4.6 million), Filipino (4.2 million), Vietnamese (2.2 million), Korean (1.9 million), Japanese (1.5 million) and Pakistani (527,000). Other groups include Thai (329,000), Hmong (320,000), Cambodian (300,000), Laotian (262,000), Taiwanese (214,000), Bangladeshi (213,000), Burmese (189,000), Nepalese (175,000), Indonesian (117,000), Sri Lankan (61,000) and Tibetan (27,000).

As we take a closer look at Asian American Christianity, it will become apparent that Christianity has a stronger presence in Asian American communities than in most Asian countries. This raises at least two questions. First, does Protestant and Catholic identification confer Asian American Christians greater social acceptance in the USA? It is uncertain how Christianity's declining status and share of the US population will affect its presence in Asian American communities. Second, is the growth of Asian American Christianity (along with Black and Latino Christianity) decentring European cultural and white racial norms in US Christianity?

Asian American Christianity Today

A survey conducted by the Pew Research Center in 2012 included queries about religious affiliation. In its report *Asian Americans: A Mosaic of Faiths*, Christians made up the largest of Asian American religious affiliations, at 42%. The unaffiliated were the next largest group of respondents, at 26% (this was the highest figure among all the racial groups in the USA). Despite very sizeable contingents of Christians and the unaffiliated, Asian Americans were also much more religiously diverse than the rest of the predominantly Christian US population and were 'largely responsible for the growth of non-Abrahamic faiths in the United States, particularly Buddhism and Hinduism'.

Buddhists accounted for about 14% of the Asian American population (white Buddhists outnumbered Asian Americans by almost two to one). East Asian Americans (Chinese, Japanese, Korean) and Vietnamese are strongly influenced by Mahayana Buddhism, Taoism, Confucianism and Christianity. Southeast Asian Americans (Cambodian, Laotian, Thai and Burmese) identify more with Theravada Buddhism. While South Asian Americans are largely Hindu, many Jains, Zoroastrians, Muslims, Sikhs and Orthodox Christians can be found among this group. Hindus (10%), Muslims (4%), other religions (2%) and Sikhs (1%) make up the remainder of the Asian American religious affiliation.

Demographics, Religious Beliefs and Practices

Asian American Christian affiliation is roughly equal between Protestant (22%) and Catholic (19%). Christianity is the majority religion among Filipino (89%) and Korean Americans (71%) and a significant minority in Japanese (38%), Vietnamese (36%) and Chinese (31%) communities. Like other Asian Americans, they are concentrated along the West Coast of the USA and in Hawaii.

In 2021, more than three million Asian Americans self-identified as Catholic. Among the six largest Asian American ethnic groups, this broke down to:

- 65% of Filipino Americans
- 30% of Vietnamese Americans
- 10% of Korean Americans
- 8% of Chinese Americans
- 5% of Indian Americans
- 4% of Japanese Americans.

Among the five million Asian American Protestants, the breakdown was as follows:

- 61% of Korean Americans (40% Evangelical, 21% mainline)
- 33% of Japanese Americans (13% Evangelical, 19% mainline, 1% other Christian)
- 22% of Chinese Americans (13% Evangelical, 9% mainline)
- 21% of Filipino Americans (12% Evangelical, 9% mainline, 3% other Christian)
- 11% of Indian Americans (11% Evangelical, 8% mainline, 2% other Christian)
- 6% of Vietnamese Americans (13% Evangelical, 9% mainline).

In 2010, 60% of mainline Protestant Asian Americans were born overseas, which matches the general Asian American population. Larger percentages of Evangelical (73%), Catholic (79%), Buddhist (79%), Hindu (96%) and unaffiliated (70%) were foreign born. A larger percentage of mainline Protestants are more than 55 years old. Furthermore, when asked whether they think of themselves as 'typical Americans' or 'very different from a typical American', only mainline Protestants had a larger percentage respond that they thought of themselves as 'typical Americans' than as 'very different'. Evangelicals scored almost as high as Buddhists and Hindus in the 'very different from a typical American' response. One can infer from this that older mainline Protestants are more acculturated than their younger and more foreign-born co-religionists.

The Pew report also provides data on the growth of Asian American Protestantism through the switching of religious affiliation. Conversion rates are higher among Japanese, Chinese and Korean Americans than among other US Asian groups, which factors into Protestant growth. Approximately 22% of Asian Americans identify as Protestant today, compared with 17% who say they were raised Protestant. However, Asian American Catholics (with a net loss of only three percentage points) and Hindus (with a net loss of only two percentage points) have experienced little net impact from switching. By contrast, Asian American Buddhists have experienced the biggest net losses from religious switching. Roughly one in five Asian Americans (22%) say they were raised Buddhist, and 2% have switched to Buddhism from other faiths (or from having no particular religion). But 10% of Asian Americans have left Buddhism, for a net loss of eight percentage points.

Asian Americans have low rates of religious intermarriage. It is striking that 94% of married Hindus have a spouse who is also Hindu. Also noticeable is that 81% of Asian American Catholics and Protestants are married to fellow Catholics or Protestants, respectively, and 70% of Buddhists are married to fellow Buddhists. Of those with no religious affiliation, 61% have a spouse who is also unaffiliated.

Asian Americans also range more widely than the total population between highly religious and highly secular. For example, unaffiliated Asian Americans tend to express lower levels of religious commitment than unaffiliated Americans in the general public (76% say religion is not too important or not at all important in their lives, compared with 58% among unaffiliated US adults as a whole). Some critics have noted, however, that the practice of family-centred cultural rituals among 'unaffiliated' Asian Americans was not adequately taken into account in these surveys. Since many understand 'religious' to mean a commitment to a church community, the religiosity of unaffiliated Asian Americans might not be measured accurately.

Asian American Evangelicals, by contrast, rank among the most religious groups in the USA when measured by weekly church attendance (76%, compared with 64% of white Evangelicals). Among Asian American Catholics the figure is 60% (compared with 39% of white Catholics who attend at least once a week). Among mainline Asian American Protestants, 42% attend weekly (compared with 25% white mainline Protestants). Overall, Asian American Christians attend services more frequently (61%) than US Christians as a whole (45%%). Asian American Christians are also more inclined than US Christians as a whole to say that living a very religious life is one of their most important goals (37% versus 24%).

The Pew survey noted that Asian American Christians, particularly Evangelicals, are also strongly inclined (72%) to believe that their religion is the one, true faith leading to eternal life. Among white Evangelicals, 49% say that their religion is the one, true faith leading to eternal life, whereas 47% say many religions can lead to eternal life. The Asian Evangelical pattern also contrasts sharply with Buddhists, Hindus and unaffiliated Asian Americans, who are relatively unlikely to make exclusive claims about true faith.

Asian American Evangelicals are also more inclined than white Evangelicals to believe that there is only one true way to interpret the teachings of their faith (53% versus 43%). Although just as likely as white Evangelicals to say that the Bible is the word of God, Asian American Evangelicals are somewhat less inclined to claim that everything in Scripture should be taken literally, word for word. Korean American Evangelicals are in this respect exceptional, since 68% say the Bible should be interpreted literally, compared with 44% of non-Korean Asian American Evangelicals who hold to this view. This is an important exception since 34% of Asian American Evangelicals are of Korean descent. This figure compares to 25% who are Chinese, 14% Filipino, 11% Indian, 10% Japanese, 2% Vietnamese and 5% others. Koreans are, nevertheless, similar to other Asian American Evangelicals on most measures of religious commitment.

Social and Political Attitudes

Asian Americans as a whole are more liberal on social and political issues than the general public. They also favour the Democratic Party (52%) over the Republican Party (32%). Asian American Christians, however, are more evenly split between the two parties. Overall, they lean Republican largely due to the strong Evangelical affinity. The Pew study reports the following breakdown of political party affiliation among Asian American religious groups:

- Protestants overall – 47% Republican, 36% Democrat
  * Evangelical – 56% Republican, 38% Democrat
  * mainline – 37% Republican, 44% Democrat
- Catholic – 42% Republican, 41% Democrat
- Buddhist – 27% Republican, 56% Democrat
- Hindu – 9% Republican, 72% Democrat
- Unaffiliated – 21% Republican, 64% Democrat.

On social issues, Asian American Christians express views that are more conservative than other Asian Americans and the wider American public. The percentages are driven by the preponderance of Asian American Evangelicals whose views are closest to those of white Evangelicals. Taking views on homosexuality as an example, 53% of all Asian Americans believe that homosexuality should be accepted by society, while 35% say it should be discouraged. By comparison, 58% among the general public say homosexuality should be accepted, while 33% say it should be discouraged by society. Asian American Evangelical opinion, however, is reversed: 65% say homosexuality should be discouraged, and 24% say it should be accepted by society. Unaffiliated US Asians lean most strongly towards acceptance of homosexuality (69%). Smaller majorities or pluralities of Asian American Catholics (58%), Buddhists (54%), Hindus (54%) and mainline Protestants (49%) also accept homosexuality.

Similarly, Asian Americans as a whole tend to support abortion rights. More than half, 54%, say it should be legal in all or most cases; 37% say it should be illegal in all or most cases. Among the general public, by comparison, 51% say abortion should be legal in all or most cases, while 43% say it should be illegal. But the majority of Asian American Catholics (56%) and Evangelical Protestants (64%) say abortion should be illegal in most or all cases. Support for legal abortion is highest among Asian Americans who are religiously unaffiliated (74%), followed by Hindus (64%), Buddhists (59%) and mainline Protestants (50%).

Black and Latino Evangelicals are also more conservative on political and social issues compared with the majority of their racial groups. But Asian American Evangelicals stand even farther apart from their group as a whole. It is possible that since 2012 (the date of the Pew survey), younger Black, Latino and Asian American Evangelicals may no longer be as conservative on abortion or homosexuality than an earlier generation, but more new data need to be collected and studied.

Surprisingly, when it comes to opinions about the size of government, Asian American Protestants, Catholics and unaffiliated are more likely than their co-religionists to prefer a bigger government that offers more services. Of Asian American Protestants, 52% prefer a bigger government, compared with about 37% of all US Protestants. The difference is starker among Evangelicals, where half of Asian American Evangelicals prefer a bigger government (51%). This is significantly more than the 20% of white Evangelicals who say the same. This appears to confirm that policies linked to the size of the US federal government such as racial equity, economic parity and immigration reform are issues that these Black, Latino and Asian Evangelicals share with their own ethnic populations – issues that have been of less interest to white Christians.

Because this snapshot of Asian American Christianity relies on a survey done more than a decade ago, it may no longer be an accurate reflection. There are indications that the emergence of Millennial and Gen-Z Asian American Christians, white Christian support of the Trump presidency and an increasingly polarised political, religious and cultural society have impacted Asian American Christianity significantly. This snapshot also does not explain how Asian American Protestantism realigned in favour of Evangelicalism. Nor does it show how Catholicism has drawn on its trans-Pacific resources and immigrant history to quietly build a large youthful generation of Asian American Catholics. We turn our attention now to some historical perspective.

Growth of Asian American Christianity

The earliest permanent Asian settlement in North America dates to 1763, when Chinese and Filipino sailors abandoned the galleon trade between the American Spanish colonies in the Philippines and Asia and established a Filipino community in Louisiana. There is evidence of Roman Catholic presence in these settlements. The first Asian American Protestants, however, are traced to the Chinese miners and merchants who were drawn to the California Gold Rush in the early 1850s. San Francisco, the hub of economic activity, became the centre of religious life for the Chinese. For the next century, the City by the Bay would be the most important intersection for Japanese, Filipino and other Asian Americans. It remains a key centre for Asian Americans today.

The first generation of Asian American converts often cited the white missionaries' compassion and their teachings about racial equality as reasons for embracing Protestant Christianity. This generation of Asian American converts and pastors proved to be far more effective at converting their own people than the white missionaries. Asian American Christian leaders were better at helping to establish missions, schools, rescue missions and community centres that assisted immigrants in adjusting to life in the USA. White women missionaries, in particular, became role models who encouraged American-born Asian women to assume leadership roles. Despite the presence of racial paternalism, they were one of the few allies of Asian Americans.

Protestant Asian Americans and their missionary allies unsuccessfully opposed discriminatory laws that proscribed Asian immigration, naturalisation and property ownership. The close relationship between the missionaries and the Asian Americans encouraged a strong identification with Protestantism. Asian Americans also formed inter-denominational organisations such as the Chinese and Japanese YMCAs, the Northern and Southern California Japanese Christian Church Federations, the North American Chinese Church Convention and the Korean Church Council of North America.

In the 1920s and 1930s, Asian American Protestants, influenced by the social gospel and liberal theology, became more socially and politically engaged. They continued to be concerned about evangelism but gave increasingly more attention to social witness. Among immigrants, much attention was given to the situation in Asia. Chinese, Japanese and Korean Christians believed that Protestantism could modernise their countries. But a heightened sensitivity about Western imperialism and the reticence of missionary agencies to relinquish control of the church in Asia generated debate among immigrants about the tensions between Asian nationalism and Christian internationalism. At the same time, a generation of American-born young people came of age. Ethnic Asian inter-church youth and young adult conferences were started. Asian American Christian collegiate student movements in the 1920s through to the 1940s confronted racial and economic injustice. Some of these students became union organisers and community activists. Others helped Asian ethnic Protestant congregations become self-supporting.

During the pivotal years between the Second World War and the passage of the 1965 Immigration Act, American-born Asian Christians built the trellises upon which Asian American Christianity today would bloom and flower. Most Japanese and a large segment of Chinese Protestants would stay in the mainline denominational structures. They supported their churches' stance on racial integration. Many even participated in the civil rights movement. But they also wanted to maintain their churches' ethnicity. The Japanese Christian Church Federation continued to organise conferences for its young adults throughout the 1950s and into the 1980s. The formation of the National Conference on Chinese Christians in America in 1955 represented an attempt to support Chinese ethnic congregations. Chinese Protestants, in particular, noted that Chinese immigration had increased significantly. To them, this justified the continuation of Chinese-speaking congregations.

The Asian American Evangelical trellis was also built during the middle decades of the twentieth century. Reacting to mainline Protestant double retrenchment from ethnic-specific ministries and traditional evangelism, neo-Evangelical Asian Americans created alternative networks. Those who remained in mainline Protestantism ignored their denominations' priorities and joined like-minded Asian American Evangelical networks. Others started independent congregations and organisations that distinguished themselves from mainline Protestantism by claiming to emphasise biblical authority and personal evangelism. The neo-Evangelicals, thus, created new opportunities and spaces for Asian American growth that mainline Protestants sought to foreclose. By the 1980s, Evangelical para-church organisations such as the Japanese Evangelical Missionary Society and Ambassadors for Christ (among the Chinese) would become more popular among Asian American Christians than the renewed emphasis on Asian American ministries within mainline Protestantism.

Since 1965, waves of Korean and Chinese immigrants have fuelled the growth of Asian American Protestantism and its realignment to Evangelicalism. Similarly, Filipino and Vietnamese immigration have dramatically increased the Asian American presence in Catholicism. Among Southeast Asian immigrants, most of whom were refugees of the Vietnam War, the psychological and philosophical upheavals of war and exile led to a significant number of conversions. In part, this was because American church groups were the most active agencies in assisting refugees in Thailand and sponsoring refugees in the USA. Though many converted to Protestant Christianity in refugee camps in Thailand during the 1970s and 1980s or after their arrival in the USA, many retain cultural elements of their older belief systems. The new immigration revitalised a demand for ethnic-specific religious organisations. None of the branches of American Christianity was adequately prepared for the explosion of ethnic and religious diversity in the 1980s and 1990s. Immigrant Asians soon overwhelmed the American-born.

As Evangelicals and Catholics (to a lesser degree) focused on evangelism and institutional growth in the 1980s and 1990s, the Asian American consciousness that inspired the mainline Protestant caucus movements was gradually muted. The term 'Asian American' was stripped of its political context and reduced to a missiological target group. As a new generation of Asian immigrant children came of age in the late 1990s, they had little historical connection with the mainline, Evangelical or Catholic Asian American baby boomers. Nevertheless, the 1992 Los Angeles uprisings, the 9/11 attack in 2001 and the most recent incidents of COVID-related anti-Asian violence have chastened Asian American Christians who earlier pivoted away from social and political issues. Reckoning with a persistent anti-Asian racism in the midst of celebratory multiculturalism as well as responding to the rising numbers of disaffected young adults might be ushering in a new degree of maturity for Asian American Protestants, Evangelicals and Catholics who seek to renew a holistic Christian social witness.

Influence in Church and Society

Historically, their proximity to American Christianity has given Asian American Christians greater influence than their numbers would indicate. Since the beginning of their mission efforts among Asian Americans and during the height of its cultural hegemony, mainline Protestantism was a channel for Asian American public witness and participation in society. White missionaries and Asian American Christians influenced by the social gospel and theological liberalism advocated for a more tolerant and inclusive multiracial society. They also created space for many Asian American women to step out of restrictive traditional roles. These goals and spaces were hard-fought victories that helped tear down segregation in favour of racial liberalism and multiculturalism. Asian American Catholics also spoke out about issues that concerned their Filipino and Vietnamese constituencies.

Asian American Evangelicals, on the other hand, paid little attention to public issues until the late twentieth century. It appears that most of their baby boomers broadly supported the progressive goals of the Asian American movement, but they focused on personal evangelism and church growth. Furthermore, the public concerns of immigrant Asian American Evangelicals diverged widely from those of American-born Asian Americans. Since the late 1990s, however, an emerging generation of Asian American Evangelicals has pressed for greater voice and fairer representation within Evangelicalism and society, even though most align themselves with public issues associated with conservative white Evangelicals. For example, Hyepin Im, founder and president of Faith and Community Empowerment, a non-profit organisation that empowers the Korean and Asian American community in Los Angeles and across the country, has been a visible presence in every US presidential administration since 2000. She has been able to engage both conservative and liberal Christian public concerns, though she volunteered for the Asian American and Pacific Islander Christians for the Biden coalition in the 2020 elections. Professor Russell Jeung, one of the founders of Stop AAPI Hate – which raised awareness of the renewed anti-Asian attacks in 2021 – was named one of *Time Magazine*'s 100 most influential leaders. Prominent sports figures like tennis star Michael Chang and professional basketball player Jeremy Lin have publicly professed their Christian faith. Lin has been very outspoken about anti-Asian discrimination. Ideologically and politically conservative Asian American Evangelicals are a significant force today. While most would support conservative social issues, few would reject the goals of racial inclusion, diversity and equality.

Asian Americans have also impacted the church in the USA. Like Latino and Native American Christians, they have broadened the church's racial composition beyond Black and white. They have also complicated the Black–white racial binary. Roy Sano, Wilbur Choy, Syngman Rhee, Jitsuo Morikawa, David Ng, Katie Choy Wong, Ella White, Paul Nagano and others rose through the ranks of mainline Protestantism, building caucuses and creating space within these denominations for Asian representation. Rita Nakashima Brock, C. S. Song, Fumitaka Matsuoka, Sang Hyun Lee, Pui Lan Kwok and others articulated contextualised Asian and Asian American mainline Protestant theologies. These theologies went beyond a liberationist perspective to engage culture and gender. Though mainline Protestantism has lost its cultural sway in the USA, Asian Americans, in general, have found it to be a more hospitable place today than it was in the mid-twentieth century. Today's Asian American mainline Protestant leaders tend to be skilfully adaptable in multiracial and cross-cultural settings.

In 2003, the Catholic Church appointed Ignatius Wang and Dominic Luong its first Asian American auxiliary bishops. There are now five active Asian American (and Pacific Islander) bishops in the USA. More than any other minority groups in the USA, Asian American and Pacific Islanders have the highest number of vocational commitments to the priesthood and religious life. Because such a high percentage of Roman Catholic Asian Americans are immigrants, one can anticipate, in the next few years, more American-born Asian Catholics gaining greater visibility.

Though racial barriers to membership of organisations historically dominated by white Evangelicals remain highest among American Christians, Asian Americans have made impressive gains in the last two decades. InterVarsity Christian Fellowship (IVCF) is one of the few Evangelical organisations to seriously address the questions of race and ethnicity in a manner that enables racial-ethnic leaders to shape the discourse. IVCF is also open to constructive engagement with social justice and religion and science discourse. Since the 1980s it has attracted a very large number of Asian American college students. It has therefore played an important role in shaping the worldviews of at least two generations of Asian American Evangelicals. Many of today's best-known Asian American Evangelical leaders, such as Ken Fong, Kathy Khang and Soong Chan Rah, have crossed paths with InterVarsity. Its president, Tom Lin, is one of the first Asian Americans to lead an Evangelical organisation. Walter Kim of the National Association of Evangelicals and Julius Kim of the Gospel Coalition have recently been appointed as heads of Evangelical organisations. Eugene Cho leads Bread for the World. Frank Yamada, formerly president of McCormick Seminary in Chicago, is now the executive director of the Association of Theological Schools. Several Asian Americans are presidents of theological seminaries.

In the past, proximity to Christianity in the USA provided a channel for social engagement and influence. While the status of American Christianity appears to be in decline, it is still a space for Asian American social participation. What seems to be changing, however, is the redefining of American Christianity by its growing racial and ethnic diversity, which includes the presence of Asian Americans.

Conclusion

Asian American Christianity is a diverse community that occupies an interstitial space in the USA. It stands apart from, yet somewhat mirrors, the broader Asian American population. It contextualises Christianity into various Asian American idioms yet simultaneously affirms a faith that claims to transcend linguistic, ethno-national and racial differences. As such, it faces a number of questions that will affect its future as a coherent religious movement.

(1) *Asian American consciousness*. Racial discrimination, Asian American cooperation and empowerment have been significant concerns for mainline Protestants and, to a lesser degree, for Roman Catholics. But these have not been perceived to be vital issues for Evangelicals. In fact, studies have shown that white Evangelicals have promoted colour-blind ideologies that work against the empowerment of racialised people. The hidden traces of 'heathen' othering still drives much of their missiological aims, creating dissonance among Asian Americans. Both have accelerated the 'silent exodus' from their Asian American congregations and have encouraged a suppression of racial identification – even in multi-ethnic settings. Respondents in mainline Protestant and Catholic multi-ethnic settings are less likely to downplay their Asian American identities. In the last 10 years, however, a new generation of Asian American Evangelicals has galvanised around anti-Asian discrimination and expressed greater ecumenical openness to mainline and Catholic Asian Americans. Between

the open letter to *Christianity Today* in 2012 and Stop AAPI Hate during the COVID pandemic, a renewal of interest in engaging Asian American consciousness seems to have appeared. What does this imply about the future of Asian American consciousness?

(2) *Inter-generational conflict and cooperation*. Related to the question of Asian American consciousness is the issue of inter-generational conflict and cooperation. Will immigrants and their offspring maintain their congregations and ministries despite the diversity of age and cultural perspectives? In the 2020 US presidential elections, informal surveys of Asian American Christians revealed a large chasm between immigrant parents, who favoured Donald Trump, and their children, who opposed him. The younger generation is also more inclined to affirm women's leadership and welcome the LGBTQ+ concerns. How will this chasm impact the younger generation's identification with Christianity? In particular, will they abandon Evangelical Christianity?

(3) *Historic memory*. How can Asian American Christians today benefit from the experiences of baby-boomer Asian American Christians? What can be retrieved from Asian American history and culture to form distinctively Asian American expressions of Christianity? Can a bridge between the historically mainline Protestants and contemporary Evangelical Asian American Protestants be built? Will Asian American Christians invest in the retrieval and retelling of their histories by supporting scholarly endeavours?

Christians represent a younger and more active segment of the growing Asian American presence in the USA. But in the face of the declining share of Christianity in American life and the ongoing fragmentation of the Asian American community, it is not clear whether Asian American Christianity will reflect this decline or be the vanguard of the renewal of a multiracial and global Christianity. The future of Asian American Christianity is uncertain, yet intriguing.

Bibliography

Burns, Jeffrey, Ellen Skerrett and Joseph M. White (eds), *Keeping Faith: European and Asian Catholic Immigrants* (Maryknoll, NY: Orbis Books, 2000).

Carnes, Tony and Fenggang Yang, *Asian American Religions: The Making and Remaking of Borders and Boundaries* (New York: New York University Press, 2004).

Iwamura, Jane and Paul Spickard, *Revealing the Sacred in Asian and Pacific America* (New York: Routledge, 2003).

Min, Pyong Gap and Jung Ha Kim (eds), *Religions in Asian America: Building Faith Communities* (Walnut Creek, CA: Altamira Press, 2002).

Yoo, David K. and Khyati Y. Joshi (eds), *Envisioning Religion, Race, and Asian Americans* (Honolulu, HI: University of Hawaii Press, 2020).

Saint Pierre and Miquelon

Danielle DeLong

The small islands of Saint Pierre and Miquelon symbolise France's final connection to its historic grasp on North America. A mere 12 nautical miles off the southern coast of Atlantic Canada's Newfoundland and Labrador, Saint Pierre and Miquelon are a territorial overseas collectivity of France and continue to be a significant resource for France with their offshore Atlantic cod and flounder. Saint Pierre and Miquelon are two of the area's eight small islands, forming an archipelago. Only Saint Pierre and Miquelon are inhabited. Of the two, the smaller island of Saint Pierre is more densely populated and functions as the islands' economic centre while Grande Miquelon is connected to Langlade (Petite Miquelon) by a sand bar and is situated just north of Saint Pierre. Saint Pierre and Miquelon is recognised as part of Europe, due to its connection with France, as well as North America, due to its geographical position.

The archipelago is home to 5,800 islanders; 90% are urban dwellers with a very large majority of the population residing in the capital city of Saint Pierre on Saint Pierre Island. The majority of islanders are French-Canadian (95%), while the remaining 5% includes Anglo-Canadians (4%) and other inhabitants (1%). The archipelago mother tongues reflect these percentages, with French being spoken by 95% of the population and English by 4%, while the remaining 1% is unidentified. In light of the strained fishery industry, the French government has been exerting significant effort to help diversify the archipelago's local economy through tourism, fish and crab farming, and agricultural ventures, including vegetables, poultry, cattle, sheep and pigs.

From the time of its discovery by explorers José Alvarez Faguendes in 1520 and Jacques Cartier in 1535 until permanent French sovereignty was established through the Second Treaty of Paris in 1815, the archipelago had been subject to a continual power struggle between the French and British over its fishery resources. Canada likewise valued the rich fishing grounds. Extensive fishing eventually threatened codfish stocks, leading Canada to impose a cod moratorium in 1992 to help stabilise the population, causing the archipelago's main industry to plummet. France resisted the moratorium, referring to the 1713 Treaty of Utrecht, which permitted French fishing around the islands, and responded with the 'Codfish

Crusade' by fishing in forbidden Atlantic waters. The fishing skirmishes eventually resolved in Canada's favour by 1994, leaving only a small area for Saint Pierre fishing boats to jig cod.

Prior to the fishing wars, the archipelago found itself at the centre of another international power struggle. Saint Pierre and Miquelon became entangled in global discord when several national powers, including Nazi Germany, France, the USA and Canada, vied for control of the islands during the Second World War once the archipelago's strategic location was recognised as an effective tool for influencing the war.

The fishing conflict between Canada and France was also not the first time that Saint Pierre and Miquelon faced threats of economic decline. The 1933 amendment to the Prohibition law of the United States' Volstead Act initiated an economic downturn, as the islands were no longer needed as a seaport for bootleg liquor operations to smuggle alcohol from Canada into the USA. In facing such economic instability, France distributed $25 million a year to the archipelago to help sustain the livelihood of the islanders. As a result, they have been commonly referred to as 'the most expensive Frenchmen'.

While the islanders strongly identify with their French roots, there is also a prevailing Acadian influence on the archipelago. The Acadians, early French settlers distinct from those in other New France colonies, were among the first people to inhabit the islands after seeking refuge during the 'great disturbance' and British deportations beginning in 1755. The removal of Acadian French settlers from their homes in New England states and Canadian Maritime provinces, where they had settled since the seventeenth and eighteenth centuries, was initiated by British victory over France during the Seven Years' War. As the Acadians refused to take a vow of allegiance to Britain's Protestant monarch and forswear the Pope, they chose to resettle on Saint Pierre and Miquelon. The Acadians brought their Catholic faith with them, accounting for the prominent Catholic influence that has been maintained to the present day.

Christianity in Saint Pierre and Miquelon, 1970 and 2020

Tradition	1970 Population	%	2020 Population	%	Average annual growth rate (%), 1970–2020
Christians	5,500	98.4%	5,500	94.4%	0.0%
Independents	0	0.0%	30	0.5%	7.0%
Protestants	50	0.9%	80	1.4%	0.9%
Catholics	5,200	94.4%	5,300	91.6%	0.0%
Evangelicals	8	0.1%	15	0.3%	1.3%
Pentecostals/Charismatics	5	0.1%	130	2.2%	6.7%
Total population	**5,600**	**100.0%**	**5,800**	**100.0%**	**0.1%**

Source: Todd M. Johnson and Gina A. Zurlo (eds), *World Christian Database* (Leiden/Boston: Brill), accessed January 2022.

The 65 years following 1755 would prove to be a tumultuous time for the Acadians. Acadian expulsion by both the French and British governments became an unfortunate pattern as they were repeatedly expelled from the islands only later to be permitted to return. This expulsion–relocation cycle continued until 1816, when they began to reside on the islands permanently. The Acadian islanders have maintained their strong ties with the Atlantic Maritime provinces ever since, with Moncton, New Brunswick, being the centre of Acadian revival, the base for the Société Nationale de l'Acadie (National Acadian Society) and the location of the Saint Pierre and Miquelon relations office. Miquelon particularly values its Acadian heritage and an Acadian memorial was erected in November 2007 to honour its historic Acadian identity.

The history of economic instability on the islands contrasts sharply with their religious constancy. The majority of the population continue to identify as Catholic, though the small minorities of Protestants, Muslims and agnostics are slowly growing. Catholic numbers have remained stable, whereas the islands' Protestant population is expected to increase in the foreseeable future. The numbers of unaffiliated Christians are decreasing just as the numbers of non-religious are on the rise. The number of Muslims has slowly increased over the last 100 years and is projected to continue. There has been a significant jump in those who identify as agnostic, with numbers projected to be close to double by 2050. A 2019 religious census suggests that the current population of 6,400 could increase to approximately 7,400 by 2050, which in turn will likely increase the number of adherents in all the religious communities.

The islands are home to several Catholic places of worship. Strong Catholic presence has been noted as early as 1689, when the Bishop of Quebec, Jean-Baptiste de Saint-Vallier, visited Saint Pierre and Miquelon from Placentia, Newfoundland, blessed a chapel and installed a priest. Joseph-Pierre de Bonnécamps and François-Paul Ardilliers were the first Jesuit missionaries to visit the islands, in 1765 after the Treaty of Paris, with authority from the Bishop of La Rochelle. The Apostolic Prefecture of Iles Saint-Pierre et Miquelon was erected in 1763 and was established as an apostolic vicariate in 1970 before merging with the Diocese of La Rochelle and Saintes in the French department of Charente-Maritime in 2018. The two parishes in Saint Pierre and Miquelon today are maintained by two priests, six female religious and two male religious. The Saint Pierre cathedral was completed by 1690, but was destroyed by a fire in 1902, and then rebuilt between 1905 and 1907 with Basque architectural influences.

Bibliography

Christian, William A., Jr, *Divided Island: Faction and Unity on Saint Pierre* (Cambridge, MA: Harvard University Press, 1969).

Fleury, Christian, 'Jersey and Saint-Pierre-et-Miquelon', *Shima: The International Journal of Research into Island Cultures*, 3:2 (2009), 32–51.

Marshall, Bill, '"Even Way Up Yonder Among the Fish": Frontiers and Islands at Saint-Pierre et Miquelon', in *The French Atlantic: Travels in Culture and History* (Liverpool: Liverpool University Press, 2009).

McDorman, Ted L., 'The Canada–France Maritime Boundary Case: Drawing a Line Around St. Pierre and Miquelon', *American Journal of International Law*, 84:1 (1990), 157–89.

Thomas, Martin, 'Deferring to Vichy in the Western Hemisphere: The St Pierre and Miquelon Affair of 1941', *International History Review*, 19:4 (1997), 809–35.

Greenland

Errol Martens

Greenland is the largest island in the world, big enough to contain Sweden, Norway, Denmark, Finland, Germany, Italy and Romania. Some 80% of the island comprises a giant icecap, more than a mile thick in some places. The ice-free area along the coast is about the size of Norway, and this is where all the towns and villages are situated. There are 13 main towns with a population of 1,000 or more, as well as 59 villages with smaller populations. Nuuk is the capital city, with a population of 18,000. Greenland is the least densely populated country in the world, with a total population of 56,823 as of January 2021. There are no roads between towns because of the great distances, mountainous terrain and deep fjords. Helicopter, aeroplane, boat and dogsled are the means of transportation. Greenland is presently a parliamentary democracy within the Kingdom of Denmark. Greenlanders attained home rule in 1979, which was then widened to self-governance in 2008, giving more control, including over international affairs.

Erik the Red was the first European to set foot on Greenland's icy shores. In 986 he led an expedition to Greenland with Icelandic settlers. Of the 25 ships that embarked, only 14 arrived. Erik named the country 'Greenland' to entice settlers to join him, although the climate in those days was warmer. Today, Greenlanders prefer to call their country Kalaallit Nunaat, meaning 'Land of the People' or 'Land of the Greenlanders'.

Early Christian History

In 1000, Leif Eriksson, son of Erik the Red, visited Norway and returned to Greenland with the first Christian missionary, a Catholic priest. By the 1100s the Norse population had grown to about 5,000, with more than 300 farms, and Catholicism became established as the main religion. This was the first Christian population in geographical North America, and they constructed the first church building. The weather gradually became too cold for farming, which might be why the entire population had vanished by the late 1400s, although research on the subject is ongoing. The Catholic presence ended with the Norsemen and did not reappear until after 1953. Today, the small number of Catholics all live in the capital city of Nuuk. Most present-day Greenlanders are descendants of people belonging to the Thule culture, who migrated to Greenland from Arctic Canada in the west around the same time the Norsemen first arrived from the east. Since Greenland is a territory of Denmark, about 13% of the population are Danes.

In Nuuk, a statue of a man looks out to sea from the top of a small hill. His name is Hans Egede. Hans sailed with his family to Greenland in 1721 to find the Norsemen and enlighten them on Reformation theology. After a fruitless search Hans turned his attention to the Greenlanders whom he encountered in the area near modern-day Nuuk. Through many trials and tribulations Hans and his family persevered in their work among the Greenlanders. However, their cultures and religious worldviews were so far apart that it was difficult for them to understand each other. The greatest challenge for Hans and his wife was Greenlandic, a polysynthetic language. Hans, however, began to have hope as he observed his sons, Niels and Poul, speaking with their Greenlandic friends. Soon they were translating his messages.

Just as they were getting some traction in the work, tragedy struck: a smallpox epidemic. Hundreds of Greenlanders died, many of whom had recently identified as Christians. Hans's wife Gertrud also perished during the terrible plague. Hans left Greenland in 1736, but his son Poul continued his work and, with Greenlandic assistants, produced the first Greenlandic translation of the New Testament in 1766. This was an important accomplishment for the sake of the church at that time, but it took various translators 150 years to finish the entire Bible. In 1999 the Danish Bible Society published the whole Bible in a modern Greenlandic translation that today is available both in book form and online. Although most North and East Greenlanders understand the West Greenlandic dialect, they are still waiting for a Bible in their own mother tongues. Initial steps have been taken to work on further translations.

Christianity in Greenland, 1970 and 2020

Tradition	1970 Population	%	2020 Population	%	Average annual growth rate (%), 1970–2020
Christians	45,300	98.3%	54,400	95.9%	0.4%
Independents	100	0.2%	930	1.6%	4.6%
Protestants	35,000	75.9%	36,000	63.5%	0.1%
Catholics	50	0.1%	140	0.2%	2.1%
Evangelicals	1,200	2.7%	2,800	4.9%	1.6%
Pentecostals/Charismatics	500	1.1%	6,200	10.9%	5.2%
Total population	**46,100**	**100.0%**	**56,800**	**100.0%**	**0.4%**

Source: Todd M. Johnson and Gina A. Zurlo (eds), *World Christian Database* (Leiden/Boston: Brill), accessed January 2022.

Another significant development during the eighteenth century was the arrival of the first Moravian missionaries, Matthaus Stach, Christian Stach and Christian David, who began a ministry on the island that continued for 157 years. By the end of the nineteenth century, the mission included six main stations with nine schools and 28 outstations with 24 schools. Due to financial challenges, the work was handed over to the Danish Lutheran State Church and all the Moravian missionaries left on 11 September 1900.

The Church of Greenland

The Church of Greenland (Lutheran Church of Greenland, Ilagiit Kaladlit Luterkussut) became semi-independent from the Church of Denmark in 2009 and came under the local government of Greenland, although it is still considered a diocese of the Church of Denmark. The Church of Greenland today has its own bishop, Sofie Petersen, and the diocese comprises 19 parishes divided among three deaneries, 40 churches or chapels and 25 vicars or priests.

Over 90% of the Greenlandic population are members of the Church of Greenland (Ilagiit in Greenlandic). Some appear to be nominal members ('I'm a Christian on paper only'). Nevertheless, in recent years churches have often been full to capacity for services and various functions. In fact, consideration is being given to the need for a third church building in the city of Nuuk, where one-third of the national population reside. Ilagiit provides a place to sing and socialise, and more of its members are feeling the need to get married as opposed to just living together. Almost all newborns are baptised in the church, and most 14-year-olds are confirmed. Ilagiit has had a major impact on the music and culture of the land.

Concerns being faced by the church in much of Greenland include homelessness, unreached youth and a need for more leaders in the church. Another concern is the ongoing impact of childhood traumas among many of its members. Today, Ilagiit is recognising this, as well as children's rights and protections. Most people in Greenland would agree climate change is real; however, some view it as a good thing because it is facilitating a longer growing season, especially in the south. In the north, some view it as a disruption to hunting, while others see it providing a longer fishing season. Whatever the outcomes, Bishop Sofie Petersen argues on biblical grounds that the nation must take responsibility to address the challenges of climate change.

Despite the very high rate of adherence to Christianity, it was apparent by the 1980s that Greenland was facing significant social problems. Alcoholism and suicide rates had become the highest ever seen in the country. Many Greenlanders believe various aspects of Danish colonisation contributed to these problems. The hasty upgrading of Greenland's infrastructure resulted in much greater access to health-care, education and modern living. However, the downside was an assault on Greenlanders' self-worth and identity. It was a matter of foreign people creating these improvement projects with little input from the Greenlanders themselves because all of it was still so new to them. At the same time, alcohol was introduced, which became the preferred self-medicating drug for addressing emotional distress. The domino effect of alcoholism continued lowering self-worth even further.

In earlier times Greenlanders survived the harshness of Arctic living through their renowned skills and understanding of the land. Survival was the mindset, not suicide. Now, as modern life came to them ever more swiftly, there were many new options. These options were popular, as life in the old days was tough, but they flooded in too quickly and contributed to a major social crisis.

New Movements

In view of the social crisis in the country, the 'free churches' of Scandinavia sensed a great need for ministry. Their missionaries started entering the country in 1953, once Greenland had changed from being a closed colony of Denmark to an official territory. It was difficult pioneer work for these 'different' Christian missionaries, who were sometimes looked down on as 'false priests'. In their early years, no one wanted to sell or rent them houses, so they built their own. These structures came to be known as *missionshus* (mission houses). The buildings served as places to meet for fellowship as well as dwellings for the missionary families. Outreach was primarily literature distribution and children's work in those days, but the work was slow and many of these missionaries left Greenland discouraged. Nevertheless, fresh recruits continued coming from Norwegian, Swedish and Danish Pentecostal churches, the Danish Apostolic Church and the Danish Covenant Church. Eventually the churches planted through the mission house ministries of these denominations came under a united fellowship called Inuunerup Nutaap Oqaluffia (New Life Church), identifying mostly as a Pentecostal movement. Faroese Brethren were also among the early pioneers of this new movement. Various other mission organisations came in, bringing distinctive perspectives and ways of ministering. Some of these arrived, gave valuable contributions and left. Others, like New Tribes Mission and Youth With A Mission, continued contributing long term.

In 1998 the two-hour feature film on the life of Christ, *JESUS*, was launched in Greenland. It was the first feature movie in history to be translated, lip-synced, into the Greenlanders' heart language. The Greenlandic translation project brought together many volunteers from the various denominations and missions, including 20 Greenlandic voice actors. The film eventually reached all of Greenland, making an impact at the spiritual level. In 2002 a Danish evangelist, Hans Berntsen, came to hold special meetings in Nuuk over the Easter holidays. When people heard he would be praying for the sick, record numbers showed up. Again, the response was unparalleled and spread through other communities, bringing another layer of impact after the *JESUS* film.

Corresponding with this spiritual awakening came a biblical counselling ministry from Canada offering courses that addressed the subject 'How to Handle the Pain of the Heart'. Through an inner healing process based on the Christian message, many were now able to experience their new life in Christ without unbearable emotional memories pulling them back into hopelessness. Hundreds have benefited from these courses all over Greenland since 2002. Today, the biblical counselling ministry is continuing under the leadership of mature and gifted Greenlanders. Likewise, the free churches are led by native Greenlanders and Inuunerup Nutaap Oqaluffia has expanded to 15 fellowships in as many towns and villages, where their outreach has considerable social impact. Another growing movement is the Jehovah's Witnesses, who claimed by 2013 to have one Jehovah's Witness for every 418 of Greenland's population.

Conclusion

Greenland has come a long way since it obtained home rule in 1979 and, like the shifting ice, continues to change. Signs of a healthier society have appeared since the 1980s, with alcoholism down by 50% and crime down by 25%. Christianity continues to be a significant part of the social landscape, with both the Church of Greenland and the new movements providing valued spiritual support and inspiration.

Bibliography

Havsteen, Sven Rune, Karen Langgård, Sofie Petersen, Hans Anton Lynge, Kennet Pedersen and Aage Rydstrøm-Poulsen (eds), *Kristendom i Grønland* (Copenhagen: Eksistensen, 2018).

Lidegaard, Mads, *Grønlændernes Kristning: Eskimoerne Og Kirken* (Nuuk: Atuakkiorfik, 1993).

Page, Jesse, *Amid Greenland Snows: Or the Early History of Arctic Missions*, 2nd edition (New York: Fleming H. Revell, 1893).

Religious Tract and Book Society for Ireland, *Greenland Missions: With Biographical Sketches of Some of the Principal Converts* (Dublin: Religious Tract and Book Society for Ireland, 1831).

Sandgreen, Otto, *Nunatsinni Oqaluffiit (Grønlands Kirker)* (Copenhagen: O. Sandgreenip atuakkiorfi, 1992).

Bermuda

Kenneth R. Ross

Bermuda, which takes its name from its discovery in the early 1500s by the Spanish sailor Juan de Bermudéz, is an archipelago consisting of seven large islands and some 170 islets and rocks, situated in the western part of the North Atlantic Ocean, approximately 1,050 km east of Cape Hatteras on the coast of North Carolina in the USA. The islands are stretched across 40 km and are connected by bridges. Hamilton, the capital, is located on Main Island, which is 22.5 km long and around 1.6 km wide. The islands are fringed by coral reefs and their beaches are famed for their beautiful pink sand. Some 60% of the population is of African ancestry, with most of the remainder being whites of British or American heritage.

English is the official language, spoken with an accent similar to that found on the Atlantic seaboard of the USA. Portuguese is also spoken, reflecting the historical influence of Portugal. Though the population is only just above 60,000, Bermuda has one of the highest population densities in the world. It has become an important offshore financial centre, with investment and insurance businesses playing a significant part in driving the national economy. Its distinctive culture includes the wearing of short, knee-length trousers for men as accepted attire for business and formal occasions. The islands came under British colonial rule in 1609. Today, Bermuda is an internally self-governing British overseas territory where the Governor is responsible for external affairs and defence but acts on the advice of the elected government in a parliamentary democracy. Racial discrimination has been a long-running concern and is one of the drivers of an independence movement. However, in the 1995 referendum on the issue, almost three-quarters of voters were opposed to independence.

With British rule came Christianity. St Peter's Church in St George's Town, built in 1619, is the oldest surviving Anglican church in the western hemisphere and has been named a UNESCO world heritage site. During the seventeenth century, nine Anglican parishes were established, each with its own church. In terms of ecclesiastical organisation, these churches fell under the jurisdiction of the Church of England Diocese of London, an arrangement that continued until 1813. At that point, episcopal supervision switched to the other side of the Atlantic as Bermuda was transferred to the Diocese of Nova Scotia in Canada, with which it remained until 1825.

There followed almost a century under the Bishop of Newfoundland. During an interlude that lasted from 1917 to 1925, the Anglican churches of Bermuda lacked episcopal supervision. Bermuda then became an extra-provincial diocese under the direct supervision of the Archbishop of Canterbury, a status which it retains up to the present day.

For most of its history the Anglican Church in Bermuda has been established by law, the British colonial government having taken responsibility for the payment of clergy stipends in 1693. However, in 1974 legislation was passed in the British parliament to allow the synod of the church in Bermuda to become fully self-governing, at the same time changing its name from Church of England in Bermuda to Anglican Church of Bermuda. Following disestablishment, the Church has continued to flourish, with almost one-fifth of the population identifying as Anglican. Under the leadership of Bishop Nicholas Dill, who was consecrated in 2013, the diocese has emphasised discipleship and training, including provision of a theological course that allows candidates to qualify as licensed lay ministers. Since 2012, the annual Nisbett Lecture has brought such prominent Anglican theologians as Alister McGrath and Rose Hudson-Wilkin to Bermuda with the aim of stimulating debate on matters of faith and encouraging mission and evangelism.

Only slightly smaller in numerical terms is the Catholic Church, with its six parish churches, each served by a resident priest. Until 1953 the Catholic Church in Bermuda was part of the Diocese of Halifax in Canada. In that year it was placed under the responsibility of the Resurrectionist order and became a vicariate in 1956. A further change of status occurred in 1967, when the Diocese of Hamilton in Bermuda was created as a suffragan diocese of Kingston in Jamaica. Catholics make a significant contribution to education, particularly through their operation of Mount Saint Agnes Academy. Today, the Diocese of Hamilton in Bermuda is a suffragan of the Archdiocese of Nassau and a member of the Antilles

Christianity in Bermuda, 1970 and 2020

Tradition	1970 Population	%	2020 Population	%	Average annual growth rate (%), 1970–2020
Christians	50,400	95.8%	55,200	88.7%	0.2%
Anglicans	22,000	41.9%	11,000	17.7%	-1.4%
Independents	4,600	8.8%	9,000	14.5%	1.4%
Protestants	11,500	21.8%	23,000	36.9%	1.4%
Catholics	7,500	14.3%	9,300	14.9%	0.4%
Evangelicals	6,200	11.8%	14,500	23.3%	1.7%
Pentecostals/Charismatics	2,900	5.5%	14,800	23.8%	3.3%
Total population	**52,600**	**100.0%**	**62,300**	**100.0%**	**0.3%**

Source: Todd M. Johnson and Gina A. Zurlo (eds), *World Christian Database* (Leiden/Boston: Brill), accessed January 2022.

Episcopal Conference of Churches. Wieslaw Spiewak has been Bishop of the Diocese since 2015. Orthodox Christians are few in number, but since 1974 the Debre Ganet Emmanuel (Immanuel Cathedral of Paradise) Ethiopian Orthodox Tewahedo Church has been worshipping in what was once the garrison chapel for the British military.

A variety of Protestant churches play their part in the life of the islands, most originating from either Britain or North America. The Methodist presence in Bermuda goes back to a visit made by the famous evangelist George Whitefield in 1748. John Stephenson, a Methodist preacher who arrived in 1799, played a major role in enabling the church to establish itself. When he was jailed for not having the required permission to exercise ministry, he continued to preach through the bars of his cell to the crowd of mostly Black citizens who gathered outside. Presbyterians also have a long history, with the Church of Scotland congregation of Christ Church, Warwick, dating back to 1719 and proudly claiming to be the oldest Presbyterian church in the western hemisphere. There is also a congregation of the Presbyterian Church of Canada, St Andrew's, which dates back to 1843 and belongs to the Presbytery of West Toronto. Christian Brethren, the Salvation Army and the Seventh-day Adventists also have a significant presence. The Portuguese community is served by a Portuguese Evangelical church in Hamilton. Most mainline Protestant churches are served by expatriate pastors from Europe or America.

Cobb's Hill Methodist Church represents Black Christian identity – a significant component in Bermuda's religious make-up. It was built in 1827 by Black Bermudans, including enslaved people, so that they would have a place to worship. Since they were occupied with their work during the day, they laboured on the construction of the church by moonlight. Today, it continues to house an active congregation, including descendants of those who worked on its construction. The African Methodist Episcopal (AME) Church has played an important role in evangelism and pastoral work, particularly among the Black community. During the period of racial segregation, St Paul's AME Church provided a place of worship for Black Christians. Today, it declares its commitment to preach a liberating and reconciling gospel, with a commitment to minister to the social, political and economic needs of the community. In 1892 it was the AME Church that took the initiative to establish the first Black high school, the Bermuda Collegiate Institute. With its 11 churches it continues to offer a vibrant ministry today, the third-largest church community in the islands and part of the First District of the AME Church along with the north-eastern states of the USA.

Christianity is inscribed on the landscape of Bermuda by the many church buildings – one of the highest densities of churches of any country in the world. There is scarcely anywhere in the islands' 54 km² where a church is not in sight. Many of the churches, across the denominational spectrum, house very active congregations today, with Sunday services complemented by midweek meetings for Bible study or Christian education as well as a wide range of community outreach projects. For example, during the COVID-19 pandemic that began in 2020, churches were active in distributing food and other necessities to those who found themselves in need. Clergy are respected figures, with wide influence in the community. Some churches broadcast their services on the radio and have a lively presence on the internet. In terms of spirituality, churches offering more informal and Charismatic forms of worship have been growing at the expense of those with more formal liturgies. Pentecostal churches have seen a growth in membership. For example, the membership of the New Testament Church of God grew from 500 in 1970 to more than 6,500 in 2015.

Inter-church relations find expression through the Joint Committee of Churches, earlier known as the Bermuda Ministerial Association. When it was founded in 1957 its membership was confined to clergy of the Protestant churches, but it became more fully ecumenical in 1966 when the Catholic Church was admitted. Taken together, Christians in Bermuda comprise almost 90% of the population and enjoy cordial relations with the small communities that adhere to other faiths: Baha'is, Buddhists, Jews, Hindus and Muslims. There is also a small but growing number of citizens who indicate that they do not belong to any religious community. Nevertheless, Christian worship and witness appear set to continue to be one of the defining features of life in Bermuda.

Bibliography

Anglican Church of Bermuda, *The Cathedral of the Most Holy Trinity, Hamilton: A Short Guide* (Hamilton: Diocese of Bermuda, 1991).

Boultbee, Paul G. and David F. Raine, *Bermuda* (Oxford: ABC-Clio Press, 1998).

Dayfoot, Arthur Charles and Roscoe M. Pierson, *Bibliography of West Indian Church History: A List of Printed Materials Relating to the History of the Churches in the English-speaking Caribbean (and Bermuda) with Annotations and Notes on Locations* (London: Hansib Publications, 2004).

Fortenberry, Brent Russell, 'Church, State, and the Space in Between: An Archaeological and Architectural Study of St. George's Bermuda' (PhD thesis, Boston University, 2013).

Hallett, A. C. Hollis, C. F. E. Hollis Hallett and Julia C. R. Dorr, *19th Century Church Registers of Bermuda* (Bermuda: Juniperhill Press, 2005).

Major Christian Traditions

Anglicans

Alan L. Hayes

The Anglican churches of the world are named for their historical connection to the Church of England, which in medieval Latin was called *ecclesia anglicana*. Forty-one national or regional church bodies are recognised by the Archbishop of Canterbury as autonomous provinces of the worldwide Anglican Communion, along with five non-autonomous, 'extra-provincial' church bodies which are formally accountable to Canterbury. In North America, three Anglican denominations are recognised members of the Anglican Communion. Two are provinces: The Episcopal Church (TEC), primarily a US denomination although it operates in 16 other countries or territories as well; and the Anglican Church of Canada (ACC). The third is extra-provincial: the Anglican Church of Bermuda (ACB), a diocese with only nine parishes in an archipelago that is a British Overseas Territory.

In addition, perhaps three dozen other families or networks of Anglican churches operate in North America, most of them quite recent, small and impermanent, and some of them with overlapping memberships. These groups understand themselves as continuing in the historic Anglican tradition but are regarded as schismatic by TEC, ACC and ACB. At least two of them appear to be reasonably sizeable and institutionally stable: the Reformed Episcopal Church (REC), which seceded from TEC in 1873, and the Anglican Church in North America (ACNA), founded in 2009 by 12 US and Canadian Anglican groupings that had already splintered off. Because many of its pre-existing groupings have maintained their identities and constitutions, ACNA functions as a cross between a denomination and an umbrella organisation. A significant sixth group of North American Anglicans, Indigenous members of the ACC, were promised self-determination in 1995, although that goal has been elusive.

Common Anglican characteristics include a claim of historical evolution from the primitive church; acceptance of the Western canon of the Bible; worship in accordance with a liturgical order; use of the Apostles' and Nicene creeds; a recognition of at least two sacraments (baptism and Holy Communion or Eucharist); a sense of mission within the social order; a threefold pastoral and liturgical ministry of bishop, priest (or presbyter) and deacon; a considerable provision for lay authority; territorial organising units called dioceses; and constitutional systems of governance.

Origins

Ministrations of the Church of England in North America began in the 1570s, in connection with projects of English colonisation promoted by Queen Elizabeth I. Before the American Revolution, the Church of England was established by law and publicly supported, at one time or another, in all or part of New York, Maryland, Virginia, North Carolina, South Carolina, Georgia and Nova Scotia. However, the colonies had no Anglican bishops. As a result, the laity exercised considerable influence in colonial Anglicanism, most thoroughly in Virginia, the most populous colony. Since then, a pattern of strong lay authority has marked North American Anglicanism in general.

After the Revolution, the Church of England in the new United States understandably repudiated all accountability to the English church and crown. It became independent and autonomous under the name the Protestant Episcopal Church in the United States of America (PECUSA). (TEC, its more common alternative name today, dates from 1967.) PECUSA created a constitution on a republican model with a president (the presiding bishop) and a legislative body (the General Convention) comprising a senior chamber (the House of Bishops) and a lower chamber (the House of Deputies) elected by the people. Similarly, each diocese within PECUSA had a bishop and a convention comprising the clergy and representatives of the laity. PECUSA maintained continuity with historic Anglicanism in several ways, most notably by its adoption of the Anglican liturgy (in an Americanised and somewhat liberalised form) and by ensuring that each of its first bishops was consecrated by three English or Scottish bishops. In the states where it had once been privileged, it was disestablished and lost much of its property, and it never recovered its strength of numbers relative to other denominations.

In the area that became eastern Canada – the northern colonies of what was then called British North America (BNA) – Anglicanism began to expand with the arrival of loyalist refugees from the American Revolution. The king began creating dioceses and appointing bishops for them, and English mission societies sent personnel and financial support. By the 1850s Canadian Anglicans were adapting several of the innovations of PECUSA that were as yet unknown in the mother Church of England,

Anglicans in North America, 1970

Region	Total population	Christian population	Anglican population	% of region Anglican	% of Christians Anglican
North America	230,992,000	211,489,000	4,395,000	1.9%	2.1%
Global total	3,700,437,000	1,225,395,000	47,394,000	1.3%	3.9%

Source: Todd M. Johnson and Gina A. Zurlo (eds), *World Christian Database* (Leiden/Boston: Brill), accessed January 2022.

notably diocesan legislative assemblies of clergy and lay representatives (Canadians called them synods instead of conventions) and the election of bishops. After several of the BNA colonies joined to create the dominion of Canada in 1867, and after Canada took over Indigenous lands all the way to the Pacific Ocean, the Church of England in Canada (CEC) was created as a national denomination in 1893. The Church of England in Canada was renamed the ACC in 1955.

The Church of England in Bermuda operated as a part of the dioceses of Nova Scotia or Newfoundland until 1879, when it created its own diocesan synod. Nevertheless, it long continued to share its bishop with Newfoundland, receiving its inaugural bishop only in 1925. It functioned as a state church until 1975, when Bermuda gave it self-government as well as its new name, the ACB.

REC was created by a secession in 1873 of Episcopal and Canadian Anglican parishes unhappy with what they saw as the Rome-ward drift of PECUSA and CEC from the Protestant principles of the Reformation. It was significantly bolstered by Black congregations from South Carolina that the PECUSA diocese in that state refused to accept for racial reasons; the REC welcomed them as equals.

ACNA was created in 2009 by Anglican traditionalists in the USA and Canada exasperated by what they saw as the increasing liberalism of TEC and ACC, evidenced by their ordination of women to the ranks of the clergy, their creation of non-traditional liturgies, their doctrinal modernism, their ordination of people in same-sex relationships, their blessing of same-sex marriages and their 'leftist' political activism. Some ACNA dioceses, however, do ordain women, and ACNA members are not all of one mind on any of these issues; some people choose churches for reasons other than theological compatibility. Many ACNA congregations represent schisms from Episcopal parish churches, resulting in dozens of lawsuits, mainly over property. Not all have been settled, but so far most (though not all) have been decided in favour of TEC.

Worship

Most Sunday services are celebrations of the Holy Eucharist (also called the Lord's Supper or Holy Communion). Some congregations, however,

Anglicans in North America, 2020

Region	Total population	Christian population	Anglican population	% of region Anglican	% of Christians Anglican
North America	368,870,000	269,524,000	2,701,000	0.7%	1.0%
Global total	7,794,799,000	2,506,426,000	99,662,000	1.3%	4.0%

Source: Todd M. Johnson and Gina A. Zurlo (eds), *World Christian Database* (Leiden/Boston: Brill), accessed January 2022.

choose on occasion to follow the order of Morning Prayer, which was far more common before the 1970s. Anglican churches use authorised liturgical texts to direct their principal worship services. In North American Anglicanism, two families of liturgical texts are in common use, one stemming from the English Reformation of the sixteenth century, the other from the Liturgical Movement of the twentieth century.

Liturgies in the Reformation tradition are typically written in dignified Tudor English that conveys a gravity that many find appealing. Service texts are almost entirely fixed. Although they make considerable use of medieval precedents, they take a Protestant turn in many ways, such as long readings from the Bible in Morning and Evening Prayer, a density of biblical phraseology and allusions, the omission of sacramental penance and language of the sacrifice of the Mass, an emphasis on divine sovereignty and human dependence, and 'exhortations' at the beginning of services explaining their purpose and Scriptural warrant (for example, 'Scripture moveth us in sundry places', 'forasmuch as Christ saith', 'an honourable estate instituted of God'). Reformation liturgies are found in the *Book of Common Prayer* (BCP), England, of 1662 in ACB, BCP (1959) in ACC, Rite I of BCP (1979) in TEC, BCP (2005) in REC and, without 'thou' and 'thee' language, BCP (2019) in ACNA.

By contrast, the Liturgical Movement, a reaction against the spirituality of the late Middle Ages (in which it included the Reformation), downplays individualistic piety and the burden of personal guilt, emphasising human initiative and cooperation with divine grace. Anglican liturgies in this family use modern, demotic language and provide a number of optional elements for every service. Most Scripture readings are short because, as the Canadian revisers explain, that is 'all most active people are likely to be able to deal with'. Liturgical Movement worship is found in Rite II of the BCP (1979) in TEC, the *Book of Alternative Services* (1985) in ACC and the Church of England book *Common Worship* (2000) in ACB. By far most Anglican churches today use these modern rites for their main services. With permission from the bishop, some congregations make other liturgical arrangements, which can variously reflect Celtic spirituality, theological liberalism, creative 'fresh expressions', youth culture or sensitivity to religious seekers.

Changes in Anglicans in North America, 1970–2020, growth rate, % per year

Region	Total population	Christian population	Anglican population
North America	0.94%	0.49%	-0.97%
Global total	1.50%	1.44%	1.50%

Source: Todd M. Johnson and Gina A. Zurlo (eds), *World Christian Database* (Leiden/Boston: Brill), accessed January 2022.

The styles of liturgical celebration are quite diverse, even in the same liturgical family. In a plain and minimalist service, the leader and people focus on the spoken word, with a minimum of ceremonial action in a simple space. A very elaborate service, by contrast, will involve choirs, lay assistants and readers, a considerable ritual including processions, the careful choreography of liturgical leaders, turnings and bowings and genuflections, the chanting of particularly sacred parts of the liturgy, and the burning of incense, all in a highly decorated space. Most services fall between these poles. In past centuries many Anglicans were scandalised by high ceremonialism, but now choices of liturgical style are widely seen as a 'thing indifferent', a matter of taste and preference. Even REC, which began in revolt against elaborate ceremony, has accommodated it.

Organisation

The basic unit of governance in the Anglican denominations is the diocese, which is defined territorially. ACNA, however, has some 'affinity-based' dioceses, representing founding constituent groups, that overlap with territorial dioceses. The bishop is the chief executive officer of a diocese, as well as its chief liturgical officer and the chief pastor. Bishops alone can ordain clergy and administer the rite of confirmation. They license presbyters and deacons to function in their diocese. They have at least some involvement, and in some jurisdictions or in some cases considerable discretion, in the appointment of parish clergy. Bishops are elected from the presbyterate, without a stipulated term.

Priests (or presbyters) usually serve as the pastoral and liturgical leaders of a parish, although they can also serve in teaching, missionary, administrative, para-church or other ministries. They can preside at the Eucharist and pronounce blessings. The priest regularly appointed to lead a parish is most generally called the incumbent but sometimes has the title 'rector' or 'vicar'. Some parishes have more than one congregation. In a majority of congregations, average Sunday attendance is less than 150, often much less. Deacons usually assist pastorally in a congregation or serve a social or institutional ministry. Liturgically, they can preach, baptise and administer marriage vows, but they cannot preside at the Eucharist. All priests have been ordained deacons first. Typically, before they are ordained, candidates for the diaconate and priesthood undertake a process of vocational discernment with clergy and lay examiners and receive formal training in a theological school or in an alternative process.

Each diocese has a council, synod or convention (different terms are used) that has some legislative and financial authority. This body includes the bishop and any assistant bishops, the clergy and representatives of the laity, who, depending on the jurisdiction and the matter under discussion, might meet together or separately. Anglicanism thus has two principles of authority, episcopal and conciliar, that can conflict. In some dioceses, particularly in the ACC, the authority of the diocesan synod is significantly weakened by the rule that the bishop must approve its decisions – in other words, has the power of veto.

The chief lay officers of a parish are called the churchwardens. The governing authority of the parish is the vestry, which includes clergy and laity (or sometimes only a select subgroup of the laity). It has authority over 'temporalia' such as budgets and elections of some lay officers, but not over 'spiritualia' such as doctrine and worship.

TEC and ACC have internal provinces: each of these is a geographical grouping of dioceses, with a provincial synod and a chief executive officer. In ACC the president of the provincial synod is always a bishop who assumes the rank of a metropolitan and is styled archbishop. The other four Anglican entities discussed here do not have archbishops. ACC also has an Indigenous archbishop without jurisdiction over any territory who can have a pastoral relationship with Indigenous clergy and parishes, but only with the permission of the territorial bishop.

Anglican provinces and dioceses are expected to operate with reasonable transparency and procedural regularity according to their constitutions and canons (church regulations) approved by their synods. TEC, ACC, ACNA and REC, which have several dioceses, have a denominational headquarters headed by a bishop whom TEC and REC call the presiding bishop, and whom ACC and ACNA call the primate. The scope of denominational governance is constitutionally limited to matters delegated by the dioceses (or, in a particular case in ACC, one of the internal provinces). Even in the areas over which the denominational governance has jurisdiction, its effective authority is limited by the practical difficulties of bringing diocesan bishops to account if they go their own way.

As with most organisations, churches are regularly financed mainly from two sources: income from endowments and property, and operating revenues. The main source of the latter is the freewill offerings of church members. Dioceses fund their work by levying an assessment on parish revenues, and the denominational headquarters levies an assessment on the dioceses. Declining memberships exacerbate financial stresses.

Those training to be Anglican priests are normally expected to earn a university undergraduate degree and then a three-year theological degree. TEC recognises 10 denominational theological schools, ACC identifies 12 and REC has one. ACNA has established none of its own but recommends seven. ACB has often made use of ACC schools but now has an arrangement with St Mellitus College in London, England. Many students, however, attend divinity schools that are not formally recognised as

Anglican, such as Duke, Yale or Harvard, or an English college, and bishops are free to recognise their credentials. Theological degree programmes are an expensive investment for students, as well as for churches, and they are most easily justified when graduates can expect full-time professional employment. Increasingly, however, Anglican churches can afford only part-time ministries, and many bishops are establishing less expensive, part-time, local alternative training processes, or otherwise lessening educational requirements.

The relations between North American Anglicanism and the global Anglican Communion are complicated. The Anglican Communion, which recognises churches in 165 countries, has no juridical authority over any of them, but it connects and supports them through certain common agencies (such as an office in London and a representative consultative council) and a meeting of bishops every 10 years or so, called 'the Lambeth Conference'. But some conservative provinces of the Anglican Communion, mainly in the global South, have an impaired relation with TEC and ACC, which are part of the Anglican Communion; instead, they fully recognise ACNA, which is not. They commonly give the rationale that TEC and ACC departed from the Scriptures and Christian doctrine when they allowed the ordination of gay clergy and bishops and the liturgical blessing of same-sex marriages. Indeed, in the early 2000s some of these conservative provinces began planting missions and churches within TEC territory, a breach of Anglican protocol, on the premise that TEC was no longer Christian. Some of these mission networks joined in creating ACNA. But their dual citizenship in both ACNA and their overseas churches has created its own set of tensions; thus, two Nigerian 'affinity-based' dioceses felt moved to exit ACNA in 2021.

Some observers suggest that theological issues are not the underlying cause of conflict, especially since ACNA is internally divided on some of them. These observers regard the issues as proxies for deeper conflicts in the Anglican Communion. For instance, TEC and ACC have developed a reputation in some parts of the Anglican Communion for colonial attitudes, financial coercion, a compromise with secularity, a politically liberal agenda and a spirit of exceptionalism. That said, however, ACNA has also been criticised in some of these areas.

Doctrine and Theology

There are two views as to whether Anglicanism is a confessional tradition: that is, one which has committed itself to a formal and public declaration of the distinctive way in which it understands the Christian faith. Those who argue that it is not confessional say that historically it has not, since its separation from Rome, embraced any doctrinal norms beyond the indispensable elements of the apostolic faith. Those who argue that it is confessional say that certain Anglican formularies, conciliar declarations, liturgical texts and additional statements do authoritatively teach a distinctive 'Anglican way'. Asserting a distinct 'Anglican way' of doctrine can be appealing in North America, where religious affiliation is a matter of consumer choice and denominations function as market brands.

Those who say that Anglicanism is confessional sometimes say that the BCP in effect lays down a law of belief, and they usually claim confessional authority for the Thirty-Nine Articles of Religion (1571). These Articles, which focus on issues that were contested in the sixteenth century, are moderately Protestant in orientation and take aim at such Catholic doctrines as papal jurisdiction, purgatory and transubstantiation. But they frequently are marked with what Anglicans have sometimes called 'holy ambiguities', and some Anglicans sympathetic to Catholic teaching have interpreted them as supporting their own position. In addition to the creeds and the Articles, ACNA and REC assert that a heterosexual understanding of marriage is essential Christian doctrine.

Those who say that Anglicanism is not confessional say that the Thirty-Nine Articles were intended only for a specific situation and note that they were never intended to control the beliefs of the laity. In this view, liturgical texts and arrangements are 'things indifferent' that are appointed for the sake of good order but do not bind the conscience. TEC, in which non-confessional views predominate, publishes in its BCP a statement known as the Chicago–Lambeth Quadrilateral, which was developed in the 1880s and proposes that in ecumenical discussions with other churches Anglicans will negotiate anything except four essentials: the Scriptures of the Old and New Testament as the revealed word of God, the Nicene Creed as the sufficient statement of the Christian faith, the sacraments of baptism and the Eucharist, and the historic episcopate. The implication of this view is that the vocation of Anglicanism is to disappear in the process of ecumenical reconciliation.

North American Anglican denominations disagree as to whether doctrinal standards for membership should be required. In some measure their different policies reflect a familiar sociological distinction between an inclusive, universalising 'church type' of religious organisation and an exclusive, selective, 'sect type'. TEC, ACC and ACB carry some of the ecclesiastical DNA of the 'church type', since in places where the Church of England was established, it had responsibility for everyone who lived within the parish boundaries. Thus, non-believers as well as believers could be church members and, indeed, in the theory of establishment, they had the greater need of the church's influence. TEC, ACC and ACB dioceses accordingly generally take the view that all baptised people are members of Christ's Church, and those who would like to be formally connected with an Anglican parish need only enrol themselves. These dioceses do, however, have a few basic rules of eligibility for vestry membership, such as taking communion in the parish church a few times every year.

By contrast, REC accepts as members only those who have been confirmed as adults by a bishop; this rite includes a personal affirmation of the Nicene Creed. ACNA congregations, which are allowed to decide their own policies for membership, typically require candidates to receive instruction, complete a discipling process and sign a covenant. Additional doctrinal, financial and lifestyle requirements may sometimes be imposed on laypeople before they can assume leadership positions.

To the extent that foundational doctrine can be distinguished from secondary theological positions and perspectives, the five major North American Anglican denominations accommodate a variety of the latter. Although all Anglicans in 1800 would have readily identified as Protestant, Anglicans today have many more choices. In fact, theological variety, at one time a scandal, is now widely seen as a mark of the virtue of comprehensiveness, although critics complain that comprehensiveness has become an excuse for a muddied denominational self-understanding.

The following are the major theological categories within North American Anglicanism. Perhaps few Anglicans fit neatly into any single one of these categories, and not everyone would agree on the characterisations given below.

- *Evangelical* has been used by Anglicans to mean 'Protestant', although in recent years its sense has merged somewhat with modern non-Anglican neo-Evangelicalism in the USA. Anglican Evangelicals understand the visible church as the fallible and mixed company of faithful and unfaithful people, rather than as the indefectible instrument of God's will, and they distinguish it from the invisible church known only to God. They do not depend on the ministrations of the visible church for their sense of their personal relationship with God. Their theological authority is Scripture, and they find greater assurance and spiritual growth in the word of God, open to all, than in the sacraments, controlled by the clergy. They mistrust church traditions not founded on Scripture. They resent clericalism, and they assign considerable leadership authority to the laity. They deny apostolic succession (the idea that the legitimacy of a church is verified by its being able to trace a line of succession from the bishops of primitive Christianity to bishops today).
    * Liberal Evangelicals (sometimes called 'open Evangelicals') interpret the Christian faith through modern knowledge and often in the context of the aspirations of modern culture.

- * Conservative Evangelicals understand the Scriptures to be inerrant, and they are wary of accommodating doctrine to modern knowledge and modern culture.
- *Anglican catholics* generally disagree with Evangelicals on the distinctives described above. That is, they do not find it useful to talk about an invisible church, and they find it most prudent to read the Scriptures through church tradition and to subordinate individual theological judgement to the voice of the church. They believe that the sacramental life of the church is required for healthy spiritual growth and that God gives divine grace through the very operation of the sacraments. They affirm apostolic succession as well as the authority of duly ordained clergy.
  - * Liberal catholics believe that the church has the authority to redefine doctrinal and theological standards in the light of modern knowledge and in the contexts of different modern cultures and that the church's sacramental life is surer and more life-giving than most theological propositions.
  - * Conservative catholics, sometimes called Anglo-Catholics, believe that the church must be directed by the deposit of faith and is required to guard and witness it, and that the substance of the deposit of faith never changes, although, in faithfulness to the tradition, it may be carefully reformulated.
- *Charismatic Anglicans* believe that, within the structure of the church, the Holy Spirit sometimes acts unexpectedly to release special spiritual gifts received in water baptism. These gifts can include speaking in unknown tongues. The experience of the power of the Holy Spirit renews our relationship with Christ and leads us into a recommitment to Christian growth, prayer and service.
- *Progressives* (or liberals) believe that Scripture cannot possibly be entirely divinely inspired in any useful sense, given its inconsistencies, absurdities and repellent immoralities. It is, instead, an anthology of fallible compositions by authors and editors expressing their experience of God. Engaging with it critically, as opposed to taking it literally, helps Christians in their spiritual growth. The moral heart of Scripture is the infinite value of every individual human being, and the church's role is therefore to proclaim and practise justice and mercy, and to apply modern knowledge to the goal of contributing to our neighbours' welfare.

With the departure of many conservatives from TEC and ACC into ACNA, traditionalists who remain sometimes feel marginalised. In ACB, conservatives and liberals coexist comfortably.

Church architecture reflects the theological variety. Gothic revival supports catholic sensibilities around tradition, dramatic sacramental action and mystery. Non-Gothic traditional styles, such as the Eastern centre-plan and Romanesque, as well as the 'auditory' church plan designed for the hearing of the word, support evangelical preferences. Anglican and Episcopal churches built after the 1950s often express modern perspectives.

Church Mission and Culture
As with other Christian groupings, North American Anglicanism embraces a mission to care for the poor, sick, marginalised, victimised and unfortunate, both at home and abroad; to sponsor schools; to evangelise the unchurched; and to advocate for social justice. Individual Anglicans prioritise different elements of this mission. With ageing members, declining numbers and financial stresses, some Anglican congregations appear to be so intent on survival that they feel less able to support a broad mission.

North American Anglicanism has earned the reputation of being highly acculturated to the settler nation-state. In Bermuda the ACB describes itself on its website as 'a part of the Bermudian way of life'. In fact, until the 1970s, ACB parish government exercised civil as well as ecclesiastical functions. In ACC, many members value its historic connection with the British crown, which may be expressed in prayers for the royal family; the display of Union Jacks; toasts to the Queen (and now the King) at synods; dedication of churches to St George, St Alban and other saints connected with Britain; and expressions of Anglophilia. TEC built, owns and manages the Washington National Cathedral, which it calls 'a spiritual home for the nation'. TEC takes some pride in the fact that, although its membership numbers have seldom risen above 2% of the general population, 11 of 46 US Presidents have been Episcopalian, a greater number than any other denomination. An indicator of TEC's identification with worldly achievement is that, according to a 2014 study by the Pew Research Center, Anglicans and Episcopalians in the USA, on average, benefit from a higher income and a higher level of education than members of any other Christian denomination. Throughout North American Anglicanism, churches celebrate civic occasions and memorials, sing patriotic anthems, mount plaques honouring former members who have fought against the country's enemies, and sometimes process and lay up battalion colours.

While many Anglicans are attracted to this ethos, others distance themselves from it. TEC and ACC have increasingly embraced a mission of social justice that has led some members to confront worldly powers and principalities, to identify with the lowly and to seek to transform the status quo. ACNA represents in part a reaction against a surrounding culture of secularism, consumerism, individualism, casual sex outside marriage, abortions of pregnancy, and degrading and brutalising forms of entertainment. Among these constituencies, whether liberal or conservative, liturgy and mission are often seen as countercultural acts.

Race and Colonialism

Since the civil rights movements of the 1960s, and particularly since the 1990s, North American Anglicans have engaged – or sometimes evaded – theologically charged and politically divisive questions of racism and colonialism. In TEC, where statistics exist, thanks to the Pew Research Center, about 90% of members are non-Hispanic white, compared with 60% of the general population. The proportion of white members is likely somewhat lower for ACC and higher for ACNA. ACB churches, however, mirror the racial demographics of the islands, about 35% white and 65% people of colour.

The North American Anglican churches are intentionally reckoning with their legacy of racism. Southern TEC and ACB churches were explicitly racially segregated until the 1950s, and northern TEC and ACC churches implicitly so. (Canada restricted Black immigration until 1962.) And racist attitudes, policies and practices persist. TEC released a report in 2021 identifying nine dominant patterns of racism in its church culture. ACC has not systematically audited church racism since a report of 1993, named for its principal author, Romney Moseley, but that report found that Anglicans of Anglo-Saxon and Celtic background – the overwhelming majority – thought of themselves as being welcoming of diversity but tended to marginalise members of 'ethnic groups', a term that they used to designate cultural groups other than their own. 'Ethnic-minority congregations', the report found, 'have survived against great odds'.

Today TEC and ACC generally require anti-racism training for clergy, lay leaders and members of denominational associations and committees. ACB has undertaken a programme of racial reconciliation centred on a sympathetic listening to one another's stories; segregation has not been practised for decades, but not all wounds are healed and not all attitudes have changed. In ACNA the College of Bishops has established a high-level group on racial reconciliation. Some southern TEC leaders have apologised for how their institutions in the past championed Jim Crow laws and 'the lost cause of the Confederacy', a narrative of the Civil War as the tragic suppression of a chivalrous Southern white aristocracy which had tried to protect and elevate an inferior Black race. In 2020 the University of the South in Sewanee, Tennessee, which is owned by 28 southern TEC dioceses, and which was founded around the time of the Civil War to promote white racial superiority, issued a statement 'categorically [rejecting] its past veneration of the Confederacy and of the "Lost Cause"'.

North American Anglicans disagree on the character of modern racism: is it embedded in social structures and institutions in ways that require systemic change, or is it what the ACNA primate has called 'a sin problem' that is best addressed by individual repentance? Indeed, some white members view racism as an issue from the past from which the churches should simply move on, and they criticise anti-racism as part of a liberal, if not Marxist, agenda.

TEC and especially ACC are also confronting their colonial attitudes towards Indigenous peoples. Both ACC and TEC participated historically in the removal of Indigenous peoples from their territories, and in attempts to erase their culture, most notably in Indian residential schools that separated Indigenous children from their families, suppressed their languages and aimed to socialise them into the white middle class. (Bermuda had no Indigenous population when Europeans arrived there.) In 1993 the ACC primate offered a formal apology for its colonial practices, and the TEC presiding bishop did so in 1997. But Indigenous Anglicans continue to experience domination, exploitation and misunderstanding from the settler colonial establishment. As a step towards reconciliation and decolonisation, ACC adopted a resolution in 1995 to create within its own structures a self-determining Indigenous church. Its progress towards that goal has been uneven.

The Future
Many are questioning whether North American Anglicanism will survive. Demographically, its constituencies are ageing. An internal TEC statistical report in 2020 led some observers to predict the demise of the denomination by 2050, and ACC, in a report of the same year, predicted its disappearance by 2040. Responses to these statistics have variously included constructive self-criticism, discouraged acquiescence, denial and hopeful calls to renewal. Although many in ACNA believe that the decline of TEC and ACC is a consequence of their departure from traditional Christianity, ACNA itself appears to be shrinking, although it is impossible to identify a clear baseline since ACNA sometimes adds, sometimes loses constituent groups under its umbrella. Some North American Anglicans hope to benefit from the influence of Anglicanism in the global South and in 'Indian country', which in many cases gives evidence of growth, creativity and energy. Some theologians offer the thought that God is not committed to any particular denomination or style of faith, and that God's people have sometimes learned to sing new songs.

Bibliography

Anglican Church of Canada Indigenous Ministries, *Our Story of Self Determination* (Toronto: Anglican Church of Canada, 2019).

Brittain, Christopher Craig, *A Plague on Both Their Houses: Conservative vs. Liberal Christians and the Divorce of the Episcopal Church USA* (London: T&T Clark, 2015).

Hassett, Miranda K., *Anglican Communion in Crisis: How Episcopal Dissidents and Their African Allies Are Reshaping Anglicanism* (Princeton, NJ: Princeton University Press, 2007).

Hayes, Alan L., *Anglicans in Canada: Controversies and Identity in Historical Perspective* (Urbana, IL: University of Illinois Press, 2004).

Prichard, Robert W., *A History of the Episcopal Church*, 3rd edition (Harrisburg, PA: Morehouse Publishing, 2014).

Independents

Jeremy Paul Hegi

Independent Christian traditions defy simple categorisation. The term 'Independent', however, does not denote a catchall category of marginal Christian traditions who do not neatly 'fit' into the historic families of the Christian faith. Instead, these groups self-identify as 'Independent' often based on historical, social and theological circumstances. Many Independent groups, such as Churches of Christ (non-instrumental), represent denominations that self-consciously separated from the historic families of the Christian faith at some point in their history. Other Independent groups, such as the Church of Jesus Christ of Latter-day Saints (LDS), trace their origins to religious movements outside and separate from historic Christian traditions. At the same time, others are Independent because their theology and practice fall outside of traditional Christian orthodoxy. For example, Jehovah's Witnesses reject Nicaean and Chalcedonian Trinitarian formulations, favouring an Arian interpretation of Jesus Christ. Finally, Christian groups can be Independents for various reasons that fall outside of those listed above. For example, Independent traditions such as the National Baptist Convention and the Church of God in Christ emerged when an ethnic minority had to create a new denomination in the face of racial prejudice. Yet despite the diverse nature of Independent Christian traditions, these groups have a commonality in their tendency to exhibit a high degree of creativity and energy in their respective interpretations of the Christian faith. As a result, Independents' respective sense of mission and identity have left a lasting imprint on both North American Christianity and the character of world Christianity.

The third edition of the *World Christian Encyclopedia* designates roughly 280 Independent Christian denominations in North America, with 248 in the USA. Of the 32 remaining groups, the majority began as US Independent denominations before being established in Bermuda, Canada and Greenland. Why does the USA have so many Independent Christian groups, especially compared with other North American nations? What is distinctive about the cultural and religious landscape of the USA that allows Independent denominations to proliferate and thrive? This essay briefly explores the political and cultural developments in the late eighteenth- and early nineteenth-century USA that allowed Independent

Christian denominations to succeed. After I establish this context, I discuss representative examples of contemporary North American Independents, many of which have roots in the USA. While African American/Black, Native American/First Nations and Pentecostal/Charismatic Christianities contain numerous Independent denominations, this volume attends to these groups in other essays. To avoid repetition, I omit them here.

North American Contexts

Three factors helped set the stage for the proliferation of Independent Christian groups in the USA: (1) the emergence of a Christian pluralism during the colonial period, (2) religious disestablishment following the American Revolutionary War and (3) the democratisation of American Christianity, epitomised by an emphasis on popular religion and voluntarism in the early nineteenth century. Europeans' patchwork efforts to establish colonies on the North American continent helped create the Christian pluralism that had emerged by the early eighteenth century. The first Christians to settle in what would become North America were Spanish and French Catholics, who began colonising North America in the mid- to late sixteenth century and early seventeenth century, respectively. Following French colonisation, British Protestants had established themselves on the east coast of the present-day USA by the mid-seventeenth century. By the early eighteenth century, a mosaic of Christian expressions existed in the American colonies. As the century progressed, a shared sense of national identity had emerged among the colonies by the beginning of the American Revolutionary War in 1775. At this time, a tolerant attitude towards Christian diversity that differed from previously inherited understandings of the relationship between the church, state and society in Europe began to characterise the colonies. In the British colonies and later the USA, this diversity of Christian expression became a normative feature of the religious landscape, setting the stage for the emergence and proliferation of North American Independent groups.

With the ratification of the US Constitution in 1788 and the Bill of Rights in 1791, federal law, through the First Amendment, would fully establish Christian pluralism as a distinctive feature of US religion. According to the First Amendment to the US Constitution, 'Congress shall make no law

Independents in North America, 1970

Region	Total population	Christian population	Independent population	% of region Independent	% of Christians Independent
North America	230,992,000	211,489,000	38,051,000	16.5%	18.0%
Global total	3,700,437,000	1,225,395,000	89,480,000	2.4%	7.3%

Source: Todd M. Johnson and Gina A. Zurlo (eds), *World Christian Database* (Leiden/Boston: Brill), accessed January 2022.

respecting an establishment of religion, or prohibiting the free exercise thereof'. This language implemented what historians often refer to as 'religious disestablishment'. Disestablishment is a condition under which state, local or even the federal government cannot officially support or promote one religious tradition over another. Disestablishment created a free religious marketplace that featured relentless competition for adherents between religious groups. As a result, old mainline Christian traditions and new Christian groups competed on a level playing field. The elimination of special taxes (such as that Baptist groups in New England had to pay to support the Congregationalist establishment) and reduced start-up costs aided the entry of new, and often Independent, groups into the religious marketplace.

By the beginning of the nineteenth century, various new energetic and creative Christian traditions had emerged on the US landscape. Groups such as the Baptists and Methodists employed innovations that eschewed long-held traditions and clerical elitism. They experimented with music, communication, organisation, religious education, revivalism and preaching. New Christian traditions thrived in a competitive marketplace that rewarded energy and innovation. Between the Christian pluralism established during the colonial period and the free religious marketplace that emerged after the Revolutionary War, a new US religious context appeared that encouraged and rewarded religious entrepreneurialism. The new free marketplace of religion, however, required individuals who felt empowered to participate in the competitive and innovative religious landscape.

An environment infused with democratic ideals predicated on an individual's agency in religious matters would complete the framework that led to the abundance and flourishing of US Independent Christian traditions. Before the Revolutionary War, a series of regional revivals in the 1730s and 1740s – primarily led by George Whitefield, an English preacher, and Jonathan Edwards, a New England theologian – infused a populist ethos into US religion. An individual's private and inward encounter with God began to define to what it meant to be a truly converted Christian in the colonial context. Such an emphasis gave laypeople a considerable degree of agency over their spiritual destinies. Regardless of their social

Independents in North America, 2020

Region	Total population	Christian population	Independent population	% of region Independent	% of Christians Independent
North America	368,870,000	269,524,000	65,115,000	17.7%	24.2%
Global total	7,794,799,000	2,506,426,000	389,474,000	5.0%	15.5%

Source: Todd M. Johnson and Gina A. Zurlo (eds), *World Christian Database* (Leiden/Boston: Brill), accessed January 2022.

standing, for better or worse, ordinary Americans could think on religious matters, interpret Scripture and organise churches for themselves. In doing so, they would collapse the distinction between clergy and laity as they refused to defer to theologians, church doctrine or orthopraxy. In this new environment, US interpreters of Christianity had little sense of limitation or boundary. Leaders with no formal training or ordination could create new religious movements by relying upon populist and democratic communication tools through vernacular language and the power of the printing press.

This democratic populist spirit finds its most explicit expression from the 1790s to the 1840s in what historians commonly refer to as the Second Great Awakening. Like the First Great Awakening, which had taken place in the mid-eighteenth century, religious revivals that emphasised popular expressions of Christianity throughout the USA, North and South, marked the Second Great Awakening. Populist revivalism, however, represents only one aspect of the Second Great Awakening. This movement also captured a democratic spirit by emphasising voluntary and self-directed organisation as the primary way a church carried out its work. As Christians across the country participated in and led religious revivals, they also gathered themselves into volunteer organisations that cut across denominational lines. Rather than relying on denominational support, these groups often followed a common pattern of self-starting and self-financing. From Sunday school unions and Bible societies to temperance movements and antislavery groups, a massive volunteer army of Christians across the USA emerged in the early nineteenth century. By relying on the democratic resources of their context, US Christians established and supported churches and organisations that often stood outside of denominational structures through their voluntaristic activity.

The confluence of a pluralistic Christian context, the development of a free religious marketplace through disestablishment, and a democratic populist ethos enacted through voluntary participation in religion gave Americans the resources and freedom to experiment with and interpret Christianity as they saw fit. This distinctive environment regularly produced and sustained Independent Christian groups. When they emerged during the Second Great Awakening, religious communities,

Changes in Independents in North America, 1970–2020, growth rate, % per year

Region	Total population	Christian population	Independent population
North America	0.94%	0.49%	1.08%
Global total	1.50%	1.44%	2.99%

Source: Todd M. Johnson and Gina A. Zurlo (eds), *World Christian Database* (Leiden/Boston: Brill), accessed January 2022.

such as the Oneida community led by John Humphrey Noyes (1811–86) and the Harmony Society founded by George Rapp (1757–1847) represented the vanguard of Independent Christianity in North America. Despite their short-lived existence, they reflected the opportunities that the new US religious landscape afforded to individuals and groups who desired to interpret religious traditions in new ways. In the nineteenth and twentieth centuries, Independent groups continued to proliferate in the US context.

In the twenty-first century, if an individual were to drive down a commercial street in an average US city, he or she would be greeted with evidence of the continued vibrancy of Independent Christianity. Upon close observation of the strip malls that populate the area, this person would find churches with names like International Church of Triumph or Come as You Are Fellowship. Groups like these self-consciously inhabit an Independent Christian identity as they interpret the faith through their immediate contexts and experiences apart from historic Christian traditions. This contemporary expression of Independent Christianity is not confined to the USA. These groups often extend their influence beyond US borders and across the North American continent. Contemporary North American Independent Christianity, with almost 300 active groups represented across the continent, continues to be a creative and energetic group of Christian traditions. To illustrate the breadth and diversity of Independent Christianity in North America, I now turn to four contemporary groups: the Church of Jesus Christ of Latter-day Saints (LDS); Jehovah's Witnesses; Churches of Christ (non-instrumental); and Christian Science (Church of Christ, Scientist).

The Church of Jesus Christ of Latter-day Saints (LDS)

The LDS church has its roots in the intense revivalism of the nineteenth century's Second Great Awakening in what was commonly referred to as the Burned-Over District in upstate New York. Joseph Smith, Jr (1805–44), the founder of the church, eagerly observed the religious enthusiasm that came with the revivals but was soon dismayed by the religious infighting they produced. Seeking the correct expression of Christianity, Smith turned to God for guidance. In a vision from God, Smith claimed that God forbade him from joining any of the denominations that participated in the revival, because they were all wrong. In the years that followed, he would continue to have a series of visions that would culminate with his discovery of golden plates outside his home in Palmyra in 1823. These plates detailed a version of what would become the Book of Mormon, an account of lost tribes of Israel in North America whom Jesus Christ visited after his resurrection and ascension in Jerusalem.

For Smith's followers, the Book of Mormon reverberated with biblical authority. It echoed biblical themes, reinterpreted biblical passages, corrected perceived errors in the Bible and filled biblical gaps. The old stories found in the Bible and the Book of Mormon would come to life for his followers as the movement sojourned into the West. In the years that followed Smith's founding of the LDS church in 1830, like the Israelites in both texts, his followers moved from place to place, always facing persecution, until eventually settling in Utah in 1847, three years after Smith's martyrdom. Their years-long journey to Utah became a recapitulation of the Exodus story: members of the LDS church were God's chosen people, led out of bondage by a prophet who would not live to see the promise of safety and flourishing fulfilled in a far-off land. Such a self-understanding drew upon the atmosphere of religious populism during the Second Great Awakening. It rejected contemporary religious conventions and distrusted traditional religious authorities.

The LDS church differentiated itself from historic Christianity in several ways. First, it reopened the closed canon of Christian Scripture and expanded the biblical narrative. For example, in the Book of Mormon, Smith claimed that Jesus visited North America and ministered to the Native Americans, whom he claimed were descendants of ancient Israelites. Second, Smith taught that soon after the 12 apostles died, a great apostasy fundamentally corrupted the teachings of Christ. Therefore, all Christianity after the apostolic period was fundamentally corrupt and did not represent the entire teaching of Jesus Christ. It would not be until his visions and translation of the Book of Mormon that the true nature and teaching of the Church could be recovered. Finally, Smith rejected Nicaean and Chalcedonian Trinitarian formulations in favour of a tritheistic position. Rather than believing in one God in three persons, he argued that the Trinity was constituted of three gods who cooperated with each other. He would continue to develop this position over the rest of his life. Smith's understanding of the Trinity and the potential destiny of individual humans placed him far outside the norms of traditional Christian orthodoxy. As an alternative to what he saw as a corrupted historic Christianity, Smith crafted an Independent religious vision that empowered the common person, rather than the religious or social elite, to participate in reconstituting the true Church.

The LDS church bases its teachings on four texts: the Bible, the Book of Mormon, Doctrines and Covenants and the Pearl of Great Price. In addition to these books of Scripture, Mormons also believe in progressive revelation. Only the current president of the church, however, can make prophetically authoritative statements that change or clarify LDS doctrine and practice. A bishop, two counsellors and the presidents of local auxiliaries called wards lead LDS congregations. These churches do not have professionally paid ministers. The entire LDS church is overseen by the 'general authorities' in Salt Lake City, Utah. This group comprises the church president, two counsellors called 'the First Presidency', the Quorum of the Twelve Apostles and the Quorum of the Seventy. The LDS church has four sacraments: baptism for the remission of sins (this includes baptism for the dead), weekly communion consisting of water and bread, and two sacraments in the temple. These final two sacraments, the endowment and sealing, bind husband, wife and their children together eternally. They both reinforce and reflect the LDS emphasis on family.

The contemporary LDS church has a significant presence across the globe, with more than 16 million members. This Independent Christian tradition continues to have a solid and growing presence in North America, with more than six million members in the USA and just under 200,000 in Canada. Since its inception in 1830, several subgroups have split off from the LDS community. The Community of Christ (formerly the Reorganized Church of Jesus Christ of Latter-day Saints) is centred in Independence, Missouri, with 170,000 members. The next largest group, the Fundamentalist Church of Jesus Christ of Latter-day Saints (FLDS), is based in Colorado City, Arizona. It has almost 100,000 members in several Western states, Mexico and British Columbia. The FLDS church continues to practise polygamy (the practice of marrying multiple spouses) despite the LDS church outlawing it in 1890.

Jehovah's Witnesses

Charles Taze Russell (1852–1916) began the Jehovah's Witnesses in 1870 (known then as 'Bible Students') when he started leading a series of small group Bible studies. Russell grew up in a Presbyterian household in Allegheny, Pennsylvania. He rejected the faith of his youth, however, as he struggled with doctrines of predestination, the trinitarian nature of God and the existence of hell. Consequently, Russell pursued his questions about religion in various contexts, from Congregationalism to Eastern religions, until he became an atheist. Russell's life changed in 1869 when he encountered Second Adventist minister Jonas Wendell (1815–73). Wendell introduced Russell to the end-time calculations of William Miller (1782–1849) and his teachings regarding Christ's second coming. Russell became enthralled with biblical prophecy teaching that Christ would return as an invisible presence on earth in 1874. Christ's spiritual return would precipitate a series of events that would culminate in 1914 with the battle of Armageddon. Jehovah (the Old Testament name for God that Russell insisted on using), Christ and an army of angels would wage war against Satan and his followers. This event, and the inevitable victory of Jehovah, would initiate 1,000 years of peace and prosperity free from suffering and injustice. The beginning of the First World War in 1914 seemed to confirm Russell's predictions for many of his followers. When Christ failed to return and physically establish God's kingdom on earth that year, however, Russell claimed that Jesus had initiated a spiritual reign in the heavens instead.

By the end of the 1870s, Russell began publishing his views in a journal he established, *Zion's Watch Tower and Herald of Christ's Presence*. Its popularity led to the growth of the movement in several states. In 1884, he incorporated the Zion's Watch Tower Tract Society, which became one of the institutional structures that helped concretise the movement. By 1893, Russell's followers had their first national assembly, in Chicago. In 1909, they established their world headquarters in Brooklyn, New York, where Russell presided as president. The following year, in 1910, Russell published his teachings in a six-volume series called *Studies in the Scripture*. These volumes, along with the Bible and the regular publication of the *Watchtower* magazine, became the central documents of Russell's movement.

After Russell died in 1916, Joseph Franklin Rutherford (1869–1942) became the organisation's new president. Rutherford continued to shape the movement's Independent identity, attacking organised religion and other expressions of Christianity as standing outside of the truth of the movement's teachings. In 1931, he officially changed the movement's name to Jehovah's Witnesses based on his reading of Isaiah 43: 10. Nathan Homer Norr (1905–77) followed Rutherford as leader of the Jehovah's Witnesses and initiated the New World Translation of the Bible that reflected the movement's doctrine. During the twentieth century, the movement continued to grow. By 2015, it had 2.8 million members in the USA and more than 8.2 million globally.

While Jehovah's Witnesses wait for the impending Battle of Armageddon, Russell's teachings encouraged them to live a distinctive lifestyle. Witnesses ought to keep themselves pure by refraining from smoking, drinking alcohol, accepting blood transfusions or associating with the government in any way. They were not to fight in a country's wars or salute its flag. These practices led to the persecution of Jehovah's Witnesses during the Second World War in Germany and the USA. Beyond leading a life marked by its ambivalence and hostility to broader culture, the movement also has high expectations that its members participate in regular evangelism. If they fail to do so, Jehovah's Witnesses threaten them with expulsion. Members often go out in pairs knocking on doors to share their faith. As a result of this focus on evangelism, Jehovah's Witnesses have continued to enjoy growth in the USA and globally.

Jehovah's Witnesses' theology departs from historic Christian doctrine on several counts. As mentioned above, they reject trinitarian theology in favour of an Arian position, asserting that Jesus is a created being who was first among God's creatures. Witnesses specifically identify Jesus with the archangel Michael, who will lead God's armies of angels to victory over the forces of Satan in the final battle of Armageddon. The movement also displays gnostic tendencies in its understanding of the resurrection, teaching that Jesus's spirit, but not his body, rose from the grave. As to the Holy Spirit, Jehovah's Witnesses believe that it lacks personal distinction and agency. Instead, they argue that the Holy Spirit represents God's impersonal active force in the world. Finally, the movement's eschatology and doctrine of humanity's final destiny represents a departure from historic Christian teachings. Russell taught that human souls were not immortal but would experience a period of 'soul sleep' after death. After the eschaton, only 144,000 of Jehovah's Witnesses would be awakened to enter heaven. At the same time, the remainder of the faithful would be resurrected to inhabit a perfect, earthly paradise. The souls who stood outside Jehovah's Witnesses would face annihilation rather than an eternity in hell.

Contemporary Jehovah's Witnesses represent one of the most ethnically diverse religious groups in the USA: 36% are white, 32% are Latinx, 27% are Black, and the remaining 5% represent other ethnicities. This Independent Christian tradition is overwhelmingly female, with almost two-thirds of its membership constituted by women. One of the most striking features of Jehovah's Witnesses is the high percentage of members who are adult converts: almost 65%. This situation not only speaks to the robust emphasis that the group places on evangelism. It also reflects how Jehovah's Witnesses have articulated a compelling identity and way of life that stands apart from the broader cultures it inhabits.

Churches of Christ (Non-instrumental)

The Churches of Christ (non-instrumental) come from the American Restoration Movement, often referred to as the Stone–Campbell Movement by scholars. This movement emerged during the revivalism of the Second Great Awakening in the USA. It was also heavily influenced by late eighteenth-century transatlantic evangelical missions culture characterised by organisations like the London Missionary Society (1795). The goal of this movement was to bring about visible unity among the various Christian denominations that inhabited the USA. Its leaders, Barton W. Stone (1772–1844), Thomas Campbell (1763–1854) and his son Alexander Campbell (1788–1866), sought to restore the practices and forms of the primitive New Testament Church. They believed they could accomplish their goal through a Common Sense reading of the Bible. Once this restoration was complete, Christians in the USA and across the globe would unite around the restored primitive Church, convert the world to Christianity and usher in the eschaton. This movement would eventually produce three denominations: Christian Churches (Disciples of Christ), Churches of Christ (non-instrumental) and Christian Churches/Churches of Christ.

As the nineteenth century progressed, the Stone–Campbell Movement rapidly grew. When it began in 1832, the movement had around 25,000 members. By 1861, it was the fourth-largest religious group in the USA, with almost 200,000 members in 29 states and two territories. At the beginning of the twentieth century, however, this Christian unity movement would fragment. Following the turbulent years of the American Civil War and Reconstruction, several congregations, located predominantly in the South, that called themselves 'Churches of Christ' left the movement. This group believed that the use of musical instruments in worship and the presence of missionary societies in the movement were extra-scriptural innovations that they could not tolerate. By 1906, because of doctrinal, regional and sociological factors, Churches of Christ officially separated themselves from Disciples of Christ, creating two streams in the Stone–Campbell Movement.

Upon their separation from Disciples of Christ in 1906, members of the Churches of Christ were predominantly Southern, rural and poor. The new denomination retained the congregationalist structure and the restorationist emphasis of the Stone–Campbell Movement, having a high view of the church and human ability. In practice, each local congregation was overseen by a plurality of elders and served by deacons who would carry out various good works. Congregations would focus on simplicity in worship with a cappella singing, an emphasis on preaching and the weekly observance of communion. Individuals joined Churches of Christ through adult baptism by immersion. The denomination was conservative in its interpretation of the Bible. It did not ordain ministers, elders or deacons because Scripture did not explicitly authorise ordination. Members abstained from drinking alcohol, dancing, playing cards, going to the theatre and wearing extravagant clothes – to resist 'the ways of the world'.

As a denomination, Churches of Christ self-differentiated from all other Christian groups, traditions and denominations. In doing so, the congregations and members of the denomination abstained from interdenominational fellowship. They believed Churches of Christ represented the fully restored New Testament Church inhabited by the only true Christians in the world. With this assumption in view, members of the denomination believed it would be wrong to partner with groups who represented a divided and thus digressive Christendom. Therefore, while the doctrine and practice of Churches of Christ mirror those of other historic Christian traditions, this denomination represents an Independent Christian group. It has historically self-identified as independent and separate from all other interpretations of Christianity.

Throughout the twentieth century, Churches of Christ proliferated. In 1906, after separating from Disciples of Christ, the denomination had 159,658 members. This number had grown to 600,000 by 1941. Churches of Christ's membership in the USA peaked at almost 1.3 million in the mid-1990s and is slowly declining. The denomination had 1.12 million members as of 2018. Outside of the USA, Churches of Christ has some 250 members in Bermuda and 7,000 in Canada. Outside of North America, however, Churches of Christ has experienced significant growth, especially in sub-Saharan Africa and India.

While the congregationalist polity of the denomination makes formal division difficult to effect or even perceive in Churches of Christ, by the early 2000s, the uniformity of this Independent Christian tradition had essentially broken down. The mechanisms that once standardised church doctrine and practice, especially denominational periodicals, no longer enjoy the widespread influence they once had. As a result, Churches of Christ has been experiencing an identity crisis in the twenty-first century. Contemporary issues like women's leadership in the church, the legacy of racism, LGBTQ inclusion and the recovery of a commitment to Christian unity have caused many of the denomination's members to question previous generations' practice, doctrine and polity. The Independent and sectarian identity that once defined and unified Churches of Christ has given way to fragmentation defined by multiple theological orientations and trajectories within the tradition.

Christian Science (Church of Christ, Scientist)

Mary Baker Eddy (1821–1910) is the charismatic figure who founded Christian Science (or the Church of Christ, Scientist) in 1879. Eddy was the youngest of six children from a traditional New England family with Congregationalist roots. She grew up during the Second Great Awakening that caused many Americans to question clerical authority, traditional church doctrines and spiritual gifts that God gave Christians. She struggled with frequent illness, and her first marriage, with George Glover (d. 1844), ended in tragedy when he died six months after their wedding. Eddy soon gave birth to her first child, whom she named George after his father. Eddy remained bedridden during the early years of his life. In 1851, she was forced to give up her son because she could no longer care for him. Two years later, in 1853, she married Daniel Patterson, a dentist interested in homeopathic medicine. The pattern of misfortune continued to plague Eddy, however, and the unhappy marriage eventually ended in divorce.

As she reflected on her life and continued to experience ill health as well as poverty, Eddy wrestled with the Reformed doctrine of her upbringing. How could she reconcile the suffering and tragedy she had experienced in her life with a loving God? In 1862, she found an answer to her question. As she was seeking relief from chronic pain, Eddy stumbled upon the writings of Phineas P. Quimby (1802–66), a leader in the New Thought Movement. Quimby believed that human illness could be cured through the mind with positive thinking. Eddy met Quimby later that year and she claimed that he healed her through his mind–body cure. Afterwards, she became one of Quimby's students, learning his philosophy and methods.

In 1866, months after Quimby's death, Eddy experienced a dramatic turning point in her life after she slipped on a patch of ice in Lynn, Massachusetts. For three days, she was bedridden. During this time, Eddy read the Bible and explored the healing miracles of Jesus. On the third day, in good biblical fashion, she recovered from her injuries. She then set out to spread the gospel of the mind–body cure grounded in the teachings and example of Jesus's healing ministry. In the years that followed, Eddy combined Quimby's philosophy with her interpretations of the Bible and developed what she called 'Christian Science'. For Eddy, 'science' referred to the underlying nature of reality and the spiritual laws that governed this reality based on her reading of Jesus Christ's life and ministry. According to Eddy, the physical world was an illusion unfolding in the mind of God. Human beings, in this cosmological scheme, were purely spiritual beings. Sin, sickness and even death were merely conditions of false belief that must be conquered through prayer and meditation. Jesus was the one who first showed human beings how to overcome false notions of material reality through his ministry.

In the years that followed her insights into Christian Science, Eddy gained a reputation as a healer and wise religious teacher. In 1875, she published her teachings in the first edition of *Science and Health*, one of the essential documents of Christian Science. Six years later, in 1881, she established the Massachusetts Metaphysical College and in 1892 she founded the Mother Church (the First Church of Christ, Scientist) in Boston, Massachusetts. By 1900, the movement had grown considerably, with Christian Science churches extending from Boston in the east to Los Angeles, California, in the west. Christian Science continued to grow in the USA throughout the twentieth century. It also drew considerable criticism over its emphasis on healing through prayer while also eschewing standard medical treatment, especially in the case of children.

This Independent Christian tradition continues to have a national and global presence, with more than 1,200 Christian Science Reading Rooms in the USA alone. It is, however, facing decline, with only 140,000 members as of 2015. Despite Christian Science's controversial nature, its founder represents someone who discovered in the Christian story the resources to escape physical pain caused by illness. Moreover, as Eddy overcame personal setbacks, she found comfort and empowerment in religion, especially as a woman living in the nineteenth century. Like other leaders of Independent Christian traditions, such as Joseph Smith, Eddy displayed an ability to create a new theological worldview through her engagement with contemporary understandings of science and metaphysics. Her ideas around mind–body cure, positive thinking and the Christian story foreshadowed the emergence of more Independent Christian movements in the twentieth and twenty-first centuries.

Conclusion

The USA has provided a fertile context for the rise and proliferation of many Independent Christian traditions. The number of Independent Christian groups, however, does not represent US exceptionalism. Instead, they arose out of the confluence of distinctive qualities that came to define US religion in the late eighteen and early nineteenth centuries: Christian pluralism, a free religious marketplace and a democratic populist spirit. These qualities favoured religious innovation and experimentation over the well-established doctrines and practices of traditional Christian traditions exported from Europe. This environment continues to give rise to new Independent interpretations in the contemporary USA.

While the preceding discussion is critical to understanding the landscape of North American Christianity and North American religion in general, it has global implications. In his book *The New Shape of World Christianity: How American Experience Reflects Global Faith* (Downers Grove, IL: InterVarsity, 2009), Mark Noll argues that the form of voluntary religion that emerged in the USA during the late eighteenth and early nineteenth centuries is a model for contemporary Christianity across the globe. In the global South (Africa, Asia and Latin America), competitive, entrepreneurial and free religious marketplaces are emerging. Mass migrations from rural areas of these continents to urban settings produce new opportunities for religious innovation as individuals are searching for new anchor points in their unsettled worlds. The contemporary world sees an explosion of Independent Christian groups in the global South, as the USA did during this Second Great Awakening. Like the LDS church, Jehovah's Witnesses and other US Independent groups, they thrive as they interpret the Christian tradition in light of their current circumstances.

Bibliography

Bushman, Richard Lyman, *Mormonism: A Very Short Introduction* (New York: Oxford University Press, 2008).

Moore, R. Laurence, *Religious Outsiders and the Making of Americans* (New York: Oxford University Press, 1987).

Penton, James, *Apocalypse Delayed: The Story of Jehovah's Witnesses*, 3rd edition (Toronto: University of Toronto Press, 2015).

Voorhees, Amy B., *A New Christian Identity: Christian Science Origins and Experience in American Culture* (Chapel Hill, NC: University of North Carolina Press, 2021).

Williams, D. Newell, Douglas A. Foster and Paul M. Blowers (eds), *The Stone–Campbell Movement: A Global History* (St Louis, MO: Chalice Press, 2013).

Orthodox

Anton C. Vrame

The Eastern Orthodox Church traces its origins in North America to two key moments. The first was in 1768, with a short-lived colony of a few hundred Greeks in New Smyrna, Florida, which was in British hands at the time. This community disbanded because of the mismanagement of the plantation owner and dispersed into St Augustine. Although they were Greek Orthodox in faith, they did not build a parish. The second was the arrival of Russian Orthodox monks in 1794 at Kodiak Island in Russian-controlled Alaska. An important member of the group was the monk Herman (c. 1750–1836), who spent the rest of his life in Alaska and was proclaimed a saint of the Orthodox Church in America in 1970. These monks were sent to minister to the Russian traders in Alaska. With a missionary spirit, the monks also began to work among the Native American population, translating and creating new texts in Native American languages. These missionaries travelled as far south as today's Fort Ross in Sonoma County, California, by the 1820s. A key figure was Innocent Veniaminov (1797–1879), later elected Metropolitan of Moscow and proclaimed a saint of the Russian Orthodox Church in 1977, who organised the communities, establishing a diocese of the Russian Orthodox Church for Alaska.

However, it was not until the late nineteenth and early twentieth centuries that Orthodox parishes began to be established in the mainland USA. As immigrants arrived and pursued economic opportunities across the country, they began settling in the major cities. The Greeks were the largest of the groups, and between 1862 and 1922 they had established 141 parishes. The first were founded in Galveston, Texas; New Orleans, Louisiana; New York City; Chicago; Boston Lowell, Massachusetts; Philadelphia; Newark, New Jersey; Birmingham, Alabama; San Francisco; and St Louis. The first Antiochian Orthodox parish was established in 1895 by Father Raphael Hawaweeny (1860–1915) in New York City. Hawaweeny would go on to become the first Orthodox bishop ordained in the USA (proclaimed a saint in 2000). One of first Serbian Orthodox parishes was established in 1892–3, in Jackson, California.

With the exception of the Russian Orthodox Church, which in 1868 had established a diocese in North America based in San Francisco following the sale of the Alaska territory to the USA, the other immigrants established parishes without official ties to ecclesiastical authorities. The patterns of immigration created the anomalous situation of multiple jurisdictions of Orthodox in North America, contrary to the tradition that would call for one ecclesiastical body for the entire nation.

The organisation of ecclesiastical dioceses began to occur in earnest in the early twentieth century as the immigrant communities grew in number. Each national group formed a diocese under their 'mother Church'. For example, the Greek Orthodox Archdiocese of North and South America was established and incorporated in 1922 by a clergy and lay group led by Archbishop Meletios Metaxakis (later Ecumenical Patriarch Meletios IV), under the auspices of the Ecumenical Patriarchate of Constantinople. Under the leadership of Bishop Tikhon Bellavin (who would go on to become Patriarch of Moscow in 1917), the Russian Orthodox Diocese (or Metropolia) would be established in New York City, moving from San Francisco in 1905. Raphael Hawaweeny was ordained as a bishop specifically to help organise the Orthodox community from the Middle East – Antiochians as they were called – as part of the Russian Orthodox Church. The Antiochian Archdiocese of North America would eventually be established in 1975, uniting the rival groups that had been established in earlier decades. It is now an Archdiocese under the Patriarchate of Antioch (Damascus, Syria).

In time, the diverse Orthodox communities understood that having separate jurisdictions was anomalous to Orthodox polity, and efforts to unite were made, especially by the time of the Second World War. This was spearheaded largely by Archbishop Athenagoras (Spyrou, later Ecumenical Patriarch) of the Greek Orthodox Archdiocese of North and South America. It was motivated by the need to be recognised as a 'legitimate religious group' by the War Department so that enlistees could receive the services of Orthodox chaplains, Orthodox military personnel could be identified as Orthodox on their dog-tags, and Orthodox clergy could be exempted from the draft.

As each group grew in size and strength, it established institutions and programmes to meet the needs of the faithful in the USA. Holy Cross Greek Orthodox School of Theology (1937), St Vladimir's Orthodox Theological Seminary (1938) and St Tikhon's Seminary (1938) were established to train

Orthodox in North America, 1970

Region	Total population	Christian population	Orthodox population	% of region Orthodox	% of Christians Orthodox
North America	230,992,000	211,489,000	4,870,000	2.1%	2.3%
Global total	3,700,437,000	1,225,395,000	139,115,000	3.8%	11.4%

Source: Todd M. Johnson and Gina A. Zurlo (eds), *World Christian Database* (Leiden/Boston: Brill), accessed January 2022.

clergy and theologians for the American context. Faculty members such as Fr Alexander Schmemann, Fr Georges Florovsky and Fr Stanley Harakas are among the best-known even today. The jurisdictions established publishing houses (such as Holy Cross Orthodox Press and St Vladimir's Seminary Press) and created newspapers and magazines (including *Orthodox Observer* by the Greek Orthodox Archdiocese and *The Word* for the Antiochian Archdiocese) to meet the needs of their populations. Especially important was making Orthodox liturgical services accessible in English for their rapidly assimilating congregations, a process that is still ongoing. The jurisdictions added departments to meet the needs of their parishes, such as sacramental registries, Christian education and youth ministries, and finance and administrative committees. They also established permanent headquarters, such as that of the Greek Orthodox Archdiocese of America, which moved from an inadequate facility in Astoria, New York, to two buildings on East 79th Street in Manhattan.

The Russian Revolution of 1917, and later the Cold War, created major problems for the Orthodox Churches tied to those countries (Russia/USSR, Serbia, Romania, Bulgaria, Albania and others). These groups were often cut off from their mother Churches, and then the Cold War led many of them to cut their ties from what was perceived as a 'Communist-occupied' Church there. This also led to the creation of 'competing' groups in the USA: those with ties to the mother Church and those without. The Russian Orthodox Metropolia in America resolved this issue by becoming the autocephalous (self-governing) Orthodox Church in America in 1970. Not until after the breakup of the Soviet Union in 1991 were attempts made to unify these groups and restore ties. The Serbian Church in the United States, which was divided into two groups because of Cold War politics, was finally reunited in 1992 – to one another and to the Patriarchate of Serbia. Perhaps, though, the most notable example is the restoration in 2007 of communion between the Russian Orthodox Church Outside Russia (established in 1919) and the Moscow Patriarchate.

The fall of communism and the challenges facing Orthodox Christians in the Middle East have led to a new 'wave' of immigrants from Eastern Europe (Romania, Serbia) and the Middle East (Palestine, Lebanon, Syria). The already established Orthodox jurisdictions in the USA have

Orthodox in North America, 2020

Region	Total population	Christian population	Orthodox population	% of region Orthodox	% of Christians Orthodox
North America	368,870,000	269,524,000	8,370,000	2.3%	3.1%
Global total	7,794,799,000	2,506,426,000	291,924,000	3.7%	11.6%

Source: Todd M. Johnson and Gina A. Zurlo (eds), *World Christian Database* (Leiden/Boston: Brill), accessed January 2022.

recalibrated some aspects of their lives to meet the needs of these immigrants – for example, by offering liturgies in the mother tongues. However, the assimilated or convert clergy might not know these languages and incorporating a new wave of immigrants into an established and assimilated community can prove challenging.

A growing segment of the Orthodox population in the USA comprises those who embraced Orthodox Christianity from other, usually Christian, communions. Many non-Orthodox embrace Orthodoxy through marriage to an Orthodox Christian. Currently, rates of 'mixed' or 'inter-Christian' marriage are as high as 65% of all Orthodox weddings. A significant historical event occurred in 1987, with the 'mass conversion' and reception of roughly 2,000 'Evangelical Orthodox' Christians by the Antiochian Orthodox Archdiocese. A group of Evangelical Protestants, largely associated with Campus Crusade under the leadership of Peter Gillquist (1938–2012), had been studying Church history and came to the realisation that the Orthodox Church was the only unchanged Church in history. Setting themselves up as an independent 'Evangelical Orthodox Church', they began to seek a relationship with the rest of Orthodoxy. After meetings with other jurisdictions, and even a meeting with Ecumenical Patriarch Dimitrios, bore no fruit, these 'Evangelical Orthodox' were received into the canonical Church through the Antiochian Orthodox Christian Archdiocese of North America by Metropolitan Philip Saliba (1931–2014).

Orthodox spirituality is closely associated with monastic life. While monastics arrived in Alaska in the 1790s, monasteries began to be established in earnest in the twentieth century. One of the first was St Tikhon's Monastery in 1905 by the Russian Orthodox Metropolia in South Canaan, Pennsylvania. A women's monastery was established in Springfield, Vermont, in 1915. Another was Holy Trinity Monastery of the Russian Orthodox Church Outside Russia in Jordanville, New York, in 1930. Holy Transfiguration Monastery (convent) was established in Ellwood City, Pennsylvania, by Mother Alexandra (the former Princess Ileana of Romania) in 1967 as part of the Romanian Episcopate of the Orthodox Church in America. The Holy Transfiguration Monastery was established in 1960. Now located in Brookline, Massachusetts, but not belonging to any of the canonical jurisdictions – it is a member of the Holy Orthodox

Changes in Orthodox in North America, 1970–2020, growth rate, % per year

Region	Total population	Christian population	Orthodox population
North America	0.94%	0.49%	1.09%
Global total	1.50%	1.44%	1.49%

Source: Todd M. Johnson and Gina A. Zurlo (eds), *World Christian Database* (Leiden/Boston: Brill), accessed January 2022.

Church of North America – this monastery is noted for its liturgical translations and iconography. The New Skete Monastery, formerly a monastic community of Byzantine Rite Franciscans and Poor Clares in Cambridge, New York, was received into the Orthodox Church in America in 1979. This monastic community is notable for their studies of the origins and evolution of the Orthodox East and their liturgical practice based on their research. In addition, this community is famous for their work with German Shepherds. A major development occurred in 1990 with the arrival of Elder Ephraim (1928–2019), the former abbot of the Philotheou Monastery on Mount Athos and student of St Joseph the Hesychast (1857–1959). Fr Ephraim began establishing monasteries across the USA, such as St Anthony's Monastery in Florence, Arizona, founded in 1995. He established 17 monasteries in the USA and two in Canada. Overall, there are 80 Orthodox monasteries in the USA.

The names of the jurisdictions reflect the national origins of that group. The Antiochian Orthodox Church was created by Arab immigrants, the Greek Orthodox Church by Greek immigrants, and so on. All Eastern Orthodox are united in faith and doctrine (the decisions of the historic Seven Ecumenical Councils being central), theology and sacraments (baptism, chrismation/confirmation, eucharist, matrimony, confession, unction and ordination). It is one faith, one Church, with many cultural expressions and administrative bodies.

The push to bring the various Orthodox jurisdictions together began in earnest in 1960 with the creation of the Standing Conference of Canonical Orthodox Bishops in the Americas, under the leadership of Archbishop Iakovos Koukouzis (1911–2005) of the Greek Orthodox Archdiocese of North and South America. This created a forum for the leadership of the jurisdictions, for common work and action. This common work took place under the auspices of various agencies, such as the Orthodox Christian Education Commission, which brought together the Christian education ministries of the jurisdictions for greater collaboration and coordination, even as each body retained its own programmes and departments. Over time, additional organisations have been created for inter-Orthodox collaboration, such as the Orthodox Christian Mission Center, International Orthodox Christian Charities and others. In 1994, in response to decisions being made globally by the 'mother Churches' to deal with the Churches in the 'diaspora', hierarchs met at the Antiochian Village in Ligonier, Pennsylvania, to discuss putting a greater emphasis on Orthodox administrative unity. The official statements from this meeting were perceived by the mother Churches as moving to create an autocephalous American Orthodox Church, even though no such statement was made. While this historic meeting was seen as a failure, after the Fourth Pre-Conciliar

Pan-Orthodox Conference convoked in Chambésy, Switzerland, in June 2009, the bishops in the USA, Canada and Central America organised as the Assembly of Canonical Orthodox Bishops of North and Central America. In April 2014, because of the diversity of the Churches in this large area, separate assemblies were organised for the USA and Canada; the Central American Churches joined the Assembly for Latin America. The goals of the Assembly of Canonical Orthodox Bishops in America are: (1) the promotion and accomplishment of Church unity in the USA; (2) the strengthening of the common pastoral ministry to all the Orthodox faithful of the region; (3) a common witness by the Church to all those outside it; and (4) the organisation of the Church in the USA in accordance with the ecclesiological and the canonical tradition of the Orthodox Church.

The Eastern Orthodox Churches, collectively as well as individually, have been active in American civil life and the public square. From the days of the Second World War when they pursued rights for Orthodox in the military, the Churches have been active in promoting their status in American society, pursuing issues in support of their populations, as well as expressing Orthodox Christian values on social issues. In the 1960s, Archbishop Iakovos of the Greek Orthodox Archdiocese marched with Martin Luther King, Jr, famously appearing on the cover of *LIFE* magazine. While today this is a matter of pride for the community, the initial reaction was more mixed. After the Turkish invasion of Cyprus in 1974, which divided the island nation, the Greek Orthodox Church encouraged its members to lobby Congress to pressure Turkey to leave the island and to restore its unity, as well as to maintain the same ratio of the sales of weapons to Greece and Turkey. The Greek Orthodox Church in America continues to speak out actively for greater freedoms for the Ecumenical Patriarchate in Constantinople (Istanbul).

More recently, Orthodox Christians and their leaders have participated in the national and local March for Life, reflecting the Church's pro-life, anti-abortion stance. The Orthodox Churches have become known for their environmental attitudes, reflecting the work of His All-Holiness Ecumenical Patriarch Bartholomew, the 'Green Patriarch'. In the aftermath of the 9/11 terrorist attacks in New York, and the destruction of the St Nicholas Greek Orthodox Church in the collapse of the World Trade Center, His Eminence Archbishop Demetrios Trakatellis of the Greek Orthodox Archdiocese took on a leadership role, talking about the effects of terrorism, but also leading the call to rebuild the parish. That church was completed and dedicated as the St Nicholas Greek Orthodox Church and National Shrine in Manhattan in 2022. During the 2020 activism around Black Lives Matter (BLM), Orthodox hierarchs spoke out on race relations. Archbishop Elpidophoros Lambriniadis of the Greek Orthodox Archdiocese marched at a rally in New York City. This act was not without controversy as some in his community did not support some aspects of the BLM agenda.

The Eastern Orthodox are fully engaged with the ecumenical movement. After the historic rapprochement between the Orthodox Church and Roman Catholic Church in 1964, the North American Orthodox–Catholic Theological Consultation, a theological dialogue between the two, was quickly established in 1965 and continues to meet (an international dialogue was not established until the 1990s). The Orthodox jurisdictions are members of the National Council of Churches in Christ in the USA, with strong participation in Faith and Order. Theologians participate in global ecumenical dialogues, representing the mother Churches.

The Eastern Orthodox Churches face similar challenges to other Christian communities in the USA. The 'baby boomers' are ageing. Concerns are ongoing about disaffiliation, especially by the young. An important emphasis, but not unprecedented, is youth ministry and religious education for the next generation. For example, the CrossRoad Institute, initiated by Hellenic College–Holy Cross Greek Orthodox School of Theology in 2003, provides an intense academic summer camp programme for juniors and seniors in high school. Finally, the Orthodox population in the USA is being affected by the religious and political polarisation of American society.

While estimates vary, the Eastern Orthodox population in the USA is thought to number between one million and two million adherents. The largest of them is the Greek Orthodox Archdiocese of America (the United States). Some estimates put the number at 600,000 adherents; official statements claim 1,500,000. Approximately 2,000 parishes in the USA belong to the canonical jurisdictions, a number that has remained stable from the 2010s. Parishes can be found throughout the USA but tend to be located in the major urban centres. Parish growth has occurred largely in the Southeastern and Western United States, reflecting general population moves out of the Northeast and Upper Midwest. While most parishes range between 100 and 200 individuals or families, some parishes are very large, such as the Annunciation Greek Orthodox Church in Houston, which has more than 5,000 adherent families.

The canonical jurisdictions in the USA are listed below by name:

- Albanian Orthodox Diocese of America
- American Carpatho-Russian Orthodox Diocese
- Antiochian Orthodox Christian Archdiocese
- Bulgarian Eastern Orthodox Diocese of the USA, Canada, and Australia
- Georgian Orthodox Parishes in the USA
- Greek Orthodox Archdiocese of America

- Orthodox Church in America
- Patriarchal Parishes of the Russian Orthodox Church (Moscow Patriarchate)
- Romanian Orthodox Archdiocese in the Americas
- Russian Orthodox Church Outside Russia
- Serbian Orthodox Church in North America
- Slavic Orthodox Vicariate
- Ukrainian Orthodox Church of the USA
- Vicariate for the Palestinian/Jordanian Orthodox Christian Communities

Two jurisdictions in the USA not in communion with the others have small populations:

- Holy Orthodox Church in North America
- Macedonian Orthodox Church: American-Canadian Diocese

In addition, it is important to take note of the Oriental Orthodox Christian Churches:

- Armenian Apostolic Church of America: Catholicosate of Cilicia
- Armenian Church of America: Catholicosate of Etchmiadzin
- Coptic Orthodox Church in the USA
- Eritrean Orthodox Tewahedo Church
- Ethiopian Orthodox Tewahedo Church
- Malankara (Indian) Orthodox Syrian Church
- Malankara Archdiocese of the Syrian Orthodox Church in North America
- Syrian (Syriac) Orthodox Church of Antioch

They are not in communion with the Eastern Orthodox Churches but have strong connections with them. Notable among them is the rapid growth of the Coptic Orthodox Church, which is receiving immigrants from Egypt.

Bibliography

Erickson, John H., *Orthodox Christians in America: A Short History*, 2nd revised edition (New York: Oxford University Press, 2008).

FitzGerald, Thomas E., *The Orthodox Church*, Denominations in America, no. 7. (Westport, CT: Praeger Publishers, 1998).

Kitroeff, Alexander, *The Greek Orthodox Church in America: A Modern History*, NIU Series in Orthodox Christian Studies (DeKalb, IL: Northern Illinois University Press, 2020).

Krindatch, Alexei, *Atlas of American Orthodox Christian Churches* (Brookline, MA: Holy Cross Orthodox Press, 2011).

Krindatch, Alexei, *Atlas of American Orthodox Christian Monasteries* (Brookline, MA: Holy Cross Orthodox Press, 2016).

Protestants

Margaret Bendroth

The story of Protestantism in North America defies easy summary. It is, on the one hand, a religious 'establishment' that has fundamentally shaped the cultural traditions and social institutions of the USA and Canada. Yet it is also one piece of an increasingly pluralistic picture, contested from within and without, tempered by internal dissent and external competition. In general, North American Protestants trace their roots to the Reformation in Europe, primarily the Reformed (Calvinist) tradition, Lutherans, Methodists and Anabaptists. (Episcopalians are ordinarily included in this category; however, churches from the Anglican Communion are dealt with separately in this volume.) But this list also includes a diverse array of 'home-grown' groups, like the Seventh-day Adventists and, many would argue, the Latter-day Saints.

White Protestantism has been profoundly affected by the theological and cultural controversies of the early twentieth century, disputes that separated denominations and congregations into two general categories, Evangelical and mainline. The categories should be used with some caution, however, as they are slippery, subjective and notoriously hard to define. There are also important exceptions, most notably the Black Protestant churches, which both overlap with the white mainline narrative and represent a unique spiritual tradition shaped by the rigours of slavery and segregation. The African Methodist Episcopal Church and the National Baptists, for example, have common historical roots with their white mainline counterparts, and share beliefs and practices around theology and church government. Yet they are also distinct in worship practices as well as spirituality and theology, and also differ from both the white mainline and Evangelicals in matters of social ethics.

This essay focuses on the story of the 'mainline'. We begin by noting that the word itself is relatively new and, among scholars of North American religion, controversial. 'Mainline' originally referred to the railroad system connecting the elite suburbs north-west of Philadelphia — thus being synonymous with wealth, social standing and old money. Exactly how the word took on a religious connotation is unclear, but by the 1960s the term was an accepted shorthand for a set of predominantly white, socially and theologically liberal denominations. In the USA, the so-called 'mainline' Protestant denominations usually include American Baptists, the Evangelical Lutheran Church in America, Episcopalians, the Presbyterian Church (USA), the Reformed Church in America, the United Church of Christ and United Methodists. As of 2014, according to the Pew Research Center, mainline Protestants accounted for approximately 14.7% of the total population, alongside Evangelicals (25.4%) and the historic Black denominations (6.5%). In Canada, the mainline includes the United Church of Canada – a merger of Methodist, Presbyterian and Congregational Churches formalised in 1925 – the Anglican Church, Lutherans and smaller bodies of Presbyterians unaffiliated with the United Church of Canada.

Why is the term controversial? The main objection is the implication that the 'mainline' denominations are the religious centre, the culturally dominant mainstream. This might have been true decades ago, when white liberal Protestants formed what historian William R. Hutchison has called a religious 'establishment'. Up through the 1970s, mainline churches supplied presidents and prime ministers, college professors and leading opinion-makers in journalism, politics and diplomacy. This is true no longer. The increasing religious diversity of the USA and Canada, as well as precipitous declines in membership and attendance, have rendered the term not only inaccurate but, in the eyes of many, blindly presumptuous. As a result, many scholars have shifted to more neutral terms, like 'old line' or 'ecumenical'. Yet the word is still useful, primarily to reflect the historical trajectory of the so-called Protestant establishment, particularly the role of mainline churches in shaping social mores and cultural values.

This essay will define and describe this Protestant family from a variety of angles, beginning with a brief historical survey. Following sections summarise recent studies of mainline beliefs and social attitudes and theories behind mainline decline.

Historical Trajectory

North American Protestantism is an uneasy duality, a religious 'establishment' built upon a dissenting, voluntary tradition. Though all of the present-day mainline denominations in the USA and Canada originated in Europe, in many cases as state-supported churches, survival on the other

Protestants in North America, 1970

Region	Total population	Christian population	Protestant population	% of region Protestant	% of Christians Protestant
North America	230,992,000	211,489,000	61,270,000	26.5%	29.0%
Global total	3,700,437,000	1,225,395,000	204,515,000	5.5%	16.7%

Source: Todd M. Johnson and Gina A. Zurlo (eds), *World Christian Database* (Leiden/Boston: Brill), accessed January 2022.

side of the Atlantic required tolerance for doctrinal diversity and constant efforts to maintain grassroots support.

In the USA, on the eve of independence, most religious adherents were Protestants, the majority of them New England Congregationalists or Anglicans in the Southern colonies. Both groups were in effect religious monopolies, established churches supported by taxation, with minimal tolerance for Baptists, Quakers or Roman Catholics. Canada's political history and settlement patterns created a more complicated situation: the Treaty of Paris in 1763 instituted a dual, bilingual establishment of French Roman Catholicism in Quebec and the Church of England in what would come to be known as Upper Canada (roughly the Province of Ontario), both under the rule of the British crown.

In the USA the Revolutionary War and the First Amendment to the Constitution led to an end of tax support for religion. The new regime was extraordinary, promising both challenge and opportunity. 'Voluntary religion', as it was called, required churches to create new mechanisms for economic support and cultural influence. They would not only have to raise their own funds, but also make a case for moral leadership in a legally secular nation.

Canada followed a different path to its own form of voluntary religion and denominational diversity. By the early nineteenth century, especially with the migration of Loyalist refugees after the American Revolution, the Anglican and Roman Catholic establishments saw a small but significant challenge from Protestants, chiefly Presbyterians, Congregationalists, Baptists and Methodists. Matters came to a head in the 1830s, in a contentious debate over the 'clergy reserves', specifically the proceeds from the sale of some 2.4 million acres of land in Upper Canada claimed by the Anglican Church (then representing about one-fifth of the population). The ultimate solution was a compromise, enacted in 1854, directing the funds to public works, in effect placing all religious groups on the same legal footing.

In both nations, the early nineteenth century saw the development of what became known as the 'benevolent empire', a vast network of schools and colleges, missionary societies and work on behalf of the poor. To a considerable degree, this extra-denominational, grassroots effort was run

Protestants in North America, 2020

Region	Total population	Christian population	Protestant population	% of region Protestant	% of Christians Protestant
North America	368,870,000	269,524,000	54,874,000	14.9%	20.4%
Global total	7,794,799,000	2,506,426,000	485,627,000	6.2%	19.4%

Source: Todd M. Johnson and Gina A. Zurlo (eds), *World Christian Database* (Leiden/Boston: Brill), accessed January 2022.

and supported by women, who comprised a consistent, solid majority of church members. Though legally disenfranchised and hampered by Victorian social convention, churchwomen proved extraordinarily adept at fundraising and building small local efforts into national ones. After the US Civil War, women's missionary organisations became a staple of North American Protestantism, and a formidable force by the early twentieth century.

Disestablishment also meant tolerating competition from other Protestant faiths, giving rise to a denominational system that has come to define mainline Protestantism in both the USA and Canada. To be sure, nineteenth-century Protestants argued, sometimes vehemently, on behalf of their own theological tenets and especially their particular polities, or systems of church government. 'Denominationalism' was a tacit agreement to accept differences in doctrine and polity – disagreements that had historically led to violence and exclusion – while standing together on what were deemed Protestant essentials.

Three basic institutional structures persist to this day. Congregationalists and most Baptists followed a simple decentralised democratic polity, giving local church members decision-making power, including the right to choose and monitor their clergy. Presbyterians and other Reformed bodies inherited from the Reformation a more formal hierarchy of local presbyteries, regional synods and a national general assembly. As with the Congregationalist/Baptist system, the Presbyterian provided oversight and credentialing of clergy, but it also took the role of a secular court system, with the authority to adjudicate in doctrinal disagreements. Methodists, an offshoot of the Anglican Church, maintained the most hierarchical polity. The Methodist Discipline gave bishops the authority to supervise clergy and to deploy them to local congregations.

For the most part, Protestants found a larger unity in common beliefs, what came to be called the 'evangelical consensus'. Before the word took on a narrower, more exclusive meaning in the twentieth century, 'evangelical' beliefs included belief in the Bible as the infallible word of God, the necessity of salvation through Christ and the responsibility of the converted to build a godly, moral world. Beyond these staples, Protestants were free to disagree over shades of meaning and the best mechanisms for promoting their beliefs. The consensus, of course, specifically excluded

Changes in Protestants in North America, 1970–2020, growth rate, % per year

Region	Total population	Christian population	Protestant population
North America	0.94%	0.49%	-0.22%
Global total	1.50%	1.44%	1.74%

Source: Todd M. Johnson and Gina A. Zurlo (eds), *World Christian Database* (Leiden/Boston: Brill), accessed January 2022.

Roman Catholics and Jews, as well as other Protestants deemed heretical or too liberal, most notably Unitarians and Universalists. Yet, on the whole, the voluntary denominational system gave religion an enormous boost, allowing Protestant churches to grow in membership and visibility. In the USA it also meant a seemingly endless possibility of variety – by current counting, the country has more than 200 different denominational bodies.

At the same time, however, the evangelical consensus was under severe duress. In the USA, the most significant break came over slavery. Three major Protestant denominations – Presbyterians, Baptists and Methodists – split into southern and northern wings in the 1840s, with theological differences amplified by angry rhetoric over the morality of 'owning' slaves or receiving donations from 'slave owners'. The damage was severe and long-lasting. While Presbyterians and Methodists reunited in the early twentieth century, Baptists are still separated and likely to remain so. Equally if not more damaging to Christian unity, the slavery debate challenged a core conviction, that the Bible's teachings were utterly clear and unambiguous to the pious reader. The truth was that both sides had marshalled the Scriptures to support their positions, each claiming their own set of competing texts.

Slavery also led to the formation of a new and distinct strain of American Protestantism, the Black church tradition. In the late eighteenth and early nineteenth centuries, Methodists and Baptists evangelised slaves with a compelling – and contradictory – message that promised spiritual redemption alongside the necessity of obedience to slave owners. For their part, African American converts not only rejected that inconsistency, they created a distinct tradition inflected by African beliefs and practices, centred on Christ as liberator and king and celebrated in ecstatic worship and song. In the North, where they were relegated to the back pews of white Protestant churches, African Americans created their own denominations – the African Methodist Episcopal (1821) and African Episcopal Methodist Zion (1821) churches – and, after the Civil War, formed their own Baptist and Methodist congregations, schools and colleges across the South. Another major Black denomination, the National Baptist Churches, USA, formed in 1895. The white mainline denominations resisted desegregation, and in the ecumenical reunions of the early twentieth century segregated their own Black members into separate conferences, most notably the Central Jurisdiction of the Methodist Episcopal Church and the Southern Conference of the Congregational Christian Churches.

The other challenge to the evangelical consensus, in both the USA and Canada, was theological. One source was biblical scholarship, originating in German universities in the early nineteenth century and filtering into North American seminaries and pulpits after the Civil War. Instead of a static and infallible word of God, the new view of the Bible emphasised its historical context and patterns of development over time. The Scriptures were not a set of immutable divine decrees but documents created by human beings wrestling with the demands of their own times and places. The so-called 'new theology' also reflected the ethical demands of the nineteenth century, as Protestants endeavoured to rework their beliefs and practices for a world increasingly shaped by the realities of scientific discovery, diverse urban populations and mounting social disorder. The significance of Jesus Christ, therefore, was not so much in his crucifixion and resurrection – his role in taking humanity's punishment for sin – as in his life and teachings, his uniquely powerful moral example. By the late nineteenth and early twentieth centuries, many Protestants had also come to understand their faith through the ethical imperatives of the social gospel, the insistence that sin and salvation were not moralistic personal categories but the framework for 'Christianising' society itself through renewal and reform.

Not everyone agreed, however. Many conservative Protestants refused to accept a historicised Bible or the idea of corporate social redemption. These dissenters came to be known as Fundamentalists (though not all accepted the category), standing for 'the faith once delivered to the saints'. That faith reflected the old evangelical consensus, but with additions, including an insistence on an inerrant Bible (not simply infallible in its teachings but free from errors of scientific or historical fact) and a system of biblical interpretation known as dispensational premillennialism, predicting an impending cataclysmic return of Christ. Opposition to evolution would also become a signal cause, fuelled by the polarisation that followed in the wake of the infamous Scopes trial in Dayton, Tennessee, in 1925. In the 1920s, these somewhat arcane doctrinal differences fuelled divisive debates primarily among northern Presbyterians and Baptists, in both cases followed by denominational schism. After the Second World War, erstwhile fundamentalists would renounce much of the world-denying separatism that had defined their cause and repurpose the old nineteenth-century term 'evangelical' to unify Protestant conservatives and differentiate themselves from moderates and liberals.

Despite the turbulence, the moderate to liberal mainline churches entered the twentieth century from a position of strength, their confidence encoded in the title of their flagship publication, *The Christian Century*, which began its publishing run in 1900. (To some, a subscription to this periodical is still a primary marker of mainline identification.)

There was good reason for optimism. The foreign missionary cause was at its height of success before the First World War, supported by the voluntary efforts of laywomen and young people answering John R.

Mott's call to 'evangelise the world in this generation'. Moreover, missionary work had grown far beyond a simple evangelistic call to conversion. Early twentieth-century Protestants proclaimed Christ through a vast network of schools and hospitals, a means of attracting converts and, more importantly, 'uplifting' non-Western societies. Indeed, North American and European Protestants rarely questioned the identification of Christianity with the fruits of Western culture, an unexamined assumption that left a decidedly ambiguous, often painful legacy, especially among Native Americans, of forced assimilation and family separation.

The other great cause of twentieth-century mainline Protestants was Christian unity. Ecumenists urged cooperation at all levels, from local councils of churches working towards the social betterment of their communities to international efforts to overcome the historic divisions of Christendom. In the USA and Canada, ecumenism was primarily a Protestant cause, aimed at reversing what many saw as the great scandal of denominational competition. The Federal Council of the Churches of Christ in America (reorganised as the National Council of Churches in 1950) was founded in 1908 with 33 member denominations, the major exceptions being Southern Baptists, Southern Presbyterians and Episcopalians. The Council's 'social creed of the churches' called for direct action to remedy the evils of the day, including the exploitation of industrial workers, especially women and children.

Ecumenical idealism also sought to overcome denominational divisions with mergers and reunions. In Canada, Presbyterians and Methodists had been pursuing unity since the late nineteenth century: the Presbyterian Church in Canada was formed in 1875 from four separated denominations, and the Methodist Church (Canada) united four groups in 1884. The creation of the United Church of Canada in 1925 was the fulfilment of long effort, harmonising historic differences in polity with a system that allowed autonomy to local congregations within a connectional system of presbyteries, regional conferences and the national General Council. The new denomination was heralded as a great success, a 'national church' representing Canadian ideals at their best.

In the USA, one major task of ecumenism was reuniting denominations divided by slavery. The Methodist Episcopal Church and Methodist Episcopal Church, South, came together, along with another smaller body, the Methodist Protestants, to form The Methodist Church in 1939. The United Church of Christ was formed in 1957, an 'organic union' of two denominations previously formed by mergers, the Evangelical and Reformed Church and the Congregational Christian Churches. Though a signal achievement, the union was marred by controversy and would prove American ecumenists' last major success.

The carnage of the First World War challenged mainline optimism but did not destroy it. Chastened by their support for a war that did little to 'make the world safe for democracy', many denominations denounced militarism and advocated pacifism. They fully supported the prohibition movement as well, convinced that alcohol was a social evil, especially as it affected the livelihoods of working men and women. During the 1920s and 1930s, under the auspices of the Federal Council of Churches, mainline churches made small steps towards racial comity, largely through efforts to promote inter-racial friendships.

The mainline churches also supported women's rights, to a degree. Though women were still the majority constituency – some two-thirds of mainline Protestant church members – they operated as an interest group, a legacy of the parallel infrastructure of women's organisations created in the post-Civil War era. Support for ordination rights grew slowly, a function of social conservatism as well as women's preference to maintain a separate power base within their denominations. Still, progress predated the rise of second-wave feminism. The United Church of Canada began ordaining women in 1930, and in the USA the Presbyterian and Methodist churches followed suit in 1956.

The years after the Second World War were in many ways the high point of mainline Protestantism's cultural power. Church membership numbers skyrocketed, along with building projects and denominational programmes. Astonishingly large numbers of people claimed belief in God and regular church attendance. Critics charged that it all amounted to 'foxhole' religion, 'the bland leading the bland' into suburban captivity. Yet in many ways, mainline churches were an important source of belonging and stability for communities undergoing rapid change.

The 1960s proved a decisive turning point. Though liberal Protestants sought to stay in step with secular culture, introducing new worship music and informal services, numbers declined precipitously – a catastrophe that historians and social scientists are still working to understand, surveyed in the penultimate section of this essay.

Mainline Beliefs and Values

Mainline Protestants are both similar to and distinct from their Evangelical cousins. The general outline of belief is the same: both affirm the existence of God, the importance and efficacy of prayer, even the possibility of heaven. Evangelicals, however, are generally more certain and more intense in their beliefs and practices. According to a recent survey by the Pew Forum on Religion and Public Life, 90% of Evangelicals are absolutely sure that God exists, as opposed to 73% of mainline Protestants; 79% of Evangelicals attest that religion is 'very important' in their lives, while 52%

of mainliners would say that same. In terms of regular church attendance, the gap between the two groups is also significant, 58% versus 34%.

Major theological differences exist as well, beginning with the use and authority of the Bible. Evangelicals regard it as the literal word of God, a sacred book without scientific or historical error. The reverse is true of mainliners, for whom the Bible is a historical text, containing timeless spiritual truths but written by fallible human beings from a specific time and place. The United Church of Christ's declaration is typical: 'We take the Bible seriously . . . not literally'.

Another dividing line has to do with religious conversion, where Evangelicals hold that a 'born again' experience is necessary for salvation. Every individual must have a personal encounter with Christ, whether in a Billy Graham crusade or in the privacy of one's home; until then, religion is not genuine. Mainline Protestants might not disagree about the importance of a personal decision but have historically relied on church institutions – Sunday school, confirmation classes – to bring individuals to faith, gradually and without coercion.

The most notorious, and often misinterpreted, differences between Evangelicals and mainline Protestants are political. In the USA, for example, the two groups are certainly distinct, but not as polarised as the nation itself. The gap is due largely to the rightward shift among Evangelicals, who were politicised in the 1970s and 1980s by organisations like the Moral Majority and Ralph Reed's Christian Coalition. They are now overwhelmingly in the Republican camp. Throughout the last century, mainline Protestants represented a moderate middle, reflecting their generally middle- to upper-middle-class constituency. Until the 1970s they were predominantly Republicans, and to a degree they remain so. Now roughly half would still identify as such, though of the 'country club Republican' variety, economically conservative and socially liberal.

Certainly, in that last respect, there is a considerable gap between the average mainline Protestants in the pews and their generally left-leaning denominational leadership; both groups, however, differ substantially from Evangelicals on key issues like abortion and LGBTQ rights, including gay marriage. Here opinion polls record directly inverse proportions. According to the Pew Forum, two-thirds of Evangelicals believe that abortion should be illegal in all or most cases and that 'homosexuality is a way of life' that society should discourage. Only a third of mainline Protestants would agree.

Still, homosexuality is a vexed issue among mainline Protestants. Many denominations actively support LGBTQ inclusion by encouraging congregations to become 'Open and Affirming' (United Church of Christ) or 'Welcoming and Affirming' (American Baptists). Since the 1970s, a constant flow of studies, reports and resolutions have affirmed that sexual orientation is a gift of God and never a bar to full Christian fellowship. Beginning with the United Church of Christ in 1975, many (though not all) mainline churches have also dropped restrictions against gay marriage and ordaining openly gay and lesbian clergy. Yet North American denominations tied to global bodies with diverse and often sharply conservative views on sexuality – Episcopalians and United Methodists in particular – remain deeply divided, even to the point of schism.

Mainline churches are more united on women's issues, including the right to ordination. Here the picture is also mixed, but certainly distinct from the prohibitions still in place in most Evangelical denominations. Moreover, it has been changing rapidly: women now account for about 20% of Protestant clergy in the USA, up from miniscule numbers as recently as 2006. That same year, Katharine Jefferts Schori became the first female bishop in the Episcopal Church. Even so, there is considerable ground to cover. Female clergy still contend with a 'stained-glass ceiling' that has kept them in smaller, often failing churches rather than major pulpits.

It is important here to point out yet again that 'mainline' and 'Evangelical' are not comprehensive categories. Not all mainliners are theological liberals, and many Evangelicals still belong to historic mainline denominations, especially those allowing for more local autonomy in decision-making. Most importantly, the categories do not even begin to account for all North American Protestants. Black Protestants, for example, are even more emphatic than Evangelicals in their certainty that God exists and that the Bible is the literal word of God. They post higher levels of church attendance and regular devotional practice and are more likely to oppose evolution and believe that the world will end soon. Yet in terms of abortion and homosexuality, they tend to split the difference between the two white Protestant camps and, not surprisingly, differ markedly from both in political affiliation – Black Protestants are overwhelmingly Democrats. In fact, regarding voting behaviour, Evangelicals and mainliners are far more similar to each other than they are to the African American churches.

Mainline Decline

A central fact of present-day mainline Protestant church life – and a consistent topic of research and debate among scholars – is its precipitous decline. The trend, which began in the 1970s, is in many respects still continuing, as a plethora of studies and statistics reveal.

The situation in Canada is the most dramatic, with the proportion of self-described Protestants falling from 41% to 27% of the population between 1971 and 2011. These membership losses are part of a general decline in church attendance in all religious bodies between the end of the Second World War and 1990 (from 67% to roughly 20%), but clearly the mainline churches are most disastrously affected. In the space of 30 years, between 1981 and 2011, the number of Canadian mainline church adherents dropped by more than 50%, and this while the population as a whole grew by 8.7 million people. The United Church of Canada has suffered some of the most acute fall-offs, losing more than half its members since the mid-1960s.

In the USA, the decline has been less dramatic, but certainly as ominous. About one-third of Americans identified as mainline Protestants in the mid-1970s; 40 years later the proportion had fallen to 1 in 10. The losses affected all the mainline denominations, but some more drastically than others: within the space of one decade, between 1960 and 1970, the United Church of Christ lost more than 12% of its membership.

Few observers failed to notice that mainline decline paralleled the rising fortunes of Evangelical and Pentecostal churches, which now account for about one-quarter of the US population (the numbers vary according to methods of computation) and about one-tenth of Canadians, a figure that has not fallen in the past several decades.

Are the two trends related? In 1972 sociologist Dean Kelley argued in his book *Why Conservative Churches Are Growing* that 'strict' faiths are intrinsically better equipped to attract and hold members. A 'costly' faith, with high standards of orthodoxy and personal morality, is simply more meaningful, more rewarding of the believer's time and effort. In contrast, Kelley argued, the liberal mainline churches were doomed to failure because they asked so little of their members. It was just too easy to walk away and never return – or to join an Evangelical fellowship where belief and behaviour mattered intensely. Kelley's argument also appeared to explain one of the most striking shifts in religious behaviour in the 1960s and 1970s: the clear attraction of Evangelical faith to younger believers.

The statistics tell a different story, however. To begin with, diffident mainline youth were not migrating to stricter, more orthodox faiths: according to sociologist Mark Chaves, only 10% of younger mainline Protestants (those born after 1970) chose to become Evangelicals. In general, mainline losses were defections from institutional religion altogether, individuals who embraced various forms of self-made spirituality or left behind any kind of religious affiliation – the group now called the 'nones'. Since the 2010s, this group has been the fastest growing in both Canada and the USA, in both cases encompassing around a quarter of the population by 2015.

There are other difficulties with the so-called 'Kelley thesis', most significantly the fact that in recent years Evangelical growth has stagnated as well. What looked like a conservative boom in the 1970s and 1980s was to a degree an index of mainline Protestant losses, perhaps even a temporary upsurge within a larger downward trend.

Many scholars contend that the mainline's problems have more to do with population demographics than a failure of will. The period of decline, in fact, tracks a downward trend in fertility among members of the largely white, middle-class liberal churches and an increase among Evangelical ones – a statistical fact, argues Chaves, that accounts for 80% of the membership differences. Mainline churches also do not benefit, as they once did, from patterns of denominational 'switching'. Rising levels of education and income among Evangelicals have allowed them to hold on to members, including young people, whom they once lost to liberal denominations. In other words, social climbing no longer requires moving up from Pentecostal to Episcopalian.

Mainline Protestants are also not likely to receive an influx of immigrant Christians from the faith's new strongholds in Asia, Africa and South America. In general, the proportion of foreign-born congregants in white Protestant churches has declined since the 1960s, and contemporary surveys show that about half of mainliners hold negative views about immigration – below that of Evangelicals (at two-thirds), but hardly a progressive trend. In terms of immigration-spurred diversity, the mainline churches are the reverse of Roman Catholicism and Pentecostalism, both of which are becoming less white and more culturally diverse. The statistical gap is an irony of history. For much of the twentieth century, mainline Protestants opposed restrictive immigration quotas and actively welcomed war refugees. In the 1970s and 1980s, liberation theologians like Gustavo Gutierrez and Paulo Freire were standards in mainline seminary education, and liberal denominations sought inclusivity by elevating persons of colour into leading positions. Yet, as recent division and upheaval among Episcopalians and United Methodists have demonstrated, global Christianity is not an easy fit for the liberal mainline, especially around culturally sensitive issues of sexuality and sexual identity. The mainline Protestant churches are more than 90% white and are likely to remain so.

Clearly, the reasons for mainline decline are complex, reflecting larger secularisation trends in Europe and North America. Whether or not Europe is a spiritual bellwether, representing the future of Christianity in other Western nations, there is no doubt that religion as a whole is facing challenging times.

Conclusion

If the mainline churches are not able to recover, much will be lost, and not just among specifically religious interests. Historically, the 'old-line' denominations have been important community institutions, and many remain so today, housing food pantries, day care centres and health clinics. They host Red Cross blood drives and addiction support groups, local artists and advocacy organisations. As attendance numbers for the Sunday morning service have fallen, non-profit groups have often reaped the benefits of large, under-used church buildings.

The loss is also to society in general. The mainline churches have long sustained the 'moderate middle' in politics and civic life, a category built on the virtues of cooperation and compromise. They have been institution builders, adept at establishing and maintaining a network of schools, hospitals and churches founded decades, even centuries, ago.

In fact, some scholars argue that in the long run the mainline churches have been astonishingly successful. Historian David Hollinger has described the 'boomerang effect' of foreign missions on the USA, as the sons and daughters of missionary families brought back knowledge of non-Western languages and cultural practices, and, even more critically, respect for their humanity. A 2010 study by Robert Putnam and David Campbell demonstrates that what we might call mainline values, particularly tolerance for religious differences and a practice of public civility, have gained broad currency in North American culture. They are still near the top of the 'feeling thermometer', measuring the general regard for religious groups by outsiders. The story is far from over, of course. Mainline churches might well benefit from their present adversity, gaining the wisdom and moral solidarity that often come with life as a religious minority – qualities that are always in short supply, and a critical necessity in the world today.

Bibliography

Chaves, Mark, *American Religion: Contemporary Trends* (Princeton, NJ: Princeton University Press, 2011).

Hutchison, William R. (ed.), *Between the Times: The Travail of the Protestant Establishment in America, 1900–1960* (Cambridge, MA: Harvard University Press, 1989).

Pew Research Center, 'America's Changing Religious Landscape', 12 May 2015 <https://www.pewforum.org/2015/05/12/americas-changing-religious-landscape>.

Pew Research Center. 'Canada's Changing Religious Landscape', 27 June 2013 <https://www.pewforum.org/2013/06/27/canadas-changing-religious-landscape>.

Putnam, Robert and David Campbell, *American Grace: How Religion Divides and Unites Us* (New York: Simon and Schuster, 2010).

Catholics

Christine Way Skinner

Geographical expansiveness and historical genesis in both colonisation and immigration make the North American Catholic Church diverse and complex. While the USA, Canada, Greenland, Bermuda and Saint Pierre and Miquelon each manifest distinct characteristics, there remains, nevertheless, an enduring unity among Catholics on the continent. An outsider to the faith attending Mass one Sunday in Greenland and the next in the Southern United States would not find the experience notably different. A Catholic would feel at home whether worshipping on the island of Bermuda or on Vancouver Island, British Columbia. In this regard, the Roman Catholic Church in North America is reflective of the universal Catholic Church.

Greenland

Leaving aside legends of St Brendan sailing to North America in the sixth century, historical accounts indicate that the first Catholic on the continent was Viking explorer Leif Erikson. Commanded by the King of Norway to bring Catholicism to Greenland, he, and an unnamed priest, established the first Catholic community there around 1000 CE. These colonies would soon become extinct and Roman Catholics would not return to Greenland until almost 1,000 years later. With colonisation by the Danish government came Lutheranism as the national religion. Following a declaration of religious freedom in 1953, a small Roman Catholic community was re-established near the capital city, Nuuk. Today, it has only 50 registered members, around 0.2% of the population. Only four are native Greenlanders; the others are foreigners affiliated with the nearby US military base. All belong to Krist Konge Kirke (Christ the King Church) and are under the jurisdiction of the Diocese of Copenhagen in Denmark. This includes a small convent of three sisters established in 1980 by the Sisters of Jesus.

The USA and Canada

The vast majority of North American Catholics live in the USA and Canada. In both countries, Catholics constitute the single largest religious community. The USA is home to more than 73.9 million Catholics, about 23% of the total population. The country is divided into 177 Latin Rite dioceses (including an Archdiocese for the Military) and 18 Eastern Catholic eparchies. A Personal Ordinariate of the Chair of Saint Peter serves Anglican clergy in both the USA and Canada who have joined the Roman communion while retaining elements of their Anglican heritage. Bishops number 433, of whom 15 are cardinals. Less-populous Canada has 14.1 million Catholics comprising around 37% of the population. It contains 59 Latin Catholic dioceses and 12 Eastern Rite eparchies. Canadians are served by 79 bishops, four of whom are cardinals. While Canadian and American Catholics share many commonalities, their cultures remain distinct and they have been formed by very different histories.

The oldest Catholic churches in the USA are the legacy of Spanish mission effort. Conquistadores entered the southern part of the continent in the 1500s with intense brutality towards the Indigenous peoples. The introduction of the faith nearly 100 years later was impeded by resistance (often violent) rooted in memories of Spanish cruelty as well as diseases they brought with them that decimated the Indigenous population. In the 1600s, Franciscan missionaries met with more success, primarily due to their strategy of converting native leaders. While missionaries condemned some of the worst excesses of the Spanish government, they also engaged in their own maltreatment of Indigenous populations. A glance at the city names in the Southwestern United States and along the California coast provides a roadmap of these missions – San Antonio, Santa Fe, San Francisco, San Diego and Los Angeles. Indigenous Catholics in the USA today number above 700,000 (approximately 3.5% of all Catholics and 20% of Native Americans). Most are concentrated in the Diocese of Gallup covering New Mexico and Arizona. Hispanic people, the largest minority in the USA, form 35% of the Catholic population. In recent years many are joining Evangelical Protestant churches, mirroring similar trends in Latin America.

Meanwhile, on the East Coast, Catholics were latecomers. At the cusp of the American Revolution in 1775, they made up only 1% of the population. Colonial British Protestants, many of whom had emigrated to the New World to escape religious persecution in Europe, had imported their fear of 'papist' religion to their new home. Fear that Catholics, overly influenced

Catholics in North America, 1970

Region	Total population	Christian population	Catholic population	% of region Catholic	% of Christians Catholic
North America	230,992,000	211,489,000	57,384,000	24.8%	27.1%
Global total	3,700,437,000	1,225,395,000	657,128,000	17.8%	53.6%

Source: Todd M. Johnson and Gina A. Zurlo (eds), *World Christian Database* (Leiden/Boston: Brill), accessed January 2022.

by Rome, would interfere with American freedom meant that they were excluded from political and civic life and were even targets of violence. Slowly, however, Catholics gained a place in mainstream America, though anti-Catholic prejudice prevailed in the USA until around the 1960s. The election in 1961 of John F. Kennedy – the first Catholic President of the USA – was a sign that it was possible to be fully Catholic and fully American. Rome, for its part, was suspicious of American Catholicism. In 1899, Pope Leo XIII condemned 'Americanism' in his encyclical *Testem Benevolentiae* and cautioned against accommodating Church teaching to accord 'with the spirit of the age'. US Catholics, such as the founder of the Paulist Fathers, Fr Isaac Hecker, and theologian John Courtney Murray, had made great efforts to understand their faith in relation to American values of pluralism, civil liberty and democracy.

Catholicism emerged quite differently in Canada. The first settlers were French Catholics, and the Church was well established by the end of the 1600s. British settlers also appeared in the seventeenth century. As in the USA, they imported their prejudice against Catholics. With the Treaty of Paris (1763), New France had become British North America and British Protestant rule was in place. Catholics were granted limited freedom to practise their religion but the French Catholic Church, which had operated freely, was in a decidedly more restricted position. When the Dominion of Canada was established in 1867, Catholics made up about 42% of the population. Being such a large minority has meant that Catholics in Canada have always been in a stronger position than their neighbours to the south. Nevertheless, anti-Catholic sentiment has been present and has flared with waves of immigration and in areas where Catholics were a smaller minority.

Saint Pierre and Miquelon

The Treaty of Paris also permitted France to retain fishing rights off the coast of Newfoundland, where they had been fishing since the early 1500s. Additionally, France was allowed to retain the islands of Saint Pierre and Miquelon in the Gulf of St Lawrence as a fishing station. Officially a self-governing 'territorial overseas collectivity' rather than a country, its residents are French citizens. Today, the population of 5,800 people is 97%

Catholics in North America, 2020

Region	Total population	Christian population	Catholic population	% of region Catholic	% of Christians Catholic
North America	368,870,000	269,524,000	88,015,000	23.9%	32.7%
Global total	7,794,799,000	2,506,426,000	1,239,271,000	15.9%	49.4%

Source: Todd M. Johnson and Gina A. Zurlo (eds), *World Christian Database* (Leiden/Boston: Brill), accessed January 2022.

Roman Catholic. The island is under the ecclesiastical jurisdiction of the French Diocese of La Rochelle and Saintes. Four churches are served by six or seven missionary priests and a community of religious women – the Sisters of St Joseph of Cluny.

Bermuda

Bermuda was the last of the North American countries to host a Roman Catholic population. Though the Portuguese and Spanish had found rest on the island for hundreds of years, it was finally colonised by the English in the 1600s. Like elsewhere, colonisers were committed to preserving the faith of England against the 'heresies' of atheists, papists and Anabaptists. Catholics in Bermuda today belong to the Diocese of Hamilton (established 12 June 1967) – a member of the Antilles Episcopal Conference. Before this, as part of British North America, Bermuda had belonged to the Diocese of Halifax-Yarmouth in the Canadian province of Nova Scotia. Thus, it was from Halifax that missionaries came in the mid-1840s – when there were just over 60 Catholics. That population increased with the establishment of a British naval base and penal colony housed on a ship moored just off the island. The percentage of Catholic prisoners rose sharply during the Irish famine as the desperately poor had turned to theft to feed themselves and their families. At the turn of the century, at the request of Catholic soldiers, a school was established by four Sisters of Charity of St Vincent de Paul from Halifax. This original school still exists and has an enrolment of about 350 students from kindergarten to grade 12. When the Diocese of Hamilton was founded, pastoral responsibility was transferred to the Congregation of the Resurrection, who continue to serve there. The diocese is divided into six parishes, each with its own church. As of 2019, around 9,300 Catholics in Bermuda comprise 14.5% of the population. At that time, they were served by three priests, two deacons and two religious women. In 2022 the sisters ended their service there. Masses are offered in English and Portuguese (who make up 25% of the Catholic community).

Leadership and Clergy Shortages

Today, the critical shortage of clergy is cause for great anxiety in the North American Church. After the Second Vatican Council (1962–5), about

Changes in Catholics in North America, 1970–2020, growth rate, % per year

Region	Total population	Christian population	Catholic population
North America	0.94%	0.49%	0.86%
Global total	1.50%	1.44%	1.28%

Source: Todd M. Johnson and Gina A. Zurlo (eds), *World Christian Database* (Leiden/Boston: Brill), accessed January 2022.

10% of priests left within the first 10 years alone. Today, the typical ratio of priests to active Catholics is 1:2,000 (exponentially more if inactive members are included). Post-pandemic estimates indicate that about 3,500 parishes have no priest.

Historically, clergy shortages in North America are not exceptional. The problem arises in every era and has sometimes been even more desperate. Frontier Catholics might have seen a priest once in their lifetimes. In the past, bishops turned to European religious communities of men and women for aid. But with a parallel shortage in Europe, bishops are turning to former mission territories where Christianity is growing – Africa and Asia especially. This has had the positive effect of creating a more diverse, global Catholicism in North America. There are, however, corresponding language and cultural barriers which can hamper effective ministry.

The restoration of the permanent diaconate has also helped. Virtually unheard of 30 years ago, permanent deacons are common in parishes today. They are usually married men with another primary career who serve the Church part time in ministries of preaching, baptising and presiding at non-Eucharistic weddings and burials. Some serve as hospital and prison chaplains. Though currently restricted to males, the Vatican is considering the question of ordaining women to the diaconate – an appealing prospect for many North American Catholics.

Bishops are also looking to the laity. The Second Vatican Council emphasised the universal call to holiness and admitted that the clergy 'were not ordained by Christ to take upon themselves alone the entire salvific mission of the Church towards the world' (*Lumen Gentium*, 31). This and the call to 'full, conscious and active participation' prompted a burgeoning of lay ministry in North America. Professionally trained lay ecclesial ministers took on roles previously held only by religious women and clergy. In the USA today, nearly 40,000 laypeople serve in paid positions in American parishes, and 312 parishes are run by pastoral administrators – deacons or laity – in the absence of a priest. Numbers are not available for Canada, but a scan of parish websites demonstrates that the situation is similar. The creation of the (US) National Association of Lay Ministry (1977) heralded the increasing recognition and institutionalisation of the role. Despite low wages and minimal job security, lay ecclesial ministers serve the Church effectively, often bridging a gap between priest and parishioners.

Women's religious orders have also experienced fundamental change. Traditionally teachers or nurses, nuns, like their counterparts in the secular world, found opportunities opening up to women. They became doctors, lawyers and theologians. Many minister to those marginalised by society (such as refugees) or by the Church (such as LGBTQ+ people). Numbers have dwindled drastically, though, and many religious orders dissolved, amalgamated or downsized – a trend expected to continue.

Evangelising and Humanising the World
Fewer sisters in teaching and nursing has meant changes for Catholic health-care providers and educators. Catholic hospitals remain the largest private health-care provider in the USA. As part of its universal health-care system, Canadian Catholic hospitals are publicly funded. Secular and ecclesial positions on medical ethics increasingly diverge, and this has raised many issues, including rights of conscience for medical professionals.

Catholic education remains strong. In the USA, Catholic elementary and secondary schools are private. Efforts to acquire government funding have been historically contentious and, apart from allowing for tax credits, very little government support has been given. The vibrancy of religious education in the USA is displayed at the annual Los Angeles Religious Education Conference – the largest of its kind in the world – drawing 40,000 participants annually. In Canada, the British North America Act that established the nation placed education in the hands of the provinces, with the caveat that they must uphold the right to denominational schools. The Charter of Rights and Freedoms of 1982 further affirmed these rights. While some provinces chose not to exercise that right, Alberta, Ontario and Saskatchewan have retained publicly funded Catholic school systems. In 1999, the United Nations Human Rights Committee declared that Canada violated Article 26 of the International Covenant on Civil and Political Rights by not offering parallel funding to members of other religious groups. While Catholics continue to be a sizeable minority, this is unlikely to change, partly because the removal of a constitutionally protected minority right by a majority is regarded as setting a dangerous precedent.

Contrary to secular criticism, Catholic schools are mostly places of free enquiry. This partly derives from the high value placed by North American Catholics on individual conscience and freedom of expression. In Canada, it might also be related to the need, as publicly funded institutions, to abide by the requirements of secular law. For instance, when the Ontario government enacted the Accepting Schools Act, which mandated support for LGBTQ+ students in all publicly funded schools, the majority of Catholic schools developed fulsome support systems. This has, unsurprisingly, been controversial, provoking claims by some Catholics that this contradicts official Church teaching.

As the practice of faith has declined dramatically and religious literacy is diminished, Catholic schools have become places of evangelisation – the primary place where children encounter Church teaching, learn prayer and even attend Mass. This has been concerning to Church leaders and requires strong parish–school partnerships to avoid schools taking on roles properly belonging to the parish. In response, a gradual metamorphosis is occurring in parish programming. Many on the continent have embraced Pope John II's 'new evangelism' focusing on inviting Catholics to reclaim their baptismal faith. An enduring opportunity for this exists when peripheral Catholics persistently return to the Church for sacraments of initiation.

As evangelisation is increasingly required *ad intra*, the nature of traditional mission *ad extra* has changed. It was only in 1908 that Rome ceased to regard North America as mission territory. But already, in the nineteenth century, Canada and the USA had begun sending out their own missionaries. Thousands travelled to serve in nearly 100 countries. The nature of missionary activity has recently undergone a radical re-evaluation due to a number of factors: the Church's modern social teaching (*Rerum Novarum* 1891 and *Quadragesimo Anno* 1931), new understandings of evangelisation and religious freedom after the Second Vatican Council, and secular post-colonial critiques. The concentration is now on human development and social justice rather than proselytising.

In both countries, social activism is vital and takes many shapes: Quebec bishops financially supporting striking asbestos workers, the Berrigan brothers destroying draft records to protest against the Vietnam War, Fr James Martin building bridges between the Church and LGBTQ+ Catholics, Dorothy Day and Peter Maurin establishing the Catholic Worker Movement, Caesar Chavez organising the United Farm Workers and Fr Moses Coady creating a cooperative movement to assist the economically depressed fishers in Nova Scotia. Church leaders speak about social issues, provide guidance for Catholic voters and occasionally take a public stand on particular issues.

The Second Vatican Council
The Second Vatican Council, held in the 1960s, was a pivotal point for the universal Roman Catholic Church. Its reforms were all-encompassing. Most significantly, the understanding of the Church changed. Notions of the Church as a perfect society, in opposition to the world, were discarded in favour of conceptions of a Christian community deeply engaged in human history, sharing in its joys and hopes, griefs and anxieties. North American bishops were a progressive voice at the Council. Archbishop Léger of Canada had significant influence in the areas of liturgy, ecumenism and ecclesiology. American John Courtney Murray as the theological adviser to Cardinal Spellman was largely responsible for the Declaration on Religious Freedom.

The Second Vatican Council was received by North American Catholics with a mix of shock and excitement. Though it was broadly welcomed, favourable reception was not universal, and this has been a source of great division in North America. Some believe the Council brought long-overdue revitalisation that still requires further implementation. Others blame it for contemporary dissent and disaffiliation. Polarisation has been consistently increasing, despite some efforts to promote ecclesial unity (such as the 1996 Catholic Common Ground Project). This division is so conspicuous in the US episcopacy that fears of schism have been raised. It was already considered 'perilous' in 1996. On the one side are bishops who favour liturgical traditionalism (even a return to the Latin Mass), oppose gay marriage and support the denial of communion to pro-choice politicians. They counsel obedience to Church teaching and lament widespread dissent (despite their vocal and public criticism of Pope Francis and their brother bishops). Many of these bishops were appointed by theologically conservative Popes John Paul II and Benedict XVI. On the other side are bishops who favour a more moderate approach. They support the Council's liturgical reforms, oppose communion bans, speak about social justice and generally allow for some moral and theological complexity among the laity. There have been liberal prelates in the USA in the past 50 years, but many of them are now elderly or have died. A scan of official publications by the United States Conference of Catholic Bishops (USCCB) suggests a transition in priorities over the past 50 years from themes of peace and social justice to concerns about theological orthodoxy and devotional practice.

Both Canada and the USA expressly support the separation of church and state. Held more in principle than in practice, this looks different in each country. Catholic inclusion in public life in the USA was a hard-won battle and Catholic politicians often still feel they must reiterate their independence from Church influence. But Catholics now hold public roles throughout the political structure and are split evenly between the two major parties, Republican and Democratic. The values of American Catholics tend to align more readily with political parties than with their faith. Historically, Catholics tended to support Democrats, whose policies corresponded with the social teaching of the Church. (Both American Catholic presidents have been Democrats.) A shift happened after the sexual revolution of the 1960s, when Democrats began supporting policies contravening Catholic moral positions on sexuality and life issues. Today, Conservative Catholics tend to focus on moral teaching, especially around sexuality, and support the Republican Party. Liberal Catholics embrace Catholic social teaching and support the Democrats. (This has had the unintended ecumenical result of aligning Catholics with Protestants of similar political affiliations.)

By contrast, in Canada, Roman Catholics have always participated at the highest levels of government. Ten of the 23 prime ministers of Canada have been Catholic. Of these, eight were members of the centrist Liberal Party. Canadian Catholics historically have tended to vote Liberal, but today they wear all political stripes.

Theological and political division within the Church, like clergy shortages, is nothing new. Historically, prelates have been embroiled in a variety of disputes – sometimes viciously so. What is new in contemporary North America is the universal access to instantaneous global communication. Through social media, the Catholic people (including their leaders) have become active participants in the American 'culture wars', making division in the Church more public than at any other time in history. Particularly active are groups like the Eternal Word Television Network (EWTN) a well-funded and neo-conservative American Catholic religious media network that has become the largest of its kind in the world. Liberal Catholics have nothing comparable. Furthermore, in 2022 the USCCB decided to close its Catholic News Service, upon which many relied for balanced reporting of ecclesial affairs.

While similar divisions exist in Canada, Canadian bishops as a collective differ from their US counterparts. More reticent about public controversy, it is hard to imagine the public episcopal disputes of the USA occurring in today's Canadian Church. (Such conflicts certainly have historical precedence, however – especially in Quebec.) Furthermore, Canadian Catholics tend to be slightly more progressive. An Angus Reid poll in 2013 found that 60–70% of Canadian Catholics hoped for a liberal successor to Pope Benedict XVI, while Americans measured at 47–51%. Bishop Remi de Roo, who died in 2022, spoke publicly in favour of women's ordination. As well, in 1968, when Pope Paul VI published the encyclical *Humanae Vitae*, forbidding all forms of artificial contraception, the Canadian Catholic bishops issued a statement reassuring Catholics that they could follow their conscience even if it differed somewhat from the vision of the encyclical.

Dissent and Disaffiliation

The promulgation of *Humanae Vitae* was a pivotal point for Catholic dissent. For many, including the North Americans who were part of the Vatican study commission, it spoke of authoritarianism, rigidity and a hierarchy disconnected from its people. Its poor reception very likely precipitated dissent in other areas. Most dissent relates to the Church's teaching on sexuality and gender (the role of women, clerical celibacy, the marriage of non-heterosexuals, divorce, birth control and abortion). The ordination of women has become particularly contentious and has many advocates among women religious.

Nothing can compare, however, to the shattering of credibility that has taken place by the scandals surrounding the Church's participation in colonialism and clerical sexual abuse. These have shaken the faith of otherwise steadfast and committed Catholics. In 2021, the discovery of more than 1,000 unmarked graves in a residential school in western Canada brought to light the horrible legacy of the Church's treatment of Indigenous people. The schools, which numbered 193 in Canada (the last of which closed as recently as 1996), were characterised by physical, emotional and sexual abuse. Parallel 'Indian boarding schools' numbered about 350 in the USA and lasted until the 1960s; 84 were administered by Catholic religious orders. The template for these schools was the Carlisle Indian Industrial School in Pennsylvania, founded in 1879 with the motto 'Kill the Indian, save the man'. In 2015 the Canadian government's Truth and Reconciliation Commission's report called this cultural genocide. Both the Canadian and US bishops have acknowledged and apologised for their roles in these schools and are making efforts towards healing and reconciliation. In 2022, a delegation of Indigenous leaders met with Pope Francis in Rome, when he issued an apology for the damage the Church caused to First Nations people and agreed to a follow-up visit that summer.

Indigenous Catholics increasingly find ways to honour their Indigenous heritage by incorporating Native images and traditional rituals into Catholic worship and by promoting Indigenous holy people such as St Kateri Tekakwitha and Nicholas Black Elk. It has been an important affirmation for Native Catholics, whose Church has for centuries not only failed to see them as holy but attempted to strip them of their culture. The legacies of North American saints remain paradoxical. When Pope Francis canonised Spanish missionary Junípero Serra, acknowledging the complicated history of Christian missionary efforts, he received mixed reactions. Some saw the canonisation as an affirmation of the Hispanic and Indigenous people while others viewed it as an attempt to sanitise colonial history.

North American Catholics are also coming to terms with a shameful history of anti-Black racism. The US Church, including religious orders of men and women, were major slaveholders in several states and operated segregated schools, hospitals, and even convents and seminaries. At least one bishop in Louisiana argued that the enslavement of Africans was divinely ordained. (He was forced by Rome to retract his letter.) Before the Civil War, no prominent Catholic leader publicly advocated the abolition of slavery and only a single bishop publicly supported the Thirteenth Amendment to the Constitution, abolishing slavery.

By the 1950s, both Black and white Catholics participated in the civil rights movement, and during the 2020 Black Lives Matter action, the

Canadian Conference of Catholic Bishops and the USCCB released statements condemning racism. Currently, six Black American Catholics are candidates for canonisation. One of these is Sr Thea Bowman, who helped found the National Black Sisters Conference, promoted Black liturgical music and gave an impassioned address on racism to the US bishops in 1989. The National Black Catholic Clergy Caucus has been instrumental in encouraging the Church to address issues of racism, which three-quarters of Black Catholics believe is essential to their faith. Significant work remains to be done. There are around three million Black Catholics in the USA. This is about 4% of Catholics. Black clergy comprise only 1% of priests and there is only one Black cardinal – Wilton Gregory (named in 2020). Canada does share the same history of slavery as the USA. In fact, since slavery was illegal in Canada, it became a refuge for escaped American slaves. However, Canadians, too, have a history of racism which they are just beginning to address.

The sexual abuse scandal has been devastating to the North American Church. The revelation during the 1980s of sexual abuse of minors and its cover-up by both Church and government in Newfoundland was the first in a series of incriminating reports that continue to emerge, exposing abuse and complicity at the highest levels of the hierarchy, including bishops and cardinals. A study commissioned by the US bishops found that between 1950 and 2002 there had been 10,667 complaints of sexual abuse against 4,392 priests and deacons. Most occurred in the 1970s and 1980s; prior to the 1960s, reports are rare. It is unclear whether this means abuse was less common or simply unreported. (In 1789, a letter from a US bishop expresses frustration that several priests sent from Europe had been charged with sexual offences.)

The hierarchy in both Canada and the USA has responded in a variety of ways – commissioning both internal and independent studies, implementing more rigorous protocols for screening clergy and lay volunteers as well as for dealing with reports of abuse, allotting monetary settlements to victims, setting up support groups for victims and, in a few cases, publishing names of credibly accused Church workers. Nevertheless, the scourge persists. Lay groups have been formed to support victims and work for ecclesial reform. Catholics – laity and hierarchy alike – are divided on their analysis. Some attribute the crisis to lax morals and, incorrectly, to homosexuality in the priesthood. Others blame clericalism, celibacy and the restriction of ordination to men. While the causes are complex, what is undeniable is that these scandals have led to an acute level of mistrust of the hierarchy.

Many people have left. Thus, not only dissent but also disaffiliation are pressing issues for Catholicism in North America. While disaffiliation is occurring across Christian denominations, Catholics are losing members most rapidly. A 2014 Pew Research study found that 12% of Catholics said that they had left the Church. Meanwhile, the number of people who identify as having no religious affiliation ('nones') has risen to about 24% from almost zero since the 1960s. Most of these are under the age of 35. Attendance at religious services, even for those who still identify as Catholic, has plummeted. From 1955 to 1998, weekly Roman Catholic Church attendance in the USA dropped from 75% to 44%, and in Canada, from 87% to 36%.

In Canada, secularisation and disaffiliation began earlier than elsewhere during what has come to be called the 'Quiet Revolution', as Québécois Catholics left the Church at an exponential rate and the Catholic Church began to hand over control of most of its schools, hospitals and other social service agencies. The province's secularity is evidenced in its 2019 law banning public employees from wearing religious symbols in the workplace.

A Global North American Church

Immigration has always been a major factor in the growth of Catholicism in North America. This is true today more than ever. The USA is the top destination for migration in the world; Canada is eighth. In Los Angeles (the most populous diocese in the USA), Sunday Mass is offered in 42 languages. In Toronto (the most populous in Canada), the number is 34. Catholic parishes often celebrate their ethnic heritage with devotional traditions from their homeland.

Each year sees more than a million immigrants enter US territory. In 2020, the foreign-born immigrant population was 85.7 million (or 26% of the total population). In 2018 the top four countries of origin were China, India, Mexico and the Philippines, but people come from all over the world. Canada's annual numbers (among the highest rate in the world) are around 300,000 people. In 2018, the country welcomed 321,045 migrants. In that same year, it accepted more refugees than any other country, including the USA. The top four countries of origin are India, China, the Philippines and Nigeria but, as with the USA, people arrive from everywhere.

Immigrant Catholics tend to be more committed to the practice of the faith than those born in North America and are a source of ministerial vocations. As well, Chinese immigrants are joining the Church at an astonishing rate. Easter adult baptisms in two Toronto-area Chinese Catholic Churches have numbered between 100 and 250 every year since at least 2007. As the ageing Catholic baby-boomers of colonial European descent disappear, their places are being filled by a new set of immigrants from

Asia and the global south where Catholicism is growing. The North American Catholic Church is becoming the global Catholic Church within North America.

As the Roman Catholic Church in North America moves forward, it will do so with new pastoral demands and a different appearance. Its solid cultural infrastructure – well suited to Europeans – will require renovation. It will proceed humbled by the revelation of its failings but perhaps purified to preach more credibly the Gospel of God's Reign that has always been at its centre.

Bibliography

Fay, Terence J., *A History of Canadian Catholics: Gallicanism, Romanism, and Canadianism* (Montreal: McGill-Queen's University Press, 2002).

Killen, Patricia O'Connell and Mark Silk, *The Future of Catholicism in America* (New York: Columbia University Press, 2019).

Reid, Angus and Reginald Wayne Bibby, *Canada's Catholics: Vitality and Hope in a New Era* (Toronto: Novalis, 2016).

Steinfels, Peter, *A People Adrift: The Crisis of the Roman Catholic Church in America* (New York: Simon and Schuster, 2004).

Tentler, Leslie Woodcock, *American Catholics: A History* (New Haven, CT: Yale University Press, 2020).

Evangelicals

Soong-Chan Rah

Defining Evangelicalism as uniquely expressed in the context of North America presents an elusive task. The label applies varyingly in different settings as a political, social, ecclesial or theological term. North American Evangelicalism does not follow the typical rules of an institution with clear boundaries of membership, leadership and structure. However, despite the movement's amorphous nature, general agreement may be determined regarding key characteristics of Evangelicalism in North America, particularly in its US iteration. These characteristics have produced a vital movement and a self-conscious tradition but also provided a problematic label for application and study in the twenty-first century.

This essay offers a snapshot of the unique expression of the current iteration of US Evangelicalism (and its larger formation and impact in North America) that emerged in the latter part of the twentieth century. The early expressions of North American Evangelicalism stressed theological distinctives. However, the identity of the US Evangelical became more aligned with sociological categories than theological boundaries. The shift in more recent years has been the identification of US Evangelical as almost exclusively a political designation, moving beyond even the sociological categories. In this essay, I use the term 'Evangelicalism' with a capital 'E' to distinguish the particular and specific expression of Protestant Christianity that becomes a distinct movement in the latter part of the twentieth century in the USA from a small 'e' evangelicalism that defines a larger movement of theologically conservative Protestantism that spans several centuries.

Theological Boundaries

Evangelicals perceive themselves in the line of orthodoxy that traces back to biblical times. Evangelicals are the inheritors of orthodox Christianity from the chosen line evident in Genesis (Adam, Abel, Seth, Enoch, Noah, Abraham, Isaac and Jacob), to the chosen nation of Israel (Moses, Joshua, David and the faithful prophets), to the new covenant community (the New Testament church) birthed in Acts 2, to the missionary efforts of the Apostle Paul, to the early church and its martyrs, to the empowered missionary activist church that succeeds the early church, to the faithful remnant in the context of the Roman captivity of the church, to the great Protestant Reformers proclaiming *sola fide* and *sola Scriptura*, to those who seek a pure faith on the canvas of a *tabula rasa*, to the chosen people seeking to establish a city set on a hill, to the experiencers of great revivals (exemplified by Whitefield, Edwards, Spurgeon and extending to Wesley and Finney), to the great missionaries of the great mission century, to the dynamic evangelists calling for personal conversion (Billy Graham) and finally to the faithful remnant who serve as cultural warriors in the midst of the collapse of Christendom. Evangelicalism transcends denominations, integrating the Lutheran, Presbyterian and Reformed churches that trace their heritage to the Protestant Reformation; the passion of the Pietists, Puritans and Pentecostals; the mission emphasis of the Moravians and the Methodists; and those who claim to seek guidance from the Bible only, such as the Baptists and the Brethren. Evangelicals will consistently read the framework of their faith back into the history of Christian orthodoxy as the inheritors and protectors of that orthodoxy.

This self-perception of orthodoxy provides strong and seemingly firm boundaries for Evangelicals but these often prove to be fluid between the various threads of Evangelicalism. A few common theological and ecclesial boundaries may be discerned, such as a high view of Scripture, a high Christology with a cruci-centric emphasis, a belief in the importance of conversion, and an active and revivalistic faith, which is all encased in a trans-denominational movement. All five of these characteristics help shape and define twentieth-century North American Evangelical Christianity in mostly theological and ecclesial terms. Evangelicals assumed that they were part of a larger historical movement with a solid theological framework and foundation. Evangelicals would place a high value on understanding their faith as an orthodox movement that is rooted in theological acuity.

Evangelicalism's theological roots, however, have particularly Western and even uniquely North American framing. For example, the desire to retain their self-perceived role of preserving orthodoxy is informed by certain intellectual assumptions. The early iteration of US democracy was influenced by Scottish Common Sense philosophy, which also played a prominent role in the formation of North American Protestantism. Scottish

Evangelicals in North America, 1970

Region	Total population	Christian population	Evangelical population	% of region Evangelical	% of Christians Evangelical
North America	230,992,000	211,489,000	47,457,000	20.5%	22.4%
Global total	3,700,437,000	1,225,395,000	111,669,000	3.0%	9.1%

Source: Todd M. Johnson and Gina A. Zurlo (eds), *World Christian Database* (Leiden/Boston: Brill), accessed January 2022.

Common Sense philosophy asserts the human capacity to attain common knowledge through rational thought. Evangelical theology rooted in this philosophy assumes a level of reasonableness and perspicuity. Even as the culture around them changes, Evangelicals assert a positive self-perception of the thought processes that formed their theology. Evangelicals would view their own epistemology as a rational system in contrast to modern liberalism's reliance on unproven hypotheses. Any potential adaptation to a changing culture, therefore, would be subsumed under the assumption that a bounded set of rational assumptions should not be challenged. The fundamental theological assertions of Evangelical faith would serve as non-negotiable tenets of orthodox faith. Truth to the Evangelical was a possessed truth, outlined by historical orthodoxy, and defined by the rational mind of the US Evangelical. Possessed truth should not be challenged, nor should it yield its lofty position to any challengers.

The colonial evangelical assumption that European Christians in the 'New World' were part of a manifest destiny to take the city on a hill from sea to shining sea became embedded in the worldview of US Christianity. Nineteenth-century evangelicals assumed they were building a new Jerusalem on the *tabula rasa* of the American canvas so they participated in civil reforms and activism. For evangelicals at this time, their God-given mission demanded the proclamation of the gospel through conversionist revivalism and a demonstration of the gospel through social action.

By the turn of the twentieth century, American Protestantism began to splinter along theological lines. Theological liberals who embraced the new science of Darwinism and questioned the literal veracity of biblical miracles were viewed as suspicious by those who viewed themselves as theologically conservative. Many liberals who identified with the social gospel movement energetically carried out justice activism as the centrepiece of their mission but de-emphasised evangelistic proclamation. In reaction, evangelicals vehemently rejected evolution and preached even stricter views of biblical inerrancy. The focus for those who identified as theological conservative evangelicals turned to the priority of global missions and personal evangelism. The proclamation of the gospel was the highest priority and orthodox faith needed to be preached faithfully.

Evangelicals in North America, 2020

Region	Total population	Christian population	Evangelical population	% of region Evangelical	% of Christians Evangelical
North America	368,870,000	269,524,000	71,102,000	19.3%	26.4%
Global total	7,794,799,000	2,506,426,000	387,026,000	5.0%	15.4%

Source: Todd M. Johnson and Gina A. Zurlo (eds), *World Christian Database* (Leiden/Boston: Brill), accessed January 2022.

The US Evangelical church in the twentieth century, therefore, was particularly concerned about the preservation of orthodox faith in face of the onslaught of secularism. Evangelicals and their fundamentalist forebears would exhibit anxiety when US culture and society assumed to be the New Jerusalem now exhibited characteristics of fallen Babylon. The postmillennial optimism of nineteenth-century American Christianity would be upended with the advent of modernity, industrialisation, urbanisation and immigration. US cities would often provide a negative example of cultural decline. The cities that had been bastions of white Anglo-Saxon Protestant faith were now home to Italian Catholics, Orthodox Greeks and Eastern European Jews. The Great Migration that resulted in the massive influx of African Americans into urban centres would also challenge the assumption of American cities as expressions of the superiority of white American Protestantism. American cities and consequently American society were believed to be under attack.

The dominant culture of Western European Protestantism feared a society no longer under the dominance of Western Europeans. The fundamentalist–modernist controversies that found expression in denominations, churches and seminaries would exacerbate this fear. As the culture around them shifted, conservative Protestants rejected the social gospel of their liberal counterparts and opted to pit Christ against the surrounding culture. To the US Evangelical, the large sweep of church history attests to the centrality of evangelical faith in the twenty-first century. As the self-perceived inheritors of historical orthodoxy, US Evangelicals would seek to preserve the integrity of the gospel in the midst of a changing world. The activist impulse to convert others remained intact, but now this impulse expressed itself as suspicion of the broader culture and seeking ways to rescue as many as possible from the wrecked, sinking vessel of the world.

To the twentieth-century Evangelical, the church needed to stand its ground against the wave of secularism that could be found not only in American society but also in other church traditions and expressions. How the Bible is interpreted in the contemporary, modern context; how evangelism is shaped by one's view of the culture; and how the church actively intersects with the culture are all important questions about the

Changes in Evangelicals in North America, 1970–2020, growth rate, % per year

Region	Total population	Christian population	Evangelical population
North America	0.94%	0.49%	0.81%
Global total	1.50%	1.44%	2.52%

Source: Todd M. Johnson and Gina A. Zurlo (eds), *World Christian Database* (Leiden/Boston: Brill), accessed January 2022.

relationship between the church and culture that begin to impact the boundaries of Evangelicalism. With a 'possessed truth' mindset and a belief in their logically derived orthodox receiving of truth, Evangelicals would seek the preservation of their worldview and theological boundaries (however shifting), sometimes at all costs.

Multiple Threads of US Evangelicalism

The US Evangelicalism (with some overlap with Canadian Evangelicalism) that emerged in the latter part of the twentieth century had multiple theological influences with some overlapping ecclesial priorities. US Evangelicalism demonstrated the initial capacity to engage multiple threads within the larger movement. These ecclesial threads would yield a common worldview that focused on the preservation of theologically conservative orthodoxy even with variation among the key aspects of their ecclesial foundations. Evangelicalism can point towards Reformed Christianity, fundamentalism, neo-Evangelicalism, Progressive Evangelicalism and Pentecostal/Charismatic as five key threads that make up the current expression of Evangelicalism. They vary in their historical narrative (albeit all are uniquely American) and even in their theological affirmations, but they provide a variety of characteristics that make up the sociological and eventually the political boundaries that define the unique expression of US Evangelicalism.

Reformed Christianity may have the longest tenure of the five threads that make up US Evangelicalism. As outlined above, the Reformed thread is expressed early in US Christian history in connection to Scottish Common Sense philosophy. The use in the founding documents of the US government of language such as 'we hold these truths to be self-evident' reveals a common philosophical approach in Reformed Christianity and American democracy. Reformed theology demonstrated a capacity to engage the larger culture of US society as certain philosophical tenets that found expression in US society also found expression in the church. Both American society and American evangelicalism were shaped by assumptions of reason and rationality. Church and culture found mutual support around this assumption. While initially viewed as a positive expression, centuries later it can be asserted that these assumptions betray forms of Eurocentric thinking that elevate white bodies above other bodies – making Reformed Christianity (as well as most expressions of early American Christianity) complicit in the sins of chattel slavery and Native American genocide.

The Reformed thread found expression in the American colonial church through recognisable stalwarts such as Jonathan Edwards, George Whitefield and Cotton Mather. They would be recognised as the key influencers of the First Great Awakening, which gave an early expression of conversionist revivalism that would come to characterise American evangelicalism. Rooted in the tight boundaries of Reformed theology, they were perceived as intellectual Christians using their capacity to reason to shape early American Christianity as well as early American society. At the same time, these key leaders had a problematic relationship with the institution of American slavery and provided a harmful acquiescence and even support for the evil institution. The Reformed thread would provide some key theological distinctives that would shape American Christianity but also reveal a dysfunctional relationship with the surrounding culture.

The second thread emerged in the early part of the twentieth century as evangelicals adopted the term 'fundamentalists' in order to distinguish themselves from theological liberals. Fundamentalists lost numerous battles in their fight against the theological liberals. Their most humiliating defeat came during the 1925 Scopes trial, as the media subjected fundamentalist beliefs to national ridicule. Fundamentalists had already begun to distance themselves from social concern, but the Scopes trial would speed what would become known as the Great Reversal, a contrast to nineteenth-century activism. A strong sense of separatism characterised fundamentalists. A typical example of fundamentalism would be the perspective of D. L. Moody, who viewed the 'world as a wrecked vessel' and evangelism as a matter of saving individuals with a lifeboat. Despite (or maybe because of) their seemingly strident separatism, fundamentalists were active in creating a network of para-church ministries, Bible schools, seminaries, radio programmes, mission agencies and periodicals, that served to provide the necessary infrastructure for fundamentalism's advancement. Fundamentalists eschewed modern society, but at the same time engaged in the structural norms and expressions of modern culture.

The third thread, of Pentecostal/Charismatics, emerged around the same time as the fundamentalist thread. The igniting spark of the modern Pentecostal movement is traced to the multi-racial Azusa Street Revival led by an African American pastor, William J. Seymour, in Los Angeles, California. Seymour would help to ignite one of the most important religious movements of the twentieth century. Unfortunately, the early expression of Pentecostalism, which demonstrated a spiritual and ecclesial unity across racial and social barriers, would not last. The movement would splinter along racial lines but also find new iterations such as the Charismatic movement, which would trace its roots to Pentecostalism but express unique ecclesial and social characteristics. Both Pentecostalism and the Charismatic movement would eventually find a home in the larger Evangelical movement in the later decades of the twentieth century. Nearly 100 years after the distinct birth of Pentecostalism, many within that movement could be categorised as US Evangelicals, particularly along social and political designations. Pentecostals/Charismatics received such a level of acceptance among Evangelicals that a Pentecostal pastor, Ted Haggard, could assume the leadership of the National Association of Evangelicals (NAE).

The fourth thread, of 'neo-Evangelicalism', built upon the existing foundations of Reformed Christianity and fundamentalism, with the Pentecostals/Charismatics eventually contributing to this thread. After the Second World War, Evangelicals began to distinguish themselves from the strident fundamentalism of the first half of the twentieth century. Neo-Evangelicals were more likely to see the culture as a tool of engagement, rather than an enemy to defeat. Neo-Evangelicals may have Reformed or fundamentalist roots, but they are more willing to use the tools of culture for such efforts as church growth, ministry effectiveness and increasing impact on American society. Neo-Evangelicals would even prefer to view their pastors as the chief executives of corporations rather than as chaplains and soul care givers.

Similar to the fundamentalists, neo-Evangelicals were effective in forming institutions and organisations. Founded during the Second World War, the formation of the NAE provided the umbrella para-church organisation that helped to shape the larger tent for neo-Evangelicalism in the latter half of the twentieth century. Specific expressions of neo-Evangelical organisations such as the periodical *Christianity Today*, Gordon-Conwell Theological Seminary, Fuller Theological Seminary, Regent College (in Canada), the Billy Graham Evangelistic Association, Young Life, World Vision and InterVarsity Christian Fellowship (the last three with substantial presence and impact in North America and the world) would also emerge in the twentieth century and provide further organisational connections. These trans-denominational efforts would translate in later iterations as a conference culture where experts would present their success stories and market a consumeristic expression of Christianity for a hungry Evangelical audience looking for effective and easily duplicated ministry success models.

Those who formerly identified with the other threads of Evangelicalism would readily identify with this larger tent. Neo-Evangelicals supported each other's ministries and developed informal and formal networks of connection that transcended denominations through these institutions. These para-church organisations evoked a common sense of mission that would unite neo-Evangelicals, even more than the decreasingly polemical statements of faith espoused by these organisations.

The fifth thread, of Progressive Evangelicals, also traces its roots to a larger evangelical ethos. Until recently, most progressive Evangelicals have not hesitated to identify themselves as Evangelicals. The main ecclesial characteristics of evangelicalism would not be rejected. The key distinctive of Progressive Evangelicals would be their affiliation with more progressive politics. In contrast to most Evangelicals holding to both a theological/ecclesial conservatism and a social/political conservatism, Progressive Evangelicals rallied around more progressive politics and eventually around their specific support for George McGovern in the 1972 presidential election. The subsequent 1973 Chicago Declaration asserted the necessity of justice and concern for the poor alongside a conversionist perspective on repentance from sin. The document sought to frame the pursuit of social concerns in the framework of evangelical language and challenged the twentieth-century fundamentalist-evangelical assertion of separatism from the world. Many of the signatories of the Chicago Declaration would lead various efforts of Progressive Evangelicals, including Jim Wallis, who published the magazine *Sojourners* and led the activist organisation of the same name. Progressive Evangelicals would express their activist faith not only through personal conversion but also social change.

Despite some seemingly profound differences, these threads would merge under the larger heading of Evangelicalism. Theological differences between Pentecostals and fundamentalists would not deter the common sense of mission that would unite Evangelicals. The broader umbrella of Evangelicalism would become a big tent that included these multiple threads in North America. However, that unity would shift away from a theological harmony to a more sociological identity that would more clearly define US Evangelicalism at the turn of the millennium.

From Theological to Sociological Identity

The range of theological opinions expressed across the spectrum of North American Evangelicalism hindered a solidifying ecclesial unity around theological commonality. Instead, unity formed around the distinct sociological attributes that began to characterise US Evangelicalism. As Evangelicalism broke from the strident fundamentalism of the first half of the twentieth century, the formation of new sociological connections helped to better define the boundaries of the movement. Evangelicals developed a sociological community bound together by the desire to preserve their perception of theological boundaries that sought to reflect historical orthodoxy. The desire to preserve the concept of conservative Christianity was often more significant than the actual theological tenets. Truth possessed became a key assumption of US Evangelicals, even if the specific truths varied between the different threads. By seeing themselves as heirs of distinct, received and even unchallengeable theological truths, US Evangelicals could assert their exceptional status and stave off challenges to the status quo of their orthodox assumptions. This particular subset of US Christianity engaged the culture in a particular way, primarily through the self-perception of exceptionalism and expectation of triumph.

With this common purpose and worldview, US Evangelicals deepened their connections through social networks and connections in the latter part of the twentieth century. Through these connections, a distinct sociological Evangelical identity would emerge. This identity is often depicted as white, middle class, suburbanite, Republican, leaving out other theologically conservative groups that did not fit these sociological categories.

During the important identity-forming stage for Evangelicals, a distinction was made between US Evangelicals and the historic Black church. Evangelical identity was sequestered in the white American space with a notable disconnect from African American Christianity. Despite parallel theological positions, the historic Black church was not seen as part of the Evangelical movement. Even the development of a uniquely African American Evangelical movement did not find traction in their intersection with the larger Evangelical movement in the USA.

In the 1960s and 1970s, African American Evangelicals emerged as a burgeoning movement. These self-identified Evangelicals held to a conservative theological framework but were often excluded from key areas of US Evangelical leadership and influence. African American Evangelicalism found itself situated between the historical and prophetic presence of the African-American church in the narrative of Western Christianity and the emergence of US Evangelicalism in the twentieth century. African-American Evangelicals presented a prophetic indictment against the cultural captivity of US Evangelicalism, which had formed clearly identifiable sociological boundaries. The process of tokenism and marginalisation that reflects US Evangelical intersection with African American Evangelicalism reveals the underlying narrative of white-centredness in the narrative of US Evangelicalism. US Evangelicalism's sociological identity as a white movement was cemented as it failed to integrate with the specific expression of African American Evangelicalism.

Racial identification served as a key marker for US Evangelicalism. Additional sociological markers would also become evident in the late twentieth century. Similar to US society, hyper-individualism became a notable characteristic as ministry efforts were geared towards reaching the needs of the individual. Hyper-individualism would also result in an increasingly materialistic and consumeristic Evangelicalism. The consumer needs of the individual would help shape the US church's populist leanings. In addition, Evangelicalism would increasingly engage a form of hyper-masculinity that would express male headship and male-centredness as a sociological tendency elevated to a theological concern. These sociological characteristics would be justified by the self-perception of a rational faith that had arrived at these sociological realities through reason and logic.

The sociological categories of US Evangelicalism would serve as firm boundaries that the wide range of theological distinctives within Evangelicalism could not. The infrastructures that were built over the course of the twentieth century helped to solidify these sociological categories. Para-church organisations could be identified as Evangelical because of the common mission and calling to reach the 'lost', usually defined as their own children (in youth programmes or in colleges and universities) or their immediate neighbours (in their homogenous neighbourhoods). The primary methods of conversion relied on the use of the sociological principle of homophily ('birds of a feather, flock together') as applied among Evangelicals as the 'homogenous unit principle', which allowed Evangelical churches to focus on 'our kind of people'. Evangelical conferences gathered the most successful and prominent Evangelical leaders to train other Evangelicals how to reach others, but mostly others who fit their sociological categories. Those who would be acknowledged as leaders of US Evangelicalism would fit these sociological categories more than even theological markers. The barriers formed by these sociological categories reveal the narrative of white-centredness within Evangelicalism and would pave the way for the next iteration of US Evangelicalism, which shifted from sociological categorisation of Evangelicalism to a political categorisation.

From Sociological to Political Identity

The distinct sociological identity that comes to define US Evangelicalism was instrumental in the transition of Evangelicalism from an ecclesial movement to a sociological movement to a political one. By the turn of the millennium, Evangelicalism was increasingly seen as a political force, particularly as expressed in the Religious Right and its relationship to the Republican Party and conservative politics. The Religious Right would emerge as the dominant expression of the Evangelical involvement in American politics and the politics of Evangelicalism would be more recognisable as a defining characteristic than any theological markers.

The rise of the Religious Right in US Evangelical history can be explained by multiple factors. The Evangelical self-perception that they are the inheritors of historical orthodoxy, the dis-ease felt by many evangelicals over societal changes (particularly around the issues of gender and sexuality), and the ability to embrace cultural tools while opposing the culture itself – all these serve as factors in the rise of the Religious

Right in the twentieth century. Evangelicals became the chief soldiers of the culture wars as they fought for pre-eminence in the public sphere over key social issues through partisan politics.

The Religious Right rose up in response to the seismic shift on social issues in the 1960s, particularly with the introduction of birth control and changing norms on pre-marital sex, homosexuality and abortion. The 1960s also witnessed the beginning of the decline of religious participation amplifying the dis-ease felt by many Evangelicals at the deterioration of American society. The Religious Right responded to these concerns in an effective way that would help swell its ranks. They would portray themselves as guardians of orthodox Christian faith and their Christian worldview, but they also would not hesitate to use the weapons of secular society to meet their goals. The overtly political expression of the Religious Right provides another example of Evangelicalism's ability to use the available tools of society to further their exclusive claim of possessed truth.

Because the world had fallen captive to secular humanism, Evangelicals needed to hang on to a God-honouring culture and worldview that was rapidly slipping away. Towards that end, the Republican Party would find issues that would tap into the evangelical sense of dis-ease with a declining culture. Conservative positions on abortion, prayer in schools and the separation of church and state would provide the necessary ammunition to bring theological conservatives into the politically conservative camp. The culture was in decline, but the tools of that culture could be co-opted. The activism of Evangelical Christianity had found an outlet, not only in the task of personal evangelism but now in the task of cultural transformation through political activism. Because evangelicals from Whitefield to Finney to McPherson to Graham had used the tools of culture to advance Christianity, the shift to use one of the most significant tools of culture – political activism – to express active, conversionist faith proved to be a smooth one.

The Religious Right captured the imagination of the majority of Evangelicals. The main outlier to the Religious Right's dominance would be among Progressive Evangelicals, who would espouse a very different political ideology. Progressive Evangelicals would focus on racial justice, care for the poor and social justice issues related to equity. While persuasive and charismatic leaders were not lacking among Progressive Evangelicals, the agenda of progressive Christianity would require greater sacrifice. The social justice and transformation bent of Progressive Evangelicals would not jibe with the strong personal salvation and holiness emphasis that ran down the middle of a conversionist, revivalist tradition. The Religious Right would be the political choice for many Evangelicals who saw an affinity with their challenge to a changing culture but also the promise of power within that culture.

The irony of using culture to change the culture they had eschewed escaped the increasingly politicised US Evangelicals. Part of the imaginative gymnastics needed to allow such paradox traces back to the long-standing narrative of American exceptionalism. This sense of US exceptionalism was tied to the sense of exceptionalism and triumphalism of the US church. The American church had brought Christian faith to the 'New World'. This winning of the Americas by the Western Christian was at the cost of Native American lives, who were deemed to be disposable by the dysfunctional theological narrative of the Doctrine of Discovery. The American church helped to build a powerful nation with a strong economy because of the successful application of the Protestant work ethic. The reality of stolen labour kidnapped from the African continent would be of secondary concern. The embedded narrative of a white-centred American Christianity that helped to build a great American nation was now at risk from a culture that rejected the possessed truth of Evangelical Christianity.

By the time of the election of Donald Trump as President in 2016, the transformation of US Evangelicalism into the political identity of a white, anti-immigrant, anti-diversity, anti-Muslim, pro-wall, pro-gun, pro-Trump masculinity was complete. The theological boundaries that had once characterised Evangelicalism, such as the centrality of the Bible for faith and life, the need for Christ for salvation, and the need for personal conversion, had been replaced with an unshakable belief in American exceptionalism, the draw of a hyper-masculine leader whose toxicity would be a necessary evil, and the need for power to win the culture wars.

Looking Forward

North American Evangelicalism has not operated with a clear central authority nor a clear central institution. Leadership of Evangelicalism has often relied on the persuasive ability of the individual and the capacity to garner popular (and populist) support for a religious expression steeped in the culture of Western individualism. Individualism and consumerism, therefore, serve as key sociological markers for Evangelical identity. Evangelicals in the latter half of the twentieth century inherited not only a theological conservatism, but also the surprisingly nimble cultural adaptability of fundamentalists. This movement that took pride in its uncompromising separatism but ultimately flourished in the twentieth century because of its adaptability.

Evangelicals viewed their faith as a truth possessed that should not diminish in light of cultural changes. The sociological identity that came to characterise their movement would become a part of the narrative of a truth possessed. The political identity of the Evangelical would be a useful tool to continue the ownership and control of truth possessed. By the turn of the millennium, there would be an increasing number of non-white evangelicals on both the global level and the local level of US society. These demographic challenges did not shake the assumed rightness of US Evangelical sociological identity. As the USA became increasingly diverse across the racial spectrum, American Christianity also became increasingly diverse. Similar to the exclusion of the Black church and African American evangelicals, non-white Christians who held to an evangelical theology were often excluded from Evangelical identity because it was captive to a sociological identity and to the stranglehold of political identity.

Non-white evangelicals who held a high view of Scripture, a high Christology and a conversionist revivalist fervour were not seen as part of the Evangelical mainstream as those theological categories no longer defined US Evangelicalism. As non-white evangelicals often pursued a different social and political agenda that included racial justice, care for the immigrant and the rights of women, the gulf between the theologically akin non-white evangelicals with their sociologically and politically defined white Evangelical cousins increased. US Evangelicalism as currently defined along non-theological boundaries may have excluded the actual heirs of evangelical orthodoxy by embracing a social and political identity over their theological and ecclesial identity.

Bibliography

Balmer, Randall, *Thy Kingdom Come: How the Religious Right Distorts the Faith and Threatens America* (New York: Basic Books, 2007).

Dayton, Donald, with Douglas Strong, *Rediscovering an Evangelical Heritage: A Tradition and Trajectory of Integrating Piety and Justice* (Grand Rapids, MI: Baker Academic, 2014).

Marsden, George, *Understanding Fundamentalism and Evangelicalism* (Grand Rapids, MI: Eerdmans, 1990).

Rah, Soong-Chan and Gary VanderPol, *Return to Justice: Six Movements that Reignited Our Contemporary Evangelical Conscience* (Grand Rapids, MI: Brazos, 2016).

Worthen, Molly, *Apostles of Reason: The Crisis of Authority in American Evangelicalism* (New York: Oxford University Press, 2013).

Pentecostals/Charismatics

Daniel D. Isgrigg

The Pentecostal/Charismatic Movement has emerged as a unique Christian tradition in the landscape of North American Christianity. These 'Spirit-filled' denominations, congregations and small groups within established churches have flourished over the past century due to their vibrant spirituality and emphasis on the gifts of the Holy Spirit – including prophecy, healing and speaking in tongues – through the empowering experience of baptism in the Holy Spirit. From humble beginnings among the poor and marginalised in North America, the various global Pentecostal/Charismatic bodies have seen exponential growth, and they now count over 644 million 'Spirit-empowered' believers worldwide. In North America, Pentecostal/Charismatic believers number more than 67 million and have distinguished themselves among the few Christian movements reporting growth in an ever more secularised society. While Pentecostal/Charismatic Christianity is a global movement, North America features prominently in its development and expansion around the world.

The first wave of renewal began in North America in the late nineteenth century when frontier Holiness evangelists preached repentance, salvation and the 'second blessing' of sanctification through the baptism in the Holy Spirit. During the 1890s, periodic episodes of Charismatic manifestations, including speaking in tongues, were witnessed in B. H. Irwin's Fire Baptized Holiness Church in the Midwest, Richard G. Spurling's Christian Union in Tennessee and North Carolina, Frank Sandford's Bible school in Shiloh, Maine, and Charles Parham's Bible school in Topeka, Kansas. Spurred on by a restorationist 'latter rain' narrative, they believed they were witnessing the last days' revival in which the gifts of the Spirit were being restored to the Church as first given to the apostles in the Book of Acts. Animated by this belief, Parham added the expectation that Spirit baptism should be accompanied by the 'Bible evidence' of speaking in tongues. As this 'apostolic faith' message made its way across the Midwestern United States, the normalisation of glossolalia as the sign of this empowerment helped to distinguish this new 'Pentecostal' movement from the Holiness movement.

However, those sparks of the nascent Pentecostal revival did not ignite a fire until an African American holiness preacher named William

Seymour started an Apostolic Faith Mission in Los Angeles, California, in 1906. In a humble two-storey building on Azusa Street, a revival broke out that quickly became ground zero for the spread of Pentecostalism across North America and eventually around the world. Under the leadership of Seymour, a prominent feature of this revival was its inter-racial ethos in which African Americans, Latinos and Whites together sought the baptism in the Spirit in services held three times a day, seven days a week. Worship at Azusa Street mixed Holiness revivalism norms with African American worship aesthetics, including singing, shouting, dancing, falling 'under the power' and altar times that went late into the night for those 'tarrying' for the baptism in the Spirit. Empowered by the Spirit, Pentecostal missionaries received calls to take the Gospel of Jesus Christ to many parts of the world, including the Middle East, Asia, Europe, South America and Africa. Even in these early years, Pentecostalism was developing a global and missionary character that has been its hallmark over the past century.

While the Azusa Street Mission was important, other revivals taking place around North America had similar Pentecostal manifestations and impacts on spreading the movement. In Toronto, Canada, in 1906, James and Ellen Hebden opened the East End Mission after Ellen had received the baptism in the Holy Spirit with speaking in tongues. Many Pentecost seekers travelled to the Hebden Mission and from there Pentecostalism spread throughout the northern USA and Canada. In 1911, Pentecost reached Newfoundland when Alice Belle Garrius opened the Bethesda Mission in the town of St Johns. The revival helped birth other Pentecostal churches that eventually became the Pentecostal Assemblies of Newfoundland and Labrador. News and testimonies of these Pentecostal outpourings carried through Pentecostal papers such as Seymour's *The Apostolic Faith* and G. B. Cashwell's *Bridegroom's Messenger* added to that early momentum.

Hispanic Pentecostalism also traces its roots to the Azusa Street Revival, where Mexican migrant workers were some of the early participants. In 1914, Romana de Venezuela, having received her baptism in the Holy Spirit in Los Angeles, returned to Chihuahua, Mexico, to begin a Pentecostal work. Assemblies of God pioneers H. C. Ball and Alice Luce also established early Pentecostal missions among Spanish-speakers in

Pentecostals/Charismatics in North America, 1970

Region	Total population	Christian population	Pentecostal/ Charismatic population	% of region Pentecostal/ Charismatic	% of Christians Pentecostal/ Charismatic
North America	230,992,000	211,489,000	14,545,000	6.3%	6.9%
Global total	3,700,437,000	1,225,395,000	57,636,000	1.6%	4.7%

Source: Todd M. Johnson and Gina A. Zurlo (eds), *World Christian Database* (Leiden/Boston: Brill), accessed January 2022.

Texas and southern California in 1917, including the Latin American Bible College. Another influential Hispanic leader was Fransisco Olazabal, who planted more than 50 Spanish-speaking Pentecostal churches in Mexico and the USA and founded the Concilio Mexicano Interdenominacional de las Iglesias Cristianas in 1923. In Puerto Rico, a revival in 1916 was led by Juan Julio Lugo, who established Pentecostal churches and founded the Pentecostal Church of God in 1920. The growth of Pentecostal and Charismatic Christianity in the early years has since expanded to become 45% of the total Christian population in Mexico today. As Latin American immigration has steadily increased in the USA, many Pentecostal denominations have established Spanish-speaking districts, some of which are among the fastest-growing segments of North American Pentecostalism.

Pentecostals in the Mainstream

In the early years of the movement, mainline Christianity paid little attention to Pentecostals, dismissing them as fanatics because of their enthusiastic spirituality and belief in tongues-speaking. Likewise, many Pentecostals eschewed social engagement because they believed in the immediacy of Christ's coming, leaving little time for social reform or political involvement. Yet, when it came to compassion ministry, Pentecostals were often at the forefront – caring for vulnerable children in orphanages, feeding the hungry through urban missions and helping women through rescue homes.

Following the Second World War, however, increasing upward mobility and institutionalisation provided stability and growth that helped Pentecostals emerge from their isolation and increased their legitimisation within the broader Christian tradition. The key shift came through the high-profile healing ministries of William Branham, Oral Roberts, Kathryn Kuhlman and A. A. Allen. The fiery evangelistic messages, the Pentecostal altar services and the spectacle of seeing dramatic miracles in real time drew thousands of mainline Evangelicals and Catholics to the healing crusades. But even more instrumental was the innovation by Oral Roberts of putting his crusades on television, where Christians from across the spectrum could see Pentecostal spirituality on display in prime

Pentecostals/Charismatics in North America, 2020

Region	Total population	Christian population	Pentecostal/ Charismatic population	% of region Pentecostal/ Charismatic	% of Christians Pentecostal/ Charismatic
North America	368,870,000	269,524,000	67,771,000	18.4%	25.1%
Global total	7,794,799,000	2,506,426,000	644,260,000	8.3%	25.7%

Source: Todd M. Johnson and Gina A. Zurlo (eds), *World Christian Database* (Leiden/Boston: Brill), accessed January 2022.

time. These nonconformist healing evangelists, particularly Oral Roberts and Jack Coe, also seized the opportunity to challenge racial norms by integrating their healing crusades at a time when Pentecostal denominations were still largely ethnically segregated. This is also true of African American independent healing and deliverance ministers such as Arturo Skinner and E. E. Cleveland, who emphasised deliverance and power evangelism, which proved to be key ingredients that drew inter-racial crowds. As urban community leaders, they led the way in social reform and addressing racism in America.

The Protestant and Catholic Renewal
The effects of the cross-pollination of Pentecostal spirituality with mainstream culture during the healing revival set the stage for a major renewal movement in Protestant and Catholic churches beginning in the late 1950s. A key moment came in 1959, when Dennis Bennett, an Anglican priest in Van Nuys, California, announced he had experienced the baptism in the Holy Spirit with speaking in tongues. Bennett's story made national news, and when pressured, he resigned from his parish in Van Nuys and was invited to a small mission parish in Seattle, Washington, St Luke's Episcopal, which, under his leadership, grew to become a centre of renewal for Christians from mainline traditions. Also joining the Charismatic Renewal were other 'Spirit-filled' ministers such as Lutheran Harold Bredesen, Methodist Tommy Tyson and Baptist John Osteen. In each case, these 'neo-Pentecostals' (later called Charismatics) introduced Pentecostal beliefs about the Spirit into their own denominations while keeping true to their theological traditions. The goal was not to leave their denominations to become Pentecostals but to renew their traditions from within. By 1970, virtually every Christian tradition had a vibrant Charismatic renewal fellowship that welcomed seekers to experience the Holy Spirit.

In the Roman Catholic Church, a great renewal movement broke out in the late 1960s on the campuses of Duquesne and Notre Dame universities, where seeking consecration and the fullness of the Spirit led to students experiencing manifestations of laughing, crying, healing and speaking in tongues. Led by Ralph Martin, Francis McNutt, and Kevin and Dorothy

Changes in Pentecostals/Charismatics in North America, 1970–2020, growth rate, % per year

Region	Total population	Christian population	Pentecostal/Charismatic population
North America	0.94%	0.49%	3.13%
Global total	1.50%	1.44%	4.95%

Source: Todd M. Johnson and Gina A. Zurlo (eds), *World Christian Database* (Leiden/Boston: Brill), accessed January 2022.

Ranaghan, the Catholic Charismatic Renewal was soon recognised by Pope Paul VI as a renewal movement marked by prayer, worship choruses, singing in the Spirit, prayer for healing and prayer for Spirit baptism, as manifested by joy and a greater desire for holiness as well as a release of the Charismatic gifts. The Catholic Charismatic Renewal Service Committee hosted yearly conferences, including the Notre Dame Conference in 1976 that gathered more than 30,000 Spirit-filled Catholics together. In 1977, Protestant and Catholic renewal leaders joined with Pentecostals for a conference on the Holy Spirit in Kansas City at Arrowhead Stadium, where more than 45,000 Charismatic worshipers gathered to testify to the wave of the Spirit that was renewing the body of Christ. The co-mingling of these various traditions who valued Charismatic spirituality helped establish Spirit-filled Christianity as a major force in North American religion in the 1980s and 1990s.

The Independent Charismatic Wave of Renewal

Following the Charismatic Renewal in Protestant and Catholic churches, new forms of independent Charismatic churches began in the 1970s. These churches drew Spirit-filled believers who had been expelled from their denominations, Pentecostals who defected over rigid denominational understandings of the Holy Spirit, and ministers from the Latter Rain Movement in Canada. While no single theology or polity holds these churches together, independent Charismatics place a priority on the exercise of spiritual gifts, both personally and in congregational worship, as the hallmarks of the Spirit-filled life. Labelled as the new 'third wave' of Pentecostalism by C. Peter Wagner, Charismatic churches experienced growth through their apostolic ecclesiology and the attractional power of Charismatic gifts for church growth. Instead of denominations, high-profile ministers serve as apostolic leaders of relational networks of churches over which they exert influence. This movement, sometimes called the New Apostolic Reformation, advanced the phenomenon of Charismatic mega-churches characterised by leaders who leverage their popularity through media.

Charismatic churches place a high priority on worship music as the primary medium for activating the Holy Spirit's work in the congregation. A central figure who shaped the form and style of the Charismatic movement was John Wimber, whose Vineyard churches became known for their expressive worship, openness to Charismatic manifestations and congregational participation in spiritual gifts. Departing from evangelical hymnody and gospel singing, Vineyard and other Charismatic churches popularised the 'praise and worship' genre of Christian music. It was this focus on worship and Charismatic phenomena that ignited a unique revival at Toronto Airport Vineyard Fellowship, led by John and Carol Arnott. Known as the Toronto Blessing, the revival was characterised by spiritual gifts, manifestations of laughing, being slain in the Spirit and bodily shaking in response to the work of the Holy Spirit. The spirituality of this revival became a major influence on independent Charismatic and Pentecostal churches across Canada and the USA in the 1990s.

Independent Charismatic Christianity is also recognised for its contribution to the growth of televangelists and the prosperity gospel in North America. In the 1970s, Christian television networks helped catapult figures like Jimmy Swaggart, Jim Bakker, Oral Roberts and Pat Robertson to national fame and provided an effective medium for the expansion of Pentecostal and Charismatic Christianity. However, a series of financial and moral scandals in the 1980s turned the public against these ministries. Yet networks like Robertson's Christian Broadcasting Network (CBN) and Paul Crouch's Trinity Broadcasting Network (TBN) continued to cultivate a growing celebrity Charismatic culture that still showcases the movement's most popular ministers and churches.

Key to the growth of Charismatic television networks was the growth of influential 'Word of Faith' ministers who popularised the prosperity gospel. A key early figure in this movement was Kenneth E. Hagin, the father of the Word of Faith Movement, who pioneered the role of faith in actualising the promises of God in the Scriptures, including health, prosperity and victory in everyday life. The Word of Faith message gained a wide influence as television networks regularly featured Word of Faith and other independent ministers such as Kenneth Copeland, Keith Butler, Paula White, Jesse Duplantis and Creflo Dollar. Christian television networks in the 1980s also helped to normalise Black aesthetics as Black Pentecostal preachers such as Reverend Ike, Fred Price, Carlton Pearson, Juanita Bynum and T. D. Jakes displayed Black church culture through the historically white medium of television. Many Black Charismatic ministers used prosperity motifs to appeal to a growing Black middle class and challenge racial stereotypes by emphasising spiritual avenues of social uplift and economic liberation for minority communities.

Unique North American Characteristics and Challenges

From its early years as a marginalised, radical religious movement, Pentecostal and Charismatic Christianity has certainly made a remarkable impact on North America's religious landscape. As the rapid worldwide growth of the movement has captured the attention of scholars of world Christianity, there is a need to consider the unique challenges and opportunities presented by the North American context. While each of the major waves of renewal is unique and diverse, this section explores some of the major themes of growth, theological orientation, inclusivity and social engagement. Each of these areas offers insights into the overall landscape of conversations taking place within the movement.

Though the movement has experienced tremendous growth globally since the 1970s, North American Spirit-empowered Christianity has not kept pace with the rest of the world. Of the 644 million global Pentecostal and Charismatic believers, only 67 million are located in North America, fourth among the six continents. Overall, Pentecostals and Charismatics in the USA have increased from 13.8 million in 1970 to 65 million in 2020 but have failed to keep up with population growth. While Pentecostals and Charismatics increased by 14 million from 2000 to 2020, their total percentage of all Christians declined from 12.1% to 10.5%. In Canada, Pentecostals and Charismatics more than tripled, from 709,000 in 1970 to 2.3 million in 2000. But growth has stagnated since, the total reaching 2.75 million in 2020. In the North Atlantic, Greenland had only a minimal Pentecostal presence in the 1950s from the Inuunerup Nutaap Oqaluffia, an independent Pentecostal church among the Inuit people. But since the 1980s, the Assemblies of God has helped boost Greenland's Spirit-empowered believers to over 6,000 (11% of the Christian population). In Bermuda, where the New Testament Church of God is influential, Pentecostals and Charismatics have grew from 5% of the Christian population in 1970 to 28% in 2020. What these numbers tell us is that the Pentecostal/Charismatic movement in North America is certainly growing, but it largely lags behind the global level of growth.

One sector that continues to see growth in North America is independent networks of Charismatic churches. Their innovative religious experiences and positive messages have attracted the middle and upper classes alike by appealing to North America's ethos of neoliberalism and self-actualisation. In these circles, the prosperity gospel has certainly flourished, but churches today can range from neo-Reformed churches that revive ancient traditions to prayer centres that welcome all kinds of prophetic and esoteric experience. While mega-churches dominate the landscape, Charismatic spirituality continues to thrive in mid-sized to small churches because of the value placed on congregational participation. This vast variety offers worshippers the ability to choose a customised worship environment, a characteristic that appeals to North Americans' individualistic culture.

A key factor driving the passing on of Spirit-empowered Christianity to the new generation is the emergence of the prayer movement in places like the International House of Prayer in Kansas City, Missouri (IHOPKC), and Bethel Church in Redding, California. These two prayer and worship movements have redefined Charismatic spirituality for a new generation through immersive worship experiences found in their 24-hour worship and prayer gatherings, healing rooms, prophecy rooms and ministry internship programmes. Places like IHOPKC and Bethel are less about expanding as franchise churches, the trend among mega-churches today. Instead, they see themselves as revival centres where they can impact younger generations to go out and renew the Church as a whole. The worship music and song-writing of these centres have become extremely popular because of their Pentecostal motifs and references to God's miraculous power to heal and deliver. Not only has the music of Jesus Culture and Bethel impacted Spirit-filled churches across North America, but its popularity has been mainstreamed through Contemporary Christian Music and is today also driving worship in many Evangelical churches.

During the 1970s and 1980s, changes in immigration laws in North America and political instability abroad led to new waves of primarily economically driven migration from the global South. Many of these immigrant groups brought their Indigenous Pentecostal or Charismatic faith with them and established diaspora churches to provide social support and cultural spirituality that helps immigrants navigate the social and economic challenges of living in North America. Coming from vibrant Pentecostal spirituality in their home countries, many immigrants are shocked at the secularism and cold spiritual climate of North American churches. Therefore, rather than assimilate into the unappealing church culture, they establish diaspora churches with the 'reverse mission' of re-evangelising North America. While first-generation immigrant churches tend to offer services in their native languages, second-generation immigrant populations tend to be English-speaking, to have a multi-ethnic make-up and to be missionally driven to minister in their primarily urban contexts.

In addition to new diaspora churches being planted, many immigrant churches are founded or supported by transnational mega-churches and Charismatic networks from the continents of Asia and Africa. With a greater emphasis on Pentecostal spirituality, healing, deliverance and the prophetic gifts than North American denominations, transnational church networks have expanded into North America with great success. The True Jesus Church, the oldest Pentecostal body in China (started in 1917), established an international branch in the USA in 1969 that has grown exponentially, with churches in more than 30 population centres in North America, including Los Angeles, Houston, New York, Miami and nearly every major city in Canada. In 1995, the Reverend Tong Liu founded River of Life Christian Church, a Chinese Charismatic mega-church that has expanded to multiple cities in North America and around the world. Each of these movements sees North America both as a mission field to reach and a base for global expansion. Similarly, Korean immigrant churches have been some of the fastest-growing immigrant congregations in North America. Korean immigrants overwhelmingly identify as Christian, and many are Charismatic, largely due to the transnational popularity of David Yonggi Cho, former pastor of Yoido Full Gospel Church in Seoul, South Korea. One Charismatic Korean church is Grace Korean Church in Los Angeles, which has planted churches across the USA and Canada and expanded its services to Spanish, Japanese and English.

African diaspora churches have also seen success as sub-Saharan immigrants have come to North America seeking education and economic opportunities. Though North America offers economic and religious freedom, assimilation is a particular challenge with the complicated racial history of America. This makes diaspora churches crucial to African immigrants, providing them much-needed cultural and religious support rather than assimilating into the moderated spirituality of North American Pentecostal churches. Transnational churches support African immigrants professionally, culturally and missionally, seeing North America as a mission field. This is true of the Ghana-based Church of Pentecost, which has planted more than 50 churches in North America. Another key transnational church is Winners Chapel, the North American branch of David Oyedepo's Nigerian mega-church that has more than a dozen congregations in North America. Winners Chapel inherited from North American evangelists in the 1980s its unique Pentecostal culture flavoured with triumphalism and the prosperity gospel. But the African diaspora is not without challenges as Africans in North America face the tensions surrounding racial attitudes.

Hispanic churches in the USA and Canada have seen significant growth. During the 1980s and 1990s, migration from Mexico and Central America increased the population of Latinx Christians in both countries. Through natural population growth, Hispanic churches are becoming multi-generational and multilingual in their expansion in North America. Spirit-filled Hispanic churches make up the largest portion of Spanish-speaking Protestants in the USA and Canada. Latin Pentecostals tend to be more socially engaged than North American churches and use the Pentecostal message to proclaim liberty and social change in their communities.

One of the primary reasons for the growth of Pentecostal and Charismatic Christianity is that it offers an experiential theology. Pentecostals draw the pattern of these experiences from the Bible, primarily from Luke–Acts, to argue that the baptism in the Holy Spirit accompanied by speaking in tongues, healing and spiritual gifts is normative for the Christian life. The supernatural orientation allows for improvisation and openness for miracles to break into the everyday spiritual, psychological and physical needs of people. Therefore, Pentecostal theology is at its heart more than a cognitive enterprise; it is experiential and affective in ways that shape praxis as much as it does doctrine. Pentecostal and Charismatic worship is participatory, characterised by exuberant expressions of praise, dance, testimony, prayer, laying on of hands for healing and exercise of spiritual gifts. Charismatics in particular place an emphasis on community participation in exercise of the charismata, as opposed to classic Pentecostals, who tend to focus on speaking in tongues as the distinctive characteristic.

Because of the historical and theological connections to nineteenth-century evangelical Protestantism, some question whether Pentecostals and Charismatics are simply Evangelicals who speak in tongues. However, this view fails to appreciate the distinctive epistemology, ecclesiology, hermeneutics, liturgy, praxis and, of course, pneumatology that shape Pentecostal theological reflection. Because of this unique theological identity, the Pentecostal movement should rightfully be considered its own distinct theological tradition. However, it should also be recognised that Charismatic Protestant, Orthodox and Roman Catholic communities tend not to differentiate themselves from the broader tradition in which they reside. Instead, they see the Spirit as a renewing force within the Church. In addition, Independent Charismatic churches individualise their theological beliefs, which range anywhere from Reformed theology to prosperity teaching. So to generalise that Pentecostals or Charismatics are subsumed under the category 'Evangelical' fails to account for the profound diversity within the movement.

One of the hallmarks of the Pentecostal and Charismatic movement is its inclusive and egalitarian ecclesiology. The 'Spirit-filled' church has always recognised the Holy Spirit's ability to call anyone to serve as a pastor, evangelist, missionary, rescue home worker or educator. The emphasis upon the universal outpouring of the Spirit in the Pentecostal narrative challenges the status quo of social roles, particularly the role of women in the church. From the beginning, Spirit-filled women have featured prominently in roles of leadership, serving as pioneering pastors, founders of denominations, evangelists, missionaries, publishers and educators around the world.

Yet, the legacy of empowerment of women in this tradition is somewhat paradoxical. Though openly supporting women in ministry, some Pentecostal denominations hold strong complementarian convictions that restrict women from lead pastoral roles and denominational leadership. In these spaces, many women have created alternative leadership avenues, such as church mothers and women's ministries, where influence over the church is less formal yet is strongly felt. Also in these contexts, women face modesty standards as well as attitudes about traditional gender roles that restrict the free agency of women. However, this is less so in independent Charismatic churches where women themselves are leaders of large ministries and many husband-and-wife couples serve together as co-pastors.

Theological training and the pursuit of higher education have long been a source of tension for Pentecostal ministry. Pentecostals shared the Evangelical critique of theology and higher criticism as the source for the erosion of truth and spiritual vitality in denominational churches. At the same time, they believed that ministers needed practical training in spiritual disciplines and ministry practices, demonstrated by the strong Bible school tradition often centred on the Bible as the primary textbook. But by the 1940s, Pentecostals had moved towards embracing higher education, as Bible schools transitioned to liberal arts education in all fields of study, not just ministry. Because of fears of secular education, Pentecostal universities became a key strategy for preserving the Pentecostal faith in the next generation. In addition, the more educated class of believers in the Charismatic Renewal helped to break down the suspicions of liberalism in higher education. Several Pentecostal colleges started regionally accredited graduate seminary education, including Oral Roberts University (1965), C. H. Mason Theological Seminary (1968), Assemblies of God Theological Seminary (1973), Pentecostal Theological Seminary (1975) and CBN/Regent University (1977). Today, Pentecostal and Charismatic universities are increasingly viewed as important for biblical, theological, practical ministerial development. This is particularly true of pastors of large and mega-church-sized congregations who are looking for deeper levels of ministry leadership training to navigate the unique challenges of large ministries.

Another factor that has shaped Pentecostal education is the founding of the Society for Pentecostal Studies in 1971. This academic society has nurtured Pentecostal/Charismatic scholarship internationally and encouraged ecumenical dialogues with other theological traditions, particularly Roman Catholics. As Pentecostal research has become more popular, Evangelical universities have recruited more Pentecostal/Charismatic doctoral candidates from around the globe, including Fuller Theological Seminary, Harvard University, Baylor University, Gordon–Conwell Theological Seminary and Tyndale University in Canada. Add to that the fact that several Pentecostal/Charismatic universities now offer PhD programmes – including Oral Roberts University, Assemblies of God Theological Seminary, Regent University and Pentecostal Theological Seminary (through Bangor University–Wales) – and it seems that Pentecostal education is truly coming of age.

The issue of ethnic and cultural diversity among Pentecostal and Charismatic churches is complicated. Compared with many other Protestant traditions, ethnic minorities represent a significant segment of the constituents in 'Spirit-filled' Christianity in North America. In fact, the largest Pentecostal fellowship in North America is the Church of God in Christ, a Black Pentecostal denomination. In addition, many predominantly white Pentecostal denominations also have vibrant ethnic populations or fellowships that have expanded due to global migration in recent decades. A great diversity also exists among Charismatic churches, which tend to be more inter-racial due to their inclusive ecclesiology, less cultural homogeneity and exuberant worship culture.

However, Pentecostal and Charismatic churches have varied responses to addressing racism within their ranks. In the early years, the movement saw threads of white supremacy that hindered the inter-racial values at Azusa Street, as was the case in the Anglo-centric ecclesiological and eschatological views of Charles Parham. That said, it was not uncommon for Blacks and whites to minister together in many early circles. But, as denominations formed in the second decade, some white groups accommodated the cultural norms of the Jim Crow era by forming mono-ethnic fellowships or distinct wings for African American ministers, in many cases overseen by white officials. During the civil rights era, African American Pentecostals were on the front lines of working towards equal rights. Mason Temple, Church of God in Christ, in Memphis, Tennessee, was at the centre of the Memphis sanitation workers strike and hosted Martin Luther King, Jr, when he made his famous 'I've Been to the Mountaintop' speech the night before his assassination. Unfortunately, many white Pentecostals did not join in the fight for racial equality or, worse, were among those who opposed these efforts. Though progress has been slow, some Pentecostal groups have worked towards reconciliation for past sins against minorities. The first significant reconciliation work was the 'Memphis Miracle' in which white Pentecostal leaders washed the feet of Black Pentecostal leaders in an act of repentance at the 1994 Pentecostal and Charismatic Churches of America meeting. More recently, the Pentecostal Assemblies of Canada made an official acknowledgement and reconciliation of its treatment of Aboriginal people in Canada. Intentional efforts in the Assemblies of God to diversify the leadership Executive Presbytery of this historically white denomination resulted in women and minorities making up the majority of the Executive Presbytery in 2021.

Conclusion

The growth of Pentecostal and Charismatic Christianity in North America is certainly a success story. From a few thousand believers in the first decade, to over 67 million today, growth in North America is on track to reach over 90 million 'Spirit-empowered' Christians by 2050. Fuelled by the attractive elements of a vibrant spirituality, inclusive ethos and hope of God's power to meet the felt needs of the human experience, Pentecostal and Charismatic Christianity appears set to continue to grow and influence the religious landscape of North America. Following the trends of the global South, the future for 'Spirit-empowered' Christianity in North America can be found in its racial diversity, opportunities for empowerment and leadership for the marginalised and its ability to innovate its methods and message to the changing society.

Bibliography

Alexander, Estrelda, *Black Fire: One Hundred Years of African American Pentecostalism* (Downers Grove, IL: IVP Academic, 2011).

Christerson, Brad and Richard Flory, *The Rise of Network Christianity: How Independent Leaders Are Changing the Religious Landscape* (Oxford: Oxford University Press, 2017).

Johnson, Todd and Gina A. Zurlo, *Introducing Spirit-empowered Christianity* (Tulsa, OK: ORU Press, 2021).

Ramirez, Daniel, *Migrating Faith: Pentecostalism in the United States and Mexico in the Twentieth Century* (Chapel Hill, NC: North Carolina University Press, 2015).

Synan, Vinson, *The Century of the Holy Spirit: 100 Years of the Pentecostal and Charismatic Renewal* (Nashville, TN: Thomas Nelson, 2001).

Key Themes

Faith and Culture

Miguel A. De La Torre

Most Eurocentric religious thinkers would argue that action flows from beliefs, from convictions, from faith. Once universal Truth (with a capital 'T') is determined by Eurocentric faith thinkers, a way of being is created, specifically in the form of a culture based on said truth being accepted. Euro-Christianity, by its very nature, has argued for a universal normativity achievable and applicable regardless of place, time, context or people group. Eurocentric culture is thus treated as the apex of civilisation precisely because it is based on Christian universal truth and virtues. Faith forged by Euro-Christian clergy, scholars and missionaries becomes the objective and universal way of being, a paragon for all of humanity regardless of their Indigenous worldviews. When accepted by those who fall short of whiteness, this truth, Euro-Christians argue, will bring forth the common good.

Once a people reach this peak of enlightenment, they have a responsibility, a calling, a mission to civilise and Christianise those stuck at a lower cultural evolutionary stage. We know they are less-than because of their ignorance, inability or stubbornness in embracing Eurocentric faith and culture. While racists of old defined all on the margins of Eurocentrism as biologically inferior (think of eugenics), today's racists expound the equality of all humans while nonetheless lamenting how many still fall short because of their cultural inferiority, which prevents them from grasping Eurocentric truth. If faith establishes culture, then converting others to superior Eurocentric thoughts and beliefs has the potential to lift them from underdevelopment, if not from primitivism. But what if Christian faith is more than laying the foundation by which Eurocentric culture functions? What if, now, Euro-Christianity becomes the means by which the colonial tendencies of Eurocentric culture are justified?

Towards the end of the nineteenth century, sociologist Emile Durkheim, in his 1893 classic *Division of Labor in Society*, argued that the beliefs and religious sentiments held in common by a community's inhabitants become the moral norms codified in shaping customs, traditions and laws. This primary function of culture becomes the protection, reaffirmation and perpetuation of faith, or what Durkheim called the 'collective or common conscience'. Sharing a collective conscience not only binds people together; this social integration exerts a coercive influence to confirm to the culture. But what if Durkheim got it backwards? What if the primary function of faith is the protection, reaffirmation and perpetuation of the culture it originally shaped? What if the relationship between faith and culture is more symbiotic? Although Durkheimian thought might have held true in explaining the geneses of cultural formation, specifically Eurocentric culture, this collective religious consciousness has evolved to serve a more encompassing function. Rather than simply binding a people together and coercing them to conform, it also – and, more importantly, spiritually – justifies the colonial legacy of invasion, theft, rape and pillage as practised by said culture even as it transgressed the original rhetoric of love that faith proclaimed.

The greatest threat to humanity has been and continues to be Eurocentric faith and culture. Since its origins, Euro-Christianity has been pitted against the human flourishing of those on its margins. Why? Because faith does more than influence culture, creating among a diverse people a sense of belonging. Faith justifies cultural atrocities. Hence, the white supremacy which had historically undergirded Eurocentric culture also undergirds Euro-Christianity, transforming any collective conscience into a global mission of enslaving those deemed to fall short of said collective. A pseudo-Euro-Christian spirituality was formed that fortified a white supremacy which justified the colonial venture. Global conquest requires a spirituality that masks the barbarism of those who self-define as enlightened.

Harm Caused by Eurocentrism

Although faith participates in the creation of culture, faith is also a self-serving construct that emerges from culture. To be born and raised within a Eurocentric ethos is to become a product of a culture in which white supremacy is closely interwoven with how the world is seen and organised. Cultural biases and prejudices are read into faith. Thus, Euro-Christians define and practise their faith subjectively, unconsciously (and at times consciously) reading into their belief system the justification for white supremacy. Claiming objectivity for their subjective Euro-Christian faith provides the means by which their subjective faith becomes objective for everyone else. Euro-Christianity lacks the hermeneutical suspicion that would enable it to investigate how culturally based white supremacy influences the faith so that it functions as an apologist for the acceptance of colonialism. Failure to examine the intersection of faith and culture, specifically Euro-Christianity and white supremacy, disregards the historical Eurocentric missionary drive to subjugate those falling short of whiteness.

Euro-Christian racialisation generates a spiritual metanarrative justifying the unearned privilege, power and profit of those benefiting from a white supremacy that accepts the colonialist order as the will of God. Think of the famous sermon given in 1630 by John Winthrop, 'A Model of Christian Charity', before reaching the promised land of New England. 'We shall be a city on a hill', he told his fellow passengers. They were on a mission from God to occupy the land belonging to a savage race. Faith justified their cultural colonial venture. 'We shall find that the God of Israel is among us', he assured fellow Puritans. The God of Israel called for the genocide of the original inhabitants of Jericho when the Hebrews first invaded someone else's land ('destroy every living thing in the city – every man and woman, both the young and the old, and every ox, sheep, and donkey' [Joshua 6: 21]). With this model in view, the fate of the Canaanites of this New World was sealed. Winthrop starts his sermon proclaiming that 'God Almighty in his most holy and wise providence hath so disposed of the condition of mankind, as in all times some must be rich some poor, some high and eminent in power and dignity; others mean and in subjection'. Euro-Christians were ordained to be lifted high and be eminent in power and dignity, while the natives were mean savages ordained for subjection. For those facing colonisation, to embrace the faith of the approaching coloniser is akin to becoming complicit with their own dispossession and decimation.

Regardless of how appealing Euro-Christianity might appear, because it is embedded in white supremacy it remains incongruent with Indigenous human flourishing. This faith has spread its culture of death by a sadistic cruelty revealed through crusades, inquisitions, religious wars and colonialism. Taking root in the so-called New World, Euro-Christianity reached new heights of human depravity. With the foundation of the USA, this savage brutality found spiritual expression and justification in a culture steeped in invasion, genocide, slavery, Manifest Destiny, Jim Crow and gunboat diplomacy.

US Manifestation of Eurocentrism

White supremacist attitudes undergirding the rise of an emerging nation took root when the first Indigenous people were killed to steal their land and when the first Africans were enslaved to produce wealth for Euro-Americans. Spiritual justifiers of these acts existed throughout US history. In their minds, invasion and enslavement were reconcilable with their interpretation of the biblical text. As the culture changed, expanded and matured, taking seriously its political rhetoric concerning liberty and democracy, faith too changed, expanded and matured, better masking its oppressive contradictions. Part of this change included an economic component. No longer was it enough for faith to justify white culture; it was also tasked with justifying the white culture of a minority of Euro-Americans, the very rich, those who today are referred to as the One Percent.

This change in how Euro-American faith is defined was a response to the economic upheavals taking place within the culture. As the Great Depression started to come to an end, the Euro-American uber-rich were frustrated by the rise of powerful labour movements and aggravated by setbacks in profits due to government regulations implemented during the New Deal. Failing to combat the economic progressiveness being ushered in by the Roosevelt administration, their spirits were uplifted when a Euro-Christian minister by the name of James W. Fifield gave the plenary address during the 1940 National Association of Manufacturers conference attended by some 5,000 heads of corporations (such as Standard Oil, General Electric, Sears Roebuck, Mutual Life and General Motors). Fifield delivered a message of salvation from the sins of Roosevelt's economic policies, preaching a Euro-Christian response to economic liberalism by advocating free enterprise and deregulation.

Fifield led Euro-Christian thought to encompass savage capitalist ideology, delegating the proselytisation of unrestrained capitalism to Euro-Christian clergy. Proclaiming the white God of capital, these ministers sought to save the soul of the nation by converting the hearts and minds of the general public to the cosmic struggle against economic liberalism. The task of outsourcing the persuasion of church congregants to capitalist ideology fell on the Euro-Christian clergy. This co-option of Euro-Christianity introduced an eleventh commandment: Thou shalt be a capitalist. Euro-Christian orthodoxy came to be understood as a culture defined by a merit-based economic system (if you work hard, you get rich) and a faith defined as a merit-based spiritual system (if you are good, you go to Heaven), all the while demonising New Deal progressive policies as 'pagan stateism'.

Soon, major Euro-American titans of industry like J. Howard Pew – the president of Sun Oil – and his brother Joseph became patrons of Fifield's ministry. With time, the Pew brothers would provide the financial backing to launch the ministry of an obscure pro-capitalist tent-revivalist named Billy Graham. Graham, receiving a call from Pew, preached against every possible progressive policy designed to alleviate human suffering: the New Deal, the Fair Deal, the New Frontier, the Great Society and civil rights. On the last issue he blasted Martin Luther King, Jr, for seeking to change laws rather than hearts. The social ills of racism would be healed with Jesus's second coming. King might dream 'that one day little black boys and girls will be holding hands with little white boys and girls', but

Graham quipped that the dream would be fulfilled only 'when Christ comes again'. Fearing a future where government strips Christians of their rights, he called Euro-Christians to elect officials sharing his apocalyptic vision.

Euro-American faith was redefined through merging a white supremacist culture with expanding the privilege, power and profit of Euro-American capitalists. This *ménage à trois* of capitalists, Euro-Christians and white supremacists eventually faced political challenges due to demographic changes at the start of the new millennium. The cultural power dynamics were threatened by a steady decline of Euro-American births, dipping for the first time below 50% of the national total; law enforcement being held accountable for what was once the uninhibited killings of persons of colour for minor law infractions; the affirmation of same-gender-loving marriages; and the unravelling of white affirmative action that had privileged and supported unqualified whites since the establishment of the Republic. Euro-Christians, who until then had a cultural and political system designed to benefit them, watched with horror as the White House ceased to be white with the election of a Black man.

Marginalised communities on the underside of Euro-American culture began to make strides in demanding a share in the nation's riches, holding Euro-America accountable for its refusal to live up to their rhetoric of 'liberty and justice for all'. A whitelash occurred in the form of electing a champion of white supremacy and Euro-American culture, demanding to make America great again, code language for 'make America white again'. Donald Trump became a cult-like figure bent on eradicating the last vestiges of progressive legislation, the last great white hope for reclaiming perceived lost territory.

Since the 1940s, Euro-Christian defence of capitalism had given rise to an American culture not only life-denying for people of colour but also damning for most Euro-Americans. By supporting Trump, many Euro-Americans followed a president whose economic system was detrimental to them. Unexamined structural racism is a powerful electoral motivator, more potent than any aspiration to form a more perfect union where Euro-Americans' own standard of living could improve. Euro-American culture and Euro-Christian faith provided spiritual cover to widespread oppression, preferring a failed state to one based on democratic principles. Telling are several polls which showed that the day after the 6 January 2021 storming of the Capitol, 45% of Republicans supported the insurrection, as 52% blamed President-elect Biden for the violent rebellion. Four in 10 Republicans expressed belief in the necessity of political violence. It is as if these Euro-Christian followers of Trump belong to a cult.

The Cult of Eurocentrism

During the 2016 presidential election, white Euro-Christians overwhelmingly supported candidate Donald Trump: 81% of white Evangelical voters cast their votes for him, as did 60% of white Catholic voters and 57% of white mainline Protestant voters. Four years of unapologetic racism ('very fine people on both sides'); authoritarian anti-democracy sentiments (storming the Capitol); ineptitude (almost 400,000 deaths from COVID by the end of his term); support for white supremacist terrorist groups ('stand back and stand by'); as well as lies, predatory sexism and self-enrichment failed to weaken his standing among Euro-Christians. Quite the contrary; his popularity among Euro-Americans increased, as indicated by the eight million more votes received in 2020!

It is as if he can stand in the middle of Fifth Avenue and shoot somebody and not lose voters! Such unquestionable obedience raises the question, 'Is the faith of the US white culture a cult?' The difference between a religious community and a cult teeters on semantics. One person's faith community, where purpose and belonging are found, can easily be described by someone else as a cult. Most are familiar with religious cults that have ended with devastating consequences, whether it be Jim Jones leading 900 followers to drink the cyanide-laced Kool-Aid, or Marshall Applewhite, whose 39 followers committed suicide so as to leave their bodily 'containers' and board the alien spaceship hidden behind the Hale-Bopp comet or, more recently, Keith Raniere's NXIVM, which notoriously attracted beautiful heiresses and actresses to personal-growth seminars only to sexually traffic them and brand them with Raniere's initials on their pelvises.

In cults, characteristically, a charismatic leader unites the community around a certain version of reality. Yale psychiatrist Robert Jay Lifton studied what at the time was deemed mind control among returning POWs held by the Chinese during the Korean War (think of *The Manchurian Candidate*). In his 1961 book *Thought Reform and the Psychology of Totalism*, he studied how authoritarian leaders exerted power similarly to cultish religious institutions. In his book he listed eight criteria by which to define what he called 'thought reform'. Steven Hassan, himself a former member of Sun Myung Moon's Unification Church cult and a current clinical professional dedicated to assisting cult members through his scholarship, published *The Cult of Trump* in 2019 arguing the forty-fifth President fits the stereotypical profile of a cult leader as outlined by Lifton.

Employing Lifton's eight criteria and building on how Hassan illustrates the parallels of cult-like behaviour by Trump's followers, we can explore the rise of a personality cult tied to US Euro-Christian culture. The first of these, milieu control, is when the leader regulates the flow of information, only trusting the news generated by allies that boosts their 'alternative facts' while labelling others as 'fake news'. Second, mystical manipulation stages a supernatural or divine experience. This can be illustrated by having ministers lay hands on the President in the Oval Office or declaring him chosen by God. Third, demand for purity promotes a world seen though a simplistic 'good versus evil' lens. Because supporters fall short of these ideals, feelings of shame and guilt are generated, followed by punishment, as witnessed through the high turnover of White House-appointed personnel. The fourth criterion, confession voiced publicly, is expected when failure to conform occurs. Confessions when voiced are neither forgiven nor forgotten but instead used by the President (who remembers every slight or betrayal) to be punished later. Fifth, sacred science, according to which the ideology and truths of the group are absolute, is invoked. For example, truths concerning climate change, minimising the consequences of the COVID-19 pandemic, or science in general are dismissed as 'hoaxes' when the cult's worldview is challenged. Sixth, loading the language is employed to teach followers thought-stopping clichés that reduce the complexities of an issue to simplistic absolutes. This is best demonstrated with terms like 'Build that wall [along the US–Mexico border]', 'Lock her [Hillary Clinton] up', 'Deep State' and 'Stop the Steal [of the 2020 election]'. Seventh, privileging doctrine over person is when the ideology of the group is privileged over the experience of the individual. This was best demonstrated when the President, shortly after losing the election, took a victory lap showcasing how his supposed actions saved lives during the pandemic even while the numbers of infections and deaths were skyrocketing. Finally, dispensing of existence holds that only group members have a right to be; critics do not. This was demonstrated by dividing blue from red states, where the latter received resources by which to combat the pandemic while the former were consistently denied federal assistance as calls to liberate those Democrat-led states were made.

All of this begs the question: Did Trump become the cult leader, or was he simply ordained to lead the already existing cult, temporarily serving as its leader? What if the cult in question is, or has historically been, truly leaderless? When exploring the cult of Trump – the intersection of faith, culture and classism – the focus usually is on one individual, usually a man. But, based on what the USA experienced during the Trump administration, the cause of cultish behaviour did not rest solely with a narcissistic con artist, a manipulator of reality gifted in his ability to sell snake oil. A cult of US Euro-Christianity, established to justify the invasion and genocide that occurred during first contact in the Western hemisphere, was incorporated into the very fabric of what would emerge as the USA. The doctrine of white supremacy (a doctrine also embraced by some people of colour) advocated by this nationalist Euro-Christian cult was incorporated into the social structures of the nation so that those who are unjustly privileged can allow the state to be racist for them, smugly clinging to the illusion that they do not have a racist bone in their bodies and demonstrating outrage if questioned about their unexamined biases.

Should we be surprised that a Trump-type figure arose to capture the imagination of Euro-Christians? Euro-Christianity is hardwired for authoritarian cult figures. What came to be a Eurocentric manifestation of the teachings of Jesus was based upon an authoritarian patriarchal structure (church) modelled on an authoritarian patriarchal family structure. As husbands are perceived to be the God-ordained head of the household, so too is the church autocratically led by ministers (mainly males) called to serve as communal spiritual fathers. Authoritarian men rule at home, at church and in the public sphere. White supremacy and the Euro-Christianity it undergirds are, and have always been, incongruent with democracy. Democratic principles like checks and balances become nuisances that are better dismantled than safeguarded. Should we therefore be surprised that Euro-Christianity, since the days of Constantine, has served as apologist for authoritarian sovereigns, crusading popes, emperors and military dictators who pledge to promote family values?

The cult of Euro-Christianity, since the first invader set foot on what would eventually become the USA, became the spiritual apologist for white nationalism: 'Caesar is Lord'. This Euro-Christian cult was never meant to be a spiritual way of being. Its *raison d'être* was to provide philosophical and theological cover for unchristian government legislation and genocidal policies, to Christianise and normalise the satanic. When all is said and done, the danger to humanity is not so much Donald Trump (that is giving him far too much credit). The real danger to humanity is and has always been Euro-Christianity.

When the faith of the people is the historical construct of a particular type of culture founded on white supremacist principles, then those born to or raised within said culture unconsciously become products of said society. A society develops in which the prevailing white supremacy is not even recognised as existing by those for whom it was constructed to protect and advance. Euro-Christianity becomes a nationalist faith that neither challenges nor threatens the injustices upon which the US social orders thrive. Believing in a morally bankrupt white Jesus trumps the praxis of living a life conforming to a message of putting the needs of the other before one's own. Through a spiritual sleight of hand, Euro-Christians profess belief in a white Jesus who asks nothing of them, a cheap grace that ignores any call to create a more just society, insisting instead on maintaining and sustaining (consciously or unconsciously) the prevailing white supremacy.

While the cult of Euro-Christianity can manifest itself through different faith traditions – or no religious tradition – it nonetheless has certain common denominators. Euro-Christianity, besides its preferential option for whiteness, justifies a partiality for hyper-individualism, stresses 'law and order', emphasises personal charity rather than public justice-building, believes that God's will is manifested within neoliberalism and market economics, and underscores an orthodoxy based on deductive reasoning over and against an orthopraxis based on an inductive methodology. Should we therefore be surprised that many within cultures comprising communities of colour abhor the faith embraced by Euro-Americans?

Authoritarian figures like Trump might arise from time to time to become the focus of adulation. Still, for most of Euro-Christian history, no gravitating individual was required for white supremacy and savage capitalism to flourish. Over the centuries, white supremacy and unjust economic structures within the USA have been successfully normalised and legitimised without the guidance of one cultic leader. What makes Trump an aberration is not his cult status; rather, the cult of Euro-Christianity has always existed within the USA without the necessary presence of a charismatic leader requiring reverence. True worship has been limited and reserved for a white God, or a white Jesus. White supremacy and unrestrained neoliberalism have been manifested through white theology and white liturgy, not necessarily a particular individual of flesh and blood. Unlike more traditional cults with a designated leader, the democratisation of the privileges reserved for the cult leader was distributed among the devotees on the basis of skin pigmentation. Those excluded from this nationalist cult, who can never belong to the dominant culture due to a lack of racial or ethnic purity, are the ones who will always remain at risk.

Reconciling the Colonised with Euro-Christianity
True, the thought of non-violent conversation seeking reconciliation is ideal. But in all honesty, those perpetuating and benefiting from the institutionalised violence embedded within Euro-American culture have lost all moral authority to paternalistically instruct those on their margins on how to seek and achieve their own liberation. And here is the difficult realisation with which to wrestle when it comes to conversations about working together for a common cause. Can one arrive at a meeting of the minds with a party who believes they have a God-given right to domesticate their non-white inferiors? Can reconciliation even be possible? Can those beaten down today by a faith and culture designed to maintain and sustain white superiority ever kiss and embrace those seeking their

subjugation? We know all too well how such efforts play out. A lull in violence might indeed ensue. But all it takes is one mis-spoken word, one act of defiance, one demonstration of independence to be smacked down again. 'Get over the past already and be a good Christian by providing forgiveness and forgetfulness so we can move on already' becomes the defensive response.

But no, we all cannot just simply get along when one party refuses to recognise the causes of violence. Susan Bro, who lost her daughter to the violence of the Unite the Right rally in Charlottesville in 2017, warned during a 2021 *New York Times* interview that 'the rush to hug each other and sing "Kumbaya" is not an effective strategy'. History teaches that we simply cannot just hug it out without assigning accountability and taking responsibility. Unity is but a consequence of justice, not the end goal.

The dominant white Euro-Christian culture, regardless of rhetoric calling for reconciliation, has neither the desire nor the will to truly seek a justice-based culture. For if they were to be successful in such an effort, it would mean the loss of their station within society. Devotees of the cult of Euro-Christianity never want to be of 'one accord' with those they deem to be undeserving of belonging. Euro-Americans prefer to simply embrace people of colour in fraternity without sacrificing the prevailing institutionalised social structures that secure their unearned power, profit and privilege. And here is why healing the division, widened during the Trump years, is such a lost cause. No historical examples exist of those benefiting from how oppressive political policies are structured renouncing their privilege for the sake of creating a more just society. Any advances made in the cause of justice usually are paid for in blood, the blood of the dispossessed.

The issue is not and never really was Trump, but the Euro-Christian faith and culture that showered him with cultish adoration. Thus, to focus solely on him ignores the Eurocentric faith and culture that can bring forth another Trump-like rogue. What is truly important is the Euro-Christianity responsible for the original rise of Trump, a pseudo-faith refashioned in his own image. He might have lost the 2020 presidential election, but his fervent supporters have only been energised by the rage of the loss of their political clout and the fear of those whom they have subjugated over the centuries. This fear and frenzy, flamed by modern-day false Euro-Christian talk-show prophets, have become a holy crusade that only deepens the level of despair which could lead to more militant future responses. Feeling betrayed by their own government, they are in danger of losing the white affirmative action that always secured their privileged space within society, making Euro-Christians the greatest threat to democracy, as witnessed during their refusal to recognise the President elect in 2021.

No doubt Trumpism continues to be based on heightened white anxiety and angst. Opportunity to explore possibilities for a more multiethnic and multiracial, justice-based culture has been lost. Diversity and a redistribution of power and wealth are defined as threats to Euro-Americans rather than solutions for the country. The future is indeed bleak. The resilience of white supremacy is enough to make anyone hopeless.

Rejecting Eurocentric Faith and Culture
For centuries, those who have suffered politically, economically and spiritually at the hands of a Euro-Christian nationalist culture looked towards their oppressors to develop an understanding of their oppression and the means by which to seek their liberation. The production of US Euro-Christian epistemology, however, is and always has been grounded in Eurocentric nativism, making those on their margins complicit with their own cultural oppression when embracing Euro-Christian faith. With the imposition of Euro-Christianity, white Euro-Americans' inclinations towards white supremacy are normalised and legitimised in the minds of the oppressed. Sadly, many – wishing to emulate the eminent white scholars of the top US research institutions – at times ironically become Euro-Christianity's most steadfast defenders. For cultures relegated to the underside of whiteness, becoming disciples of Euro-Christianity means complicity with the inhumanity visited upon non-whites by US Christian nationalism. The uncritical embrace of Euro-Christianity silences any attempt to decolonise, making disenfranchised faith leaders complicit with their people's oppression. Euro-Christianity, unjustifiable in a postcolonial world, pursues its own liberation from the historical damage inflicted in the name of civilising and Christianising non-whites.

We are thus left asking, Can we come together, heal our divide and learn how to live in peace without the prevailing racism and ethnic discrimination? Can the disenfranchised keep coming forward in good faith, seeking to convince those who refuse to listen? Those who refuse to examine their own faith tradition, which justifies all sorts of bloodletting? Seeking solutions for the existing institutional violence visited upon different races, ethnicities and faith traditions lies with those historically responsible for benefiting from said violence. Salvation of the faith and culture can begin only with the turning away from 'sin' that is the repudiation and rejection of the cult of Euro-Christianity, an act I fear most Euro-Americans – even those who are neither Euro-Christian nor religious – are unwilling to make.

Proof of an unwillingness to repent was demonstrated by white Christians during the 2020 election, in their refusal to rebut and renounce Trumpism. In disproportionate numbers they came out and voted for the one who affectively wrapped himself in the flag (culture) and cross (faith).

They voted for their white Euro-Christian beliefs and the unearned privileges flowing from said beliefs. If all this is true, are we, as an encompassing culture, condemned to the consequences of the prevailing Euro-Christian cult that continues to advance the failed policies of white supremacy? Is there any hope for those who for generations bowed their knees before the white Jesus of genocide, slavery, manifest destiny, gunboat diplomacy, colonialism and all manner of oppressive political structures? Can a new way of being as a culture even be possible? The only hope is the total repudiation and rejection of Euro-Christianity and the economic, political and cultural symbols it holds up. What is needed, if we wish to survive as a culture, is for whites to get 'saved'. Their salvation is made possible when they crucify their white supremacy, their white theology and their white Jesus. Only by nailing all that provides them with unearned privilege to that old, rugged cross can a semblance of resurrected hope arise. The white Jesus leads to death, destruction and damnation. Euro-Americans, for the sake of their own salvation and liberation, must follow the Jesus of the disenfranchised, the Jesus of the dispossessed, the Jesus of the disinherited. To continue clinging to the white Jesus will only bring forth further death.

Bibliography

De La Torre, Miguel A., *Burying White Privilege: Resurrecting a Badass Christianity* (Grand Rapids, MI: Eerdmans, 2018).

De La Torre, Miguel A., *Decolonizing Christianity: Becoming Badass Believers* (Grand Rapids, MI: Eerdmans, 2021).

Hassan, Steven, *The Cult of Trump* (New York: Free Press, 2019).

Kruse, Kevin M., *One Nation Under God: How Corporate America Invented Christian America* (New York: Basic Books, 2015).

Lifton, Robert Jay, *Thought Reform and the Psychology of Totalism: A Study of 'Brainwashing' in China* (Chapel Hill, NC: University of North Carolina Press, 1989 [1961]).

Worship and Spirituality

Grace Eun-Sun Lee

History has shown myriads of ways in which various cultures and people groups have survived waves of colonialism and immigration through religious practices. In North America, specifically in Canada and the USA, the pursuit of God among Christian communities has been interwoven with the pursuit of freedom. Land has come to symbolise the time, space and rights that allow worship to be freely expressed. North American worship and spirituality are shaped by one's desire to freely express one's devotion while affirming one's uniqueness within a community that provides safety and acceptance.

Not all forms of worship have enjoyed liberty of expression. Historically, the First Nations of North America have faced many struggles in their homeland, fighting for the existence of their cultures, languages and people groups against the force of colonialism. Even when they came to adopt the Christian faith, their Indigenous traditions and rituals were condemned as heathen, pagan and occultic.

Another group that historically struggled to find acceptance in the North American Church was the Black Church. Forced to migrate across the Atlantic Ocean against their will, African Americans survived slavery as well as injustices in the exchange of trade, culture and religion between Africa and the Americas. They were separated from their motherlands and ancestral cultures and stripped of their individuality and their personhood. Yet through the Christian faith, an African American spirituality was born, as witnessed by vibrant expressions of song and dance as communal worship of the God of liberation. For both the Native Americans and the African Americans, even when they were oppressed by the impacts of colonialism, the Christian faith anchored a new source of hope. The power of the gospel took hold, transforming a spirituality originally rooted in animism.

In recent history, North American spirituality has been fuelled by immigrants, who arrived often after great sacrifice, leaving their native communities and identities behind for the pursuit of a better life. Continual immigration from Latin America, Africa, Oceania and Asia has led to these cultures finding a home in different places in North America. The influx of immigration led to the exponential growth in diaspora churches of various denominations, including Catholics, Charismatics, Orthodox and Pentecostals.

Language also reflects which culture dominantly influences the spirituality of the community. Many immigrant churches have multiple services, conducted in their mother tongue, in English, or bilingually to cater for the different generations represented. Furthermore, these churches have become the hubs for community and solace, places of nostalgia and belonging where languages and cultures intersect. Corporate expressions of worship are more evident within the collectivist-oriented communities, where there are intentional moments of interaction with one another during the service or worship ritual. Verbal responses are expected during the preaching. Dancing is not merely a performance to be watched but a communal offering of praise.

Out of the immigrants' struggles in a working society that values individualism, communal worship becomes a signpost of loving God and others. The Christian community provides a haven of acceptance and belonging. It also serves as a place to practise hospitality. Simultaneously, there is a theological emphasis on a God who sees people in their struggles and delivers them from oppression. There is a collective remembrance of the freedom God has brought thus far, whether it is from spiritual or political bondage. There is also a collective cry for a fullness of freedom not yet achieved in society.

In the same way that each denomination emphasises certain doctrines and practices, particular ethnic communities highlight various Christian themes and express them uniquely through their cultures. Multiethnic worship pioneer Sandra Maria Van Opstal has observed how each group underscores and responds to distinct attributes of God. While African American spirituality highlights freedom and remembrance of God's power, Latino worship celebrates the presence of the Holy Spirit with radical joy. While the Asian American community expresses intimate devotion in their reverence towards the sacrifice and servanthood of God, the Western community exuberates adoration especially through the works of creation and nature. Though the list is not exhaustive, these diverse worship expressions demonstrate the repertoire of Christian doxology, pointing towards the multifaceted character of God.

First Nations: The Jesus Way
Though many have rejected Christianity as 'the white man's religion', a growing movement among the First Nations is following and embracing the 'Jesus Way'. Denominations like the Lutherans, Anglicans/Episcopals, Methodists and American Baptists have been involved with the Indian Ecumenical Movement (IEM) for several decades. Unfortunately, Native

leadership is absent in much of mainstream Evangelicalism, as Native culture is rejected as incompatible with biblical orthodoxy. The rejection of Native culture is a stumbling block to the Native American community, preventing them from encountering Jesus as Creator, as they gradually lose their language, culture and customs. Over centuries of missionary work, when many Natives became Christians, they participated in Christian practices that reflected mainly Euro-American forms of worship. As Native Christian communities have been marginalised, misunderstood and oppressed for their spirituality, their Indigenous expressions have been denied a chance to flourish.

In recent decades, an emerging group of Native Christian leaders has sought to decolonise the gospel and contextualise it in a way that is true to their Indigenous practices. Such leaders as Kaitlin B. Curtice, Terry LeBlanc and Richard Twiss raise awareness of the Native Christian community's presence and promote innovative worship and spirituality that are rooted in their cultures and that honours their histories. In his book *Rescuing the Gospel from the Cowboys: A Native American Expression of the Jesus Way* (Downers Grove, IL: InterVarsity Press, 2015), Richard Twiss notes that a disparity exists between the First Nations and more recent immigrants in the North American Church as each group seeks to find a place of belonging in the greater Church community.

Among First Nation Christians, Jesus is worshipped as the one and only Creator of heaven and earth, and all living things. The people of the First Nations have deep reverence for creation, which includes the earth, trees and all creatures. The varied beauty of creation only points to deeper revelation of the one Creator. Through nature, the wonder and mystery of the transcendent and the supernatural enhance the corporate spiritual experience. For example, as trees, while outliving generations, are interconnected with one another by their roots, the First Nations reflect on how the trees also connect them to their ancestors and their communities. First Nation Christians have deep appreciation of their histories and an awareness that each person is connected to a tribe, and each tribe carries a unique heritage. In the same way that individual trees have intertwining roots, each person's history is intertwined with the history of creation. All living matter shares the commonality of dwelling under the grace of the Creator and the privilege of responding in the creation song.

In First Nation communities, remembrance is a gift that is to be shared. Thus, ceremonial rituals and storytelling are essential to cultivate remembrance. In specifically remembering one's ancestors, the sense of identity is secured, and legacies of predecessors are honoured. Stories, considered sacred and thus treasured by an individual or a tribal community, range from testimonies of suffering to those of liberation in the radiance of the

Son who came to dwell among the Natives. The stories and poetry the Native Christians share are received as gifts to be tended, especially in the face of resistance. The beauty and power of storytelling come in the form of reverence towards the Creator's sovereign purposes and direction. Furthermore, when it comes to biblical narratives, Native Christians are attentive to the way Jesus engages with natural substances, like healing the blind man using spit and dirt.

The First Nations love to engage in worship with their hearts through music and dance. Traditional intertribal powwows have become a festive celebration of drumming, singing and dancing, a social event with food and fellowship. Dancing has become a way to pray, or, as Twiss puts it, 'dancing our prayers'. Drums play a pivotal role in the Native music, reflecting the heartbeat of the whole community. Songs unify the community in a sensory experience to connect them to the deeper meaning of the Christian faith. In addition to drums, sweat lodges have been repurposed for prayers and petitions of healing and blessings. The sweat lodge ritual is where humanity, in all its frailty, encounters the divine Creator and receives healing, mercy and forgiveness through the powerful name of Jesus Christ. Often the aroma of burning sage, sweet grass or cedar accompanies prayer to symbolise prayers ascending to God.

In redeeming and cultivating their Christian identity, the First Nations of North America have come together in various collaborations, adopting the posture of journeying together as followers of the Jesus Way. Their solidarity honours their ancestral roots and provides hope for deeper connection with God and each other. Representing diverse denominational and tribal backgrounds, their initiatives also partner with other Native Christian communities around the world in the discourse and work of Christian contextualisation and evangelism.

Black: Wholistic, Whole-body Worship
African American spirituality traces its roots to Africans of various backgrounds in terms of tribe, language and belief, who acclimated into North American soil and assembled into one collective group. Their Christian faith has been refined as they navigated the economic, political and cultural turmoil of recent history while keeping a corporate faith. The vibrancy of their devotional practices empowers individuals to anchor themselves in God and in their communities as embodied human beings worthy of dignity and respect.

Adopting the wholistic worldview, all aspects of worship, including the liturgy, reflect a connectedness and inter-relatedness in which the worshipper engages the whole self with God and others. This wholistic mindset is rooted in traditional African spirituality, where all of life is deemed sacred, with religious implications. The worshipper participates physically with the total self, body and voice, in response to the movement of the Holy Spirit. Thus, Black worship can be characterised as Spirit-filled, celebratory and dynamic. Worshippers celebrate what God has done in bringing them this far and for the promise of the Holy Spirit still dwelling in their midst, empowering them to express powerful modes of worship through vocal improvisation, dance and the arts. The working of the Holy Spirit in the individual and the community is manifested by the physical responses, especially through dance. Their dances consist of running, clapping and the waving of hands as they improvise through various rhythms and melody. Each person expresses gratitude and joy in their own unique way, from exclamations to proclamations, from shouting to chanting, humming and moaning.

The majority of the Black church in North America consists of Protestants, mostly Baptists. There are about three million African American Catholics in the USA, around the same number as belong to the African Methodist Episcopal Church. Just as there is no single African culture, there is no single Black church culture with one style of worship. Worship practices are exchanged between the Catholic and Protestant circles. Black Catholic congregations have adopted numerous Black Protestant traditions in their liturgies, like dance, shouts and gospel music. In New Orleans, the birthplace of jazz, Black Catholic parishes innovated the Gospel Jazz Mass to incorporate indigenous Black music into their liturgies and prayers.

In addition to serving as a gathering place for Sunday service, the African American church fulfils spiritual, political and prophetic purposes for the welfare of the community. The church has served various purposes, including being a source of education, political engagement, arts and social gatherings. It is a place of refuge amid the stresses of life and discrimination from the wider society. Personhood is restored in the presence of others who share similar experiences of oppression. The Word of God, preached and applied in the practical, everyday life, engages with issues of social justice and equality. Church services are where people experience liberation in solidarity, expressing and enacting it through dynamic, bodily movements and vocal spontaneity.

Community is essential in Black worship. All are family, and the community strengthens one's sense of belonging. While Black worship is considered a corporate act of celebration, the uniqueness of their expression is that one's individuality is encouraged even within the currents of collectivism. Thus, improvisation is evident in songs and dances, where the congregation encourages others to 'sing your song'. Through physical, vocal and communal modes of worship, creativity is unleashed in the freedom provided by the safe refuge within the faith community.

One distinguishing feature of African American worship is the call–response pattern, which resonates with their communal worldview. Whether it is in the way they preach, pray or engage with music, each component of worship is an event where the preacher and every member of the congregation is in dialogue with one another. Every worshipper participates in the proclamation of God's Word, responding with phrases like 'Preach it!', 'Amen!', 'Hallelujah!', 'Praise the Lord!' or non-verbal acts like humming, nodding the head, waving the hand, clapping or snapping the fingers. Prayer is also a dialogical event in which the participants' active responses demonstrate the unified leading of the Holy Spirit.

One of the gifts the Black church contributed to other American churches was exemplifying what it means to lament. Historically, the roots of Black spirituality have turned laments into songs of prayers. In *A Time for Sorrow: Recovering the Practice of Lament in the Life of the Church* (Boston, MA: Hendrickson, 2019), six scholars have reflected on the spiritual significance of lament especially for contemporary times. Emmett G. Price III, an expert on Black music and culture and Christian worship, published his chapter as a separate excerpt during the time of the COVID-19 pandemic and the aftermath of the murder of George Floyd. He challenged and exhorted the global church to join in an honest act of lamenting, which consists of complaints, vulnerability, confession and praise, for the hope of healing together and repositioning grief towards the glory of God.

Latino/Latina: Passionate Spirituality

The Latino community carries a complex history shaped by European colonialism in the Americas. When the USA expanded into the western and southern regions, indigenous Latinos became citizens. However, as minorities, the Latino communities were impacted by conquest and by migration. Though their proficiencies differ, most Latin communities in North America are bilingual, in English and Spanish or Portuguese, as language has served to provide strong connection to one's sense of ethnic self-identity.

Their religious faith, whether Catholic, Evangelical Protestant, Pentecostal or traditional African religion, plays an integral part in forming the Latin identity. The Christian faith is lived out in the context of communities. The Latin culture is intergenerational and community oriented, deeply committed to family while branching towards other ethnic and cultural communities within its vicinity.

The experience of the fullness and freedom of the Holy Spirit is an emphasis among Latino Pentecostals, Evangelical Protestants and Charismatic Catholics. The manifestations of the Holy Spirit and the exercise of spiritual gifts are two distinct characteristics in the fast-growing Latin spirituality that embraces the supernatural. Their worship can be characterised as 'prophetic', where the church community intentionally discerns the need of the moment and acts in faith to minister with great passion and expectation. Mercy ministries and outreaches of the Latin faith communities integrating the proclamation of the gospel with works of justice and compassion are fuelled with passion and the empowerment of the Holy Spirit.

Latin spirituality is marked by passion. Worship is primarily affective, with free expression of feelings and emotions in response to what the Holy Spirit is saying or doing. This freedom to respond with one's whole heart is manifested through various religious events like Holy Week, passion plays, *posadas* or the *quinceañera*. Many Latinos express the fiesta spirit – in the Christian context, fiesta can be experienced through ritual and religious drama where God's mighty character and deeds are proclaimed and celebrated. Fiesta worship consists of joy, enthusiasm and spontaneity. Humour, laughter, applause, dance and hugs are various means of the corporate interactions that occur within a worship service. Latinos embrace physical touch and use their bodies to express the fiesta spirit, through handshakes, *abrazo* or embrace, or holy kiss.

It is worth noting that the fiesta acknowledges the difficulties and struggles of life, particularly in the area of oppression and marginalisation. The celebration comes from the gratitude of simply being alive. The celebratory liturgical elements of worship point to the hope and liberation the gospel brings to living purposeful lives. The sharing of *testimonios* has become an occasion to testify of God's goodness and to express thanksgiving for answered prayers. The community joins to celebrate the Holy Spirit's continual presence at work in ministering to them and among them. The church, with the fullness of emotions and the liveliest actions, gathers as one extended family to praise God with joyous music and expressive art.

The Latin style of music uniquely captures their history. Through music, Latino believers pour out their hearts and souls. Congregational singing is an important part of the service that encourages a high level of participation, whether it is through dancing, the lifting of hands or exclaiming a shout of praise. The *coritos*, which are short praise songs with lyrics derived from the Scriptures and Hispanic-style music, are the most popular type of congregational songs circulating in Hispanic communities.

Prayer plays a significant part in the worship service. Often the prayers are spontaneous and without time limit. Before the presence of God, burdens are openly shared for corporate petition. Catholic churches incorporate incense, images and other artistic forms to cultivate the worship environment *ambiente*. More initiatives within the Hispanic community incorporate traditional instruments, like the Spanish guitar and maracas, and rhythms. Brazilian gospel music has gained momentum as a musical genre in its native land. Its influence is spreading over Latin America and to North America.

Asian North American: Emerging, Collective Spirituality
Though the presence of English-speaking Asian Christians is growing, the Asian North American (ANA) community still forms a cultural minority whose collective Christian identity is still maturing. Fuller Theological Seminary Professor Russell Yee, examining its history in comparison with other ethnic cultures, considers the ANA worship culture to be in its young, emergent phase, not yet fully developed nor understood.

When describing ANA spirituality in his book *Worship on the Way: Exploring Asian North American Experience* (Valley Forge, PA: Judson Press, 2012), Yee mentions five dominant groups of Asians representing distinctive histories and cultures: (1) East and Southeast Asians, (2) South Asians, (3) Native Hawaiians and Pacific Islanders, (4) Asians in Mexico, Central America and the Caribbean, and (5) North, Central and West Asians. He notes that efforts to create a collective Asian identity are more active in the USA than in Canada.

While ANA groups vary in their immigration narratives, a common struggle they share is that every individual and community has to navigate between various cultures, especially between the two dominant cultures surrounding them, that of their Eastern, Asian heritage and their Western, American environment. The phrase 'East meets West' describes the clash of the two dominant cultures, further defining the Asian North Americans as a bicultural minority.

Much of ANA worship culture has been impacted by Western Christianity. Many Asian communities can trace their Christian heritage to Western missionary activities that occurred in Asia or is occurring in North America. Many bilingual congregations sing translated Western hymns and gospel songs. The physical migration from Asia to America parallels the shift of spirituality as ANA believers leave their animistic or traditional worldviews rooted in Taoism, Buddhism or Confucianism to adopt Westernised contemporary forms of Christian devotion. The exception would be Filipino Christians, as the Philippines is considered a Christian nation with Roman Catholics and Protestants. Western evangelisation provided the ANA church with an expanded Christian repertoire, including theology, songs and evangelism. Consequently, many of the religious practices and rituals associated with Asian culture have been dismissed.

As the ANA church develops in its collective identity, the task of embracing Indigenous traditions honouring one's ethnic culture and the Christian faith lies ahead. Questions remain as to how to incorporate the rich disciplines of prayer like silence and stillness, meditation, chants, incense and bells. The communion table is a great opportunity to celebrate ANA culture, though not without controversy. Yee shares a personal example where in celebrating with the Southeast Asian American community, he uses rice to decorate the table to express Jesus as the 'rice of life' and intentionally chooses a variety of tropical drinks for the communion cup. Yee gives another example where a Japanese American presider serves *senbei* crackers and hot green tea. Rather than appealing to the dark colour of grape juice to reflect the blood of Christ, the presider appeals to the warmth of the tea to reflect the warm nature of blood.

As young as the ANA church might be, Yee affirms the many gifts it has to offer in corporate worship spaces: traditional music and dances, traditional instruments, sharing stories and wisdom proverbs, promoting beauty through architecture, furnishings and decor. Festivals and rituals that honour ancestors and bless the next generation serve healing purposes, especially in the acts of forgiveness and reconciliation between the different generations.

Contemporary Christian Music and Gospel

By the late 1990s, contemporary Pentecostal and Evangelical worship in North America began to receive other forms of worship from all around the world. Since then and into the beginning of the twenty-first century, British Christian songs have been sung in many churches in the USA and Canada. Prominent British songwriters include Graham Kendrick, songwriter of 'Shine, Jesus, Shine', Martin Smith, Matt Redman and Tim Hughes. Following the British influence, music from Australia had the next greatest impact on contemporary worship culture, specifically through Hillsong Church in Sydney. Since the early 2000s, Hillsong's global branding of its contemporary worship spread beyond Australia and America, especially under Darlene Zschech's leadership as the music director from 1995. Hillsong's robust rock-music style attracted youth and young adults.

As North America was receiving fresh forms of contemporary worship from overseas, a new generation of American and Canadian songwriters emerged from the late 1990s. From Grand Saline, Texas, Christopher Tomlin is renowned for his hit songs 'How Great Is Our God' (2004) and 'Amazing Grace (My Chains Are Gone)' (2008). His songs are frequently sung in Evangelical settings. Canadian contemporary Christian artists also reached the Billboard charts and music industry, like Amanda Lindsey Cook, known for her single 'You Make Me Brave' (2014) with Bethel Music. Other well-known Canadian Christian artists include Matt

Maher, a Catholic worship leader who wrote 'Lord I Need You' (2015), and Starfield, a band from Winnipeg, Manitoba, that won Gospel Music Association Canada Covenant Awards.

The USA is known as the second-largest Spanish-speaking country in the world. There has been a move among Spanish-speaking communities not only to translate English songs into Spanish but to release their own originals that honour the rich Latino musical heritage. Rising contemporary artists include Blanca, Danny Gokey, Evan Kenneth Craft, Christine D'Clario and Mariah McManus from Mosaic MSC.

The Native Christian communities are revitalising their languages, re-establishing their ancestry and family systems, and redeeming their music, dance and various arts to glorify the Creator God in a way that is authentic to their heritage. Some notable Native Christian artists who produced songs and received recognition from the Native American Music Award Association include Ben Miller, Terry and Darlene Wildman, and Jan Michael Looking Wolf. The band Broken Walls led by Jonathan Maracle was among the first to innovate a new genre of worship music that fused the contemporary style with traditional Native sounds, rhythms and instruments.

In Asian American communities, people from the diasporas compose songs in their own native languages. Much of their resources were English contemporary worship songs that were translated into various Asian languages. However, unlike the other ethnic groups that sought opportunities to promote songwriters or worship leaders to the spotlight, the initial efforts of the Asian American community prioritised the local church community, providing new songs that blended contemporary, English-speaking styles with ethnic Asian languages. Often these worship leaders and songwriters are not known beyond their geographic location.

African American communities continue to innovate new musical forms while remaining true to their gospel roots. Gospel music has served a crucial part in the Pentecostal movement and, furthermore, Pentecostalism spread the influence of contemporary Christian music, which includes the genre of gospel music. Distinguished gospel artists include Cece Winans, Fred Hammond, Israel Houghton and Kirk Franklin. Dante Bowe, a member of Bethel Music and Maverick City Music Collective, is a rising artist who bridges the gospel and contemporary Christian genres. Rap and hip-hop also made their way into the contemporary Christian genre. In 2013 Christian rapper Lecrae became the first hip-hop artist to win the Grammy Award for Best Gospel Album.

Since the 2000s, the increase of publishing companies and commercial entities like Passion Conference, Maranatha! Music, and Capitol Christian Music Group have equipped the Christian music industry to produce more music. While many associate contemporary music with spotlights and a concert-like atmosphere, the worship space has also been shifting towards more intimate settings, such as living rooms. Such worship initiatives as Housefires, United Pursuit and Upper Room have a more acoustic musical style.

With the advancement of social media platforms like YouTube, worship songs are readily distributed between North America and to the rest of the world. In light of recent crises like the COVID-19 global pandemic and the Ukraine war, Christian music has made national and global impact by providing hope, encouragement and inspiration to promote peace and reconciliation in times of conflict and distress. In 2020, two songs – 'The Blessing' and 'Way Maker' – topped the worship music charts in North America and became popular as the worship anthems during the global pandemic.

First introduced in North Carolina on 1 March 2020, before its official release, 'The Blessing', written by Kari Jobe, Cody Carnes and Elevation Worship, became a viral sensation during the initial months of the pandemic. Since then, over 100 YouTube renditions by digital choirs and translations have been produced from more than 128 countries around the world. Based on the Aaronic blessing from the Book of Numbers, the song that was launched from a Baptist Evangelical church in the USA became an expression of solidarity that connected churches and nations together.

Another song that impacted the North American church during the pandemic and in the wake of racial tensions was 'Way Maker'. The song is unique in that it originated from Nigeria, written by Osinachi Kalu Okoro Egbu, also known as Sinach. 'Way Maker' had global influence, being translated into more than 50 languages. Known as the godfather of Christian contemporary music, Michael W. Smith and another American Christian group, LeeLand, released renditions of the song, which then expanded its influence, especially among North American Evangelicals. Worship music produced from the Global Church is slowly making its appearance, impacting North American society through the help of media and American Christian worship leaders.

Collaboration among Christian artists has increased in recent years. Canadian Catholic worship leader Matt Maher has written music with many American Protestant Evangelicals to build bridges between Christian traditions. The album *Old Church Basement* is a collaborative project between Maverick City and Elevation Worship that won the 2022 Grammy Award for Best Contemporary Christian Music Album. Such collaborative endeavours not only accelerated the spread of contemporary Christian music throughout North America but also demonstrated the unity of the Christian faith and the strengthening of the North American Church.

Conclusion: Culturally Diverse Worship

As North America continues to come to terms with a more diverse society, endeavours to diversify expressions of worship in local Christian contexts increase. Christian ministries and networks, across many different traditions, are intensifying their work on cultural engagement. Their aim is to honour and incorporate the diversity represented in the local and global church into regular church services. With vast resources of theology, media and exposure to diverse contexts, the North American Church has great potential to reflect the Global Church in worship practices and dynamic spirituality. From a faith perspective, this can be a taste of the glory of God as described in Book of Revelation, in which a great multitude from every nation, tribe, people and language will gather to worship God forever.

Bibliography

Curtice, Kaitlin B., *Native: Identity, Belonging, and Rediscovering God* (Downers Grove, IL: InterVarsity Press, 2020).

Lim, Swee-Hong and Lester Ruth, *Lovin' on Jesus: A Concise History of Contemporary Worship* (Nashville, TN: Abingdon Press, 2017).

Maynard-Reid, Pedrito U., *Diverse Worship: African-American, Caribbean, and Hispanic Perspectives* (Downers Grove, IL: InterVarsity Press, 2000).

Van Opstal, Sandra Maria, *The Next Worship: Glorifying God in a Diverse World* (Downers Grove, IL: InterVarsity Press, 2016).

Yee, Russell, *Worship on the Way: Exploring Asian North American Christian Experience* (Valley Forge, PA: Judson Press, 2012).

Theology

Dhawn B. Martin

Four doctrinal loci order this essay: Scripture, Trinity, kingdom and eschatology. Though far from exhaustive when tasked with surveying this region, each locus highlights ruptures marking the theological landscapes of Canada and the USA. These ruptures simultaneously reflect and provoke questions of authority, access, power, identity, place and language amid talk of the divine. As an example: who (the Triune God, theologians, colonisers) or what (Scripture, sociopolitical institutions) defines concepts such as 'traditional' and 'disruptive'? This question is but one in a field of enquiry as vast as the acreage from Montreal to San Jose, California. Amid such vastness, the aforementioned doctrines offer theological landmarks of a sort. More precisely, they form a confessional quadrilateral that is at once bounded, yet porous, akin to the diversity of North American interpretations of Christianity.

In systematic, and typically more Eurocentric, expositions, prolegomena serve as ports of entry. They map terrains to be covered, track elements of methodology and post epistemological boundaries. Across dusty and recent pasts, however, many 'first words' failed to dissect structures of colonisation, systems of exploitation and economies of extraction that privileged certain voices at the expense of others. Said failures blocked access to the sacred as demarcated by biases both implicit and explicit.

A prolegomenon disrupted, however, attests to the dynamisms of North American theological endeavours. It speaks neither first nor last words definitively, but rather to the threefold form of the Word and to the pluriform expressions of divine revelation. It seeks to attend to the spectrum of lived Christianities that populate the region, cognisant that no one document can encompass the vitality of these evolving faith systems. Thus a prolegomenon disrupted is less a 'first words' than an 'other words' method.

These other words accentuate the contested reality of Christianity in North America. Across borders national, state and theological, notions such as conservative, liberal, heretic, literal, metaphoric, social justice, Bible-based, orthodox, mainline, progressive, secular, eco-spirituality, true believer, end-times and 'spiritual, but not religious' attempt to coexist. Often, however, they compete for sanctified validation.

Amid such contestation, this essay approaches Scripture, Trinity, kingdom and eschatology as confessions both concentrated and expansive. As concentrated expressions of faith, these doctrines crystallise theological resonances across difference. It is key, however, to remain mindful that resonances co-opted by human drives for empire-making have risked and continue to risk calcification into ideology or idolatry. (See the incisive analyses of empire's lingering strategies by Asian American Anglican theologian Kwok Pui-Lan.) As expansive invitations, then, these doctrines point to dissonances and multiplicities inspired by that singularity called the Christ event. Such resonances and dissonances speak to the past, present and future of theological reflection.

Any review of Christian theology in North America, therefore, need reference not only those histories rooted in the Doctrine of Discovery and practices of slavery, but also twenty-first-century wrestling with rising populist sentiments and anti-immigrant rhetorics, alongside continuing racist and misogynistic practices. Theology does not occur in a vacuum. An incarnational exercise, Christian theology attends to bodies and the environs they inhabit. It is imperative, then, to interrogate norms forged through socio- and theo-political structures that have centred and de-centred peoples across the centuries.

Extensive interrogation exceeds the bounds of this essay. That said, the below doctrinal discussions are informed by the work and insight of those that trouble privileged discourses. Examples of this troubling include the blurring of binaries (think gender codes and labels separating 'civilised' and 'uncivilised') and the challenging of white supremacies (think the multi-vocal articulations of First Nations, Indigenous and Native wisdoms along with the #MeToo and Black Lives Matter movements). The sections that follow are informed also by the projects of liberation, post- and de-colonialism, feminism, postmodernity, intersectionality, queer theory, multi-religious dialogue and deep ecology – to name but some. Such projects disrupt first words moored within exclusivist sedimentations.

A few 'other words' are necessary. First, though somewhat neatly contained in sections, no doctrine is extricable from others or from the expanse that is Christian theology. This inter-relatedness echoes the perichoretic vibrancy of Trinitarian revelation. Second, the names and items included in certain parenthetical notes suggest relevant scholarship or examples. While clearly not extensive, these notes offer readers possibilities to engage further with themes articulated in a sentence or paragraph.

Sola Scriptura?

Scripture alone ... or is it? The question is profoundly salient as it draws us to consider the nature, role, content, status and interpretation of Scripture in North American contexts. These considerations link closely to the functioning of norms and sources in theological reflection, whether such functions are expressly delineated or not. No discussion of the normative is complete, of course, without discussing who or what wields power in setting the criteria of normativity. But before the broader category of norms and sources, we turn to the 'what' of Scripture.

Examinations of the nature of sacred texts infuse efforts to name the 'what' of Scripture. Some Christian theologies see such efforts as complicated by the histories and processes of canonisation. Others do not. And while orality was the medium communicating the stories of the Jesus movement prior to print technologies, the patterns, practices and communities enlivening oral traditions are engaged differently. Across the continuum of engagement, First Nations, Indigenous and Native American Christian theologies accentuate the role of spoken words. The act of attending to words woven across histories, rituals, geographies and kinships challenges colonial quests to categorise and control the sacred along with its textuality. (For broader conversation on American Indian religious traditions, read the works of theologian/activist George E. Tinker, citizen of the Osage [wazhazhe] Nation.) In another register, one influenced by the European-inflected Reformed tradition, the spoken word is emphasised as pivotal to the human–divine encounter. A threefold revelation, the Word spoken, alongside the Word written and revealed, attests to the gratuity of Divine love addressing the existential condition.

But just what is this Word? Responses vary. Numerous theological systems affirm Scripture as the Word of God. Beyond that consensus (which is far from unanimous across the region), debate ensues as to whether this Word is one inspired or directly dictated, whether humanly redacted and therefore fallible, or divine and thus inerrant ('Cambridge Declaration Heritage and Resources' from the Alliance of Confessing Evangelicals). The tussle over authorship – be it a writ wholly divine, wholly human or wholly hybrid – inevitably leads to the issue of the authority of Scripture.

Does Scripture stand alone and therefore ultimate? Is it revelation *in toto* or ongoing? Does Scripture eclipse, if not erase, experience, tradition and reason? Again, responses vary and the continuum of engagement is vast. For some theologies tied to Reformed sensibilities, to confess *sola scriptura* is to exalt this text as 'final authority' ('The Statement on Social Justice and the Gospel'). *Sola* here tends to be bound to the methods and meanings of literalism. For others, to confess *sola scriptura* is simultaneously to confess *sola gratia*, *sola fides* and *solus Christus*. This simultaneity, in its more fluid expressions, touches upon the ineffability of things sacred as manifest in God's gift of grace, faith and self (in Christ).

Whether alone or in the company of other theological confessions, the 'what' of Scripture inspires myriad approaches. Take, as an example, the Jesus Seminar, which is committed to excavating the 'authentic' sayings and deeds of Jesus from the strictures of 'orthodoxy' narrowly conceived. It is a project influenced, in many ways, by Bultmann's demythologising, with its search for a biblical kerygmatic core that speaks to human realities. In recent decades, the Jesus Seminar has broadened its scope to include the Paul Seminar, the Christianity Seminar and the God Seminar. Each seminar seeks to chart not only the historical trajectories of the Christian phenomenon but also the roles human drives, communities and language play in these histories.

Be it embraced as the capitalised Word, the lower-case word mired in the glories and foibles of humanity, or a W/word that invites continued and open-ended enquiry, the 'what' of Scripture is inextricable from the 'how' of reading Scripture. How we read and are read by sacred texts is far from a neutral exercise. It is a process of interpretation, a process bearing within it the imprint of our contexts in all their intersectionalities.

Matters of interpretation, or hermeneutics, are deeply rooted in questions not only of the 'what' of Scripture and its authority, but also of access. Here we engage the 'who' of Scripture. Who 'gets' to read and interpret Scripture? Whose voice, intra-textual as well as extra-textual, is not only recognised, but also heard and legitimated?

The opening centuries of North American Christian biblical interpretation followed the cadences of Eurocentric models. For example, some schools of theological thought were influenced by nineteenth-century German theologian Friedrich Schleiermacher. In the twentieth and twenty-first centuries, the syncopations of alternative biblical interpretation disrupted, countered and elaborated on earlier models.

Fernando F. Segovia traces the evolutions of seven 'grand models of interpretation', from the historical-critical to the most recent, 'global-systemic'. The proliferation of interpretative paradigms highlights the vitality of biblical scholarship since the 1970s – including projects informed by the theories and theologies of liberation together with de- and post-colonialism. And though 'grand' might appear weighted by colonising or 'meta' trappings, Segovia calls biblical interpreters to readings cognisant of the overlapping, intersectional and ever-emerging techniques of critique.

In the evolving exercise of biblical interpretation, liberative praxes, alongside hermeneutics of suspicion, carved out spaces of textured difference and sociocultural nuance. Methodological emphases shifted. Analyses of narratives shaped by liberation movements and the communities they energised burgeoned, as did critiques noting that numerous theologies (explore the thought of Black liberation theologian James H.

Cone) and the Scriptures they centre constitute 'texts of terror' (feminist biblical scholar Phyllis Trible) to bodies and souls deemed other by gender and race codes. These and other articulations, such as womanist theologies, continue to approach the task of hermeneutics as one neither perfunctory nor innocuous. On the contrary, hermeneutics of 'survival' (womanist theologian Delores S. Williams) and 'ambivalence' (womanist biblical scholar Shanell T. Smith) not only upend theological strategies limiting access to sacred texts, but also reconsider Scripture's influence, function, participation in and construction by diverse communities.

Taken together, the 'what', 'how' and 'who' questions suggest that Christian Scripture is a complex amalgam. Whether viewed through lenses of literalism or analogy, whether taken as article of blind faith or object of critical reflection, it appears that a multi-perspectival approach to these sacred texts is unavoidable. Yet appearances can be deceptive.

Systems can be found across North America – theological and other – that perpetuate practices minoritising already minoritised biblical critique. Such systems eschew pluralities of interpretations, identifying theological openness as dangerous, or even truth-destroying (see works by R. Albert Mohler, Jr, president of the Southern Baptist Theological Seminary). Tightly clinched hermeneutical circles remain impervious to proposals that the meaning-making processes of sacred texts might be both divine and human endeavours. Other perspectives, of course, flourish.

The production of meaning through and by texts, be they sacred or not, draws upon religious, political, sociocultural, racial, class and gender constructs. One examination of this productivity is Vincent L. Wimbush's work with 'scripturalisation', whereby language, theologies, race structures, power dynamics and various 'Scriptures' contribute to and sustain societal normativities. Here we find ourselves once more at the question of who or what defines the 'traditional' and the normative. Building on Wimbush's work, Tat-siong Benny Liew and Jacqueline M. Hidalgo speak to the mutable ways (Christian) Scripture, as communal product and potential vision of identity, shapes collective praxis.

The theme of normativity ushers us back to the topic of norms and sources. Various theological frameworks recognise, if not celebrate, a diversity of sources, from experience to psychoanalysis, from literary criticism to climate sciences, from consideration of global citizenship to practices of equity and social justice. A few examples provide a glimpse of the breadth, though not depth, of these sources.

Within Catholicism, certain orders embrace the perennial tradition/ philosophy. Franciscan Richard Rohr, for instance, weaves the perennial tradition across theological, contemplative and activist methods. It is necessary, however, to state that definitions of 'perennial' vary. Within and beyond the Catholic tradition, controversies swirl across North America concerning the scope, meaning and reliability not only of philosophy but also of science as theological resources. Despite seemingly innumerable controversies, however, appeals to expanding horizons of thought, study and embodied experience continue. These horizons extend from the dissection of gender and sexuality constructs (see the queer theology of Asian American Episcopal priest Patrick S. Cheng) to work with trauma studies (explore the thought of theologian Shelly Rambo).

Akin to the ambiguous character of the *sola* in relation to Scripture, enquiry into the limits or expanses of theological resources is similarly contested. Some streams of enquiry pivot on the issue of 'appropriateness', developing criteria for what does and does not constitute viability. Whether tied to a solitary *sola*, enveloped in a chorus of *solas* or bursting at the hermeneutical seams, the discussion of sources tends both to emerge from and to substantiate a particular understanding of the Divine. Next, then, we turn our attention to the doctrine of the Trinity.

Trinity and Other Multiplicities

As the section on Scripture highlights, words, along with the systems they populate, are generative. 'In the beginning' evokes images of infinite sacred possibilities to some and to others details a single line of Divine revelation given to a particular people. Language and its interpretations rarely stand by passively. Perhaps no language or, more precisely, no single word is more charged than 'God'. Elizabeth A. Johnson has demonstrated that the symbol of God 'functions'.

In Christian imaginaries, the symbol of Trinity articulates the grace-filled mystery of God's gift of Godself to creation. Trinity 'functions'. It is irreducible and elusive, yet intimate and existential. It points to confessional horizons wherein the tangibles and intangibles of faith spark creative engagement with God and the world. Across these endless horizons, a mere two 'functions' guide our examination of this symbol in North American theological systems: identity formation and boundary-marking.

Questions of identity, divine and human, are woven intricately across theologies that attend to the Triune God as experienced by Christian communities. So, too, the markings of boundaries, be they concerned with navigating the three-in-one relationships, demarcating what constitutes 'orthodoxy' or imagining the breadth and depth of community. Consider the Orthodox 'diaspora' in North America. A diverse body united by rich tradition, ecclesial structure and confessional theology, the Orthodox Church disavows the '*filioque*' ('and the Son') clause added to the Nicene Creed in the eleventh century. The question of 'procession' – whether the Holy Spirit proceeds from the Father (East) or from the Father and the

Son (West) – speaks not only to Divine realities, but also to the ordering of human relationships, both ecclesial and political. The *filioque* dispute contributed to the Great Schism, rupturing Roman and Byzantine Christianities. The rupture remains, yet efforts exist to foster what His All-Holiness Ecumenical Patriarch Bartholomew describes as a 'dialogue of love' striving towards ecumenical unity. While central to a faith marked by the Triune, love and unity often elude Christian confessions and the communities they build.

The ancient confession of Trinity as one essence/substance in three persons is concise. Yet the concision befuddles, beguiles and inspires – as divine mystery is wont to do. Hence Anselm's description of the Triune as 'three I know not what'. Expressing the inexpressible tests not only the capaciousness of language, but also human impulses to define absolutely and thereby 'manage' God. If God-in-three-persons can be controlled, so, too, the bodies, identities and personhoods of finite entities – and with greater ease.

Aware of the ever-consuming possibilities of idolatry, different theological strategies subvert human desires to corral the Divine. One persistent depravity presents as the twisting of the three-in-one confession into rigid calculation. This calculus tends towards weighted transactions whereby either the one or the three is overvalued. Efforts to overturn theological exchange rates include stressing the metaphoric character of language about God. Resonant efforts like apophatic or negative theologies disrupt accretions of certitude through processes of 'unknowing'. Theological unknowing, ancient and contemporary, clears away detritus that would confine the Divine in reductive designs. Akin to apophasis, Christian mystical theologies discover through *unio mystica* dynamisms and deconstructions that unravel theological pretensions. Such deconstructions continue the work of dismantling various towers of Babel in their twenty-first-century architectures.

While deconstruction serves counter-idolatry purposes, theology is a kataphatic enterprise, as well. It dares to speak … and speak … about the Divine. Thus, Trinity is never a solitary utterance. God-talk about perichoresis, pneumatology, soteriology and incarnation swirl about it.

Karen Baker-Fletcher, in her Trinitarian work, foregrounds the choreographies of the perichoretic. Baker-Fletcher discovers in dancing – Divine and human – movements towards creativity and justice in a world awash with needless violence. In this relational and womanist theology, the Holy Spirit animates (Christic) resurrection activisms in and for the Creator's beloveds. In moves both deconstructive and constructive, Grace M. Jantzen rethinks (via Feuerbach) incarnational possibilities, or 'becoming divine'. These possibilities challenge theologies and philosophies predicated on systems of violent totality. Jantzen's 'feminist religious symbolic' focuses on human becoming, a becoming that acts in love (and not through death-drives) for the world. Through different doctrinal loci, Baker-Fletcher and Jantzen locate a for-the-world imperative as integral to the horizons of divine–human encounter.

The linking of human identity formations to a for-the-world imperative reflects the import of justice and community to the Christian imaginary, a theme to which we will return in the kingdom section. What is more, numerous theologies ground the *pro mundi* impulse of human ethics in the *pro nobis* revelation of the Triune God. Social Trinitarianism, as an example, develops analogies from the three-in-one relationships of love, equity and solidarity to (re)configure human communities.

The overlay of divine and human projects, however, is not without critics. Linn Marie Tonstad argues that social Trinitarianism claims too much – or perhaps too little – in extracting practical 'how to's of community from the Trinity. Utilising strategies from queer theory, Tonstad also critiques Trinitarian theologies that embed sexed and gendered roles within the doctrine together with themes of submission (Son to Father) and death (on the cross). As alternative to theologies that repeat constrictive tropes, Tonstad accentuates resurrection and its limitless transformations. This resurrection Trinitarianism professes 'polyfidelity' to multiple sources and discourses as well as God's ongoing gift of self.

The linking of 'polyfidelity' to Trinitarian discourse is unsurprising, as themes of multiplicity frequently accompany reflection on Triune revelations. Amid the fields of comparative theology and inter-religious dialogue, the doctrine of the Trinity opens a gratuitous site of transformation, community and unbounded welcome. Take as illustrations the research of Michelle Voss Roberts and John J. Thatamanil. Voss Roberts, through comparative analysis of figures from Christianity and Hinduism (Mechthild of Magdeburg and Lallesvari, respectively), names 'dualities' as spaces of difference. It is not opposition but possibilities upending oppressions that define these spaces. The Trinity, as read by Voss Roberts via Mechthild, attests to the fluid, overflowing character of divine love. Human identities and communities participate in this flow by relationships of solidarity, service and cooperation. Working across expanses of hospitality, Thatamanil draws on theological and philosophical strands from Hinduism, Christianity and Buddhism to detail a 'speculative' articulation of Trinity as 'Ground', 'Singularity' and 'Relation'. Thatamanil's speculations, rooted in a Trinitarian imaginary, embrace religious diversity not as problematic reality to overcome, but as fecund locus of dialogue and reception. Divine multiplicity, in these theologies, exceeds dogmatic boundaries.

As the three-in-one transcends reductive calculus, so, too, does it render boundaries – of language, tradition, identity and community – porous. The symbol of Trinity functions. It nurtures individual and collective horizons of being and doing. In the following section we look at that collective form of being addressed in Christian imaginaries as the kingdom.

Kingdom(s) – Sacred and Not So

'Thy kingdom come' conveys a plurality of yearnings, some grounded in prayer and petition, others in human projects and projections. The *basileia*, as preached in parables or enacted in the overturning of money-changers' tables, propels the vision of the biblical Jesus. This vision, according to some theologies, destabilises exploitative identities, policies and structures. To others, the kingdom is less concerned with transforming daily life than with the elimination of worldly obstacles such that 'God may be all in all' (1 Corinthians 15: 24–8). An endless symbolic reservoir, God's kingdom (*basileia tou theou*) 'functions' in ways both inspirational and critical. These two functions serve as entry points to discuss the *basileia*, the doctrinal scope of which invites diverse engagements.

The theological task understood as one of critique that participates in transformation, for example, informs the theologies of John B. Cobb, Jr and Kathryn Tanner. In Cobb's process theology, the powers of creativity and persuasion, not coercion, pulsate across the 'commonwealth of God', fostering critiques of unjust systems and prompting acts towards the common good. The common good here attends to justice-based and ecological sustainability. In Tanner's Christocentric theology, an economy of unconditional grace circulates within and emanates from the Trinity. This economy marks the *basileia* and shapes human wrestling with and reform of systems of deprivation, injustice and greed.

As suggested by Cobb's and Tanner's works, efforts to flesh out the kingdom reflect the theological impulses mobilising them, impulses drawn in varying degrees from Scripture, tradition, experience and/or a multitude of other sources. Often these impulses coalesce around ethical, *pro mundi* imperatives. The justice imperative ascribed to kingdom discourses, for example, inspired the social gospel movement that blossomed in the nineteenth century and flourished in the early twentieth century across Canada and the USA. The kingdom's call to transform the whole life of peoples – spiritual, social, political, psychological, economic – energised the theologies of Walter Rauschenbusch and the Reverend Dr Martin Luther King, Jr. The movement sputtered as global crises mounted, systemic sin ravaged and theological realism came to the fore. Each of these, in differing ways, challenged the movement's more 'utopian' hopes and refrains. Nevertheless, certain social gospel themes continue to energise 'liberal' North American theologies, as detailed by social ethicist and theologian Gary Dorrien.

A somewhat similar arc of delayed kingdom realisations thwarted by the intransigencies of sin marks the work of progressive Evangelicals. In a 2018 article, for instance, David P. Gushee re-evaluates the theological framework he and Glen H. Stassen detailed in their earlier text, *Kingdom Ethics*. *Ethics* emphasised a hope-filled and -fuelled vision of human participation in realising basileic calls to justice. Yet when confronted by the realities of existential suffering, a theological hope tied to Euro-American and twentieth- and twenty-first-century notions of success and guaranteed end(s) appears, Gushee acknowledges, rather hollowed out. What is more, such a gutted hope might lead to despair when confronted by catastrophic horizons such as global warming. Where potential despair looms in Gushee's turn to a more confessional, less results-oriented theology, John Fea locates 'fear', 'power' and 'nostalgia' as driving forces in Evangelical politics and theology since the 1970s. Fea, working within the tradition, encourages Evangelicals to resist theo-political lures that jettison the good news of God's salvation for 30 pieces of silver.

The blurring of religion and politics is not, of course, simply an Evangelical issue. As traced across the field of political theology, concepts of God, particularly the scope and exercise of divine power, permeate Euro-American political systems. From Constantine's 'conversion' to practices of the divine right of kings to notions of God-sanctioned national sovereignty, the appetites of empire and conquest tapped into missionary zeal, propelling Christianity to become a global phenomenon. Case in point, the pervasive allusions to civil religion in the USA (see the work of historian of religion Charles H. Long). Whether interpreted as benign, beneficial or destructive, the collusions of Manifest Destiny, American exceptionalism and 'city-on-a-hill' references (Matthew 5: 14) fund a US national identity grounded in myths of divine origin, purpose and sanction. These myths echo the cry of 'kingdom come'. One query, however, remains ambiguous: whose kingdom?

The merging of political and theological kingdom designs both contribute to and arise from a 'diseased and disfigured' Christian imagination, as analysed by Willie James Jennings. Individual and collective identities formed by this imagination seek to acquire mastery and control. Such acquisitive drives – past and present – rank bodies, lands and human possibilities along a racialised spectrum, a spectrum dominated by constructs of whiteness. The now disavowed 'Indian' residential and boarding school systems of Canada and the USA attest to the devastations wrought by theologies of conquest and conversion. And while denominational confessions of and apologies for participation in these systems are crucial

('The Apologies', United Church of Canada), the basileic imperative of justice demands ongoing work to de- and reconstruct Christian imaginations. Developing practices of 'belonging', proposes Jennings, entails one way to reconstruct Christian imaginations.

The symbol of God's kingdom functions – at times as impetus towards expansions of the common good, civil rights and practices of belonging, at other times as blueprint distorted by human quests. Thus, when exploring the doctrine of *basileia tou theou*, critical elements to review include (sacred) words and the worlds they create. These worlds span across the now and not yet. They foretell in-breakings of Divine grace in this moment and promises of future peace and communion with God. They offer glimpses of an end without end, to eschatological potentialities that motivate endless theological reflections and to which we turn next.

Eschatology and Other Edgy Topics

Eschatos, that edge where the now and not-yet of grace fully realised intersect, proves provocative. It conjures images ranging from the bucolic to the catastrophic, from the harmonious catnap of lion with lamb to the blood-soaked battle at Megiddo (Armageddon) glorified in the *Left Behind* series. The cries for the coming of God's kingdom remain palpable, perhaps inevitably when the Book of Revelation saturates Christian 'end-time' rumination and ruination. Then why, you might wonder, separate kingdom and *eschatos*?

It is, admittedly, artificial to disentangle the two – artificial and yet, as illustrated in the last section, a temptation indulged when human power drives override divinely promised possibilities. Amid these possibilities kingdom imagery is integral but not ultimate. Thus, while some kingdom aspirations foment ideological captivity, continued theo-political fascination with the basileic points to the alluring scope of the eschatological. It spans from here to eternity. Its visions depict politics-as-usual collapsing before the *basileia tou theou*, a communal reality wherein God shall be all in all and the last shall be first. It speaks of salvation/wholeness and to God's redemptive creativity – *pro nobis*. In short, then, eschatology is hope. What is more, for some theological systems hope encompasses the breadth and depth, the breath and life of Christianity.

Eschatological hope catalyses. The catalytic conversions it sparks run the gambit from the transformative to the apocalyptic, from the revolutionary to the reactionary, and from social-justice mobilisations to religiously sanctioned escapism. As indicated earlier, hope has and continues to fund movements towards social, political and theological reform across North America. That said, embedded as it is in Christian imaginations skewed towards privileging white experiences and power, hope bears theological ambiguities, particularly for communities marginalised by legacies and redeployments of Empire.

Excavating the escapist tendencies of a hope forged in Eurocentric worldviews, Miguel A. De La Torre calls for a praxis of 'hopelessness', practices that navigate the in-betweenness of Holy Saturday. Shorn of beatific horizons that obscure the atrocities of current oppressions, hopelessness engages in 'civil initiative' that addresses injustice. It functions as critique of and resistance to the cold comforts of a still-colonising status quo. Where De La Torre interrogates hope as problematic opiate of mass (white Christian) inaction, Catherine Keller tracks the destructive impulses accompanying the 'apocalypse habit' pervading Euro-American narratives and mind-sets.

Portents of apocalypse, latent or activated, permeate North American contexts. For confirmation, survey various media that dabble in post-apocalyptic scenarios. As Keller notes, end-is-nigh proclamations galvanise, for good and for ill. At their worst, such proclamations peddle in dualisms, identifying an 'evil' that must be overcome by the 'righteous'. They tend to prophesy ultimate victory – however protracted or gory the battles – a victory assured by transcendent powers. The apocalypse habit validates aggressions, past and present, against so-named 'others'. To thwart the habit's doomsday violences, Keller proposes a 'counter-apocalyptic' approach. This approach attends to strands within apocalypticism committed to uprooting injustice, alleviating suffering and participating in (divine) possibilities. What is more, it practices an 'apocalyptic mindfulness' that acts in caring solidarity with earth, all species and neighbours.

Be it hopeless or counter-apocalyptic, the eschatological threads in De La Torre and Keller decry not-just-yet, happy-ending theologies detached from the existential now of exploitative systems. Relatedly, Keller and De La Torre reject complacency, complicity and nihilism as human responses to potentially world-ending political and theological stratagems. Activism, echoing the justice imperatives noted earlier, grounds these theological models. This grounding is far from isolated. As sketched from Trinity to kingdom to eschatology, these theological confessions affirm that however nigh the end, God's *pro nobis* love invites *pro mundi* practices.

Conclusion

For all its fire-and-brimstone posturing, the apocalyptic functions as both religious and secular symbol. It partakes in expansive, even edgy possibilities. In Christian contexts, these possibilities attest to transformations of the divisive, cruel and oppressive into the peaceable, compassionate and just. Recognised or not, these transformations reveal the Incarnate's continuing work – fully divine, fully human – throughout creation, from alpha and (to) omega. The eschatological, then, is not simply an edgy end, nor is 'in the beginning' a one-time creative Word. As such, the eschatological is wondrously and disruptively conjunctive. It is now and not yet, an ending and beginning. It is perhaps fitting, then, to conclude with a doctrine confessing an end without end. Fitting in that the Christianities practised in North America beget infinite worlds of meaning, possibility and action.

Bibliography

De La Torre, Miguel A., *Decolonizing Christianity: Becoming Badass Believers* (Grand Rapids, MI: Eerdmans, 2021).

Johnson, Elizabeth A., *Quest for the Living God: Mapping Frontiers in the Theology of God* (New York: Continuum, 2008).

Kärkkäinen, Veli-Matti, *A Constructive Christian Theology for the Pluralistic World*, 5 vols (Grand Rapids, MI: Eerdmans, 2013–17).

Keller, Catherine, *Face of the Deep: A Theology of Becoming* (London: Routledge, 2003).

Thatamanil, John J., *Circling the Elephant: A Comparative Theology of Religious Diversity*, Comparative Theology/Thinking Across Traditions (New York: Fordham University, 2020).

Social and Political Context

Jim Wallis

United States

We start with a paradox – religion in general, and Christianity in particular, has been far more influential on the society and politics of the USA throughout its history than on those of other Western nations like France, the UK or Germany over that same period – and this is especially true in the twentieth and twenty-first centuries. At the same time, the USA has since its founding emphasised freedom of religion and a legal separation between church and state, which is more formally called disestablishment. Indeed, the First Amendment to the US Constitution, which was adopted as part of the Bill of Rights in 1791, formalises these two intimately related commitments. The first two clauses of the First Amendment read: 'Congress shall make no law respecting an establishment of religion, or prohibiting the free exercise thereof'. By contrast, many other Western nations have an official state church, or did until far more recently. While most of these nations also have laws protecting religious freedom, religion has become less and less influential on the culture and politics (deeply connected of course) of those countries, and survey data consistently show a significantly higher percentage of the population is atheist than in the USA. The separation of church and state does not require the segregation of religious and moral values from public life – indeed, the legal separation can strengthen the integration of faith values into public life, even politics.

The principal theory that resolves this seeming contradiction revolves around both theological and practical rationales for freedom of conscience with respect to religious conviction. Many of the colonies were founded by Protestant Evangelicals and were heavily influenced by their theology. Prominent among them were Reformational Protestants, Congregationalists, Methodists, Baptists and even Anabaptists. One commonality between many of these groups was the idea that to be genuine, faith must be personal, voluntaristic – that is to say, it must be freely chosen by the individual believer. As such, establishing a particular religion or Christian church as the state church with the sanction and support of the government constitutes an unacceptable form of coercion. Or, to think about it another way, the government establishment of religion has the effect of weakening rather than strengthening personal faith and religion.

Many of the nation's founders, like Thomas Jefferson and James Madison, were by contrast heavily influenced by the more secular philosophy of the Enlightenment. Yet it led them to the same conclusion as many more-religious people with respect to the separation of church and state, and for much the same reason. These founders believed in the freedom of conscience, which must include religious freedom and the separation of church and state, not because they necessarily wished to see Christianity or any particular religion flourish, but because they believed that government's job was to protect and serve earthly rights, and it lacked the power to change human religious convictions – and, further, that a pluralistic, religiously tolerant society where the government did not favour a particular sect or set of beliefs would be a more stable, open and peaceful society.

The result of the USA having officially separated church from state for more than 200 years is that a wide panoply of religious beliefs has always been present and continues to change and diversify in the twenty-first century. Even as this century has seen a marked decline in formal membership in houses of worship, which fell below 50% in the USA for the first time in 2021, belief in God or some form of higher power remains higher than in most Western nations. At the same time, a lack of government-sanctioned religious belief has never stopped Christians and believers of other faiths from bringing their faith-derived values to their thinking about public policy. As such, there has always been a push and pull of a wide variety of religious traditions attempting to influence federal, state and local governments to pass laws that comport with their faith values. As we will discuss below, the white Evangelical embrace of former President Donald J. Trump was perhaps the most dramatic and incongruous recent example of white Christians attempting to support and privilege their religious preferences through an alliance with temporal political power, though it remains to be seen whether the Trump era augurs a change in the fortunes of the white Evangelical Religious Right or merely a continued rise to ascendancy in political influence, or even ultimately to a fall in their impact and influence.

Impact of the Great Awakenings

Some historians say that spiritual activity cannot be called revival until it changes something, not just in people's inner lives but in society. Revivals often occur when politics fails to address the most significant moral issues of the day. Social movements then rise up to change politics, and these movements throughout US history have, until quite recently, generally had spiritual foundations. The politics and society of the USA were deeply impacted by Christian revival movements that occurred primarily inside the white church, one in the mid-eighteenth century, one in the early nineteenth, and one from the latter half of the nineteenth century to the early part of the twentieth, which have come to be called the Great Awakenings. The First Great Awakening, that of the 1730s and 1740s, is often credited with helping to pave the way for a political awakening that in turn led to the independence movement which culminated in the American Revolution and the formation of the USA. The Second Great Awakening, that of the early 1800s, embraced the clear call for the abolition of slavery that preceded the Civil War. The Third Great Awakening saw white Evangelical Christians play an important role in ushering in the progressive era, the social gospel movement and the New Deal. Some of the specific social reforms of this era included child labour law improvements, the settlement house movement, the career of social work, youth organisations such as the YMCA, and the temperance movement, which would eventually, if temporarily, succeed in making alcohol illegal, with major societal and political impacts. Another result of the Third Great Awakening was the populist presidential campaigns of William Jennings Bryan. The mid-twentieth-century civil rights movement, whose moral authority and leadership came primarily from Black churches, could and should be regarded as a Fourth Great Awakening, with political and social impacts at least as important as any of the others, and ultimately greater, especially in the impact of American religion around the world.

White Supremacy and US Christianity

It is, sadly, impossible to discuss the current political and social context of Christianity in the USA without looking at the way racism, America's original sin, has impacted Christianity since colonial times and continues to do so today. It is, lamentably, a matter of historical fact that the USA was established as a white society, founded upon the genocide of another race and then the enslavement of yet another. This statement, which I have often made, is also my most controversial. Yet such a statement is neither 'outrageous' nor 'courageous' – though it has been called both – but merely a historical statement of fact. The historical record of how white Europeans conquered North America by almost destroying the native population and how they first built the colonies, and then constructed their new nation's economy, on the backs of kidnapped Africans who had been turned into chattels can hardly be denied. Rather, the 'original sin' of the nation became foundational to it, and Christianity has been used by white Christians at every step of the way to justify or excuse the genocides, atrocities, plunder, enslavement and violent oppression.

Racism originates in domination of one group of human beings over another and provides the social rationale and philosophical justification for debasing, degrading and doing violence to people on the basis of colour. Many have pointed out how racism is sustained both by personal attitudes and by structural forces. Racism can be brutally overt or invisibly institutional, or it can be both. Its scope extends to every level and area of human psychology, society and culture – and of course, therefore, both economics and politics. Prejudice might be a universal human sin, but racism is more than an inevitable consequence of human nature or social accident. Rather, racism is a system of power and oppression for a social and economic purpose.

In the USA, the original purpose of racism was to justify slavery and its enormous economic benefit and to legitimise the genocide of the Indigenous population. The particular form of racism, inherited from the English to justify their own slave trade, was especially venal, for it defined the slave not merely as an unfortunate victim of bad circumstances, war or social dislocation but, rather, as less than human, as a thing, an animal, a piece of property to be bought and sold, used and abused.

The slave did not have to be treated with any human consideration whatsoever. Even in the founding document of the US nation, the famous constitutional compromise defined the slave as only three-fifths of a person. The professed high ideals of Anglo-Western society could exist side by side with the profitable institution of slavery only if the humanity of the slave was denied and disregarded. Sadly, white Christianity provided that moral cover, with bad theology concocted around the so-called 'Curse of Ham' as an argument for Black people's supposed inferiority, and passages like Paul directing slaves to obey their masters given outsized importance and emphasis, disregarding the emerging equality in early Christian communities. Indeed, white supremacy has shaped Christianity in the USA in the same way that white supremacy has shaped the rest of US history, society and politics. Even in the question of whether and how to evangelise slaves and Native Americans, we see brutal economic and political considerations impacting ostensibly religious decisions. For example, as conversions of enslaved people to Christianity became increasingly common in the nineteenth century, pro-slavery clergy worked with slave masters throughout the South to emphasise a version of Christianity that suppressed the liberating teachings of Jesus and focused on the virtues of submission and obedience to authority. Slaves were deliberately discouraged from reading the Bible, and even denied the ability to read it, and to avoid the teachings of Jesus in particular, as they might be seen or used to create and inspire the impulse towards their freedom. Keeping parts of the Bible or Christianity hidden has always been a strategy to prevent the Scriptures from inspiring movements of freedom, dignity, equality and justice.

The Black Church

It is impossible to understand the current social and political context of US Christianity without discussing the key role played by the Black church throughout American history. The history of the Black church in the USA – in other words the multitude of denominations and individual congregations made up mostly of Black parishioners and their role as the key community institution for many Black people still today – goes back to around the time of the American Revolution. Starting in the late eighteenth century, in the decades after the First Great Awakening, the efforts of white Baptist and Methodist missionaries contributed to increasing numbers of enslaved Black people in the American South converting to Christianity. While many were only officially permitted to worship in white-controlled settings where the liberating message of the Bible was suppressed by the slave masters and many white clergy, historians have documented the emergence of an 'invisible institution' – underground churches where enslaved Black people could freely mix a liberatory brand of Christianity with rhythm, song and beliefs brought from Africa by either them or their ancestors.

In the meantime, a parallel Black Christian tradition was developing in the Northern states where slavery was abolished in the decades after US independence, with free Black churches forming their own denominations like the African Methodist Episcopal (AME) Church, as well as Black congregations forming as part of existing, predominantly white denominations. These Northern churches were deeply involved in the abolition movement, and many also provided aid and refuge for escaped enslaved people as part of the Underground Railroad. In the decades following emancipation in 1863 and the end of the Civil War in 1865, Black churches became the key community institution for Black people in the North and the South, a refuge from the daily reality of white supremacy and the myriad manifestations of structural racism in US society. That status as a place of refuge, inspiration and support continues to this day for many Black Americans.

As the central institution in the lives of many Black Americans, Black churches always played an important role in shaping and reflecting the human needs and social and political priorities of their parishioners. This phenomenon was most visible and famous in the twentieth-century civil rights movement, when preachers like Dr Martin Luther King, Jr, inspired a broad movement of Black Americans and multiracial allies to end Jim Crow laws and for the first time pass federal legislation to guarantee the civil rights and the voting rights of Black Americans. Before, during and since the civil rights movement, the Black church pulpit has historically been a place of prophetic truth-telling about the realities that Black people experience in their own country. Indeed, the Black church has often been one of the only places where such truths are ever told.

Black preachers have had the pastoral task of nurturing the spirits of people who feel beaten down week after week. Strong and prophetic words from Black church pulpits are often a source of comfort and affirmation for Black congregations. For example, Black liberation theology, pioneered by Dr James Hal Cone, helped articulate and systematise within a theological framework the idea that God has a specific message of liberation for Black Americans stemming from God's love for all oppressed people and the divine passion for justice. As noted in his Union Seminary obituary, Cone 'upended the theological establishment with his vigorous articulation of God's radical identification with black people in the United States'. Black church theology and the Black church's leadership in the civil rights movement have gone on to influence political and social movements in other nations, like the anti-apartheid struggle in South Africa.

Black churches have also played a key role in mobilising voters in their communities. 'Souls to the Polls' – voting drives that occur after Sunday worship on early-voting days in the weeks immediately preceding elections – play a crucial role in Black voter turnout, which alone can prove decisive in close local, state and even national elections. The runoff elections in Georgia for two US Senate seats in January 2021 offer an important example. It gave Georgia its first Jewish senator and its first ever Black senator in Jon Ossoff and Rafael Warnock, both of whom would not have prevailed in their races without the strong support they received from Black voters. Senator Warnock rose to prominence as the head pastor of the historic Ebenezer Baptist Church in Atlanta, a church that was led by Dr Martin Luther King, Jr, during the twentieth-century civil rights movement, and his father before him – a position the Reverend Warnock retains even as he also serves as a US senator.

White Evangelicals and Politics

After the successes of the three Great Awakenings in mobilising mostly white Christians for significant social and political changes, the twentieth century saw white Evangelical Christians increasingly turning away from the social implications of the gospel and embracing a private, individual faith where eternal salvation from personal sin is the overwhelming focus. The mandate to bring the surrounding society closer to the biblical articulation of God's kingdom became less emphasised, and the school of apocalyptic eschatology which taught that the Second Coming of Jesus Christ would soon whisk all true believers off the Earth gained influence.

In my life story, I will never forget the elder in my family's Evangelical Plymouth Brethren congregation telling me in the 1960s that I should stop insisting on discussing racism in church: 'Son, you've got to understand: Christianity has nothing to do with racism; that's political, and our faith is personal'. I have found his words to be sadly emblematic of the tendency of the majority of white Evangelicals, as well as many other white Christians, to abdicate responsibility for addressing many systemic social issues, and none more so than racism.

In the 1970s, some Evangelicals, myself among them, were able to push back against this retreat from the key social issues of our time and start a real conversation about the social and political implications of US Christianity – a conversation that continues to this day. Its apex was perhaps the release in 1973 of the Chicago Declaration of Evangelical Social Concern, a document that emerged from convening a group of mostly young Evangelicals, including Black Evangelicals, the first Evangelical feminists, some global Evangelical leaders, but also some of the leading establishment white Evangelical leaders at the time. When it was released, the Chicago Declaration gained great attention in Evangelical schools and seminaries, and it was a significant national news story. Until 1980, people who worked on it were often referred to as the 'young Evangelicals' in a 'new Evangelical' movement.

Around 1980, however, a political assault and takeover was successfully executed by the Republican right wing, and the 'Religious Right' was born. White Evangelicals, in particular, were targeted by a far-right movement steeped in racism and were deliberately politicised. It is now painfully clear that the Evangelical world was strategically and politically co-opted, not by more conservative Evangelical leaders, but by political operatives from the Republican Party who saw a real opportunity to take over the Evangelical world by making particular appeals to 'conservative social issues'.

This is not hyperbolic rhetoric. Those right-wing political operatives – such as Richard Viguerie, Paul Weyrich, Kevin Phillips and Terry Dolan – would later say much about how they recruited white Evangelicals. They approached fundamentalist leaders like Jerry Falwell and Pat Robertson and offered to make them household names if they gave them their mailing lists. The Republican activists created new organisations like the Moral Majority, with Falwell and Robertson as the public figures and the political operatives behind the scenes making the strategy.

The story that most of the Religious Right tells about itself is one where the Supreme Court's 1973 decision in *Roe* v. *Wade*, which made abortion legal in all 50 states, was the animating principle behind the Religious Right's formation – specifically that outrage over the decision spurred Evangelicals to start a movement to eventually overturn it. Religion scholar Randall Balmer did a great service when he published the definitive article

('The Real Origins of the Religious Right', *Politico Magazine*, 27 May 2014) on the origins of the Religious Right, which wholly debunks the *Roe* v. *Wade* myth. The truth that Balmer has meticulously documented is that the movement that would become the Religious Right got its start in fierce opposition to desegregating private religious schools and seized upon opposition to abortion as an energising issue only a full six years after *Roe* v. *Wade*, as a more palatable rallying cry that could help them defeat Jimmy Carter's 1980 re-election campaign.

The 1980 election was a watershed moment in that, from that point forward, the Religious Right was largely successful in tying white Christianity generally, and white Evangelicalism in particular, ever more tightly to the Republican Party, around a stated message of socially conservative opposition to abortion and, later, same-sex marriage. That alliance, which persists to this day, has sadly also found all too many (primarily white) Christians increasingly distorting or ignoring clear biblical imperatives around poverty, immigration and peacemaking in order to conform their theology to the political orthodoxy of the modern Republican Party. The alliance between political operatives and faith leaders, I would argue, has caused far too many Americans' politics to shape their faith, when it should be the other way around – the moral convictions derived from religious belief should dictate the public policies to be supported or opposed.

The administration of George W. Bush, who was President from 2001 to 2009, provides a twenty-first-century example of how heavily white Evangelical Christianity has influenced and been influenced by US society and politics. Bush came into office after an extraordinarily close election that was ultimately resolved by a five-to-four decision of the US Supreme Court, with the Court's five conservative justices at the time essentially determining the election for the Republican candidate. He campaigned and entered office with a promise to govern as a 'compassionate conversative'. His governance, however, soon revealed his administration to have conventional Republican priorities, chief among them a large tax cut that benefited mostly the wealthy.

The terrorist attacks of 11 September 2001 changed everything. They led President Bush down an aggressive foreign policy path in terms of launching the wars in Afghanistan and Iraq, but more problematically they also empowered a more aggressive and warlike theology among many of the President's Christian supporters. Despite the opposition of almost every major Christian body in the world, who believed the invasion of Iraq would launch a 'war of choice' that would be both unnecessary and unjust, Bush found strong support from conservative Christians from all branches of US Christianity. Indeed, the way the war was consistently couched in the language of a 'righteous cause' and a 'just war' against 'evildoers' – the way the President talked about 'mission' and even 'divine appointment' of the USA and its leaders to lead 'the war on terror' and 'rid the world of evil' – seemed to many Christians who opposed the war to confuse the roles of God, church and nation. The issue here is the danger of political idolatry, of replacing biblical theology with a nationalist religion.

The politicisation of white Evangelical Christians in the USA reached a new high in the overwhelming and largely uncritical support for Donald Trump, whose personal immorality clashed so incongruously with the professed moral values of most white Evangelicals that much of the world was utterly astonished at how enthusiastically most white Evangelical voters and leaders took to him. As Joe Scarborough, a former Republican member of Congress and host of a popular cable news show, put it in 2017, in expressing his consternation at the warmth of President Trump's reception by white conservative Christians, 'You look in Matthew, and go through the Beatitudes. Every single Beatitude. You go through Jesus's teaching, what he says he wants people to be. Donald Trump is the antithesis of just about every single thing that Jesus Christ said in the Sermon on the Mount'. Many white Evangelical leaders who supported President Trump claimed the strong support he enjoyed from their parishioners was primarily a function of his professed opposition to abortion and commitment to nominating judges who likewise held anti-abortion views, as well as his commitment to protecting their religious freedom, but polling data from the Public Religion Research Institute and others told a very different story: that antipathy to immigration and refugees, and racial and cultural resentment, were the strongest predictors of support for Trump. The teachings of Jesus had seemingly been fully abandoned in favour of white American ethnocentrism, with a standard-bearer who seemed to embody the worship of money, sex and power, all 'idols' to which Christianity throughout history has consistently tried to provide an alternative.

Along with the 81% of white Evangelical voters who supported Trump's candidacy in 2016, he also won the votes of 60% of white Catholic voters and 57% of white mainline Protestant voters. Those numbers eroded somewhat in his unsuccessful re-election campaign in 2020, but the relative closeness of the election compared with what most polls had forecast, and the resilience of Trump's support among the majority of white Christian voters despite (or perhaps because of) four years of racist and xenophobic rhetoric and policies, leaves Christianity as practised by Americans who identify as white at a crossroads.

The future of white Christianity in the USA is likely to be a continued struggle of two competing visions of both the gospel and the nation's future. The joining of a faithful remnant of white Christians alongside and behind the leadership of Black and brown Christians to help realise a new multiracial Christianity shaped primarily by Black church theology might help make the USA, for the first time in its history, a truly multiracial democracy. The more white Christians instead side with the Christian nationalist vision recast by Donald Trump and his most ardent white Evangelical supporters, the more likely it becomes that, in a future where white people will no longer be a majority in the USA by the 2040s, white minority rule, propped up by the structures and systems that have been in place since the nation's original sin, could persist for many decades to come. In such a future, the influence of the First Amendment's establishment clause might wane to the point that an ethno-nationalist distortion of Christianity moves closer and closer to becoming a state church devoted to white minority rule.

More Non-white Expressions of Christianity
Outside the boundaries of white Christianity and the Black church, something else has been happening to Christianity in the USA in recent decades. Patterns of human migration and the unprecedented growth of Christianity in the global South have combined in a way that makes US Christianity both less white and less Western with every passing year. As Wesley Granberg-Michaelson documents at length in both *From Times Square to Timbuktu: The Post-Christian West Meets the Non-Western Church* (Grand Rapids, MI: Eerdmans, 2013) and *Future Faith: Ten Challenges for Reshaping Christianity in the 21st Century* (Minneapolis, MN: Fortress Press, 2018), drawing upon the work of the *Atlas of Global Christianity* (Edinburgh: Edinburgh University Press, 2009), nearly the only churches in the USA that are growing rather than declining comprise Christians who are born outside the USA and/or are people of colour. To put it more simply, immigrants are the future of Christianity in America.

The impacts of this demographic as well as cultural change in US Christianity on US politics and society, which mirrors the larger demographic change in the USA that will result in a majority non-white nation within about 20 years, are complex and in many respects unpredictable. Nonetheless, we can draw a few conclusions. First, the broader phenomenon of changing US demographics, creating a future that is less and less white, is a dynamic that lies beneath so many political debates in the USA, perhaps none more so than the decades of debate over how to reform the nation's hopelessly broken immigration system. As US churches undergo a parallel transformation, with Hispanics comprising 71% of the growth of US Catholics since 1960 and nearly 10 million Protestant Hispanic Christians in the USA, nearly 85% of whom are Evangelical or Pentecostal, congregational and denominational leadership in many churches, including the US Catholic bishops, has become increasingly active in lobbying Congress and the White House for humane and comprehensive immigration reform.

There is a temptation to draw simplistic conclusions about the politics of Hispanic Christians in the USA based on President Trump's demonstrated hostility towards immigrants, particularly in his rhetoric around the US–Mexico border and his signature 2016 campaign promise to 'Build the Wall'. It is important to note, however, that unlike white Evangelicals and Black Christians, there is a less pronounced preference for one political party over the other among Hispanic Christian voters. It is even too simple to say that Hispanic Christians are socially conservative but pro-immigration. Indeed, the two crucial political and social facts of Hispanic Christianity in the USA are that it is growing and that it is highly diverse, both theologically and politically.

The same is true when looking at the political and social context of Asian American Christians. Because 'Asian American' is itself such a wide designation, the expressions of Christianity in the Asian American community are necessarily varied and diverse. For example, while the majority of Filipino Americans are Catholic, most Korean Americans are Protestant. As with Hispanic Christians, the social and political attitudes of Asian American Christians vary based on nation of origin (or nation of ancestry for US-born Asian Americans), along with the particular expression of Christianity practised by that person or community. One observable trend that the data do show is common to Asian American and Hispanic Evangelicals is a tendency towards social conservatism and more support for Republican than Democratic political candidates, compared with Black Christians as well as non-Evangelical Asian American and Hispanic Christians. It is, however, worth noting that the skew towards the Republican Party is much less pronounced among Hispanic and Asian American Evangelicals than it is among white Evangelicals. It is also true that the political loyalties of mainline Protestant and Catholic Asian Americans are fairly evenly divided between the two major parties, in a way that mirrors the political leanings of white Catholics and mainline Protestants.

Canada

Canada contrasts with its southern neighbour in many ways, with its comparatively secular society and politics marking one of the key distinctions. Canada has not always been as secular as it is now, but since the end of the Second World War the decline in the population's religiosity has been steady, with a particularly sharp decline from the 1950s to the 1970s and again in the early 2000s. One way of measuring this phenomenon is by looking at weekly religious service attendance, which has gone from 67% of Canadians attending a religious service at least once per week in 1947 to less than 20% who do so today. One thread in common with the USA, however, is that recent immigrants to Canada are significantly more likely to be religiously observant than people born in Canada, with one study suggesting foreign-born Canadian residents of large cities attend religious services at roughly twice the rate of those born in Canada.

The book *Religion and Canadian Party Politics* by David Rayside, Jerald Sabin and Paul E. J. Thomas (Vancouver: University of British Columbia Press, 2017) identifies three broad divisions or axes around which religion generally, and Christianity specifically, have intersected with Canadian politics and society throughout the nation's history: 'the denominational divides that were prominent historically and continue to echo in a few provinces; the advocacy by social conservatives seeking to resist the secularization that has so strikingly reshaped society since the Second World War; and conflicts over how to accommodate the immigration-driven diversification of faith communities since the 1970s'.

The denominational divides have been seen principally in the conflict between Protestants of various denominations and Catholics throughout Canadian history, which have often been connected to historically rooted cultural, linguistic and regional differences going all the way back to the colonial legacy of French Catholics and English Protestants. The legacy of government funding for Catholic schools throughout much of the country was thus a source of great contention for many decades and still shows up in some political debates to this day, with one example being debates over whether and to what extent state-funded Catholic schools may deviate from provincial curricula when these conflict with Church teachings.

Socially conservative Christians are active in Canada, with some similarities to their US counterparts and some key distinctions. They have been animated by similar issues, such as opposition to abortion and same-sex marriage, and one can see a similar alliance between socially conservative Catholics and Evangelical Protestants that characterises the US Religious Right – an alliance that has among other things eroded some of the earlier Catholic–Protestant political division. However, the key distinction is that the Canadian Religious Right has never been as closely allied and identified with a political party in the way that the Republican Party has largely captured religious conservatives in the USA, though, broadly speaking, religious social conservatives are certainly more likely to vote Conservative. Part of the issue is a higher level of societal support for both abortion rights and LGBTQ rights in Canada than in the USA, which has required politicians wishing to court the votes of social conservatives to tread carefully and use less direct rhetoric for fear of alienating more voters than they attract. Conservative politicians have found more success courting social conservatives recently in debates around sex work and euthanasia.

Another similarity between the political and social context of Christianity in the USA and Canada is a strong tradition of progressive Christianity which has seen its influence wane since the 1980s relative to the Religious Right. Progressive Christians in mainline denominations like the United Church of Canada have played an important role in advocating for immigrants, fighting poverty and confronting Canada's own colonial legacy with respect to the oppression and genocide of Indigenous people. Both church statements and practices and government policies show that discussions and decisions in relation to Indigenous tribes and populations in Canada are much further along than they are in the USA – and church education and advocacy have been part of that.

The increase in the immigration of ethnic religious minorities has occasioned periodic political debates such as the controversy in the 1990s over whether the Royal Canadian Mounted Police would allow Sikh members to wear turbans or, more recently, over how and whether to accommodate the practices of some Muslim immigrants like the face-covering niqab. Nevertheless, anti-immigrant sentiment *per se* has not received the same salience and level of partisan polarisation that one sees in Western Europe or the USA. Instead, upwards of 80% of Canadians agree that the economic impact of immigration is positive.

Conclusion

The political and social context of Christianity in North America is impossible to capture fully in a short essay such as this one. As such, I have tried to keep the focus on the most important trends and divides that help explain both religion and politics in the USA and Canada. In the USA, the current social and political context of Christianity is inextricably interwoven with the nation's original sin of slavery and Native genocide, in the historical support for and opposition to the structures of white supremacy, and how that has rippled through both all our religious denominations and the two major political parties. Though Canada has not been spared from some of the same debates and effects, the differences in the nation's history and population have led to a more secular population today, with a Religious Right that, while active, has not found nearly as potent an alliance with conservative-party politics as we see in the USA.

Let me venture a bold prediction – not often found at the end of an academic essay. On the one hand, if the conformity and complicity with white ideology and idolatry continue in the white churches, those churches will attract fewer and fewer people from the next generation – even younger white people – and most of those denominations will either die or become more and more dormant. On the other hand, if a genuine repentance (meaning a 'turning around') occurs among some, in response to the racial reckoning that emerged during the COVID-19 pandemic, a new American church could be the result, with a white remnant church that embraces the leadership of Black, Brown and Asian Christians. This could help provide the moral compass and theological roadmap towards the USA becoming truly 'united' for the first time, becoming the genuinely multiracial democracy inspired by its earliest stated principles and implemented by the changing demographics in the country. The white churches will either join those white supremacist forces who seek to prevent those changing demographics from changing democracy through carefully structured minority rule, or they will join and help churches of colour to lead the spiritual pilgrimage towards a nation where minorities are the majority – like the rest of the world.

Bibliography

Granberg-Michaelson, Wesley, *From Times Square to Timbuktu: The Post-Christian West Meets the Non-Western Church* (Grand Rapids, MI: Eerdmans, 2013).

Rayside, David, Jerald Sabin and Paul E. J. Thomas, *Religion and Canadian Party Politics* (Vancouver: UBC Press, 2017).

Wallis, Jim, *America's Original Sin* (Grand Rapids, MI: Brazos, 2016).

Wallis, Jim, *Christ in Crisis? Reclaiming Jesus in a Time of Fear, Hate, and Violence* (New York: HarperOne, 2020).

Wallis, Jim, *The Great Awakening* (New York: HarperOne, 2008).

Mission and Evangelism

Allen Yeh

North America is an incredibly diverse region, despite some superficial characteristics that could lead to an assumption of homogeneity. One obvious characteristic is its apparent monolingualism, or the phenomenon that English can be used nearly everywhere across Canada and the USA, an area of nearly 12.4 million square kilometres. This belies the great ethnic and cultural diversity that manifests itself across this vast terrain, and while English might mostly be the primary language spoken on the continent, hundreds of secondary or tertiary languages are also spoken.

Select History of North American Missions

While the evangelisation of North America began with the sixteenth-century arrival of the Spanish conquistadors in Florida on the East Coast and California on the West Coast and the arrival of the Pilgrims in 1620 at Plymouth, Massachusetts, missions proper began with John Eliot (1604–90), the 'apostle to the Indians'. His Algonquin Bible (1663) was the first complete Bible printed in the Western hemisphere. He was followed by other luminaries among the Native Americans such as David Brainerd (1718–47) and Jonathan Edwards (1703–58), both of whom ministered among the Stockbridge Indians in western Massachusetts. Evangelism did not stop with Native Americans, however: Edwards, along with George Whitefield, launched the First Great Awakening, which led to revival and religious fervour across the Eastern seaboard, from New England (Edwards' region) to Georgia (Whitefield's domain), among the white British colonists. Western Massachusetts later became an important location for the inspiring of American missionaries abroad at the Haystack Prayer Meeting (1806) at Williams College, where Samuel Mills, James Richards, Francis LeBaron Robbins, Harvey Loomis and Byram Green (collectively called 'The Brethren') committed to overseas missionary work with the eventual establishment of the American Bible Society and the American Board of Commissioners for Foreign Missions (1810). The 1806 meeting was considered the seminal moment when US American foreign missions were born. Their first missionaries to be commissioned and sent out were Ann and Adoniram Judson, from Salem, Massachusetts, to India and Burma, in 1812–13.

However, 30 years before the Judsons, the first overseas missionary from the USA was a freed Black slave, George Liele (1750–1820; alternatively spelled Lisle or Leile). He set sail from Savannah, Georgia, in 1782 and made his way to Jamaica. It must be noted that both the Judsons and Liele identified as Baptists, which was a frequent feature of US missionary work. This also highlights a lacuna in North American mission studies, namely the work of African American missionaries.

Meanwhile, on the West Coast, the Spanish were at work establishing 21 Catholic missionary stations (1769–1833). The Franciscan order was dedicated to helping the poor, and with its linking of the missions via El Camino Real (the Royal Highway – today US Highway 101), they created the backbone of what would become the State of California. Leading this charge was Fr Junípero Serra (1713–84), nicknamed 'The Apostle of California', who was canonised as a saint by Pope Francis in 2015. Building on his work establishing his five mission stations in the Mexican region of Sierra Gorda, he took those same principles and applied them to setting up the first nine of the California missions. In contrast to Protestant missions, which tended to go into Indigenous communities ('centrifugal mission'), these mission stations were set up to invite the Indigenous people into their community compounds to educate and Christianise them ('centripetal mission').

The nineteenth century was an age of Romanticism and an age of heroes. This so-called 'Great Century of Missions' spurred on by William Carey's *Enquiry* (1792) brought on a global revival of Protestant missions. Perhaps the most famous US missionary during this time was E. Stanley Jones (1884–1973). Serving at the tail end of the Great Century, he made a name for himself as the 'Billy Graham of India'. As a Methodist, he advocated for inter-religious dialogue, especially with his famous book *The Christ of the Indian Road* (1925).

On the home front, the Second Great Awakening (beginning in the late eighteenth century but lasting well into the nineteenth century) expanded beyond the scope of the First Great Awakening in that geographically it encompassed more than just the Eastern seaboard, and not just mainly the upper classes. This evangelistic revival especially impacted African American churches and female church attendance. Many of the societal reforms of this era had to do with racial rights, abolitionism, women's rights and temperance, all of which were tied to a spiritual revival in Christian morality. The Second Great Awakening can also be characterised in this spirit of Romanticism, but in the sense of emotional fervour, the exercising of spiritual gifts and an optimistic post-millennial theology that the Kingdom of God would continue to cover the whole world as Christianity heads towards the eschaton.

The twentieth century brought a sea change in missionary work, not least because of the end of the Great Century of Missions. Following the World Missionary Conference at Edinburgh, 1910, 'the birthplace of the modern ecumenical movement', US Christianity split between the fundamentalists (who rejected European ideas like Darwinism and biblical criticism) and the modernists (who welcomed these new ideas, especially hard sciences and social sciences). Unfortunately, this meant that the former claimed evangelism while the latter claimed social justice and environmental concern. Missions, then, took on two faces: fundamentalists, from among whom the Neo-Evangelical movement emerged, and ecumenists, who tended to be mainline Protestants. The loss of social justice efforts among the fundamentalists became known as 'The Great Reversal'. There was also a shift of eschatology to a more pessimistic premillennial theology, that the world would get worse before Jesus returns. This made sense as a response to two World Wars, the Great Depression, the Holocaust, nuclear weapons and secular modernism, and led to more of an entrenched and defensive mentality among North American Christians. One result of this was the attempt to just save souls rather than redress social injustices.

In the early twentieth century, the fundamentalists drew inspiration from people like Dwight L. Moody (1837–99), who worked out of western Massachusetts and was probably the most seminal figure of the Third Great Awakening. Moody's signature event was the revivalistic evangelistic crusade. By the mid-twentieth century, Neo-Evangelicals had largely replaced the fundamentalists as a less exclusive, gentler, more social justice-embracing version of conservative Christianity (in essence, they reversed the Great Reversal). The face of the Neo-Evangelicals was the most prolific evangelist in history, Billy Graham (1918–2018). He and his fellow Neo-Evangelicals set up seminaries like Fuller and Gordon-Conwell, magazines like *Christianity Today*, para-church organisations like the Lausanne Movement, and evangelistic crusades reaching thousands of people. They utilised new technologies like radio, television and air travel to great evangelistic effect. Graham himself remained the adviser to 12 successive US Presidents, from Truman to Obama (1945–2016), wielding arguably greater political influence than any other religious leader in US history. The Ecumenists, however, went the direction of the World Council of Churches. The second-ever Assembly of the WCC was held in the Chicago suburb of Evanston in 1954 and addressed issues and tensions of the Cold War, racism and disunity. Another feature of mainline Protestantism was the advent of the social gospel, propounded by Baptist theologian and pastor Walter Rauschenbusch (1861–1918). This movement emphasised not just personal sins but also systemic injustices. However, despite their differences, both the Neo-Evangelicals and the mainline Protestants (as evidenced by Lausanne and the WCC, respectively) believed in both evangelism and social justice, unity, caring for creation, and did indeed associate with European organisations. In fact, going back to the roots of Edinburgh 1910, despite the fact that it was held in the UK, the main architect and visionary was John R. Mott, an American, so its spirit – especially Mott's watchword, 'the evangelisation of the world in this generation' – was thoroughly American in its foundations.

Missions Today

While missions and evangelism certainly cannot be claimed to originate from North America, since the early twentieth century this continent – and particularly the USA – has collectively sent out the greatest number of missionaries worldwide. (It must also be acknowledged that the USA has received more missionaries than any other country as well, though still far fewer than the number it has sent out). The reasons for this relate to: (1) education, (2) para-church organisations and (3) denominations. A further major factor is multi-ethnicity, to which substantial attention is devoted below.

(1) While Bible institutes largely fell out of favour after fundamentalism morphed into Neo-Evangelicalism, the rise of seminaries (stand-alone divinity schools unattached to universities) and the CCCU (the Council for Christian Colleges and Universities) led to an embrace of Christian integration – the idea that Evangelicals were more willing to engage with hard sciences, social sciences, environmental concern and social justice (for example, the Bible Institute of Los Angeles became Biola University – no longer an acronym – broadening the scope of its education and insisting that 'all truth is God's truth'). CCCU institutions all have a commitment to mission, and in fact in 2022 a new Evangelism Commission was established to ensure the schools carry forth their stated purpose. Fuller Theological Seminary in particular had a profound impact on not just US missions, but world missions. The founder of its School of World Mission (SWM, now School of Intercultural Studies), Donald McGavran, wrote *The Bridges of God* in 1955 and launched the Church Growth movement that led to a worldwide Evangelical embrace of the Homogeneous Unit Principle as part of missionary strategy. Wheaton College became known as the premier Christian college in America, with some of its 'famous sons', Billy Graham and C. René Padilla, contributing greatly to the global Lausanne Movement (to this day, Wheaton has a Billy Graham Center for Evangelism, and Padilla is synonymous with 'integral mission'). Asbury Theological Seminary in Kentucky has its own famous missionary alumnus and named its E. Stanley Jones School of World Mission and Evangelism

after him. And although this is not a seminary, the Overseas Ministries Study Center, formerly located across the street from Yale Divinity School and now housed at Princeton Theological Seminary, is a major centre for missiological research.

In more ecumenical educational spheres, theological consortia sometimes have stellar missions programmes in their midst as well, such as the Association of Chicago Theological Schools, comprising 11 theological institutions of higher learning. Of particular note is Stephen Bevans at Catholic Theological Union, who is particularly known for contextual theology, and Trinity Evangelical Divinity School, which has its Hiebert Center for World Christianity and Global Theology. Every year the Association jointly holds the Chicago World Mission Institute conference. Boston has the Boston Theological Institute (BTI), a consortium of 10 theological schools, two of which are worth highlighting here: Boston University with Dana Robert, and Gordon-Conwell Theological Seminary with Todd Johnson. Both have major mission study centres, respectively the Center for Global Christianity and Mission, and the Center for the Study of Global Christianity. The BTI annually holds the Orlando E. Costas Consultation on World Mission and Ecumenism. The Graduate Theological Union comprises nine theological schools in Berkeley, California, and is dedicated to inter-religious dialogue. Two of the greatest missiological archives today are at the Yale Divinity School Library and Union Theological Seminary, New York. The greatest collection of Baptist archives is housed at Mercer University in Georgia.

Canada – because much more secular (as well as much less populous) – has fewer Christian colleges and universities (11 in total, five of which are Catholic). Its most prominent seminary is Tyndale in Toronto, which was named after one of the pioneers of English Bible translation, showing its commitment to mission.

(2) One of Donald McGavran's 'all-star' faculty that he recruited for his SWM was Ralph Winter. Winter was arguably the most cutting-edge missiological thinker of his generation. Fuller could not contain him, which led him to leave and found the US Center for World Mission (now renamed Frontier Ventures). Among Winter's many contributions was an admiration of William Carey's advocacy of para-church organisations ('sodalities') as opposed to ecclesial structures ('modalities') as apparatuses to send out missionaries. Para-church organisations have since dominated the US missions landscape. Most secular universities now have campus ministries such as Bill and Vonette Bright's Campus Crusade for Christ (now simply 'Cru'), InterVarsity Christian Fellowship (IVCF) and Navigators. Every Tribe, Every Nation and Wycliffe Bible Translators aim to translate the Bible into every language on earth. Organisations to end

global child poverty include Compassion International and World Vision, the largest US-based international relief and development organisation. Billy Graham's son Franklin runs Samaritan's Purse, one of the largest humanitarian aid organisations. Ministries like Focus on the Family arose with James Dobson at its helm, to evangelise families. Christian publishers, particularly of the Dutch Calvinist variety, were established in the Midwest, such as Zondervan, Eerdmans, Baker and InterVarsity Press, often with strong missional emphases. The IVCF also hosts (since 1946) the largest undergraduate missions conference in the world, Urbana (named after the original location where it was held, the University of Illinois at Urbana-Champaign; now it is held in Indianapolis). These turned certain cities in the USA into Christian ministry 'hotspots', including Colorado Springs, Colorado; Orlando, Florida; Grand Rapids, Michigan; and Chicago, Illinois.

Academic missiological societies also exist, such as the Association of Professors of Mission (which led to the American Society of Missiology), the Evangelical Missiological Society, Missio Nexus and the Yale–Edinburgh Group on World Christianity and the History of Mission (founded by renowned missiologists Lamin Sanneh and Andrew Walls). A number of mission studies periodicals are published, including the *International Bulletin of Mission Research*; *International Journal of Frontier Missiology*; *Missiology: An International Review*; and *Evangelical Missions Quarterly*. All these various para-church initiatives function to further Christian mission.

(3) While North America perhaps does not have the abundance of multi-nationalities that other continents have, it does have a preponderance of church denominations (many, of course, imported from Europe, but also many that are of the USA's own making). Four in particular are worth noting for their global missional influences.

First, Los Angeles is often recognised as the birthplace of global Pentecostalism, as it originated from the Azusa Street Mission in that city. An African American preacher, William J. Seymour (1870–1922), led this revival from 1906. Some would point even further back, to his teacher, Charles Fox Parham, at Bethel Bible College in Topeka, Kansas, in 1900. Others, like Swiss theologian Walter Hollenweger, would advocate a polycentric thesis, with a number of mini-Pentecosts (with no connection to foreign missionaries) springing up all over the world at the same time, such as Wales (1903–4), India (1904–5), Chile (1906–7) and Korea (1907). Regardless, Pentecostalism has had a strong history in the USA, from Canadian radio evangelist Aimee Semple McPherson's (1890–1944) Foursquare Church, to televangelist Oral Roberts (1918–2009), to John Wimber's (1934–97) Vineyard Church and the Signs and Wonders Movement. Today, the Assemblies of God Church has been a major source of the worldwide spread of Pentecostalism, especially that originating from North America, not the least because of its empowerment of women and people of colour.

The second denomination worth highlighting is one that is more homegrown. The Southern Baptist Convention (SBC) has been a major sender of missionaries, especially through its Foreign (now International) Mission Board. So convinced are they of the role of missions in their life that they almost changed their name to Great Commission Baptists in 2012. Perhaps the most high-profile pastor in the SBC has been Rick Warren, pastor of Saddleback Community Church in Southern California, the nation's largest SBC church congregation. He wielded such influence that he could host a US presidential debate (Obama versus McCain in 2008) and his bestselling book *The Purpose-Driven Life* and PEACE plan have left indelible marks, working to eradicate the five biggest problems in the world as he sees them: Spiritual Emptiness, Self-Serving Leadership, Poverty, Disease and Illiteracy. This is holistic mission rather than simply evangelism.

Third, though the US tends to be seen as a Protestant nation, the single largest denomination remains Roman Catholicism. Catholic missions from the USA took on increased impetus after the publication of Pope Pius XII's encyclical *Mystici Corporis* (1943), which especially inspired laypeople. This kind of mission often took on a north–south axis as dioceses in North America were paired with their counterparts in Central and South America. Perhaps the Catholic Church's most famous extension arm for mission in North America is in Maryknoll, located in upstate New York. Collectively, these ministries comprise the Catholic Foreign Mission Society of America, the publishing house Orbis and others, and Maryknollers are sometimes known as the 'Marines of the Catholic Church' due to their ability to minister in the roughest areas on earth. Orbis's most famous book is probably Gustavo Gutiérrez's *A Theology of Liberation*, which again highlights the North American–South American connection. In 2003, the Mexican and US bishops issued a pastoral letter titled 'Strangers No Longer: Together on the Journey of Hope' to re-emphasise the joining of the Americas in the Catholic mind. It actually makes sense that Pentecostals and Catholics are two of the largest churches and mission forces in North America, given that Hispanics are the largest ethnic minority group and tend towards Pentecostalism or Catholicism.

Fourth, the work of the Church of Jesus Christ of Latter-day Saints (LDS) must be acknowledged. It is one of the few North American-birthed major religions and it is a force for missions, as all male members are required to go on a two-year missions trip, usually when aged 19–20. They have spread the LDS faith far beyond the borders of the USA, especially in

Africa and Latin America. It also employs creative methods of evangelism, such as running the theme park Polynesian Cultural Center in Hawaii, which also serves to raise funds for its missions. Other religions that fall into this home-grown category include Jehovah's Witnesses, who often go door to door distributing the *Watchtower* magazine.

Finally, although these might not be huge senders of missionaries from North America, their collective weight from other countries in global mission makes them worth mentioning: Orthodox and Anglicans. The Orthodox Christian Mission Center (OCMC) in St Augustine, Florida, is the hub of Orthodox missions-sending in the USA. And the Anglicans have the Anglican Mission in the Americas (AMiA), the missional arm of the Anglican Church in North America (ACNA), which was derived from the split within the worldwide Anglican communion over the LGBTQ issue. This caused the more conservative faction to form ACNA (as opposed to the more progressive Episcopal Church in the United States and the Anglican Church in Canada) and align with the Anglican dioceses in Africa, which also tend to be more conservative. In sum, the Anglicans in North America tend to partner globally with Africa, and the Catholics in North America tend to partner globally with Latin America.

Ethnic Diversity and Missions

North America displays an ethnic diversity that makes for a global mix right in its midst. Soong-Chan Rah wrote in *The Next Evangelicalism: Releasing the Church from Western Cultural Captivity* (Downers Grove, IL: InterVarsity Press, 2009) that – while the centre of gravity of Christianity has indeed shifted from the West to the Majority World – the centre of gravity of Christianity in North America has shifted to ethnic minorities and immigrants. The USA and Canada are two of the most multi-ethnic countries in the world, particularly in the major metropolitan areas. Toronto is the most culturally diverse city in the world. However, the USA remains the only Westernised country in the world that has stayed majority Christian, largely because of Rah's observation above. Some of the ethnic groups in North America are great mission senders; others are major receivers of mission. And some are a fairly even mix of both.

Jewish Americans

The fundamentalism of the early twentieth century, with its concomitant pre-millennial dispensationalism (eschewing the more optimistic post-millennialism of the Great Century of Missions and the social gospel from the late 1800s), favoured literal, ethnic Jews and a modern-day State of Israel. This was a particularly US theology, coming from John Nelson Darby in the nineteenth century and solidified in the pages of

C. I. Scofield's Reference Bible (1909). The idea that Jews still had a role to play in the end times as a fulfilment of biblical prophecy was further stoked after the Second World War by Allied sympathy towards the plight of the Jews after the Holocaust and by the fact that New York City had the world's largest Jewish population – even more than Israel. Jews also largely ran all the major Hollywood studios in California, which added to media coverage. Therefore, US missions work had a strong theology of Jewish evangelism, through organisations like Jews for Jesus and Chosen People Ministries.

African Americans

In contrast to the white, Southern theology that drove Jewish evangelism and support of Israel was a parallel Black, Northern theology that drove a social racial consciousness. Though Black Americans have a solid history of sending and being overseas missionaries (not just George Liele but also others like Lott Carey and Betsey Stockton), much of this was curtailed with domestic struggles through the years. Martin Luther King Jr (1929–68) was a Baptist preacher who was (re-)named for the father of the Protestant Reformation (his birth name was Michael) but influenced by Rauschenbusch's social gospel. However, he really made a name for himself with his prophetic speech-making in becoming the father of the civil rights movement.

The USA has long had a racial reckoning coming, through its legacy of enslavement and Jim Crow laws. Some may find it ironic that Black enslaved who were brought over from Africa would have embraced the faith of their enslavers, but the same Bible that drove the white enslavers to justify their exploitation of land and bodies buoyed Black slaves to give them hope of liberation. This theme was picked up by James Cone (1938–2018) of Union Theological Seminary in New York City. He was the author of *A Black Theology of Liberation* (1970), which emphasised Old Testament themes of exodus from enslavement and prophetic justice, as opposed to white theology, which mainly was spiritual rather than physical, and individualistic rather than systemic. Another African American worth noting was the evangelist Tom Skinner (1942–94). At the Urbana 1970 student missionary conference, he picked up on Cone's themes and boldly proclaimed, 'We need to go out into the highways and the byways and tell people what true liberator is. The Liberator has come!'

Though African American overseas missionaries number less than 1% of the total US overseas force, there are signs that this percentage is increasing. One system that might have to change, however, is the fundraising model ('faith missions', a legacy of Hudson Taylor, among others), which does not work as well in communities of colour.

Hispanic Americans

Many of the most well-known Latin American *evangélicos* were trained or taught in the USA, namely Ecuadorian C. René Padilla (1932–2021) at Wheaton College; Peruvian Samuel Escobar (b. 1934), who taught at Palmer Seminary alongside Ron Sider (founder of Evangelicals for Social Action – now called Christians for Social Action); and Puerto Rican Orlando Costas (1942–87), who was educated at Nyack and Garrett-Evangelical Seminary and later taught at Andover Newton Theological School in Boston (following in the footsteps of Adoniram and Ann Judson; Orlando and Rose Costas were even commissioned as missionaries on the Judson bench in Salem). These three men were all Baptists and were speakers at the first Lausanne Congress in 1974. This shows the close ties and porous borders between North America and its southern neighbours, and that the influence went both ways: they influenced John Stott, the architect of the Lausanne Covenant, to include *misión integral* (holistic mission, that is, not separating evangelism and social justice), which is a hallmark of the Lausanne Movement today. Most North American mission organisations require anyone who signs up with them to sign and affirm the Lausanne Covenant. Hispanic Americans also contribute to domestic missions; for example, Al Padilla (b. 1954) heads the Center for Urban Ministerial Education, the downtown Boston campus of Gordon-Conwell Seminary. Many initiatives also seek to reach Hispanics to further their theological and pastoral education, such as Centro Latino at Fuller Seminary, the Hispanic Theological Initiative at Princeton Seminary, Hispanic House at Duke Divinity School, and AETH (Association for Hispanic Theological Education) founded by Justo González (b. 1937).

Asian Americans

Koreans are renowned worldwide for their overseas missionary efforts and fervour, and Korean Americans no less so. This is often bolstered by their legendary Charismatic prayer life. Chinese and Chinese Americans also have their fair share of evangelistic endeavours, Japanese American churches often embrace the Wesleyan Holiness movement and Filipino Americans bring in a Catholic social consciousness as well. Today, with increasing frequency, Asian Americans are leading major missions and evangelism organisations in North America. Examples include the chief executive officer of the Lausanne Movement, Michael Oh; the executive director of American Baptist International Ministries (the modern name for the American Baptist Foreign Mission Society), Sharon Koh; the executive director of Christians for Social Action, Nikki Toyama-Szeto; the executive director of Canadian Baptist Ministries, Jennifer Lau; the president of the National Association of Evangelicals, Walter Kim; coordinator of Mission to the World (Presbyterian Church in America), Lloyd Kim; and the president of InterVarsity, Tom Lin. This, despite Asian Americans comprising only about 5% of the US population.

Native Americans

Though the Native peoples of North America (Natives or Indians in the USA; First Nations in Canada) were largely decimated through European warfare and disease (estimates are that more than 90% of the continent was depopulated), the land remains, though not in perhaps as recognisable a form. Notable Native North American Christians include Terry LeBlanc (Mi'kmaq-Acadian), Randy Woodley (Keetoowah Cherokee), Ray Aldred (Cree), Mark Charles (Navajo) and the late Richard Twiss (Sicangu Lakota Oyate). Some books worth highlighting include Twiss's *One Church, Many Tribes* (Ventura, CA: Regal Books, 2000), Woodley's *Shalom and the Community of Creation* and Charles's *Unsettling Truths: The Ongoing, Dehumanizing Legacy of the Doctrine of Discovery* (co-authored with Soong-Chan Rah; Downers Grove, IL: InterVarsity, 2019). Charles also has the notable distinction of being the first Native man ever to run for US President, in 2020. The refocusing of mission on reconciliation – both ethnic and ecological – is a hallmark of Native theology. Creation Care especially is an ethic that is ingrained in the Native worldview and offers a huge contribution to missiological literature. It must be noted that many of the above mentioned are Canadian. In many respects Canada does a much better job of honouring Native communities than the USA.

Women

Although gender is not the same as race, there are some parallels and points of resonance between the two. One example is Rosemary Radford Ruether (b. 1936), a Catholic theologian who taught at Yale, who emulated James Cone's achievement in Black Theology by producing a feminist liberation theology, with the publication of books such as *Sexism and God-Talk: Toward a Feminist Theology* (Boston, MA: Beacon Press, 1993). Women have historically outnumbered men two-to-one on the mission field. As with African Americans, much of this was curtailed by domestic struggles, particularly related to the Second World War and suffrage. Nonetheless, North American women have had tremendous successes on the mission field, both at home and abroad. Ironically, one of the reasons for this is and was complementarianism, which holds that a woman should not hold certain church offices (particularly those of pastor and elder) and/or preach. Many women who have felt called to preach the gospel – but who have felt disbarred from doing so domestically – have gone overseas instead. In an irony, the Southern Baptist Convention (one of the most complementarian denominations) sees its patron saint of missions as Lottie Moon, even taking a Christmas offering in her name every year that is hugely successful in funding international missionary efforts. And the Convention does the same with Annie Armstrong and its annual Easter offering in her name.

Postcolonial Critique

An extensive literature exists about the colonial nature of mission, or at least its complicity with colonialism. This is a fair critique, especially considering that the 'Great Century of Missions' was the age of maritime travel which carried missionaries, as well as colonists, to nations around the world. Therefore, to parse where one ends and the other begins is confusing, to say the least.

Today, the ease of short-term missions due to air travel leads to a further problem, namely the phenomenon sometimes known as 'voluntourism'. This is when missionaries from the West go to the Majority World for a few days, or even up to a few months, to have a missionary experience. It is often acknowledged that the experience is more beneficial to the missionary than to the people to whom they are sent. Certainly, in order for many young people to determine if they are called to long-term missionary service, they have to try it out for a while, and even if they ultimately decide they are not called, at least they have a changed (hopefully in a positive sense) perspective on other people groups. However, the acknowledgement of the benefit to the missionary does not mitigate the fact that often the target cultures are harmed. This could take the form of material goods brought into the country that rob local businesses of income. Or it could be 'poverty porn' (an actual phrase), where photographs are taken of poor people overseas and used in shiny brochures in the West to appeal for financial support. Or it could foster Majority World dependence on Western funds. And sometimes, spending an extended time overseas does not necessarily mean that Westerners learn a respect for the local people; they might be just as prejudiced as before if they have not learned to listen.

There has even been a shift in language. Michael Stroope, in his book *Transcending Mission* (Downers Grove, IL: InterVarsity Press, 2017), calls for a moratorium on the word 'mission' because it is not a biblical word, but instead was originally an Iberian colonial word (*misión* in Spanish and *missão* in Portuguese), 'terms in wide use to describe the diplomatic and military activities of Iberians in foreign lands'. Words like 'crusade' (as in Billy Graham Crusade, or Campus Crusade for Christ) have also fallen out of favour, as they conjure up images of the warfare of the medieval Crusades. Another example is United World Mission's changing the name of its Spearhead programme to Avance to adopt less militaristic language.

With the USA being the most powerful country in the world, avoiding words that might evoke fears of colonialism seems wise.

In contrast, the idea of the Three-Self Church (developed by American missiologist Rufus Anderson and British missiologist Henry Venn) remains valid: national churches ought to become self-governing, self-sustaining and self-propagating. This idea still has not completely taken hold, even though it is two centuries old. And even more importantly, a 'fourth self' is now called for: self-theologising. This is for the purpose of having Majority World Christians write theologies that are relevant to their own contexts. Thankfully, some US American publishers like Zondervan are championing these efforts and distributing them worldwide.

Conclusion

Some common themes that might be seen in North American missions include the role of Baptists (Liele, the Judsons, Latino *evangélicos*, MLK, the SBC); the empowerment of people of colour and women; the historical gravitational pull towards New England (Brainerd, Edwards, Haystack) and a North Atlantic partnership (Edinburgh 1910, Lausanne, World Council of Churches, Yale–Edinburgh); and the structural apparatuses of denominationalism and para-church organisations, both of which serve as effective vehicles for missions and evangelism work.

Bibliography

Dries, Angelyn, *The Missionary Movement in American Catholic History* (Maryknoll, NY: Orbis, 1998).

Moreau, A. Scott, *Evangelical Dictionary of World Missions* (Grand Rapids, MI: Baker Academic, 2000)

Robert, Dana L., *American Women in Mission: The Modern Mission Era 1792–1992* (Macon, GA: Mercer University Press, 1997).

Stearns, Richard, *The Hole In Our Gospel* (Nashville, TN: Thomas Nelson, 2010).

Woodley, Randy S., *Shalom and the Community of Creation: An Indigenous Vision* (Grand Rapids, MI: Eerdmans, 2012).

Gender

Susan M. Shaw

Gender is not something we have but is something we do. Gender is the behaviours a society expects of people based on perceptions of their biological characteristics, and so gender is something we learn to perform – how to move, how to dress, how to speak, how to relate to other people based on our perceptions of their gender. In the dominant culture in North America, gender is divided into two categories: male and female. This is called the gender binary, and almost all people are assigned to one of these two categories at birth. Our internal sense of gender – our gender identity – however, might or might not fit with our gender assignment. People whose sense of gender identity fits more or less well with their gender assignment are denoted cisgender. People whose sense of gender identity does not fit with their gender assignment are transgender, gender non-binary, gender non-conforming or any of a number of other gender identities.

The gender binary plays an important role in reinforcing sexism, the system of oppression that maintains a hierarchy with men over women. This hierarchical structure is known as patriarchy. This system is pervasive, affecting and supported by social institutions like government, education, media, health-care, family and religion. The gender arrangements of patriarchy, the ways in which beliefs, relationships and institutions force people into patterns of behaviour, compel patterns of constraint, discrimination and oppression that appear in many Christian institutions in North America as limitations on women's religious leadership, restrictions on women's control of their own sexuality and fertility, gender violence, and condemnation of transgender and gender non-binary people. It also limits the scope of acceptable masculinities, boxing men into stereotypical roles of patriarchal authority and dominance. These arrangements also reinforce and are reinforced by heteronormativity, the assumption that everyone is heterosexual and the social practices that underpin this assumption (forms that ask for mother and father, wedding paraphernalia for bride and groom, etc.) and heterosexism, the system of oppression that maintains heterosexual dominance through norms, laws, policies and practices (such as excluding LGBT people from ordination or, until recently, from marriage).

People, however, do not simply go along with their oppression; they also resist. Feminism is, as feminist scholar bell hooks puts it, a movement to end sexist oppression. Feminism is an analytical tool that helps us identify, name, explain and contest sexism and patriarchy. It suggests ways to transform social structures to move towards a society that is inclusive, equitable and just for all people. Feminism recognises that sexism is not simply a matter of individual men mistreating women; rather, it is systemic, woven into the fabric of society, and therefore requires systemic solutions that transform ideologies, languages and institutions, including religion. In North America, many Christian churches actively engage in feminist work and resistance to sexist oppression. Often the divide between conservative and progressive Christian churches is stark, especially around issues of gender.

Feminism also recognises that gender does not work on its own but, rather, shapes and is shaped by other forms of social difference such as race/ethnicity, sexuality, ability, social class, age, national origin and religion. Intersectionality reminds us that as we analyse problems and propose solutions we must keep in mind that we cannot talk about gender apart from its intersections. So, for example, in the 2016 and 2020 presidential elections in the USA, we saw that White Evangelical women overwhelmingly supported Donald Trump, while Black women supported Hillary Clinton and Joe Biden. An intersectional lens helps us tease apart the reasons for this significant difference.

In North America, Christianity is a force for both oppression and liberation for women and LGBTQ people. Many conservative denominations, such as the Southern Baptist Convention (SBC), the nation's largest Protestant denomination, believe in women's subordination. The SBC asserts that because man was first in creation and woman was first in the Fall, women are to submit to male headship in the family and church. Therefore, women should not be ordained or serve as pastors. Similarly, the Lutheran Church Missouri Synod believes that Scripture teaches women should keep silent in the churches, and thus women cannot be pastors. A number of these denominations, like the Presbyterian Church of America, have embraced complementarianism, the idea that God has created ontologically equal but distinct gender roles for women and men that define responsibilities in home and church. While the Catholic Church explicitly excludes women from the priesthood, it is more egalitarian in many other social relations.

Most conservative Christian churches and the Catholic Church teach that diverse sexualities are sinful. Many reject LGBTQ people from church membership, and most exclude LGBTQ people from church leadership. Most also prohibit pastors from performing same-sex weddings or allowing same-sex couples to use church facilities for ceremonies. In recent years, however, a number of Evangelical churches have begun to show some openness to LGBTQ people, although sexuality remains a highly divisive topic in many Christian denominations.

Significant numbers of Canadian Evangelicals also disapprove of homosexuality, same-sex marriage and abortion rights. For example, the Evangelical Missionary Church of Canada believes marriage is between a man and a woman, and the husband is the head of the home. The Christian Right in Canada is significantly smaller and less influential than in the USA. Only 10–15% of Canadians identify as Evangelicals. Additionally, while conservative Evangelicals in Canada tend all to agree on issues of reproduction and sexuality, they differ much more on other social issues than do their American counterparts.

While the Canadian system of government provides less opportunity for conservative Christians to promote their social agenda, Christian churches in the USA have enormous influence and often push governments towards control of women and of LGBTQ people. Reproductive rights, particularly access to abortion, are highly contested in the USA, with religious groups exerting enormous influence. Believing that life begins at conception, conservative Christians, including Protestants and Catholics, have advocated for greater restrictions on abortion access with the ultimate goal of overturning *Roe* v. *Wade*, the 1973 Supreme Court decision that made abortion legal in the USA. Black churches in the USA are deeply divided over abortion, with issues of race and class complicating the discussion.

As many laws and Supreme Court decisions have granted more rights to women and LGBTQ people, Christian conservatives have promoted broader latitude for religious exemptions. For example, conservative Christians in the USA have argued that Christian business owners with convictions against same-sex marriages should not be required to provide services such as wedding cakes or photography to gay and lesbian couples. A Supreme Court decision exempts employers from providing contraception coverage under the Affordable Care Act if employers hold religious convictions against contraception.

Despite these and other beliefs and practices of Christian churches in North America, many expressions of Christian faith offer support and empowerment to women and LGBTQ people. Even in churches that teach women's submission and exclusion from formal leadership, women find affirmation in the many ways they serve and lead, and many women who profess male headship in the home describe much more pragmatic and egalitarian family relationships in practice. Women often find deep communities with other women and participate in personally meaningful experiences in their communities of faith. Many women gain leadership skills in their work with women's ministries and many of the behind-the-scenes activities essential to the functioning of churches. In Pentecostal traditions, churches often expect women to stay within certain gender roles. Yet many women have leadership roles, for example, in the Foursquare church, and women have prominent roles in Pentecostal institutions of higher education. People across denominations who challenge church stances and practices have also formed para-church groups to offer support and advocate for change. For example, Catholics for Choice promotes reproductive rights, and Christians for Biblical Equality urges egalitarianism among Evangelicals. Some women in the Church of Jesus Christ of Latter-day Saints (LDS) formed Feminist Mormon Housewives, a blog, podcast and Facebook group for women to discuss issues from more liberal points of view. Among many progressive churches, women and LGBTQ people participate, serve and lead in every capacity, and churches are engaged in activism on behalf of disenfranchised groups of people.

Diversity and disagreement characterise Christian thinking about gender in North America. The following sections examine five important contemporary topics about gender that are central in North American Christianity: women in church leadership, women's bodies and sexuality, gender violence, transgender lives, and masculinities.

Women in Church Leadership

The role of women in church leadership is highly contested across Christian groups within North America. While some churches exclude women from any kind of leadership that implies authority over men, others are fully egalitarian, welcoming women into leadership in every role. Conservative Protestant churches and the Catholic Church exclude LGBTQ people from leadership, and even some mainstream Protestant churches that are open to women's leadership disallow leadership by LGBTQ people. On the other hand, a small but growing number of denominations have begun to affirm leadership by LGBTQ people.

Many Evangelicals believe that the Bible teaches that women are to submit to men. They believe that men should be the heads of households and the pastors of the church. Many believe that women's God-ordained role is in the home as wife and mother, and some go so far as to suggest women should not work outside the home at all. The Church of Jesus Christ of Latter-day Saints (LDS) excludes women from the priesthood and extols motherhood as women's highest calling. Catholics and progressive Protestants are much more likely to support gender equality in the home and society. For example, the United Methodist Church affirms the equality of women and men in the home, workplace and church.

Some denominations have a long history of ordaining women; others have embraced the practice more recently; and many still exclude women from ordination. The first woman ordained in the USA was Congregationalist Antoinette Brown in 1853. The African Methodist Episcopal Zion Church began ordaining women in the late 1880s, although it did not elect its first woman bishop until 2008. The United Church of Canada ordained its first woman minister in 1936. The first ordination of a Southern Baptist woman was in 1964, but the issue of women in ministry became central in the battle between fundamentalist and moderate Southern Baptists in the 1980s and, with the triumph of fundamentalists and exodus of moderates from the denomination, the Convention took official stances opposing women's ordination. The moderate groups that left the Southern Baptist Convention – the Cooperative Baptist Fellowship and the Alliance of Baptists – support the ordination of women. Seventh-day Adventists in North America also support ordination of women. The Catholic Church, however, does not ordain women as priests, although the Women's Ordination Conference, a grassroots feminist Catholic organisation, advocates for the ordination of women to the priesthood.

Perhaps even more contentious than the issue of women's ordination is the question of the role of LGBTQ people in the churches of North America. Many denominations that accepted women's ordination decades ago still struggle over LGBTQ issues and, within denominations that expressly oppose diverse sexualities and gender diversity, some people and groups are pushing for change.

In the USA, the United Church of Christ was the first Christian denomination to support ordination of LGBTQ people and the first to consecrate same-sex partnerships and endorse marriage equality. The first gay man was ordained in the church in 1972. The United Church of Canada recommended ordination of gay men and lesbians in the late 1980s, and a significant number of members left the church in the ensuing controversy. The first gay man was ordained in the Church in 1992. The Episcopal Church authorised ordination of lesbians and gay men in 1994, followed by the Evangelical Lutheran Church in America in 2010 and the Presbyterian Church (USA) in 2011. In 2020, the United Methodist Church, unable to reach consensus over LGBTQ ordination and same-sex marriage, decided to split.

Many Evangelical churches continue to oppose any acceptance of LGBTQ people, although surveys suggest that younger generations are much more likely to be accepting of LGBTQ people and to support non-discrimination protections and marriage equality than their elders. Within many denominations, groups challenging anti-LGBTQ beliefs and practices have formed. In 1972, American Baptists Concerned for Sexual

Minorities was the first Baptist group to offer support and advocacy for LGBTQ Baptists. In 2003, the group helped form the Association of Welcoming and Affirming Baptists to bring Baptists across the country together to work for change. Similarly, DignityUSA is a Catholic group working for LGBTQ acceptance in the Church, and Affirmation works for support among the LDS.

Feminist and queer theologies are also challenging traditional gender and sexuality norms in the church in North America. Feminist theologies arose in the 1960s alongside the broader women's movement. These early works focused on reinterpreting the biblical text to argue for the full inclusion of women in the life of the church, rewriting church history to recover women's presence and leadership in the church, and challenging church doctrines that subordinated women. Theologising and reading the Bible from their own social locations, Black women developed womanist theology to capture the intersections of gender and race. Likewise, other women of colour constructed contextual theologies that reflected the specificities of Indigenous, Asian American and Latina experiences. *Mujerista* theologies, for example, reflect Latinas' struggle for liberation and daily survival. Lesbian and gay theologies argued for a place for lesbians and gay men in the church and, as queer theory developed in academia as a direct challenge to heteronormativity, queer theologies arose to confront heterosexism in the church. Rather than simply arguing for inclusion, queer theologies contested the very foundations of theology as rooted in heteronormativity and complicit in the maintenance of the subordination of LGBTQ people in church and society.

In 2012, the Vatican criticised American nuns' Leadership Conference of Women Religious for doctrinal problems because it had questioned the Church's teachings on homosexuality and the male priesthood. The Conference is an umbrella association of women's religious communities and represents 80% of Catholic sisters in the USA. The Vatican accused them of promoting radical feminist themes, focusing too much on social justice and disagreeing with the bishops. Nuns organised a bus tour through nine states to call attention to their social justice work and advocate for policy change to address issues of wealth inequality and poverty. Eventually the Vatican dropped its investigation of American nuns.

Women's Bodies and Sexuality

Central to any discussion of gender is the role of bodies and sexuality, because both are central in the ways gender is constructed and functions to constrain women and LGBTQ people. In North America, gender, bodies, sexuality and Christianity intersect in a number of issues, including purity culture, abortion access and reproductive justice, and queer sexuality.

Purity culture is a movement among conservative Christians that emphasises the dangers of girls' and women's sexuality and promotes abstinence outside traditional heterosexual marriage. The movement makes girls and women responsible for men's sexuality and suggests that the bodies and sexuality of girls and women are a stumbling block for boys and men. The movement has spawned an entire industry of books, purity curricula, purity music, purity rings and purity balls that reinforce these ideas for young women (and young men) and lead to a great deal of shame, fear, guilt and anxiety for those who internalise purity culture's messages. In addition to its messages about sexuality, purity culture also expects hyper-femininity of women and hyper-masculinity of men; requires women to submit to male headship; and teaches that God has ordained specific gender roles for women and men. While purity culture is a product of White Evangelicalism, some Christian communities of colour have imported it.

Closely related to purity issues are North American Christian perspectives on abortion and reproductive justice. Abortion may be the most divisive issue churches in North America face. In many ways, the fight over abortion has been key to the politicising of conservative Christianity and the energising of the Christian Right in the USA. Anti-abortion advocates argue that human life begins at conception and so abortion is tantamount to murder. The anti-abortion movement has created interesting alliances of Catholics and Evangelical Protestants who engage in protesting, lobbying and campaigning to limit abortion access and, in the USA, ultimately to overturn *Roe* v. *Wade*. In the USA and Canada, some anti-abortion activists have even resorted to violence, ranging from blocking access to clinics to bombing clinics and murdering abortion providers.

For most progressive Christians, the issue of abortion is much more complicated and is seen within a larger framework of reproductive justice. Reproductive justice is a term growing out of the work of feminists of colour who recognise abortion is only one of a number of intersecting issues that constrain and control women's bodies and lives – race, poverty, access to reproductive health-care, gender violence and education. Reproductive justice advocates for systems in which women have control over their own bodies and reproduction and can make their own decisions about whether and when to have children. Progressive Christians understand abortion within a theological framework that values women's full humanity and ability to make decisions. For example, the statement from the Evangelical Lutheran Church in America on abortion recognises differences of opinion among Christians on the issue while calling for compassion for women making decisions about pregnancies and advocating for social issues that make pregnancies untenable to be addressed.

One of the measures that research has shown to reduce unintended pregnancies is contraceptive access. Yet a number of Christians in North America oppose contraception. Traditionally, the Catholic Church has prohibited use of contraceptives, but in recent decades some conservative Protestants have also decried contraception. The 'full quiver' movement argues that married couples should have as many children as God gives them. Hobby Lobby owner David Green opposes birth control because he believes that many contraceptives are abortifacients. Green successfully persuaded the US Supreme Court to exempt businesses from the Affordable Care Act's requirement to provide insurance coverage for contraception if their owners have religious convictions against birth control.

Evoking almost as much controversy in the churches of North America is the issue of queer sexuality. Many churches, including the Catholic and Orthodox Churches, most Evangelical and Pentecostal churches, and some mainline churches, teach that homosexuality is sinful. Some of these churches have even advocated 'conversion therapy', a discredited practice of trying to change someone's sexual or gender identity. These churches have also often been active in political advocacy in opposition to marriage equality and antidiscrimination protections for LGBTQ people. For example, evangelist Franklin Graham claimed that the US Supreme Court's decision that extended employment protections to LGBTQ people was an infringement on religious liberty.

Evangelical Lutheran churches in Canada reflect the divide among North American Christians over diverse sexualities. The Evangelical Lutheran Church in Canada (like its sister denomination in the USA, the Evangelical Lutheran Church in America) welcomes LGBTQ people and blesses same-sex unions. The Lutheran Church–Canada, a smaller and more conservative denomination, believes marriage is reserved for one man and one woman, and homosexuality is sinful; LGBTQ people are excluded from ministry. The Black church in the USA also struggles with the issue of diverse sexualities. On the one hand, historically, Black churches have opposed homosexuality and, on the other, they have led in social justice movements, and LGBTQ people have been active members of congregations. Even within the United Church of Christ, the most progressive Christian denomination in the USA, with a long history of supporting LGBTQ people, some local churches still oppose diverse sexualities.

Gender Violence

Gender violence is a particularly vexing problem in the North American church. Gender violence is violence that targets people based on gender, and in the church clergy abuse scandals reflect the larger social contexts of gender violence. While stories had circulated for years about abuse by

Catholic priests in the USA, the first to gain prominence was in Louisiana in 1985, when a priest pleaded guilty to 11 counts of molesting boys. He eventually confessed to abusing more than 300 children. Not until 2002, however, did the extent of the problem become visible, when the *Boston Globe* published an exhaustive story about abuse cases in the Boston area. After that, victims around the country began to come forward and file lawsuits against various Catholic dioceses. These stories exposed the Church's culture of cover-up, simply moving predatory priests from parish to parish. In 2019, Pope Francis acknowledged the sexual abuse of nuns by Catholic priests and bishops.

In 1988, Barbara Blaine, a survivor of abuse by a priest, founded the Survivors Network of Those Abused by Priests (SNAP). SNAP began as a way for survivors of clergy abuse to support one another. After the *Boston Globe* story, the organisation was overwhelmed by survivors coming forward. Now the organisation works to expose abusers and Church officials who shield them, to hold Church institutions accountable, and to reform laws that enable abusers.

Following the eruption of #MeToo in 2017, #ChurchToo trended as people posted their experiences of abuse at the hands of trusted and often prominent pastors, evangelists and youth ministers. Activist Tarana Burke had begun the MeToo hashtag to help girls of colour talk about abuse about a decade before actor Alyssa Milano's 2017 tweet, 'If you've been sexually harassed or assaulted write "me too" as a reply to this tweet'. Within days of Milano's tweet, millions of people responded. Shortly after, Emily Joy and Hanna Paasch launched the #ChurchToo conversation that led to thousands of people telling their stories of sexual abuse within the church, including those of teenage girls raped by youth pastors and young daughters abused by church-going fathers, gay teenagers shamed, and wives beaten by church leaders. In 2018, when a mega-church pastor confessed he had sexually assaulted a teenage girl two decades earlier and asked for forgiveness, his church gave him a standing ovation. A 2019 exposé by the *Houston Chronicle* revealed hundreds of cases of abuse by Southern Baptist pastors and a denomination unwilling to address the problem. In 2021, a global Evangelical organisation acknowledged that its founder, who had died the previous spring, had engaged in widespread sex abuse. While these scandals have led to some soul-searching among churches, few structural changes have been made to prevent abuse and ensure accountability for predatory clergy.

Gender violence also includes violence against LGBTQ people. In recent years, a number of Christians, including pastors, in the USA have called for executions of LGBTQ people. Many churches condemn LGBTQ people, calling them an 'abomination' and declaring they will go to hell.

Many hate groups that profess Christian beliefs target LGBTQ people. In particular, the Westboro Baptist Church in Topeka, Kansas, has created a 'ministry' of anti-LGBTQ hate, picketing funerals and supportive churches with signs that read 'God hates fags' and other abhorrent messages.

Another form of gender violence closely connected to North American churches is sex trafficking. Many churches are involved in ways to end trafficking and to support survivors, although some instances are highly problematic. For example, a number of Christian anti-trafficking organisations prioritise evangelism as part of their work with survivors of trafficking, or they are also anti-abortion and anti-LGBTQ. Sometimes their work reflects 'White saviourism', an approach by which White people make themselves feel better or superior by rescuing women, especially Women of Colour, without addressing the underlying structures of racism that disadvantage Women of Colour and create situations that make them vulnerable to trafficking and other problems. The very real problem of sex trafficking and well-intentioned but often problematic involvement of Christian organisations in anti-trafficking also likely made many Christians vulnerable to believing QAnon's false claims about child trafficking among Democratic politicians and business leaders. QAnon is a White supremacist, anti-Semitic conspiracy theory that took hold in the USA during the presidency of Donald Trump and eventually contributed to the 2021 insurrection. One of its key tenets is that the USA is run by a cabal of Satan-worshipping paedophiles who operate a child-trafficking ring. Many conservative Christians followed QAnon, and even more were influenced by QAnon's falsehoods as these lies and disinformation crept into the mainstream.

Many churches, however, are actively involved in efforts to end gender violence. The Evangelical Lutheran Church in America's 'Social Message on Gender-Based Violence' argues, 'Gender-based violence is an ancient sin that for thousands of years has harmed countless women, children and men. It is a sin that Christians need to recognise, understand and confront, for our religious history also bears its stain.' The Alliance of Baptists states, 'The church must be proactive and not keep silent on the reality of sexualized violence … Because we are called to stand alongside one another in suffering – "when one member suffers, all suffer together" (1 Corinthians 12: 26) – the Alliance of Baptists recognizes its call to not only help those who have been victimized but also to proactively oppose patterns of behavior which enable the perpetuation of sexual violence'.

Transgender Lives
In recent years, Christian churches in North America have begun to grapple with the place of transgender people in church and society.

Transgender, gender non-binary and gender non-conforming identities challenge dominant notions of gender as fixed and determined at birth. Many Christians, however, believe that gender is a binary created by God, and so transgender identity is an affront to the divinely ordained order. The Catholic Church maintains that gender is binary and is set at birth. The Assemblies of God asserts that humans are created in the image of God as male and female. In 2016, the Church of God passed a resolution stating that Scripture does not allow people to 'self-identify as the gender they wish to be, rather than the biological sex to which they were born' and requiring that churches maintain rest-rooms, locker rooms and other such facilities for exclusive use by men and women according to their biological sex and the sex identified on the birth certificate. Many churches exclude transgender people from leadership and ordination. During the 2020 COVID-19 pandemic, a Baptist pastor in Canada came out as transgender during a Zoom sermon. A month later, her church fired her. Additionally, many Christians back political efforts to pass 'bathroom bills'. Bathroom bills are legislation that limits access to public rest-rooms according to sex as defined by biology or birth certificates. Advocates for transgender people consider these bills discriminatory. Another recent battleground over transgender rights is in girls' and women's sports. A number of Christian groups have become involved in opposing participation by transwomen and girls in athletic competition with other women and girls. The Alliance Defending Freedom, a conservative Christian group of lawyers who promote conservative defences of religious liberty, in 2019 filed a lawsuit on behalf of three cisgender girls who, the suit says, missed out on opportunities because of the participation of transgender athletes.

Other Christian churches in North America, however, have welcomed and supported transgender people. In 2012, the Episcopal Church voted overwhelmingly to approve ordination of transgender people. The United Church of Canada welcomes people of all gender identities. In 2018, the Presbyterian Church USA voted to welcome transgender people in all aspects of church life. A number of churches have specific organisations that offer support for transgender, as well as lesbian, gay, bisexual and queer people, such as the Association of Welcoming and Affirming Baptists, the Disciples LGBTQ+ Alliance and Affirm United in the United Church of Canada.

Masculinities

During the Second Industrial Revolution (from the mid-1800s to the early 1900s), as people left agrarian life for manufacturing jobs in cities, factory work produced a gendered division of labour, with men engaging in paid work outside the home and women doing unpaid work inside the home.

In the harsh environment of industry, men quickly learned to be tough and unemotional. As fathers left boys at home with mothers, a social fear (mostly among White people) developed that, by spending so much time with mothers, boys would become soft and feminised. This fear, coupled with the threat of a burgeoning first wave of the women's movement, led to a crisis in masculinity and a moral panic that sons would become gay. One of the answers to this problem was organised sports as a way to shape boys into masculine heterosexual men. Some corners of Christianity also became concerned with this problem and developed 'muscular Christianity' in response. This movement emphasised White Western notions of manliness and hardened boys against immoral influences. This strain of muscular Christianity has persisted into the twenty-first century among many Christian traditions. The contemporary movement for 'biblical manhood' relies on stereotypical understandings of masculinity – strength, fortitude, resolve – and exhorts men to protect and provide for women and children. Within this movement, fear of a new crisis of masculinity has arisen, leading to an even more macho version of Christian masculinity that appears in artists' renderings of Jesus as a biker or beefed-up boxer, sermons by tough-guy pastors, and church-sponsored mixed martial arts (MMA) watch parties. While these images of a new muscular Christianity purport to attract men to Christian faith by showing them they do not need to be feminised to follow Jesus, they also serve to maintain patriarchal control of women by reinforcing messages of male dominance.

Masculinity, however, is contested terrain for the Christian churches of North America, and many Christian leaders across all genders call for an inclusive masculinity that expands notions of who men are and what they can express. Inclusive masculinity also embraces feminism and works for equity and justice for all genders. Rather than relying on cultural stereotypes about masculinity, these churches draw from their understanding of the gospel and particularly the example of Jesus, who preached peace, acceptance and love.

Undoubtedly, gender is at the centre of controversy in the Christian churches of North America. Young people, however, seem much more open to gender and sexual equality than older generations, even among conservative Christians. While churches are likely to continue to debate gender and sexuality for the foreseeable future, change is already underway to create more inclusivity and welcome in the church in North America.

Bibliography

Barr, Beth Allison, *The Making of Biblical Womanhood: How the Subjugation of Women Became Gospel Truth* (Ada, MI: Brazos Press, 2021).

Kim, Grace Ji-Sun and Susan M. Shaw, *Intersectional Theology: An Introductory Guide* (Minneapolis, MN: Fortress Press, 2018).

Muir, Elizabeth Gillan, *A Women's History of the Christian Church: Two Thousand Years of Female Leadership* (Toronto: University of Toronto Press, 2019).

Peterfeso, Jill, *Womanpriest: Tradition and Transgression in the Contemporary Roman Catholic Church*, Catholic Practice in North America (New York: Fordham University Press, 2000).

Session, Irie Lynne, Kamilah Hall Sharp and Jann Aldredge-Clanton, *The Gathering, A Womanist Church: Origins, Stories, Sermons, and Litanies* (Eugene, OR: Wipf and Stock, 2020).

Religious Freedom

Paul Marshall

The United Nations' North American Geoscheme – consisting of the USA, Canada, Bermuda, Greenland, and Saint Pierre and Miquelon – makes sense spatially but comprises unlike entities with respect to religious freedom. The latter three have local characteristics but are not fully self-governing and, by history and current law, their freedoms also reflect the practices of their original European colonisers, the UK, Denmark and France, respectively. In North America, restrictions affecting Christians are often distinct from those in other parts of the world, especially outside the West. There is a wide range of freedom: for example, no need for entities to register as a recognised religion, even for tax benefits; well-established freedoms for core religious institutions, such as churches; and strong safeguards for the roles of clergy, including chaplains. With the exception of health restrictions during the COVID-19 pandemic, religious practices such as prayer and worship continue freely. There are no ongoing attacks on congregations and no overt or explicit religious discrimination. Specific instances of anti-Christian violence have occurred, such as the killings of students at Umpqua Community College in Roseburg, Oregon, on 2 October 2015. And, of course, Al Qaeda and the Islamic State have regarded their killings in the West, including in North America, as attacks on Christian 'Crusaders'. But these are not pervasive patterns. The US Federal Bureau of Investigation's 'Hate Crime' statistics for 2019 categorise only 12% of religiously based hate crimes as against Christians, far below the percentage of Christians in the population.

However, surveys by the Pew Research Center show that restrictions on religious freedom have increased in the twenty-first century in most of the West, including North America, and these affect Christians as well as others. Many of these restrictions are tied to cultural and intellectual changes leading to 'secular' or 'post-Christian' societies and to what have been described as 'culture wars'.

Changing View of Secularity
North America's increasing religious diversity has undercut the previous privilege of Christian groups and led to more stress on state religious neutrality and to secularity. While the term 'secular' has a range of

meanings, including referring simply to non-confessional states, one more recent usage, growing since the nineteenth century, characterises and often advocates for a state – and, in some cases, for a society – emptied of religious influence. This concept of secularism has resulted in increased pressure to exclude religion from political and social life. Religion is then said to be private, or else should be required to be private: not merely in the sense that might refer to a company, university, school or charity as private rather than public, but as something more akin to 'intimate', something that should be kept behind walls and not allowed to impinge on public life. Hence, many calls for religious toleration and openness often imply restricting the scope of religion in society; religion may be tolerated because it is held to be personal and, therefore, largely irrelevant to public life.

One striking example occurred in a 2010 case before the US Court of Appeals for the Ninth Circuit as to whether the large Christian humanitarian organisation World Vision was in fact a religious organisation. World Vision's employees needed to sign a statement of faith upon beginning employment, and this had to be renewed each year. In a dissent, Judge Marsha Berzon asserted that in order to determine whether an organisation is religious, 'we ask *only* whether the primary activity of a purportedly religious organisation consists of voluntary gathering for prayer and religious learning' (emphasis in original). She remarked that most of World Vision's work was humanitarian relief, 'providing potable water, emergency medical, and vocational training … that is on its face, secular'.

This is despite the fact that the USA's and Canada's founding documents stress the broad significance of religion. The first paragraph of the American Declaration of Independence refers to the 'Laws of Nature and of Nature's God' and holds that 'all men are created equal, that they are endowed by their Creator with certain unalienable Rights'. Equality is held to stem from the fact that God has created us. More recently, the Preamble to the 1982 Canadian Charter of Rights and Freedoms states that 'Canada is founded upon principles that recognise the supremacy of God and the rule of law'.

The assertion that religion should be excluded from public life leads to what Charles Taylor describes as a public arena 'allegedly emptied of God, or of any reference to ultimate reality'. This exclusion in turn undercuts the belief that the church, or religious institutions generally, might be independent sources of authority whose freedom should be zealously guarded. Consequently, governments are more inclined to believe that they can and should regulate religious bodies more extensively. Also, if the state becomes involved in larger swaths of society, as it is doing in North America, then religion tends increasingly to be restricted. Adapting the American language of the separation of church and state, wherever the state goes, the church is pressured to leave.

Changing View of Religious Freedom

This reduction of the understanding of religion, coupled with the remaining influence of Christian belief in the responsibility and authority of human beings as *imago Dei*, leads to an increasing emphasis on human autonomy. Many policy debates in North America are now predicated on the notion of a sensate, autonomous and expressive self. Consequently, Christian or other religious beliefs that would restrict some areas of human autonomy may be treated as repressive. This often comes to the fore with Christian social service agencies and in matters sexual and medical.

These changing patterns can be shown in the shifting treatment of the US Religious Freedom Restoration Act (RFRA). The 1990 case *Employment Division, Department of Human Resources of Oregon* v. *Smith* concerned Native Americans who had been fired for using peyote, a long-standing liturgical practice of the Native American Church. In its decision, the US Supreme Court held that the applicants' religious freedom had not been violated since the law in question was a general law forbidding psychedelics and was not aimed at religious practitioners *per se*.

A widespread bipartisan outcry followed this verdict and, in response, in 1993 Congress passed the RFRA. The push for this legislation was led by prominent Democrats such as Chuck Schumer in the House, where it passed unanimously, and the late Senator Ted Kennedy in the Senate, where the vote in favour was 97–3, and it was signed into law by President Clinton. RFRA held that 'Government shall not substantially burden a person's exercise of religion even if the burden results from a rule of general applicability'. However, in 1997 the Supreme Court held that RFRA applied only to the federal government, not to the states, and so began a process of passing laws at the state level modelled on RFRA.

By the early decades of the twenty-first century, when it appeared that they might provide religious exemptions from abortion, same-sex marriage, transgender and euthanasia laws and the like, such state laws frequently were denounced as bigoted and discriminatory. In the space of some 20 years almost identical laws had gone from being passed unanimously in the US House of Representatives as uncontroversial and necessary defences of religious freedom to being labelled as bigotry.

In early 2021, the Equality Act was introduced in Congress. It adds 'sexual orientation' and 'gender identity' to the list of grounds on which one may not discriminate. It also expands the list of 'public accommodations' – those institutions and services to which the law applies – to include 'any establishment that provides a good, service, or program'. This could include private religious schools, a religious family renting out a room at home and, potentially, houses of worship themselves. Recognising that this could introduce major infringements on religious freedom, the bill specifically adds that RFRA 'shall not provide a claim concerning, or a defence to a claim under' the new law. In this area of law, RFRA would be negated.

The issues here are not, *per se*, one's judgements on sexual identity and the like but on the degree to which people are allowed to differ in their views. The complex interests involved make it difficult to define what counts as an actual restriction on religious freedom, and these matters are in continual dispute. Indeed, opposing sides in a conflict might each claim that it is their own religious freedom that is at stake. These new restrictions affect primarily conservative churches and Christians with traditional beliefs on family, life and sexual issues, such as conservative Catholics, Evangelicals and Orthodox Christians.

United States

In the USA, formal legal guarantees of religious freedom are strong and churches and other religious groups receive several tax benefits. One recurring theme is the dangers of an 'establishment of religion', sometimes referred to as 'separation of church and state', although the latter phrase does not appear in the Constitution. Hence, controversies continue about whether having a cross or monument containing the Ten Commandments on public land is illegal. Similar concerns have arisen over prayers at events such as high school football games or whether religious groups can run after-school programmes or rent space in state schools. The courts are sometimes unclear but generally hold to a standard of whether the offending item implies any official government endorsement of religion. Thus, for example, teachers must stay clear of any implied religious endorsement while working, but school students are free to do a wide range of religious things on school premises. Similar concerns arise as to whether government funding can go to private religious schools or social-service agencies. The courts have generally held that it can, as long as such funding is also given to similarly situated secular organisations.

Legal protections for churches themselves are very strong. In the 2012 case of *Hosanna-Tabor* v. *EEOC*, the US Supreme Court held unanimously that federal discrimination laws do not apply to a religious organisation's selection of its religious leaders. This has become known as the 'ministerial exception'. The same Court's decision in the similar 2020 case *Our Lady of Guadalupe School* v. *Morrissey-Berru* was seven-to-two in the school's favour. The decision held that this exception applied even to a person who did not have the formal title or training of a religious leader.

Given this strong concern to safeguard church autonomy, the more closely a Christian organisation is connected to a church, the more likely it is to receive robust legal protection.

The situation of religious bodies such as schools, universities, hospitals, charities, social agencies and media organisations that are not directly tied to churches is more complex. Debate is ongoing over who might count as a 'minister' and whether these organisations may restrict their staff, or at least some of them, to those who uphold the religious mission and beliefs of the organisation. These restrictions might cover not only creedal statements but also moral standards. Many such organisations insist that their faculty, staff and perhaps students and others whom they serve follow codes of moral conduct, often involving sexual ethics. The courts usually have held that this is permissible. Indeed, in the 2014 *Burwell* v. *Hobby Lobby Stores* case, the Supreme Court held that even 'closely held' for-profit corporations could be considered as 'persons' under the Religious Freedom Restoration Act and thus could properly have religious freedom claims.

When the issue involves third parties – such as hospitals, universities or social agencies – the situation is more complex. Institutionally, controversy surrounds both, for example, whether a Catholic hospital can refuse to perform abortions and, individually, whether doctors, pharmacists, counsellors or nurses who work or volunteer in secular agencies may secure religious objections to certain procedures. Similar questions are arising with respect to euthanasia and gender identity concerns. Meanwhile, religious student groups have been denied status as recognised clubs by public universities if they require that their leaders subscribe to the groups' beliefs and conduct, though the courts usually have sided with the religious groups.

One ongoing example involves Catholic charities, which provide adoption and foster care. They typically require that a child go to a home that has a mother and a father who are married. In 2006, Catholic Charities of Boston, one of America's oldest adoption agencies, was told that in order to continue to be licensed it would have to place children with same-sex couples or be found in violation of state laws barring discrimination on the basis of sexual orientation. Catholic leaders asked the state for a religious exemption but were refused, and so the charity was forced to shut down its adoption services. Similar closures have happened in San Francisco, Washington, DC, Illinois and elsewhere. In *Fulton* v. *Philadelphia* in 2021, the US Supreme Court found in favour of a Catholic charity but only on narrow procedural grounds.

In addition, a range of cases concerning individuals providing commercial services have been tried. In 2013, the Supreme Court of New Mexico ruled that a Christian photographer could be compelled to photograph a lesbian wedding. Similar actions have been pursued against owners of cake and flower shops who have refused to lend their services to same-sex weddings. Note that the focus here was on the nature of marriage: those who have refused services with respect to marriage have usually said they would provide services for gay clients in matters of birthdays and the like.

One particular set of religious freedom tensions surfaced sharply in 2020 and 2021 in disputes with respect to the COVID-19 pandemic and government restrictions on church services and other in-person religious gatherings, including weddings and funerals. Several churches, based on a separationist view of church and state, violated what most observers thought were reasonable and constrained governmental rules.

The vast majority of Christian and other religious bodies accepted that, in an emergency, governments may take steps, such as limiting worship services, that they could not in normal circumstances. But in several instances, governments overstepped proper bounds, particularly in placing restrictions on churches that they had not placed on similarly situated secular bodies. In some cases, the Justice Department's Office of Civil Rights intervened and the Attorney General warned that 'Government may not impose special restrictions on religious activity that do not also apply to similar nonreligious activity'.

Many of these issues are still unfolding, particularly with respect to religious objections to being involved in activities that would violate people's consciences. This appeared starkly in the 2015 *Obergefell* v. *Hodges* case before the Supreme Court, in which the Court found a constitutional right to same-sex marriage. When Solicitor General Donald B. Verrilli Jr, who had argued for the US government in favour of same-sex marriage, was asked whether institutions that refused to accept this new definition of marriage could lose their tax-exempt status, he responded 'It is – it is going to be an issue'. Chief Justice John Roberts said in his dissent: 'Today's decision ... creates serious questions about religious liberty ... The majority graciously suggests that religious believers may continue to "advocate" and "teach" their views of marriage. The First Amendment guarantees, however, the freedom to "exercise" religion. Ominously, that is not a word the majority uses.'

Canada

As in the USA, restrictions on religious freedom affecting Christians in Canada are often distinct from those in other parts of the world, especially outside the West. The country has neither ongoing attacks on congregations nor overt or explicit religious discrimination. Formal legal guarantees of religious freedom are strong. The Constitution of Canada, specifically the Canadian Charter of Rights and Freedoms, guarantees freedom of conscience, religion, thought, belief, opinion and expression, and guarantees that every individual has the right to equal protection and benefit of the law without discrimination based on religion. The Canadian Charter allows 'reasonable limits' on the exercise of religion only if such restrictions can be 'demonstrably justified in a free and democratic society'. Religious groups are not required to register but need to do so if they want tax-exempt status, and such status also provides other tax benefits. Groups that have tax-exempt status must be non-political, though this matter is legally disputed.

Before the passage of the 1982 Canadian Charter of Rights and Freedoms, there were no specific constitutional guarantees of religious freedom, but religious freedom was assumed to be a fundamental and necessary condition of social and political life. Following the passage of the Canadian Charter, developments have occurred similar to those in the USA, particularly concerning the degree to which religious beliefs may be involved in public discussions and decisions. In the earlier years after the Charter's passing, an expansive view of religious freedom was the norm, reflecting previous assumptions. The Supreme Court of Canada's 1985 decision in *R* v. *Big M Drug Mart* maintained, 'The essence of the concept of freedom of religion is the right to entertain such religious beliefs as a person chooses, the right to declare religious beliefs openly and without fear of hindrance or reprisal, and the right to manifest religious belief by worship and practice or by teaching and dissemination'. However, as with secularisation trends in the USA, a stronger tendency to regard religion as something private that should not intrude into public space is taking hold. The courts have given little or no legal force to the Charter's declaration that 'Canada is founded upon principles that recognize the supremacy of God'.

Accordingly, the recent trends in the USA described above – the privatisation of religion, standards properly applicable to the state being applied to private religious institutions, the broadening of non-discrimination limits and the reluctance to allow people to be exempt on grounds of conscience and religion from participating in actions to which they object – have occurred in Canada as well, and in many respects have gone farther. The sometimes heavy-handed restrictions on congregations that occurred in the USA because of the COVID-19 pandemic also featured in Canada.

These trends are shown most clearly in the treatment of religious institutions. For example, in 2018, Curtis Clark, then the Province of Alberta's Deputy Minister of Education, threatened religious schools with defunding and de-accreditation if they did not remove various faith statements from their school policies. Items that were held to be in violation of the Province's School Act and were to be removed included reference to 'The unchangeable and infallible truth of the Word of God', which statement allegedly violated the School Act requirement that diversity must be respected.

In the Province of British Columbia, the Irene Thomas Hospice, a 10-bed facility operated by the non-profit Delta Hospice Society, maintained that medical assistance in dying (MAID) went against its principles. Instead, the Society's charter mandates that its staff provide 'compassionate care and support for persons in the last stages of living'. But the local health authority mandated that any hospice that received more than 50% provincial funding for its beds must offer MAID and ordered the hospice to comply. The hospice declined, lost funding and in 2021 was forced to issue layoff notices to all clinical staff.

The most striking case has been Trinity Western University (TWU), whose disparate treatment over time, somewhat like with RFRA in the USA, illustrates changing views of religious freedom in recent decades. In 2012, TWU, the largest private Christian university in the country, proposed starting a law school. Since its founding, TWU has had a community covenant upholding a traditional Christian understanding of marriage, in particular that members of the community should voluntarily abstain from 'sexual intimacy that violates the sacredness of marriage between a man and a woman'. After extensive litigation, Canada's Supreme Court ruled that this covenant was discriminatory and that, hence, the Bar Associations of Ontario and British Columbia had a legitimate 'public interest' in denying accreditation for TWU law school graduates. The Court held that being 'required by someone else's religious beliefs to behave contrary to one's sexual identity … is degrading and disrespectful'. The result is that graduates of the proposed law school would be denied licences to work as lawyers in Ontario and British Columbia. While the court recognised that a legitimate religious freedom interest existed on the part of the School, it held that the 'public interest' demanded that this religious freedom interest be overridden.

This case was remarkably similar to legal challenges brought when TWU had sought to create a teacher training college in 2001. In that case, official bodies had argued that because of TWU's covenant, any graduating teachers would be likely to discriminate on the basis of sexual orientation. However, in that instance, Canada's Supreme Court decided eight to one in favour of TWU. Despite the forceful decision in a strikingly similar case, in 2018 the same Court abandoned this strong precedent. In order to avoid following the precedent, the Court resorted not to constitutional law *per se*, but instead argued that the government and government-accredited bodies must be concerned not only with the actual rights recognised under the Charter of Rights and Freedoms but also with what it called 'Charter values', which were also held to be embodied in the Charter. Here a constitutional bill of rights was transmuted into a set of 'values' whose source and legal nature are obscure and which are then applied to non-governmental institutions. The effect is that societal institutions come to be considered somewhat as governments writ small and subject to the same rules.

This application of proper governmental obligations to private organisations, including religious ones, has affected a range of government programmes. One has been the Canada summer jobs programme. The Canadian government gives funding to organisations to provide summer jobs for students and, in recent years, has included among its funding criteria that the applicant organisations must support 'Charter values'. These 'values', which are nowhere written down, appear to include access to abortion and other issues on which religious groups differ. Hence, the funding has depended not on only what the organisation would actually use the funds for, an issue in which the government clearly has a legitimate interest, but also on what the organisation believes. This means that the government would discriminate in its distribution of state funds based on a judgement about whether the recipient agrees with current government 'values' and policies, which are often opposed by some religious groups.

Quebec

Similar issues have arisen in the predominantly Francophone Province of Quebec, but here they encounter additional features that reflect a more French *laïcite* mindset that is often highly secular. This has led, as in France, to a focus on restricting the display of religious symbols in public since they are held to contravene public values and, also as in France, these restrictions seemed to be aimed primarily at Muslims but were written in general terms to apply to all religions.

In 2019, Bill 21 was passed, which prohibits certain government employees from wearing religious symbols while exercising their official functions. It defines a religious symbol as 'any object, including clothing, a symbol, jewellery, an adornment, an accessory, or headwear, that (1) is worn in connection with a religious conviction or belief; or (2) is reasonably considered as referring to a religious affiliation'. Among the categories of employees included in the law are the President and Vice Presidents of the National Assembly; administrative justices of the peace; certain municipal court employees; police, sheriffs and deputy sheriffs; certain prosecutors and criminal lawyers; and certain principals, vice principals and teachers, among others. The law also requires anyone seeking certain provincial government services to do so with 'face uncovered'. It exempts provincial employees working prior to the implementation of the law, but they lose their right to wear religious symbols upon changing jobs or receiving a promotion. Given its likely violation of the Charter, the law invokes the 'notwithstanding clause', a provision of the Charter that permits a government to override specific constitutional protections for a period of five years, after which the override may be renewed.

Other religiously discriminatory features in Quebec have drawn less attention. Private child-care providers in Quebec are eligible for public subsidies, but those that teach any religious beliefs or practices, such as opening with prayer, are automatically disqualified.

Greenland, Bermuda, and Saint Pierre and Miquelon

The legal structures of Greenland, Bermuda, and Saint Pierre and Miquelon reflect the patterns of their 'parent' countries, Denmark, the UK and France, respectively, but often with slight legal variations. Frequently the local customs and intimate relations in these small populations soften any potential legal restrictions.

In Greenland, *de jure* discrimination exists among Christians in that the Church of Greenland, which is Lutheran, is a diocese of the Church of Denmark, which is a state-established church and thus has privileges and state support not available to other Christian group or to non-Christian groups. In 2009, jurisdiction over the Church of Greenland was removed from the Danish parliament and given to the government of Greenland. As a result, the Church of Greenland has a degree of independence from the mother church, but it still retains certain privileges.

In Denmark itself, religious bodies other than the Church of Denmark that wish to be registered in order to receive tax and other benefits must have at least 150 adult members, and congregations must have at least 50 adult members. However, given Greenland's small and scattered population, these limits are often waived.

In 2021, probably out of concern about Islamist radicalism, discussion was initiated of a draft Danish law asking all religious groups to produce a Danish-language version of their sermons and messages. In Greenland, Greenlandic is the sole official language, though most people also speak Danish, but the law could be a burden for smaller groups. In November 2020, the Danish Prime Minister admitted that she could not assure that an exemption would be approved for religious groups in Greenland and the Faroe Islands, another Danish territory.

Bermuda is a British Overseas Territory, which means that governing powers are divided between the Government of Bermuda and that of the UK. It is internally self-governing, while the King is the sovereign; the UK government handles defence and foreign affairs and is required to maintain good governance. The Anglican Church of Bermuda, the largest religious grouping, is not part of any Anglican ecclesiastical province and so is directly under the authority of the Archbishop of Canterbury.

There is a right of conscientious objection to any association with military activities, even non-combatant ones. Sunday is a public holiday and, with some exceptions, shops may not open on Sundays or other public holidays. Any school that receives government aid must begin the school day with collective worship that should not 'be distinctive of any particular religious group' but commonly includes the Lord's Prayer. Parents may withdraw their children from such collective worship. The history of slavery and of legal and informal racial discrimination limited religious freedom for non-whites, whose effects may be learned from the 'Enslaved Struggle for Religious Freedom Bus Tour'. While the legal situation is not clear, it is possible that the common law offence of blasphemy against the Christian religion is still part of Bermudan law.

Controversy remains ongoing over same-sex marriage, which has included the unusual argument that maintaining a definition of marriage that disadvantages those who believe in same-sex marriage discriminates against them on the grounds of their creed, contrary to the Constitution.

Saint Pierre and Miquelon is an integral *collectivité* of France and, like modern Quebec, its view of religious freedom is shaped by that country's secular outlook of *laïcite* in which, in principle, religion is excluded from public life. In practice, the French government relaxes such restrictions when it believes it needs to do so, and this happens in these islands, where local ties and customs are strong. While state functionaries such as public-school teachers are forbidden to wear religious garb or symbols at work, in fact primary education is mostly parochial and run by the Roman Catholic Church.

In 2021, probably also out of concern about Islamist radicalism, the French government was considering a range of measure that could impact religious freedom, including a ban or severe restrictions on home schooling. Additional proposals include new obligations to register and re-register for certain tax benefits, and stricter accounting mechanisms that could prove onerous for smaller organisations.

The Future

While North America remains largely religiously free, restrictions have been increasing, and the patterns of a more aggressive secularism described above suggest that they might continue to do so. Fears about this were articulated in 2020 by US Supreme Court Justice Samuel Alito, a conservative Catholic, who stated, 'It pains me to say this, but in certain quarters, religious liberty is fast becoming a disfavored right. And that marks a surprising turn of events. Consider where things stood in the 1990s and, to me at least, that does not seem like the Jurassic Age...' He lamented, referring to RFRA, 'Today that wide support has vanished ... For many today, religious liberty is not a cherished freedom. It's often just an excuse for bigotry and it can't be tolerated ... The question we face is whether our society will be inclusive enough to tolerate people with unpopular religious beliefs.'

Bibliography

Buckingham, Janet Epp, *Fighting Over God: A Legal and Political History of Religious Freedom in Canada* (Montreal: McGill-Queen's University Press, 2014).

Cardus, *An Institutional History of Religious Freedom in Canada,* 2nd edition (online 2020) <https://www.cardus.ca/research/law/reports/an-institutional-history-of-religious-freedom-in-canada>.

Corvino, John, Ryan T. Anderson and Sherif Girgis, *Debating Religious Liberty and Discrimination* (New York: Oxford University Press, 2017).

Hertzke, Allen D. (ed.), *Religious Freedom in America: Constitutional Roots and Contemporary Challenges* (Norman, OK: University of Oklahoma Press, 2015).

Waldman, Steven, *America's Long, Bloody, and Ongoing Struggle for Religious Freedom* (San Francisco: HarperOne, 2019).

Inter-religious Relations

Peter C. Phan

North America, in United Nations' usage, comprises the USA, Canada, Greenland, Bermuda, and Saint Pierre and Miquelon. This essay will focus on inter-religious relations in the USA and Canada, with the lion's share of attention given to the former, and takes 'relations' to mean both theological dialogue and institutional initiatives. It discusses inter-religious relations between the Christian churches on the one hand and the other two Abrahamic religions – namely, Judaism and Islam – and the major Eastern religions, including Buddhism and Hinduism, on the other.

Inter-religious Relations in the USA
The need for inter-religious relations in the USA is best expressed by the title of Diana L. Eck's 2001 book, *A New Religious America: How a Christian Country Has Become the World's Most Religiously Diverse Nation*, a result of the Pluralism Project she directed at Harvard University beginning in 1991. The USA has been called a 'Christian country', and the moniker is still justified since Christianity is the most prevalent religion in that country.

The US religious landscape has, however, changed significantly, especially after the 'new immigration' precipitated by the Immigration and Nationality Act of 1965, also known as the Hart–Celler Act, which abolished the National Origins Formula that favoured people from Northern and Western Europe and opened the doors to immigrants from the other parts of Europe, Africa and Asia. With these newcomers from Asia and Africa came various religions, such as Hinduism, Buddhism, Jainism, Sikhism, Zoroastrianism, Islam, and African and Afro-Caribbean religions. Of course, several of these religions had been represented at the World's Parliament of Religions in Chicago in 1893 (renamed in 1993 as the Parliament of the World's Religions), the first attempt at creating a global dialogue of faiths. However, religious diversity displayed at the 1893 Parliament was, for most Americans, just a curious assortment of far-away religions. Today, thanks to migration and globalisation, it has become a fact of life. In 1955, the sociologist Will Herberg published a book on the American religious diversity of his day with a simple title: *Protestant, Catholic, Jew*. As of 2021, not only Christian churches and Jewish synagogues but also Muslim mosques, Buddhist pagodas, Hindu mandirs,

Sikh gurdwaras, Jain derasars, Zoroastrian gujaratis, Confucian temples and Daoist miaos dot the American landscape in both urban and rural areas. Multiculturalism and religious pluralism have become the norm.

This does not mean that religious pluralism is widely accepted. On the contrary, exclusion of people ('strangers') other than the Protestant Anglo-Saxon core 'native' population has long been part of the American story and the general practice. In the seventeenth century, Jews, Catholics and Quakers were told by the Puritans of Massachusetts to leave. Jews who streamed into the USA from Eastern Europe and Russia during the late nineteenth and early twentieth centuries were said to constitute the 'Jewish invasion' and were deemed unassimilable and incapable of adopting the American ideals. Moreover, Asian exclusion was the federal policy throughout the nineteenth century. In 1882, the Chinese Exclusion Act was passed to ward off the 'Yellow Peril from Asia'. At the beginning of the twentieth century, the Asiatic Exclusion League was formed to promote the right to exclude 'strangers' and 'invaders' from America and to protect 'white Protestant supremacy'.

In the past, even when immigrants were admitted, the melting-pot model was imposed on them, demanding that they shed their cultural and religious heritage and be assimilated into Anglo-Saxon, Protestant America. Today, by contrast, cultural and religious pluralism not only recognises the validity of retaining one's cultural and religious traditions but also, unlike relativism, rejects mere tolerance (the 'intolerance of tolerance') and requires that all members of society engage with one another in their differences, understand how the others live and believe differently, undertake dialogue to define the roles of diverse religions in American society and participate actively in building a multicultural and multireligious society. It is here that inter-religious relations come into play.

Christians and Jews

The number of Jews currently living in the USA is estimated at between five and eight million, accounting for 2–3% of the US adult population. When the Dutch yielded Recife, Brazil, to the Portuguese in 1654, the latter carried with them the anti-Jewish policies of the Iberian Peninsula and forced the Jews to leave. The first group of Jewish families, mostly Sephardic Jews, migrated in 1654 to the Dutch settlement of New Amsterdam and were welcomed by the Dutch West India Company for the economic benefits they allegedly would bring. New Amsterdam fell into British hands in 1664 (and was renamed New York); colonial authorities allowed the Jews to establish a synagogue in 1695 and function according to the Portuguese and Spanish Sephardic traditions.

After the American Revolution, Jews enthusiastically embraced the First Amendment to the new nation's Constitution, which prohibited Congress from establishing a national religion or limiting the free exercise of religion by citizens, as an affirmation of the right to religious freedom. However, despite the non-establishment clause, Protestants vigorously promoted the shaping of America as a 'Christian nation', appropriating the Jewish notion of being God's Chosen People, especially during the Second Great Awakening (roughly 1790–1840).

Between 1881 and 1914, about two million Ashkenazi Jews migrated to the USA, mainly from Eastern Europe and Russia, to escape pogroms. As the Jewish population increased dramatically, anti-Semitism and anti-Judaism became widespread. Jews (and Catholics) were considered racially inferior, prone to crime and harmful to American identity. The World's Parliament of Religions in Chicago in 1893, mentioned above, provided Catholics and Jews the first opportunity to appear alongside Protestants as equals. After the First World War, Catholics, Jews and Protestants found common cause in ameliorating the social and economic condition of war victims and poor people. The National Catholic Welfare Conference, founded in 1919, collaborated with the Central Conference of American Rabbis, founded in 1889, to support legislation for more humane working conditions. However, anti-Semitic/anti-Judaic and anti-Catholic bigotry did not abate, and in 1928 the National Conference of Christians and Jews (now known as the National Conference for Community and Justice) was founded to combat racial and religious discrimination, especially through communication and education by means of its Religion News Service.

The Second World War and the Holocaust (Shoah) pushed American Christians to fight against anti-Semitism and anti-Judaism, and the term 'Judeo-Christian', first coined in Germany (*Judenchristlich*) to refer to Jewish converts to Christianity, was now used to underline the common religious heritage between Jews and Christians. Military chaplaincy during the war also enabled Catholic priests, Jewish rabbis and Protestant ministers to work side by side as equals. In the post-war era, Protestant America moved towards greater acceptance of Catholicism and Judaism. Another factor binding Christians and Jews together was the struggle in the early 1960s for the civil rights of African Americans. Jewish collaboration with Christians in the civil rights movement was sustained by the perception that American racism was a parallel to the Nazi persecution of Jews. One tragic exception is the case of the Catholic priest Charles Coughlin, who spewed vicious anti-Semitic venom on his popular radio broadcasts during the 1930s.

More than any other event, the Holocaust has challenged Christians in America to re-examine their past attitudes towards Jews. The horrors of the

Holocaust raise the question of Christianity's responsibility for it, either through failures to show solidarity with the Jews and actively oppose Nazi policies or, more fundamentally, by the promotion of centuries-long anti-Semitism and anti-Judaism in Christian theology and worship.

Theologically, relations between Jews and Catholics in the USA have been deeply influenced by the Second Vatican Council (1962–5). The twenty-first general council of the Catholic Church marked a decisive turning point in its unequivocal rejection of both anti-Semitism and anti-Judaism. The Second Vatican Council's most important document on the relations of the church to non-Christian religions is the declaration *Nostra Aetate*. The declaration is composed of five paragraphs, the last two on Jews and Judaism. *Nostra Aetate* affirms that the Church is like wild olive branches grafted onto the good olive tree that is Judaism; that the Jews remain very dear to God; that the Jews should not be spoken of as rejected or accursed; and that all forms of discrimination and persecution, especially anti-Semitism, must be condemned. Thus, the Council highlights the deep historical and theological roots of Christianity in Judaism, rejects the charge of deicide against the Jews, defends the permanent validity of God's covenant with God's Chosen People, denies supersession, and condemns anti-Semitism and anti-Judaism, all pivotal issues in Jewish–Christian dialogue and theology.

The Second Vatican Council gave birth to numerous institutions, centres and works of scholarship for the study of Jewish–Christian relations around the world, especially in the USA. The Vatican's organisation for Jewish–Christians relations is the Commission of the Holy See for Relations with the Jews, which is responsible for two standing dialogues between the Holy See and the international Jewish community, one with the International Catholic–Jewish Liaison Committee and the other with the Chief Rabbinate of Israel. It has issued two important documents, *Notes on the Correct Way to Present Jews and Judaism in Preaching and Catechesis in the Roman Catholic Church* (1985) and *We Remember: A Reflection on the Shoah* (1988). The Pontifical Biblical Commission in 2002 released *The Jewish People and Their Sacred Scriptures in the Christian Bible*. Another significant official document is *Bearing Faithful Witness: Statement on United Church–Jewish Relations Today*, a declaration of a joint commission of the Chief Rabbinate of Israel and the Holy See's Commission for Religious Relations with the Jews (2003).

Despite the enormous variety of theological views held by its constituent churches, the World Council of Churches (WCC), a fellowship of about 350 mainline Protestant and Orthodox denominations, at its first assembly, in 1948, produced the document *The Christian Approach to the Jews*, which condemned anti-Semitism as 'a sin against God and man'. However, the same assembly called for a redoubling of efforts to convert Jews. This view of Christian mission to Jews is no longer held by the WCC, though it remains much disputed among its members, as are the significance of the State of Israel and the Israel–Palestinian conflict. In 1947, the WCC met with the International Council of Christians and Jews, founded in 1946, in Seelisberg, Switzerland, and issued *An Address to the Churches*, which included the 'Ten Points of Seelisberg' and anticipated in many respects by some 20 years the discussion of Christian anti-Semitism and ways to overcome it. The WCC's Commission on Faith and Order published *The Church and the Jewish People* in 1967, and in 1971 the WCC established a sub-unit for Dialogue with People of Living Faiths and Ideologies, with a desk for Jewish–Christian dialogue. In 1979, the WCC issued an important document, *Ecumenical Considerations on Jewish–Christian Dialogue*, followed in 1988 by *The Churches and the Jewish People: Towards a New Understanding*. More recently, *Ecumenical Considerations for Dialogue and Relations With People of Other Religions: Taking Stock of 30 Years of Dialogue and Revisiting the 1979 Guidelines*, an overview and assessment of its many dialogues, was published by the WCC in 2004.

The above-cited documents from both the Second Vatican Council and the WCC merit careful study because they have been influential guideposts for Jewish–Christian relations in the USA. The United States Conference of Catholic Bishops (USCCB) includes a Committee on Ecumenical and Interreligious Affairs (CEIA), which has played a significant role in promoting Jewish–Christian relations. CEIA's Secretariat for Catholic–Jewish Relations issued *Guidelines for Catholic–Jewish Relations* in 1967 (with a revised edition in 1985) and *Criteria for the Evaluation of Dramatizations of the Passion* (1988). Another important document is *Reflections on Covenant and Mission*, issued in 2002 by the consultation of the National Council of Synagogues and the delegates of CEIA. In 2009 this statement was deemed to be in need of clarification, and CEIA jointly issued a short statement, along with the Committee on Doctrine, entitled 'A Note on Ambiguities Contained in *Reflections on Covenant and Mission*', which stated that it is necessary to affirm the Church's belief that 'Jesus Christ in himself fulfils God's revelation begun with Abraham and that proclaiming this good news to all the world is at the heart of her mission' (no. 6). Another committee of the USCCB, the Committee on the Liturgy, published *God's Mercy Endures Forever: Guidelines on the Presentation of Jews and Judaism in Catholic Preaching* in 1988.

At the institutional level, numerous centres for the study of the relations between Judaism and Christianity were founded after the Second Vatican Council. These centres in the USA form the Council of Centers on Jewish–Christian Relations, whose goal is to enhance mutual understanding between Jews and Christians. It is composed of some 30 regular and five affiliate (overseas) members and maintains official liaison with the American Jewish Committee, the Anti-Defamation League, the National Council of Synagogues and CEIA. The Council is dedicated to research, publication, educational programming and inter-religious dialogue that respect the religious integrity and self-understanding of the various strands of the Jewish and Christian traditions.

Theological scholarship on Jewish–Christian relations in the USA, by both Christians and Jews, is more abundant and developed than for any other inter-religious relation. The major themes for Jewish–Christian dialogue include the Jewish identity of Jesus, anti-Semitism and anti-Judaism in the New Testament and Christian tradition, the eternal permanence of God's covenant with Israel, supersessionism, the Holocaust, Christian mission to the Jews, and the State of Israel. These themes figure prominently in *Dabru Emet* (2000), an eight-point statement that was offered as a basis for a theological dialogue between Jews and Christians by Jewish scholars Tikva Frymer-Kensky, David Novak, Peter Ochs, David Fox Sandmel and Michael A. Signer, who also edited the book *Christianity in Jewish Terms* (2000). The Christian Scholars Group on Christian–Jewish Relations joined the dialogue with the volume *Seeing Judaism Anew: Christianity's Sacred Obligation* (2005).

Christians and Muslims

After Christianity and Judaism, Islam is the third-largest religion in the USA. According to a 2017 study by the Pew Research Center, the 3.45 million Muslims in the USA comprised about 1.1% of the total US population and were divided into three groups: Sunni (65%), Shi'a (11%) and non-denominational Muslims (24%). American Muslims are one of the most racially diverse religious groups in the USA, with no majority race: 25% Black, 24% white, 18% Asian, 18% Arab, 7% mixed race and 5% Hispanic. Among Black American Muslims, the Moorish Science Temple and the Nation of Islam have played key roles. Half of American Muslims are native-born, most of whom are African Americans. An estimated 10–20% of the slaved people brought to colonial America from Africa were Muslims, though the practice of Islam was strictly banned on the plantations. From the 1880s to 1914, thousands of Muslims immigrated to the USA from the Ottoman Empire and British India. The Muslim population grew dramatically in the second half of the twentieth century, with immigration from Southeast Europe, the Middle East, Africa, South Asia and Southeast Asia.

Relations between Christians and Muslims in the USA, not unlike those between Christians and Jews, have been shaped by various factors and have moved from hostility to dialogue. David D. Grafton, writing in *The Routledge Handbook on Christian–Muslim Relations* (London: Routledge, 2018), helpfully classifies Christian attitudes towards Islam throughout American history into four types. The first, 'Cultural despotism', portrayed Muslims as barbaric and backward, as was done as early as 1698 by Cotton Mather (1663–1728) and later by Samuel Zwemer (1867–1952), and depicted Muhammad as a false prophet, a warmonger and a sexual deviant, as was done by the Anglican Humphrey Prideaux in 1697 and more recently by Jerry Falwell, Pat Robertson and Franklin Graham. Secondly, 'Humanistic pluralism', under the influence of the Enlightenment and Deism in the eighteenth century, proposed an opposite image of Muhammad – as a great political leader and a religious genius, as was done by Thomas Jefferson (1743–1826) and Washington Irving (1783–1858). In the nineteenth century, under the influence of Orientalism, this humanistic tendency went further and presented Islam as a mystery religion, as was done by Ralph Waldo Emerson (1803–82) and Henry David Thoreau (1817–62) of the Transcendentalist movement and Helena Blavatsky (1831–91) and William Q. Judge (1851–96), the founders of the Theosophist Society. Finally, Islam was given public recognition at the World's Parliament of Religions in Chicago in 1893, represented by Alexander Webb, an American convert to Islam. The third type, 'Evangelical biblicism', uses the Bible as the primary reference point to interpret the function of Islam in American history. Cotton Maher, mentioned earlier, popularised the idea of Muslims as 'Gog and Magog', the enemies of God's people (Ezekiel 38–9) and even as the Antichrist (Revelation 20: 8). Jonathan Edwards (1703–58), a leading theologian of the First Great Awakening, identified Islam as 'the kingdom of the false prophet'. In the nineteenth and twentieth centuries, American Christians who adopted millennialism interpreted the locusts rising from the smoke in Revelation 9: 3 to refer to Islam and Muhammad. Lastly, 'Inter-religious dialogue' is the most recent stage in Christian–Muslim relations.

The impetus for the fourth type of relations between Christians and Muslims in the USA was given by the Second Vatican Council's *Nostra Aetate*, no. 3, which states that the Church has 'high regard' for Muslims, since Islam and Christianity share many beliefs. However, the Council also acknowledged that over the centuries 'many quarrels and dissensions' have arisen between Christians and Muslims but it 'now pleads with all to forget the past and urges that a sincere effort be made to achieve mutual understanding' and to work together 'to preserve and promote peace, liberty, social justice, and moral values'. During the Council, Pope Paul VI in 1964 instituted the Secretariat for Non-Christians, which Pope John Paul II renamed the Pontifical Council for Interreligious Dialogue (PCID) in 1988, which included the Commission for Religious Relations with Muslims. One of the important documents issued by the PCID is *Guidelines for Dialogue between Christians and Muslims* (1990). For their parts, American Protestant churches were inspired by the WCC's Sub-Unit for Dialogue with People of Living Faiths and Ideologies, which was disbanded in 1991 and replaced with the Office of Inter-Religious Relations within the General Secretariat. One significant document issued by this office is *Issues in Christian–Muslim Relations: Ecumenical Considerations* (1992).

Christian–Muslim inter-religious relations in the USA were immensely complicated by two events. The first is the 11 September 2001 attacks on the Twin Towers of the World Trade Center in New York and on the Pentagon in Washington by 19 Muslim hijackers, followed by the 'War on Terror' and the US war in Afghanistan and Iraq. These terrorist and military activities exacerbated the polarisation between the World of Islam and the West and between Christians and Muslims. The second is Pope Benedict XVI's lecture 'Faith, Reason and the University' at the University of Regensburg on 12 September 2006. In the course of his speech, Benedict made a number of comments about Islam's lack of harmony between faith and reason and its use of violence to spread itself. These comments created a diplomatic incident and violent reactions in several parts of the Islamic world. Fortunately, they also prompted a positive scholarly response. On 12 October 2006, 38 scholars from different countries addressed an open letter to Benedict, also signed by several top Muslim leaders, in which several errors in his speech were corrected. On 13 October 2007, 'A Common Word between Us and You' was addressed by 138 Muslim scholars to Pope Benedict and 26 leaders of major Christian bodies, in which several common points between Christianity and Islam, especially the oneness of God and the command to love God and neighbour, are presented as a basis for a dialogue between the two religions.

'A Common Word' was a common text for numerous dialogues between Christians and Muslims at the academic and popular levels. These dialogues strengthened an earlier initiative, the Building Bridges Seminar, launched by Archbishop of Canterbury George Carey and continued by his successor, Rowan Williams. After Williams's retirement, responsibility for the Building Bridges Seminar was taken over by Georgetown University, a Jesuit institution in Washington, DC, where the Prince Alwaleed bin Talal Center for Muslim–Christian Understanding is based. Another important centre in the USA is the Duncan Black Macdonald Center at Hartford Seminary in Connecticut.

David Grafton, in his *Routledge Handbook* essay, notes that Christian–Muslim relations in the USA will continue to be influenced by three factors: US foreign policy towards Muslim-majority countries, the battle over American identity within an increasingly diverse population, and racism. To these may be added American policies towards the State of Israel, the treatment of Christian minorities in Muslim-majority countries and the issue of mission-conversion of Muslims to Christianity.

Christians and Buddhists

Buddhism came to the USA in the nineteenth century with the arrival of immigrants in large numbers from East Asia, especially China, following the 1849 California Gold Rush. In 1882 the Chinese Exclusion Act, which suspended Chinese immigration for 10 years, reduced the number of Buddhist immigrants. Buddhism was also brought in the nineteenth century by Japanese immigrants (especially to Hawaii) and Koreans. The first time Buddhism was publicly introduced to America was at the World's Parliament of Religions in 1893, where Theravada Buddhist leader Anagarika Dharmapala from Sri Lanka and Zen Buddhist Shaku Soyen from Japan, as well as other Buddhist leaders, appeared on stage with Christian leaders. The 1965 Immigration and Nationality Act opened the door to other Buddhists of other countries, especially Sri Lanka, Thailand, Cambodia, Taiwan and Vietnam.

Currently, Buddhism is the fourth-largest religion in the USA, making up about 1% of the adult population. About two-thirds of US Buddhists are Asian Americans, according to 2019 Pew Research Center estimates. All the major traditions of Buddhism are represented in the USA, including Theravada, Mahayana (especially Zen, Pure Land and Soko Gakai International) and Tibetan Buddhism. Whereas immigrant Buddhists focus on preserving the distinctive characteristics of their own Buddhism, American Buddhist converts prefer to 'braid' and intermingle many streams of Buddhism and have given rise to what is called 'American Buddhism'.

American Buddhists have also recognised the need to appreciate other religions, especially Christianity. So far, most Buddhist inter-faith relations have focused on Buddhist–Christian dialogue. In 1987, the Society for Buddhist–Christian Studies was founded to serve as a coordinating body supporting activities related to the comparative study of, and the practical interaction between, Buddhism and Christianity, whether by groups or individuals. It has an official journal, *Buddhist–Christian Studies*. Among Catholics, the first Buddhist–Christian dialogue took place among monks of both faiths. In the USA, the North American Board for East–West Dialogue was formed in 1978, later becoming Monastic Interreligious Dialogue. Numerous Buddhist–Christian conferences were organised, notably at Gethsemani Abbey, the monastery of the American Cistercian monk Thomas Merton. On the Buddhist side, Masao Abe and the Dalai Lama are the most famous partners in dialogue. The Christian side is represented by numerous eminent scholars of Buddhism, both Catholic and Protestant. The topics for dialogue are wide-ranging, including monastic practices, yoga and the 'no-self', and the divine kenosis.

A major development in Buddhist–Christian dialogue in the USA is 'socially engaged Buddhism', which seeks to interpret and live Buddhist teachings in ways that relieve social, political, economic and environmental suffering and injustice. The movement was initiated by the Vietnamese Zen Buddhist master Thich Nhat Hanh and has been favourably received in America.

Christians and Hindus
Hinduism is the fifth-largest religion in the USA, with about three million members, comprising around 1% of its total population. Most American Hindus are immigrants from South Asia, mainly India, who came to the USA after the Immigration and Nationality Act of 1965. Except for the Transcendentalists Henry David Thoreau and Ralph Waldo Emerson and the psychologist William James (1842–1910), American Christians before the twentieth century, especially missionaries, had an overwhelmingly negative view of Hinduism as polytheism and idol worship. A significant change occurred after the arrival at the Chicago World's Parliament of Religions of Swami Vivekananda (1863–1902), who introduced the Advaita Vedanta tradition to the USA. Today, Hindu concepts such as karma, veganism, reincarnation, meditation, yoga and Ayurveda have entered the US mainstream and are also believed and practised by non-Hindus. Another Hindu who had a great impact on America, especially on the African American struggle for freedom and human rights, is Mohandas K. ('Mahatma') Gandhi. Gandhi's concept and practice of *satyagraha* ('grasping truth') – that is, non-violent resistance to injustice – profoundly influenced the thought of Reinhold Niebuhr, Howard Thurman and Martin Luther King, Jr.

American Catholics' attitude towards and dialogue with Hinduism is guided by the following affirmation from the Second Vatican Council: 'In Hinduism people explore the divine mystery and express it both in the limitless riches of myth and the accurately defined insights of philosophy. They seek release from the trials of the present life by ascetical practices, profound meditation and recourse to God in confidence and love' (*Nostra Aetate*, no. 2). One Hindu practice that has become popular with American Christians is yoga, and, more precisely, the mental and physical hatha yoga. Theological dialogue with Hinduism in the USA takes the form of comparative theology. In 1998, the International Society for Krishna Consciousness, under the direction of Anuttama Dasa, and the USCCB's Secretariat for Ecumenical and Interreligious Affairs, under the direction of John Borelli, set up an annual Christian–Vaishnavite meeting. Finally, the academic peer-reviewed *Journal of Hindu–Christian Studies* is dedicated to Hindu–Christian dialogue.

Inter-religious Relations in Canada

Like the USA, Canada has no established Church, and the government of Canada is officially committed to religious freedom and religious pluralism. In 2018, the total population of Canada was estimated at 35.9 million. According to the 2011 census, which has the most recent data available on religion, approximately 67% of the population self-identified as Christian. Roman Catholics constitute the largest Christian group (38% of the total population), followed by the United Church of Canada (6%), Anglicans (5%), Baptists (1.9%) and Christian Orthodox (1.7%). Presbyterian, Lutheran and Pentecostal groups each constitute less than 2% of the population. The Church of Jesus Christ of Latter-day Saints estimates its membership at 190,265. Approximately 3% of the population is Muslim, and 1% is Jewish. Buddhists, Hindus, Sikhs, Scientologists, Baha'is and adherents of Shintoism, Taoism and Aboriginal spirituality together constitute less than 4% of the population. Approximately 24% of the population lists no religious affiliation.

Given Canada's general acceptance of multiculturalism and religious pluralism, inter-faith dialogue is widely practised by a number of churches and church organisations and is strongly supported by the Canada Council of Churches and the Canadian Conference of Catholic Bishops. Inter-faith dialogue in Canada is carried out either bilaterally or multilaterally, the former between one Christian church and another non-Christian tradition (for example, between the Catholic Church and Islam), the latter among more than two different religious traditions (for example, among Christians, Jews and Muslims).

The oldest bilateral relations in Canada are those between Christians and Jews. The Canadian Council of Christians and Jews was founded in 1947. The other major Jewish–Christian organisation is the National Tri-Partite Liaison Committee, jointly sponsored by three bodies, the Canadian Council of Churches, the Canadian Conference of Catholic Bishops and the Canadian Jewish Congress. In the twenty-first century, Christian–Muslim relations have been strengthened by the establishment of the Christian–Muslim National Liaison Committee by the Canadian Council of Churches, the Canadian Conference of Catholic Bishops and the Council of Muslim Communities of Canada.

In 1984, a Buddhist–Christian dialogue group was jointly sponsored by a number of Christian churches and the Buddhist Council of Canada and its affiliates. This group has published a book of guidelines for dialogue,

Awakened Heart: Buddhist–Christian Dialogue in Canada. Relations with Hindus have also attracted attention. Hindu–Catholic dialogue is co-sponsored by the Canadian Conference of Catholic Bishops and the Hindu Federation of Canada, the International Society of Krishna Consciousness and other members of the Hindu community. In 2016, the Catholic–Hindu Dialogue of Canada published a photo essay providing an overview of the dialogue meetings and its members, as well as its goals and aims.

Conclusion

Inter-religious relations between Christianity and other religions in North America have made a dramatic turn since the middle of the twentieth century. In the cases of Judaism and Islam, unspeakable acts of violence in the remote past and in recent times have compelled Christians to re-examine their traditional teachings and attitudes towards them. In the case of other Asian religions, especially Hinduism and Buddhism, better scholarship on them and shared living with their followers have produced a greater appreciation of their teachings and practices. Hostility has been replaced by friendship, wholesale condemnation by sincere dialogue. Though a return to mutual enmity is always possible, the prospect for further progress in inter-religious relations in North America is more than good.

Bibliography

Berthrong, John, 'Interfaith Dialogue in Canada', *Ecumenical Review*, 37:4 (October 1985), 462–70.

Hammer, Juliane and Omid Safi (eds), *The Cambridge Companion to American Islam* (Cambridge: Cambridge University Press, 2013).

Kessler, Edward, John Pawlikowski and Judith Banki (eds), *Jews and Christians in Conversation: Crossing Cultures and Generations* (Cambridge: Orchard Academics, 2002).

Lefebure, Leo D., *Transforming Interreligious Relations: Catholic Responses to Religious Pluralism in the United States* (Maryknoll, NY: Orbis Books, 2020).

Thomas, David (ed.), *Routledge Handbook on Christian–Muslim Relations* (London: Routledge, 2018).

Immigration and Xenophobia

Jung Eun Sophia Park

In North America, immigration can be a benchmark for understanding contemporary Christianity in relation to social justice and xenophobia. Since the first group of European immigrants arrived and settled on the continent, Christianity, as the dominant religion, has been constructed and understood within a society that practises policies against non-European immigrants. The immigration story of non-European Christians and their lived experiences have largely gone unheard. In the past they had been invisible and regarded as 'the other'. The situation in the present is similar.

After removing the bar against non-European immigration in Canada in 1962 and in the USA in 1965, North America has become home to a great diversity of churches. Furthermore, due to globalisation and the neoliberal economy, more people migrated, and cosmopolitan cities such as New York, San Francisco, Toronto and Vancouver have become final destinations of a global cohort of immigrants, refugees and exiles. Now, in the twenty-first century, the Christianity of North America faces the task of building a sense of unity in Christ while fully acknowledging and addressing cultural difference and embracing the other.

As a way to comprehend the contemporary multicultural Christianity in North America, I apply the concept of borderlands, because a borderland indicates the liminal space where many different kinds of cultural expression are encountered, which can lead to unease, conflict and even violence. Yet, hope for transformation also arises. The process of creating the liminal space of encounter with the other invites Christians to fully understand the nature of xenophobia, which comes from the fear of the unfamiliar and the foreign other.

Immigration and Fear of the Other

Certain biases and fear of others, such as immigrants, people of colour and Indigenous peoples, has been pervasive in the entire history of mainstream North American culture and, more specifically, within the structure of the church. Christianity in North America has reflected and reacted to immigration in both the past and the present, which often results in racial injustice or the division of people and their particular communities. In the context of the global COVID-19 pandemic, the existential threat of climate change and frequent environmental crises, levels of anxiety about others have increased.

North American society is organised according to three main strata: the top, the middle and the bottom. The top are white residents and new white immigrants, and in the near future assimilated (light-skinned) Latin Americans and a few individual Asian Americans/Canadians will be included. The middle group is composed of most Latin Americans/Canadians and Northeast Asian Americans/Canadians, such as Japanese, Koreans and Chinese. The bottom is collectively composed of Blacks, which includes most Africans and African Americans/Canadians, dark-skinned Latin Americans and Southeast Asians. During the pandemic, the division among these groups of people deepened, and xenophobia – which has been manifested as discriminatory violence, verbal assaults and racial impositions – has become more obvious, not only between whites and non-whites but, more intricately, among different groups of people of colour. For instance, during the pandemic, Asians and Asian descendants experienced hostility and violence, demonstrated through the rise of hate crimes against Asians. Brutal attacks on elderly Asians occurred all over North America. The media broadcast that older Asians were being attacked, mostly by young African Americans as well as by white Americans.

The Black Lives Matter movement, founded in 2013, raised social consciousness of systemic violence and incarceration of Black people, particularly by law enforcement, white police officers and court officials. In 2020, George Floyd, a Black man, lost his life in consequence of extreme police brutality. Footage of his death soon proliferated across both social media and mass media. Soon afterwards, people across the USA marched for the movement, which spread into a global protest against gun violence, police brutality and systemic racial injustice. Deep-seated injustice against the Black population in America is regarded as xenophobia, carried in the psyche of society, not just relegated to white society. Those who are caught by anxiety and fear of the other manifest hatred or anger against a specific ethnic group, eliciting a series of actions or thinking processes of discrimination, violence and its contorted justification.

In addition, members of a Christian community can be diverse. It is common to find different ethnic groups within a local church, and not much pastoral effort to create a vital intercultural community has been made. Also, gaps exist between the immigrant contingents and following generations in an immigrant ethnic church; usually, the second or the third generation of immigrants are quite different from the first generation in terms of their level of assimilation and accessibility to the mainstream culture.

The situation that exacerbates dissonance and disconnection among members in a congregation reveals a crucial characteristic of the borderland. It is clear that needs differ according to each generation of immigrants. For first-generation immigrants, urgent needs are a community that gives them a sense of belonging, information to settle in a new environment and the opportunity to worship in their native language. The following generation might need more spiritual support in comprehending their hyphenated identities or developing self-confidence as an ethnic minority. Because of language barriers, different generations find it difficult to engage and communicate with each other. In many Korean congregations, for example, first-generation immigrants offer education programmes about Korean language and culture for their children.

As a borderland, North American Christianity, which has been shaped by various types and ways of immigration, exhibits a certain anxiety and discomfort in relation to the other. Immigration creates a borderland, where different cultures encounter one another, often creating high levels of tension and violence.

Immigration and Social Justice

Today we live in the global market system, which emphasises free trade and a capital-centred neoliberal economy. The global economy operates in order to maximise capital and for it, the labour force flows from the global South to North America. The disparity between the rich and the poor is heightened as many people residing in the global South who suffer from poverty try to move to North America for better opportunity, education, safety and quality of life. In the church, we encounter large numbers of immigrants, including exiles and refugees. Although immigration stories are diverse in terms of time, place of origin and immigration status, the current immigration crisis creates moral demands for Christians in North America. The anti-immigration policy, especially for immigrants crossing the Mexico–US border, challenges North Americans through Christ's commandment of love for all neighbours and the moral imperative for social justice.

First of all, during the Trump era, the USA proclaimed an anti-immigration policy against South and Central Americans, who are mostly Christians, causing turmoil. Many families have been separated, and many children have been sent to retention centres, separated from their parents and families. Also, many people who were rejected when they attempted to cross the border legally chose to come to North America through dangerous desert routes, crossing rivers and encountering traffickers. In countless cases, those who take the risk and illegally cross the border end up losing their lives along the way.

The border sites between the USA and Mexico have become violent and dangerous places. Many Christians have responded to the situation, both personally and communally, serving at the border areas and supporting those who are held at the border waiting for acceptance by the US government. For example, Maryknoll lay missionaries lead the Friends Across Borders project, which accompanies and empowers those who are dislocated. Similarly, Catholic women religious built shelters for those who need help at border towns and cross the border, feeding asylum seekers who stay on the Mexico side of the border, even during the pandemic. Local churches collect daily necessities such as water, socks or toilet paper and send them to those who stay at the border sites.

Remarkably, the Sanctuary Movement in the San Francisco Bay area, which transported refugees from Central America, especially Guatemala, to safe areas and sheltered them in churches in the 1980s, restarted the same initiative as a response to the current immigrant crisis. The New Sanctuary Movement offers refuge to immigrant families being torn apart by the US Immigration and Customs Enforcement regulation. This movement invites parishioners at local parishes to practise prophetic hospitality, hosting immigrants and refugees at their homes.

On the border site, Christian communities express the spirituality of hospitality through rituals. Each December, Christians volunteer at the border area and perform the ritual La Posadas, in which they re-enact the story of Mary and Joseph searching for shelter in Bethlehem. In towns along the US–Mexico border, candlelit processions from both sides come together at the border. Hands reach through the fence in a touch of humanity, believing love stands beyond the laws of immigration. This ritual rekindles the spirit of hospitality as a Christian virtue and social ethics in the global world, expressing the apocalyptic hope for a new order of humanity and that of the church. Genuine hospitality stands at the liminal space between hostility against foreigners and strangers, and the welcoming spirit that is ready to sit together at the dinner table with an unknown figure. In Christian tradition, sitting at the table with a stranger brings faith that the unknown figure would be the Divine, as told in the Emmaus story in Luke 24: 13–36.

In the current crises of immigration and border crossing, most North American churches universally proclaim the importance of the humanitarian value of hospitality, and Christian ethics of social justice, while critically questioning the function of the borders. The Catholic worker communities in the USA and Canada support immigrants who have lost their family or need support, embodying the Catholic social teachings and standing against injustice. Also, many Christian universities proclaim the campus as a 'sanctuary', protecting the DACA (Deferred Action for

Childhood Arrival) and any undocumented students. As the North American churches have walked through the pass for justice, the current immigration crisis gains more attention now as a moral imperative to take an action.

Another disheartening reality of global immigration to North America is human trafficking. Many Christian organisations have created networks to fight against it, protecting the women and children who have fallen victim to trafficking. Human trafficking is a global crime in which human beings are bought and sold for physical and sexual slavery, mainly pertaining to victims who are forcefully moved from the global South to North America, Western Europe or East Asia. One of the most powerful groups fighting against human trafficking is the US Catholic Sisters Against Human Trafficking (USCSAHT), a national network. The USCSAHT envisions a world free of modern-day human slavery through a network of services advocating for victims, preventing any action of human trafficking and educating people about the issue. Especially USCSAHT as a member of Talitha Kum International is connected to a global network of women working to end human trafficking. Human trafficking, which results in forced dislocation of many women and children, brings huge moral concerns, and many churches pay close attention to it as a specific type of immigration, emphasising the feminisation of poverty.

Flourishing theological reflections may be found in the current immigration crises. These reflections pay attention to the reality of global migration, the voices of immigrants, exile and the dislocated as well as promoting a spirituality of hospitality and solidarity. The immigration theology emphasises the ordinariness or mundane holiness of Christian living, looking for the incarnated God among the immigrants and strangers. In Genesis 12: 1, God called Abraham to leave for the land that God will show. Theologians have sought from the Bible and systematic theology the spirituality of social justice in relation to voluntary and enforced immigration. The Hebrew Scriptures have been especially utilised as a text to indicate the life of immigrants as sojourners. Social ethics for slaves and foreigners in the Torah has become a centre of immigrant theology. Especially for Hispanic immigrants, due to the vast numbers and complicated cultural history in relation to the land of the USA, particularly in the states of Texas and California, comes the challenge of the notion of prophetic or radical hospitality, which stands for humanity and economic equity.

Fear of the Other Within

Historically, Christianity in North America began with immigration from Europe. The first significant immigration to and settlement of North America, which is one of the main parts of Christian history, involves genocide against the people of the First Nations. The first European settlers took the land from the First Nations through one-sided treaties, relegating the Indigenous peoples to reservation areas with poor living conditions. By definition, genocide denotes the deliberate killing of a large number of people from a particular nation or ethnic group with the aim of destroying that nation or group. The church practised its 'mission' upon them, in the midst of building the church, imposing cultural assimilation into the 'white' Christian culture in the name of 'civilisation'. More penetrating cultural oppression and violence robbed Indigenous culture, language, historical understanding and native heritage.

Indigenous children, for example, were forced to leave their hometowns and relocate to Christian residential schools, often enduring years of physical and sexual abuse by administrators, teachers, preachers and church authorities. Indigenous students suffered from malnutrition, physical abuse and emotional humiliation. In 2021, a report surfaced that on one old Canadian residential school site, hundreds of children's bodies were found. After examination, the children were shown to have died from malnutrition and illness.

Today, Indigenous people still suffer from the effects of oppression and marginalisation in society. Often the media cover the innumerable Indigenous women who have gone missing, yet there remains a vacant response in terms of discovering what happened to them and what their stories might be. Also, we need to better discern the reality that Indigenous spirituality and spiritual practices are often used as a commodity. Spiritual practice such as the sweat lodge and the vision quest have become commercialised, and their sacred stories and songs are now purchased, watered down and manipulated for economic gain and easy consumption.

It is hopeful that the church acknowledges this painful past in the grace of conversion, and in the efforts manifest through church publications across a variety of denominations. Canadian churches are more advanced than those in the USA in acknowledging the church's misbehaviour against the First Nations people. National Aboriginal Day is celebrated on 2 June, and many people participate in the ceremony together. In churches, an Aboriginal Day of Prayer is observed either on this day or on the previous Sunday. Native songs, narratives and dance are appropriated in some Christian worship services and their spiritual traditions and cultures are performed according to their respective traditions. It is remarkable that the United Church of Canada officially announced the Apology to First Nations Communities in 1986, and since then, its congregations have made efforts to receive forgiveness and to reach reconciliation.

Regarding immigration and fear of the other within the society of North America, it is essential to mention African Americans as the other on an individual and collective level. Despite African American Christians having been a momentous force in North American church history as well as immigration history, their narrative has often been ignored. This has led African Americans to proclaim their status as exiles in their own land. In North America, African Americans are descendants of those who immigrated from West Africa as slaves when human slavery was legal in North America. Since then, the Black church has evolved with many acts of faith and resistance, piety and protest. Although the African American church has been fundamentally shaped by regional differences – north and south, east and west – the church has inspired the wider church and society by its spirit of resilience, grace, healing and justice. Black leaders such as the Reverend Martin Luther King, Jr, have paved a discernible foundation of social and racial justice and spirituality in North America. Black theology has gained a central position in North America, and the freedom and liberation that Black theology addresses is rooted in the civil rights movement, affirming the Black Lives Matter movement today.

Multicultural Practice

North America's religious landscape is still dominated by Christianity, but the composition of Christianity has changed. The increasing number of 'nones', who do not claim membership in any particular religious denomination, practise instead various other forms of spirituality or adopt an entirely secular life. This is a relatively new phenomenon. In 2021, nones represent 30% of the US population, which is similar to the proportion of Roman Catholics. Their rapidly increasing numbers signify a declining number of Christians. Thus, it is plausible that the future of the church in North America might heavily rely on new immigrants from Asia, Africa and Latin America. The church of the future in North America might present itself as a church of colour, with diverse ethnic and racial backgrounds.

Regarding multicultural practices in the church, we can find three different patterns. The first is to share church space with other ethnic groups. Walking on the street of a cosmopolitan city in North America, it is easy to find a church building that is shared among many immigrant ethnic groups. For example, in downtown Los Angeles, St Basil Catholic parish offers Masses in numerous different languages. The Mass in English is at 10 a.m., Korean at noon, then Spanish in the afternoon. Each congregation does not necessarily encounter the others and practise fellowship, but the clergy of each group meet regularly in order to share pastoral information. Each community belongs to one parish, yet it has financial independence. This type of co-habitation becomes one of the most common types of multicultural practices of faith.

The second type is similar to the first one in sharing the space, yet church members often cross the denominational divisions. A congregation with a big church building rent out the space to an ethnic church. Very often, the renting congregation shares the worship space and other spaces such as the office, library and kitchen with one or two other ethnic groups, not counting denominations. In Alameda, California, a Baptist church shares its building with a Korean Presbyterian congregation and a Mongolian non-denominational congregation with different worship times. Ethnic churches worship in their native languages as well as sharing information for new immigrants to settle in the new country.

The third type is an independent ethnic church. Many communities begin with renting at an existing, so-called 'white-centred' church, and later they purchase a church building independently. For example, San Jose, California, is home to many Vietnamese churches that practise their faith, fully appreciating Vietnamese culture. Also, large groups of immigrant churches from Mexico and other Latin American countries may be found. St Elizabeth in the Oakland diocese in California is a famous parish with strong Mexican cultural components. On Sunday, hundreds of Latinx people gather and worship together with beautiful songs in Spanish. Similarly, parishes in New Mexico and Texas provide Spanish worship or bilingual services. Many Catholic parishes that have Hispanic Masses practise the Quinceanera, a rite of passage for 16-year-old girls and an important ritual along with the sacrament of confirmation.

While even today immigrants from Europe easily become part of the North American church, so-called coloured ethnic minority groups remain separated and somehow alienated. However, practising their faith according to their respective cultures and maintaining similar forms of worship as are practised in their origin countries offer spiritual comfort and nourish their faith. In Asian Catholic parishes, Lunar New Year's Day or Full Moon festivals are implemented at Sunday Mass, with memorial services for the dead. Ancestral worship rites, which are one of the most important Asian cultural and Confucian elements, are infused in the Asian Catholic church services.

It is hard to deny that a particular ethnic church remains alienated. However, it is true that new immigrants and exiles look for a community and often a local church that provides new immigrants with a sense of community. Local churches and church members recruit attendees by helping new immigrants to settle in their new homes. In other cases, immigrants of Christian faith yearn for a worship space that shares the culture and language of their country of origin. In the case of the latter, the church needs to provide more care rather than passively encountering those immigrant Christians.

On a special occasion to celebrate cultural diversity, it is not usual to observe each community dressing up in their traditional attire, singing and dancing while bringing their ethnic food. However, such events raise critical questions: who are the agents of this celebration, and what is the goal of it? Or more specifically, to whom does each group exhibit their cultural heritage? Christianity in North America has yet to create a spirituality that cultivates a sense of unity among ethnically diverse groups through education and praxis. Interestingly, people experience creative connection or oneness through music, rituals or popular devotion practised among the people. While North American liturgy is heavily logocentric, using words, Latin American liturgy possesses more melody and songs. In this multicultural habitus, some songs, such as 'Pan de Vida', become popular throughout all Christian churches, and it is becoming more common to sing that song during Mass across the USA and Canada.

Devotion to Our Lady of Guadalupe is gaining more popularity among Catholic people, highlighting the motherly love of the Virgin Mary for immigrants and Indigenous peoples. In almost every parish in the USA and Canada, Catholics celebrate the Feast of Guadalupe, re-enacting how the Virgin Mary appeared to Juan Diego, the Indigenous Mexican farmer. Beginning in 2016, the US Conference of Catholic Bishops has named the Feast of Our Lady of Guadalupe a day of prayer in solidarity with immigrants and refugees. After midnight on 11 December, mañanitas are sung to honour Our Lady of Guadalupe. At the Mission Dolores in San Francisco, the whole congregation celebrates the Mañanitas, serving Mexican food to all participants, including children who come from all over the Bay Area of San Francisco.

Although I mentioned some examples of people celebrating together through certain rituals and devotions, arguably the current situation does not yet show enough intercultural engagement or unity in diversity. Rather, it remains segmented as differing cultures, each group practising their faith in their own way but not discovering a way to worship together interculturally. Christians are still walking towards the borderlands where they will be able to worship together, while appreciating cultural difference. To reach this goal, the church will need to provide various ways to engage in intercultural worship and fellowship, not just bringing food and sharing greetings. The task is to live as the Body of Christ, fully admitting difference without any sense of discriminatory bias or judgement, creating a sense of oneness in Christ and building a spirit of unity.

The Church as a Bridge

Mexican-American feminist Gloria Anzaldua, in her seminal book *The Borderlands*, suggests that the function of the borderland is to be a bridge.

In the era of cultural diversity and cross-cultural movements, one of the most important plans of action is to build bridges between different churches with different cultural and ethnic backgrounds, or between diverse members within the same church denomination. People complain that immigrant churches are not willing to engage with the mainstream white church. However, it is imperative to reflect and consider whether there is a sense of mutual need, rather than just pulling ethnic churches into assimilating into mainstream cultures and churches.

Also, in the global era, many immigrant churches are more inclined to serve the suffering people of the world. If each immigrant church is organically related to other communities, the collective community can work on advocating for the concerns of the greater North American Church so that faith communities in North America work for global social justice and solidarity. For example, Burmese-American churches in California offer special prayers for peace in Myanmar in light of political warfare. If this community had more connection with other local churches, the prayer and social action to support Myanmar would be more influential. When a small worship community creates a bridge, the space as the borderland will be the global centre, breaking the rigid notion of the centre and the margin, no matter what marginality it carries. This way of bridging to connect between a local church in North America and any place in the globe provides a new paradigm of the church in which the sense of centre and margin is subverted. When we hear more direct voices of suffering, we can build a human connection which can grow into global friendship based on mutual respect.

The church as a borderland can provide a more collaborative or mutual project to promote healing and reconciliation within the wider North American Church through bridging communities in this way. In Canada, groups of Asian Canadian women and Aboriginal and Native women gather together to create a liminal space for social justice. Together, they follow a path of truth and reconciliation towards a shared future of harmony and peace in Canadian society. These inter-religious or inter-spiritual dialogues of racialised marginal women, including the Us Too Roundtable Movement, contribute to the growth of the women's spirituality in diversity within unity and build multitudes of bridges. Their connection would break the traditional structure of divided ethnic faith communities, overcoming the separation among minority groups.

Postmodern philosopher Jacques Derrida describes hospitality as the only poetic work in the world. For example, in 2015, Christian communities invited Syrian refugees to their annual picnic and rented a room to serve as a mosque for the month of Ramadan in the town of Leamington in Ontario, Canada. Valley Park Middle School in North York, Toronto, provides space for Muslim students to have Friday prayers under the direction of an imam during school hours. Muslim and Jewish teenage girls unite to serve the homeless in the city, and children's education programmes are carried out in the immigrant Korean United Church. These efforts to bridge people and communities together beyond cultural and religious difference bring a sense of peace and justice. These encounters break the barriers of religious sectarianism and form an integral part of real people's ordinary lives, creating a sense of a more globalised church. When immigrant religious identities continue to hybridise and multiply, they break down rigid boundaries, creating a new sense of community.

As a borderland, this movement or action can create discomfort. When the 2006 annual meeting of the Toronto Conference of the United Church of Canada took place on the theme of 'Journeying as Pilgrims in a Multi-Faith World', groups of Koreans protested about the opening worship service being performed by a Buddhist monk. Feelings of discomfort and confusion in the space of inter-religious encounter can motivate a person to pursue freedom, while discovering greater depths to their faith.

Always, the action of kindness enlightens the spirit of solidarity with other marginal groups. During the COVID pandemic, the Korean Immigrant Women for Mission group, which belongs to the United Methodist Church in the USA, sent handmade masks to Native American reservation sites, shelters and new immigrants. Korean senior women who are good at sewing gathered together and made thousands of handmade masks for others. Asian women in immigrant churches engaged in solidarity with an Aboriginal women's group, borrowing Native peoples' myths, symbols and songs to use in their own worship services. All such endeavours create a new sense of what the church of the future can be, where the centre and margin do not exist any longer, and reconciliation and new friendship are created.

Conclusion

In the twenty-first-century global era, the Christianity of North America can be characterised as increasingly multicultural due to the growth of immigration. The multicultural Church as a borderland becomes a liminal space where many different cultural elements meet, bringing anxiety and often violence, yet carrying the possibility of creating a new way of being church, embracing the others in the spirit of Christ. The North American Church as a borderland experiences dissonance and separation. Yet a new way of forming the church as a borderland would bridge the divisions and allow for mutual solidarity, pointing towards social justice and reconciliation. Fully acknowledging the racial injustice, cultural diversity and multiple crises faced by immigrants, the Christians of North America must respond to the call for social justice. By the grace of the Holy Spirit, it is a moral demand that Christians in North America learn to embrace the other, finding splendour in all the differences we bear.

Bibliography

Anzaldua, Gloria, *Borderlands/La Frontera: The New Mestiza* (San Francisco, CA: Aunt Lute Books, 1987).

Brock, Rita Nakashma, Jung Ha Kim, Kwok Pui-Lan and Seung Ai Yang (eds), *Off the Menu: Asian and Asian North American Women's Religion and Theology* (Louisville, KY: Westminster John Knox, 2007).

Brunsma, David (ed.), *Mixed Message: Multicultural Identities in the 'Color Blind' Era* (London: Lynne Rienner, 2006).

Carroll, M. Daniel R., *Christians at the Border: Immigration, the Church and the Bible* (Grand Rapids, MI: Baker Academic, 2008).

Myers, Ched and Matthew Colwell, *Our God Is Undocumented: Biblical Faith and Immigrant Justice* (Maryknoll, NY: Orbis, 2012).

Christian Nationalism

Daniel D. Miller

Present-day American Christian nationalism represents arguably the most potent and culturally and politically visible Christian expression in the contemporary North American context. While the application of this term to social and political analysis in North America has not been typical, it has gained increased currency in the US context over the course of the twenty-first century precisely because it highlights the potent convergence of White nationalism, Christian identity, an impulse towards organised violence, and nostalgia for a mythic America imagined to exist before the social, political, religious and demographic tumult of the 1960s and the decades that have followed. Showing troubling signs of exportation to Canada, it represents the mainstreaming or banalisation of political and social impulses long present in the USA and aims at the (re)establishment of a 'Christian nation'. The political impulses, and the potential violence, at the heart of what has become a mainstream expression of North American Christian identity was vividly displayed in the insurrection at the US Capitol on 6 January 2021. As that event attests, Christian nationalism is not merely an expression of a distinctive political ideology, religious belief or personal religiosity, but a populist-nationalist movement that aims to maintain and exercise political authority in the USA by all means necessary.

'Values Voters' to Christian Nationalists
A shift from a focus on so-called 'values voters' at the turn of the twenty-first century to recognition of the presence and significance of Christian nationalism is discernible in analyses of religion and politics in the USA. This shift marks a movement away from a narrow focus on the political behaviour of White Evangelical Christians to a recognition of the broader scope of Christian nationalism, increasing recognition of its specifically populist and nationalist dynamics, and calls for a shift in analytical perspective from religious and political belief to a more robust understanding the social dynamics of political and religious identity. Viewed from within this shifted perspective, Christian nationalism emerges not as a novel or nascent phenomenon, but one that has been operative throughout the twenty-first century.

Typical of the time, analyses of the role of religion in the 2000 and 2004 presidential elections focused heavily on the significance of White Evangelical Christians as 'values voters'. This was particularly true of the 2004 election, in which George W. Bush received 78% of the White Evangelical vote after campaigning on a 'values' platform appealing to social issues of concern to that voting bloc and emphasising his own personal moral and religious views. Unsurprisingly, analysts attributed Bush's widespread Evangelical support largely to voters' perception of shared religious belief and social values. Following this explanatory logic, Bush overwhelmingly garnered White Evangelical support because his personal narrative of faith resonated with them, his expressions of personal morality were consistent with their own beliefs, and the policy positions he advanced were consistent with their moral and religious convictions. The apparent explanatory value of such analyses was strengthened not only by many White Evangelicals' own accounts of their support for Bush and the Republican Party in the period, but also by the stark contrast of this support to Evangelicals' widespread condemnation of President Bill Clinton in the context of his affair with Monica Lewinski and Clinton's subsequent impeachment. In this context, prominent Evangelical leaders argued forcefully that observant Evangelicals and other Christians could not support Clinton because his personal morality was at odds with Evangelical religious and ethical values.

The lead-up to, and outcome of, the 2016 presidential election demonstrated the insufficiency of such analyses, which had seemed so compelling in the context of the 2000 and 2004 presidential elections. In marked contrast to Bush, Donald Trump espoused no strong personal faith narrative, demonstrated a fundamental biblical illiteracy and had no significant personal connection to a Christian tradition. Of even greater significance, he lacked virtually all the personal moral characteristics Evangelical leaders had argued, in the context of the Clinton scandals, were absolutely essential for presidential leadership and support from Christian voters. Compounding this contrast, Trump self-consciously eschewed the appeals to values that had figured prominently in Bush's 2004 campaign, instead explicitly and nakedly embracing a populist and nationalist agenda.

Yet, despite these marked differences, Trump carried a historically high percentage (81%) of the White Evangelical vote. Further, many of the same prominent Evangelical leaders who had opposed Clinton and supported Bush on the basis of 'values' now publicly supported Trump. Particularly noteworthy was the fact that, in doing so, these leaders advanced the same kinds of utilitarian moral arguments they had explicitly rejected on theological grounds in the context of the Clinton scandal. While they articulated their support for Trump in theological terms, then, they adopted exactly the opposite political-theological rationales they had embraced at the turn of the century.

The contradictory moral and theological arguments advanced by Christian thinkers in the contexts of the Clinton, Bush and Trump presidencies undermine the cogency of analyses based on such arguments or beliefs as the 'values voters' discourse. Opposition to Clinton and support for Bush, on the one hand, and support for Donald Trump, on the other, cannot be analytically reconciled at the level of religious or moral belief, political theology or the like. Such analyses are overly rationalistic, relying too heavily on the role of belief and intellection and overestimating their significance as explanations of shared social behaviour. In contrast to these approaches' lack of explanatory value, an approach highlighting the significance of contemporary Christian nationalism, understood as a complex social identity, provides a much more cogent explanation. Donald Trump garnered massive support from White Christians (this was not limited to Evangelicals) not despite his populist-nationalist rhetoric and policies but because of them. The overwhelming support for Trump on the part of White Christians reveals the existence of a strong populist-nationalist identity with which his rhetoric and policy positions readily resonated.

Christian Nationalism's Nature and Scope

Populism takes shape around a visceral, felt sense of who is numbered among the 'real' or 'authentic' 'people' (Latin *populus*) within a given population, while nationalism takes shape around a felt sense of who the true or authentic members of the 'nation' really are. Within the context of an established and stable political state like the USA or Canada, nationalism also expresses a sense that only members of the authentic nation ought to wield social, cultural and political authority within the state. Despite their analytical distinction, populism and nationalism are often articulated together in concrete social and political contexts, which is unsurprising given the traditional overlap of such concepts as 'people', 'nation' and 'race'. In their typical coincidence, populism and nationalism are co-articulated in a populist nationalism that takes shape around a shared sense of the 'national people', which includes only a subset of residents, or even political citizens, within the geographical borders of the state. Within this frame, populist nationalism takes shape around the intuition that all and only those recognised as members of the authentic people are members of the true nation, while those who properly ought to wield power and authority are also, and only, members of the true or authentic people.

Populist nationalism expresses a visceral, felt sense of social, political and cultural identity rather than a consciously held or even logically consistent political ideology – or, in the case of Christian nationalism, theology. It expresses an intuitive, deeply held, non-rational sense of who are properly members of the national people. Further, like all social identities, populist-nationalist identities are complex, coalescing in the intersections of multiple axes of identification. Reflecting this, they take shape around idealised prototypes of members of the national people, who are perceived as properly embodying these complex constellations of identity.

As the term suggests, American Christian nationalism takes shape around a clear sense that the USA is properly a 'Christian nation'. But awareness of the formal characteristics of populist nationalism alerts us to the fact that the sense of Christian identity operative and expressed within contemporary Christian nationalism involves much more than standard measures of personal religiosity or religious belief, extending beyond these to incorporate a prototypical image of the 'real' or 'authentic' American. A survey of studies of Christian nationalism yields a very specific, but notably consistent, profile of this imagined prototypical American: real Americans are White, cisgender, heterosexual, Protestant, English-speaking, US-born, of northern European descent, affirmative of patriarchy (if not male) and politically and socially conservative. Following a clear populist-nationalist logic, only those perceived to embody this prototype are 'real' Americans, regardless of political citizenship or residency status.

While it has been tempting for many to dismiss American Christian nationalism as a fringe social phenomenon limited to the margins of American society, contemporary analyses reveal that slightly more than half of Americans are at least sympathetic to, even if they do not fully identify with, the perspective of Christian nationalism and its felt sense of authentic American belonging. This makes evident the fact that, while a majority of White American Evangelicals can be counted as Christian nationalists, Christian nationalism extends well beyond White Evangelicalism. Indeed, reflecting the complexity of Christian identity as constructed within Christian nationalism, it is not even limited to those demonstrating high levels of Christian religiosity or even to those who explicitly identify as Christian. Additionally, though Donald Trump very effectively tapped into the widespread Christian nationalist sentiment pervading much of the American electorate, his successful bid for the presidency and the rabid support he continues to command vividly highlight that Christian nationalism was a potent force within the American electorate long before his presidential bid. Trump's electoral success should therefore be understood as a metric of pre-existing, widespread Christian nationalist identity, rather than the inauguration of something socially or politically novel within the context of US electoral politics.

Christian Nationalism's Increased Visibility

Recognition of this fact highlights the analytical mistake in attempting to understand American religion and politics in the rationalistic terms of religious belief or 'values'. Instead, analyses informed by an awareness of the dynamics and complexities of Christian nationalist identity reveal that the idealised real-American prototype at the heart of Christian nationalism has shaped the entirety of twenty-first-century US politics, including the 2000 and 2004 presidential elections. While American Christian nationalism, and its violent, militaristic potential, are more evident post-2016 than they were in 2000, it is clear in retrospect that it was operative in that earlier period as well. But this assertion raises crucial questions: if Christian nationalism has long been operative within the USA, how was it able to escape notice for so long? How can we explain its increased visibility in recent years?

The idealised real-American prototype has always shaped a dominant strain among competing understandings of American identity. For most of American history, US immigration law, social customs, expansionism, colonialism and myriad domestic laws favoured those perceived as embodying the real-American prototype, ensuring their hegemonic occupation of positions of cultural, economic and political authority, while also ensuring that all others occupied socially, economically and politically peripheral positions within the body politic. This *de facto* structuring of the American social body was justified and legitimised through a narrative of American greatness, according to which the USA gained its position of global prominence due to the divinely favoured efforts of 'real' Americans.

This narrative naturalised prototypical 'real' Americans' traditional occupation of positions of social and political authority – essentially, they occupied such positions because they deserved to do so, having faithfully carried out a divine mission and forged a great nation. This naturalisation marks the disavowal of the violence of an American founding built on practices of settler colonialism, chattel slavery and misogyny, and actively maintained through more than two centuries of subsequent legal, cultural, institutional and religious legitimation of ongoing marginalisation and subordination. While millions of Americans who did not fit the real-American prototype experienced the oppressive force of this narrative for centuries, those who benefited from it experienced it only as a confirmation of proper social order.

To be sure, this social order faced historical challenges, resulting in significant gains on the part of some marginalised populations (such as the granting of citizenship to African Americans and Native Americans, and the extension of suffrage to women). Overall, however, the social and political effects of such gains were successfully contained through machinations intended to blunt their force. This began to change significantly in the 1960s and 1970s. The social and political effects of diverse civil rights movements (the African American civil rights movement, the women's movement, the LGBTQ+ rights movement) combined with significant demographic shifts, due in large measure to the effects of the 1965 Hart–Cellar Act removing immigration quotas based on national origin, provoked a significant backlash against the normative Christian nationalist framing of American identity.

The emergence of the Religious Right in the 1980s, a novel social and political movement marking the coalescence of previously disparate conservative Protestant and political identities and grounded in the normative Christian nationalist vision of America, highlights the backlash against these developments. Despite this backlash, however, the social and political changes that spurred the formation of the Religious Right at the end of the twentieth century accelerated and gained increasing visibility in the first two decades of the twenty-first. A range of significant developments, such as the election of the first African American US President, the recognition of marriage equality, the formation of ongoing social justice movements demanding equality in other social and political domains, the increasingly secular character of the US population and the spectre of America's impending shift to a 'majority minority' demographic constitution, posed ever-greater challenges to the normative Christian nationalist structuring of the American body politic.

By the second decade of the twenty-first century, such social and political developments had precipitated a power-devaluation crisis among those fitting the traditional real-American prototype. That is, the changes within the American body politic, combined with increasing recognition and political representation on the part of those groups traditionally marginalised within it, came at the cost of the diminution of the overall social and political authority and power of imagined 'real' Americans. Given such Americans' historically hegemonic social and political position, this displacement manifests in a deeply felt sense of aggrieved victimhood, as the loss of social position and authority that are theirs by right. This sense of aggrieved victimhood is strengthened by the America-as-Christian-nation founding myth, which operates not only as a legitimating founding narrative, but as a declensionist narrative outlining America's fall from prior greatness as a result of 'real' Americans' social and political displacement. Like other narratives of decline, this narrative is simultaneously a redemptive narrative outlining the path back to American greatness: the restoration of 'real' Americans to their rightful place of social and political authority within the American body politic.

It is crucial to register the phenomenological nature of Christian nationalists' sense of loss and grievance. It is not a matter of any systematic political ideology or political theology. Indeed, it is not primarily a matter of belief or intellect at all. Rather, in keeping with the insights of political and social psychologists, sociologists and theorists of identity, it manifests as a deeply felt affective sense that members of the American body politic are fundamentally out of place. The non-rational nature of this sense of fundamental displacement, which is granted *post facto* legitimation through the articulation of political ideology and theology, explains the coalescence of disparate social groups and identities within the shared social identity provided by Christian nationalism, a phenomenon that defies reasonable explanation when analysed in terms of political or theological belief.

Christian nationalism gains its contemporary visibility as a visceral backlash against all of these social and political changes, the affective sense of displacement they provoke, and the populations perceived to be responsible for this displacement. It aims at the restoration of 'real' Americans' rightful social and political authority. The 'Christian nation' imagined within Christian nationalism and to which Christian nationalists call for a return is a body politic that is properly ordered in a hierarchical fashion, with those perceived as embodying the real-American prototype at the top and all others in subordinate positions. As long as the Christian nationalist social imaginary operated as the *de facto* norm structuring the American body politic, it operated invisibly, forming the unseen background against which American social and political life proceeded. The departure from that norm, effected in the power-devaluation of Christian nationalism, thrust that background into the social and political foreground, effectively rendering visible what had been socially invisible for many. While the dynamics of hegemonic Christian nationalism have always been all too apparent to those marginalised by it, the developments of the twenty-first century have led to its increased visibility for those who had not previously been aware of its operation. What has appeared to many analysts of American 'religion and politics' as a new social and political phenomenon is in fact only the emergence into increased visibility of a social and political identity that goes back to the founding of the USA and beyond.

Christian Nationalist Governance
Despite its anti-establishment, anti-elitist, anti-government rhetoric, all typical features of populism, American Christian nationalism is deeply invested in achieving state power and gaining access to its institutions and mechanisms, as evident in both the 2016 and 2020 US presidential elections. Within this frame, the lead-up to the 2016 presidential election and the subsequent presidency of Donald Trump are notable not because

they are unique, but because they vividly illustrate the patterns typical of populist governance. These can be examined through a consideration of political polarisation and radical majoritarianism.

Populist nationalism produces a radically polarised social and political space, defined by an opposition between the national people and the political party representing them as the purported majority, on the one hand, and minority groups and parties who are not numbered among the national people, on the other. Within American Christian nationalism, this logic is expressed in the sense that the 'American people' for whom Christian nationalists speak are limited to those who fit the real-American prototype around which the movement takes shape, effectively claiming majority status for that narrow subset of Americans.

Two features within this process mark the shift from a straightforward claim of numerical majority status to radical majoritarianism. The first is that polarisation is coupled with the denial of minority groups' or parties' social or political legitimacy as such. Expressing the exclusivist logic of the national people outlined above, only those recognised as fitting the real-American prototype have a legitimate role in the governance of the state. The purported minority status of those not recognised as 'real' Americans, by way of contrast, is such as to effectively disqualify them from an equal place in social or political life, even to the point of positioning them as political enemies, an outcome that is entirely typical of populist nationalisms elsewhere.

The second feature marking contemporary Christian nationalism as a majoritarian phenomenon is the decoupling of claims to majority status from empirical reality. As previously noted, the impending majority-minority constitution of the US population is a significant contributor to the power-devaluation crisis driving Christian nationalism. The empirical reality is that by the mid-twenty-first century, those embodying the real-American prototype will no longer represent a numerical majority of the population. Yet this shift will not displace Christian nationalists' claims to represent the majority of the 'American people'. This is because, insofar as only those embodying the real-American prototype are 'real' Americans within the Christian nationalist imaginary, their phenomenological, affective social and political perception will continue to be that they represent the majority will of *real* Americans, the empirical constitution of the US population notwithstanding. Claims to majority status, then, are increasingly unmoored from an actual numerical majority, so that Christian nationalism is rapidly coming to express a 'minoritarian majoritarianism' effectively working to enact minority rule within the USA.

The permanent imposition of this minority rule is entailed by the unique logic of elitism and representation within populist nationalism.

While Christian nationalists deploy anti-elitist rhetoric typical of other populist movements, such rhetoric belies the complex elitism at its heart. On the one hand, the 'establishment' against which Christian nationalists routinely rail is expansive, encompassing all out-groups who are not recognised as embodying the real-American prototype, with the effect that the 'elites' opposed by Christian nationalism include many people and groups who would not qualify as elite in any empirical sense. On the other hand, Christian nationalism often coalesces around leaders who might themselves occupy elite social and/or political positions. Acceptance of such leaders is not dependent on their not being elites, but on their being the right kind of elites – that is, whether they themselves embody the real-American prototype. The easy assumption of anti-elitism as a defining feature of populism, and expressed within Christian nationalism, therefore needs to be carefully re-examined.

Similar considerations apply with regard to representation. Populist nationalism typically presents itself as an expression of the pure, unmediated will of the people and, following this logic of immediacy, often deploys an anti-representational rhetoric. That is, insofar as it expresses the will of the national people directly, it has no need for mediating representational mechanisms. In concrete terms, this is why populist nationalists, in power, tend to eschew established institutions and procedures of representation, proportionality and the protection of minority rights. Despite some scholars' suggestions that populism represents the apotheosis of democracy, this rejection reveals populist-nationalist movements to be fundamentally anti-democratic in nature, given the roles of these mechanisms and procedures in ensuring the full political participation of a plurality of political subjects. As with elitism, however, populist denials of representation belie a much more complex reality. While populist nationalism aims at a more immediate identification of representative and represented than is allowed within formal democratic procedures and institutions, representation nevertheless remains fundamental to its operation. In a markedly Hobbesian fashion, populist nationalism takes shape around an 'incarnational' model of representation, according to which the populist leader is perceived not as a mere representative of the national people but as the embodiment of the people's will as such. In this capacity, authority to act is effectively ceded 'upward' to the leader as the incarnational representative of the people in an expression of political verticalisation. Insofar as the person of the leader, rather than any supra-personal institution or body, plays this incarnational, representative role, this incarnational representation also expresses a dynamic of political personalisation.

The full significance of populist nationalism's radical majoritarianism, elitism and operative practices of representation is evident in their transformation of one of the defining features of advanced democracies: elections. Within a populist/nationalist imaginary, elections are transformed from a means of discerning the majority will expressed within a heterogenous population of voters or of adjudicating differences inherent within a diverse, pluralistic electorate into exercises in the acclamation of the political leader as national people's incarnational representative. Elections are therefore experienced as a means not of leader selection but of leader acclamation, with the effect that, once in power, political leaders are, properly speaking, invested rather than elected. Conversely, any electoral exercise in which the populist-nationalist leader could be removed from power can only register as an illegitimate effort to disenfranchise or otherwise displace the national people from their rightful places of authority within the body politic.

Contemporary Christian nationalism in the USA provides a textbook illustration of these and other defining characteristics of populist-nationalist governance. While Christian nationalism predates the presidential candidacy of Donald Trump, he was swept into the presidency by fomenting the aggrieved sense of power-devaluation at the heart of Christian nationalism and, once in power, actively sought to weaken, ignore and otherwise bypass the institutions and mechanisms of US representative democracy. The populist-nationalist dynamics of incarnational representation have been evident in the fanatical, unshakeable support of Trump on the part of his followers, for whom he does, indeed, embody the will of 'real' Americans in his person and presidency. This incarnational understanding and the election-cum-installation dynamic it inaugurates were also evident in Trump's efforts to utilise the mechanisms of the US state, particularly the Department of Justice, to overturn the results of the 2020 US presidential election and remain in office.

Violence undertaken to preserve power and/or to counter all those not recognised as belonging to the body of national people follows logically from the dynamics of governance within populist nationalism. Within the context of contemporary Christian nationalism, these dynamics culminated in the attempted insurrection at the US Capitol on 6 January 2021, during which supporters of President Donald Trump attempted to prevent the certification of the 2020 presidential election. Ongoing investigations into the events of that day have revealed how close the tragedy that occurred, which led to the deaths of people, came to being even greater, with the Vice President of the United States and key members of Congress, including the Speaker of the House, having been evacuated to safe locations minutes before the insurrectionists reached them. While these events, described by the US FBI as an act of 'domestic terrorism', shocked many Americans and surprised many commentators, they were not surprising, but entirely predictable. Going further, they decisively undermine the arguments of those who dismiss the significance of contemporary Christian nationalism by suggesting that it merely represents one distinctive ideological perspective among others within the pluralistic space of a contemporary democracy.

Rethinking 'Christian' Nationalism

An examination of contemporary Christian nationalism also raises a significant methodological/theoretical issue related to discussions of 'religion and politics'. Such discussions often presuppose the distinctively modern conceptions of 'religion' and 'politics' long operative within Western scholarship. That is, they typically proceed on the assumption, often implicit, that 'religion' names a domain that is essentially personal and private in nature, while 'politics' names a social domain that is shared and public in nature. On such a schema, the respective domains of religion and politics are essentially and inherently distinct, with the consequence that analyses often devolve into being reductive concerning the scope of their legitimate (or illegitimate) interactions.

Contemporary Christian nationalism demonstrates the insufficiency of such approaches. While studies reveal evidence of Christian nationalist identity or sympathies among a majority of Americans, they also reveal that not all of those Americans demonstrate high degrees of individual religiosity. Given such data, it has proven tempting to dismiss Christian nationalism as not being about Christianity at all, but as reducing to a question of politics alone. Though such approaches have some intuitive appeal, such reduction is problematic. The descriptor 'Christian' in Christian nationalism is informative, capturing real and significant features of the movement, not the least of which is the stubborn datum that almost all who identify or sympathise with Christian nationalism affirm that the USA is, or ought to be, a 'Christian' nation. It is crucial to understand that within the Christian nationalist imaginary, Christian identity is so tied to this real-American prototype that only those perceived as embodying it constitute authentic or real Christians.

Such considerations should lead to the shift from a methodological approach reducing religion to individual religiosity or personal belief to one that understands Christian identity as a complex, full-blooded social identity. An analysis of Christian nationalism reveals an expression of religiosity that is inherently public and political, as opposed to being merely private and individual. This expanded conception of religiosity can accommodate the fact that the typical Christian nationalist would likely reject the assertion that their support for Christian nationalist positions, regardless of their levels of personal practice or adherence, registers anything other than 'Christian' identity. Rather, they are likely to suggest that such support represents a fundamental expression of their Christian identity, measures of personal religiosity notwithstanding. Indeed, most Christian nationalists would likely reject the notion that one could maintain an authentic Christian identity (as they experience it) and not support Christian nationalist policies and positions. If an affirmation of Christian nationalism is itself experienced as a public form of religiosity, then many Christian nationalists' low levels of individual religiosity do not reveal that Christian nationalism is not really Christian, but instead that Christian nationalism represents a particular public and political expression of Christian identity. Further, in keeping with the analysis above, Christian nationalism represents a public and political expression of Christian identity within which militarism and violence find natural expression.

Bibliography

Jones, Robert P., *White Too Long: The Legacy of White Supremacy in American Christianity* (New York: Simon and Schuster, 2020).

Miller, Daniel D., *Queer Democracy: Desire, Dysphoria, and the Body Politic* (London: Routledge, 2022).

Seidel, Andrew L., *The Founding Myth: Why Christian Nationalism Is Un-American* (New York: Sterling, 2019).

Stewart, Katherine, *The Power Worshippers: Inside the Dangerous Rise of Religious Nationalism* (New York: Bloomsbury, 2019).

Whitehead, Andrew L. and Samuel L. Perry, *Taking America Back for God: Christian Nationalism in the United States* (Oxford: Oxford University Press, 2020).

Ecology

Cynthia Moe-Lobeda

The story of ecology and Christianities in the land that became known as North America begins long before Christianity was born and long before the term 'ecology' or North America existed. The story goes back to the biblical creation stories, their anthropocentric interpretation throughout time and the platonic hierarchical dualism that informed Christianity as it arose from Judaism. The saga continues with the beliefs and practices of Christian communities as those unfolded and changed throughout two millennia in relationship to the Earth. Those beliefs and practices were highly varied. However, by the time Christianity landed on the shores of Turtle Island (as North America was known to many Indigenous peoples), dominant streams of Christianity – including those that arrived as part of the colonisation of the continent – saw the other-than-human aspects of creation as far below humans in the dualistic hierarchy of being that Christianity inherited from platonic philosophy.

Dualism aligned spirit and reason with good and saw matter (including the Earth) as either evil or relatively insignificant compared with humans, as well as having value primarily as resources for human use. The hierarchy placed Earth farthest from God and male human beings of dominant classes at the top and closest to God. Many scholars have argued (beginning with the famous essay by historian of medieval science Lynn White, published in *Science*) that these assumptions helped lay the groundwork for modernity's relentless onslaught against the other-than-human parts of creation. Eco-feminist scholars have uncovered the extent to which this hierarchy, linking women more closely to the Earth, also linked the domination of woman with the domination of the Earth, sanctifying both.

With the advent of European colonisation and conquest, 'race' emerged both as a social construct and as another dimension of the hierarchy. Non-European people ranked lower than Europeans in their inherent worth and rights. Kelly Brown Douglas, in a brilliant essay on American exceptionalism, demonstrates the origins of white supremacy in the first-century tract *Germania*, penned by the Roman historian Tacitus. This trajectory is integral to the ecology and Christianities story because, as demonstrated by Willie James Jennings and others, the divine mandate to subdue and use the 'natural world' was theologically linked to a divine mandate to subdue and conquer dark-skinned people. Exploitation and conquest of land was inseparable from the presupposed white supremacy that marked the conquest of Indigenous peoples and the kidnapping and enslavement of African peoples. Contemporary attention to ecology by Christian communities plays out against this backdrop, although much of Christian environmentalism in the USA does not recognise these roots.

Recent decades have seen a conscious and explicit turn to 'creation care' and more recently to environmental justice and eco-justice as integral dimensions of faith in many parts of North American Christianity. There is no singular beginning point of this turn. Rather, it has many beginning points, much as a river with multiple headwaters. Here we note those intersecting tributaries.

For many, the story of ecology and Christianity starts with developments in the secular world, beginning with Rachel Carson's *Silent Spring* in 1962 and other disquieting warnings: the aforementioned essay by Lynn White; the Club of Rome's *Limits to Growth* in 1972; the 1992 Earth Summit in Rio de Janeiro; and appeals by scientists and environmental groups for religion to take on the environmental crisis. Examples include the 1990 'Open Letter to the Religious Community' sent by 34 internationally renowned scientists stating that 'Efforts to safeguard and cherish the environment need to be infused with a vision of the sacred' and the 1992 Union of Concerned Scientists' 'Warning to Humanity', signed by some 1,700 of the world's leading scientists, including over half of the living Nobel Laureates in the sciences. An earlier tributary feeding into contemporary ecological consciousness in North American Christianities is early American natural theology (studying the natural world to understand God) and the related reverence for 'nature' as locus of spiritual enlightenment that emerged in the mid-nineteenth century.

For others, the story begins not even in North America, but with dawning awareness in the global ecumenical community that humans were dangerously damaging Earth's life-support systems – waters, soils, atmosphere and other aspects of the ecosystems on which life depends. Significant moments were the famous speech by theologian Joseph Sitter at the World Council of Churches (WCC) 1961 assembly in New Delhi calling for Earth-honouring Christology and an emphasis on cosmic redemption, and the WCC's series of consultations on 'Justice, Peace, and the Integrity of Creation', which culminated at its 1990 assembly in Seoul, Korea. The move at these events to declare that all of creation bears the image of God prompted the formation of the Evangelical Environmental Network in 1993, partly to counter that claim. Meanwhile, Pope John Paul II, in his 1990 World Day of Peace appeal, called on Catholics to prioritise environmental concern. The declaration by the leader of Orthodox

Christianity worldwide, Ecumenical Patriarch Bartholomew (now known as the 'Green Patriarch'), that wanton environmental destruction is a sin reverberated around the globe. The WCC was at the forefront of this ecumenical movement and was one of the first civil society organisations to insist on holding social justice together with concern about climate change, pointing to its disproportionate and disastrous consequences for people of the global South.

Another powerful tributary is the environmental justice movement led by people of colour to combat environmental racism, a movement in which some parts of Christianity played a key role. Many attribute the birth of this movement to the struggles against toxic dumping launched by local churches, faith leaders and other civil rights leaders in Warren County, North Carolina, beginning in 1982. The United Church of Christ through its Commission on Racial Justice helped to organise protests blocking trucks from dumping the waste and finally produced a seminal document called 'Toxic Waste and Race', demonstrating that the most statistically significant factor indicating the location of toxic waste facilities was race. Two other highly formative moments in the environmental justice movement as it impacted Christian environmentalism were the 1990 founding of the Indigenous Environmental Network and the First National People of Color Environmental Leadership Summit in 1991. The latter, involving some 600 people of colour, marked a shift in the racial make-up of the US environmental movement. This seminal gathering was supported by mainline church agencies through the Eco-Justice Working Group (formed in 1986) of the National Council of Churches of Christ in the USA (NCC). The Summit produced the Principles of Environmental Justice, now internationally recognised. It was followed in 1993 by the Black Church Environmental Summit organised in part through the NCC's Eco-Justice Working Group. In 2014, Green the Church was formed to encourage Black congregations to fight climate change, build power for political and economic change, and strengthen their communities through sustainable energy and food justice initiatives.

Closely related to the environmental justice movement and arising at the same time was the eco-justice movement in Christian theology and institutions. It insists that gender, racial and economic justice are inseparably linked to the well-being of Earth's ecosystems. This movement arose from the trajectory in Christianity which holds that God calls people not only to acts of compassion but also acts of justice. Said differently, the call to 'love your neighbour as yourself' entails not only compassionate service to neighbours in need but also seeking to dismantle social injustice that is harming neighbour or self. This understanding grounded the social gospel movement of the early twentieth century and the later civil rights movement. Eco-justice builds on this by claiming that humans are to love what God loves, which is all people and all of creation. Neighbour-love as a biblical and theological norm is not only justice-seeking and self-respecting, but also Earth-honouring. The eco-justice movement in the church, with the faith-rooted climate justice movement as a part of it, was born out of these grounds wed to the realisation that environmental destruction disproportionately damages impoverished people and people of colour. On Turtle Island, perhaps the most influential and emblematic document articulating eco-justice theology and actions is Pope Francis's 2015 encyclical *Laudato Si'*. It illumines links between unfettered capitalism, poverty and the wealth gap and devastation of Earth's ecosystems. The Pope calls for transformation of social systems that maintain these travesties and the dominant ideologies justifying them.

The joint impact of the appeals by global church leaders noted above and the growing environmental justice and eco-justice movements was powerful in the USA. It helped catalyse the formation of the National Religious Partnership for the Environment, a joint effort of the NCC's Eco-Justice Working Group, the Environmental Justice Program of the US Conference of Catholic Bishops, the Coalition on the Environment and Jewish Life, the Evangelical Environmental Network and the inter-religious GreenFaith.

Since the 2010s, climate justice has become a focal point of ecological concern in some circles of Christianity in North America. Here, the leadership and impetus are coming especially from frontline communities both in North America and around the globe. This movement is ecumenical, inter-faith, globally linked and engaged with non-religious groups. It arises from the reality of climate debt and climate colonialism – the fact that the people most devastated by the fury of climate change and the pollution and pain generated by fossil-fuel industries are also the people least responsible for the greenhouse gases that cause the climate catastrophe. The emphasis is on justice for these people. This movement and its call for climate justice insist that the wealthy nations and sectors most responsible historically for climate change should bear the economic costs of mitigation and adaptation, and should assume more responsibility for dramatically lowering greenhouse gas emissions.

The religious climate justice movement cries out for systemic change – change from advanced global capitalism with its dependence on fossil fuels and on maximising profit, consumption and growth despite terrible costs to the people and lands exploited in the process. Where the church in North America is entering into climate justice work, it does so inspired by church partners and others of the global South. As demonstrated in global ecumenical bodies such as the World Council of Churches and the Lutheran World Federation, the climate justice movement is closely aligned with other movements for human rights, a more equitable financial and economic architecture, food sovereignty, water justice, food justice, racial justice and peace.

One final tributary in the river of ecology and Christianities in North America arises in the theological academy and its question 'What has religion to do with ecology?' A seminal moment in that enquiry was a series of 10 sponsored conferences at Harvard University and organised by Mary Evelyn Tucker and John Grim from 1996 to 1998, the proceedings of which were subsequently published as a series of books. Countless later publications and conferences have explored this question in varied forms. Responses to it suggest that religion offers at least the following gifts: mechanisms for repentance and turning in a new direction; a call to serve a good greater than self or tribe; moral values such as care for the vulnerable, compassion and the goodness of creation; critique of idolatry; an understanding of the human vocation; moral vision; a discourse of lament and resources for it; language that might wake people up and express the depths of their feelings; and a horizon of hope.

Diversity and both constructive and damaging conflict mark the story of Christianities and ecology on Turtle Island. Conflicts are theological and political, reflecting the diversity within Christianity on this continent. Conflict has been particularly prominent within Evangelical Christianity, especially along theo-political lines, mirroring the diversity within Evangelical culture. Some sectors of it are fomenting climate denial and denouncing environmentalism, while others are highly engaged in the fight against climate change.

Nevertheless, to a remarkable degree, communions across the Christian spectrum are joining hands in the quest for Earth-honouring forms of Christianity and Earth-honouring societies, albeit grounded in divergent theologies, theories of change and political outlooks. In short, in the pursuit of ecologically sustainable human societies, Christianity composes a changing, emerging, tumultuous and hope-filled terrain. That terrain may be seen in three distinct but closely related dimensions of Christian faith life: theology and theological ethics; the internal life of faith communities; and their activity in seeking social change in the broader society.

With this brief overview in place, we move on in the next sections to consider the ecology–Christianity nexus in these three aspects of faith. But first, a brief word about misleading words and assumptions is in order. The word 'Christianity' tends to suggest a singular monolithic religious tradition. I assume, to the contrary, that Christianity is in fact Christianities – a vast, multivalent cacophony of traditions, voices, forms of worship and stances on any given theological or moral issue. To speak only of 'Christianity' in the singular risks universalising either the dominant forms of Christianities or perhaps the form with which one is most familiar. Obscured in this dangerous universalising are particular or little-known Christianities that often do not come to mind with reference to 'Christianity'. In this essay, I occasionally use 'Christianities' instead of 'Christianity' to remind the reader of this rich plurality.

'North America' as the label for this continent can reinforce a false notion that the historically significant story of this land and people on it begins with the landing of Europeans who christened it 'North America'. 'Turtle Island', a name for the continent used by many Indigenous peoples of this land, suggests a longer and less exclusive story. For this reason, I use 'Turtle Island' at times rather than 'North America'.

Ecology and environmentalism in North America often are assumed to be largely the interest and work of white people and middle- or upper-class people. This is not the case. As pointed out by eco-womanist Christian ethicist Melanie Harris and environmental historian Dianne D. Glave, widespread understandings of environmentalism in North America are deficient and misleading if they do not include the significant contributions of Black, Brown and Indigenous/First Nations people and peoples.

Ecology in Three Dimensions of Christian Faith Life

Many ecologically aware voices in North American Christianities recognise that for ecological healing to begin, people of the high-consumption industrialised world must make radical changes in how we live in order to reduce our devastating impact on Earth's fragile biosphere and ecosystems. We must diminish vastly our greenhouse gas emissions, our consumption of the world's goods and our production of toxins and other wastes. For ecologically attuned Christians, this response is understood as an integral dimension of Jesus's call to love neighbour as self in the current context. Such radical social re-formation is not a matter simply of change at the individual or household level. It also entails change in social systems. In fact, ecological well-being wed to social justice happens in the dance between change in consciousness/worldview (including theology), change in individual and institutional behaviour, and change in social structures, including public policy. None of these three arenas of change works alone; they require each other. The following sections corollate these arenas to three dimensions of life in Christian faith: theologies, the internal life of the church and the role of the church in society.

Eco-reformation in Theology

Central Christian doctrines have been rethought and reshaped to challenge Earth-damaging aspects of Christian beliefs. Christianity's turn to the Earth is as theologically varied as are Christianities. Different ecclesial communions and persons within them approach eco-theology from varied theological stances. The theological diversity is, however, giving rise to a striking degree of collaboration. Uniting the theological moves summarised here is the shift from medieval and modern Christianity's emphasis on human–human relations and human–God relations to realising the moral and spiritual significance of the relationships between humans and the Earth and between God and the Earth. This entails a move from valuing the other-than-human parts of creation primarily for their utility to humans to valuing them as inherently of infinite worth to God aside from their utility to humans. The eco-theological awaking or eco-reformation involves shifts in understandings of sin, salvation, cosmology, the work of Jesus Christ, the role of the Holy Spirit, the nature of God, the purpose of human life and more. A few illustrations will suffice.

Theology of God
Many Christian traditions conceive of God as a white, male monarch located in heaven above and concerned with spiritual life, not material life. Ecological theology has recognised that such a God image not only elevates white men over other humans but also subordinates the concerns of material life to trans-worldly spiritual concerns. Eco-theologians draw upon the Bible and Christian teachings throughout the ages to reclaim images of a God who is dwelling within creation itself and cherishing it, speaking through the winds and water; is multi-gendered or non-gendered; is made flesh not in a white person but in a dark-skinned Palestinian Jew named Jesus; and is lowly rather than kingly.

Theological cosmology
Cosmology refers to theories or models of the universe – often unconscious – reflecting cultural assumptions about the nature of the world. Troubling for earth-honouring Christianities have been centuries of perceiving the earth as a mere stage for the great human–divine drama at best and corrupt, godless and evil at worst. Humans strive to rise above the earthly world towards the supernatural realm of the spirit. This understanding became deeply entrenched in the Western psyche for centuries.

Yet, a strong ecological motif running through the Bible has been unearthed and revived in recent decades. The ecological motif shows that God is the power of life itself, present within Earth's creatures and elements, including humanity. The Hebrew scriptures (what Christians call the Old Testament) show God, people and Earth inextricably linked together. The other-than-human world exists in its own right, not only as resources for human beings or as companions to them. Moreover, it has both revelatory power and moral standing. Many theologians have explored the theological implications of our unfolding scientific discoveries of the cosmos, including the vast and complex interdependence of ecosystem parts. Some scholars look to the rich potential of sacramentalism within Christian traditions, claiming that the Earth itself is a sacrament. As such, the Earth reveals God's immanence in creation and takes on infinite inherent worth.

Theological anthropology
Who we think we are matters. Are we a part of the Earth or apart from it? Are we divinely mandated to have dominion over the Earth and use it for our good alone? Or are we Adam, made from *Adamah* (Hebrew for Earth), 'mud creatures' made of dust and moisture, here to live in communion with all that is and to keep, cultivate and protect the Earth? Both understandings of the human have been derived from the biblical creation stories. ('Mud creatures' is the interpretation of the Hebrew *Adam* by second-century theologian and church leader Irenaeus of Lyons.)

A central anthropological concern is the perceived dualism between nature and humans discussed earlier. Entrenched throughout Western history, this dualism privileges reason, men and spirit over emotion, women, animals and matter. Many eco-theologians argue that to achieve sustainable Earth–human relations, we must move beyond thinking in these dualistic and hierarchical terms. Instead, we must redefine humans as a part of – rather than apart from – Earth's ecosystems.

Closely related is the widely perceived mandate associated with the creation of humans in Genesis: to dominate or subdue the rest of creation. Eco-theologians have reinterpreted the mandate in Genesis 2 not to subdue the Earth, but to work and till it, to steward it and serve it (Genesis 2: 15). Other eco-theologians critique the stewardship anthropology, noting that the Earth does not need humans but, rather, humans are a species utterly dependent upon other species to care for us. According to this interpretation, humans are kin with all other life forms and must exist in deep, reciprocal, mutually beneficial relationship with them.

Along with the above concern is a tendency to see humans as the only part of creation within which God dwells. The re-emergence of panentheism, the belief that God exists both within and beyond every part of nature, offers a compelling response. Panentheism draws on biblical texts and classical and medieval theologians who understood all of creation to be the dwelling place of the divine.

Soteriology (theology regarding salvation)
Many traditional soteriological interpretations do not include all of creation in salvation, reserving salvation for humans – or, rather, some

humans – alone. Eco-theologians have reconsidered this doctrine. Individual salvation is bound up in the liberation of all creation, they argue. Salvation includes dismantling systems of power and privilege that oppress most humans and destroy the life-sustaining balance in Earth's ecosystems. Redemption, or salvation, should be understood as the consummation of *shalom* – a world of life in its fullness with justice and joy for all of creation.

Hamartiology (theology regarding sin)

The deeply entrenched doctrine of original sin carries problematic ecological implications that eco-theologians have worked to redress. An anthropogenic understanding of God's curse upon the Earth in response to humankind's original sin results in the perception of a tarnished and corrupt natural world. The fall of 'nature', according to this interpretation, accompanies the fall of Adam and Eve. If the present fallen world is mired in sin, then believers look for paradise to be restored at a future time and in another place.

In response, eco-theologians are reinterpreting the doctrine of sin. For some this is as simple as including heedless environmental destruction as sin. For others this approach is too simplistic. Sin is not only individual, but also systemic, manifesting itself personally, social structurally and globally. Modern societies, in damaging Earth's capacity to sustain life, are perpetrating structural sin. Structural sin is enabled by inter-related power structures. It defies the moral agency of individuals and is passed from generation to generation through processes of socialisation unless recognised and renounced. These features of structural sin help explain the failure of US society in general to recognise the magnitude of the Earth crisis and our culpability in it. Sin, thus understood, extends beyond disorientation with God, to distorted and dysfunctional relationships with self, others and the Earth.

Eschatology

Eschatology concerns the end times in Christian theology – in short, the fates of individuals, humankind and all of creation. A troubling eschatology for the Earth is one that sees Earth as destined to be abandoned when humans (or, rather, some humans, according to this eschatology) rise to heaven. This licenses rampant ecological exploitation, because conservation is seen as pointless. Alternatively, and equally troubling, an end to the Earth is interpreted by some as God's doing, allowing humans to wash their hands of any responsibility for its destruction.

However, Christian traditions, from the outset, have housed far less fatalistic and more Earth-honouring eschatologies. The second-century

Irenaeus of Lyons, for example, held that all of creation is destined for union and communion with God. Likewise, many contemporary eco-theologians argue that to hope for the 'kindom' of God means to act in such a way now as to realise it. ('Kindom of God' is a term used by many feminist, womanist and eco-theologians to replace the patriarchal image of 'kingdom of God'.) We can and should elect now to live in terms of what we envision as new possibilities for human society and Earth's well-being. Ecological eschatologies assume that the 'already and not-yet' reign of God does not exist without the other-than-human parts of creation.

These and other theological reconstructions give rise to significant change in the life of the church. The dynamic flows also in the opposite direction. The greening of the church engenders further theological exploration.

Eco-reformation in the Church's Internal Life

To many Christians, Christian eco-practices are unknown or irrelevant. Many others, however, embrace 'greening Christianity', eco-reformation or ecological faith with energy, hope, creativity and tenacity. This section explores the turn to Earth-honouring forms of Christianity as they shape the internal life of the church. Nearly every major denomination in the USA has issued statements calling Christians to care for creation, or 'Earth-keeping', as inherent in allegiance to God. In line with these statements, many churches are beginning to honour creation during worship and to attune the deep symbolism and meaning-making acts of liturgy to the other-than-human world. The mission of Earth healing is seen as an extension of Christ's healing activities. The Earth is celebrated as sacramental, and humans' voices 'join in the hymn of all creation'.

The ecumenical and global Season of Creation movement is illustrative. It proposes and resources a new season alongside Pentecost, Lent, Advent, Epiphany and the other seasons of the church year – namely the season of 'Creation'. In this season the Earth is celebrated as a sacred planet, Christians unite with the rest of creation in praising the Creator, and they confess sins against creation. The project's website offers liturgies, lectionary readings, music, children's themes and sermon ideas. Resources such as this offer a glimpse into the vibrant movement to reshape worship along ecological lines. The emerging 'wild church movement', worshipping outdoors, invites people to reconnect with the other-than-human parts of creation as kin, as sacred and as beloved companions in God's story.

Biblical scholars are developing eco-hermeneutics in their study and teaching of the Bible. An early undertaking in eco-hermeneutics is the five-volume *Earth Bible* series, edited by Australian scholar Norm Habel. This effort seeks to reflect with Earth as a subject in Scripture and to perceive from Earth's perspective. The series offers hermeneutical principles for this new field of biblical interpretation. Conversion to Earth-honouring faith and lifeways beckons Christianities to explore more fully and bring to public use the biblical testimony that God speaks through creatures and elements of Earth and calls them to 'testify', 'witness', 'minister' (Psalm 104: 4), convey God's message (Psalm 104: 4) and praise God (Psalm 148).

Sunday-school curricula and adult-education curricula around creation care have blossomed in the last two decades. Graduate and undergraduate courses in theology and religious studies are developing programmes in 'ecology and religion' under various rubrics. A Green Seminary Initiative provides networking opportunities for seminaries committed to greening Christianity, and the American Academy of Religion's unit on religion and ecology is vibrant.

In line with these movements in worship and education, many congregations and colleges, universities and seminaries with ties to the church have embarked on projects to lower their carbon footprints. Some worshipping communities, for example, take on plastic reduction, transition to renewable energy, integrate environmentally sustainable food practices into their programmes, build water collection projects and urban agriculture, or encourage automobile-free transportation to worship. A few seminaries and colleges have built windmills, geo-thermal heating, composting projects and gardens. Others have converted as much as possible to organic and locally produced food. Some eco-theologians predict that these developments in theology and church life are only the early stages of a vast eco-reformation to which the church is now called. This internal re-formation is mirrored in the work of the church in the broader society.

Eco-reformation through Church Engagement in Social Change

Many Protestant, Catholic and Orthodox communions in North America hold that the church gathered in worship, education and community is not for its own sake: it is for the sake of the world. They understand the church to be created by God through Christ and empowered by the Holy Spirit to bear witness to and participate in God's creating, liberating and healing activity in the world. The 'greening' of internal church life, then, is for the healing of the world. How, from this perspective, is God calling Christianities in North America to bring God's creating, healing, liberating love into the ecological and social realities of our day? How is the church responding to that call?

We have said that a rapid and radical societal shift to Earth-honouring ways of life will require change in the arenas of consciousness/worldview (including theology), household and institutional behaviours and broader social structures. Change in the structures of society might seem daunting and unattainable. Moving rapidly from a society based on fossil fuels to one based on renewable energy is no small feat. Holding major global corporations accountable for the environmental and social consequences of their drive to maximise profit – often regardless of the cost – might seem nearly impossible. Partly for this reason, Christians, at least in North America, in their efforts to be a healing presence in the world, have tended to be more engaged in social services, individual actions and charitable giving than in action towards radical structural change. And yet, action aiming at structural change as a way of heeding God's call to 'love your neighbour as yourself' (Matthew 22: 39) is indeed integral to Christianity at its best. The abolition of slavery and the civil rights movement are prominent examples. Today, in the face of a society and a global economy dashing madly ahead towards ecological devastation, some Christian communities are stepping up to the plate of leadership for social structural change.

In the formidable arena of structural change towards Earth-friendly societies and environmental justice, Christian communities are engaged in diverse but complementary forms of action. They seek change in varied societal structures, including public policy and governance, business corporations and institutions of civil society. Admittedly, the church (with a few exceptions) arrived late onto the scene of leadership towards more ecologically sustainable and equitable societies. The climate crisis, and especially its disproportionate impact on people and peoples least responsible for greenhouse gas emissions – low-consuming people the world over – is propelling increasing numbers of North American Christian communities into social change work.

In these endeavours, as in other historic movements towards the common good, the church is joining hands with other sectors of civil society. Moreover, the efforts are decidedly ecumenical, inter-faith and transnational. They may be seen as the embodiment or practice of the theological changes noted above. Here we sketch in broad strokes diverse forms of Christian engagement in the quest for structural change that will lead to sustainable Earth–human relations. In each arena, we merely illustrate a rich and growing movement.

Theologians, other church leaders and national or regional church bodies in North America have joined global networks and church leaders on other continents in calling public attention to the climate crisis and other ecological crises as spiritual and moral emergencies. Many suggest also that addressing these crises in ways that build more equitable and ecologically sane societies will require drawing deeply on the wellsprings of moral wisdom and spiritual strength, not only within the church but within other religious and wisdom traditions.

Countless faith-based ministries and organisations have sprung up to mobilise communities around specific environmental issues. Some employ faith-based community organisers to build people's power for bold action on climate change. Other environmentally oriented faith-based groups focus not on community organising but on public policy advocacy. Christian public policy advocacy networks have been active in North America at the local, state/provincial, national and international levels for decades. The years since 2010 have seen this activism expand from concern with social issues to include climate policy, energy policy, sustainable agriculture, food justice, water justice and other environmental issues, often because of their impact on already marginalised people.

Movement-building is another dimension of the church's engagement in ecologically oriented social change. Ecclesial communions are helping to inspire, found and develop social movements towards ecological well-being and environmental justice. A recent example is the role of faith communities in major climate marches. The inter-faith community was the largest contingent in San Francisco's 2018 Climate March and was significant in the New York City mobilisation. Noteworthy (and noted above) was the United Church of Christ's role in the birth of the environmental justice movement in North America. The Green Sisters, a coalition of Catholic women religious, is an inspirational force in the worldwide movement to counter the rapidly disappearing diversity in seeds.

Finally, the historical work of Christian communities in divestment from exploitative industries and in advocacy for corporate social responsibility has expanded to include ecological concerns and divestment from fossil fuels. According to GreenFaith, at least '130 religious institutions with assets of over US$24 billion have committed to full or partial fossil-fuel divestment'.

Conclusion

Christianities on Turtle Island have brought invaluable religious resources to the world's efforts to reverse the ecological devastation that threatens Earth's web of life and especially its most vulnerable members. A shared commitment to the Earth as beloved by God and as worthy of human reverence instead of human exploitation, and a commitment to justice for people least responsible for ecological damage but most endangered by it, is bringing together in common cause Christian communions with each other, other faiths and civil society groups with shared aims. That inter-faith and religious–secular collaboration has been central to the effectiveness of Christian ecological work.

I close with a word from my beliefs grounded in my position as a liberationist, eco-feminist Lutheran Christian. The urgency of the

Earth crisis and the reality that climate change is killing and displacing countless 'neighbours' on this continent and around the globe – particularly economically impoverished 'neighbours' who are least responsible for having caused the climate disaster – call Christianity to deeper and stronger forms of prophetic and practical leadership. This is because Christianity is rooted in God's call to love neighbour as self and, in the face of injustice, neighbour-love as a biblical and theological guide for life bears a fierce and tender commitment to dismantle injustice and to build societies that enable Earth's ecosystems to flourish and all people to have the necessities for life with justice and joy.

I am convinced that all religious traditions – including Christianity – are called now to draw upon the depths of their resources for moral-spiritual power to engage this life-saving work. Hope and moral-spiritual power lie in a trust that the sacred source of life, known in Jewish, Christian and Muslim traditions as God, is flowing through all things and will bring about healing and liberation despite all evidence to the contrary. As professed by Hadewijch of Brabant, a fourteenth-century poet and mystic, God's love 'will never cease in all the endless age to come'. Nor will that love cease in bringing the entire world into its destiny of life according to God's reign of love. The Sacred Source who called this world into being loves it with a love beyond human imagining that will never die. That love cannot be taken from us by any force in heaven or Earth. This does not mean waiting for God to make things right; it means, rather, throwing ourselves (to the extent that we are able) into the work of justice-seeking, Earth-relishing neighbour-love aimed at moving communities, societies and their economies away from extraction and exploitation into more just, sustainable and compassionate ways of living together on this good Earth.

Bibliography

Chavis, Benjamin, *Toxic Waste and Race* (New York: United Church of Christ, 1987).

Gould, Rebecca Kneale and Laurel Kearns, 'Ecology and Religious Environmentalism in the United States', in John Corrigan (ed.), *The Oxford Encyclopedia of Religion in America* (Oxford: Oxford University Press, 2018).

Harris, Melanie L., *Ecowomanism: African American Women and Earth-Honoring Faiths* (Maryknoll, NY: Orbis, 2017).

McFague, Sallie, *Models of God: Theology for an Ecological, Nuclear Age* (Philadelphia, PA: Fortress Press, 1987).

Moe-Lobeda, Cynthia, *Resisting Structural Evil: Love as Ecological-Economic Vocation* (Minneapolis, MN: Fortress, 2013).

Media

Zachary Sheldon and Heidi A. Campbell

The history of Christianity is intimately tied to the history of media, from the Roman codex to architecture to the printing press, and on through radio and film to the internet. Individual Christians, their churches and para-church organisations have long made use of distinct and popular media forms and affordances to accomplish their goals. From the spread of the gospel to the formation of churches and the facilitation of Christian community, media have always played a part in defining the faith. Especially in North America, media have been influential in spreading Christianity, complicating its ties to politics and culture, and reshaping church culture and the communal identities and practices of Christians across the continent.

This essay takes a topical approach to examining the history of Christianity and media in North America. Moving from the printing press and into the electronic age with radio, film, television and ultimately the internet, it illustrates the lasting impact that media have had on the development and character of the Christian faith in North America across denominations and perspectives. Following this history, the essay engages approaches from 'digital religion studies', which specifically seeks to understand intersections between new media, digital technology and religion. The essay concludes with an overview of current trends in research in digital religion and their relation to the study of media in North American Christianity.

The Printing Press

The relationship between Christianity and media is as old as the faith itself. Jesus and his disciples lived, taught and wrote at a time of great transition in the history of the alphabet, paper and other media for writing. In North America the development of Christianity was intimately tied to the invention of the printing press, which facilitated Martin Luther's break with Rome, the establishment of Protestantism and, in time, the Puritan flight to the New World. A printing press arrived in the USA in 1638, and in time print media proliferated in North America, although Canada's own print industry was not firmly established until the 1830s. Thus, a line can be traced from the printing press's influence on religion to the power of media in North America and its developing culture. Catholicism and various branches of Protestantism flourished in the New World, representing diverse theologies, approaches to the Bible and ministerial emphases. These diverse perspectives helped shape the religious use of developing media into the mass, electronic era, beginning with radio.

Radio

Some of the earliest adopters of radio were Christian religious broadcasters who saw the medium as a tool for amplifying Christianity's presence in industrialised society. Radio lent itself well to the spread of local messages to a mass audience; the format was not unlike how church sermons already functioned, but with a drastic increase in the number of potential listeners. Associations of religious broadcasters emerged across the USA, including the Bible Institute of Los Angeles and Moody Bible Institute in Chicago. Early radio regulations enabled stations to give airtime to religious broadcasters, and religious programming was some of the most popular content across the country. Many of these stations even made significant headway into Canada, partially inspiring the Royal Commission on Radio Broadcasting to measure and combat the influence of the USA on Canadian media. Initially, religious broadcasters tended to represent mainline Protestantism and Catholicism, but increased federal regulation decreased the amount of free airtime given for religious causes, thus encouraging preachers and churches desiring airtime to fundraise to purchase broadcasting time.

Consequently, Evangelical strains of Christianity flourished in this new, mass media environment. Aimee Semple McPherson stands out as an exemplar. Opposing stereotypes of traditional preaching and Bible exposition, she brought a penchant for theatrics to her Los Angeles Pentecostal congregation. In contrast to mainline Protestant preachers like Harry Emerson Fosdick, who believed in using radio to promote nonsectarian social reform, McPherson and other Evangelicals used the radio's possibilities for entertainment and interpersonal connection to advance particular causes and theological views. McPherson's weekly sermons included large-scale dramas and attracted such crowds and financial support that her organisation, the Church of the Foursquare Gospel, was able to build the coliseum-like Angelus Temple in Los Angeles in 1923 and establish its own commercial radio station, KFSG, in 1924. Others, like Baptist Charles E. Fuller, adopted a more conversational tone that personalised his old-fashioned gospel message to individual listeners. This, too, had its marketing appeal, and donations from listeners enabled Fuller to purchase prime-time distribution and led to the syndication of his *Old-Fashioned Revival Hour,* directly inspiring the tactics of later televangelists.

Mainline Protestant and Catholic broadcasters still made an impact via the radio in this era. Father Charles Coughlin, based near Detroit, accrued nearly 30 million weekly listeners to his radio show at the outset of the 1930s, for instance. But in general, non-Evangelical broadcasters seemed to follow one of two paths, both of which led to the diminished effectiveness of their message and the size of their audience. Some simply lost out stylistically to Evangelical preachers: maintaining non-sectarian principles minimised the distinctiveness of such messages, and the lack of a need to accrue advertisers deprived these programmes of the entertainment value present in much evangelical broadcasting. Other liberal Christian and Catholic broadcasters became overtly political, thus violating standards of the Federal Communications Commission and the National Association of Broadcasters and leading to their cancellation. Such was the fate of Father Coughlin's programme in the wake of anti-Semitic comments made at the outset of the Second World War.

Christian radio persists today, and some minority Christian traditions like Orthodox Christianity have made significant gains in utilising broadcasting to reach especially new converts to the tradition. Radio continues to help Christian churches, organisations and preachers reach unprecedented numbers of people. Historically, as the first electronic mass medium, radio's use by various Christian groups set the stage for their use of other, related media, including film and television.

Film

Like radio, film was a mass and prominent medium that prompted diverse responses from North American Christians. Biblical and religious stories were some of the earliest put to celluloid, including silent versions of *The Ten Commandments* (1923) and *Ben-Hur: A Tale of the Christ* (1925). But Hollywood was as apt to film gangster stories as it was biblical epics, such that the medium's mass popularity quickly led to worries from pastors and priests over objectionable content in films and the medium's potential negative ideological influence.

Where Protestants – and especially Evangelicals – maintained a distinct advantage in the realm of radio, the emerging film industry found itself uniquely shaped by Catholic influences. When the US Supreme Court ruled in 1915 that protections of free speech did not extend to motion pictures, it opened the door for active censorship of the movies. Catholics had an early and prominent 'in' through Jesuit father Daniel A. Lord, who in 1929 created an independent code of social and moral standards to govern the content of motion pictures. In 1930 Lord met with several Hollywood studio heads, and his standards were adopted as the official Production Code that dictated appropriate and objectionable content in films. The Production Code restricted instances of profanity, blasphemy, sex and violence; banned depictions of inter-racial marriage, ridicule of clergy and nudity; and provided guidance on sensitively depicting subjects like sedition, marriage, theft, rape and murder. The Production Code was largely symbolic until 1934 and the establishment of the Production Code Administration (PCA), organised as an official certifier of Hollywood films. Without the PCA's approval, a film was unlikely to be released. Ostensibly a secular organisation supported by Hollywood's own studios – the heads of which were predominantly Jewish – the Code's morality was undergirded by Catholic theology. Thus, Catholic morality shaped the industry actively involved in shaping US popular culture.

The institutional power of the Catholic Church and its theology also made its impression on film through the National Legion of Decency, or Catholic Legion of Decency, established in 1933. This organisation acted as an independent check on the already heavily Catholic PCA. After a film received PCA approval, it was submitted to the Legion of Decency, which placed its own stamp of approval on films before their general release. Failure to receive such approval could prove detrimental to a film's financial prospects through the Legion's reliance on the authority of the Church: the Legion's condemnation of a film forbade America's 20 million Catholic parishioners from attending it. Thus, Catholics were, for a time, able to exercise a large measure of theologically based control over the moral content of Hollywood cinema and North American culture. The organisation still exists, but over time its influence waned; some condemnations were perceived as endorsements for some films, weakening the organisation's institutional hold over the viewing habits of parishioners and the film industry itself.

Protestant independence led to denominational and organisational infighting that crippled any attempts at Catholic-like influence over motion pictures. Because Protestants had no single governing authority, distinct denominations and sometimes individual churches created their own standards for combating immorality in Hollywood. Generally, Protestant groups adopted one of two perspectives on film: a pietist concern for content or a structuralist concern for message. For some, morality in film needed to be regulated on the basis of its content. Films were censored or boycotted on the basis of sex, swearing, violence or depictions of other kinds of immoral conduct. For others, it was the overall message of a film that was the measure of its appropriateness. Some immoral content in a film could be tolerated, so long as the larger message of the film was in line with Christian social and moral values. So, while a film about a drug addict would be ignored wholesale by pietists concerned with the morality of its content, structuralists might accept the film provided its moral focused on the negative consequences of drug use and offered a positive social perspective on its own immoral content. Both perspectives emphasised the Protestant understanding of individuality and freedom and sought to train believers in discernment rather than relying on industry or government censorship.

Christian responses to and involvement in film also highlight the development of a Christian media industry parallel to that of mainstream, secular media. Some evangelists, pastors and Christian creatives showed their distinctiveness from Hollywood by establishing their own film studios and distribution networks. A similar phenomenon has occurred with Christian music, radio, television and other merchandising, but Christian film has, especially of late, increased its mainstream presence. Though not limited to Protestantism, many of these parallel Christian industries share with radio a particularly Evangelical bent. Famed evangelist Billy Graham started his film studio Worldwide Pictures in 1951, producing family-friendly and evangelical-style films. Later Christian productions sought to incorporate elements reminiscent of popular films, including rock soundtracks and higher production values; the apocalyptic *A Thief in the Night* (1972) persists as an exemplar here. In the early 1990s, Christian film capitalised on the emergence of digital filmmaking technologies, making animated and live-action film production cheaper and more accessible to amateurs, perhaps most notably with the animated series VeggieTales (1993–2018), an early innovator in digital animation.

But it was actually an independent Catholic production that brought the most attention to the potential of Christian cinema: Mel Gibson's *The Passion of the Christ* (2004). Gibson's retelling of Jesus's last day on earth earned an R-rating (restricted to adult audiences) for its violence, featured dialogue exclusively in ancient languages and was told from a distinctly Catholic theological perspective. Yet its appeal at the box office seemed to cross denominational lines, and its worldwide gross of over US$622 million pointed to the presence of an audience for religiously based cinema that Hollywood had ignored. In the wake of Gibson's unprecedented and unpredicted success, Christian filmmaking received renewed attention, and some mainstream studios established subsidiaries to create films for the religious market. No studio-produced or independent Christian film has duplicated Gibson's feat, but Christianity has maintained a steady presence in both Hollywood and independent film production across the USA and Canada ever since. Evangelical films like *Facing the Giants* (2006) and *Courageous* (2011), both from Sherwood Pictures, and films like *The Other Side of Heaven* (2001), which portrayed the story of a Church of Jesus Christ of Latter-day Saints missionary, helped bring Christian cinema to newfound prominence.

Television

Unlike with radio and film, Christians were slow to adopt the fledgling medium of television. Though it emerged in the 1930s, religious broadcasters made relatively little use of it until the 1950s, when Archbishop Fulton J. Sheen transitioned his long-running popular radio show into an eventually Emmy-winning television programme in 1951. Others representing Protestant and Evangelical denominations followed suit, such that by the 1970s religious television had supplanted radio as the primary location of electronic media engagement in North American Christianity. With this, the era of 'televangelism' arrived, which would contribute significantly to the growth of some pastors as celebrity-like figures in Christian culture.

As a medium that utilised the latest technology to create an attractive, accessible package, religious television helped establish and grow a number of Christian ministries, as well as the reputations of those involved with them. Not unlike radio, a smaller and consistent Catholic presence was dominated by Protestant, especially Evangelical, stations and programmes. In addition to simply televising worship services or Mass, innovators in religious television made use of the medium's secularly established formats for shows as starting points to innovate in the presentation of religious messaging. Christian variety programmes were an early prime-time innovation of Oral Roberts in the late 1950s, and in the 1970s and 1980s Christian talk shows and worship programmes expanded on this through combining preaching and filmed corporate worship with celebrity guests, skits and special musical numbers.

Religious television used the fundamental dramatic principles of the televisual medium and a technological sophistication that matched the best of secular broadcasting at the time to heighten the drama and entertainment value of its programming. Doing so attracted massive audiences and helped contribute to the growth of worldwide broadcasting and evangelism networks. The Christian Broadcasting Network, founded in 1960 by Pat Robertson, was among the earliest and most successful of these televisual ministries in the USA. Trinity Broadcasting Network followed in 1973, PTL Television Network in 1974, and others like Christian Television Network, Daystar and Catholic Faith Network in the ensuing decades. Likewise, in Canada, Crossroads Christian Communications was established in 1962, with other networks following in subsequent decades. Many flagship programmes for these networks led to significant fame and attention for their hosts and pastors and helped establish an 'expansionary' mindset for Christian broadcasters, in which a televangelism ministry was simply a starting point for spin-off ministries that could be supported by the fundraising efforts of the main broadcast. Early televangelists in the USA like Oral Roberts, Jimmy Swaggart, Robert Schuller, Pat Robertson,

Jim and Tammy Faye Bakker, and Jerry Falwell, to name just a few, built broadcasting networks, television stations, universities and even theme parks off the funds accrued by their broadcasting efforts, while also supporting missionary and other ministry initiatives across the globe.

If televangelism emerged from television's development in the broader secular culture, its use as a fundraising platform enabled a conservative Christianity to feed back into the popular and political culture of the USA, with a much smaller impact in Canada. Jerry Falwell's Moral Majority, founded in 1979 as a political action committee dedicated to pro-life and other pro-family values, served to unite a number of conservative Christian pastors, televangelists and congregants around conservative causes and politicians. While Christian involvement in US politics already had a long history, Falwell's efforts and the support of other televangelists and related funding operations galvanised conservatives across the nation and helped lead to the establishment of the Christian Right as a significant political force. Some, including Billy Graham, critiqued the movement for politicising the gospel and deviating from the initial evangelistic efforts of televangelists and Christian broadcasting. The Moral Majority was disbanded in 1989, but the movement's contributions to the rise of a conservative wing of American politics remain, and thus illustrate just how impactful conservative televangelists really were.

Throughout the 1980s and 1990s, though, the character of televangelism shifted. Charismatic movements not aligned with mainstream Protestant or Evangelical denominations took to the airwaves, popularising preachers like Benny Hinn, T. D. Jakes, Joyce Meyer, Joel Osteen, Paula White, and Kenneth and Gloria Copeland. This new televangelism commanded a tremendous audience with captivating worship, faith healings and an emphasis on the financial and material rewards of Christian faithfulness that critics would label the 'prosperity gospel'. 'Televangelism' as a term ultimately became equated with this movement, and its most prominent televangelists became flashpoints for controversy regarding the authenticity of a faith steeped in American consumer culture. The financial success and material wealth of many preachers associated with this movement have made them a favourite of critiques by other Christians and the secular media regarding the perceived lavishness of their lifestyles. Several own private planes, multiple homes and expensive cars, and their churches and broadcasting ministries have considerable financial and other material assets. Yet while detractors see such things as evidence of charlatanism or deceit, adherents recognise these as blessings from God.

Perhaps the greatest consequence of Christianity's relationship with television has been the rise of pastors as celebrities and public figures in American culture. Certain pastors and ministries have always gained some measure of fame in America, but television amplified this phenomenon in significantly public ways. With millions of viewers tuning in, televangelists did the work of spreading the gospel and growing ministries and were recognised for their distinct styles and abilities as the hosts of television shows whose popularity rivalled that of some mainstream, secular programmes. This enabled greater potential for outreach, as well as new possibilities for Christian voices to speak into and about American culture, empowering figures like Pat Robertson and Jerry Falwell to take active roles in American politics. Conversely, however, many powerful preachers found themselves engaged in scandalous and widely reported controversies that undercut their success and tarnished their reputations as well as their ministries. In the 1980s and 1990s in particular, such controversies included tax-evasion investigations, affairs and other sexual misconduct. More recently, controversy has enveloped some televangelists like Kenneth Copeland and Jim Bakker for broadcasting misinformation regarding COVID-19, including marketing of unproven faith-based healing regimens for the virus. Ironically, then, the same televisual medium that enabled significant growth and success for Christian ministries and celebrity pastors has also been the mechanism by which their controversies have been exposed and reported. Worth noting is that this particular storm of controversies did not touch Canadian religious broadcasting with the same level of furore. Rather, the 1990s and early 2000s saw the establishment of new Christian television networks in Canada and the continuation of long-running programmes like *100 Huntley Street* with minimal interference.

In the twenty-first century, televangelism has also contributed to some more positive and curious developments in the relationship of Christianity and media. For example, Joel Osteen's Lakewood Church in Houston, Texas, is the largest church in America and is intensely media-savvy and media-focused in its operations, and others have followed this model. Thus, Christian television broadcasting remains alive and well across North America, on both the airwaves and dedicated cable networks. Though televangelists today are more likely to be critiqued or even lampooned in mainstream and secular culture, the history of televangelism demonstrates key ways that Christians have used television to interact with and shape American culture, especially in politics. Beyond traditional mass media industries, though, Christians are finding new and significant ways to share the faith and engage others via the internet.

Internet
Religious groups, content and resources have been a part of the internet landscape almost from its founding. Contrasting with how religious institutions and denominations have dominated the use of mass media like

radio, film and television, early Christian and other religious content online was created by individuals or groups of individuals who were able to connect via the fledgling medium. Thus, Christian communities flourished in the early internet era, but they also provoked questions regarding the status of traditional religious authority online and what kind of spirituality was promoted by the internet. These are the kinds of questions taken up by the field of digital religious studies. Digital religion as a field of study points to how digital media and spaces are shaping and being shaped by religious practice. This necessarily involves the study of the internet and, in today's converged media environment, the internet's inter-relations to other digital media platforms like cell phones, blogs, social media and even video games. In considering these various media, digital religious studies asks how religion, religious groups and religious individuals have used digital technologies like the internet to express their faith and how religion itself might be changing through the influence of digital media. Of course, these questions are applicable to a variety of religions and contexts. In American Christianity, two consequences of digital technology stand out – the emergence and popularity of church online and the role of digital religious creatives in shaping the American worship context.

As early as the mid-1980s, computer hobbyists, governmental researchers and individuals with early internetworking connections brought their spirituality into online discussion forums. Religious discourses arose on bulletin board systems (BBSs) under a 'create your own religion' discussion forum, and in 1984 Usenet began to be split into a number of specialised hierarchies to accommodate the growing number of special-interest network users, including 'alt.religion', 'soc.religion' and 'talk.religion'. In the early to mid-1990s the internet was a heavily text-based medium, so most religious interaction online happened on bulletin boards, newsgroups and email lists. For example, Ecunet, an ecumenical Christian email listserve (www.ecunet.org), became a very active email-based group seeking to build a conversational Christian community across denominational lines. The rise of websites in the 1990s led to numerous religious websites and even the establishment of various virtual churches and temples, including The First Church of Cyberspace (www.godweb.org), established by American Presbyterians in 1992 as the first virtual non-denominational online church, which ran weekly services via a chat forum for more than a decade.

By the late 1990s, multitudes of different religious online groups and resources began to surface. Often created by religious individuals rather than institutions, these led to discussions about whether the internet promotes individualised spirituality over communal affiliations. Sites like Beliefnet (www.Beliefnet.org) sought to create a 'multi-faith e-community' offering e-devotionals and access to sacred texts from different faith traditions, allowing individuals to 'pic-n-mix' between different religious traditions and sources. Online religious communities also continued to rise in popularity, some focused on theological discussion or religious study, others offering prayer and support or providing a common ground for affirming religious identity.

The early 2000s saw a debate emerge among religious leaders about how religion online, especially individualised information-seeking and engagement, was changing religious culture. Clergy and religious leaders reflected on the extent to which they needed to adapt or to take control of the internet and culture in such a way as to recoup authority they saw as having been undermined by online practices. Within internet studies, debates arose regarding whether the internet encouraged diversity of religious dialogue as a place where people could build bridges or whether people gravitated to the same groups online as offline, reinforcing religious ghettos and stereotypes. Another debate was whether the internet empowered individuals and was going to be a good thing for religion and even political and social culture, or whether it threatened offline authority. In the 2000s many religious congregations were beginning to see the importance of having a digital presence to be able to connect to spiritual information-seekers online, as well as how the internet could extend their mission and outreach with things like online fatwa sites and bringing official and unofficial religious leaders together to answer questions generated from religious dialogue online.

The 2010s saw significant changes in the technology influencing how people practise religion online. One example is the evolution of cyberchurches from a broadcast style of communication to more virtual interactive environments. Early cyberchurch entities were often websites set up by independent groups seeking to replicate or mirror some feature of church life online through their design or the resources they offered, such as providing a place to leave prayer requests. Then cyberchurches emerged, attempting to emulate aspects of offline church services online using technologies such as IRC chat, podcasts or RealAudio players for sermons, singing and limited engagement between congregants. The rise of the virtual world saw many groups embracing Second Life or other platforms to create a more interactive online worship experience, such as the Anglican Cathedral in Second Life and the Church of Fools. Now, the internet has become a tool to extend a church's offline ministry to the online context. Many multisite churches also have internet campuses, offering satellite services via various iPhone and Facebook apps. Cyberchurches continue to raise interesting questions about the implications of replicating offline church online or the extent to which the internet offers an opportunity to reflect on what constitutes church for a specific community. Furthermore, experimentation and variation on these tactics emerged throughout the COVID-19 pandemic, building on nearly 40 years of churches in America and abroad doing church online.

Now, in an era of social media, we also see that Jesus has his own Facebook page, the Buddha tweets and you can download a variety of religious mobile phone apps that can help you pray towards Mecca or connect with the Pope. We also see religious groups leveraging the advantages of social media, such as the innovative work of the United Church of Canada. At the same time, the desire to avoid problematic moral content has led religious groups to create religiously framed versions of various social media applications for their specific communities, such as GodTube.com, a Christian-filtered version of YouTube. As new media have become embedded in our daily patterns, our technology helps extend our abilities to integrate spirituality in our everyday lives in new ways.

In addition, Christianity and religion on the internet have also been significantly shaped by the impact of religious digital creatives, or RDCs. These are individuals with technological skills that grant them a level of public prominence in media contexts and thereby influence within religious institutions. They might be app designers, webmasters or technical directors at churches whose technical expertise uniquely positions them to exercise some authority over how Christianity and specific churches are engaged with and perceived online and beyond. One example to illustrate the phenomenon and power of RDCs is that of 'Confession: A Roman Catholic App', released in 2011. Created in conjunction with advisers and leaders of American Catholicism, the app was designed as a preparatory guide for adherents but not as a replacement for face-to-face confession. Still, the app showed the influence of technology and technological experts in contemporary American Christianity, even eliciting a response from the Vatican approving of the app but offering guidance for its use. RDCs occupy diverse roles as digital entrepreneurs, spokespersons and strategists who use their technical skills to contribute meaningfully to the growth and image of their respective churches.

North American Christianity's use of electronic media and the internet thus involves more individuals in the performance and maintenance of their faith and the faiths of others. As a uniquely flexible tool, the internet has encouraged the growth of new forms of worship, empowered technical and creative individuals in their contributions to the faith, and built new forms of community via networked connections and online spaces. While these changes have occurred throughout the world, North American Christianity has been at the forefront of many innovations in the use of digital media to impact worship and other practices of the faith.

Conclusion

From mass media industries to the power and authority of individuals in the internet era, Christians in North America have always negotiated the use and role of media in the faith. As Christianity's proliferation was innately tied to emerging media forms like the book, it is no surprise that North American Christians have engaged media as tools for spreading and defining the faith in their specific cultural context. In closing, this essay surveys developing areas of research from digital religious studies and their relation to the study of media and Christianity in North America.

Digital religion has been characterised by four 'waves' of research. The first focused on enthusiastically describing new aspects of cyberspace and their relation to religion and religious communities while theorising about the expansive possibilities that the internet offered to religious groups. The second employed a more realistic perspective to categorise trends within internet studies and the use of the internet in religious contexts. A third wave turned towards theoretical and interpretive research to identify methods, tools and larger theoretical frameworks and themes for the study of religion and new media. The fourth and current wave incorporates perspectives from critical approaches to media and emphasises the integration and negotiation of religious beliefs, practices and identities into studies of how life 'online' and 'offline' have often merged in the contemporary media sphere.

North American culture has in many ways been shaped by its media. Christianity in this context is no different. North American culture has also been marked by an innate instability, a constant sense of growth in the effort to achieve a better, more representative democracy. As this culture has shifted and changed, so too has the relationship of Christianity to that culture. As such, the fourth wave of critical digital religion scholarship is a timely intervention in the continued study of the history and use of media in North American Christianity.

Bibliography

Campbell, Heidi A. (ed.), *Digital Religion: Understanding Religious Practice in New Media Worlds* (London: Routledge, 2013).

Hendershot, Heather, *Shaking the World for Jesus: Media and Conservative Evangelical Culture* (Chicago, IL: University of Chicago Press, 2004).

Hutchings, Tim, *Creating Church Online: Ritual, Community and New Media* (London: Routledge, 2017).

Romanowski, William D., *Reforming Hollywood: How American Protestants Fought for Freedom at the Movies* (Oxford: Oxford University Press, 2012).

Schultze, Quentin, *Televangelism and American Culture: The Business of Popular Religion* (Grand Rapids, MI: Baker Book House, 1991).

Conclusion

The Future of Christianity in North America

Robert Chao Romero

> As a Latino growing up as the son of an undocumented pastor, my experience was much different from those who surrounded me. I felt that I could not identify with my peers and I always felt out of place. My white peers accepted me in the way that I stood in right by being [part of their denomination], but I was not accepted because of my skin color, my race, or my father's undocumented status. I wanted to believe in what my family and church taught me as truth but I slowly drifted away from my beliefs as a result of the testimony I received from the Anglo church and their members. Even to this day those same Protestants refer to us as 'wetbacks, beaners, and spics.' I find myself conflicted with my identity.

This note was written to me by a student in a religious studies course on the history of the Brown Church. His conflict of cultural and religious identity reflects several of the notable demographic and sociological trends discussed in this volume and presages the future of Christianity in the USA. As the North American church has diversified through immigration from Latin America, Asia and Africa in recent years, a reactionary movement of white Christian nationalism has arisen that conflates the church with US civil religion and rejects immigrant Christians as undesirable newcomers and even illegitimate believers. One result is that millions of Latino young adults, as well as millennials and GenZ of all cultural backgrounds, are fleeing the church, repelled by the increasingly explicit equation of Christianity with white nationalism. Perhaps unsurprisingly, and despite their loud and vocal presence in the popular US imagination, this brand of white Evangelical Christianity is in sharp numerical decline.

At the same time, however, the opposite pole of progressive Euro-American Christianity is likewise experiencing a strong downturn. Some elements of this politically progressive expression of Christianity limit faith to social activism, while de-emphasising personal transformation and deep spiritual encounter with the Holy Spirit. The fundamentalist–modernist debates of a century ago seem to have reached the end of a road as their contemporary denominational progeny do not seem to possess within themselves what is required to successfully address the pressing problems and spiritual hunger of our current day. A symptom of all of this is the flight of millions of 'nones', such as my student, from organised religion and church affiliation, largely across generational lines. People feel that there must be something more than Christianity as a Sunday morning reiteration of a conservative or progressive political talk show. As in the days of Jesus of Nazareth, however, hope sometimes springs from unexpected and forsaken places such as 'Galilee of the Gentiles', and the rapidly growing immigrant church holds much promise for the future revitalisation of Christianity in North America.

Decline of Euro-American Christianity

White Christian nationalism is part of a long historical tradition of North American religion tracing back to the founding of the USA, as well as the theology of Manifest Destiny that fuelled its westward expansion. As reflected in the following prayer of Baptist minister Isaac Kolloch from 4 July 1878, the intertwining of white nationalism, race, class and US civil religion is nothing new:

> We believe, O Lord, that the foundations of our government were laid by Thine own hand; that all the steps and stages of our progress have been under Thy watch and ward … We meet together today to celebrate the anniversary of our national birth, and we pray that we may be enabled to carry out the divine principles which inspired our noble sires and others, and we pray that … capital may respect the rights of labor, and that labor may honor capital; that the Chinese must go … and good men stay.

Kolloch intoned these insidious words in San Francisco as part of the anti-Chinese campaigns of the late nineteenth century that culminated in the passage of the Chinese Exclusion Act of 1882. Sadly, white worker unions played a central role in the Sinophobic movement and portrayed Chinese immigrant labourers as a racially and culturally inferior cheap labour force with which they could not compete. After Kolloch's endorsement of the Workingman's Party in 1878, it is said that white working-class attendance in his church skyrocketed and, drawing upon his newfound religious and political acclaim, Kolloch became the eighteenth mayor of San Francisco the following year.

It is perhaps obvious to state, but the Make America Great Again (MAGA) movement, under the leadership of Donald Trump and white Evangelical figures such as Franklin Graham, Paula White and Jerry Falwell, Jr, have followed the same time-tested civil religion playbook of Isaac Kolloch and others. According to civil religion, religious clergy work in symbiotic relationship with a narrowly defined civil community and bring assurances of God's favour. A civil community is defined by a set of religious understandings and practices, and also sometimes a racial or ethnic component. Membership in the civil community is established by birth, and those of the civil community define themselves in relation to 'outsiders' and 'enemies'. Following this framework, MAGA defines its own civil community as those of white European descent and appeals particularly to the disaffected class of white workers. Mexican, Latino, Muslim and Asian immigrants are outsiders and enemies who threaten the 'American dream'. As chaplains of the empire, Graham, White, Falwell and even some Latino Evangelical pastors, such as Guillermo Maldonado and Samuel Rodriguez, have brought false assurances of God's favour to Trump's movement through their various expressions of public support. Given the rapid numerical decline of white Evangelical Christians in the past decade, coupled with their high median age of 56 years, it is evident that this brand of Christianity is in the early stages of collapse. Nonetheless, because it is a time-tested, effective tool of white identity politics, white Christian nationalism will no doubt continue to be a powerful political subdenomination of Evangelicalism in the coming decades.

At the opposite religious and political pole, a movement of progressive Christianity has surfaced in recent years to challenge the rise of white Christian nationalism. Largely expressed through the mainline denominational descendants of the fundamentalist–modernist debates, some elements of this politically progressive expression of Christianity stress the social implications of the gospel, while de-emphasising personal experiences of radical spiritual encounter with the Holy Spirit. In recent years, progressive Christians have championed issues such as immigration reform, eco-activism, the ordination of women, LGBTQ civil rights and marriage equality. Though found in some strands of Evangelicalism, progressive Christianity is largely associated with mainline denominations such as the Episcopal Church, the United Methodist Church, the United Church of Christ and the Evangelical Lutheran Church in America. Similar to their more conservative Evangelical counterparts, white mainline Protestants have also experienced a steady decline in numbers, coupled with a median age of 50. Without significant intervention, this downturn will likely continue into the next several decades.

Though these two poles of Euro-American Protestant Christianity by no means represent the full denominational spectrum of Christianity in North America, the political and cultural divisions they represent are to be found within most other Christian denominations, including the Roman Catholic Church. A bellwether of these conflicts and increasing discontent with institutional Christianity is the flight of millions from organised religion and church affiliation, as well as the dramatic drop in regular church attendance, largely along generational lines. For tens of millions of millennials and GenZ, the politically tainted religious approaches of their parents and grandparents are insufficient. Neither Christianity as a frame for progressive activism bereft of deep spiritual encounter, nor Christianity as a proxy for religious nationalism and personal self-fulfilment, is sufficient to meet the deepest spiritual hungers of the coming generations. Owing to factors such as age structure and religious switching, such trends of religious disaffiliation will continue into the next several decades unabated, and it is estimated that the numbers of religiously unaffiliated will increase to 26% of the entire US population by 2050. This translates into 111 million individuals.

Notably, the Canadian church has experienced similar trends in secularisation and the decline of Christian affiliation. Among Canadians born in the period 1980–99, only 32% self-identify as Christian, as opposed to 85% of older adults. As a consequence of such religious trends, the Anglican Church of Canada sadly predicts that it might have no members by 2040. By 2050, moreover, it is projected that only 60% of all Canadians will claim a Christian denominational affiliation and 26% will identify as religiously unaffiliated. The remaining nations of North America, Greenland, Bermuda, and Saint Pierre and Miquelon, will retain overwhelming Christian majorities over the next several decades owing to smaller, more stable populations and the deep entrenchment of the Christian faith.

Immigration and Diversity

At the same time that North America is experiencing such an overall marked collapse in formal religious identification, it is also experiencing a diversity explosion, reminiscent of John's vision of the New Jerusalem, with people from every language, tongue, tribe and nation. The USA is in the early stages of a profound racial and ethnic *mestizaje*, in which cultural groups from every continent on the globe are freely mixing in a historically unprecedented way. From 2010 to 2020, the multiracial population of the USA grew 276%, to 33.8 million people; the Black or African American population increased from 38.9 million to 46.9 million; the American Indian and Alaska Native population increased from 5.2 million in 2010 to 9.7 million in 2020 – an 86.5% increase. The Hispanic/Latino population climbed by 23% to 62.1 million; and the Asian American community, comprising people having origins in East Asia, Southeast Asia or the Indian subcontinent, increased to 24 million. The white population, itself also comprising diverse ethnic origins in Europe, the Middle East and North Africa, remained the largest racial or ethnicity group in the USA, with 204.3 million people identifying as white alone and another 31.1 million reporting white in combination with another group. However, the 'white alone' population decreased by 8.6% from 2010. The Census Bureau projects that the multiracial population will triple by 2060, and it is estimated that as much as 20% of the entire US population will be mixed race by 2050. In fact, in the near future, the growth of the mixed-race population will outpace that of Asians, Latinos, whites, Blacks and Native Americans.

In the decades to come, these cultural demographic trends will continue to become more pronounced. By 2060, the white population will shrink by 20 million, though it will still constitute the single largest ethnic/cultural group, at 32% of the total US population. During the same period, the number of foreign-born individuals will grow to 69 million, or roughly 14–17% of the total US population. This represents the highest proportion of foreign-born persons since the height of European immigration to the USA in the late nineteenth century. By 2060, moreover, non-Hispanic whites will comprise only 36% of those under 18 years of age, the Asian and Hispanic descent populations will double in size, and the multiracial population will triple. The demographic future of the USA is written on the wall. The USA is in a profound pluralistic transition. Canada is similarly on a fast track to diversity as nearly half of its entire population will be foreign-born by 2031.

These demographic changes are driven by several major factors that also hint at the future of Christianity in the USA. First is the ageing of the US population. Within the next decade, baby boomers will all be older than 65, and older adults will come to outnumber children for the first time in US history. Second, the USA is also experiencing falling fertility rates. As a consequence of this shift towards an increasingly older population and declining birth rates, there will be a need to turn to international migration in order sustain the labour force, economy and market demand. The end result is that immigration will soon become the primary driver of population growth. Immigrants will increasingly sustain the USA socially, economically and even religiously.

This rapid trend towards cultural diversity is reflected in the changing demographics of the US church. The North American church is 'browning' as white representation is in decline and all other ethnic groups are together increasing. Immigration from places such as Latin America, Africa and Asia is fuelling this rapid ecclesial change and, in fact, one in three American Evangelicals is now a person of colour. Accordingly, approximately a quarter of all Christians in the USA come from firstgeneration immigrant families. As part of these rapid changes, grassroots expressions of church are gradually replacing the formal structures and practices of Euro-American Christendom.

These domestic trends coincide with the fact that the global pendulum of Christianity has already swung in the direction of Africa, Latin America and Asia. The expression that Christianity is a 'white man's religion' is already not true. By 2050, moreover, it is estimated that the majority of Christians in the world will live in Africa, Asia and Latin America, with four out of every 10 Christians residing in sub-Saharan Africa. The present and future face of the Church of Jesus of Nazareth is 'brown', and Christianity is returning to its historical origins as a faith of the marginalised born in the Near East. In the decades to come, Christian immigrants from Latin America, Africa and Asia will redefine the US church in practice, polity and theology.

Christian immigrants from the Majority World often bring with them a vibrant personal faith driven by radical dependence on Jesus made necessary by suffering and the struggle to survive. There is an *'abuelita faith'*, or 'grandmother's faith', that has been tested and purified by many testimonies of God's faithfulness and passed down to successive generations. Such radical belief is often associated with the rapid global spread of Protestant Pentecostalism, as well as with Charismatic Catholic Christianity in Africa and Latin America, but this characteristic of Southern Christianity transcends formal Pentecostal denominational affiliation. Global theologians also bring distinct perspectives that have the potential to address many of the burning spiritual and social questions facing the North American church. Calvin and Zwingli have good things to say, but little poignance for pressing issues of race and culture. The faith of immigrants will revitalise the US church in many ways that are presently unforeseen. From such faith, revival can spring.

The Rise of the Brown Church

Stated another way, Christians from the global South bring distinct community cultural wealth and spiritual capital to the waning US church. The Euro-American church is coming close to the end of its spiritual rope and does not possess within itself the cultural resources to save itself. In biblical terms, John the Seer refers to this community cultural wealth as the 'glory and honour of the nations' (Revelation 21: 26). According to John, every ethnic group of the world possesses distinct 'glory and honour' that are of eternal value for the service of God, the church and the world. This cultural treasure or 'glory' is a reflection of the glory of God in and through each of us as God's unique children. From this perspective, contrary to some white Christian nationalist discourse, God does not make 'shithole' countries, and those of every ethnic community possess equal dignity in God's eyes. The 'glory and honour' of the nations can be understood to include not only tangible aspects of ethnic culture, such as food, music, dance, literature and architecture, but also the distinct lenses and perspectives that every ethnic group brings to the world and to the church.

As an example of the latter, the Latin American church offers the US church the benefit of half a millennium of theological reflection around issues of racial justice. Though spiritual deconstruction and reconstruction related to race are largely new phenomena within the Euro-American church, Latinos have been wrestling with such questions for many years as part of the Brown Church – the prophetic ecclesial community of Latinas/os which has contested racial and social injustice in Latin America and the USA for the past 500 years. In every such instance of injustice, the Brown Church has risen to challenge the religious, socioeconomic and political status quo. Collectively, the Brown Church has challenged such great evils as the Spanish Conquest and Spanish colonialism, the *sistema de castas*, Manifest Destiny and US settler colonialism in the Southwest, Latin American dictatorships, US imperialism in Central America, the oppression of farm workers, as well as the current exploitation and marginalisation of undocumented immigrants. It is significant to note that the Brown Church has comprised an ecumenical body of Roman Catholic and Protestant followers of Christ who have worked both in cooperation with, and in prophetic witness to, official ecclesiastical authorities and institutions. The Brown Church has been a repository of 500 years of Latino community cultural wealth that may be applied for the benefit of the US church.

As a strategy of survival, the Brown Church has decolonised its Christology and largely resisted the North American bifurcation of the gospel into personal and social, announced and embodied. Latino/a theologians such as Orlando Costas, Virgilio Elizondo and Elizabeth Conde-Frazier have emphasised the marginalised socioeconomic and political roots of Jesus the Galilean. Galilee was in fact far from the centre of religious, political and economic power in Jerusalem and most Galileans, like Jesus, were poor, bilingual and spoke with an accent. They were oppressed by Roman colonisers as well as by the elites of their own people and shunned as cultural 'mixed breeds' or 'mestizos'. Galilee was the 'hood' or 'barrio' of Jesus's day, and the Brown Church takes comfort in knowing that Jesus of Nazareth, seen as a marginalised Galilean himself, relates to the suffering of the Latino community and marginalised communities of the USA of every ethnic background. Galilee represents not only the Latino immigrant communities of East Los Angeles, San Antonio and Miami, but also the most disenfranchised Black and white communities of urban centres and the rural South; suffering Southeast Asian communities in Long Beach and Wisconsin; as well as the First Nations of North America living in urban and suburban cities and sovereign Indigenous communities. In the economy of Latina/o theology, Jesus the Galilean is big enough to hold the suffering of us all.

Within a Latino theological understanding, the 'good news' of Jesus is also holistic, with equally profound personal and social implications. From the distinct treasury of experience and theological reflection of the Brown Church, Latino theologians have resisted the false modernist–fundamentalist tendencies to dichotomise the gospel as either social justice or personal salvation. According to René Padilla and the framework of *misión integral*, or holistic mission, Christianity involves 'the mission of the whole church to the whole of humanity in all its forms, personal, communal, social, economic, ecological, and political'. Nothing and no one is left out of the salvation of Jesus the Messiah.

Moreover, the gospel is like a plane with two wings. One wing involves its verbal proclamation and the other its embodiment in social responsibility and love of neighbour. If either wing is missing, as is often the case in many North American ecclesial models, the plane does not fly. As Padilla wrote:

> The proclamation of the gospel (kerygma) and the demonstration of the gospel that gives itself in service (diakonía) form an indissoluble whole. One without the other is an incomplete, mutilated (mutilado) gospel and, consequently, contrary to the will of God. From this perspective, it is foolish to ask about the relative importance of evangelism and social responsibility. This would be equivalent to asking about the relative importance of the right wing and the left wing of a plane. (David C. Kirkpatrick, 'C. René Padilla and the Origins of Integral Mission in Post-War Latin America', *Journal of Ecclesiastical History* 67:2 (April 2016), 351–371; 353, 368)

These examples of Latino Christology and soteriology are but a small sampling of the distinct cultural treasure and wealth that the Latin American immigrant church brings to North America. If one extends this reflection to consider the vastness of the combined community cultural wealth brought by immigrant churches from Africa, Asia, Latin America and the Middle East, it is easy to become quickly overwhelmed. Asians represent the fastest-growing immigrant group in the USA, and Black immigrants, at more than four million, have increased by 30% in the past decade. Given their critical mass and distinct spiritual practices rooted in vital faith, Asian and Black Christian immigrants will no doubt have a deep impact upon the future of North American Christianity. Their ethnic churches will draw curious onlookers and participants searching for authentic faith beyond a white paradigm, and their second-generation integrated church plants will offer spiritual homes for many cross-cultural families in the coming years. Characterised by theological orthodoxy, Asian and Black immigrant churches will also swing the doctrinal pendulum in the general direction of historic Christian faith. Known for evangelistic zeal, some African and Asian churches might also pioneer models of evangelisation among the increasing population of white religious 'nones'. In the face dramatic change, declining white churches and denominations might also turn to immigrant churches for models of revitalisation in theology and worship, as well as for future leadership.

Cultural Diversity: Challenge and Possibility

A sense of hope quickly rises when one imagines the diverse 'glory and honour' of the global South as metaphorical jasper, sapphire, agate, emerald, onyx, jacinth, chrysolite, beryl, topaz, gold and silver, and contemplates the potential the immigrant church possesses for transforming not only the North American church, but all of society. It is like a dress rehearsal for Heaven and the New Jerusalem, as described in the Book of Revelation:

> After this I looked, and there before me was a great multitude that no one could count, from every nation, tribe, people and language, standing before the throne and before the Lamb. They were wearing white robes and were holding palm branches in their hands. And they cried out in a loud voice: 'Salvation belongs to our God, who sits on the throne, and to the Lamb'. (Revelation 7: 9–10)

Although it may be said that the Holy Spirit is birthing such dramatic cultural changes, the structures and theologies of local churches, denominations, seminaries and Christian colleges and universities largely reflect the church of 50 years ago and another era. Existing ecclesial structures trace their lineage to times of slavery, Jim Crow segregation and the white flight of the 1970s and 1980s, when the glory and honour of non-Anglo cultures went unrecognised and were in fact often deliberately excluded. In order to pave the way for the ethnic and cultural reformation of the US church, church leaders must first acknowledge this past and do the hard work of coming to understand the ways in which white normativity has shaped ecclesial leadership, structure and practice. This does not mean the complete eradication of Euro-American church systems, but it does require reclaiming the glory and honour of Euro-American church traditions, sifting racial sin, and rebuilding the North American church based upon the diverse cultural treasures of the various ethnic groups which will comprise the US church in the coming decades. The Black Church is owed a critical seat at this table and discussion, for it has championed racial justice in North America for centuries. Another important question for exploration is how immigrant churches will learn from, and relate to, both the Black and Native American Churches that have borne the racial burden and heat of the day for people of colour throughout the history of the USA.

The philosophical commitment to 'colour-blindness' that is found in many Euro-American churches is at once both a help and a hindrance to reaching this future. In a positive sense, many within the North American church today would affirm that all people are equal and created in the image of God, regardless of cultural heritage. This aspect of contemporary Christian colour-blindness obviously aligns with scriptural truth and represents a big improvement from that of 60 years ago, when many white Christians confidently argued that they were racially superior to all other ethnic groups and that God condoned the 'segregation of the races'. This sense of 'colour-blindness' lines up squarely with Paul's words in the book of Galatians:

> So in Christ Jesus you are all children of God through faith, for all of you who were baptized into Christ have clothed yourselves with Christ. There is neither Jew nor Gentile, neither slave nor free, nor is there male and female, for you are all one in Christ Jesus. If you belong to Christ, then you are Abraham's seed, and heirs according to the promise. (Galatians 3: 26–9)

At the same time, however, it is also common to find a deficient view of colour-blindness in US churches. This view posits unbiblically that cultural diversity is unimportant to both God and the church. It flows from faulty theology that lacks understanding of the positive value of what John describes as the 'glory and honour of the nations'. By God's design, every ethnic group of the world possesses distinct community cultural treasure and wealth for the benefit of the church and the world. Theological colour-blindness is harmful because it overlooks non-white community cultural wealth and does not appreciate the critical leadership benefits that flow from diverse cultural representation. It thereby deprives the North American church of the diverse leadership that will be required in order to successfully navigate the present and future of race relations in the USA. Claiming to not 'see' colour easily becomes an excuse by some to dismiss out of hand cultural perspectives with which they disagree and to deny the need for cultural diversification as an urgent matter requiring proactive solutions.

Although the immigrant church holds much promise for the future of Christianity in North America, immigrant churches also possess 'ticking time bombs' that, if left unchecked, might sabotage the potential for long-term revival of the US church. Examples include the prosperity gospel and Christian nationalism that were exported from the USA in recent years and that many immigrants carry back with them. Many immigrants also bring with them belief structures, practices and financial dependencies which have yet to be 'decolonised', or untethered from the Euro-American church and its power structures. Moreover, it is all too easy for many immigrants to assimilate dangerous US theologies through their denominational and social ties. Nationalistic theologies are easily absorbed through media sources, such as the Trinity Broadcasting Network and Fox News, which are always just a click away. That being said and the USA aside, in accordance with traditional Christian doctrine, and as a theological corollary to the 'glory and honour of the nations', immigrant families also bring their own patterns of personal, generational and cultural sin that wreak havoc in churches and in families all on their own (Romans 3: 23; Revelation 21: 27).

These promises and dangers of the immigrant church speak to the vital importance of healthy Christian education and theological formation. Fortunately, such efforts have long been underway by immigrant-led grassroots organisations. One example is the Association for Hispanic Theological Education (Asociación para la Educación Teológica Hispana, AETH). Founded in 1992 by noted theologian Justo Gonzalez, AETH is a network of dozens of Latino seminaries and Bible institutes in the USA, Canada, Puerto Rico, Latin America and the wider Caribbean that are dedicated to the promotion and improvement of Hispanic theological education. AETH sponsors annual conferences, communities of practice and monthly *conversatorios* and partners with the Association of Theological Schools to create unique on-ramps into theological education for the Hispanic church community. Substantively, AETH focuses upon the preparation of believers for holistic mission and creates theological content with practical application to day-to-day life and ministry in the Latino community.

Conclusion

In sum, fuelled by an ageing constituency and political division, the days of Euro-American Christianity are waning. Jesus as proxy for partisan political skirmishes on the right or left strays far from the historic Christian message, and the effects are manifest in the downward spiral of white evangelical Christianity, mainline Christianity and even Euro-American Catholicism. Notwithstanding such numerical decline, the two brands of white nationalistic Christianity and progressive Christianity will likely continue to contest with one another in the coming decades because they represent powerful interests and are fuelled by significant financial resources. Dissatisfaction with these two dominant church approaches is expressed most clearly along generational lines as millions of young adults are rejecting formal religious affiliation. Ecclesial hope springs, however, from the diversity explosion which will increasingly define North American church life and society. Christian immigrants from Africa, Latin America, Asia and the Middle East possess thriving faith and vast treasuries of community cultural wealth which hold promise to revive the church of North America and address the most divisive cultural and political issues of the future.

Bibliography

Barna, George and David Kinnaman, *Churchless: Understanding Today's Unchurched and How to Connect with Them* (Carol Stream, IL: Tyndale Momentum, 2016).

Conde-Frazier, Elizabeth, *Atando Cabos: Latinx Contributions to Theological Education* (Grand Rapids, MI: Eerdmans, 2021).

Frey, William H., *Diversity Explosion: How New Racial Demographics Are Remaking America* (Washington, DC: Brookings Institution Press, 2014).

Olupona, Jacob and Regina Gemignani, *African Immigrant Religions in America* (New York: New York University Press, 2007).

Yong, Amos, *Renewing the Church by the Spirit: Theological Education After Pentecost* (Grand Rapids, MI: Eerdmans, 2020).

Appendices

Christianity by Country

The table that begins overleaf provides a quick-reference, country-by-country listing for Christianity and its major traditions for all the countries that appear in this volume. These statistics are found in the *World Christian Database* (see Methodology and Sources) and all figures relate to 1970 and 2020. Small numbers are left unrounded to distinguish known small populations from zero but do not represent precise estimates.

The columns are as follows:

- Country (name of country in English)
- Region in which country is located
- Total population of country (United Nations estimate, 1970, 2020) and total numbers and percentage of population in each tradition
- Percentage mean annual growth rate, 1970–2020.

The last page of the table presents regional totals.

Christianity by Country

Country	Region	Tradition	1970 Population	%	2020 Population	%	Growth rate (%), 1970–2020
Bermuda	North America	Total population	52,600	100.0%	62,300	100.0%	0.3%
		Christians	50,400	95.8%	55,200	88.7%	0.2%
		Anglicans	22,000	41.9%	11,000	17.7%	-1.4%
		Independents	4,600	8.8%	9,000	14.5%	1.4%
		Protestants	11,500	21.8%	23,000	36.9%	1.4%
		Catholics	7,500	14.3%	9,300	14.9%	0.4%
		Evangelicals	6,200	11.8%	14,500	23.3%	1.7%
		Pentecostals/Charismatics	2,900	5.5%	14,800	23.8%	3.3%
Canada	North America	Total population	21,374,000	100.0%	37,742,000	100.0%	1.1%
		Christians	20,185,000	94.4%	23,952,000	63.5%	0.3%
		Anglicans	1,177,000	5.5%	570,000	1.5%	-1.4%
		Independents	761,000	3.6%	1,305,000	3.5%	1.1%
		Orthodox	561,000	2.6%	1,220,000	3.2%	1.6%
		Protestants	4,133,000	19.3%	2,900,000	7.7%	-0.7%
		Catholics	9,066,000	42.4%	14,100,000	37.4%	0.9%
		Evangelicals	2,566,000	12.0%	2,085,000	5.5%	-0.4%
		Pentecostals/Charismatics	709,000	3.3%	2,750,000	7.3%	2.7%
Greenland	North America	Total population	46,100	100.0%	56,800	100.0%	0.4%
		Christians	45,300	98.3%	54,400	95.9%	0.4%
		Independents	100	0.2%	930	1.6%	4.6%
		Protestants	35,000	75.9%	36,000	63.5%	0.1%
		Catholics	50	0.1%	140	0.2%	2.1%
		Evangelicals	1,200	2.7%	2,800	4.9%	1.6%
		Pentecostals/Charismatics	500	1.1%	6,200	10.9%	5.2%
Saint Pierre and Miquelon	North America	Total population	5,600	100.0%	5,800	100.0%	0.1%
		Christians	5,500	98.4%	5,500	94.4%	0.0%
		Independents	0	0.0%	30	0.5%	7.0%
		Protestants	50	0.9%	80	1.4%	0.9%
		Catholics	5,200	94.4%	5,300	91.6%	0.0%
		Evangelicals	8	0.1%	15	0.3%	1.3%
		Pentecostals/Charismatics	5	0.1%	130	2.2%	6.7%

Country	Region	Tradition	1970 Population	%	2020 Population	%	Growth rate (%), 1970–2020
United States	North America	Total population	209,513,000	100.0%	331,003,000	100.0%	0.9%
		Christians	191,202,000	91.3%	245,457,000	74.2%	0.5%
		Anglicans	3,196,000	1.5%	2,120,000	0.6%	-0.8%
		Independents	37,285,000	17.8%	63,800,000	19.3%	1.1%
		Orthodox	4,309,000	2.1%	7,150,000	2.2%	1.0%
		Protestants	57,091,000	27.2%	51,915,000	15.7%	-0.2%
		Catholics	48,305,000	23.1%	73,900,000	22.3%	0.9%
		Evangelicals	44,883,000	21.4%	69,000,000	20.8%	0.9%
		Pentecostals/Charismatics	13,833,000	6.6%	65,000,000	19.6%	3.1%
North America	North America	Total population	230,992,000	100.0%	368,870,000	100.0%	0.9%
		Christians	211,489,000	91.6%	269,524,000	73.1%	0.5%
		Anglicans	4,395,000	1.9%	2,701,000	0.7%	-1.0%
		Independents	38,051,000	16.5%	65,115,000	17.7%	1.1%
		Orthodox	4,870,000	2.1%	8,370,000	2.3%	1.1%
		Protestants	61,270,000	26.5%	54,874,000	14.9%	-0.2%
		Catholics	57,384,000	24.8%	88,015,000	23.9%	0.9%
		Evangelicals	47,457,000	20.5%	71,102,000	19.3%	0.8%
		Pentecostals/Charismatics	14,545,000	6.3%	67,771,000	18.4%	3.1%

Methodology and Sources of Christian and Religious Affiliation

Todd M. Johnson and Gina A. Zurlo

Unless otherwise designated, the demographic figures in this book, both in the colour section and in the tables throughout, are from the *World Christian Database* (Leiden/Boston: Brill). This essay offers a concise explanation of methods and sources related to the database. It is adapted from longer treatments in Todd M. Johnson and Brian J. Grim, *The World's Religions in Figures: An Introduction to International Religious Demography* (Oxford: Wiley-Blackwell, 2013) and Todd M. Johnson and Gina A. Zurlo, *World Christian Encyclopedia*, 3rd edition (Edinburgh: Edinburgh University Press, 2019). The *World Christian Database* (*WCD*) includes detailed information on 45,000 Christian denominations and on religions in every country of the world. Extensive data are available on 234 countries and 13,000 ethno-linguistic peoples, as well as on 5,000 cities and 3,000 provinces. Information is readily available on religious activities, growth rates, religious literature, worker activity and demographics. Sources are evaluated and reviewed on a weekly basis by a professional staff dedicated to expanding and updating the *WCD*, and the database is updated quarterly.

The Right to Profess One's Choice

The starting point of this methodology is the United Nations 1948 Universal Declaration of Human Rights, Article 18:

> Everyone has the right to freedom of thought, conscience and religion; this right includes freedom to change his religion or belief, and freedom, either alone or in community with others and in public or private, to manifest his religion or belief in teaching, practice, worship and observance.

Since its promulgation, this group of phrases has been incorporated into the state constitutions of a large number of countries across the world. This fundamental right also includes the right to claim the religion of one's choice, and the right to be called a follower of that religion and to be enumerated as such. The section on religious freedom in the constitutions of very many nations uses the exact words of the Universal Declaration, and many countries instruct their census personnel to observe this principle. Public declaration must therefore be taken seriously when endeavouring to survey the extent of religious and non-religious affiliation around the world.

Religious Demography

The origins of the field of religious demography lie in the church censuses conducted in most European societies. For many years and in many countries, churches produced the most complete censuses of the population. They achieved this largely by recording baptisms and funerals. These data, however, were seen not as referring to specific religious communities, but rather to the larger homogeneous societies. With the decline of national churches in Europe beginning in the nineteenth and continuing into the twentieth century, governments began tracking births and deaths, eventually replacing churches as the main bodies collecting detailed information on human populations. Although thousands of sources for international religious demography are available, ranging from censuses and demographic surveys to statistics collected and reported by religious groups themselves, little has been done by scholars in religion, sociology, or other disciplines to collect, collate and analyse these data.

Sources

Data for religious demography fall broadly under five major headings:

1. Censuses in which a religious question is asked

In the twentieth century, approximately half the world's countries asked a question related to religion in their official national population censuses. Since 1990, however, this number has been declining as developing countries have dropped the question, deeming it too expensive (in many countries each question in a census costs well over US$1 million), uninteresting or controversial. As a result, some countries that historically included a religion question have not done so in their censuses since 1990. National censuses are the best starting point for the identification of religious adherents, because they generally cover the entire population.

2. Censuses in which an ethnicity or language question is asked

In the absence of a question on religion, another helpful piece of information from a census is ethnicity or language. This is especially true when a particular ethnic group can be equated with a particular religion. For example, over 99% of Somalis are Muslim, so the number of Somalis in, say, Sweden is an indication of a part of the Muslim community there.

Similarly, a question that asks for country of birth can be useful. If the answer is 'Nepal' there is a significant chance that the individual or community is Hindu. In each of these cases the assumption is made (if there is no further information) that the religion of the transplanted ethnic or linguistic community is the same as that in the home country.

3. Surveys and polls

In the absence of census data on religion, large-scale demographic surveys such as MEASURE (Monitoring and Evaluation to Assess and Use Results) and Demographic and Health Surveys (DHS) often include a question about the respondent's religious affiliation. In some instances, demographic surveys by groups such as UNICEF (the United Nations Children's Fund) include a religious affiliation question. Demographic surveys, although less comprehensive than a national census, have several advantages over other types of general population surveys and polls. DHS are highly regarded by demographers and social scientists, and provide valuable nationally representative data on religion. Surveys can also be commissioned in light of a dearth of data on a particular subject and results can be used to search for correlations between different variables.

4. Scholarly monographs

Every year, scholars publish hundreds of monographs on particular religions or religions in particular countries or regions. Such monographs differ from other sources in that they attempt to provide an overall profile of religion in an area or country, bringing to light local sources of quantitative data as well as qualitative information that provides layers of context and background.

5. Religion statistics in yearbooks and handbooks

Religious communities keep track of their members, using everything from simple lists to elaborate membership reports. The most detailed data collection and analysis is undertaken each year by some 45,000 Christian denominations and their 4.7 million constituent churches and congregations of believers. The latter invest over US$1.1 billion annually for a massive, decentralised and largely uncoordinated global census of Christians. In sum, they send out around 10 million printed questionnaires in 3,000 different languages, covering 180 major religious subjects reporting on 2,000 socio-religious variables. This collection of data provides a year-by-year snapshot of the progress or decline of Christianity's diverse movements, offering an enormous body of data from which researchers can track trends and make projections. Statistics collected by religious communities often enable researchers to distinguish between two categories of religionists – practising and non-practising – based on whether or not they take part in the ongoing organised life of the religion.

In addition to the above categories, there are governmental statistical reports, questionnaires and reports from collaborators, field surveys and interviews, correspondence with national informants, unpublished documentation, encyclopaedias, dictionaries and directories of religions, print and web-based contemporary descriptions of religions, and dissertations and theses on religion. The best practices in determining the religious affiliation of any population utilise as many sources as possible.

Affiliation

There are at least two different perspectives on what it means to be a Christian: professing Christians and affiliated Christians. Utilising the United Nations Universal Declaration of Human Rights as a foundation, 'professing Christians' means all those who profess to be Christians in government censuses or public-opinion polls, that is, who declare or identify themselves as Christians, who say 'I am a Christian' or 'We are Christians' when asked the question 'What is your religion?'

However, not all those who profess to be Christians are affiliated to organised churches and denominations. Therefore, 'affiliated Christians' are those known to the churches or known to the clergy (usually by names and addresses) and claimed in their statistics, that is, those enrolled on the churches' books or records, with totals that can be substantiated. This usually means all known baptised Christians and their children, and other adherents; it is sometimes termed the 'total Christian community' (because affiliated Christians are those who are not primarily individual Christians but who primarily belong to the corporate community of Christ), or 'inclusive membership' (because affiliated Christians are church members). This definition of 'Christians' is what the churches usually mean by the term (and thus the *WCD*), and statistics on such affiliated Christians are what the churches themselves collect and publish. In all countries, it may be assumed with confidence that the churches know better than the state how many Christians are affiliated to them. This therefore indicates a second measure of the total Christians that is quite independent of the first (government census figures of professing Christians).

Children

The family is by far the most important instrumentality through which individuals acquire personal, cultural and social self-identification. In consequence, children of church members are more likely to remain members than those whose parents are not church members. Children of ardent and practising Christians usually are, to the extent that their years permit, ardent and practising Christians. However, many churches do not enumerate children under 15 years. One reason is that it has been widely noted that most conversion crises occur in the 13–20-year age group in Christian families or in majority Christian contexts. On this view, therefore, children who have not yet reached 15 cannot reasonably be expected to be practising and believing Christians. The *WCD* takes the opposite view: children and infants also can properly be called Christians, and can actively and regularly (to the extent of their ability) practise the Christian faith. Consequently, where Christian denominations do not count children in their membership rolls, their membership is reported in our adult category. A total community figure is calculated (in the absence of any additional information from the denomination) by adding in the average number of children reported in United Nations statistics for the given country. Thus, the total community figures are comparable from one denomination to the next whether or not they count children in their membership.

Choice of Best Data Available

Religious demography must attempt to be comprehensive. In certain countries where no hard statistical data or reliable surveys are available, researchers have to rely on the informed estimates of experts in the area and subject. Researchers make no detailed attempt at a critique of each nation's censuses and polls or each church's statistical operations. After examining what is available, researchers then select the best data available until such time as better data come into existence. In addition, there are a number of areas of religious life where it is impossible to obtain accurate statistics, usually because of state opposition to particular tradition(s). Thus it will probably never be possible to get exact numbers of, for example, atheists in Indonesia or Bahá'í in Iran. Where such information is necessary, reasonable and somewhat conservative estimates are made.

Reconciling Discrepancies in Survey Data

There are post-survey strategies that help general population surveys better reflect the actual composition of a particular country. For instance, if in a survey of 1,000 people, 60% were women and 40% were men, but we know that women and men are each 50% of the country's total population based on a recent census, then each woman's response on the general population survey would be weighted down by a factor of 500/600 and each man's response would be weighted up by a factor of 500/400. Such adjustments are called weighting.

Other adjustments made to general population surveys may require taking into account that they are meant to be representative of only adult populations. Therefore their results require adjustments, particularly if some religious groups have more children than others in the same country. This requires either a complete roster of members of each household or some other way to estimate the number of children living in the household with the adults. When a complete roster is unavailable, most estimates of religious affiliation of children assume that they have the same religion as their one of their parents (usually assumed by demographers to be the religion of the mother). Differences in fertility rates between religious groups are particularly useful in estimating religious differentials among children. This is because demographic projections include children, who will increase the size of their religious community. It may introduce some bias to the degree that the father's religion is more likely to be the religion of the children than that of the mother.

Example: Coptic Church in Egypt

At times, the results from government censuses and information from religious communities can be strikingly different. For example, in Egypt, where the vast majority of the population is Muslim, government censuses taken every 10 years have shown consistently for the past 100 years that a declining share of the population declare themselves as or profess to be Christians. In the most recent census, some 5% identified as Christian. However, church estimates point to a percentage figure three times larger (15%). This discrepancy may be due to overestimates by the churches or attributed, at least in part, to social pressure on some Christians to record themselves as Muslims. Further, according to news reports, some Egyptian Christians have complained that they are listed on official identity cards as Muslims. It also might be that church reports include Egyptian Christians working as expatriates outside of Egypt, while the census does not, or that the churches simply overestimate their numbers.

Such a lack of clarity is compounded by media reports and even Egyptian government announcements repeatedly claiming that Christians make up 10% or more of the country's approximately 80 million people, despite the fact that the census repeatedly reports only 5%. The highest share of Christians found in an Egyptian census was in 1927 (8.3%). Figures for Egyptian Christians declined in each subsequent census, with Christians seemingly making up 5.7% of the Egyptian population in 1996. The report from the most recent census, conducted in 2006, does not, however, provide data on religious affiliation, but a sample of the 2006 census data is available through the Integrated Public Use Microdata Series, International (IPUMS). They sample the same Christian share (about 5%) as the latest Egyptian Demographic and Health Survey, with a sample size of 16,527 women aged 15–49 years.

According to the Pew Forum's analysis of Global Restrictions on Religion (see www.pewforum.org), Egypt has very high scores for government restrictions on religion as well as high scores for social hostilities involving religion. These factors might lead some Christians to be cautious about revealing their identity. Regardless of the actual number, it is very likely that Christians are declining as a proportion of Egypt's population, even if their absolute numbers are not falling. On the one hand, Christian fertility in Egypt has been lower than Muslim fertility. On the other, it is possible that large numbers of Christians have left the country, although a 2012 study by the Pew Forum on the religious affiliation of migrants around the world has not found evidence of an especially large Egyptian Christian diaspora.

Dates of Statistics

It is important, in changing situations, to know the exact date (year, perhaps also month and sometimes even day) to which particular statistics apply. This methodology compares government statistics on religion with statistics from religious communities themselves; but in doing so, it must be remembered that a government census (or a public-opinion poll) is almost always taken on a single, known day, whereas, by contrast, religious statistics are compiled over a lengthy period – perhaps three, four or even five years from the local grassroots counting of heads to final compilation of totals by a large denomination or church. Denominational totals published in 2020 therefore probably refer to the situation in 2017, 2016 or even 2015.

Counting Pentecostals

Three types of Pentecostals
For the purpose of understanding the diverse global phenomenon of Pentecostalism, it is useful to divide the movement into three kinds, or types. First are denominational Pentecostals, organised into denominations in the early part of the twentieth century. Second are Charismatics, individuals in the mainline denominations (primarily after the mid-twentieth century). Third are Independent Charismatics, those who broke free of denominational Pentecostalism or mainline denominations to form their own networks. A more detailed treatment can be found in Todd M. Johnson and Gina A. Zurlo, *Introducing Spirit-Empowered Christianity: The Global Pentecostal and Charismatic Movement in the 21st Century* (Tulsa, OK: Oral Roberts University Press, 2020).

Pentecostals (Type 1)

Pentecostals are defined as Christians who are members of the explicitly Pentecostal denominations whose major characteristic is a new experience of the energising ministry of the Holy Spirit that most other Christians have considered to be highly unusual. This is interpreted as a rediscovery of the spiritual gifts of New Testament times and their restoration to ordinary Christian life and ministry. Classical Pentecostalism usually is held to have begun in the United States in 1901, although most scholars have moved to a 'multiple origins' theory of the birth of modern Pentecostalism, emphasising early activity outside of the Western World. For a brief period, Pentecostalism expected to remain an interdenominational movement within the existing churches, but from 1909 onwards its members increasingly were ejected from mainline bodies and so forced to begin new organised denominations.

Pentecostal denominations hold the distinctive teachings that all Christians should seek a post-conversion religious experience called baptism in the Holy Spirit and that a Spirit-baptised believer may receive one or more of the supernatural gifts known in the early church: the ability to prophesy; to practise divine healing through prayer; to speak (glossolalia), interpret or sing in tongues; to sing in the Spirit, dance in the Spirit, pray with upraised hands; to receive dreams, visions, words of wisdom, words of knowledge; to discern spirits; and to perform miracles, power encounters, exorcisms (casting out demons), resuscitations, deliverances, or other signs and wonders.

From 1906 onwards, the hallmark of explicitly Pentecostal denominations, by comparison with Holiness/Perfectionist denominations, has been the single addition of speaking in other tongues as the 'initial evidence' of one's having received the baptism of the Holy Spirit, whether or not one subsequently experiences regularly the gift of tongues. Most Pentecostal denominations teach that tongues-speaking is mandatory for all members, but in reality today not all members have practised this gift, either initially or as an ongoing experience. Pentecostals are defined here as all associated with explicitly Pentecostal denominations that identify themselves in explicitly Pentecostal terms, or with other denominations that as a whole are phenomenologically Pentecostal in teaching and practice.

Among Protestants (coded as 'P-') are Pentecostal denominations such as the Assemblies of God. Sub-categories of Oneness, Baptistic, Holiness, Perfectionist and Apostolic were retained from earlier research. Each minor tradition within Pentecostalism is considered to be 100% Pentecostal (all members of Pentecostal denominations are counted as Pentecostals).

Charismatics (Type 2)

Charismatics are defined as Christians affiliated to non-Pentecostal denominations (Anglican, Protestant, Catholic, Orthodox) who receive the experiences above in what has been termed the Charismatic movement. The Charismatic movement's roots go back to early Pentecostalism, but its rapid expansion has been mainly since 1960 (later called the Charismatic renewal). Charismatics usually describe themselves as having been 'renewed in the Spirit' and as experiencing the Spirit's supernatural and miraculous and energising power. They remain within, and form organised renewal groups within, their older mainline non-Pentecostal denominations (instead of leaving to join Pentecostal denominations). They demonstrate any or all of the *charismata pneumatika* (gifts of the Spirit), including signs and wonders (but with glossolalia regarded as optional).

Type 2 recognises the existence of Pentecostal individuals within the Anglican, Roman Catholic, Orthodox and Protestant traditions. These are designated 'Charismatic' and evaluated by country as Catholic Charismatics, Anglican Charismatics and so on, designating renewal within an existing tradition. For example, the beginning of the Charismatic movement in Anglican churches is described by Episcopal priest Dennis Bennett in *Nine O'Clock in the Morning* (Alachua, FL: Bridge-Logos, 1970). Traditions are assessed to determine what percentage of adherents identify themselves as Charismatics, ranging from 0% to 100%. Self-identification percentages for Charismatics were calculated by contacting renewal agencies working within denominations.

Independent Charismatics (Type 3)

While the classification and chronology of the first two types is straightforward, there are thousands of churches and movements that 'resemble' the first two types but do not fit their definitions. These constitute a third type and often predate the first two types. For lack of a better term, these are called 'Independent Charismatics'. Part of the rationale for this term is the fact that they are largely found in the Independent category of the overall taxonomy of Christians. Thus, Type 3 includes Pentecostal or semi-Pentecostal members of the 250-year-old Independent movement of Christians, primarily in the global South, of churches begun without reference to Western Christianity. These Indigenous movements, although not all explicitly Pentecostal, nevertheless have the main features of Pentecostalism. In addition, since Azusa Street, thousands of schismatic or other Independent Charismatic churches have come out of Type 1 Pentecostals and Type 2 Charismatic movements. They consist of Christians who, unrelated to or no longer related to the Pentecostal or Charismatic denominations, have become filled with the Spirit, or empowered by the Spirit and have experienced the Spirit's ministry (although usually without recognising a baptism in the Spirit separate from conversion); who exercise gifts of the Spirit (with much less emphasis on tongues, as optional or even absent or unnecessary) and emphasise signs and wonders, supernatural miracles and power encounters; but also do not identify themselves as either Pentecostals (Type 1) or Charismatics (Type 2). In a number of countries they exhibit Pentecostal and Charismatic phenomena but combine this with rejection of Pentecostal terminology. These believers frequently are identified by their leadership as Independent, Post-denominationalist, Restorationist, Radical, Neo-Apostolic or 'Third Wave.'

Thus, the third type is Independent Charismatics (also known in the literature as neo-Charismatics or neo-Pentecostals), who are not in Protestant Pentecostal denominations (Type 1), nor are they individual Charismatics in the traditional churches (Type 2). Type 3 is the most diverse of the three types and ranges from house churches in China to African Initiated Churches to white-led Charismatic networks in the Western world. It includes Pentecostals who had split off from established Protestant denominations (Type 1) and who were then labelled as Independent. Independent churches formed by Charismatic leaders (Type 2) who founded new congregations and networks are also included. Some Independent Charismatics speak in tongues, but healing and power evangelism are more prominent in this type than in the other two.

Three types together
One difficulty that has plagued all researchers and historians of Pentecostalism is what to call the overarching movement. Some have used 'Pentecostalism' or 'Global Pentecostalism', while others have used 'Charismatic'. Still others have used 'Pentecostal and Charismatic'. David Barrett originally used the lengthy phrase 'the Pentecostal and Charismatic Renewal of the Holy Spirit', which he later shortened to 'Renewal'. He then coined the term 'Renewalist' to refer to all three waves or types. For the purposes of this series, we use the term 'Pentecostals/Charismatics' to refer to all three types.

A demographic overview of Pentecostals/Charismatics (all types) illustrates the complexities of both the spread of the movement across the countries of the world and the striking diversity of the churches themselves. While current ways of understanding Pentecostals, Charismatics and Independent Charismatics reveal a global movement of immense proportions, perspectives on classification, counting and assessment of the movement are likely to continue to evolve. In the meantime, hundreds of millions of Christians across all traditions will continue to participate in the movement – bringing vitality in some denominations and schism in others. They will also promote social transformation in some communities and show little participation in others. What is certain is that, for the foreseeable future, Christianity as a whole will continue to experience the growth pains of this global phenomenon.

Counting Evangelicals

Any effective and comprehensive method for counting Evangelicals must take into consideration denominational affiliation, self-identification and theology. The results of counting Evangelicals are directly related to denominational membership figures. Strictly speaking, denominational affiliation means official membership on a church roll.

Method 1: Individuals in denominations that are 100% Evangelical

The first category of Evangelicals includes individuals who are found in denominations that are coded 100% Evangelical. That is, membership of an Evangelical council (national, regional or global) is assessed for every denomination and those denominations that have Evangelical affiliations are classed as 100% Evangelical. Consequently, 100% of the members of these denominations are considered Evangelical. Using this method alone, the *WCD* estimates there are 200 million Evangelicals in the world. As of 2020, the nine largest 100% Evangelical denominations in the world were all Protestant, and the five largest 100% Evangelical denominations were found in Brazil, Ethiopia, Nigeria and Indonesia, reflecting the global scope of the movement.

Method 2: Individuals who self-identify as Evangelical in non-100% Evangelical denominations

For those denominations not identified as 100% Evangelical, an estimate is made of the percentage (0–99%) of members who self-identify as Evangelical. Self-identification percentages for Evangelicals in non-100% Evangelical denominations are verified by contacting key figures within each denomination, and each estimate is sourced in documentation housed at the Center for the Study of Global Christianity.

Adding together figures from both 100% and partially Evangelical denominations gives a total of 386 million Evangelicals worldwide. Looking at both 100% and non-100% Evangelical denominations reveals that the movement has a significant presence beyond Western Protestantism. Some of the denominations with the most Evangelicals are within Anglicanism in the global South, such as the Anglican Church of Nigeria and the Church of Uganda. Chinese house churches (classified as Independents) taken together constitute the denomination with the third most Evangelicals globally. The United Kingdom (the Church of England) and the United States (the Southern Baptist Convention), however, are still important locations of the movement.

Method 3: Evangelicals not affiliated with any denomination (Unaffiliated Evangelicals)

To date, no studies have addressed directly how many Evangelicals are denominationally unaffiliated. However, two well known realities (in Western Christianity in particular) appear to provide indirect evidence for this undocumented trend. The first is reflected in recent research indicating the unaffiliated are not uniformly non-religious. The Pew Research Center reported that 68% of America's unaffiliated believe in God. It is reasonable to assume that a notable proportion of Christians is among the ranks of the unaffiliated by virtue of Christianity being the largest religion in many of the countries studied. The second reality is the acknowledged fact that unaffiliated Christians often attend and are active in churches, including Evangelical churches, without becoming official members. These unaffiliated Christians profess allegiance and commitment to Christ but do not maintain church affiliation.

Dynamics of Change in Religious Populations

The question of how and why the number of religious adherents changes over time is critical to the study of international religious demography. It is more complex than simply 'counting heads' via births and deaths – a well established area in quantitative sociological studies – but in addition involves the multifaceted areas of religious conversion and migration. The migration of religious people has only in the past few years become a more researched area of demographic study, and issues surrounding religious conversion continue to be under-represented in the field. Data on religion from a wide range of sources – including from the religious communities themselves, as well as governments and scholars – must be employed to understand the total scope of religious affiliation. Given data on a particular religion from two separate points in time, the question can be raised, 'What are the dynamics by which the number of adherents changes over time?' The dynamics of change in religious affiliation can be reduced to three sets of empirical population data that together enable enumeration of the increase or decrease in adherents over time. To measure overall change, these three sets can be defined as follows: (1) births minus deaths; (2) converts to minus converts from; and (3) immigrants minus emigrants. The first variable in each of these three sets (births, converts to, immigrants) measures increase, whereas the second (deaths, converts from, emigrants) measures decrease. All future (and current) projections of religious affiliation, within any subset of the global population (normally a country or region), will account for these dynamics, and the changes themselves are dependent on these dynamics.

Births

The primary mechanism of global religious demographic change is (live) births. Children are almost always counted as having the religion of their parents (as is the law in Norway, for example). In simple terms, if populations that are predominantly Muslim, for example, have more children on average than those that are predominantly Christian or Hindu, then over time (all other things being equal) Muslims will become an increasingly larger percentage of that population. This means that the relative size of a religious population has a close statistical relationship to birth rates.

Deaths

Even as births increase their memberships, religious communities experience constant loss through the deaths of members. Although this often includes tragic, unanticipated deaths of younger members, it most frequently affects the elderly members. Thus, changes in health care and technology can positively impact religious communities if members live longer.

Births minus deaths/total fertility rate

The change over time in any given population is most simply expressed as the number of births into the community minus the number of deaths out of it. Many religious communities around the world experience little else in the dynamics of their growth or decline. Detailed projections rely on a number of estimated measures, including life expectancy, population age structures and the total fertility rate. This means that any attempt to understand the dynamics of religious affiliation must be based firmly on demographic projections of births and deaths.

Converts to

It is a common observation that individuals (or even whole villages or communities) change allegiance from one religion to another (or to no religion at all). Unfortunately, one of the problems in studying conversion is the paucity of information on it. Reliable data on conversions are hard to obtain, for a number of reasons. Although some national censuses ask people about their religion, they do not directly ask whether people have converted to their present faith. A few cross-national surveys do contain questions about religious switching, but even in those surveys it is difficult to assess whether more people leave a religion than enter it. In some countries, legal and social consequences make conversion difficult, and survey respondents might be reluctant to speak honestly about the topic. In particular, Hinduism is for many Hindus (as is Islam for many Muslims) not just a religion but also an ethnic or cultural identity that does not depend on whether a person actively practises the faith. Thus even non-practising or secular Hindus may still consider themselves, and be viewed by their neighbours, as Hindus.

Converts from

Conversion to a new religion, as mentioned above, also involves conversion from a previous one. Thus, a convert to Islam is, at the same time, a convert from another religion. In the twentieth and twenty-first centuries, the most converts from Christianity were and continue to be found largely among those in the Western world who have decided to be agnostics or atheists.

Converts to minus converts from

The net conversion rate in a population is calculated by subtracting the number of 'converts from' from the number of 'converts to'. Conversion to and conversion from will likely continue to play a role in changing religious demographics in the future.

Immigrants

Equally important at the international level is how the movement of people across national borders impacts religious affiliation. Once religious communities are established through immigration they often grow vigorously (for a time) via high birth rates.

Emigrants

In a reversal of nineteenth-century European colonisation of Africa, Asia and parts of the Americas, the late twentieth century witnessed waves of emigration of people from these regions to the Western world. The impact on religious affiliation is significant.

Immigrants minus emigrants

In the twenty-first century, international migration continues to have a significant impact on the religious composition of individual countries. One can try to anticipate the way in which expected immigration and emigration trends will affect a country's population over time. One profound change to be expected is the increase of religious pluralism in almost every country of the world. Increasing religious pluralism is not always welcomed and can be seen as a political, cultural, national or religious threat.

The six dynamics discussed above determine changes in religious demographics. Gains are the result of three positive dynamics: births, conversions to, and immigration. Losses are the result of three negative dynamics: deaths, conversions from, and emigration. The net change in religious demographics is the result of gains minus losses. The balance of dynamics can be reflected in any proportions (for example, mainly births for gains, mainly conversions from for losses) but can also be represented by pairing the gains and losses by type: births versus deaths, converts to versus converts from, and immigrants versus emigrants. In each case, the net change (either positive or negative) will be the difference between the two. This means that any attempt to understand religious affiliation in the past, present or future must be firmly based on demographic dynamics. A proper awareness of these dynamics and their significance is thus vital both for undertaking and for interpreting studies of the future of religion.

Measuring Growth Rates

The rates of growth, increase, decrease or decline of membership in many congregations can readily be measured from their annually reported statistics. This has been done by obtaining the statistics for two different years, where possible five years apart (to minimise the effects of roll-cleaning and other annual irregularities), usually 2000–5 and 2010–15, and working out the average annual growth rate as a percentage. Great care must be taken in such computations to ensure that the statistics used are measuring exactly the same entity (especially geographically) for each of the two years concerned. Growth, as a percentage increase or decrease per year, must be measured by dividing any annual increase by the identical category of total. Thus a church, for example, in a particular country with 500,000 total adherents (including children) in 2010 which grows to 600,000 total adherents (including children) in 2015 shows an increase of 600,000 minus 500,000 = 100,000, which divided by 5 = 20,000 a year, which divided by the mean membership of 550,000 gives an increase rate of 3.64% per year. In practice, the methodology follows a more accurate method by using the 1970 to 2015 figures for each denomination to arrive at average annual growth rates.

There are different ways of measuring the growth of a religious body. First, one can measure either adults only, or total community including children. Secondly, the growth rate of a church or religious grouping can be measured over a single day, or a month, a year, a decade, or 50 years – and all will yield differing results. This survey is concerned primarily to measure long-term rates. A growth rate measured for a specific religious body over a two- or three-year period may not be sustained over a decade.

Projecting Religious Populations

The starting point of future studies is natural growth of the total population of the country or region of interest, using demographic projections as a baseline. Three major areas beyond natural growth are utilised to improve the projections. First, birth and death rates vary among religious communities within a particular country. Secondly, increasing numbers of people are likely to change their religious affiliations in the future. Thirdly, immigration and emigration trends will impact a country's population over time. The highest-quality projections for religious communities are built on cohort-component projections that use differential rates for each religion: age-specific fertility rates by religion, age structure in five-year age-and-sex cohorts by religion, migration rates by religion, and mortality by religion.

Unfortunately, this kind of detail is not yet available for many countries (half of censuses do not ask a question about religion). Fortunately, the process of filling in missing data using demographic and smaller-scale general population surveys is underway, and as these data become available through the Pew–Templeton Global Religious Futures Project, researchers will have access to these data through the *World Religion Database*, where they will be archived in full, with summary results available at the Pew Forum's website. In the meantime, projections cannot solely rely on the cohort-component method. Instead, they use a hybrid projection method. First, the 2020 religious composition of each country is established as the baseline. Then, utilising the United Nations medium variant cohort-component projections of populations for five-year periods up to 2050, future religious shares are modestly adjusted from the 2020 baseline. Adjustments are based on analysis of past differential growth rates of religious groups, factoring in historical patterns of religious switching and possible future attenuation of past trends. Finally, these projections take into account how immigrants might alter the future religious composition of country populations.

Ethno-linguistic People Groups

A problem for social science research is the lack of available survey and polling data in non-Western countries. While the United States and many European countries have a long history of engaging in this kind of research, many often more underdeveloped countries can be difficult to access and/or speak languages difficult for Western researchers. The *WCD*'s method directly addresses this methodological challenge through its additional taxonomy of the world's ethnic groups, which are paired with religious statistics.

A 'peoples' taxonomy must take into account both ethnicity and language. The approach taken in 'Ethnosphere' in Part 8 of the *World Christian Encyclopedia* (2nd edition, 2001) was to match ethnic codes with language codes, which produced over 13,700 distinct ethno-linguistic peoples. Not all combinations of ethnicity and language are possible, but nevertheless every person in the world can be categorised as belonging to an ethno-linguistic people (mutually exclusive). For example, there are ethnic Kazaks who speak Kazak as their mother tongue and ethnic Kazaks who speak Russian as their mother tongue. These, then, are two separate ethno-linguistic peoples.

The work of determining the religious breakdown of ethno-linguistic peoples was begun in the 1970s in Africa, where many Christian churches reported the ethnic breakdown of their congregations. Utilising data gathered by religious bodies and in government censuses, estimates of religious affiliation for all peoples was completed in the mid-1990s and published in the second edition of the *World Christian Encyclopedia*. These data continue to be updated and published in the *World Christian Database* and *World Religion Database*.

Each distinct ethno-linguistic group in a country is assigned varying shares of the 18 categories of religion. For example, the Japanese in Japan are reported as 56% Mahayana Buddhist, 23% various New religionist, 10% agnostic, 3% atheist, 2% Shinto and 1% Christian. Each group is traced throughout the world with the assumption that whatever their religious breakdown is in their home country will be the same abroad. This allows researchers to locate Christian people in predominantly non-Christian countries. For example, the *WCD* reports that Pakistan – a Muslim-majority country – is also home to over 2 million Christians. While Christians are found among majority-Muslim people groups (for example, Punjabi at 4% Christian), they are also present in the country as ex-pats, such as French (65% Christian) and British (70% Christian).

Conclusion
There are a variety of issues related to finding and choosing the best data sources of religious affiliation. Censuses are generally accepted as the most reliable, but there are times when they fail to present the full picture, for example because they omit certain regions of a country or because they do not ask clear or detailed questions about religion. General-population surveys can often fill the gap, but, depending on their quality, they may

also have some bias. At times, religious groups may have very different estimates of their sizes than are found by censuses and surveys, but for some types of data, such as denominations of Protestantism, estimates by the groups may be the best information available. Finally, for religions such as Islam, Hinduism, Buddhism and Judaism, subgroup information is routinely missing from censuses and surveys. Estimates for the subgroups of these religions often rely on indirect measures, such as ethnic groups likely to adhere to a particular subgroup or expert analysis of multiple ethnological and anthropological sources. Thus, it is important to take into consideration many different kinds of data in order to arrive at the best estimate of a particular religious population in a country.

Index

#ChurchToo, 345
#MeToo, 140, 298, 345

Aaronic blessing, 295
Abbaye Val Notre-Dame, 62
Abe, Masao, 370
Abel (biblical), 245
Abernathy, Ralph, 93
abolition of slavery, 241, 312, 409
Aboriginal Day of Prayer, 379
Aboriginal(s), 47, 269, 372, 379, 383–4
abortion, 46, 67, 70, 136, 138, 153, 160–1, 194, 216, 227–8, 240, 254–5, 316–18, 321, 339, 342–3, 346, 352, 354, 358
Abraham, 157, 245, 362, 366, 378
abstinence, 343
abuse, 18, 33, 43, 47, 49, 94–6, 103, 114, 118, 140–1, 241–2, 313, 344–5, 379
Abyssinian Baptist Church, 110
Acadia Divinity College, 34
Acadians, 169–70, 334
Accepting Schools Act, 237
activists, 72, 83, 120, 155, 162, 316, 343
Acts (Book of), 245, 258, 266
Adam (biblical), 245, 405–6
Adamah, 405
adoption, 37, 107, 184, 354
adult(s), 13, 43, 45, 95, 159, 162–4, 191, 205–6, 243, 293, 359, 363, 370, 408, 416, 427, 430–1, 437, 448–9, 458
Advaita Vedanta, 371
Advent Review, 73
Advent, 12, 65, 73, 150, 179, 203, 219, 341, 407
Adventist(s), 12, 65, 73, 150, 179, 203, 219, 341
affiliation(s), 36, 57, 60, 64, 67, 88, 99, 103, 105, 112, 120, 149, 153, 157–8, 160, 190, 217, 228–9, 239, 242–3, 251, 358, 372, 420, 428–30, 432, 437, 445–7, 449–50, 454–60
Affirming Baptists, 342, 347
Affordable Care Act, 339, 344
Afghan(s), 317, 369
Afghanistan, 317, 369
Africa(ns), 11, 13, 15, 17–19, 56, 58, 66, 68, 70, 77, 79–90, 92, 97, 101–3, 107–8, 110–12, 125–7, 177, 179, 198, 207, 209, 219, 223, 228, 230, 236, 241, 248, 250, 253, 256–9, 261, 265–6, 269, 275, 285–6, 288–90, 294, 312, 314–15, 325, 329, 331–2, 334, 341, 362, 364, 367, 371, 375, 379–80, 390–1, 399, 427, 430–2, 434–5, 437, 453, 457, 460
African American(s), 19, 79, 81–7, 102–3, 110–12, 198, 223, 228, 248, 250, 253, 257–9, 261, 269, 285–6, 288–90, 294, 325, 329, 332, 334, 364, 367, 371, 375, 379–80, 390–1, 430
African Methodist Episcopal (AME) Church, 68, 77, 81–3, 92, 97–8, 110–11, 179, 219, 289, 314
African Methodist Episcopal Zion (AMEZ) Church, 80, 92, 97, 111, 341
Afro-Caribbean(s), 66, 86, 362
agnostic(s), 112, 170, 457, 460
agriculture, 145, 410
Akron, Ohio, 85
Al Qaeda, 350
Alabama, 88, 97–8, 211
Alameda, California, 381
Alaska, 64, 67, 71, 74, 211, 214, 430
Alaskan Native(s), 430
Albania, 213
Alberta, Canada, 30, 237, 356
alcohol(ism), 41, 174
Aldred, Ray, 26, 334
Algonquin Bible, 324
Algonquins, 52
Allegheny, Pennsylvania, 203
Allen, A. A., 260
Allen, Richard, 110
Alliance Defending Freedom, 347
Alliance of Baptists, 341, 346
Alliance of Confessing Evangelicals, 299
Alpharetta, Georgia, 96
altar(s), 259–60
Amazing Grace, 293
American Academy of Religion, 408
American Bible Society, 324
American Board of Commissioners for Foreign Missions (ABCFM), 324
American Jewish Committee, 367
American Orthodox Church, 215
American Restoration Movement, 205
American Revolutionary War, 54, 89, 184, 198, 221, 233, 314, 364
Amish, 74
Amsterdam, Netherlands, 77, 363

An, Choi Hee, 128
Anabaptist(s), 47, 83, 219, 235, 310
Anaheim Hills, California, 69
ancestor(s), 30, 74, 134, 287, 293, 314
Ancient Near East, 90
Anderson, Indiana, 78
Anderson, Rufus, 336
Andover Newton Theological School, 333
angels, 203, 205
Angelus Temple, 413
Anglican Church in North America Episcopal (ACNA), 183, 185–95, 331
Anglican Church of Bermuda (ACB), 183, 185–6, 188, 190, 192–4
Anglican Church of Canada (ACC), 183, 185–6, 188–90, 192–5
Anglican communion, 183, 189, 219
Anglican Consultative Council (ACC), 183, 185–6, 188–90, 192–5
Anglican Council of Indigenous People (ACIP), 28
Anglican(s), 11, 26, 28–9, 40, 44, 54, 86, 89, 98, 111, 177–8, 183–91, 193–5, 219–22, 233, 261, 286, 298, 331, 360, 368, 372, 421, 430, 452, 454
Anglo-Saxon(s), 135, 194, 248, 363
Anglophilia, 193
Anglophone Canada, 26, 41, 43–4, 50, 52, 55, 58, 110
Anglophone West Indian(s), 110
animals, 73, 405
animism, 285
Annunciation Greek Orthodox Church, 217
Anselm, 303
anthropology, 405
Anti-Defamation League, 367
anti-Semitism, 364–5, 367
Antichrist, 368
Antilles Episcopal Conference, 178, 235
Antiochian Orthodox Church, 211, 214–15
Antwerp, Ohio, 77
Anzaldua, Gloria, 382
apartheid, 315
apocalypse, 308
apostasy, 202
Apostolic, 38, 53, 74, 85, 150, 170, 175, 190, 202, 258–9, 262, 451, 453
Apostolic Assembly of Faith, 150
Apostolic Prefecture of Iles Saint-Pierre, 170
Appalachian Mountains, 109
apparitions, 67
Applewhite, Marshall, 278
Appomattox, Virginia, 91
Arab(s), 215, 367
Archbishop of Canterbury, 178, 183, 360, 369
Archbishop of Quebec City, 61
Archdiocese of Nassau, 178
Archdiocese of St John, 43
Archdiocese of San Antonio, 99

archives, 328
Arctic, 29, 173, 175
Argentina, 137, 147
Arizona, 64–5, 67, 71–2, 82, 145, 203, 215, 233
Arkansas, 88
Armageddon, 203, 205, 307
Armenian Orthodox Church, 74
Armenian(s), 74–5
Armstrong, Annie, 335
Arnott, Carol, 263
arts, 127, 268, 289, 294, 348
Ashkenazi Jews, 364
Asian American Christians, 155–6, 159–61, 163–4, 320
Asian(s), 11–12, 15–16, 19, 46, 86, 95, 102, 104, 108, 110, 112, 129–30, 148, 152, 155–67, 286, 292–4, 298, 302, 320, 323, 333–4, 342, 363, 367, 370, 373, 375, 381, 383–4, 429–31, 433–5
Asiatic Exclusion League, 363
assassination, 269
Assemblies of God (AOG), 70, 78, 83, 108, 150–2, 259, 264, 268–9, 329, 347, 451
Association for Hispanic Theological Education (AETH), 333, 437
Association of Chicago Theological Schools, 328
Association of Theological Schools (ATS), 77, 120, 166
Assyrians, 91
Astoria, New York, 213
asylum seekers, 377
atheist(s), 49, 112, 203, 235, 310, 448, 457, 460
Athenagoras, Archbishop, 212
Atlanta, Georgia, 84, 95–6, 98, 315
Atlas of Global Christianity, 319
attendance, 15, 41, 43–4, 63, 96, 148, 159, 187, 220, 226–9, 231, 321, 325, 428, 430
Augsburg, Germany, 77
Augustine, 53, 145, 211, 331
Australia(n), 15, 41, 49, 293, 407
Ayurveda, 371
Aztec(s), 66, 99
Azusa Street Revival, 70, 151, 250, 259, 269, 329, 452

Babel, 93, 303
baby boom, 41
Babylon, 91, 248
Baha'i(s), 180, 372
Baker, Ella, 93
Baker-Fletcher, Karen, 303–4
Bakker, Jim, 263, 419
Bakker, Tammy Faye, 418
Ball, H. C., 259
Balmer, Randall, 316–17
Bande FM, 62
Bangladeshi, 156
Bangor University, 268

baptism(s), 29–30, 90, 113, 147, 183, 190, 203, 206, 215, 238, 243, 258–9, 261–2, 266, 445, 451, 453
Baptist(s), 15, 34, 38, 45, 47, 68, 76–7, 79–80, 82–5, 87–9, 92–5, 97, 105, 109–11, 140–1, 150, 170, 197, 199, 219–25, 227, 246, 261, 286, 289, 295, 301, 310, 314–15, 325–6, 328, 330, 332–4, 336, 338, 341–2, 345–7, 372, 381, 413, 428, 451, 455
Barbados, 110
Barrett, David B., 453
Barth, Karl, 127, 137
Bartholomew, Patriarch, 216, 303, 400
Bass, Diane Butler, 142
Bates, Daisy, 93
Bath, Danai, 347
Baylor University, 268
BC Native Ministries, 32
Bear, Cheryl, 124
Beatitudes, 318
Beausejour, Manitoba, 31
Bebbington, David W., 93
Bell, Rob, 142
Bellavin, Bishop Tikhon, 212
Ben-Hur, 414
Benbow, Candice, 98
Benedict XVI, Pope, 239–40, 369
Bennett, Dennis, 261, 452
Berkeley, California, 155, 328
Berlin, Wisconsin, 77
Bermuda, 11, 17, 177–80, 183, 185, 193, 195, 197, 207, 232, 235, 264, 350, 359–60, 362, 430
Bermuda Collegiate Institute, 179
Bermuda Ministerial Association, 180
Berntsen, Hans, 176
Berrigan, Daniel and Philip, 238
Berzon, Judge Marsha, 351
Bessette, Alfred, 55
Bethel African Methodist Episcopal Church, 82, 110
Bethel Bible College, Kansas, 329
Bethel Church, 70, 264
Bethel Music, 293–4
Bethel School of Supernatural Ministry (BSSM), 70–1
Bethesda Mission, 259
Bethlehem Baptist Church, Minnesota, 85
Bevans, Stephen, 328
Bialecki, Jon, 71
Bibby, Reginald, 48
Bible Belt, 88, 94
Bible Institute of Los Angeles (BIOLA), 413
Bible Society(ies), 173, 200, 324
Bible(s), 15, 27, 36, 40–1, 73, 80, 88, 90, 93–5, 107, 113, 115–16, 118, 120–1, 123, 127, 133–4, 140, 159, 173, 180, 183, 186, 200, 202–4, 206, 208, 222–4, 227–8, 246, 248, 250, 256, 258, 260, 266, 268, 297, 313–14, 324, 328–9, 332, 340, 342, 368, 378, 404, 407, 413, 437
Biden, President Joe, 132, 143, 165, 277, 338
Big M Drug Mart, 356
Bill of Rights, 198, 310
Billy Graham Crusade, 335
Birch River, Manitoba, 36
Birmingham, Alabama, 93, 211
Birmingham Jail, 93
birth(s), 29, 43, 66, 120, 139, 141, 147, 207, 240, 245, 250, 254, 259, 277, 289, 326, 329–30, 332, 337, 344, 347, 355, 400, 410, 429, 431, 435, 445–6, 451, 455–9
Black American Muslims, 367
Black Bermudans, 179
Black Catholics, 242, 289
Black Church Environmental Summit, 400
Black Lives Matter (BLM), 143, 216–17
Black Theology of Liberation, 332
Black Theology, 332
Black-fishing, 129
Blaine, Barbara, 345
Blanca, 294
blasphemy, 360, 415
Blavatsky, Helena, 368
Blessed Assurance, 80
blind, 28, 31–2, 119, 220, 288, 301, 436
blood, 204, 231, 281–3, 293, 307, 396
Blue Zones, 73
Boebert, Lauren, 69
Bolz-Weber, Nadia, 142
bombing(s), 343
Bonhoeffer, Dietrich, 137
Boogaloo Boys, 132
Book of Alternative Services, 186
Book of Common Prayer (BCP), 186, 190
Book of Mormon, 201–2
Book of Numbers, 295
Book of Revelation, 296, 307, 435
Borelli, John, 372
Boston, Massachusetts, 102–4, 106, 108–10, 208, 211, 290, 328, 333–4, 345, 354, 444
Boston College, 104
Boston Globe, 345
Boston Theological Institute (BTI), 328
Boston University School of Theology, 106, 109, 328
boundaries, 26, 190, 245–6, 248–9, 252–3, 256–7, 297, 302, 304–5, 319, 384
bourgeoisie, 55
Bourgeoys, Marguerite, 55
Bourget, Bishop Ignace, 55
Bowe, Dante, 294
Bowman, Sr Thea, 242
Boy Scouts, 41
Boyd, Brady, 69
Brainerd, David, 324
Branham, William, 260
Brazil, 74, 86, 109, 292, 363, 454

Brazilian(s), 86, 109, 292
Bredesen, Harold, 261
Brethren Churches, 36, 45, 83, 175, 179, 246, 315, 324
Briand, Olivier, 54
Briggs, William, 84
Brigham Young University, 72
Britain, 45, 54, 169, 179, 193
British Columbia, 32, 35–6, 41, 47, 49, 203, 232, 321, 357
British India, 367
British North America Act, 237
British Overseas Territory, 183, 359
Bro, Susan, 282
Brock, Nakashima, 165
Broken Walls, 124, 294
Brookline, Massachusetts, 214
Brooklyn, New York, 105, 109–10, 204
Brown Church, 427, 433–4
Bryan, William Jennings, 92, 312
Budd, Henry, 29
Buddhist Council of Canada, 372
Buddhist(s), 48, 60, 65, 81, 157–60, 180, 362, 370–3, 384, 460–1
Buettner, Dan, 73
Buffalo, New York, 103
Build the Wall, 320
Building Bridges Seminar, 369
Bulgaria, 213
bulletin board systems (BBSs), 420
Bultmann, Rudolf, 300
Burke, Tarana, 345
Burleigh, Harry T., 82
Burmese-Americans, 383
Bush, Peter, 34
Bush, President George W., 13, 138, 140, 152, 317, 387
business, 139, 177, 335, 339, 344, 346, 409
Butler, Keith, 263
Bynum, Juanita, 263
Byzantine Rite Franciscans, 215
Byzantine(s), 215, 303

C. H. Mason Theological Seminary, 268
Calgary, Canada, 47
California, 64–5, 67–71, 73–5, 145, 155, 161–2, 208, 211, 233, 250, 259–61, 264, 297, 324–5, 328, 330, 332, 370, 378, 381, 383
California Gold Rush, 161, 370
Calvillo, Jonathan E., 67
Calvinists, 219, 329, 432
Cambodians, 156–7
Cambridge Declaration Heritage and Resources, 299
Campbell, Alexander, 205
Campbell, David, 231
Campbell, Thomas, 205
Campus Crusade for Christ, 109, 214, 335
Canaanites, 275

Canada Council of Churches, 372
Canadian Baptists of Atlantic Canada (CBAC), 34
Canadian Charter of Rights, 19, 351, 356
Canadian Conference of Catholic Bishops, 242, 372–3
Canadian Jewish Congress, 372
Cane Ridge, Kentucky, 89
Cannon, Katie Geneva, 128
Cano, Gerardo Valencia, 57, 215–16
Canterbury, 178, 183, 360, 369
Cape Hatteras, North Carolina, 177
capitalism, 125–6, 129–30, 276–7, 281, 401
Carey, Archbishop of Canterbury George, 369
Carey, Lott, 332
Carey, William, 325
Caribbean(s), 66, 70, 86, 102, 104, 107, 109–12, 126, 129, 292, 362, 437
Carlisle Indian Industrial School, 241
Carnes, Cody, 295
Carter, Jimmy, 317
Cartier, Jacques, 168
Cashwell, G. B., 259
caste, 142, 413–14, 417
cathedral(s), 55, 70, 105, 170, 179, 193, 421
Catholic Action Team, 105
Catholic Charismatic Renewal Service Committee, 262
Catholic charities, 354
Catholic Climate Covenant, 105
Catholic Common Ground Project, 239
Catholic Faith Network, 417
Catholic Foreign Mission Society of America (Maryknoll), 330
Catholic Legion of Decency, 415
Catholic News Service, 240
Catholic PCA, 415
Catholic Theological Union, 328
Catholic Worker Movement, 238
Catholic(s), 11–12, 17, 26, 29–31, 33, 40–5, 48, 50, 52–61, 63, 65–8, 70, 76–81, 85–9, 98–105, 108–10, 112, 128, 134–41, 143, 145–51, 156–61, 163–5, 169–70, 172, 178, 180, 190, 198, 217, 221, 223, 230, 232–44, 248, 260–2, 267–8, 278, 286, 289–92, 294–5, 301–2, 318–21, 325, 328, 330–1, 333–4, 338–45, 347, 353–4, 360, 362–6, 370–3, 377–8, 380–2, 399, 401, 408, 410, 413–17, 422, 429, 432–3, 437, 452
cattle, 168
Cayuga, 31
celebrations, 147, 185
celibacy, 240, 242
Celie, 130
censorship, 414, 416
Census Bureau, 145, 156, 431
census(es), 40, 67, 98, 144–5, 149, 156, 170, 372, 431, 445–50, 456, 459–61

Central America, 15, 129, 216, 266, 292, 376–7, 433
Central Asia, 156
Central Conference of American Rabbis, 364
Central Jurisdiction of the Methodist Episcopal Church, 223
Centre d'études Missionnaires, 56
Centre Street Church, Calgary, 47
ceremony(ies), 30, 35, 116, 119, 137, 187, 339, 379
Chalcedon, 197, 202
Champlain, Samuel de, 52
Chang, Michael, 165
chants, 161, 293
chapel(s), 36, 42, 56, 62, 70, 78, 83, 85, 170, 174, 179, 266
chaplain(s), 29, 44–5, 58–9, 91, 212, 236, 251, 350, 364, 429
Charbonneau, Joseph, 57
Charente-Maritime, Saint Pierre and Miquelon, 170
charisma(s), 17, 38, 41, 46–7, 70–1, 75, 102, 135–6, 150–1, 180, 198, 207, 249–51, 255, 258, 260–70, 278, 286, 333, 418, 432, 450, 452–3
Charismatic(s), 17, 38, 41, 46–7, 70–1, 75, 102, 135–6, 150, 180, 198, 249–51, 258, 260–70, 286, 333, 418, 432, 450, 452–3
charity, 53, 55, 235, 275, 281, 351, 354
Charles, Mark, 115–16, 334
Charleston, South Carolina, 90
Charlotte, North Carolina, 282
Charlottesville, Virginia, 282
Chauvin, Derek, 143
Chaves, Mark, 229
Chavez, Caesar, 238
Cheng, Patrick S., 302
Cherubim and Seraphim church, 87
Chicago, Illinois, 80–7, 151, 166, 190, 204, 211, 252, 316, 326, 328–9, 362, 364, 368, 371, 413
Chicago Declaration of Evangelical Social Concern, 316
Chicago World Mission Institute, 328
Chihuahua, Mexico, 259
children, 18, 20, 41, 44, 59, 69, 75, 78, 89, 92, 112, 118, 121–3, 129, 146, 148, 164, 174–5, 195, 203, 207–8, 225, 237, 254, 260, 326, 343–6, 348, 354, 360, 376, 378–9, 382, 384, 407, 431–2, 446–9, 456, 458
Chile, 329
China, 46, 50, 56, 243, 265, 370, 453
Chinese, 12, 17, 45, 108, 156–9, 161–3, 243, 265, 278, 333, 363, 370, 375, 428, 454
Chinese Exclusion Act, 363, 370, 428
Chippewa, 78, 129
Cho, David Yonggi, 266
Choctaw, 124, 129
Choi, Hee An, 128
choirs, 82, 187, 295
choruses, 82, 262

Chosen People Ministries, 332
Choy, Wilbur, 165
Christ the King Church, Greenland, 232
Christian and Missionary Alliance (CMA), 32–3
Christian Brethren, 179
Christian Broadcasting Network (CBN), 263, 268
Christian Century, 134, 224
Christian education, 180, 213, 215, 437
Christian media, 142, 416
Christian Methodist Episcopal (CME), 97–8
Christian Nazism, 137
Christian Reconstructionists, 69
Christian Reformed Church (CRC), 37
Christian Revival Crusade (CRC), 37
Christian Right, 85, 339, 343, 418
Christian Scholars Group, 367
Christian Science, 101, 201, 207–9
Christianity Today, 83, 134, 167, 251, 326
Christians for Biblical Equality, 340
Christmas, 335
Christology, 246, 257, 399, 434
Church of Christ, 78, 201, 207–8, 220, 225, 227–9, 341, 344, 400, 410, 429
Church of Denmark, 174, 359
Church of England, 177–8, 183–6, 190, 221, 455
Church of England in Canada (CEC), 185
Church of Fools, 421
Church of God, 70, 78, 85–6, 97, 109, 111, 180, 197, 260, 264, 269, 347
Church of God in Christ (COGIC), 70, 97
Church of Greenland, 174, 176, 359
Church of Jesus Christ of Latter-day Saints (LDS), 12, 65, 67, 71–3, 197, 201–3, 209, 219, 330, 340, 342, 372, 416
Church of Scotland, 179
Church of the Foursquare Gospel, 413
Church of the Nazarene, 150
Church, Casey, 124
Churches of Christ, 105, 197, 201, 205–7, 225, 400
cities, 13–15, 75, 77, 84–5, 96, 101–3, 106–7, 109–11, 115, 122, 130, 138, 148, 205, 211, 248, 265, 274, 283, 298, 308, 312, 321, 329, 342, 347, 374, 433, 444
citizen(s), 45, 93, 126, 130, 145, 179–80, 189, 234, 290, 299, 301, 364, 388–90
Citizens for Public Justice, 45
citizenship, 189, 301, 389–90
City Seminary New York, 110
Civil War(s), 91, 93, 121, 194, 206, 222–3, 226, 241, 312, 314
civilisation, 138, 273, 379
Clark, Curtis, 356
clergy, 20, 30–1, 53–4, 57–8, 68, 79–82, 84, 86, 91, 103, 105–7, 111, 113, 116, 140, 178, 180, 184–5, 187–9, 194, 200, 212–14, 221–2, 228, 233, 235–6, 240, 242, 273, 276, 313–14, 344–5, 350, 380, 415, 421, 428, 447

Cleveland, E. E., 261
Cleveland, Ohio, 85
climate change, 13, 20, 67, 71, 106, 174, 279, 400–2, 410–11
clinics, 231, 343
Clinton, Hillary, 279, 338
Clinton, President Bill, 352, 387
clubs, 41, 45, 82, 354
Coady, Fr Moses, 238
coalitions, 106, 155
Cobb, John B., 305
Coca-Cola, 85
Codfish Crusade, 168
Coe, Jack, 261
coffee, 73
cohorts, 459
Cold War, 108, 213, 326
colleges, 42, 56–7, 76, 93, 104, 134, 149, 221, 223, 254, 268, 328, 408, 435
Colombia, 150
colonial(ism), 25–7, 30–2, 52, 54, 64–6, 78–9, 87–8, 101, 106, 118, 125, 155, 177–8, 184, 189, 194–5, 198–9, 233, 238, 241, 243, 247, 249, 273–5, 283–5, 290, 298–300, 310, 312, 321–2, 335–6, 363, 367, 390, 401, 433
Colorado, 64, 67–9, 98, 329
Colorado City, Arizona, 203
Colorado Springs, Colorado, 68–9, 98, 329
Colored Methodist Episcopal Church, 92
Columbus, Christopher, 17
Columbus, Ohio, 81
combat, 276, 279, 360, 364, 400, 413, 415
Committee on Ecumenical and Interreligious Affairs (CEIA), 366–7
Common Word, 369
communion, 77, 79, 113, 183, 185, 189, 191, 203, 206, 213–14, 218–19, 233, 239, 293, 307, 331, 402, 404–5, 407–8, 410
communism, 57, 136, 213
Community Empowerment, 164
Community of Christ, 203
Community of Creation, 334
community(ies), 14, 17, 20, 25, 28–9, 31, 38, 51–5, 57, 60–2, 67, 69–76, 79–81, 83–5, 92, 96, 99, 105–7, 116–20, 122, 131, 137, 144, 149–50, 153–4, 159, 161–2, 164, 166–7, 179–80, 201, 203, 211–12, 214–17, 231–2, 235, 238, 245, 252, 261, 267, 273, 278, 285–94, 302, 304–5, 314, 320, 325, 330, 334, 350, 357, 364, 373, 375–6, 380–4, 399, 408, 410, 412, 420, 422, 428–30, 432–4, 436–8, 445–8, 456, 458
compassion, 49, 138, 153, 161, 260, 291, 308, 317, 343, 357, 400, 402, 411
competition, 50, 59, 151, 199, 219, 222, 225, 347
Concilio Mexicano Interdenominacional de las Iglesias Cristianas, 260
Conde-Frazier, Elizabeth, 433
Cone, James, 111, 127, 129, 301, 315, 332, 334

Confederacy, 91, 194–5
Conference of Catholic Bishops, 239, 242, 366, 372–3, 382
Conference of Churches, 179
confession, 17, 59, 89, 136, 189–90, 215, 279, 290, 297–8, 300, 302–3, 306, 308, 351, 422
conflict(s), 26, 33, 101, 103, 107, 122, 169, 188–9, 240, 295, 321, 353, 374, 402, 427, 429
Confucian(ism), 50, 157, 292, 363, 381
Congregation Notre-Dame, 55
Congregation of the Holy Cross, 55
congregation(s), 31, 33–7, 40, 44, 46–7, 55–8, 61, 63, 76, 79–87, 90, 102, 106–11, 113, 142, 147–8, 150–1, 153, 163, 179–80, 185–7, 191, 193, 199, 203, 206–7, 213, 219, 221–3, 225, 227, 258, 262, 264, 266, 268, 289–92, 310, 314–15, 319, 330, 344, 356, 359, 376, 379, 381–2, 400, 413, 421, 446, 453, 458, 460
Congregational Christian Churches, 223, 225
Congregational Church, 79, 81, 84
Congregationalist(s), 31, 40, 76, 79, 83, 199, 221–2, 310
Congress, 61, 132, 198, 216, 310, 318, 320, 333, 352, 364, 372, 395
Connecticut, 101, 369
conservative(s), 12–13, 17, 19, 32–4, 36, 43, 46, 57, 68–70, 76, 78, 83, 85, 88, 92, 95, 97, 100, 103–7, 134–43, 160, 164–5, 189, 192, 194, 224, 227–30, 239–40, 245, 247–9, 252–5, 297, 316–18, 320–2, 326, 331, 338–40, 343–4, 346–8, 353, 360, 389, 391, 418, 428–9, 448
Constantine, 126, 280, 306
Constantinople, 212, 216
constitution(s), 42, 50, 85, 183–4, 188, 198, 221, 237, 241, 310, 313, 353, 355–60, 364, 393, 444
contemporary Christian music (CCM), 142
contextualisation, 119–20, 288
Continental Pietist (Moravian), 111, 174
controversies, 219, 248, 302, 353, 419
conversion(s), 27, 53, 79–80, 89, 93, 99, 108, 124, 138, 158, 163, 214, 225, 227, 246–7, 249, 252, 254–7, 306–7, 313, 344, 370, 379, 408, 448, 451, 453, 455–8
Cook, Amanda Lindsey, 293
Cooperative Baptist Fellowship, 341
Copeland, Gloria, 418
Copeland, Kenneth, 263, 419
Copenhagen, Denmark, 232
Coptic Orthodox Church, 218
Cosby, Frances (Fanny), 80
Costas, Orlando, 328, 333, 433
Costas, Rose, 333
Cote Reserve, Saskatchewan, 36
cotton, 15, 89
Coughlin, Charles, 364, 414
Council of Churches, 83, 134, 217, 225–6, 326, 336, 365, 372, 399–401

Council of Muslim Communities of Canada, 372
counselling, 176
couples, 68, 139, 268, 339, 344, 354
COVID-19, 11–12, 75, 113, 141–2, 164, 167, 180, 278–9, 290, 295, 323, 347, 350, 355–6, 374, 384, 419, 422
cowboys, 287
Craft, Evan Kenneth, 294
creation, 28, 53, 55–6, 82, 92, 124, 127, 185, 213, 215, 225, 236, 274, 286–7, 302, 309, 327, 334, 338, 398–9, 401–2, 404–8
Creation Care, 334
Creator God, 294
Cree New Testament, 34
Cree, 26, 29–30, 34, 334
creeds, 183, 190
Creole(s), 109
crime, 12, 138, 176, 350, 364, 375, 378
crisis(es), 19–20, 43, 91, 98, 103, 128, 140–1, 175, 207, 242, 295, 305, 348, 375–8, 384, 391, 393, 399, 406, 409, 411, 448
crops, 15
CrossRoad Institute, Boston, 217
Crossroads Christian Communications, Canada, 417
Crow, Jim, 194, 269, 275, 314, 332, 435
crucifixion, 224
crusade(s), 105, 109, 168, 214, 227, 260–1, 275, 282, 326, 335, 350
Cuban Ecclesial Reflection (REC), 183, 185–8, 190–1, 384, 419
Cuban(s), 128, 145
cults, 278, 281
curriculum, 57, 59
Curse of Ham, 313
Cursillos de Cristiandad, 99
Curtice, Kaitlin B., 287
customs, 147, 273, 287, 359–60, 377, 390
Cyprus, 216

d'Youville, Marguerite, 55
Da Graça, Marcelino Manuel, 111
Dabney, Robert Lewis, 90
Dalai Lama, 370
Damascus, Syria, 212
dance, 15, 41, 43–4, 56, 63, 96, 114, 116–17, 119, 148, 159, 183, 187, 199, 201, 216, 220, 226–9, 231, 238, 243, 246, 267, 281, 285, 288–9, 291, 293–4, 321, 325, 379, 403, 412, 415, 422, 428, 430, 432, 437, 451
Danish Apostolic Church, 175
Danish Bible Society, 173
Danish Covenant Church, 175
Danish Lutheran State Church, 174
Daoist(s), 50, 363
Darby, John Nelson, 331
Darwin, Charles, 92, 133, 247, 326
Dasa, Anuttama, 371

David, Christian, 174
Day, Dorothy, 238
Daystar, 417
Dayton, Tennessee, 224
de Gaulle, President Charles, 58
De Jesus, Wilfredo, 151
De La Torre, Miguel A., 308
deacons, 86, 93, 187, 206, 235–6, 242
death, 18, 28, 50, 53, 56, 74, 93, 98, 127–8, 135, 205, 208, 275, 278–9, 284, 304, 375, 395, 445, 455–6, 458–9
debate(s), 60–1, 95, 155–6, 162, 178, 221, 223–4, 228, 299, 319, 321–2, 330, 348, 352, 354, 421, 427, 429
Debre Ganet Emmanuel, Bermuda, 179
debt, 126, 401
Declaration of Independence, USA, 116, 351
decolonisation, 32, 122–3, 195
Deep State, 279
dehumanisation, 115, 127, 334
Deism, 368
Delaware, 88
Delgado, Teresa, 128
deliverance, 50, 261, 265
Deloria, Vine, 129
Delta Hospice Society, 357
democracy, 66, 172, 177, 226, 234, 246, 249, 275, 278, 280, 282, 319, 323, 394–6, 423
Democrat(s), 46, 67, 70, 83, 94, 97, 139, 143, 153, 160, 228, 239, 279–80, 320, 346, 352
demographics, 13, 25, 70, 77, 103, 152, 194, 230, 319, 323, 431, 444, 457–8
demons, 19–20, 63, 67, 94, 116–17, 128, 230–1, 236, 247, 249–50, 268, 279–80, 282–3, 286, 290, 295, 356, 375, 387, 389, 396, 398, 400, 419, 451–2
Denmark, 90, 172–5, 232, 350, 359
denominations, 12, 25, 31, 35–7, 40–2, 45–6, 60–1, 75–80, 82–3, 85–7, 91, 97, 102, 105–8, 110–11, 114–15, 120–2, 139–40, 150–1, 163, 165, 175–6, 183–4, 187, 190–1, 197–8, 201, 205–6, 219–20, 223, 225–31, 243, 246, 251, 258, 261–2, 265, 267, 269, 286, 314, 321–2, 334, 338–41, 365, 379, 381, 412, 415, 417–19, 429, 435, 444, 446–8, 450–4, 461
Department of Indian Affairs, 18
Department of Justice, 395
deportation, 169
depression, 42, 68, 92, 105, 276, 326
Derrida, Jacques, 383
Detroit, Michigan, 78, 81, 85, 414
Dett, Nathaniel, 82
development, 16, 26–7, 30, 32–3, 38, 45, 48, 57–8, 68, 78, 102, 110, 114, 120, 136–7, 139, 141, 174, 197, 200, 215, 221, 224, 238, 253, 258, 268, 273, 329, 356, 371, 391–2, 408, 412, 416, 418–19
devil, 119
devotees, 281–2

Dharmapala, Anagarika, 370
dialogue, 13, 61, 100, 152, 217, 268, 290, 298, 303–4, 325, 328, 362–3, 365, 367–73, 383, 416, 421
diaspora, 113, 215, 265–6, 285, 294, 302, 450
dictators, 280, 433
Diego, Juan, 233, 382
DignityUSA, 342
Dill, Bishop Nicholas, 178
Diocese of California, 74
Diocese of Copenhagen, 232
Diocese of Gallup, 233
Diocese of Halifax-Yarmouth, 235
Diocese of Hamilton, 178, 235
Diocese of La Rochelle, 170, 235
Diocese of Montreal, 55
Diocese of Quebec, 53
diocese(s), 56, 61, 66, 104, 183–5, 187–91, 194, 212, 233, 330–1, 345
Disciples LGBTQ+ Alliance, 347
Disciples of Christ, 78, 206–7
discrimination, 15, 68, 70, 84, 94, 149, 165, 177, 337, 341, 344, 350, 353, 355–6, 359–60, 364–5, 375
disease, 17, 101, 233, 306, 330, 334
disestablishment, 178, 198–200, 222, 310
dispensationalism, 331
divinity, 32, 34, 77, 106, 188, 328, 333
divorce, 42, 132, 208, 240
Dobson, James, 69, 329
doctors, 236, 354
Doctrine of Discovery, 17, 115–16, 256, 298, 334
doctrine(s), 16–18, 20, 48, 72, 90, 94, 115–16, 188–92, 200, 202–5, 207–9, 215, 222, 256, 267, 279–80, 286, 297–8, 302, 304, 307, 309, 334, 342, 366, 403, 406, 437
dogma, 304
Dolan, Terry, 316
Dollar, Creflo, 263
Dominica, 150
Dominican Republic, 107
Dominican University College, 61
Dominicans, 62, 104, 107
Dorrien, Gary, 306
Dorsey, Thomas, 82
Douglas, Kelly Brown, 398
Douglass, Frederick, 81
Dranes, Arizona, 82
dreams, 451
Drew Theological School, 106
drums, 288
Du Mez, Kobes, 140
Dubois, Theodore, 82
Duke Divinity School, 333
Duncan Black Macdonald Center, 369
Duplantis, Jesse, 263
Duplessis, Maurice, 57–8
Durkheim, Emile, 273
Dutch, 41, 129, 329, 363
Dwyer, Dave, 104

Eagle Forum, 85
Earth Bible, 407
Earth Summit, 399
East Asia, 155, 157, 370, 378, 430
East End Mission, 259
East Greenlanders, 173
Easter, 63, 65, 73, 81, 109, 135, 138, 155–6, 176, 193, 203, 211, 213, 215–18, 233, 243, 248, 292, 324–5, 335, 362–4
Eastern Europe, 213, 248, 363–4
Eastern European Jews, 248
Eastern Orthodox Church, 65, 73, 135, 211, 215–18
Eastern University, 109
Ebenezer Baptist Church, 315
ecclesiology, 34, 238, 262, 267, 269
Eck, Diana, 106
Eco-Justice Working Group, 400–1
ecology, 11, 298, 398–9, 402–3, 408
Ecuador, 333
Ecumenical Association of Third World Theologians (EATWOT), 127
Ecumenical Council(s), 215
Ecumenical Patriarch Bartholomew, 303, 400
Ecumenical Patriarch Dimitrios, 214
Ecumenical Patriarch Meletios IV, 212
Ecumenical Patriarchate of Constantinople, 212, 216
ecumenism, 40, 82–3, 86, 105–6, 127, 180, 190, 212, 214–17, 220, 223, 225, 239, 268, 286, 303, 326, 328, 371, 399–401, 407, 409, 420, 433
Ecunet, 420
Eddy, Mary Baker, 101, 207
Edinburgh, Scotland, 26–7, 35, 319, 326–7, 336, 444
Edmonton, Canada, 33, 37
education, 17, 42, 47, 49, 53–5, 57–9, 61, 63, 74–5, 79, 92, 105–6, 108–11, 113, 119, 126, 130, 136, 148, 152, 155, 175, 178, 180, 193, 199, 213, 215, 217, 230, 237, 266, 268, 289, 322, 328, 333, 337, 340, 343, 356, 360, 364, 367, 376, 382, 384, 408, 437
Edwards, Jonathan, 199, 249, 324, 368
Eerdmans, 319, 329
egalitarianism, 95, 340
Egbu, Osinachi Kalu Okoro, 295
Egede, Gertrud, 173
Egede, Hans, 173
Egede, Niels, 173
Egede, Poul, 173
Egypt, 218, 449–50
Eklutna, Alaska, 74
El Camino Real, 325
El Paso County, Colorado, 69
El Salvador, 104, 107

Elaw, Zilpha, 97
Elder Ephraim, 215
elderly, 12, 41, 239, 375, 456
elders, 31–2, 38, 121, 206, 341
elections, 67, 94, 132, 152–3, 165, 188, 315, 338, 387, 390, 392, 395
Elevation Worship, 295
Eliot, John, 101, 324
elites, 54, 91, 202, 394, 433
Elizabeth I, 184
Elizondo, Virgilio, 433
Elk, Nicholas Black, 241
Ellwood City, Pennsylvania, 214
emancipation, 58, 314
Emerson, Ralph Waldo, 368, 371
Emet, Dabru, 367
Emmanuel College, Toronto, 44
Emmanuel Community, Quebec, 62
Emmanuel Gospel Center, Boston, 110
empire, 90, 126, 221, 298, 306, 308, 367, 429
employment, 43, 55, 84–5, 189, 344, 351–2
empowerment, 129, 164, 209, 258, 267, 291, 330, 336, 339
England, 41, 55, 77, 101, 109, 169, 177–8, 183–6, 188, 190, 199, 207, 221, 235, 275, 324, 336, 455
English Bible, 120, 328
English Reformation, 186
English-speaking First Nations, 120
English-speaking Hispanics, 147
Enns, Peter, 142
Enoch (biblical), 245
Enon Tabernacle Baptist Church, 110
Enslaved Struggle for Religious Freedom Bus Tour, 360
entrepreneurs, 422
environment, 60–2, 85, 101–2, 105–6, 121, 126, 130, 199–200, 209, 216, 264, 291–2, 326, 348, 375–6, 399–403, 406, 408–10, 413, 420–1
Environmental Justice Program, 401
Epiphany, 407
Episcopal Church (USA), 68, 77, 80–2, 92, 105, 110–11, 150, 183–4, 193, 219, 223, 225, 228, 289, 331, 341, 347, 429
episcopate, 190, 214
epistemology, 247, 267, 283
Equal Rights Amendment (ERA), 85, 87
equality, 14, 20, 84–5, 93–4, 108, 110, 161, 165, 269, 273, 289, 313, 340–2, 344, 348, 351–2, 391, 429
Equality Act, 352
Erik the Red, 172
Erikson, Leif, 172, 232
Eritreans, 87
eschatology, 205, 297–8, 307–8, 315, 326, 406
Escobar, Samuel, 333
Espinosa, Gaston, 70
Eternal Word Television Network (EWTN), 103, 240

ethics, 48, 59, 73, 93–4, 109, 111, 133, 136, 141, 219, 237, 304, 306, 354, 377–8, 402
Ethiopian Orthodox Tewahedo Church, 179
Ethiopian(s), 86–7, 179, 454
ethnicity, 67, 88, 109, 145, 148, 151, 162, 165, 338, 430, 445, 460
Eucharist, 29, 61, 183, 185, 187, 190, 236
Euchee, 124
Euro-American(s), 116, 146, 151, 155, 287, 306, 308, 429, 431–3, 435–7
Eurocentrism, 15–16, 30, 38, 249, 273–4, 280, 282–3, 297, 300, 308
Europe(an), 11–12, 16–18, 25, 30, 40, 42–3, 47, 54–5, 65–6, 71, 78, 82, 86, 88, 99, 101–4, 125–6, 129, 145, 149, 156, 168, 172, 179, 195, 198, 209, 213, 219–20, 225, 230, 233, 236, 242–4, 247–8, 259, 290, 299, 312, 322, 326–7, 334, 350, 362–4, 367, 374, 378–9, 381, 389, 398, 403, 429–31, 445, 457, 459
Evangelical Environmental Network, 399, 401
Evangelical Fellowship of Canada (EFC), 45–6
Evangelical Free Church of America, 83
Evangelical Hispanics, 148–9
Evangelical Lutheran Church, 78, 105, 220, 341, 343–4, 346, 429
Evangelical Mennonite Church, 36
Evangelical Missionary Church of Canada, 339
Evangelical Orthodox Church, 214
Evangelical(s), 17, 36, 40–1, 44–8, 50, 60, 65, 68–70, 76–8, 83, 85–9, 91–7, 99–100, 102–3, 105, 107–13, 126, 130, 134, 136, 138–43, 148–51, 158–61, 163–6, 179, 192, 214, 219–20, 225–30, 233, 245–57, 260, 265, 267–8, 278, 287, 290, 293, 295, 299, 306, 310–11, 315–21, 326–8, 331, 333, 338–41, 343–6, 353, 368, 386–9, 399, 401–2, 414, 416–18, 427–9, 431, 454–5
Evangelicalism, 17, 41, 46, 83, 88–9, 93, 95–6, 108, 110, 126, 134, 136, 141, 149–50, 161, 163–4, 245–6, 248–9, 251–7, 287, 317, 331, 343, 429
evangelisation, 237–8, 292, 324, 327, 435
evangelism, 33–4, 47, 96, 108, 113, 144, 149, 153–4, 162–4, 178–9, 204–5, 238, 247, 250, 255, 261, 288, 292, 324, 326–7, 330–3, 336, 346, 417–19, 453
evangelist(s), 29, 36, 89, 105, 108, 134, 176, 179, 225, 246–7, 251, 258, 260–1, 263, 266–7, 325–6, 329, 332–3, 344–5, 413, 416–19, 435
Evans, Clay, 84
Evans, Faith, 111
Evanston, Illinois, 326
Eve (biblical), 406
evil, 34, 138, 226, 250, 256, 279, 308, 318, 398, 404
evolution, 41–3, 52, 58–9, 89, 92, 103, 133, 145, 183–4, 198–9, 213, 215, 221, 224, 228, 233, 239, 243, 247, 273, 300, 307, 314, 347, 364, 421

exile, 57, 142, 163, 374, 376, 378, 380–1
exodus, 64, 91, 94, 112, 202, 332, 341
exorcism(s), 451
explorers, 18, 47, 88, 168
Exvangelicals, 100
Ezekiel, 368

Facebook, 340, 421–2
Fair Deal, 276
faith, 67, 106, 111, 150, 157, 164, 209, 217, 259, 263, 273–5, 319, 369, 384, 401, 410, 417
Falwell, Jerry, 85, 316, 368, 418–19, 428
families, 41, 44, 55, 64, 72, 77, 110, 112, 114–15, 121–2, 175, 183, 186, 195, 197, 217, 231, 235, 329, 363, 376–7, 431, 434, 437, 448
Famille Marie-Jeunesse, Quebec, 62
famine, 145, 235
Faroe Islands, 359
Father Divine, 111
Fea, John, 306
fear, 13, 48, 66, 75, 123, 143, 233, 248, 282–3, 306, 321, 343, 348, 356, 374–5, 379
Feast of Our Lady of Guadalupe, 382
feasts, 36–7
Federal Communications Commission, 414
Federal Council of Churches, 83, 226
Federal Council of the Churches of Christ in America (FCC), 225
female(s), 53, 57, 90, 94, 97–8, 170, 205, 228, 325, 337, 347
feminism, 106, 226, 298, 338, 348
feminist theology, 334
fertility, 230, 337, 431, 449–50, 456, 459
festivals, 293, 381
Feuerbach, Ludwig, 303
Fifield, James W., 276
Filipino(s), 43, 155–7, 159, 161, 163–4, 292, 320, 333
finance, 53, 188, 213
Finke, Roger, 50
Finland, 172
Finney, Charles Grandison, 79–80, 101, 246, 255
fire, 170, 258, 308
First Amendment, 198, 221, 310, 319, 355, 364
First Baptist Church, Indiana, 85
First Church of Christ, Scientist, Boston, 208
First Congregational Baptist Church, Chicago, 83
First Congregational Church of Columbus, Ohio, 81
First Corinthian Baptist Church, Harlem, 111
First Great Awakening, 89, 200, 249, 312, 314, 324–5, 368
First National People of Color Environmental Leadership Summit, 400
First Nations, 18, 33, 47, 116, 120–1, 198, 241, 285–8, 298–9, 334, 379, 403, 433
First Nations Alliance Churches of Canada, 33

fishing, 129, 168–9, 174, 234
Fletcher, James C., 106, 303–4
floods, 145
Florence, Arizona, 215
Flores, Archbishop Patrick, 99
Florida, 88, 98–100, 145, 211, 324, 329, 331
Florovsky, Fr Georges, 213
Flotow, Von, 82
Floyd, George, 94, 98, 143, 290, 375
Focus on the Family, 45, 69, 329
Folster, Stewart, 35
Fong, Ken, 166
Fontaine, Mary, 35
food, 85, 91, 117–18, 130, 146, 180, 231, 288, 382, 400, 402, 408, 410, 432
Foote, Julia, 97
Fordham University, 104
foreigners, 232, 377–8
forgiveness, 19, 282, 288, 293, 345, 379
Fort Ross, 211
Fosdick, Harry Emerson, 134, 413
Founding Fathers, 91
Fourth Great Awakening, 312
Fox, Vicente, 329, 367, 437
Fox News, 437
fragmentation, 167, 207
France, 29, 49, 53–4, 56, 58, 60, 78, 80, 89, 168–9, 234, 310, 350, 358–60
Francis, Pope, 27, 52–3, 77, 92, 103–4, 107, 147, 155, 161, 211–12, 215, 233, 239, 241, 261, 301, 324–5, 345, 354, 374, 377, 382, 401, 410, 428
Franciscans, 52, 104, 215, 233, 301, 325
Francophone Canada, 40, 52, 55–6, 60–1, 63
Franklin, Kirk, 294
Fraser Valley, 47
Fraternal Council of Negro Churches, 82–3
Free Constitutional Church (FCC), 225
Free Quebec, 58
Freedom Schools, 83
Freire, Paulo, 230
French-Creole, 109
French Diocese of La Rochelle, 235
French Huguenots, 59
French Jesuits, 101
French Revolution, 41
friend(s), friendship, 84, 373, 377, 383–4
Friends (Quakers), 89, 221, 363
Friends Across Borders, 377
Frobisher, Martin, 29
Frymer-Kensky, Tikva, 367
Full Gospel Church, 266
Fuller Theological Seminary, 134, 251, 292, 333
Fuller, Charles E., 413
Fulton, Archbishop, 417
Fundamentalist Church of Jesus Christ of Latter-day Saints, 72–3, 203
fundamentalist(s), 12, 72–3, 83, 86, 105, 109, 133–4, 203, 224, 247–8, 250–2, 256, 316, 326, 341, 427, 429, 434

funding, 36, 121, 237, 321, 335, 353, 356–8, 418
funerals, 346, 355, 445
future, 14, 16, 18, 20, 38, 53, 58, 62, 64, 67, 137, 144, 153–4, 166–7, 170, 230, 270, 277, 282–3, 298, 307, 318–19, 348, 375, 380, 383–4, 406, 427–8, 431–2, 434–6, 438, 454–5, 457–9

Galatians, 436
Galilee of the Gentiles, 428
Gallup, 233
Galveston, Texas, 211
gambling, 92
Gandhi, Mahatma, 371
gangs, 414
Gardner, Reverend Tyshawn, 97
Garrett-Evangelical Seminary, 333
Garrius, Alice Belle, 259
Gateway Church, Texas, 96
Gauvreau, Michael, 40
Gaye, Marvin, 111
gender, 11, 17, 20, 79, 85, 90, 94, 127–9, 165, 240, 254, 268, 277, 298, 301–2, 304, 334, 337–8, 340–8, 352, 354, 389, 400, 404, 407
General Association of General Baptists, 83
General Electric, 276
General Motors, 276
Geneva, Switzerland, 77, 128
genocide, 18–19, 114, 124, 129, 241, 249, 275, 279, 284, 312–13, 322, 379
GenZ, 427, 430
geography, 25, 36
Georgetown University, 369
Georgia, 88, 90, 95–6, 98, 147, 184, 315, 324–5, 328
German Shepherds, 215
German(s), 65, 137, 215, 223, 300
Germania, 398
Germany, 89, 137, 169, 172, 204, 310, 364
Gethsemani Abbey, Kentucky, 370
Ghana, 87, 108, 266
ghettos, 84, 421
Giglio, Louie, 96
Gillquist, Peter, 214
Girl Guide troop, 41
Gladden, Washington, 127
Glave, Dianne D., 403
Glendale, California, 75
global South, 14, 16, 27, 70, 106–7, 189, 195, 209, 244, 265, 270, 319, 376, 378, 400–1, 432, 435, 452, 454
global theology, 328
global warming, 306
globalisation, 16, 113, 362, 374
glossolalia, 258, 451–2
Glover, George, 207
God Seminar, 300
God-Talk, 334
Godse, Nathuram, 302
GodTube, 422

Gog, 368
Gokey, Danny, 294
gold, 161, 370, 435
Gonzalez, Justo, 437
Gordon, Adoniram Judson, 109–10, 251, 268, 326, 328, 333
Gordon College, 109
Gordon-Conwell Theological Seminary, 110, 251, 328, 333
gospel, 34–5, 47, 62–3, 80–2, 100, 105, 110–11, 119, 124, 127, 133, 162, 164, 166, 179, 208, 224, 244, 247–8, 259, 262–4, 266, 285, 287, 289, 291–2, 294, 299, 305, 312, 315, 318, 326, 331–2, 334, 348, 400, 412–13, 418–19, 429, 433–4, 436
Gospel Jazz Mass, 289
Gospel Music Association Canada, 294
government(s), 18–19, 28, 35, 37, 42, 45–6, 51, 53–4, 57, 60, 69, 89, 92, 100, 112, 114, 121–2, 126, 129, 138, 146, 152–3, 156, 161, 168, 174, 177–8, 185, 193, 199, 219, 222, 233, 237, 240–2, 276–7, 280, 282, 310–11, 321–2, 339, 351–3, 355, 357–60, 372, 392, 416, 420, 445, 447, 449–50, 455, 460
grace, 111, 128, 186, 266, 280, 287, 293, 299, 302–3, 305, 307, 379–80, 385
Grace Korean Church, Los Angeles, 266
Graduate Theological Union, Berkeley, 328
Grafton, David D., 368
Graham, Billy, 108, 134, 227, 246, 251, 276, 325–6, 329, 335, 416, 418
Graham, Franklin, 141, 344, 368, 428
Grammy Awards, 294–5
Granberg-Michaelson, Wesley, 319
Grand Rapids, Michigan, 319, 329
Grand Saline, Texas, 293
Grande Miquelon, 168
Grande Noirceur, 58
Grant, Jacquelyn, 128
Grant, John Webster, 40
grassroots, 221, 341, 431, 437, 450
Gravel, Raymond, 63
Great Awakenings, 95, 101, 312, 315
Great Depression, 68, 92, 276, 326
Great Migration, 110, 248
Great Reversal, 250, 326
Great Society, 276
Greek Orthodox Church, 215–17
Greek(s), 112, 211–13, 215–17, 248
Green, Byram, 324
Green, David, 344
Green Patriarch, 216, 400
Green Seminary Initiative, 408
Green Sisters, 410
GreenFaith, 106, 401, 410
Greenland, 11, 17, 172–6, 197, 232, 264, 350, 359, 362, 430
Gregory, Wilton, 242
Grey Nuns, 55

Gribben, Crawford, 69
Grim, John, 402
Groulx, Canon Lionel, 57
Grove City College, 109
Guadalupe, 66, 99, 105, 147, 353, 382
Guatemala, 104, 107, 377
guitar(s), 43, 292
Gulf of St Lawrence, 234
Gushee, David P., 306
Gutierrez, Gustavo, 230

Habel, Norm, 407
Hadewijch of Brabant, 411
Haggard, Ted, 69, 250
Hagin, Kenneth E., 263
Haiti, 104–5, 109, 111
Haitian(s), 104–5, 109, 111
Hale-Bopp comet, 278
Halifax, Nova Scotia, 178, 235
Hamer, Fannie Lou, 93
Hamilton, Bermuda, 177–9, 235
Hammond, Fred, 294
Hammond, Indiana, 85
Hanh, Thich Nhat, 371
Harakas, Fr Stanley, 213
Harlem, 111
Harmony Society, 201
Harper, Fletcher, 106
Harper, Stephen, 46
Harris, Melanie, 403
Harris, Michael Wesley, 82
Harrison, Beverly, 127
Hart-Cellar Act, 108, 391
Hartford Seminary, 369
Harvard Divinity School, 106
Harvard University, 268, 402
Hawaii(an), 64–5, 67, 70, 107, 156–7, 292, 331, 370
Hawaweeny, Father Raphael, 211–12
Hawthorn-Mellody, 85
Haystack Prayer Meeting, 324
HBO (Home Box Office company), 50
healing, 30, 36, 55, 70–1, 75, 80, 119, 121–4, 176, 208, 241, 258, 260–2, 265–7, 282, 288, 290, 293, 380, 383, 403, 407–9, 411, 418–19, 451, 453
Healing Hearts Ministry, 36
Healing the Land Publishers, 119
health, 20, 42, 53, 63, 73, 116, 121–2, 128, 130, 175–6, 208, 231, 237, 263, 337, 343, 350, 357, 437, 446, 450, 456
heaven, 116, 204–5, 226, 276, 287, 404, 406, 411, 416, 435
Hebden, Ellen, 259
Hebden Mission, 259
Hebrew Scriptures, 378
Hecker, Fr Isaac, 234
hegemony, 48, 50, 90, 135, 164
hell, 89, 203, 205, 345

Hellenic College, 217
Henderson-Espinoza, Robyn, 128
Herberg, Will, 135, 362
hermeneutics, 267, 300–1, 407
heroes, 325
heterosexuals, 72, 240
Hidalgo, Jacqueline M., 301
Hiebert Center for World Christianity and Global Theology, 328
High Low Food (Hi-Lo), 85
Hill Methodist Church, Bermuda, 179
Hillsong Church, Sydney, 293
Hindu Dialogue of Canada, 373
Hindu Federation of Canada, 373
Hindu(s), 157–8, 362, 371–3, 446, 456
Hinduism, 48, 65, 81, 112, 157, 304, 362, 371, 373, 457, 461
Hinn, Benny, 418
Hispanic American Freethinkers, 99
Hispanic House, 333
Hispanic Theological Education, 333, 437
Hispanic(s), 16–17, 67, 88, 98–100, 104–5, 107–8, 112, 144–54, 194, 233, 241, 259–60, 266, 291, 319–20, 330, 333, 367, 378, 381, 430–1, 437
Hmong, 156
Hobbesian, 394
Hobby Lobby, 354
Hoklotubbe, Dr T. Christopher, 124
holidays, 144, 176, 360
Holiness churches, 76, 83, 109, 216, 258–9, 303, 333, 451
Hollenweger, Walter, 329
Hollinger, David, 231
Hollywood, California, 332, 414–16
Holocaust (Shoah), 326, 332, 364–5, 367
Holy Cross Greek Orthodox School of Theology, 212, 217
Holy Cross Orthodox Press, 213
Holy Spirit, 70–1, 205, 258–9, 261–3, 266–7, 286, 289–91, 302–3, 385, 404, 408, 427, 429, 435, 451, 453
Holy Transfiguration Monastery, 214
Holy Trinity Monastery of the Russian Orthodox Church Outside Russia, 214
Holy Week, 291
homeless, 61, 174, 384
homosexuality, 153, 160–1, 227–8, 242, 254, 339, 342, 344
Honduras, 104, 107
Hopkins, Dwight, 98
hospice, 357
hospital(s), 53, 57, 62, 130, 145, 225, 231, 236–7, 241, 243, 286, 304, 354, 377–8, 383
hospitality, 62, 130, 286, 304, 377–8, 383
Hospitallers of St Augustine, 53
hostility, 95, 136, 204, 320, 368, 373, 375, 377
Houghton, Israel, 294
Houghton College, 109

house church(es), 108, 453–4
House of Bishops, 184
House of Deputies, 184
households, 340
Houston Chronicle, 95, 345
Houston, Texas, 94–6, 151, 217, 265, 345, 419
How Great Is Our God, 293
Hudson-Wilkin, Rose, 178
Hughes, Tim, 293
Huguenot(s), 59, 89
human rights, 237, 444, 447
Humanae Vitae, 43, 240
humanism, 99, 255
Hummingbird Ministries, 35
hunger, 428, 430
hunting, 174
Huntsville, Alabama, 98
Hurons, 52–3
Hutchison, William R., 220
hymns, 43, 80, 119, 124, 292

Iakovos, Archbishop, 215–16
Iannaccone, Laurence, 50
Iberia(n), 335, 363
Idaho, 64, 67, 69, 71
identity, 17–20, 32, 37, 42–3, 47, 52, 60, 66–7, 72, 124, 129, 136, 147, 150–1, 155, 170, 175, 179, 197–8, 201, 204–5, 207, 230, 245, 252–4, 256–7, 267, 287–8, 290, 292, 297, 301–2, 304–6, 337, 344, 347, 352–4, 357, 364, 367, 370, 386, 388–92, 396–7, 421, 427, 429, 449–50, 457
ideology, 18, 55, 125, 255, 276, 279, 298, 322, 386, 389, 392
idioms, 142, 166
Iglesia Juan 3:16, Bronx, 107
Ike, Reverend, 263
Ilagiit Kaladlit Luterkussut, 174
Iliff School of Theology, 129
Illich, Ivan, 105
Illinois, 76–7, 80, 329, 354
Illinois Street Church, 80
illiteracy, 330, 387
illness, 207–9, 293, 379
Im, Hyepin, 164
imagery, 126, 130, 132, 307
imagination, 20, 59, 255, 280, 306–7, 427
imago Dei, 131
Immaculate Conception, 56, 78
Immanuel Cathedral of Paradise, 179
immigrant(s), 13–15, 43, 48, 59, 66, 70, 75, 78–9, 86, 88, 100, 105–6, 109, 111–12, 116, 128, 134, 138, 141, 145–7, 161–5, 211–15, 218, 243, 256–7, 265–6, 285–7, 298, 320–2, 331, 362–3, 370–1, 374–8, 380–4, 427–9, 431–7, 455, 458–9
immigration, 13, 16–17, 20, 42, 46, 48, 60, 64–7, 71, 74, 86–7, 89, 98, 108, 112, 135, 145, 152–3, 155, 161–3, 194, 212, 230, 232, 234, 243, 248, 260, 265, 285, 292, 317–22, 362, 370–1, 374, 376–80, 384, 390–1, 431, 457–9
Immigration Act, 86, 162
imperialism, 125, 162, 433
Inca(s), 53, 308
incarnation, 53
inclusivity, 135, 230, 264, 348
income, 188, 193, 230, 335
inculturation, 35
independence, 54, 58, 116, 177, 203, 221, 239, 282, 312, 314, 351, 359, 415
Independent(s), 11, 197–205, 207, 209, 263, 267, 450, 452–3
India, 18, 30–1, 50, 76–8, 80, 85–6, 110, 114, 116, 118, 120–2, 126, 156, 159, 195, 207, 241, 243, 286, 299, 306, 324–5, 329, 334, 363, 367, 371, 430
Indian Ecumenical Movement (IEM), 286
Indian(s), 18, 30–1, 76–8, 80, 85–6, 110, 114, 116, 118, 120–2, 126, 156, 159, 195, 241, 286, 299, 306, 324–5, 334, 430
Indiana, 76–8, 80, 85
Indigeneity, 116
indigenous, 12, 16–18, 25–38, 47, 52–4, 64, 66, 74–5, 78, 88, 114–24, 126, 129–30, 183, 185, 188, 195, 233, 241, 265, 273, 275, 285, 287, 289–90, 292, 298–9, 322, 325, 342, 374, 379, 382, 398–400, 403, 433, 452
Indigenous Environmental Network, 400
Indigenous Pathways, 37, 120
Indigenous Water Protectors, 116
individualism, 11–12, 51, 126, 194, 253, 256, 281
Indonesia, 127, 156, 448, 454
Industrial Revolution, 347
industrialisation, 102, 108
inequality, 84, 108, 110, 342
inerrancy, 247
infant(s), 448
Influence Church, Anaheim, California, 69
infrastructure, 91, 97, 175, 226, 244, 250, 254
injustice, 97, 116, 162, 204, 280, 285, 305, 308, 326, 371, 374–5, 377, 384, 400, 411, 433
Inner City Youth Alive, 36
Innocent, Archimandrite, 211
instability, 169–70, 265, 423
Institutional African Methodist Episcopal Church of Chicago, 81
Integrity of Creation, 399
inter-religious dialogue, 304, 325, 367–8
Interfaith Center of New York, 106
intermarriage, 37, 151, 158
International Church of the Foursquare Gospel, 329, 340, 413
International Church of Triumph, 201
International Eucharistic Congress, 61
International House of Prayer in Kansas City (IHOPKC), 264–5
International Orthodox Christian Charities, 215

International Peace Mission, 111
International Society for Krishna Consciousness, 371, 373
intersectionality, 131, 298, 338
InterVarsity Christian Fellowship (IVCF), 45, 109, 165, 251, 329
InterVarsity Press, 98, 287, 329, 331, 335
intolerance, 146, 363
Inuit, 264
Inuunerup Nutaap Oqaluffia, 175–6, 264
Iowa, 76
Iqaluit, 29
Iran, 448
Iraq, 317, 369
Ireland, 65, 89
Irenaeus of Lyons, 405, 407
Irish, 66, 85–6, 88, 102, 105, 146, 235
Iroquois, 52
Irving, Washington, 368
Irwin, B. H., 258
Isasi-Diaz, Ada Maria, 128
Islam, 44, 48, 50, 59, 89, 138, 350, 359–60, 362, 367–9, 372–3, 457, 461
Islamic State, IS, ISIS, 350
Israel, 91, 201–2, 245, 275, 294, 331–2, 367, 370
Istanbul, Turkey, 216
Italy, 65, 172

Jackson, California, 211
Jackson, Joseph H., 83
Jackson, Mahalia, 82
Jackson, Reverend Jesse, 84, 93
Jacobs, Adrian, 31
Jains, 157, 362–3
Jakes, T. D., 263, 418
Jamaica, 110, 178, 325
James, William, 371
Jamestown, Virginia, 145
Jantzen, Grace M., 303
Japan, 56, 156–9, 161–3, 266, 293, 333, 370, 375, 460
Japanese, 156–9, 161–3, 266, 293, 333, 370, 375, 460
Japanese Evangelical Missionary Society, 163
Japanese YMCAs, 162
Jarrell, Texas, 99
jazz, 82, 127, 289
Jefferson, Thomas, 311, 368
Jenkins, Philip, 70
Jennings, Willie James, 306–7, 398
Jericho, 275
Jerusalem, 71, 201, 247–8, 430, 433, 435
Jesuit Post (blog), 104
Jesuit(s), 52–3, 101, 104, 170, 369, 414
Jesus Culture, 265
Jesus Seminar, 300
Jesus Way, 286–8
Jeung, Russell, 165
Jewel Foods, 85

Jewish relations, 366–7
Jews, 103, 134–5, 150, 180, 223, 248, 331–2, 363–7, 372
Jobe, Kari, 295
jobs, 14, 68, 84, 145, 347, 358–9
Joh, Wonhee Anne, 128
John Paul II, Pope, 59–60, 136, 238–9, 368, 399
Johnson, Elizabeth A., 302
Johnson, Hall, 82
Johnson, Todd, 328
Joint Committee of Churches, Bermuda, 180
Jones, Charles Colcock, 90
Jones, E. Stanley, 325
Jones, Jim, 278
Jordanville, New York, 214
Journal of Hindu-Christian Studies, 372
Journal of NAIITS, 120
journalists, 45
Jovanovich, Harcourt Brace, 128
Joy, Emily, 345
Judaism, 50, 59, 73, 134, 362, 364–7, 373, 398, 461
Judge, William Q., 368
judgement(s), 115, 353, 358, 382
Judson, Adoniram, 324, 333
Judson, Ann, 333
Jurassic Age, 361
justice, 14, 16–17, 45, 58, 82–3, 85, 92, 95–8, 104, 106, 111, 115–16, 120, 126, 136, 143, 152–3, 162, 165, 193, 204, 238–9, 247, 252, 255, 257, 277, 280–3, 285, 289, 291, 297, 299, 301, 303–8, 313, 315, 317, 326–7, 332–3, 342–4, 348, 355, 358, 360, 364, 368, 371, 374–8, 380, 383–5, 391, 395, 399–403, 406, 409–11, 433–5

Kahului, Hawaii, 70
Kamloops, British Columbia, 30
Kansas, 76–7, 80, 258, 262, 264, 329, 346
Kansas City, Missouri, 262, 264
Kaskaskia, Illinois, 78
Kateri Tekakwitha, 29–31, 52, 241
Kayin (Karen), 129, 303
Kazaks, 460
Keetoowah Cherokee, 119, 124, 334
Keller, Catherine, 308
Keller, Timothy, 109
Kelley, Dean, 229
Kelly, Kate, 72
Kendrick, Graham, 293
Kennedy, President John F., 103, 146, 234
Kennedy, Senator Ted, 352
Kentucky, 78, 88–9, 98
Kenya, 108
KFSG radio (KFSG), 413
Khang, Kathy, 166
Kidwell, Clara Sue, 129
killing(s), 95, 128, 277, 350, 379, 411
Kim, Grace Ji-Sun, 128

Kim, Julius, 166
Kim, Lloyd, 334
kindergartens, 45
Kindom of God, 407
King, Reverend Dr Martin Luther, 19, 83, 87, 93–4, 96, 98, 216, 269, 276, 305, 314–15, 332, 371, 380
kingdom, 119, 172, 204, 297–8, 304–8, 315, 325, 368, 407, 455
Kingdom Ethics, 306
kings, 178, 302, 306–7
Kingston, Jamaica, 178
kinship, 299
kneeling, 146
Kodiak Island, 211
Kollman, Jack, 74
Kolloch, Isaac, 428
Kool-Aid, 278
Korea, 15, 45–6, 86, 108, 127–8, 156–9, 162–4, 266, 278, 320, 329, 333, 370, 375–6, 380–1, 384, 399
Korean Americans, 157–8, 320, 333
Korean Church Council of North America, 162
Korean Immigrant Women for Mission, 384
Korean United Church, 384
Korean War, 278
Korean(s), 15, 45, 86, 108, 128, 156–9, 162–4, 266, 278, 320, 333, 370, 375–6, 380–1, 384
Koukouzis, Archbishop Iakovos, 215
Krist Konge Kirke, 232
Kuhlman, Kathryn, 260
Kumbaya, 282
Kwok, Pui Lan, 165
Kyung, Chung Hyun, 128

La Posadas, 377
La Rochelle, Bishop of, 170
labour, 18, 57, 81, 88, 107, 126, 256, 276, 312, 347, 376, 428, 431
Labrador, 168, 259
Lac Ste Anne, 30
laity, 56, 99, 103–6, 113, 140, 184, 187–8, 190, 200, 236, 239, 242
Lakotas, 78
Lallesvari, 304
Lambeth Quadrilateral, 190
land, 11, 14, 16, 18, 26, 40, 52, 55, 66, 77, 88–9, 91, 114–15, 117–19, 123, 145, 172, 174–5, 202, 209, 221, 275, 285, 292, 297, 332, 334, 353, 370, 374, 378–80, 398–9, 403
Langlade, 168
language(s), 15–16, 29, 37, 52–4, 58–9, 74–5, 105, 114, 119–21, 123, 144–7, 150–1, 155, 173, 175, 177, 186, 195, 199–200, 211, 214, 231, 236, 243, 249, 252, 265, 277, 279, 285–8, 290, 294–7, 300–3, 305, 317, 324, 335, 338, 352, 359, 376, 379–81, 402, 416, 430, 445–6, 460
Laotians, 156–7
Las Asambleas de Dios, 151

Latin America(ns), 13, 56, 58, 66, 68, 70, 102, 106–9, 126, 141, 145, 150–1, 209, 216, 233, 260, 285, 292, 331, 333, 375, 380–2, 427, 431–4, 437
Latin American Bible College, 260
Latin American Council of Christian Churches, 151
Latin Mass, 239
Latino(s), 17, 98–100, 108, 145, 148, 156, 160–1, 165, 259, 286, 290–1, 294, 333, 336, 427, 429–31, 433–4, 437
Latinx, 66–8, 70, 128, 130, 205, 266, 381
Latter Rain Movement, 262
Laudato Si', 401
Lauritzen, Stephanie, 72
Lausanne Covenant, 333
Lausanne Movement, 326–7, 333, 336
Laval University, 54, 61
Law, Cardinal Bernard Francis, 103
law(s), 50, 69, 103, 130, 145, 169, 178, 184, 190, 198, 237, 243, 277, 281, 310, 312, 350–3, 356–60, 375, 390, 456
lawyers, 236, 347, 357–8
Lay, Humberto, 108, 236, 242
Lay Involvement for Evangelism (Campus Crusade for Christ) (LIFE), 216
laypeople, 53, 56–8, 191, 199, 236, 330
leadership, 13, 25–6, 28, 31, 33, 38, 53, 57, 71–2, 81–4, 90, 97, 99–100, 103–4, 107, 120, 140, 146–9, 153, 162, 176, 178, 191, 207, 212, 214–16, 221, 227, 245, 250, 253, 256, 259, 261, 267–70, 287, 293, 312, 315, 319, 339–40, 342, 347, 387, 400, 409, 411, 428, 435–6, 453
Leadership Conference of Women Religious, 342
Leamington, Ontario, 383
Lebanon, 213
LeBlanc, Terry, 47, 119, 287, 334
Lecrae, 97, 294
Lee, Jarena, 97
Lee, Sang Hyun, 165
LeeLand, 295
Left Behind, 307
Legend, John, 111
Lent, 407
Leo XIII, Pope, 234
Lesage, Jean, 57
Lewinski, Monica, 387
LGBTQ (LGBTIQA), 13, 68, 72, 75, 94, 97, 106, 109, 129, 139, 142, 207, 227, 236–8, 321, 331, 338–42, 344–7, 391, 429
Liberal Party, Canada, 240
liberalisation, 42
liberation, 58, 68, 98, 106, 111, 127–8, 155, 165, 230, 263, 281, 283–5, 287, 289, 291, 298, 300, 315, 330, 332, 334, 338, 342, 380, 406, 410–11
Liberation Methodist Connexion, 68
Liberation Theology, 111

Liberia, 108
liberty, 42, 60, 69, 90, 94, 139, 141, 234, 266, 275, 277, 285, 344, 347, 355, 360–1, 368
Liberty Conference, 69
Liele, George, 325, 332
Liew, Tat-siong Benny, 301
Lifton, Robert Jay, 278
Ligonier, Pennsylvania, 215
Lin, Jeremy, 165
Lin, Tom, 166, 334
literacy, 63, 237, 330, 387
literature, 47, 91, 175, 334–5, 432, 444, 453
Liturgical Movement, 186
liturgy, 74, 89, 184, 187, 194, 238, 267, 281, 288, 366, 382, 407
Liu, Reverend Tong, 265
lobbying, 80, 84, 139, 320, 343
Loma Linda University School of Health, 73
London, Ontario, 14
London, UK, 177, 188–9, 205, 368
Long Beach, California, 433
Long, Charles H., 306
Long, Robert Aaron, 95
Loomis, Harvey, 324
Lord, Daniel A., 414
Lord I Need You, 294
Los Angeles, California, 70, 75, 151, 164, 208, 233, 237, 243, 250, 259, 265–6, 329, 380, 413, 433
Los Angeles Religious Education Conference, 237
Louisiana, 66, 88, 161, 211, 241, 345
Louisville, Kentucky, 78
Lowell, Massachusetts, 103, 211
Luce, Alice, 259
Lugo, Juan Julio, 107, 260
Lugo, Luis, 100
Luhrmann, Tanya, 71
Lumen Gentium, 236
Luong, Dominic, 165
Lutheran Church Missouri Synod, 338
Lutheran Church of Greenland, 174
Lutheran World Federation, 402
Lutheran(s), 17, 40, 76–80, 87, 89, 105, 174, 219–20, 232, 246, 261, 286, 338, 341, 343–4, 346, 359, 372, 402, 410, 429
Lynn, Massachusetts, 208

McCaulley, Esau, 98
McCormick Seminary, 166
MacDonald, Most Reverend Mark, 28
McGee, F. W., 82
McGill University, 55
McGrath, Alister, 178
McKenzie, Bishop Vashti Murphy, 98
McLaren, Brian, 142
McManus, Mariah, 294
McNutt, Francis, 261
McPherson, Aimee Semple, 255, 329, 413

Madison, James, 311
Magog, 368
Mahayana Buddhism, 157, 370, 460
Maher, Matt, 295
Main Island, Bermuda, 177
Maine, 101, 258
mainline churches, 17, 40, 76, 94, 106, 220, 224, 226, 228–31, 344
Mainse, David, 45
Make America Great Again (MAGA), 428–9
Malaysia(n), 156
Maldonado, Guillermo, 429
male(s), 236, 280
malnutrition, 121, 379
Mance, Jeanne, 53
Manchuria, 74
Manhattan, New York, 17, 109, 213, 216
Manifest Destiny, 275, 306, 428, 433
Manito Sahkahigan, 30
Manitoba, 29, 31, 36, 294
map(s), 77, 297
Maracle, Jonathan, 124, 294
Maranatha Music, 294
marginalised, 16–17, 66, 123, 127, 192–3, 236, 258, 263, 270, 277, 287, 308, 390, 392, 410, 432–3
Maria Chapdelaine, 56
Marian apparitions, 67, 99
markets, 85
marriage, 37, 43, 46, 63, 68–70, 72, 74, 95, 97, 107, 109, 139, 151, 153, 158, 185, 187, 189–90, 194, 207–8, 214, 227–8, 239–40, 277, 317, 321, 337, 339, 341, 343–4, 352, 355, 357, 360, 391, 415, 429
Mars Hill, 140
Martin, Fr James, 238
Martin, Ralph, 261
Martin, Sallie, 82
martyr(s), 53, 202, 245
Marx, Karl, 195
Maryknoll, 330, 377
Maryland, 65, 88, 184
masculinity, 253, 256, 343, 348
mass, 11, 43, 48, 53, 56, 62, 79, 84, 86, 101–2, 108, 110, 112, 117, 121, 128, 135–6, 142, 148, 186, 209, 214, 232, 238–9, 243, 289, 308, 375, 380–2, 413–14, 417, 419, 423, 434
Massachusetts, 74, 101, 103, 208, 211, 214, 324, 326, 363
Massachusetts Metaphysical College, 208
Mather, Cotton, 249, 368
Matovina, Timothy, 99
Matsuoka, Fumitaka, 165
Matthew, Apostle, 306, 318, 409
Maui County, Hawaii, 65
Maurin, Peter, 238
Maverick City Music Collective, 294
Mecca, 422
Mechthild of Magdeburg, 304

media, 12, 15, 48, 53, 63, 84, 96, 104, 113, 139–42, 144, 148, 201, 240, 250, 254, 260, 262, 295–6, 308, 315, 332, 337, 354, 375, 379, 394, 412–14, 416–20, 422–3, 429, 437, 449
medical assistance in dying (MAID), 357
medicine, 31, 117, 208
meditation, 208, 293, 371
mega-church, 76, 85, 94, 96, 100, 110, 135–6, 140–2, 262, 264–6, 268, 345
Megiddo, 307
membership, 14, 34, 47, 83, 85, 90, 94, 97, 107, 116, 180, 183, 188, 190–1, 193, 205, 207, 220, 223, 226, 228–30, 245, 338, 372, 380, 429, 446–8, 454, 456, 458
Membertou, Saqamaw, 29–30
Memphis Miracle, 269
Mennonite Brethren, 36, 45, 83
Mennonite Central Committee, 36
Mennonite Church Canada (MCC), 36
Mennonite(s), 35–6, 45–6, 77, 83
Mercer University, 328
merchants, 161
Merton, Thomas, 370
Metaxakis, Archbishop Meletios, 212
Metaxas, Eric, 141
Methodist Episcopal Church, 68, 77, 81–2, 92, 110–11, 219, 223, 225, 289
Methodist(s), 31, 40, 68, 76–7, 79–83, 87, 89–90, 92, 97, 105–7, 110–11, 115, 179, 199, 219–23, 225–6, 228, 230, 246, 261, 286, 289, 310, 314, 325, 340–1, 384, 429
methodology (methods), 114, 118, 121–2, 124, 127, 132, 208, 229, 254, 270, 299, 301, 331, 423, 441, 444
Metropolia, 212–14
Mexican Revolution, 145
Mexico, 19, 64, 66–7, 88, 98–9, 129, 203, 233, 243, 259–60, 266, 279, 292, 320, 354, 376–7, 381
Meye, Steve, 418
Meyer, Joyce, 418
Meyer, Marshall T., 418
Miami, Florida, 99, 265, 433
Michigan, 76–9, 329
Middle America (Midwest), 76, 78, 87, 107
Middle East, 65, 75, 108, 112, 138, 155–6, 212–13, 259, 367, 430, 434, 437
migrant(s), 13–15, 41, 43, 48, 59, 65–6, 70, 75, 78–9, 86, 88, 100, 102–12, 116, 128, 134, 138, 141, 145–7, 161–5, 211–15, 218, 243, 256–7, 259, 265–6, 285–7, 298, 319–22, 331, 362–3, 370–1, 374–8, 380–4, 427–9, 431–7, 450, 455, 458–9
migration(s), 13, 15–17, 20, 42, 46, 48, 60, 64–7, 70–1, 74, 79, 86–7, 89, 98, 101–2, 104–12, 135, 145, 152–3, 155, 161–3, 194, 209, 212, 221, 230, 232, 234, 243, 248, 260, 265–6, 269, 285, 290, 292, 317–22, 362, 367, 370–1, 374, 376–80, 384, 390–1, 431, 455, 457–9

Milan, Italy, 345
Milano, Alyssa, 345
military, 41, 44, 54, 68, 71, 101, 108, 126, 132, 179, 212, 216, 232–3, 280, 335, 360, 364, 369
Miller, Ben, 294
Miller, William, 73, 203
Mills, Samuel, 324
Minneapolis, Minnesota, 85, 143, 319
Minnesota, 76–9, 87
minorities, 85, 94, 170, 269, 290, 322–3, 331, 342, 370
miracle(s), 55, 71, 208, 247, 260, 267, 269, 451, 453
Miranda, Reverend Jesse, 152
Missing and Murdered Indigenous Women, 122
missiology, 32
Mission Dolores, San Francisco, 382
Missionaries of the Immaculate Conception, 56
Missionary Alliance, 15, 32, 45
missionary(ies), 15–16, 27, 29, 32–6, 45, 47, 52–3, 56–8, 63, 66, 70, 78, 91, 98, 100–1, 105–6, 113, 121, 144, 154–5, 161–4, 170, 172, 174–5, 187, 205–6, 211, 221–2, 224, 231, 233, 235, 238, 241, 245–6, 259, 267, 273–4, 292, 306, 314, 324–7, 329–33, 335, 339, 371, 377, 416, 418
Mississippi, 88–9
Missouri, 76–8, 203, 264, 338
Mistawascis, 35
mixed martial arts (MMA), 348
mobility, 260
models, 162, 251, 300, 308, 404, 434–5
modernisation, 136
modernity, 57, 112, 248, 298, 398
Mohawk, 29, 31, 53
Mohler, R. Albert, 141, 301
monastery(ies), 62, 214–15, 370
Monastic Interreligious Dialogue, 370
Moncton, New Brunswick, 170
money, 50, 118, 219, 305, 318
Mongolian(s), 381
monks, 211, 370
Mont Royal, Quebec, 56
Montana, 64, 67–8, 71
Montreal, Archbishop of, 57–8, 62
Montreal, Canada, 32, 42, 53, 55–9, 61–2, 297
Moody, Dwight Lyman, 80, 250, 326
Moody Bible Institute, 413
Moody Church, Chicago, 85
Moon, Lottie, 335
Moon, Sun Myung, 278
Moore, Beth, 95–6, 140
Moore, Lecrae, 97
Moore, Russell, 94, 96, 141
Moorish Science Temple, 367
Moral Majority, 69, 85, 227, 316, 418
morality, 50, 126, 135, 140, 223, 229, 318, 325, 387, 415

moratorium, 168, 335
Moravian(s), 111, 174, 246
Morikawa, Jitsuo, 165
Mormon(s) (cf. Church of Jesus Christ of Latter-day Saints), 47, 71–2, 101, 201–2, 340
Moroni (angel), 71
Morris, William, 353
mortality, 459
Mosaic MSC, 294
Moscow Patriarchate, 213, 218
Moscow, Idaho, 69
Moscow, Metropolitan of, 211
Moseley, Romney, 194
mosques, 48, 362
Mother Alexandra, 214
Mother Church (Christian Science), 208
mothers, 41, 78, 128, 267, 348
Mott, John R., 327
Mount Athos, Greece, 215
Mount Cashel Orphanage, Newfoundland, 43
Mount Saint Agnes Academy, Bermuda, 178
movements, 12, 14, 38, 56, 58, 85, 90, 101, 104, 106–7, 109, 111, 113, 135, 162–3, 176, 194, 197, 200, 209, 250, 258, 264, 266, 276, 289, 298, 300, 303, 307, 311, 313, 315, 344, 383, 391, 394, 400–2, 408–10, 418, 446, 452
Muhammad (Prophet), 368
murder, 17, 92, 94, 122, 143, 290, 343, 415
Murray, John Courtney, 234, 238
music, 45, 69, 80–2, 96, 111, 113, 121, 124, 142, 144, 149–51, 153, 174, 199, 206, 226, 242, 262, 265, 288–95, 343, 382, 407, 416–17, 432
Muslim National Liaison Committee, 372
Muslim(s), 49, 60, 106, 138–9, 150, 152, 155, 157, 170, 180, 256, 322, 358, 362, 367–70, 372, 384, 411, 429, 445, 449–50, 456–7, 460
Mutual Life, 276
My Chains Are Gone, 293
Mya, Francis Ah, 383
Myanmar, 383
Mystici Corporis, 330
myths, 139, 306, 384

Nagano, Paul, 165
NAIITS Learning Community, 120
Nakota Sioux, 30
Nation of Islam, 367
National Acadian Society, 170
National Assembly of Quebec, 63
National Association for the Advancement of Colored People (NAACP), 83
National Association of Broadcasters, 414
National Association of Evangelicals (NAE), 83, 250–1
National Association of Lay Ministry, 236
National Association of Manufacturers, 276
National Baptist Churches, 223
National Baptist Convention (NBC), 97

National Baptist Convention of America (NBCA), 97
National Black Catholic Clergy Caucus, 242
National Black Sisters Conference, 242
National Catholic Welfare Conference, 364
National Conference of Christians, 364
National Convention of Gospel Choirs, 82
National Council of Churches (NCC), 134, 217, 225, 400
National Council of Churches of Christ in the USA (NCC), 400–1
National Council of Synagogues, 366–7
National Football League (NFL), 97
National Fraternal Council of Negro Churches, 82
National Hispanic Christian Leadership Conference (NHCLC), 149, 152
National Household Survey, 47, 60
National Indigenous Council, 32
National Latino Evangelical Coalition, 108
National Legion of Decency, 415
National Origins Formula, 362
National Religious Partnership, 401
National Team Company, 85
National Tri-Partite Liaison Committee, 372
nationalism, 18–20, 57, 135, 137, 162, 222, 280, 283, 336, 386, 388–90, 392–7, 427–30, 436
Nationality Act, 362, 370–1
Native American Contextual Movement, 119
Native American Expression of the Jesus Way, 287
Native American Music Award Association, 294
Native American(s), 16–19, 78, 86, 101, 114, 117, 119–24, 129, 165, 198, 202, 211, 225, 233, 249, 256, 285, 287, 294, 299, 313, 324, 352, 384, 390, 431, 435
Native Ministries of Ontario, 32
Native Ministry Circle, 35
native(s), 16–19, 32–3, 35, 40–1, 45, 47, 52–4, 78–9, 86, 101, 105, 114–24, 129–30, 134, 149, 156, 163, 165, 176, 184, 186–7, 189, 198, 202, 211, 225, 232–3, 241, 249, 255–6, 265, 267, 275, 279, 285–8, 292, 294, 298–300, 304, 312–13, 318, 322, 324, 334, 352, 363, 367, 376, 379, 381, 383–4, 390, 406, 430–1, 435
nature, 11, 16, 28, 31, 58–9, 75, 89, 102, 126, 137, 142, 197, 202–3, 208–9, 238, 245, 273, 286–7, 293, 298–9, 313, 320, 326, 335, 351, 355, 358, 374, 392, 394, 396, 399, 404–6
Navajo(s), 38, 65, 334
Nazareth, Israel, 126, 428, 432–3
Nazi(s), 169, 364–5
Nebraska, 76
Negro Spirituals, 82
neighbours, 48, 93, 234, 254, 308, 333, 376, 400, 411, 457
Nepal, 156, 446
Nephites, 71
Netflix, 50

networks, 102, 106, 108, 112, 134–5, 140, 163, 183, 189, 251–2, 262–5, 296, 378, 409–10, 416–19, 450, 453
Nevada, 64, 68, 71
New Amsterdam, 363
New Apostolic Reformation, 262
New Brunswick, 170
New Delhi, India, 399
New England, 41, 55, 77, 101, 109, 169, 199, 207, 221, 275, 324, 336
New Friendship Baptist Church, 84
New Frontier, 276
New Hampshire, 101
New Jersey, 101, 211
New Jerusalem, 248, 430, 435
New Life Church, 69, 175
New Life Covenant, 151
New Light Evangelicalism, 89
New Mexico, 64, 67, 233, 354, 381
New Orleans, Louisiana, 82, 211, 289
New Sanctuary Movement, 377
New Skete Monastery, 215
New Smyrna, 211
New Testament Church of God, 180, 264
New Thought Movement, 208
New World Translation of the Bible, 204
New York, 65, 67, 69, 71, 73, 86, 101–12, 184, 201, 204, 211–17, 265, 282, 328, 330, 332, 363, 369, 374, 410
New York Times, 282
New Zealand, 41, 119
Newark, New Jersey, 211
Newfoundland, Bishop of, 178
Newman Centers, 104
newspapers, 55–6, 213
Ng, David, 165
Nicene Creed, 190–1, 302
Nicholas, Archbishop of Japan, Hieromonk, 74, 178, 216, 241
Niebuhr, Reinhold, 127, 133–4, 371
Nigeria(n), 86–7, 108–9, 189, 243, 266, 295, 454
Nikon, Patriarch, 74
Nisbett Lecture, 178
Noah, 245
Nobel Laureates, 399
Noll, Mark, 91, 209
Nones, 112
nonreligious, 355
Norr, Homer, 204
Norsemen, 172–3
North Africa, 430
North American Chinese Church Convention, 162
North American Institute for Indigenous Theological Studies (NAIITS), 119–20, 124
North American Orthodox-Catholic Theological Consultation, 217
North Atlantic Ocean, 177
North Carolina, 88, 177, 184, 258, 295, 400

North Dakota, 76, 78
North Point Community Church, Georgia, 96
Northeastern United States, 101–2
Norway House Cree, 29
Norway, 172, 232, 456
Nostra Aetate, 365, 368, 371
Notre Dame University, 261–2
Notre-Dame-du-Cap, Quebec, 56
Nova Scotia, 177, 184–5, 235, 238
Novak, David, 367
Noyes, John Humphrey, 201
nun(s), 55–7, 62, 236, 342, 345
Nunaat, Kalaallit, 172
nurses, 58, 236, 354
nutrition, 73, 121, 379
Nuuk, Greenland, 172–4, 176, 232
Nyack College, 109, 333

Oakland, California, 381
Obama, President Barack, 138–9, 152, 326, 330
Obergefell v. *Hodges*, 355
Oberlin College, 79
Oceania, 285
Ochs, Peter, 367
Oglala, 78–9
Ohio, 76–7, 79, 81, 85
oil, 43, 116, 276, 279
Ojibwe, 78–9, 120, 124
Oklahoma, 88
Olazabal, Fransciso, 260
Olivet Baptist Church, Chicago, 83
One Belt, One Road (OBOR), 88, 94
Oneida, New York, 201
Ontario, 14, 32, 34, 221, 237, 357, 383
Operation Breadbasket, 84–5
oppression, 15, 18–19, 50, 125, 128, 277, 283, 286, 289, 291, 308, 312–13, 322, 337–8, 379, 433
Oral Roberts University, 268, 450
orality, 50, 126, 135, 140, 223, 229, 299, 318, 325, 387, 415
Orange County, California, 68
orders, 104, 145, 201, 236–7, 241, 280, 297, 301, 330, 333, 377, 388, 457
ordination, 13, 20, 31, 61, 68, 94, 97, 105, 107, 185, 189, 200, 206, 215, 226, 228, 240, 242, 337–8, 341–2, 347, 390, 429
Oregon, 64, 67–8, 71–2, 74, 350, 352
Oriental Orthodox Christian Churches, 218
orientalism, 368
Orlando, Florida, 128, 329
Orlando E. Costas Consultation, 328
orphanages, 260
Orthodox Christian Education Commission, 215
Orthodox Christian Mission Center (OCMC), 331
Orthodox Observer, 213

Orthodox Theological Seminary, 212
Orthodox(y), 17, 40, 65, 73–4, 76–7, 86, 112, 126–7, 135, 157, 179, 197, 211–18, 248, 267, 286, 302, 331, 344, 353, 365, 372, 399, 408, 414, 452
orthopraxy, 200
Osage, 129, 299
Ossernenon, New York, 52
Ossoff, Jon, 315
Osteen, Joel, 418–19
Osteen, John, 261
Ottawa, 31, 61
Ottoman Empire, 367
Ouellet, Cardinal Marc, 61
Our Lady of Guadalupe, 147, 353, 382
Our Lady of the Cape, Quebec, 56
outreach, 37, 56, 104, 113, 175–6, 180, 291, 419, 421
Oxford University Press, 67, 69
Oyate, Sicangu Lakota, 334
Oyedepo, David, 266

Paasch, Hanna, 345
Pacific Islander(s), 156, 165, 292
Pacific Northwest, 41, 64, 69
Padilla, Al, 333
Padilla, C. René, 327, 333, 434
Pakistan, 156, 460
Palestinian(s), 126, 404
Palmer Seminary, 333
Palmyra, New York, 71, 201
Pan de Vida, 382
Pan Orthodox, 86
pandemics, 51
paradigms, 300
Parham, Charles Fox, 70, 258, 269, 329
parish(es), 44, 52, 54–6, 59, 63, 74, 81, 85–6, 102–5, 109, 113, 147–50, 170, 174, 177–8, 183, 185, 187–8, 190–1, 193, 211–13, 216–17, 235–6, 238, 243, 261, 289, 314, 318, 345, 377, 380–2, 415
Park, Marquette, 84
Parliament of World Religion, 87
parliament(s), 46, 63, 80–1, 86–7, 172, 177–8, 359, 362, 364, 370–1
Parsis (Zoroastrians), 157, 362–3
partnership(s), 61, 80, 106–7, 110, 138, 153, 238, 336, 341, 401
Passion Conference, 96, 294
pastors, 36, 45, 68, 93, 95–6, 109, 123, 142, 150, 162, 179, 251, 267–8, 338, 340, 345, 348, 414, 416–19, 429
Patriarch of Moscow, 212
Patriarchate of Constantinople, 212
Patriarchate of Serbia, 213
patriotism, 133
Paul, Apostle, 245
Paul VI, Pope, 43, 240, 262, 368
Paulist Fathers, 234

peace, 14, 42–3, 85, 93, 111, 119, 136, 204, 239, 283, 295, 307–8, 311, 317, 330, 348, 358, 368, 383–4, 399, 402
Pearson, Carlton, 263
Peers, Michael, 29
Pelly Fellowship Chapel, Saskatchewan, 36
Pennsylvania, 101, 107, 109, 203, 214–15, 241
Pentagon, 369
Pentecostal Assemblies of Canada (PAOC), 33–4
Pentecostal Assemblies of Newfoundland, 259
Pentecostal Assemblies of the World, 78, 86
Pentecostal Church of God, 260
Pentecostal Theological Seminary, 268
Pentecostal(s), 17, 33, 41, 45–7, 65, 68, 70–1, 76–8, 82–3, 86–7, 98–103, 107–9, 111, 135–6, 150–2, 175, 180, 198, 229–30, 246, 249–52, 258–69, 286, 290, 293–4, 329–30, 340, 344, 372, 432, 450–3
peoples, 14–15, 17–18, 25–37, 40, 52, 66, 77–9, 88, 116, 120, 126, 129, 144–5, 155, 195, 233, 298, 305, 334, 374, 379, 382, 384, 398–9, 403, 409, 444, 460
Pepsi-Cola, 85
percussion, 129
persecution, 65, 75, 149, 204, 233, 364–5
Personal Ordinariate of the Chair of Saint Peter, 233
Peters, Andrej, 77, 174
Petersen, Bishop Sofie, 174
Petite Miquelon, 168
Pew Research Center, 88, 99–100, 157–61, 193–4, 220, 226–7, 243, 276, 350, 367, 370, 450, 455, 459
Philadelphia, Pennsylvania, 102, 110, 147, 219, 354
Philippines, 70, 104, 161, 243, 292
Phillips, Kevin, 316
philosophy, 33, 38, 49, 208, 246, 249, 301–2, 371, 398
Pietists, 83, 246
piety, 111, 138, 186, 380
pilgrimage, 30, 56
Pius XII, Pope, 330
Placentia, Newfoundland, 170
Plains, Georgia, 29
Plains Cree, 29
plantations, 90–1
Pluralism Project, 106
pluralism, 48, 54, 86, 106, 198–9, 209, 234, 363, 368, 372, 457
Plymouth Brethren, 315
poetry, 127, 288
pogroms, 364
Pokagon Band Potawatomi, 124
Poland, 65
police, 60, 94, 111, 126, 128–30, 143, 322, 358, 375
politicians, 19, 141, 153, 239, 321–2, 346, 418

Politico magazine, 317
politics, 13, 18–20, 46, 91, 94, 97, 137, 144, 213, 220, 231, 251, 254, 306–7, 310–11, 313, 317, 319–22, 386, 389–90, 392, 396, 412, 418–19, 429
polity, 96, 100, 207, 212, 222, 225, 262, 432
polls, 48, 145, 149, 227, 277, 315, 318, 446–8
polygamy, 73, 203
Polynesian Cultural Center, 331
Polynesian(s), 331
polytheism, 89, 371
Pond, Dr Negiel Big, 124
Pontifical Council for Interreligious Dialogue, 368
poor, 55, 57, 84, 92, 94, 98, 105, 108, 127, 130, 193, 206, 215, 221, 235, 240, 252, 255, 258, 275, 325, 335, 364, 376, 379, 433
Poor Clares, 215
Pope Alexander VI, 17
Pope Benedict XVI, 240, 369
Pope Francis, 147, 239, 241, 325, 345, 401
Pope John Paul II, 59–60, 136, 238–9, 368, 399
Pope Leo XIII, 234
Pope Pius XII, 330
Portugal, 177
Portuguese, 66, 102, 109, 129, 177, 179, 235, 290, 335, 363
poverty, 65, 84, 122, 124, 128, 130, 208, 317, 322, 330, 335, 342–3, 376, 378, 401
power, 12, 14, 19, 28, 46, 48–9, 54, 57, 85, 88–9, 112, 115, 126, 129–30, 133–4, 136–7, 140–1, 153, 164, 168–9, 188, 193, 199–200, 202, 209, 222, 224, 226, 245, 255–6, 258–9, 261–2, 264–5, 267, 270, 275–8, 282–3, 285–6, 288–9, 291, 297, 299, 301, 305–8, 311, 313, 317–18, 330, 336, 339, 359, 377–8, 388, 391–5, 400–1, 404–6, 408, 410–12, 415, 419, 421–3, 429, 433, 436–7, 450–3
Prague, Czech Republic, 77
prayer, 14, 29, 38, 53, 62, 81, 111, 113, 116–17, 147, 151, 186, 193, 208, 226, 237, 255, 262, 264–5, 267, 288–91, 293, 305, 324, 333, 350–1, 353, 359–60, 379, 382–4, 421, 428, 451
preach(er), 34, 50, 54, 56, 70, 80, 84, 89–90, 97, 107, 113, 179, 187, 199, 206, 236, 244, 247, 258, 263, 276, 286, 289–90, 305, 314–15, 329, 332, 334, 348, 366, 379, 413–14, 417–19
preaching, 50, 56, 80, 90, 113, 206, 236, 276, 286, 366, 413, 417
Precious Lord, 82
pregnancy, 49, 194
Presbyterian Church of America, 338
Presbyterian Church of Canada, 179
Presbyterian Church of the United States, 91
Presbyterian Church USA, 347
Presbyterian(s), 12, 15, 34–5, 40, 47, 76–81, 83, 89–91, 105, 109, 150, 179, 203, 220–6, 246, 334, 338, 347, 381, 420

Presbytery of West Toronto, 179
president(s), 12, 58, 72, 132, 138–9, 152, 193, 234, 256, 278–9, 282, 311, 317–18, 320, 326, 334, 352, 358, 387, 391, 395
Price, Fred, 263
Price III, Emmett, G., 290
Prideaux, Humphrey, 368
priest(s), 20, 29–30, 54, 56, 58, 61–3, 72, 86, 98, 104–6, 147–8, 165, 170, 172, 174–5, 178, 183, 187–8, 232, 235–6, 242, 261, 302, 338, 340–2, 345, 364, 414, 452
Primate of the Anglican Church, 29
prime ministers, 46, 359
Prince Alwaleed bin Talal Center for Muslim-Christian Understanding, 369
Princess Ileana of Romania, 214
Princeton Theological Seminary, 106, 328, 333
printing, 200, 412
prison(s), 92, 235–6
privacy, 227
Production Code Administration (PCA), 415
Progressive National Baptist Convention (PNBC), 97, 111
Prohibition, 169
prophesy, 308, 451
prophet(s), 12, 38, 71, 114, 135, 202, 245, 253, 264–5, 282, 289, 291, 314–15, 332, 368, 377–8, 411, 433
proselytising, 238
prosperity, 18, 42, 47, 204, 263–4, 266–7, 418, 436
Protestant Episcopal Church in the USA (PECUSA), 184–5
Protestant Reformation, 77, 149, 246, 332
Protestant(s), 11, 17, 32, 40–1, 44–6, 54–5, 58–60, 64–9, 71, 76–83, 85–9, 94, 99, 102–3, 105–10, 112–13, 133–7, 139–42, 148–52, 156–65, 169–70, 179, 184–6, 190, 198, 214, 219–30, 233–4, 239, 245–8, 256, 261–2, 266–7, 278, 289–90, 292, 295, 310, 318–21, 325–6, 330, 332, 338–40, 343–4, 362–5, 371, 389, 391, 408, 412–18, 429, 432–3, 451–4, 461
protests, 72, 84, 98, 143, 156, 400
Proud Boys, 132
proverbs, 293
Provo, Utah, 72
PTL Television Network, 417
Public Religion Research Institute, 99, 318
publishing, 76, 134, 204, 213, 224, 294, 330
Puerto Rican, 103–5, 107–8, 145, 150, 333
pulpits, 223, 228, 315
Punjabi, 460
Puritans, 101, 246, 275, 363, 412
Putnam, Robert, 231

QAnon, 132, 346
Quadragesimo Anno, 238
Quaker(s) (Friends), 89, 221, 363

Quebec City, 52–3, 55–6, 59, 61–2
Quebec, Canada, 32, 40–1, 43, 52–63, 170, 221, 238, 240, 358–60
Queen Elizabeth I, 184
queen(s), 184, 193
questionnaire(s), 447
Quimby, Phineas P., 208
Quinceanera, 381
Quinn Chapel AME, 83
Quorum of the Seventy, 203
Quorum of the Twelve Apostles, 203

Raboteau, Albert, 90
race, 79, 92, 94, 98, 102, 126–7, 129–30, 139, 143, 145, 148, 156, 165, 194, 216, 275, 301, 312, 334, 338–9, 342–3, 367, 388, 398, 400, 428, 431–3, 436
racism, 11–12, 15, 18–19, 92, 97, 115, 120, 125–6, 128–30, 138, 143, 152–3, 164, 194–5, 207, 241–2, 261, 269, 276–8, 283, 312–14, 316, 326, 346, 364, 370, 400
Radha, 126
radicalism, 359–60
radio, 45, 84, 113, 142, 180, 250, 326, 329, 364, 412–14, 416–17, 420
Rah, Soong-Chan, 115, 166, 331, 334
railway, 15
rain, 121, 258, 262
Ramadan, 383
Ramage, David, 86
Rambo, Shelly, 302
Raniere, Keith, 278
rape, 140, 274, 415
Rapid City, South Dakota, 119
Rapp, George, 201
Rauschenbusch, Walter, 127, 133, 305, 326, 332
Ravi Zacharias International Ministries (RZIM), 96–7
Rayside, David, 321
Reagan, President Ronald, 138, 152
RealAudio players, 421
reality, 18, 20, 35, 52, 59, 63–4, 72, 98, 133, 142, 208, 256, 278–9, 297, 304, 307, 314, 346, 351, 378–9, 393–4, 401, 411, 451, 455
rebellion, 277
Recife, Brazil, 363
reconciliation, 11, 18–19, 28, 33, 47, 127, 190, 194–5, 241, 269, 281–2, 293, 295, 334, 379, 383–4
Reconciliation Commission, 28, 47
reconstruction, 69, 91, 206, 407
Red Cross, 231
Red Lip Theology, 98
Redding, California, 70, 264
Redeemed Christian Church of God (RCCG), 109
Redeemer City-to-City, 110
Redeemer Presbyterian Church, New York, 109

Redman, Matt, 293
Reform Era, 89–90
Reformation, 77, 101, 149, 173, 185–6, 219, 222, 246, 262, 310, 332, 404, 407
Reformed Church, 37, 45, 220, 225
Reformed Episcopal Church (REC), 183, 185–8, 190–1
refugee(s), 13, 20, 106, 138, 141–2, 163, 184, 221, 230, 236, 243, 318, 374, 376–7, 382–3
Refus global, 57
Regent University, 268
regime(s), 46, 52, 55, 58–9, 221, 419
Regina, Saskatchewan, 33, 37
regulations, 188, 276, 413
Reid, Angus, 240
relief, 92, 208, 329, 351
Religion News Service, 364
religiosity, 60, 133–4, 159, 320, 386, 389, 396–7
religious affiliation, 60, 64, 88, 99, 149, 157–8, 190, 229, 243, 358, 372, 437, 445–7, 449–50, 455–60
religious diversity, 59, 65, 75, 102, 106, 112, 135, 163, 220, 304, 350, 362
religious freedom, 12, 49, 232, 238, 266, 310–11, 318, 350, 352–7, 360, 364, 372, 444
Religious Freedom Restoration Act (RFRA), 352–3, 357, 361
religious identity, 43, 52, 150, 386, 421, 427
religious liberty, 60, 94, 139, 141, 344, 347, 355, 360–1
Religious Liberty Commission, 94, 141
Religious Right, 45, 254–5, 311, 316–17, 321–2, 391
Relocation Act, 122
renewal, 17, 32, 102, 109, 150, 167, 195, 224, 258, 261–3, 268, 452–3
Reorganized Church of Jesus Christ of Latter-day Saints, 203
repentance, 195, 252, 258, 269, 323, 402
Republican Party, 132, 160, 239, 254–5, 316–17, 320–1, 387
Rerum Novarum, 238
research, 11, 34, 48–9, 61, 67, 88, 99, 106, 119, 138, 145, 151, 157, 172, 193–4, 215, 220, 228, 243, 268, 283, 304, 318, 328, 344, 350, 367, 370, 412, 420, 423, 446, 448, 451, 453, 455, 459–60
resources, 33, 50, 63, 113, 118, 125–6, 128, 136, 147, 151, 161, 168, 200, 209, 279, 294, 296, 299, 302, 352, 398, 402, 404, 407, 410–11, 419–21, 432, 437
respondent(s), 156–7, 446, 457
Reston, Virginia, 99
restoration, 30, 80, 205–6, 213, 236, 258, 352, 354, 391–2, 451, 453
resurrection, 28, 71, 201, 205, 224, 235, 303–4
retirement, 369

revival(s), 44, 70, 79–80, 89–90, 96, 101, 107, 122, 151, 170, 193, 199–201, 205, 246–7, 249–50, 255, 257–61, 263, 265, 276, 311, 324–6, 329, 413, 432, 436
revolution, 41–3, 52, 58–9, 89, 103, 145, 184, 198–9, 213, 221, 233, 239, 243, 307, 314, 347, 364
Revolutionary War, 198–9, 221
Rhee, Syngman, 165
rhetoric, 138–9, 223, 274–5, 277, 282, 298, 316, 318, 320–1, 388, 392, 394
Rhode Island, 101
rhythm, 82, 94, 289, 292, 294, 314
Ricardo, Father Alberto, 107
Richards, James, 324
rights, 17, 19, 49–50, 58, 60, 68, 72, 75, 80, 83–5, 87, 92–4, 96–7, 106, 109, 129, 135, 138–9, 160, 162, 174, 194, 198, 216, 226–7, 234, 237, 241, 257, 269, 276–7, 285, 307, 310–12, 314–15, 321, 325, 332, 339–40, 347, 351, 355–8, 364, 371, 380, 391, 394, 398, 400, 402, 409, 429, 444, 447
Rio de Janeiro, Brazil, 399
rites, 72–3, 116, 147, 186, 381
ritual(s), 11–12, 17, 27–31, 41, 44, 48–9, 53, 59, 62, 82, 87, 91, 93, 98–9, 108, 111, 114, 124, 126, 131, 137, 153, 159, 176, 180, 186–8, 193, 199, 203–4, 207–8, 214, 219, 223, 227, 229–30, 241, 250, 260–8, 270, 274–7, 280, 283, 285–93, 296–7, 299, 305, 311, 323, 325, 330, 332, 372, 376–83, 399, 404, 409, 411, 420–2, 427–30, 432–4, 451
River of Life Christian Church, California, 265
rivers, 50, 177, 376
Robbins, Francis LeBaron, 324
Robert, Dana, 328
Roberts, Chief Justice John, 355
Roberts, Michelle Voss, 304
Roberts, Oral, 260–1, 263, 268, 329, 417, 450
Robertson, Pat, 85, 263, 316, 368, 417, 419
Rodriguez, Samuel, 429
Roe v. *Wade*, 316–17, 339, 343
Rohr, Richard, 301
Roman Catholic(s), 12, 40, 42–4, 50, 80–1, 85–7, 128, 136, 161, 165, 217, 221, 223, 230, 232, 235, 238, 240, 243–4, 261, 267–8, 292, 330, 360, 372, 380, 422, 429, 433, 452
Roman Empire, 90
Romana de Venezuela, 259
Romanesque, 193
Romania, 172, 213–14
Romanian Episcopate of the Orthodox Church, 214
Romanticism, 325
Rome, Italy, 55, 185, 189, 234, 238, 241, 399, 412
Romney, Mitt, 72
Roo, Remi de, 240
Roof, Wade Clark, 50

Roosevelt, First Lady Eleanor, 92
Roosevelt, Franklin D., 92
Roseburg, Oregon, 350
Ross, Denise, 211
Ross, John, 211
Royal Canadian Mounted Police, 322
Royal Commission on Radio Broadcasting, 413
Ruether, Rosemary Radford, 128, 334
Russell, Charles Taze, 101, 203
Russia, 74, 112, 211–14, 363–4, 460
Russian Orthodox Church Outside Russia (ROCOR), 74, 213–14
Russian Orthodox Church, 74, 211–14
Russian Revolution, 213
Rutherford, Joseph Franklin, 204

sabbath, 73
Sabin, Jerald, 321
sacraments, 35, 183, 190, 203, 215, 238
sacrifice, 42, 57, 123, 186, 255, 285–6
Saddleback Community Church, California, 150, 330
Said, Edward, 155, 297, 400
St Alban, 193
St Andrew's church, Bermuda, 179
St Anne de Detroit, Michigan, 78
St Anthony's Monastery, Arizona, 215
St Basil Catholic, 380
St Brendan, 232
St Clair, Michigan, 77
St Francis-Xavier mission, Quebec, 53
St Francis, South Dakota, 77
St George, 193
St Jerome's church, New York, 105
St John's, Newfoundland, 43, 259
St Joseph the Hesychast, 215
St Kateri, 29–31, 241
St Louis, Missouri, 77–8, 81, 83, 85, 211
St Mellitus College, 188
St Nicholas Greek Orthodox Church, 216
St Nicholas Orthodox Church, 74
St Paul, Minnesota, 77
Saint-Paul University, 61
St Peter's Basilica, Rome, 55
St Peter's Church, Bermuda, 177
Saint Pierre and Miquelon, 11, 17, 168–70, 232, 234, 350, 359–60, 362, 430
St Stephen, Minnesota, 77
St Tikhon's Monastery, 214
St Tikhon's Seminary, 212
Saint-Vallier, Jean-Baptiste de, 170
St Vladimir's Seminary, 112, 212–13
saints, 12, 30, 52, 65, 67, 71–2, 77, 147, 193, 197, 201, 203, 219, 224, 241, 330, 340, 372, 416
Sakacewescam, 29
Salem, Massachusetts, 324, 333
Salguero, Gabriel, 108
Saliba, Metropolitan Philip, 214

Sallman, Warner, 15
Salt Lake City, Utah, 72, 203
Salvation Army (TSA), 36–7
San Antonio, Texas, 99, 233, 433
San Diego, California, 233
San Francisco, California, 155, 161, 211–12, 233, 354, 374, 377, 382, 410, 428
San Francisco State University, 155
San Jose, California, 297, 381
sanctification, 258
sanctions, 126
Sanctuary Movement, 377
Sandford, Frank, 258
Sandmel, David Fox, 367
Sandy-Saulteaux Spiritual Centre (SSSC), 31–2
sanitation, 121, 269
Sankey, Ira, 80
Sano, Roy, 165
Santa Clara County, California, 65
Santa Fe, New Mexico, 233
Saskatchewan, 29, 36, 237
Saskatoon, Saskatchewan, 35
Satan, 203, 205, 346
Savannah, Georgia, 325
Scarborough, Joe, 318
schism(s), 183, 185, 224, 228, 239, 303, 452–3
Schlafly, Phyllis, 85
Schleiermacher, Friedrich, 300
Schmemann, Fr Alexander, 213
schools, 18–19, 29–32, 35, 38, 41–2, 45–7, 55–9, 61, 76–7, 83, 91, 102, 104, 106, 120–2, 134, 145, 148, 162, 166, 174, 188, 193, 195, 221, 223, 225, 231, 237–8, 241, 243, 250, 255, 268, 300, 316–17, 321, 328, 353–4, 356, 379, 437
Schori, Katharine Jefferts, 228
Schumer, Chuck, 352
science, 49–50, 61, 92, 99–100, 114, 127, 138, 165, 190, 201, 207–9, 237, 240, 247, 273–4, 279, 301–302, 310–11, 326, 355–6, 367, 398–9, 459
scientists, 46, 101, 144, 155, 226, 399, 446
Scientologists, 372
Scopes trial, 92, 224, 250
Scotland, 89, 119, 179
Scottish Common Sense, 246, 249
scripture(s), 93, 115, 159, 186, 189–90, 192, 200, 202, 204, 206, 223, 246, 257, 263, 291, 297–302, 305, 313, 338, 347, 378, 404, 407
Sears Roebuck, 276
Seattle, Washington, 261
Second Great Awakening, 89, 95, 101, 200–2, 205, 207, 209, 312, 325, 364
Second Life, 421
Second Treaty of Paris, 168
Second Vatican Council, 43, 58, 147, 235–6, 238–9, 365–6, 368, 371
Second World War, 57, 68, 92, 107, 134, 162, 169, 204, 212, 216, 224, 226, 229, 251, 260, 320–1, 332, 334, 364, 414

sect(s), 65, 190, 248, 311
sectarianism, 384
secular(ism), 40–1, 45, 48–9, 51–2, 60, 63, 69, 96, 98, 146–7, 159, 189, 194, 221–2, 226, 230, 236–8, 243, 247–8, 255, 258, 265, 268, 297, 308, 311, 320–2, 326, 328, 350–1, 353–6, 358, 360, 380, 391, 399, 410, 415–19, 430, 457
security, 130, 132, 236
seekers, 186, 259, 261, 377, 421
Segovia, Fernando F., 300
segregation, 18–19, 82–4, 91–3, 179, 194, 219, 435–6
seminary(ies), 44–5, 54, 58, 66, 77, 94, 106, 109–12, 134, 141, 148, 166, 212–13, 223, 230, 241, 248, 250–1, 268, 292, 301, 315, 326, 328, 332–3, 369, 408, 435, 437
Senegalese, 87
Seoul, South Korea, 266, 399
Sephardic Jews, 363
Serbia(n), 211, 213
Serbian Orthodox Church, 211
sermon(s), 12, 96, 151, 275, 318, 347–8, 359, 407, 413, 421
Seth, 245
settlement(s), 52, 81, 161, 221, 242, 363, 378
Seven Ecumenical Councils, 215
Seventh-day Adventist(s), SDA, 12, 65, 73, 179, 219, 341
sex, 46, 68–70, 72, 95, 97, 107, 109, 122, 139–40, 147, 185, 189, 194, 254, 317–18, 321–2, 338–9, 341, 344–7, 352, 354–5, 360, 415, 459
sexual abuse (children), 94–6, 140, 241–2, 345, 379
Seymour, William J., 70, 250, 259, 329
Shakyamuni Buddha, 126
sheep, 168, 275
Sherbrooke University, 61
Shiloh, Maine, 258
Shintoism, 372, 460
ship(s), 84, 172, 304
Shoah (Holocaust), 326, 332, 364–5, 367
Shug Avery, 130
Shuttlesworth, Fred, 93
Siberia, Russia, 74
Sicangu Lakota, 116, 124, 334
sickness, 208
Sider, Ron, 333
Sierra Gorda, Mexico, 325
Signer, Michael A., 367
Signs and Wonders Movement, 329
Sikhs, 48, 322, 362–3
Silk, Mark, 64
sin, 28, 72, 89, 95, 114, 119, 143, 195, 208, 224, 252, 283, 305–6, 312–13, 315, 319, 322, 346, 365, 400, 404, 406, 435, 437
Sinach, 295
singing, 14, 80, 93, 117, 206, 259, 262, 288, 291, 382, 421
Sioux Valley, Manitoba, 36

Sisters of Charity of St Vincent de Paul, 235
Sisters of Jesus, 232
Sisters of Mercy, 104
Sisters of St Joseph of Cluny, 235
Sitter, Joseph, 399
Skinner, Arturo, 261
Skinner, Tom, 332
slavery, 12, 72, 79, 90–1, 125–6, 200, 219, 223, 225, 241–2, 249–50, 275, 284–5, 298, 312–14, 322, 360, 378, 380, 390, 409, 435
slaves, 91, 179, 223, 242, 313, 332, 378, 380
Smith, Christian, 50
Smith, Joseph, 71–3, 101, 201–2, 209
Smith, Martin, 293
Smith, Michael W., 295
Smith, Shanell T., 301
social action, 104, 115, 247, 333, 383
social consciousness, 333, 375
social justice, 115, 299
social services, 42, 57, 81, 102, 243, 352, 409
sociologists, 50, 392, 445
Sojourner Truth, 101
Sojourners, 252
soldiers, 47, 235, 254
Somalis, 445
Song, C. S., 165
Sonoma County, California, 211
soteriology, 303, 434
soul(s), 62, 133–4, 137, 144, 152, 205, 251, 276, 345
South Africa, 85, 108, 127, 315
South America, 15, 100, 107–8, 212, 215, 230, 259, 330
South Asia, 155, 157, 367, 371
South Canaan, Pennsylvania, 214
South Carolina, 88, 90, 184–5
South Dakota, 76–7, 119
South Korea, 127, 266
Southeast Asia, 155, 157, 163, 293, 367, 375, 430, 433
Southern Baptist Convention (SBC), 76, 88, 94–6, 140–1, 150, 330, 334, 336, 338, 341, 455
Southern Baptist Theological Seminary, 301
Southern California Japanese Christian Church Federations, 162
Southern Christian Leadership Council, 84
Southern Conference of the Congregational Christian Churches, 223
Southern Presbyterians, 91, 225
Southern United States, 88, 99, 232
Southlake, Texas, 96
Soviet Union, 75, 213
Spain, 99, 145
Spanish American Bible Institute, 107
Spanish Conquest, 433
Spanish-language, 144, 146–7, 150
Speaker of the House, 395
Spiewak, Bishop Wieslaw, 179
Spirit Lake, 30

Spiritual But Not Religious (SBNR), 49
spiritual(Ity), 31, 49, 82, 275, 330, 379
Springfield, Vermont, 214
Spurgeon, Charles, 246
Sri Lanka, 370
Stach, Christian, 174
Stach, Matthaus, 174
Standard Oil, 276
Standing Conference of Canonical Orthodox Bishops, 215
Standing Rock Reservation, 116
Starfield, 294
Stark, Rodney, 50
Stassen, Glen H., 306
statistics, 17, 84, 194–5, 228–9, 350, 441, 445–8, 450, 458, 460
Stephenson, John, 179
stereotypes, 263, 413, 421
stewardship, 405
Stiller, Brian, 45
Stockbridge Indians, 324
Stockton, Betsey, 332
Stone-Campbell Movement, 206
Stone, Barton W., 205
Stop AAPI Hate, 165, 167
stories, 17–18, 72, 95, 133, 140, 194, 202, 233, 251, 287–8, 293, 298–300, 344–5, 376, 379, 398, 405, 414
Stott, John, 333
stress, 44, 62, 89, 175, 188, 193, 245, 281, 289, 295, 303, 350–1, 429
Stroope, Michael, 335
student(s), 12, 45, 47, 55, 71–2, 86, 117, 148–9, 155, 162, 166, 188–9, 203, 208, 215, 235, 237, 261, 332, 350, 353–4, 358, 378–9, 384, 427–8
subjugation, 281
suffering, 50, 93, 99, 130, 204, 208, 276, 287, 306, 308, 346, 371, 383, 432–3
suicide, 33, 46, 174–5, 278
Sulpician community, 53
summer camp, 45, 217
Summer, Donna, 111
Sun Oil, 276
Sunday school, 41, 45, 80, 93, 200, 227
Sunni(s), 367
Sunsum Sore (spiritual churches), 87
supernatural, 70, 266, 279, 287, 291, 404, 451–3
Supreme Court (US), 316–17, 339, 344, 352–5, 360, 414
Supreme Court of Canada, 43, 49, 356–7
survey(s), 47, 49, 60, 64, 84, 157, 159, 161, 220, 226, 230, 297, 308, 310, 341, 350, 389, 423, 445–50, 456–7, 459–61
survival, 57, 69, 108, 128, 175, 193, 220, 301, 342, 433
Survivors Network of Those Abused by Priests (SNAP), 345
sustainability, 105, 305
Swaggart, Jimmy, 263, 417

Swami Vivekananda, 371
Sweden, 49, 172, 445
Swedish Mission (KMA), 30
switching (religious), 149
Switzerland, 216
Sydney, Australia, 293
symbols, 60, 99, 132, 243, 284, 358–60, 384
synagogues, 362, 366–7
syncretism, 119
synod(s), 78, 178, 185, 187–8, 193, 222, 338
Syria(ns), 212–13, 383

Tacitus, 398
Taiwan, 156, 370
Talitha Kum International, 378
Tanner, Kathryn, 305
Taoism, 157, 292, 372
Taylor, Breonna, 94
Taylor, Charles, 60, 351
Taylor, Hudson, 332
teachers, 18, 38, 45, 49, 58, 236, 353, 357–8, 360, 379
Tebow, Tim, 97
technology, 100, 108, 138, 417, 420–2, 456
Tejanos, 98
Tekakwitha, St Kateri, 241
Telemundo, 144
televangelism, 149, 417–19
television, 45, 103, 113, 240, 260, 263, 326, 412, 414, 416–20
Ten Commandments, 414
Tennessee, 70, 88–9, 98, 194, 224, 258, 269
terrorism, 216, 395
Testem Benevolentiae, 234
testimonies, 120, 151, 259, 287, 432
Texas, 70, 88, 96, 98–100, 138, 145, 211, 260, 293, 378, 381, 419
texts, 16, 27, 35, 37, 186, 190, 201–3, 211, 223, 265, 267, 296, 299–301, 308, 336, 344, 388, 405, 420–3, 448
Thai(s), 156–7
Thailand, 163, 370
Tharpe, Rosetta, 82
Thatamanil, John J., 304
The Blessing, 295
theologians, 98, 106, 123, 127, 136, 142, 178, 195, 200, 213, 217, 230, 236, 297, 378, 404–9, 432–4
theological education, 106, 113, 333, 437
theology, 11, 16, 28, 30, 32, 34–5, 38, 61, 81, 89, 94–5, 98, 103, 106, 109, 111, 127–9, 136, 140, 147, 162, 173, 197, 205, 212, 215, 217, 219, 224, 246–7, 249, 257, 262, 266–8, 281, 284, 292, 296, 298, 302–6, 310, 313, 315, 317–19, 325–6, 328, 330–2, 334, 342, 365, 371, 378, 380, 388–9, 392, 399–404, 406, 408, 415, 428, 432–3, 435–6, 454
theory, 92, 94, 143, 190, 298, 304, 310, 342, 346, 451

Theosophist Society, 368
Theravada Buddhism, 157, 370
Thibault, Pierre, 62
Third Great Awakening, 312, 326
Third World Liberation Front, 155
Thirteenth Amendment, 241
Thirty-Nine Articles of Religion, 190
Thomas, Paul E. J., 321
Thoreau, Henry David, 368, 371
Thornwell, James Henley, 90
thought reform, 278
Three-Self Church, 336
Thurman, Howard, 371
Tibetan Buddhism, 156, 370
Time magazine, 165
tithing, 98
tobacco, 15, 89
tolerance, 93, 146, 221, 231, 363
Tomlin, Christopher, 293
tongues, 70, 168, 173, 214, 258–61, 266–7, 451, 453
Tonstad, Marie, 304
Topeka, Kansas, 258, 329, 346
Torah, 378
Toronto, Canada, 17, 43–7, 60–1, 179, 243, 259, 263, 328, 331, 374, 383–4
Toronto Airport Vineyard Fellowship, 263
Toronto Blessing, 263
Toronto Conference of the United Church of Canada, 384
torture, 138
tourism, 168, 335
Tower of Babel, 93
toxic waste, 400
trade, 78, 122, 129, 161, 211, 216, 285, 313, 369, 376
traders, 78, 211
tradition(s), 12–14, 17, 20, 25–32, 34–8, 42, 46–7, 50, 54, 56, 58–9, 61–2, 64, 68, 71, 73–5, 77, 79–80, 94, 96, 99–102, 105–6, 111–13, 120, 133, 135, 140, 142, 144–7, 149, 163–4, 183, 185–6, 189, 192–3, 195, 197, 199, 201–3, 205–7, 209, 212, 216, 219–20, 223, 236, 239, 241, 245, 248, 255, 258, 260–2, 264, 267–9, 281, 283, 285, 288–90, 292–5, 297, 299, 301–2, 305–6, 311, 314, 322, 340, 342–4, 348, 353, 357, 363, 367, 370–3, 377, 379, 382–3, 387–8, 390–1, 402, 404–6, 409, 411, 413–14, 419–21, 428, 437, 441, 448, 451–3
trafficking, 122, 346, 378
training, 31–3, 35, 45, 71, 85, 148, 178, 187–9, 194, 200, 268, 351, 353, 357
Trakatellis, Archbishop Demetrios, 216
Transcendentalist(s), 368, 371
transformation, 20, 58, 61, 105, 255–6, 304–5, 308, 319, 374, 395, 401, 427, 454
Trappists, 62

trauma, 53, 114, 118, 121–2, 124, 174, 302
travel, 82, 90, 100, 117, 121, 211, 238, 259, 326, 335
treaties, 379
Treaty of Paris, 54, 168, 170, 221, 234
Treaty of Utrecht, 168
Tribal Nations, 115, 118, 120
tribe(s), 79, 116–17, 175, 201, 287–8, 296, 322, 334, 402, 430
Trible, Phyllis, 301
Trinitarianism, 304
Trinity Broadcasting Network (TBN), 263, 417, 437
Trinity Evangelical Divinity School, 328
Trinity Western University (TWU), 357
True Jesus Church, 265
True Love Waits, 95
Truman, President Harry, 326
Trump, President Donald J., 12, 94–5, 98, 100, 132, 140–1, 143, 152, 161, 256, 277–83, 311, 318–20, 338, 346, 376, 387–9, 392, 395, 428–9
Truth and Reconciliation Commission (CVR), 28, 47
Tucker, Mary Evelyn, 402
Tudor English, 186
Tulsa, Oklahoma, 450
turbans, 322
Turcotte, Jean-Claude, 62
Turkey, 216
Turtle Island, 398, 401–3, 410
Twin Towers of the World Trade Center, 369
Twiss, Katharine, 117
Twiss, Richard, 116, 119, 124, 287–8, 334
Tyndale University, 268, 328
Tyson, Tommy, 261

Uganda, 454
Ukraine, 295
Umpqua Community College, 350
unaffiliated, 64, 69, 112, 157–61, 170, 220, 430, 455
unchurched, 47, 193
Underground Railroad, 314
Unification Church, 278
Union of Concerned Scientists, 399
Union of Soviet Socialist Republics (USSR), 213
Union Theological Seminary, 111, 315, 328, 332
Unitarians, 223
United Church of Canada, 31, 40, 220, 225–6, 229, 307, 322, 341, 347, 372, 379, 384, 422
United Church of Christ (USA), 78, 220, 225, 227–9, 341, 344, 400, 410, 429
United Daughters of the Confederacy, 91
United Farm Workers, 238
United House of Prayer, 111
United Methodist Church, 68, 105, 107, 220, 228, 230, 340–1, 384, 429

United Missionary Church (UMC), 68
United Nations (UN), 90, 129–30, 159, 237, 350, 362, 394, 444–8, 459
United Nations Children's Fund (UNICEF), 446
United Nations Educational Scientific and Cultural Organization (UNESCO), 177
United Nations Human Rights Committee, 237
United Pentecostal Church, 78
United States Conference of Catholic Bishops (USCCB), 239–40, 242, 366, 371
Universal Declaration of Human Rights (UDHR), 444, 447
Universalists, 223
University of Alabama, 97
University of British Columbia, 321
University of California, 155
University of Illinois, 329
University of Regensburg, 369
University of Toronto, 44
Univision, 144
Upper Midwest, 76, 78, 80, 217
uprisings, 164
urban, 32–3, 35–7, 43, 46–8, 56–7, 60, 81, 83–5, 97, 101–5, 108–11, 122, 148, 168–9, 209, 217, 224, 226, 248, 253, 260–1, 265, 322, 329, 332–3, 363, 408, 433
Urban Indigenous Ministries (UIMs), 37–8
Urban League, 83
Urbana-Champaign, Illinois, 329
urbanisation, 57, 101, 103, 108, 110–11, 248
Ursuline Convent, 53, 103
US Catholic Sisters Against Human Trafficking (USCSAHT), 378
US Census Bureau, 145, 156
US Court of Appeals, 351
US Religious Freedom Restoration Act, 352
Usenet, 420
Utah, 64, 67, 71–3, 202–3

V Encuentro, 148
Vaishnavite(s), 372
values, 32–3, 42–3, 49, 56, 63, 89, 95, 102, 147, 154, 170, 216, 220, 231, 234, 239, 269, 280, 286, 310–11, 318, 343, 358, 368, 386–8, 390, 402, 415–16, 418
Van Nuys, California, 261
Van Opstal, Sandra Maria, 286
Vancouver, Canada, 17, 32–3, 35–6, 46–7, 232, 321, 374
Vancouver Island, 232
Vancouver School of Theology, 32
Vatican, 43, 58, 67, 69, 103, 136, 147, 235–6, 238–40, 342, 365–6, 368, 371, 422
Vatican II, 103, 136
Vedanta, 371
vegetarianism, 73
VeggieTales, 416

veneration, 30, 195
Venezuela, 259
Veniaminov, Innocent, 211
Venn, Henry, 336
Vermont, 101, 214
vernacular(s), 43, 136, 145, 200
Vernon Park Church, Chicago, 83
Verrilli Jr, Donald B., 355
Vesey, Denmark, 90
victims, 20, 43, 95, 242, 345, 364, 378
video, 72, 420
Vietnam, 85, 104, 135, 156–7, 159, 163–4, 238, 370–1, 381
Vietnam War, 163, 238
Vietnamese, 156–7, 159, 163–4, 371, 381
Viguerie, Richard, 316
Villanova University, 104
Ville-Marie, Montreal, 53
Vineyard Church, 71, 262–3, 329
violence, 20, 84, 92, 103, 126–8, 130, 143, 164, 222, 234, 277, 281–3, 303, 308, 313, 337, 340, 343–6, 350, 369, 373–6, 379, 384, 386, 390, 395, 397, 415–16
Virgin Mary, 53, 66, 382
Virgin of Guadalupe, 66, 99, 105
Virginia, 88, 91, 98–9, 184
virtue, 51, 60, 191, 231, 273, 313, 377, 455
Vivekananda, Swami, 371
Vladimir, Archbishop, 112, 212–13
vocations, 56, 58, 243
Vodou, 104
volunteers, 175, 242
Voss Roberts, Michelle, 304

Wagner, C. Peter, 262
Wakamne, 30
Wales, 268, 329
Walker, Alice, 128, 130
Wallis, Jim, 142, 252
Walrond, Michael A., 111
Wang, Ignatius, 165
Wanzer Dairy, 85
War on Terror, 369
war(s), 41–2, 44, 54, 57, 68, 79, 82, 91–3, 107–8, 110, 121, 126, 130, 133–4, 138, 162–3, 169, 194, 198–9, 203–4, 206, 212–13, 216, 221–4, 226, 229–30, 238, 241, 251, 260, 278, 295, 312–14, 317–18, 320–1, 326, 332, 334, 364, 369, 414
Wariboko, Nimi, 109
Warnock, Reverend Rafael, 315
Warren, Kristy-Nabhan, 67
Warren, Rick, 150, 330
Warren Avenue Congregational Church, Chicago, 84
Warren County, North Carolina, 400
Warwick, Bermuda, 179
Washington, 64, 67, 261
Washington, Booker T., 92
Washington, DC, 19, 132, 354, 368–9
Washington National Cathedral, 193
Watchtower magazine, 204, 331
water, 58, 116, 138, 168, 203, 317, 351, 377, 379, 399, 402, 404, 408, 410
Way Maker, 295
Wayne, John, 140
wealth, 27, 88, 103, 111–12, 125, 129, 219, 275, 283, 305, 317, 342, 401, 418, 432–4, 436, 438
weapons, 216, 255, 326
Webb, Alexander, 368
websites, 236, 420–1
weddings, 90, 214, 236, 338, 355
Wells, Ida B., 92
Wendats, 53
Wendell, Jonas, 203
Wenski, Archbishop Thomas, 99
Wesley, John, 246
Wesleyan church, 86, 111, 333
West, Ralph D., 94, 96
West Africa, 66, 380
West India Company, 363
West Virginia, 88
Westboro Baptist Church, 346
Westerdahl, John, 73
Westminster Theological Seminary, 109
Weyrich, Paul, 316
Wheaton College, 83, 333
White, Ella, 165
White, Ellen, 73
White, Lynn, 398–9
White, Paula, 263, 418, 428
White Anglo-Saxon Protestant (WASP), 135, 248
White Earth Chippewa, 129
White House, 277, 279, 320
Whitefield, George, 179, 199, 246, 249, 255, 324
whites, 46, 79, 85, 98, 144, 148, 152, 177, 259, 269, 277, 283–4, 360, 375, 431
Wiconi International, 117
Wildman, Darlene, 121, 294
Wildman, Terry, 120, 124
Willard, Frances Elizabeth, 80
Williams College, 324
Williams, Delores S., 128, 301
Williams, Rowan, 369
Willow Creek Community Church, 85, 140
Wilson, Douglas, 69
Wimber, John, 262, 329
Wimbush, Vincent L., 301
Winans, Cece, 294
Winners Chapel, 266
Winnipeg, 33, 37, 47, 294
Winthrop, John, 275
Wisconsin, 76–9, 433
wisdom, 118, 231, 293, 298, 409, 451
witnessing, 56, 258
Wittenberg, Missouri, 77
Wolf, Jan Michael Looking, 294

womanist theology, 125–8, 301, 303, 342, 403, 407
women, 13, 20, 30, 33, 35, 41, 53, 57–8, 61, 63, 72, 74, 80, 85, 87, 89–91, 93–5, 98, 105, 108, 111, 122, 127–30, 140, 151, 162, 164, 185, 205, 207, 214, 222, 224–6, 228, 235–6, 240–1, 257, 260, 267–9, 325, 330, 334, 336–43, 346–8, 377–9, 383–4, 390–1, 398, 405, 410, 429, 448–50
Women's Christian Temperance Union (WCTU), 80
Wong, Katie Choy, 165
Woodburn, Oregon, 74
Woodley, Randy, 119, 124, 334
Woods River Baptist Association, 80
Word of Faith Movement, 263
World Christian Database (WCD), 444, 447–8, 454, 460
World Christian Gathering of Indigenous People, 119
World Council of Churches (WCC), 326–7, 336, 365–6, 399–401
World Day of Peace, 399
World Missionary Conference (Edinburgh 1910), 326
World Trade Center, 216, 369
World Vision, 251, 329, 351
World War I, 82, 204, 224, 226, 364
World Youth Day, 60–1
worldview(s), 166, 173, 209, 247, 249, 252, 255, 273, 279, 288, 290, 292, 308, 334, 403, 408
Worldwide Pictures, 416
worship, 11–16, 28, 32, 34–5, 37–8, 48, 56, 60, 63, 69, 81, 85, 90, 96, 102, 109, 116–17, 119, 121, 123–4, 136–7, 142, 150–1, 170, 179–80, 183, 186, 188, 206, 219, 223, 226, 232, 241, 259, 262, 264–5, 267, 269, 281, 285–96, 311, 314–15, 318, 346, 350, 353, 355–6, 360, 365, 371, 376, 379, 381–4, 402, 407–8, 417–18, 420–2, 435

Wounded Knee, South Dakota, 117
Wyminga, Shannon, 35
Wyoming, 64, 67, 71

Xavier, Francis, 53
xenophobia, 12–13, 15, 374–5

Yakima, 120, 124
Yale Divinity School, 106, 189, 278, 328, 334, 336
Yamada, Frank, 166
Yee, Russell, 292
Yellow Peril, 363
yoga, 371
Yoido Full Gospel Church, 266
Yonkers, New York, 112
Young, Brigham, 72
Young Life, 251
Young Men's Christian Association (YMCA), 312
youth, 36, 41, 45, 48, 60–2, 72, 74, 148–9, 161–2, 174–5, 186, 203, 213, 217, 229, 254, 293, 312, 345
Youth Mass, 62
Youth With A Mission (YWAM), 175
YouTube, 295, 422
Yuchi, 124

Zacharias, Danny, 34
Zacharias, Ravi, 96–7, 140
Zen Buddhist Shaku Soyen, 370
Zhen Yesu Jiaohui (True Jesus Church), 265
Zoom, 347
Zoroastrian(s), 157, 362–3
Zschech, Darlene, 293
Zuni, 38
Zurich, Kansas, 77
Zwemer, Samuel, 368
Zwingli, Ulrich, 432